Table of Contents

The Foodservice Industry

CONSIDERED AMERICA'S FIRST FINE-DINING RESTAURANT,
Delmonico's (above) began life as a small café and pastry shop in New York's financial district run by two brothers from Switzerland. The café had six small matching tables and chairs made of pine. Business grew quickly and required the brothers to expand their café. They soon had the first American restaurant. Culinary firsts introduced by the brothers included presenting diners with a menu, offering private dining rooms, and creating innovative dishes such as eggs Benedict, baked Alaska, lobster Newberg, and the Delmonico steak. With an emphasis on the highest quality ingredients, some grown on their own farm, and great customer service they achieved enormous fortune and worldwide fame. (More details of the history of Delmonico's are included on the timeline in this chapter.)

Delmonico's is just one of many success stories in the foodservice industry. Where did it all start? The history of foodservice is fascinating, ever evolving, and a mirror of the social, political, and economic times of the world in which we live.

Perhaps no other industry is as pervasive as the foodservice industry, which touches the lives of all of us on a daily basis. Those employed in the industry—from research and development scientists, food technologists, farmers, processors, manufacturers, distributors, suppliers, and truckers to those who work in office, plant, and school cafeterias, hotels, hospitals, correctional facilities, the military, in-flight foodservice, formal restaurants, hotel dining rooms, coffee shops, family restaurants, specialty and ethnic restaurants, and fast-food outlets—can be very proud of the invaluable service they provide to us.

The statistics underscore the size and scope of the industry. Ranked number one among private-sector employers, foodservice directly employs more than 12.7 million people. One-half of all adults in the United States have worked in the foodservice industry at some time during their lives. Foodservice is the largest employer of ethnic groups, minorities, women, workers with disabilities, and entry-level workers. The millions of jobs provided and created by the industry, the training and teaching of responsibility and skills, and the opportunities provided to develop self-esteem and for promotion to management and ownership combine to make this industry an exciting, rewarding, and dynamic career choice.

There are more than 945,000 foodservice locations in the United States, with 2010 sales predicted to be over $580 billion annually. Almost 70 billion meal and snack occasions are provided in restaurants and school and work cafeterias each year. The restaurant industry's share of the food dollar was 25 percent in 1955, compared with 49 percent today. The National Restaurant Association's *Restaurant Industry Pocket Factbook* describes the magnitude of this industry (Figure 1).

Foodservice industry
All establishments where food is served outside of the home

Today the **foodservice industry** is defined in its broadest sense to mean all establishments where food is regularly served outside the home. Such establishments include formal restaurants, hotel dining rooms, coffee shops, family restaurants, specialty and ethnic restaurants, and fast-food outlets. Foodservices that operate in schools, colleges, and universities; hospitals, nursing homes, and other health care settings; recreational facilities; transportation companies; the military; correctional facilities; office buildings and plants; convenience stores, supermarkets, service delis, and department stores; and community centers and retirement residences are also included.

The history and development of organizations within the foodservice industry, embedded in the timeline presented in this chapter, are intended to give the reader a perspective on, and an appreciation for, foodservices today. The timeline is not meant to be comprehensive but to provide highlights of the most critical developments in the long history of foodservice.

Why study the history of the foodservice industry? As George Santayana, philosopher, essayist, poet, and novelist, said, "Those who cannot remember the past are condemned to repeat it." History not only provides people with an opportunity to learn from past mistakes, but also can show which of the seeds that were sown blossomed into successes and why. As Radford University's Department of History Web site states, "The study of history provides a window into the past that provides understanding of the present-day, and how individuals, nations, and the global community might develop in the future. Historical study instructs how societies came to be and examines cultural, political, social, and economic influences across time and space" (http://www.radford. edu/~hist-web/index.htm; accessed 9/23/10). This is certainly true of the foodservice industry.

The systems approach concept is based on the idea that complex organizations are made up of interdependent parts (subsystems) that interact in ways to achieve common goals. The systems concept is applied to foodservice organizations.

Managers face decisions about how to organize foodservice departments for the efficient procurement, production, distribution, and service of their food and meals. Many options are available based on the type of food purchased, where the food is prepared in relation to where it is served, the time span between preparation and service, and the amount and kind of personnel and equipment required.

Foodservices with similar characteristics are grouped as particular types of production or operating systems. Each of the four types of foodservice operating systems found in the United States today is described with its identifying features, advantages, and disadvantages. The typical foodservice organizations that use each type are also identified.

2010 Restaurant Industry

Pocket Factbook

2010 Industry Sales Projection	$580 billion	
		2010 Sales (billion $)
Commercial		$ 530.4
Eating places		388.5
Bars and taverns		18.8
Managed services		40.9
Lodging place restaurants		26.9
Retail, vending, recreation, mobile		55.2
Other		$ 49.7

Restaurants
An Essential Part of Daily Life

- Restaurants will provide more than 70 billion meal and snack occasions in 2010.
- On a typical day in America in 2010, more than 130 million people will be foodservice patrons.
- 44% of adults say restaurants are an essential part of their lifestyles.
- 65% of adults say their favorite restaurant foods provide flavor and taste sensations that can't easily be duplicated in their home kitchens.

Restaurants
Small Businesses with a Large Impact on our Nation's Economy

- Restaurant-industry sales are forecast to advance 2.5% in 2010 and equal 4% of the U.S. gross domestic product.
- The overall economic impact of the restaurant industry is expected to exceed $1.5 trillion in 2010.
- Every dollar spent by consumers in restaurants generates an additional $2.05 spent in the nation's economy.
- Each additional dollar spent in restaurants generates an additional $0.82 in household earnings throughout the economy.
- Every additional $1 million in restaurant sales generates 34 jobs for the economy.
- Eating-and-drinking places are mostly small businesses. Ninety-one percent have fewer than 50 employees.
- More than seven of 10 eating- and drinking-place establishments are single-unit operations.
- Average unit sales in 2007 were $866,000 at fullservice restaurants and $717,000 at quickservice restaurants.

Restaurants
Cornerstone of Career Opportunities

- The restaurant industry employs about 12.7 million people, or 9% of the U.S. workforce.
- The restaurant industry is expected to add 1.3 million jobs over the next decade, with employment reaching 14 million by 2020.
- Nearly half of all adults have worked in the restaurant industry at some point in their lives, and more than one in four adults got their first job experience in a restaurant.
- Eating-and-drinking places are extremely labor-intensive — sales per full-time-equivalent non-supervisory employee were $75,826 in 2008. That's much lower than most other industries.
- One-quarter of eating- and drinking-place firms are owned by women, 15% by Asians, 8% by Hispanics and 4% by African-Americans.
- Eating-and-drinking places employ more minority managers than any other industry.
- The number of foodservice managers is projected to increase 8% from 2010 to 2020.
- Fifty-eight percent of first-line supervisors/managers of food preparation and service workers in 2008 were women, 14% were of Hispanic origin and 14% were African-American.

Restaurant Industry
Share of the Food Dollar

 25% — 1955

 49% — Present

Total Restaurant Industry Employment

- 11.2 million — 2000
- 12.7 million — 2010*
- 14 million — 2020*

* Projected

Restaurant Sales
1970–2010
Food-and-Drink Sales
(Billions of Current Dollars)

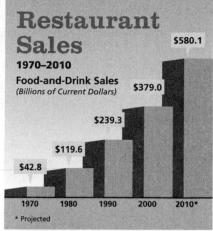

- $42.8 — 1970
- $119.6 — 1980
- $239.3 — 1990
- $379.0 — 2000
- $580.1 — 2010*

* Projected

Restaurants by the Numbers

- **$1.6 billion** Restaurant-industry sales on a typical day in 2010.
- **40** Percent of adults who agree that purchasing meals from restaurants and take-out and delivery places makes them more productive in their day-to-day life.
- **73** Percent of adults who say they try to eat healthier now at restaurants than they did two years ago.
- **57** Percent of adults who say they are likely to make a restaurant choice based on how much a restaurant supports charitable activities and the local community.
- **78** Percent of adults who say they would like to receive restaurant gift cards or certificates on gift occasions.
- **59** Percent of adults who say there are more restaurants they enjoy going to now than there were two years ago.
- **52** Percent of adults who say they would be more likely to patronize a restaurant if it offered a customer loyalty and reward program.
- **$2,698** Average household expenditure for food away from home in 2008.
- **29** Percent of adults who say purchasing take-out food is essential to the way they live.
- **54** Percent of adults who say they would be likely to use an option of delivery directly to their home or office if offered by a fullservice restaurant.
- **78** Percent of adults who agree that going out to a restaurant with family or friends gives them an opportunity to socialize and is a better way to make use of their leisure time than cooking and cleaning up.
- **63** Percent of adults who say the quality of restaurant meals is better than it was two years ago.
- **56** Percent of adults who say they are more likely to visit a restaurant that offers food grown or raised in an organic or environmentally friendly way.
- **70** Percent of adults who say they are more likely to visit a restaurant that offers locally produced food items.

1200 17th St. NW, Washington, DC 20036 | (202) 331-5900 | E-mail: askus@restaurant.org | www.restaurant.org

Figure 1 The *Restaurant Industry Pocket Factbook*.
Source: Courtesy of National Restaurant Association (www.restaurant.org)

This description should provide a basis for managers to decide on the type of operation suitable for a particular situation.

Despite the numerous types of foodservices in operation in the United States today, the fact that they are more alike than they are different should be emphasized. All are concerned with providing good, safe food to meet the specific needs and desires of people served outside the home and to operate in a financially sound manner.

KEY CONCEPTS

1. Religious orders, royal households, colleges, and inns were among the earliest organizations to practice quantity food production.

2. Seventeenth-century foodservices were established in colleges and hospitals or were places to meet to conduct business or socialize.

3. Advances in the fields of microbiology, physics, and industrial engineering led to improvements in how food is produced.

4. The restaurant industry, as we know it today, had its beginnings in France.

5. Innovative and visionary pioneers of the commercial foodservice sector introduced many new foods and concepts that continue to enjoy widespread use today.

6. World Wars I and II had a major impact on foodservice operations throughout the twentieth century.

7. Several pieces of key legislation have affected both fine-dining and school foodservice programs in the past and continue to do so today.

8. The popularity of automobile travel was the stimulus for the quick service, drive-in, drive-through, and fast-food concepts.

9. The economic conditions in the country have a major impact on the foodservice industry in all sectors.

10. The successful foodservice operators of the future will continue to learn from the past and build on the foundations that have been laid by those who went before.

THE HISTORY OF FOODSERVICE

A FOODSERVICE INDUSTRY TIMELINE
5th Century

■ **KEY CONCEPT: Religious orders, royal households, colleges, and inns were among the earliest organizations to practice quantity food production.**

England Although religious orders and royal household foodservices are far different from those we know today, each has made a contribution to the way in which present-day foodservice is practiced.

Abbeys that dot the countryside, particularly in England, not only serve the numerous brethren of the order, but also thousands of pilgrims who flock there to worship. The space provided for food preparation indicates the scope of their foodservice operations (Figure 2). At Canterbury Abbey, a favorite site of innumerable pilgrimages, the kitchen measures 45 feet wide.

Records show that the food preparation carried out by the abbey brethren reaches a much higher standard than food served in the inns. The vows the brothers have taken do not diminish their appreciation for good food. Food is grown on the abbey's grounds, and lay contributions are provided liberally for the institution's table. The strong sense of stewardship in the abbeys leads to the establishment of a detailed accounting system. These records show that a specified per capita per diem food allowance is in effect creating an effective early-day cost-accounting system.

The royal household with its hundreds of retainers and the households of nobles, often numbering as many as 150 to 250 persons, also necessitates an efficient foodservice. The differing degrees of rank results in different food allowances within these groups. In providing for these various needs, strict cost accounting is necessary, and this, perhaps, marks the beginning of the present-day scientific foodservice cost accounting.

Figure 2 Twelfth-century double octagonal kitchen of Fontevraud Abbey, Val-de-Loire, France.

There are often two kitchens. The cuisine de bouche provides food for the monarch, the principal courtiers, officials and their immediate servants; the cuisine de commun prepares food for everyone else. Unless an important banquet is being prepared, the two kitchens probably produce similar food. In the castle kitchen, the cook and his staff turn the meat (pork, beef, mutton, poultry, or game) on a spit and prepare stews and soups in great iron cauldrons hung over the fire on a hook and chain that are raised and lowered to regulate the temperature (Figures 3 and 4).

Almost all of the kitchen staff is male. A woman's place is certainly not in the kitchen. Even though there is no official record of female kitchen staff before 1620, a few women certainly work as ale wives, hen wives, and the like. Because labor is cheap and readily available, a large staff of male workers are employed to prepare the food. Rank is evident in the division of

Figure 3 A royal barbeque at Stirling Castle in Scotland.
Source: Courtesy of Kathleen Watkins, Norwich, England.

Figure 4 Stews and soups cooked in great iron cauldrons.
Source: Courtesy of Kathleen Watkins, Norwich, England.

labor. The head cook might wear a gold chain over handsome clothing and present his culinary creations to his employer in person. The pastry cook and the meat cook do not rate as high, but they are esteemed for their contributions. The average scullion often has scarcely a rag to wear and receives broken bread and the privilege of sleeping on the hearth through the chilly winter nights as his wage (Figure 5).

The diet of the royal household is very largely dependent on meat and, during Lent, on fish. Many castles have their own gardens that provide fresh vegetables, herbs, and fruit. The gardener often receives no pay unless he is able to produce sufficient fruits and vegetables.

The present-day foodservice manager would be appalled by the kitchens in these medieval households in their disregard for sanitary standards in food storage, preparation, and handling. A clutter of supplies, which overflows from inadequate table and shelf space to the wooden plank floors, and are handled by children and nosed by dogs, is the background for the preparation of elaborate creations for the table (Figure 6).

Figure 5 A kitchen worker brings in chicken for preparation.
Source: Courtesy of Kathleen Watkins, Norwich, England.

Figure 6 Windsor Castle kitchen.
Source: Courtesy of the Library of Congress.

10th Century

Sung Dynasty, China   A restaurant culture is established in the cities of Kaifeng and Hangchow.

12th Century

Europe   Through the Middle Ages at European colleges and universities, hostels are the accepted arrangement for student living. On the continent, students manage these hostels. At Oxford, England, however, hostels are endowed to provide board and lodging for students unable to pay these costs for themselves. At least to some degree, the university manages these endowed hostels—a policy that continues today.

14th Century

Ming Dynasty, China   Tourism becomes a popular pastime; restaurants are in demand; take-out food and catering also flourish.

16th Century

Constantinople   The first cafés are established to sell snacks and drinks and are places where educated people meet to share ideas and discoveries.

17th Century

KEY CONCEPT: Seventeenth-century foodservices were established in colleges and hospitals or were places to meet to conduct business or socialize.

America   Public houses in Colonial America are popular gathering places for men to drink beer. A limited selection of food is sometimes available.

Colonial colleges in the United States provide residence halls with dining rooms for all students. Administrators, generally clergymen, are responsible for their operation. They dispatch their duties prayerfully and thriftily—not always with student approval! Later, with an interest in and therefore a shift toward German educational procedures, which do not include housing as a school responsibility, some colleges lose interest in student living situations. As a result, sororities and fraternities without faculty supervision assume the feeding and housing of large groups of students. In many cases, this also leads to the problem of providing adequate diets for all students.

KEY CONCEPT: Advances in the fields of microbiology, physics, and industrial engineering led to improvements in how food is produced.

1676

France   The discovery of bacteria as the cause of food spoilage leads to improved practices in food storage and in food preparation.

1688

London   Edward Lloyd's coffeehouse is referenced in a London newspaper. It is the place for merchant ship owners and maritime insurance agents to meet and conduct insurance transactions. In 1771 the ownership of the coffeehouse is transferred to professional insurance underwriters and becomes the world-famous Lloyd's of London.

1698

London Two thousand coffeehouses are doing a booming business.

1751

Philadelphia The first hospital is established in the Colonies. Meals in early-day hospitals are simple to the point of monotony, and no attempt is made to provide any special foods or therapeutic diets. Menus in an eighteenth-century American hospital, for example, include mush and molasses for breakfast on Monday, Wednesday, and Friday, varied by molasses and mush for supper on Monday, Wednesday, Thursday, and Saturday. Oxtail soup and black bread appear on occasion.

1762

New York Fraunces Tavern opens at the corner of Pearl and Broad streets where it still operates. Meals from the tavern are regularly sent to George Washington's quarters nearby.

1765

KEY CONCEPT: The restaurant industry, as we know it today, had its beginnings in France.

Paris The word *restaurant* is first used. The cook shops of France are licensed to prepare ragoûts, or stews, to be eaten on the premises or taken to inns or homes for consumption. The shops have *écriteaux,* or menus, posted on the wall or by the door to whet the interest of the passerby. The story goes that one *boulanger,* a bouillon maker, added a sheep's-foot soup (he calls it a *restaurant* or restorative soup) to his menu, contending that this was not a ragoût and, therefore, did not violate the rights of the *traiteurs,* or cook shopkeepers. In the legal battle that follows, the French lawmakers sustain his point, and his new business is legalized as a restaurant. The word *restaurant* comes from the French verb *restaurer,* which means "to restore" or "to refresh." It is said that the earliest restaurants had this Latin inscription over their doorway: *Venite ad me qui stomacho laoratis et ego restaurabo vos*—Come to me all whose stomachs cry out in anguish, and I shall restore you!

1782

Paris The first restaurant is established. A *traiteur* named Beauvilliers opens La Grande Taverne de Londres, converting his take-out shop by listing dishes available on a menu and serving them at small tables during fixed hours.

1784–1833

France The first star chef, Antonin Careme, cooks for Czar Alexander of Russia, King George IV of England, Talleyrand of France, and others. He becomes known as the "Cook of Kings and King of Cooks."

1789

Paris The modern restaurant industry is launched following the French Revolution. Since the Middle Ages, laws had restricted the selling of certain foods by specific tradesmen. The relaxation of these laws allows chefs for the first time to offer complete individually prepared, portioned, and priced dishes to order by anyone who could afford them.

1794

New York At the corner of Wall and Water Streets, the Tontine Coffee House opens and becomes a hangout for speculative investors who later found the New York Stock Exchange.

Early 19th Century

■ **KEY CONCEPT: Innovative and visionary pioneers of the commercial foodservice sector introduced many new foods and concepts that continue to enjoy widespread use today.**

Scotland Industrial catering is begun by Robert Owen, a Scottish mill owner, near Glasgow during the early nineteenth century. He so improves working conditions for his employees that his mill becomes a model throughout the industrial world. Among other things, it contains a large kitchen and eating room for employees and their families. Prices for meals are nominal, and so begins the philosophy of subsidizing meal service for employees.

1800s

United States Many employees provide free or below-cost meals to their employees.

1804

Philadelphia Milk, butter, pork, and soap are produced on the Philadelphia Hospital grounds for consumption in the hospital. Also, cows, calves, and pigs are sold for income. Salary for a husband and wife serving as steward and matron is $350 for nine months of service.

1811

France Nicolas Appert discovers how to preserve food by canning.

1819

United States Advances in the understanding of the laws of physics result in the replacement of open hearths with iron stoves and many refinements to the kitchen equipment. Many cooks resist the change from open-hearth cooking to the enclosed iron stove. The wood is expensive, requires storage space, and makes the kitchen dirty.

1824

New York Swiss-born Giovanni Del-Monico retires from his career as a sea captain and opens a wine shop.

1825

Philadelphia The soda fountain is born. A pharmacist offers his customers seltzer water remedies at his drugstore.

1826

New York to Berne, Switzerland Giovanni Del-Monico sells his business and returns to Switzerland to join his brother in the candy and pastry business. They then decide to move back to New York. They invest $20,000 in the new business.

1827

New York Adapting to American customs, the brothers change their last name to the English version, Delmonico, and open a small café and pastry shop called Delmonico and Brother with six small pine tables and matching chairs where they serve pastries, coffee, chocolate, bonbons, orgeats, wines, liquors, and fancy ices.

1830

New York The Delmonico brothers expand into the building next door and create the very first restaurant or public dining room ever opened in the United States. They model their business after those that were proliferating in Europe and hire French cooks who have immigrated to the United States. Innovations introduced by the brothers include a bill of fare (now called a menu), new foods (such as eggplant, artichoke, endive, and subtle French sauces), a courteous staff, and better cooking than even in the homes of the most wealthy New Yorkers.

1831

New York Needing more help, the Delmonicos are joined by their 19-year-old nephew Lorenzo, who for the next 40 years guides the business to a status and reputation that has never been matched. Food is served on fine china, and the menu includes many European imports and the best wines and rare champagnes.

1832

London Charles Babbage, a mathematician/philosopher/inventor/mechanical engineer, in his book *On the Economy of Machinery and Manufactures*, argues that the key to business success is a systematic approach to design. This is considered the first publication on operations research.

1833

United States The coal stove is patented. Coal is cheaper than wood, requires less storage space, but is dirtier when burned (Figure 7).

1834

New York The Delmonicos purchase a 220-acre farm on Long Island where they grow vegetables not yet found in America for the restaurant. They also purchase a lodging house.

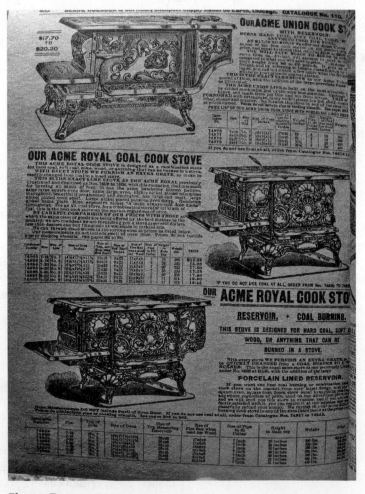

Figure 7 An early coal-burning stove.

1835

London Charles Babbage designs and builds the first programmable computer (then called an analytical engine).

New York A huge fire destroys much of lower New York, including Delmonico's.

1836

New York The Delmonico brothers remodel the lodging house and reopen their restaurant there just two months after the fire. Later this year they begin to build a new restaurant.

1837

New York The new Delmonico's is 3-1/2 stories high. The first and second floors house large saloons (dining rooms) that are luxuriously decorated. The third floor houses the kitchen and several private dining rooms. The wine cellar has vaults for 16,000 bottles of French wine. The entrance to the restaurant features marble columns imported from Pompeii. Delmonico potatoes become a menu item favorite.

1845

New York Another fire sweeps through New York, destroying the Delmonicos' lodging house but not the restaurant. They decide to build a brand new hotel.

1846

New York The Delmonico Hotel opens as the first major hotel in the United States to operate on the European plan (the room and meals are priced separately). Under the American plan, a guest pays one price for room and board. The hotel soon becomes world famous.

1849

France The first school lunch is offered in canteens.

California The cafeteria is born. The cafeteria is a further step in the simplification of restaurant foodservices. This style of self-service came into being during the Gold Rush days of 1849 when the "forty-niners" demanded speedy service. Regarded as an American innovation, its popularity extends throughout the United States. The word *cafeteria* is Spanish for coffee shop.

1850

London The Reform Club of London hires noted chef Alexis Soyer to provide a sanitary and efficient foodservice setup that includes the recent innovations of gas stoves, water baths, and refrigeration.

Washington, D.C. President Millard Fillmore puts a gas stove in the White House kitchen, and the cooks refuse to use it.

1853

New York School foodservice is started in the United States when the Children's Aid Society of New York City opens an industrial school in an effort to persuade children from the slums to see "instruction in industry and mental training," and food is offered to all who come.

1855

Turkey The beginning of dietetics. Dietetics, as a hospital service, has its beginning at the time of the Crimean War (1854–1856). Florence Nightingale, whom dietitians, as well as nurses, revere and honor as the pioneer of their profession, establishes a diet kitchen to provide clean, nourishing food for the ill and wounded soldiers in Scutari (now Uskudar), Turkey. Until then, foods of questionable quality were poorly cooked in unsanitary conditions and served at irregular intervals (Figure 8).

Alexis Soyer (who, as noted earlier, was a chef who had worked with the Reform Club of London) contributes greatly to Nightingale's efforts when he offers to serve without pay as manager of the barracks hospital kitchen. Soyer's plan for operating the kitchen is as efficient as modern-day practice.

Figure 8   A Statue of Florence Nightingale.

1856

New York Seeing that the city center is moving north, Lorenzo Delmonico sells the hotel and opens another new restaurant across from City Hall.

1862

New York Continuing to move north, Delmonico converts a mansion across from Union Square into the most luxurious restaurant New Yorkers have ever seen.

1865

New York Lorenzo Delmonico opens his fourth restaurant. Each restaurant draws a different clientele: 14th Street draws "society"; Chambers Street, politicians, merchants, lawyers, and brokers; South William Street, bankers and shipping magnates; and Broad Street, stockbrokers and specialists.

England The novelist Victor Hugo starts offering hot lunches to school children at his home in exile.

1868

Chicago The Pullman dining car is added to the already luxurious sleeper cars on American railroads. Menus feature local produce, and trained waiters and chefs create an upscale mobile dining experience for those who can afford it.

1869

United States Campbell's introduces condensed soup.

1872

Providence, Rhode Island The first mobile lunch wagon, which is horse-drawn, is introduced by food vendor Walter Scott.

United States Blackjack® chewing gum is first sold.

1876

New York Delmonico's continues to move north. They close the 14th Street restaurant and open at 26th Street near Madison Square. The new restaurant is five stories high and features silver chandeliers, mirrored walls, mahogany furniture, a central fountain, a ballroom, and a banquet hall. The four restaurants operated by the Delmonico family now have 400 employees. Lobster à la Newberg is invented at the 26th Street restaurant. Baked Alaska is first served here.

Topeka, Kansas At the Atchison, Topeka, & Santa Fe railroad depot, Fred Harvey opens his first restaurant.

1882

New York Delmonico's raises the price of a Delmonico steak from $0.75 to $1.00 as inflation hits the country.

1886

United States   Coca-Cola® first appears on the scene.

1888

New York   The Pine Street Delmonico's closes because of decreased business.

1889

United States   Calumet® baking powder and McCormick® spices are first sold.

1890

United States   Knox® gelatin, Lipton® tea, and peanut butter are introduced.

1891

New York   A brand new 8-story high Delmonico's opens, featuring electric lights for the first time.

1893

New York   The Broad Street Delmonico's lease expires, and it is closed. Eggs Benedict is created at one of the other Delmonico restaurants.

1894

United States   Hershey® bars, chili powder, and Sen-Sen® first appear.

1895

New York   Charles Delmonico introduces the "alligator pear" or avocado, which has been newly imported from South America.

1896

United States   Triscuits®, Cracker Jack®, Tootsie Rolls®, and shredded coconut are developed.

1897

United States   Grape-Nuts® and Jell-O® make their appearance on shelves.

New York   Delmonico's continues to move north, opening a new restaurant at 44th Street. At this restaurant, smoking is allowed in the dining room and an orchestra plays while people eat. These are both "shocking" changes at the time.

1898

United States   The tray is invented, as are graham crackers and shredded wheat.

20th Century

KEY CONCEPT: World Wars I and II had a major impact on foodservice operations throughout the twentieth century.

United States   The twentieth century witnesses many changes in college and university foodservices in the United States. A shift occurs from the laissez-faire policy of early-day administrators to a very strict one in the late nineteenth century. Until World War II, colleges provide separate dining halls for men and women. Not only do students have their dietary needs satisfied, but they are also trained in the "social graces." Seated table service with students serving in rotation as hostess or host and as waiter or waitress is the accepted procedure in many residence hall dining rooms. Although this service may still be found in some colleges and universities today, it is the exception rather than the rule.

Gradually, with the influx of GI students into American schools of higher education after World War II (1939–1945), the more formal seated service and leisurely dining give way to the speedy informality of cafeteria service. This service style makes it possible to meet student demands for greater menu variety and to cater to the food preferences of various ethnic groups that make up the student body. Also, with coeducational residences and dining halls now commonly found on the college campus, the dietary requirements of both men and women in the same dining hall can be met by cafeteria or self-service. Student food habits also change as a result of increasing concern for physical fitness and weight control. Foodservice managers attempt to comply with this need through suitable menu selections. For example, salad bars, pasta bars, potato bars, and vegetarian bars are standard in most campus dining halls.

Growing knowledge about nutrition and concern about the poor state of health of many draftees during World Wars I and II result in an emphasis on the importance of wise food selection and the need for nourishing school lunches at little or no cost to the students. This decade sees significant improvements in the school lunchroom movement throughout the country.

Changes in hospital foodservice during this century include the introduction of centralized tray service and mechanical dishwashing, establishment of a separate kitchen for special diet preparation and later elimination of such kitchens, and the advent of frozen foods and their use in food preparation. Also, pay cafeterias for staff and employees and separate dining areas for these two groups are introduced during this period. Employing qualified dietitians to administer dietary departments and "therapeutic" dietitians for "special diet" supervision becomes the usual practice.

1902

Philadelphia The automat first appears. This innovative foodservice is opened by Horn and Hardart. Patterned after a "waiterless" restaurant in Berlin, it combines features of a cafeteria with those of vending. Individual food items are displayed in coin-operated window cases from which customers make their selections. This "nickel-in-a-slot" eatery provides good food and high standards of sanitation for nearly 50 years, drawing customers from every walk of life. For many people, it becomes a haven, especially during the Great Depression years, beginning with the stock market crash in 1929, the years of the automat's greatest success. After World War II, the automat's popularity declines as a more affluent society seeks greater sophistication in dining.

1904

St. Louis, Missouri Hamburgers are first served at the World's Fair. However, the actual invention of the hamburger is hotly contested.

1910s

United States Crisco®, Oreos®, fortune cookies, and French dip sandwiches are introduced. Sugar costs $.04/pound, eggs are $.14/dozen, coffee is $.15/pound, and canned beer and iced tea have not been invented yet.

1912

Providence, Rhode Island Roadside diners are developed because lunch wagons have become so numerous that they block the roads. A law is passed that they must be off the roads by 10 a.m., so many park their wagons permanently in empty lots.

1914–1919

World War I Delmonico's Restaurant operations suffer financially from the changes in eating habits and the economic conditions caused by the war in Europe. In addition, the descendants of the brothers and owners begin to fight legal battles over ownership.

1916

Coney Island, New York A nickel hot dog stand is established and grows to become Nathan's Famous®, with revenue of $29.8 million a year and 370 locations in the United States and overseas today.

1919

■ **KEY CONCEPT: Several pieces of key legislation have affected both fine-dining and school foodservice programs in the past and continue to do so today.**

New York *Prohibition:* The last Delmonico's restaurant is sold on the day that Prohibition is enacted. The new owner is no longer able to serve wine, use wine in cooking, or serve wild game in New York. The wealthy no longer eat at Delmonico's but hire private cooks, stock their own wine cellars, and enlarge their kitchens. The middle class find their entertainment at dance halls, private clubs, and burlesque houses rather than restaurants.

United States The speakeasy is spawned. The passage of the Volstead Act, the Eighteenth Amendment to the Constitution, which prohibits the manufacture, sale, and distribution of alcoholic beverages in the United States, has a major and lasting impact on commercial foodservice. With the loss of alcohol in the menu mix, everyone begins to get serious about the food served. Concerned restaurateurs gather in Kansas City, Missouri, and found the National Restaurant Association (NRA). Many landmark establishments go bankrupt while, at the same time, a new breed of operation is spawned—the speakeasy. Two of the most famous "speaks," the Coconut Grove in Los Angeles and New York's 21 Club, become known not only for the bootleg liquor served, but for the quality of food as well. The legendary Musso-Franks Grill is founded during this time (shown in a 1928 picture, Figure 9); and, as the Musso & Frank Grill, it is still in operation (as it appears today, Figure 10).

United States The franchise concept is inaugurated. The first A&W root beer stand was opened by Roy Allen and Frank Wright, pioneers of the franchise concept in the foodservice industry. At one time, they had more than 2,500 units; most were franchised.

1920s

United States Wonder Bread®, Wheaties®, frozen foods, Kool-Aid®, po' boy sandwiches, and Gerber's® baby food appear on grocery store shelves.

Figure 9 Musso-Franks Grill in Hollywood in 1928.
Source: Photograph by *hollywoodphotographs.com.*

Figure 10 Musso & Frank Grill in Hollywood as it looks today.
Source: Photograph by *hollywoodphotographs.com.*

1921

■ **KEY CONCEPT: The popularity of automobile travel was the stimulus for the quick-service, drive-in, drive-through, and fast-food concepts.**

Dallas–Fort Worth, Texas The first drive-in restaurant opens. As mass quantities of automobiles hit the roads, J. G. Kirby, a candy and tobacco wholesaler, opens the Pig Stand on the Dallas–Fort Worth Highway. Service at the barbecue-themed Pig Stand is provided by waitresses who jump up on the protruding running boards of the automobiles—therefore they become known as carhops (Figure 11). This same year, Billy Ingram and Walter Anderson start their White Castle operation with a $700 investment. They sell bite-size hamburgers for 5 cents each. Ingram was a pioneer of many fast-food concepts still in use today, such as strict product consistency, unit cleanliness ("White" in the name stood

Figure 11 Carpenter's Drive In at Sunset and Vine.
Source: Photograph by *hollywoodphotographs.com.*

Figure 12 The first White Castle hamburger stand.
Source: Courtesy of Todd Murray.

for cleanliness), coupon discounts, heat-resistant cartons for carryout orders, and folding paper napkins. White Castle hamburgers were the first "sliders" (Figure 12).

New York Delmonico's is raided by "Dry Agents," who arrest a waiter and a manager for serving vodka and gin in violation of the Volstead Act.

1923

New York The last Delmonico's closes, and the final dinner is served with mineral water as the beverage.

1925

Massachusetts During the 1920s and 1930s, restaurants evolve from being luxuries to necessities. Perhaps no one takes better advantage of the growing popularity of automobile transportation than Howard Dearing Johnson of Wollaston, Massachusetts. Johnson takes a bankrupt pharmacy in Quincy, Massachusetts, and converts it into a soda fountain serving a trio of ice cream flavors he had developed. After expanding his menu to include such quick-service items as hamburgers and hot dogs, Johnson sets his sights on opening more units. Without the capital to do this, he decides to franchise. By 1940, there are 100 Howard Johnson's franchises and 28 ice cream flavors.

1926

Los Angeles *The beginning of gimmicks to attract restaurant customers:* The Brown Derby, a restaurant building shaped like a derby hat (Figure 13), opens and is the restaurant where the Cobb salad is invented.

Figure 13 The Brown Derby.
Source: Courtesy of the California Historical Society.

1927

Washington, D.C. At approximately the same time that Johnson is watching traffic on the highway, a 26-year-old from Utah is watching pedestrian traffic in Washington, D.C., on a hot July day. J. Willard Marriott sees that the thirsty masses have no place to go for a cold drink. With a $3,000 investment, he and his future wife, Alice, open a nine-stool A&W root beer stand (later called The Hot Shoppe). It grosses $16,000 the first year. (This is the beginning of the Marriott Corporation, currently a multi-billion-dollar foodservice and lodging empire; Figure 14.)

Figure 14 J. Willard Marriott in front of one of his Hot Shoppes in 1948.
Source: Photograph from Ollie Atkins Photograph Collection, George Mason University Archives.

1930s

United States Bisquick®, tacos, Fritos®, Spam®, Krispy Kreme® donuts, Kraft macaroni and cheese, and canned sodas make their debut.

1933

United States The repeal of Prohibition helps to boost fine-dining restaurants and deluxe supper clubs featuring live entertainment. Theme restaurants with fun, but outrageous, gimmicks often thrive. Trader Vic's, Romanoff's, Chasen's, El Morocco, Lawry's Prime Rib, the Brown Derby, and the Pump Room are among those that become the haunts of the rich and famous.

United States The first federal legislation designed to assist and direct school foodservices is enacted, providing loans to help communities to pay labor costs for preparation and service of lunches in schools. The impetus for this legislation is the rejection rate (due to poor nutrition) from the military during World War I.

1935

United States The federal government is authorized to donate surplus farm commodities to schools to assist the school lunch program. A noon meal becomes a common part of school activities.

1937

Washington, D.C. The airline catering business begins. Marriott supplies box lunches to passengers on Eastern, Capital, and American Airlines leaving Hoover Field (currently the site of the Pentagon) and calls its division "In-Flite Catering." Full meals are supplied later on, delivered in special insulated carriers, and placed onboard by a custom-designed truck with a loading device attached to the roof.

1940s

United States M&M's®, Cheerios®, corn dogs, nachos, cake mixes, loco moco, Whoppers®, chicken-fried steak, and seedless watermelon first appear.

1940

San Bernardino, California McDonald's arrives on the scene. The face of fast food is changed forever just 50 miles east of Los Angeles in the then-sleepy little town of San Bernardino. Brothers Mo and Dick McDonald open a 600-square-foot facility that violates a basic rule of restaurant design by exposing the entire kitchen to the public. The 25-item menu generates $200,000 in annual sales. Twenty carhops are needed to service the 125-car parking lot. But, faced with increasing competition and the constant turnover of carhops, the brothers make the dramatic decision to eliminate the carhops, close the restaurant, convert to walk-up windows, and lower the hamburger price from 30 cents to 15 cents. After a few months of adjustment, annual sales jump to $300,000. (By 1961, the McDonalds had sold 500 million hamburgers, and they sold the company to Ray Kroc for $2.7 million. Today, McDonald's has about 31,000 units spread over 118 countries serving 50 million customers each day with annual revenues of more than $23.5 billion.)

1941

Los Angeles Competition increases. A former bakery delivery man in Los Angeles secures a hot-dog cart with $15 cash and a $311 loan against his Plymouth automobile. Carl N. Karcher makes $14.75 on his first day in business. The hot-dog cart evolved into a drive-in barbecue joint and then a quick-service operation featuring hamburgers and chicken sandwiches. (Some 50 years later, the Carl's Jr. chain would ring up $640 million in sales and number 640 units.) Carl Karcher contributed air conditioning, carpeting, piped-in music, automatic charbroilers, salad bars, nutritional guides, and all-you-can-drink beverage bars to the fast-food concept.

1944

United States Howard Johnson closes 188 restaurants, leaving only 12 open because of the war.

1946

United States The National School Lunch Act is passed. Through this act, funds were appropriated as may be necessary

> to safeguard the health and well-being of the nation's children and to encourage the domestic consumption of nutritious agricultural commodities and other food, by assisting the States, through grants-in-aid and other means, in providing an adequate supply of food and other facilities for the establishment, maintenance, operation and expansion of non-profit school lunch programs. (P. L. 396-79th Congress, June 4, 1946, 60 Stat. 231.)

States were required to supplement federal funding as set forth in Section 4 of the act, and lunches served by participating schools were obligated to meet the nutritional requirements prescribed. Although the National School Lunch Act allowed Type A, B, and C meals, the Type A lunch is the only one now served under the federal school foodservice program and is referred to as "the school meal pattern".

1948

Baldwin Park, CA In-N-Out Burger, the first drive-through hamburger stand, is founded. The idea of a speaker box where customers can order is unique. The company's fundamental philosophy from the beginning is, "Give customers the freshest, highest quality foods you can buy and provide them with friendly service in a sparkling clean environment."

1949

The Good Humor Man is a favorite in every neighborhood starting in 1949. Ice cream is peddled from bicycles and later vans playing a well-recognized tune.

Figure 15 Dining at Schwab's Drug Store soda fountain in Hollywood in 1945.
Source: Photograph by *hollywoodphotographs.com*.

1950s

United States   The drugstore soda fountain counter (Figure 15) and the coffee shop become the "in" places to be. In the 1950s, coffee shops begin to proliferate, particularly in Southern California. Tiny Naylor's, Ships, Denny's (formerly Danny's), and the International House of Pancakes (now IHOP) had their beginnings during this time. Spinoffs from the McDonald's fast-food concept include Taco Bell, Burger King, and Kentucky Fried Chicken (now KFC), each with similar success stories. In New England in 1950, an industrial caterer named William Rosenburg opens a doughnut shop featuring 52 varieties of doughnuts, and Dunkin' Donuts is born. In the late 1950s, pizza moves from being served in mom-and-pop, family-run eateries to the fast-food arena. Pizza Hut opens in 1958 and is followed within a few years by Domino's and Little Caesar's.

TV dinners, Tex-Mex, ranch dressing, smoothies, instant pudding, beefalo, and Rice-a-Roni® appear on the scene.

1951

San Bernardino, California   Glen Bell, feeling competition from the McDonald brothers, adds tacos to the menu of his Bell's Burgers. At 19 cents each, they are a hit, so he opens three Taco Tia restaurants featuring his tacos. Spinoffs from Bell's and Taco Tia include Baker's Drive-In, Del Taco, Naugles, Denny's, Der Wienerschnitzel, El Taco, and Taco Bell. Also founded in this year are Burger King and El Torito.

1959

Waikiki, Hawaii   Chuck's Steakhouse is founded and features the first salad bar.

1960s

United States   Innovative marketing concepts are introduced in new chains such as T.G.I. Friday's, Arby's, Subway, Steak and Ale, Victoria Station, Cork 'n Cleaver, Black Angus, Red Lobster, Domino's Pizza, Hardee's, Tim Horton's, Blimpie,

Benihana, H. Salt, Long John Silver's, Red Robin, Steer 'n Stein, Chick-fil-A, Sirloin Stockade, Old Spaghetti Factory, and Wendy's. And, Gatorade® (a drink developed for the Florida Gators) and buffalo wings are introduced.

1966

United States The Child Nutrition Act authorizes the School Breakfast Program and the Special Milk Program to further help alleviate inadequate nutrition in childhood.

1967

United States The Big Mac® is developed to satisfy the appetites of hungry construction workers in Pittsburgh.

1970s

United States The rising popularity of ethnic foods, television shows featuring cooking instruction, women entering foodservice management and back-of-the-house executive positions, some interest in health foods and vegetarianism, and the beginnings of California cuisine. Egg Beaters®, Jelly Bellies®, and the Egg McMuffin® make their appearance.

1971

Seattle, Washington Starbucks makes its debut. Named after the first mate in Melville's Moby Dick, Starbucks now has more than 10,000 locations.

1972

Ithaca, New York A social conscience comes to the restaurant industry: Moosewood Restaurant is opened by a group of friends as a community cooperative venture. The menu is vegetarian and ethnically diverse.

United States A very big year for restaurant openings: Popeye's, The Cheesecake Factory, Gladstone's 4-Fish, Baker's Square, Ruby Tuesday, Captain Tony's Pizza and Pasta, Super Popeye's Fried Chicken, and Cousin's Subs are all founded.

1973

United States McDonald's adds the Egg McMuffin to its menu. Miguel's Mexican restaurant is started in Corona, California.

1974

United States The Federal Conditions of Participation Regulations specifies:

Condition of participation dietetic services: The skilled nursing facility provides a hygienic dietetic service that meets the daily nutritional needs of patients, ensures that special dietary needs are met, and provides palatable and attractive meals. A facility that has a contract with an outside food management company may be found to be in compliance with this condition provided the facility and/or company meets the standards listed herein. (Committee on Nursing Home Regulation, Institute of Medicine (U.S.). *Improving the Quality of Care in Nursing Homes.*

(Washington D.C.: National Academy Press, 1983.)

The services of registered dietitians (RDs) are required to ensure that dietary service regulations are adequately met and administered. Part-time or consultant RDs may be employed by small nursing homes; full-time registered dietitians are needed in the larger, skilled nursing homes.

1975

United States The owners of Miguel's open Miguel's Jr., a fast-food restaurant serving homestyle Mexican foods. Joining them in the Mexican food business are Chili's, El Pollo Loco, and Casa Gallardo.

1976

Cupertino, California Steve Wozniak and Steve Jobs start Apple Computer in a garage and personal computers come into being.

1977

Los Alamitos, California The Claim Jumper chain is founded.

1978

United States Opening this year are Chuck E. Cheese, Ben & Jerry's, Au Bon Pain, and Barnaby's Family Inn.

1980s

United States The Yukon Gold potato and spaghetti squash are developed. Applebees, Fuddruckers, TCBY, Farmer Boys, Buffalo Wild Wings, Lindey's Restaurant, Figaro's, Papa Aldo's, Chesapeake Bagel, Olive Garden, Islands, Ruby's Diner, L & N Seafood Grill, Dave & Busters, Quiznos, Papa John's Pizza, Rubio's, Bruegger's Bagels, Panda Express, Hooters, Miami Subs, Chin Chin's, Copeland's New Orleans Restaurant, Blackjack Pizza, Café Express, Juan Pollo, Hooker Hamburgers, Papa Murphy's Pizza, American Café, Culver's, and Starvin' Arvin's all open their doors.

KEY CONCEPT: The economic conditions in the country have a major impact on the foodservice industry in all sectors.

United States The economic downturn is both good and bad for the restaurant industry. On the positive side, progress is made with environmental and solid-waste proposals and health and nutrition mandates. On the negative side, poor economic conditions lead to unbridled expansion, overleveraged buyouts, employee buyouts, a rash of bankruptcy filings, system-wide restructurings, downsizing, and job layoffs. General Mills opens its Olive Garden chain in 1982 and China Coast in 1990. PepsiCo Inc. acquires Taco Bell, Pizza Hut, and Kentucky Fried Chicken to make it an industry powerhouse.

Casualties of the 1980s include Sambo's, Flakey Jake's, and D-Lites of America. Some believe that government regulations that pass during this decade are the most harmful since Prohibition. Meal deductibility is reduced to 80 percent from 100 percent, the FICA tax-on-tips mandate is instituted, and the Americans with Disabilities Act and the Family Leave Bill go into effect.

United States The Omnibus Reconciliation Act of 1980 reduces the reimbursement rate to schools for the first time and changes the income eligibility standard for students who can receive free or reduced-price meals.

1981

United States Further adjustments are made to help achieve reductions in federal spending. School foodservice managers work creatively to adjust to these changes while maintaining an attractive meal program that meets nutritional guidelines and appeals to students.

1983

Chicago Cell phones first appear.

April 23–July 11, 1985

United States Coca-Cola introduces New Coke® and puts its 99-year-old formula in a bank vault until consumers demand the resurrection of Coke Classic.

1985–1989

United States Chick-fil-A Dwarf House, El Torito Grill, Boston Market, Cinnabon, California Pizza Kitchen, Beef O Brady's, Cici's Pizza, Copeland's Cheesecake Bistro, Carrabba's Italian Grill, Charley's Grilled Subs, Chevy's, Truett's Grill, Manhattan Bagel, 5 and Diner, Back Yard Burgers, Champps, Coldstone Creamery, Koo Koo Roo, Outback Steakhouse, Roy's, Auntie Anne's, Hogi Yogi, Market Broiler, Jose's Mexican Food, Abuelo's, and Buffalo Southwest Café join the foodservice industry lineup.

Late 1980s

United States Public school enrollment drops dramatically, but spending continues to climb. School foodservice directors switch from operating subsidized departments to self-supporting ones. Some of the changes that are made in an effort to make the switch include implementing centralized food production; raising prices for paying students; attracting more paying students to the program to offset free and reduced-price lunches; offering more high-profit, fast-food-style, à la carte items; and reaching out to service community programs, such as Meals-on-Wheels, senior citizen and day care centers, and community "soup" kitchens.

1990–1994

United States The FlavrSavr tomato and Sun Chips are developed. Jamba Juice, Caribou Coffee, Pufferbelly Station Restaurant, Zaxby's, Baja Fresh, Kenny Rogers Roasters, Pat & Oscars, Pretzel Maker, Logan's Roadhouse, Bullets Burgers, BD's Mongolian Barbeque, Juice Stop, PF Chang's China Bistro, New World Coffee, Texas Roadhouse, Roadhouse Grill, Chipotle Mexican Grill, Atlanta Bread Company, Buca di Beppo, Pasta Pomodoro, Juice It Up, Buck's Pizza, and Xando all open.

Value wars, environmental concerns over packaging waste, and the public's increasing interest in nutrition and freshness are all issues that have been faced by the industry in the recent past. Operators have responded in various ways to each challenge by offering low-price loss leaders, reducing packaging, and offering lower fat, healthier alternatives prepared in front of customers.

Perhaps the post–World War II baby boom generation and the resulting population bulge have influenced the growth of the foodservice industry as much as any other factor in recent years. As this generation raised on fast food matures, it continues to seek more sophisticated fast-food dining. Many foodservice trends that seemed to be new at the time are in reality, as J. Woodman said, "One more repeat in a cyclic phenomenon, wrapped up in a new language and viewed by a new generation" (Woodman, J.: Twenty years of "400" translates into light years of change for food service. *Restaurants and Institutions*, 1984; 94(15): 98).

Chipotle Mexican Grill opens in 1993 and states that it is seeking ingredients that are not only fresh but sustainably grown and naturally raised with respect for the animals, the land, and the farmers who produce the food.

1995

Provo, Utah Teriyaki Stix, a healthy Japanese fast-food restaurant, opens with locations primarily in Utah and Idaho. Also opening this year are Zuka Juice and Haru. Baked Lays® potato chips first appear.

Berkeley, California School foodservice gets a nutritional boost from the establishment of an Edible Schoolyard, a one-acre garden and kitchen classroom supplying fruits, vegetables, herbs, and flowers. Alice Waters, chef and author, is the developer of the concept. The idea catches on, and vegetable gardens are seen in schoolyards across the nation.

1996–1999

United States McDonald's introduces its Arch Deluxe® burger in an attempt to capture the adult market. The quarter-pound burger is topped with peppered bacon, cheese, lettuce, tomato, mustard, and mayonnaise on a potato-sesame roll. Customers were turned off by the high price, unconventional ads, and high caloric content. The company spends over $300 million in marketing, research, and production for the product. The product is gradually discontinued and is no longer offered today.

United States Joining the restaurant lineup are Cosi, Bahama Breeze, Crescent City, ETX, Montana Mike's, Rockfish Seafood Grill, Fleming's Steakhouse, Biaggi's, Grand Lux Café, Brio Tuscan Grille, and Coyote Canyon—and in New York, a new Delmonico's is opened by owners who spend $1.5 million to recreate the Old World atmosphere of the originals.

21st Century

■ **KEY CONCEPT: The successful foodservice operators of the future will continue to learn from the past and build on the foundations that have been laid by those who went before.**

United States Residence hall dining offers longer hours of service, fewer restrictions on the number of services allowed, and greater flexibility in board plans, including a "pay as you eat" plan, rather than having to pay a set rate in advance.

In addition to residence hall dining, a diversity of other campus foodservices is a familiar pattern today. Student union buildings have, for example, set up creative and innovative units catering to students' changing food interests and demands. Commercial fast-food companies are a major competitor for student patronage in many college towns. Some universities contract with these companies to set up and operate food units on campus.

Hospital foodservices, faced with tighter budgets, have brought more innovations and changes for greater operating efficiency and increased revenues to hospital food and nutrition departments. Some of the innovations that have been implemented include increasing nonpatient, in-house cafeteria volume; marketing catering services; use of professional chefs to improve menus; contracting professional and food production services to smaller operations; and creating new services, such as diet workshops for the public, room service, and take-home employee and patient meals. Patients are being offered more personalized foodservice, allowing them to eat what they want to eat and when.

2005

New Orleans, Louisiana The Edible Schoolyard concept comes to New Orleans with the goal of instilling in children a lifelong appreciation of the connections between food, health, and the environment.

2007

San Francisco, California School foodservices face increasing pressures to produce and serve nutritious food. The Edible Schoolyard spreads to San Francisco. For schools where there is no available land for a garden, Woolly Pockets, small gardens that can hang on a wall, have been developed (Figure 16).

Figure 16 Woolly Pockets, small wall hanging gardens.
Source: Courtesy of Suthi Picotte, Picotte Photography.

2009

United States Restaurant customers demand more variety, safer and more nutritious foods, faster and more convenient service, and better quality. McDonald's tries to maintain a competitive edge by offering even faster service using warming trays that hold more food and software upgrades to speed up ordering in attempts to shave seconds off food delivery time. California enacts menu labeling legislation mandating that all chain restaurants with 20 or more units provide customers with nutritional information, either calorie counts on the menu or more detailed information in brochures. By 2011, the calorie counts will have to be printed on the menu. IHOP and Applebee's Neighborhood Bar and Grill have calorie information on their menus. Some Jack in the Box restaurants have the information framed on the wall near the counter. California Pizza Kitchen had the calorie counts on the menu but removed them when customers complained.

Restaurants are using social media (Facebook, Twitter, MySpace, and others) to recruit employees, generate traffic, and solicit feedback on menu changes. Karaoke, artisanal pizzas, tapas, and more reasonable prices are some of the concepts being used to lure customers from the competition.

Fast-food chains continue to grow globally and offer concepts unique to the country in which they are operating. For example, McDonald's uses touch-screen kiosks for ordering in Europe; home delivery in Asia; wine and Caprese salad on the menu in France; and Spam in Hawaii.

Trendy lunch trucks satisfy customers' appetites for quality, convenience, and value by offering an upscale menu, often prepared by well-known chefs (Figure 17). Because the lunch truck is cheaper to operate and maintain than a restaurant facility, prices can be lower without sacrificing food quality, and they are not just for lunch anymore. Dinner at the "lunch" truck is a popular event that has made it necessary to drop "lunch" from the name. Social media, such as Twitter, is used to determine the current location of one's favorite truck. To eliminate the chase around town to find one's favorite truck, portable food courts are the latest development in the Twitter-fueled gourmet food truck craze. A few changes have occurred since that first lunch wagon appeared in 1872!

Figure 17 A trendy lunch truck.
Source: Courtesy of Peter Barrett.

SUMMARY

The Delmonico's story is illustrative of the importance of history. It is an American success story in every sense. Growing from the small six-table bakery/café to multiple restaurant and hotel operations that became synonymous with excellence in food and service, the keys to their success are still relevant today: (1) The customer must be pleased; (2) the ingredients must be absolutely the best obtainable and of the highest quality; (3) pay little heed to (and indeed, even relish) complaints about the steepness of the prices; but (4) let the least hint of criticism about your food or service bring instant, personal, and complete attention. In addition to these precepts, it is clear that the Delmonico family paid constant attention to the smallest details, watched the changes in society and their community carefully, were never satisfied with the status quo, were creative and innovative, invested in the future, and were very hard working. The demise of the business can be attributed to the loss of the leadership provided by the family, prohibition, and the changing social and financial conditions of the time.

The foodservice history timeline presented in this chapter shows that religious orders, royal households, colleges, and inns were among the earliest organizations to practice quantity food production. During the seventeenth century, foodservices were established in colleges and hospitals or were places to meet to conduct business or to socialize.

Several advances in the fields of microbiology, physics, and industrial engineering led to improvements in how food is produced. The restaurant industry, as we know it today, had its beginnings in France. Innovative and visionary pioneers of the commercial foodservice sector introduced many new foods and concepts that continue to enjoy widespread use today.

World Wars I and II had a major impact on foodservice operations throughout the twentieth century.

Several pieces of key legislation have affected both fine-dining and school foodservice programs in the past and continue to do so today. The popularity of automobile travel was the stimulus for the quick-service, drive-in, drive-through, and fast-food concepts. The economic conditions in the country have a major impact on the foodservice industry in all sectors. The successful foodservice operators of the future will continue to learn from the past and to build on the foundations that have been laid by those who went before.

APPLICATION OF CHAPTER CONCEPTS

In order to provide "real life" applications of the concepts presented in this text, a case study is included at the end of the chapter. The scenarios are real, and the data presented are factual and current. Critical-thinking questions are supplied at the end of the case study scenario that will require students to engage in some higher-order thinking skills and, in some cases, further outside research.

"During the sixties, college campuses became centers of debate and scenes of protest more than ever before. Great numbers of young adults, baby boomers, reaching military draft age and not yet voting age (minimum voting age did not become 18 until 1971), caused a struggle which played out on many campuses as the country became more involved in the Vietnam War." (http://kclibrary.lonestar.edu/decade60.html; accessed 9/23/10)

Confrontations between large universities and the towns in which they were housed grew intense. In Madison, Wisconsin, the 35,000-student university was blamed for the deterioration of inner-city housing, the development of hippy ghettoes, the trashing of retail stores in the university commercial areas, and expansion of the university's tax-exempt property. At the same time students were demanding to live where and how they pleased, eat what and when they pleased, and come and go as they pleased.

In 1970, the University of Wisconsin–Madison, addressed the students' specific demands for more flexibility in meal plans and better food and privacy when dining. The board plan was replaced by meal tickets based on a three-level point system. With the points, students were able to eat in any residence hall or snack bar on campus. If they ran out of points, they would have to pay cash.

Because of the high wages paid foodservice workers at the time ($2.45 to $4/hour), more convenience foods were incorporated into the menus. This allowed for the closing or consolidation of some of the university's kitchens. The number of employees was reduced through attrition and transfers to other departments. Losses in china and silverware caused the foodservice to change to disposables. Because hours of service were a sore point with students, consideration was given to staying open 24 hours a day. If this were to happen, there would be a greater need for single-portion packets for off-hour use.

CRITICAL-THINKING QUESTIONS

1. What social, political, or economic trends may have caused the University of Wisconsin–Madison foodservice to make the changes it did in 1970?
2. How could the foodservice have addressed the students' demands for dining privacy?
3. What labor-saving solutions might have been used other than buying convenience foods?
4. Do you see a dichotomy between an attempt to offer "better food" and the incorporation of convenience foods into the menu?
5. How do the student demands in the 1960s differ from those of today? How are they the same?
6. What are ramifications of operating the university foodservice 24 hours a day?
7. Why would a 24-hour-a-day operation consider using single-portion packets in the off hours?
8. In your opinion, how could your university foodservice improve in today's economic climate?
9. What are the positives and negatives of the use of disposables?
10. What social, political, and economic trends are affecting university foodservices today?

CHAPTER REVIEW QUESTIONS

1. Based on what you have read in this chapter, why can it be said that all change is inevitable and cyclical?

2. Where did quantity foodservice get its start?
3. How have present-day lifestyles made an impact on commercial and on-site foodservices?
4. What unique concepts has the fast-food industry introduced to foodservice?
5. What major legislation established the National School Lunch program? How has the program changed over the years?
6. Where did foodservice cost accounting get its start?
7. What sciences led to the improvements in methods used in on-site foodservice, and what were these changes?
8. Taking a look at the Web sites of the restaurant chains that opened in the late 1990s, what do you see as a trend?
9. What is different about today's fine-dining restaurants when compared to Delmonico's?
10. What are the socioeconomic and political conditions and demographic changes that have influenced the foodservice industry in the past, and what is the impact they currently have today?

SELECTED WEB SITES

www.aw-drivein.com   (A&W Restaurant)
www.fastcasual.com   (Ideas and trends for the fast casual restaurant)
www.foodtimeline.org/food1.html   (Culinary history timeline)
www.godecookery.com   (History of food and feasts of the Middle Ages and Renaissance)
www.hollywoodphotographs.com   (Hollywood photograph collection)
www.kraftfoodscompany.com   (Kraft Foods)
www.mcdonalds.com   (McDonald's Corporation)
www.merrell-inn.com   (Historic Merrell Inn)
www.mediapost.com   (Media, Marketing, Advertising Professional's Resource)
www.neenah.org   (Future Neenah, a nonprofit civic development group)
www.nraef.org   (National Restaurant Association Educational Foundation)
www.nytimes.com   (*New York Times*)
http://restaurant.org   (National Restaurant Association)
www.restaurantchains.net   (Chain restaurant information)
http://sca.gmu.edu   (George Mason University Libraries)

The Systems Approach

Erwinova/Shutterstock

THIS CHAPTER BEGINS WITH THE CURRENT STATUS OF

the foodservice industry. The factors affecting the growth of some segments and the trends and challenges the industry faces are discussed. The trends that are

From Chapter 2 of *Foodservice Management: Principles and Practices*, Twelfth Edition, June Payne-Palacio, Monica Theis.
Copyright © 2012 by Pearson Education, Inc. Published by Pearson Prentice Hall. All rights reserved.

shown provide some basis for anticipating the future. These trends should alert managers to the demands that new developments and changes in this field may bring, so that they can prepare to meet them.

The systems approach is based on the idea that complex organizations are made up of interdependent parts (subsystems) that interact to achieve common goals.

Managers face decisions about how to organize foodservice departments for the efficient procurement, production, distribution, and service of their food and meals. Many options are available based on the type of food purchased, where the food is prepared in relation to where it is served, the time span between preparation and service, and the amount and kind of personnel and equipment required.

Foodservices with similar characteristics are grouped as particular types of production or operating systems. Each of the four types of foodservice operating systems found in the United States today is described with its identifying features, advantages, and disadvantages. The typical foodservice organizations that use each type are also identified. This description should provide a basis for managers to decide on the type of operation suitable for a particular situation.

KEY CONCEPTS

1. Socioeconomic trends and demographic changes continue to affect the foodservice industry.

2. To provide customer satisfaction and to run a financially sound operation, a foodservice manager must possess an awareness of current trends.

3. A number of challenges face the industry that will require innovative solutions.

4. The foodservice industry is vast and complex. The wide range of establishments in the industry may be classified into three major categories: commercial, on-site, and military. Each of these three may then be further categorized by type of operation.

5. The mission of a foodservice organization is the foundation on which all decisions should be made.

6. Systems theory evolved from earlier management theories such as scientific management, the human relations movement, operations research, and general science theory.

7. A system is a set of interdependent parts that work together to achieve a common goal. A foodservice organization is a system.

8. The systems model and some key systems definitions are important for developing an understanding of systems thinking.

9. The four major types of foodservice operations in existence today are conventional, ready-prepared, commissary, and assembly/serve. These classifications are based on differences in location of preparation, amount of holding time and method of holding cooked food, the purchase form of the food, and labor and equipment required.

10. Each of the four major types of foodservice operations has distinct advantages and disadvantages.

STATUS OF FOODSERVICE TODAY

Foodservice in the United States today is a complex and fast-changing industry, one that has expanded rapidly in the last half-century. It ranks as the number one retail employer with more than 13 million workers. A conservative estimate is that 47 percent of meals consumed are planned, prepared, and served outside the home in one of the estimated 945,000 establishments that exist in the United States.

FACTORS AFFECTING GROWTH

■ **KEY CONCEPT:** **Socioeconomic trends and demographic changes continue to affect the foodservice industry.**

The growth in patronage of foodservices may be attributed in part to socioeconomic trends and other demographic changes.

1. **The changing status of women** has had an influence on the workforce. In 1970, approximately 43 percent of women over 16 years of age were working, and in 1993, 59 percent of women in that age group were in the workforce. Today, two-thirds of the industry's employees are women, seven out of ten supervisors in food preparation and service occupations are women, and one-fourth of all eating-and-drinking-place firms are owned by women.

2. **The large number of single-person households** has an impact on the foodservice industry. Single people tend to spend a larger portion of their food budget on meals away from home than do family groups.

3. **Population growth in the United States seems to be slowing**. If this trend continues, there will be fewer young people and an increasing number of older persons in our society. The average age of the U.S. population, now nearly 36 years (it was 23 in 1900, 30 in 1980, 35 in 1996 and is expected to be 37 in 2010 and 39 in 2030), will continue to increase as the number of babies born remains low and the life span of adults continues to lengthen. These facts seem to indicate a need for more retirement and health care facilities, an older target market for restaurants, and a change in the age groups in the labor market.

4. **An increase in the Asian and Hispanic populations**, in which "married with children" units make up more than one-third of households, has led to a decrease in the number of meals eaten away from home. Hispanics spend more per week on groceries and visit the supermarket more often than any other ethnic group.

5. **The shift from manufacturing to technology and service industries** has created more office jobs and white-collar workers. In-plant feeding is down, and contract foodservice in business offices is increasing. The shortened work week of recent years has added leisure time and promoted the recreational foodservice segment of the industry.

6. **The awakened interest in the health and well-being of people and concern about improving the nutritional status of individuals** has also had an impact on foodservice. In fact, much research is being conducted and reported by the media concerning the impact of nutrition on health. People are becoming generally more knowledgeable about nutrition and food safety. As a result, most types of foodservices, from schools and colleges to airline and commercial operations, are offering healthier menu choices.

7. **The shortage of qualified foodservice personnel** is an internal factor that is having an impact on the industry. If the labor crisis continues, it may affect the foodservice system chosen and the form in which food is purchased by the operation.

All these factors have helped shape the foodservice industry into what it is today. Managers must always be alert to societal trends and have the ability to adjust their operations to the changing situation in order to be competitive and successful in this market.

TRENDS IN FOODSERVICE

KEY CONCEPT: **To provide customer satisfaction and to run a financially sound operation, a foodservice manager must possess an awareness of current trends.**

The National Restaurant Association assists restaurant owners and managers in identifying trends by surveying professional chefs each year. In 2009, 1,800 chefs were surveyed, and the top 5 trends they identified were:

1. **Sustainability**—This means using environmentally friendly practices and local sources for produce, meat, and seafood. The three main reasons for this trend are the desire for freshness, the increasing cost of transportation of products, and support for local communities and businesses.
2. **Nutrition**—Everyone is interested in improved nutrition, but there is particular focus on kids' meals, superfruits, half portions, and gluten-free and allergy-conscious meals.
3. **Simplicity and smaller portions**—During this time of economic uncertainly, consumers are looking for lower prices but good quality. This means simpler dishes and smaller portion sizes.
4. **Locally produced wine and beer**—combined with culinary/savory cocktails and artisan liquor.
5. **Liquid nitrogen freezing/chilling**—This is the hottest trend in preparation methods, followed by braising, sous vide, smoking, and oil-poaching confit.

In general, economic factors, issues of time, and concerns about safety and health appear to be the driving forces behind predictions of trends in the foodservice industry. Consumer prognosticators observe that many of today's hard-working consumers have fewer dollars to spend and a greater appreciation for value and convenience. Higher costs for gas, education, home energy, health care, and increasing interest rates on consumer debt have resulted in less discretionary income. In addition, the findings of a research survey were that two thirds of adults do not feel there is enough time in the day to meet all of their commitments. So, pressed for time and with less disposable income, food consumers seek dining experiences that are value-priced, convenient, or provide a psychological lift.

With increasing rates of heart disease, diabetes, and obesity and the media focus on food safety issues, the food that consumers eat is no longer simply a source of enjoyment and sustenance but a potential source of danger as well. Foodborne illnesses (such as mad cow disease, *Escherichia coli*, *Listeria*, and bird flu), the presence of pesticides and genetically modified ingredients, threats of terrorism in the food chain, artificial ingredients (such as trans fats), and the consumption of excess and/or unhealthy choices are of increasing concern. One trend-predicting company has stated that food safety and healthfulness are two of the most important issues that food chains and companies face in the coming years.

What, when, and where we eat is of vital interest to those in the foodservice industry. Foodservice operators who stay on top of emerging trends have a better chance of attracting and satisfying customers and thus boosting sales and beating the competition. However, predicting trends is not always an easy task. Fads in foodservice are common. In contrast to a trend, which grows and matures, a fad is a fleeting interest. Fads are usually fun innovations that add interest and excitement, whereas trends are fueled by such present conditions as the state of the economy and changes in lifestyles.

The National Restaurant Association identified 14 innovations that address some of the issues and challenges facing the foodservice industry today:

1. More energy-efficient equipment designed to reduce energy costs
2. Self-service options such as kiosks, tabletop ordering systems, and other self-service devices (including a self-serve ice cream dispenser the size of a vending machine that makes 96 varieties of ice cream—a customer can select ice cream type, flavors, and mix-ins through a touch screen and in 45 seconds receive the custom-made scoop)

3. Smaller restaurants and smaller, multitasking, high-volume equipment (such as combi ovens and half-size ovens/holding cabinets) to address skyrocketing real estate and construction costs

4. Electronic inventory management including handheld barcode scanners

5. Faster cooking equipment including a combi oven that can bake up to 32 loaves of bread in 10 minutes

6. More use of **sous vide** (pronounced "soo veed," which is French for "under vacuum"), a method of cooking food in plastic bags at lower temperatures to reduce food costs, conveniently prepare items, and improve flavor

7. On-the-spot training of employees using PDAs, cell phones, iPods, and MP3 players to improve productivity

8. Use of management software to do scheduling, matching staffing with customer flow

9. Increased use of environmentally friendly materials (made from recycled materials or from renewable resources and biodegradable) for disposable ware

10. Spill-free, leak-proof, dripless, take-out containers and in-house dispensers

11. Safer, more comfortable, and more fashionable shoes and safer, antimicrobial, and lighter floor mats to avoid costly slip-and-fall worker compensation claims

12. Whole- and multigrain products including rolls, rice, pasta, pita, cereals, and wraps that meet the USDA's new dietary guidelines

13. Trans-fat-free oils that are also low in saturated fat with a long fry life to address increasing customer demand for healthy options and keep food costs low

14. Bold, spicy flavors and cooking styles including Caribbean-, African-, and Indian-inspired dishes to satisfy the changing American palate

Sous vide
Food is precooked and vacuum packed for longer shelf life

Ongoing research reveals the following selected facts about the status of the industry:

- In 2010, the foodservice industry will operate more than 1 million units and post sales of $577 billion.
- More than 50 percent of all consumers visit a foodservice on their birthdays, making this the most popular occasion to eat out, followed by Mother's Day and Valentine's Day.
- August is the most popular month to eat out, and Saturday is the most popular day of the week for dining out.
- Roughly three out of four foodservice operators have an e-mail address for customer response or comment.
- Roughly half of table-service restaurant operators have a Web site.
- Three out of five table-service restaurant operators report having access to the Internet at the unit level.
- Roughly one-third of table-service restaurant operators plan to allocate a larger proportion of their budget to food safety.
- Hot sandwiches are more popular than cold ones.
- Americans are growing accustomed to ethnic items on nonethnic restaurant menus, and their taste for ethnic flavors is growing. Ethnic foods are growing immensely within noncommercial/health care foodservice. The most popular ethnic food choices are Mexican/Hispanic, Asian, and Italian; however, regional and demographic differences exist. For example, Chinese/Asian/Indian entrées appeal especially to baby boomers, upper-income individuals, and residents of the Western states.
- Customers want increased food variety, speed of service, and convenience. Consumers are demanding more variety, with 58 percent agreeing that they would prefer a greater variety of food and beverages.
- Pizza is big! Ninety-four percent of the population of the United States eats pizza, with approximately 3 billion pizzas sold each year. Children between the ages of 3 and 11 prefer pizza to all other foods for lunch and dinner. Each man, woman, and child eats an average of 46 slices (23 pounds) of pizza a year. Consumers are choosing pizzas that are more sophisticated in the way they look and taste. Sixty-two percent of the pizzas purchased are topped with meat.
- In the fast-food (quick service) segment of the industry, diet foods do not work, larger portions do work, value pricing is in, and the burger business is down but not out.

Even though consumption of French fries is down 10 percent, customers are replacing them with fried onion rings and desserts.

- For the first time in a long time, grocery and retail food dollar sales are exceeding foodservice revenues. More meals are being eaten at home, prepared from convenience items purchased in a grocery store.
- Even though two-thirds of Americans report eating healthier, the sheer amount of food consumed is at an all-time high.
- Consumption of red meat, poultry, and fish is also up, but leaner products have kept fat consumption down.

In response to these facts, current macro trends include an increase in the number of chain restaurant outlets, particularly steak houses (points of access); an increase in the use of technology; expansion of menus to include more sandwiches and fast Mexican, Asian, and fresh foods; **family value marketing** and **value pricing**; fast-food operations located within large discount stores; **multiple-branding** where several restaurant chains operate at the same location; and grocery store food products that are "fresh," fully cooked, seasoned (bold flavors), ready-to-eat, value-added, and shelf stable; that require no cleanup and leave minimal packaging waste; and that are resealable, portion controlled, and will not spill/spoil/crush in transit.

Among the various segments of the market, the following trends that follow these macro trends are emerging:

- Correctional foodservice is expanding rapidly as prison populations increase and the use of the **cook/chill method** continues to grow (Figure 1). Some estimate that by the year 2025, half of the prison population will be over 50 years of age. The need to provide more nutritional counseling, special diets, and healthy food choices will need to be balanced with cost effectiveness.
- The fine-dining restaurant business is down, but interest in cafés and bistros is increasing. Casual eateries continue to soar in popularity in response to burgeoning consumer demand for healthy, freshly prepared options. Operations such as Baja Fresh and Chipotle Mexican Grill have fused high-quality ingredients, upscale dishes, and quick service that seems to satisfy all of the current consumer demands.

Family value marketing

Pricing to appeal to family budgets

Value pricing

Pricing such that consumers feel they have received good value for amount paid

Multiple-branding

When several restaurant chains operate, or brand name products are sold, at the same location

Cook/chill method

Food production method in which food is prepared and cooked by conventional or other methods, then chilled and refrigerated for use at a later time

Figure 1 A cook/chill production facility.
Source: Courtesy of Chester-Jensen Company, Chester, PA.

- Recreational facility foodservices are expanding with **upscale menus**.
- School foodservice faces budget battles and legislative changes with an increase in the use of brand-name foods (**branding**) and the development of a business mentality.
- Hospital foodservice is employing **benchmarking** statistics to justify costs, introducing "grab-and-go" food in the staff cafeteria, espresso bars, limited patient menus, restaurant-style menus, comfort foods, and **satelliting** (selling food to other facilities).
- Foodservice in the lodging sector is incorporating mini-marts, ethnic fare, simpler foods, healthier selections, and buffets.
- College foodservice will see more self-service, grab-and-go options (including pizza), extended hours of operation, authentic vegetarian dishes, and full-flavored ethnic choices. The number one request in colleges and universities is for more chicken, followed by pizza, then Mexican food.
- Military foodservice faces base closings but also better food quality, consistency, and pricing with more branding, catering to civilian personnel, high-energy nightclubs, kiosks, and mini-units.
- Foodservice in nursing homes will serve to sicker and younger patients with more convenience products, more ethnic foods, more liberal diets, and a room service option. There is some movement back to preselect menus.
- Quick-service restaurants are offering the nutritional content of their menu on their Web sites, some with customized versions of food items. Some chains are testing programs to offer fresh fruit, milk, salads, and low-fat options of menu items.

The addition of new and exciting menu items will remain an important competitive tool in all foodservice segments. Food trends include specialty coffees; entrée salads; high-flavor condiments; spicy food with Mexican pegged as the next biggest ethnic cuisine after Italian; specialty desserts; **comfort foods**, such as meat loaf, roast chicken, mashed potatoes, and fruit cobbler; pasta; and beef. A number of industry experts predict that trends on the way out are bagels, black serving plates, and 20-word menu titles. Taking their place will be such trends as the three S's—soups, sandwiches, and salads—as well as authentic foods and dining environments, manufacturer-chef partnerships, speed scratch cooking, tea, regionalized ethnic foods, and non-meal-period opportunities, such as high tea. One business expert sums it up with, "It's now all about the 4-F's—family, food, fast, and fun!" To this list could be added a fifth F—fresh.

Sociological predictions that Americans will face even longer work hours and there will be more dual-income families in the years ahead have led more and more foodservice operators to offer what are called **home meal replacements** (HMRs) or **meal solutions**. HMRs run the gamut from gourmet meals, healthy dinners for two, comfort food entrées, bagged salads, bakery items, components that may include sauces ready to be poured over pasta (so-called dump-and-stir cooking), to groceries such as fresh produce and milk. Take-out stations are turning up in fullservice dining venues such as the Outback Steakhouse. Foodservices in hospitals, businesses, industry, and colleges are natural settings for the HMR market, as are supermarkets that are now offering a bevy of heat-and-serve fare either prepared on-site or delivered from a nearby commissary. Two recent supermarket strategies have included in-store chefs who cook food to order while you wait and the issuance of weekly menus so customers know to drop by on Tuesday for beef stew or Friday for chicken Kiev.

The **display cooking** trend in upscale restaurants is finding its way into on-site foodservices (Figure 2). Kitchenless, storage-free designs, where all food is displayed and prepared in full view, appeals to all the senses as customers see, hear, smell, and taste as food goes from raw to cooked.

In the noncommercial sector, whether to operate the foodservice with **in-house management** or to use a **contract foodservice** company continues to be an important and difficult decision to make. After years of cutting the bottom line to control food and labor costs, contractors are shifting their focus to improving promotions, services, and price–value perceptions. Those who choose to stay with or return to in-house management cite the opportunity to increase revenue, improve quality and control, and stamp the operation with a unique signature as the reasons.

Upscale menus

Fancier, more expensive foods, often with a gourmet appeal

Branding

The use of nationally or locally labeled products for sale in an existing foodservice operation

Benchmarking

The Total Quality Management measurement tool that provides an opportunity for a company to set attainable goals based on what other companies are achieving

Satelliting

Selling and/or delivering food to other facilities

Comfort foods

Foods associated with the comfort of home and family; includes traditional American dishes

Home meal replacements

Prepared or partially prepared foods to take home

Meal solutions

Prepared or partially prepared foods to take home

Display cooking

Restaurant design where the kitchen may be viewed by the diners

In-house management

Foodservice within an organization operated by the organization

Contract foodservice

Foodservice within an organization operated by an outside company

Figure 2 A custom-built island of cooking equipment allows for the ultimate in display cooking.
Source: Courtesy of the Montague Company, Hayward, CA.

CHALLENGES FACING THE INDUSTRY

■ **KEY CONCEPT:** **A number of challenges face the industry that will require innovative solutions.**

The top challenges facing the industry in the coming years are:

- The economy/recession
- Competition
- Building/maintaining sales volume
- Recruiting and retaining employees
- Labor costs

Some suggestions to address these challenges in the next 25 years have been made by executives in the industry. They include the following:

- Offering better pay and benefits (including health care, child care subsidies, and flextime) and promoting advancement opportunities to minorities who may lack work experience
- Supplier-managed shared labor pools available to operators on an as-needed basis
- Special event teams that travel with menus, decorations, and entertainment from institution to institution
- Supplier-managed systems to track products through the entire production/packaging/distribution/usage cycle
- Robotic equipment programmed for cleaning services and available for lease
- Loading docks on roofs with delivery by Hovercraft

CLASSIFICATION OF FOODSERVICES

■ **KEY CONCEPT:** **The foodservice industry is vast and complex. The wide range of establishments in the industry may be classified into three major categories: commercial, on-site, and military. Each of these three may then be further categorized by type of operation.**

The foodservice industry is broad and encompasses a wide range of establishments. They may be classified into three major groups:

- Commercial (restaurants, supermarkets, convenience stores, delis, snack bars, and other retail food establishments)
- Noncommercial (sometimes called institutional or on-site)—business, educational, governmental, correctional, or other organizations that operate their own foodservice
- Military

Scope of Services. Within each of these types of foodservice organizations, a broad **scope of services** is offered. The phrase *scope of services* in foodservice operations refers to the number and types of business units offered through individual foodservice operations. The scope is typically a mix of retail and non–revenue-generating units. For example, food and nutrition departments in hospitals offer patient meal and nutrition services. Both of these are typically non–revenue-generating units. These same departments, however, likely offer at least one retail unit. The most common of these is the employee/visitor cafeteria, where prices may be set to generate revenue for the entire department. Other retail units include satellite cafés, food courts, coffee kiosks, and vending and catering services. (Figure 3 includes several examples of scopes of services for a variety of foodservice operations.)

It is important for a foodservice manager to recognize the scope of services offered by a foodservice to gain an appreciation for the complexity of the department. Knowledge of the scope will also help the manager understand the financial status of the department and the opportunities to contain costs or generate revenue. Menus, production methods, and service

Scope of services
The number and types of business units offered by individual foodservice operations

Large Urban Hospital		
Patient Services	Retail	Nutrition Services
Tray Service	Employee/Visitor Cafes	Inpatient MNT/Ed
Room Service	Vending	Outpatient MNT/Ed
Nourishments	Catering	Community Education
	Satellite Units	Research Diets
	–Kiosks	

Community-based Hospital			
Patient Services	Employee Foodserv.	Community Foodserv.	Nutrition Services
Tray Service	Cafeteria	Mobile Meals	Inpatient MNT/Ed
Room Service	Vending	Child Care Ctr	Outpatient MNT/Ed
Nourishments	Catering	Adult Care Ctr	Community Education

School		
USDA Child Nutrition Program	Retail	Other
Breakfast	A la Carte	Employee Meals
Lunch	Vending	Catering
After School Snacks	Food Court	
Summer Feeding		

College/University	
Resident Halls	Retail
Dining Halls	Kiosks
Room Service	Faculty Executive Dining
	Delis
	Convenience Stores

Figure 3 Examples of scope of services of four foodservice organizations.

styles will vary among the various units, which will in turn influence how each unit needs to be managed. Finally, the food manager must understand the needs of each unit to allocate effectively limited resources among the units during the budget planning process. Also, within each of these groups, there are myriad types of foodservice establishments; each of these establishments has its own objectives, goals, and type of organization and management. Although they may seem widely divergent, each is concerned with providing a foodservice to some segment of the public. There is a commonality among them that can be identified for the purpose of grouping them into specific types of foodservice operations.

FOODSERVICE OPERATIONS

The Nature of Foodservice Management

■ **KEY CONCEPT:** The mission of a foodservice organization is the foundation on which all decisions should be made.

Mission statement

A summary of an organization's purpose, customers, products, and services

Objectives

Specific and measurable goals or targets of an organization

All organizations have a mission that evolves from their reason for existence. A written **mission statement** is rapidly becoming a common document for guiding organizational decision making. To achieve this mission effectively, the organization must then develop specific targets or **objectives**. For example, a foodservice organization's mission might be to satisfy customers by serving high-quality, nutritious food at reasonable prices while achieving a desired profit for the organization. The objectives in this case might be such benchmarks as percent of customers marking satisfied and above on a rating scale, increase in total sales and number of customers, number of "regular" customers, and net profit. It is the responsibility of management to achieve the organization's objectives.

A generic definition of management is that it is the effective, efficient integration and coordination of resources to achieve the desired objectives of the organization. *Managerial effectiveness* may be measured by how well the organization achieves its objectives over time. *Efficiency*, in contrast to effectiveness, is a measure of short-term objectives. If a foodservice paid $1 for a head of lettuce and used an entire head for an individual salad, we would surmise that a lot of lettuce was being wasted. This is a comparison of input of lettuce to output of one salad—an inefficient use of resources, a short-term measure. The effectiveness measure would be to produce a high-quality, nutritious salad at a reasonable price in order to satisfy potential customers and return a profit to the organization.

Some of the functions performed by foodservice managers include the following:

- Selection, orientation, and provision of ongoing training and supervision of staff
- Monitoring of staff workload and performance and designation of assignments appropriately
- Development and control of operational and capital budgets
- Preparation of financial reports
- Ensuring quality, safety, and sanitation of all food prepared

Each of these functions is discussed in more detail.

Of prime importance to any organization in this increasingly competitive world is how well it is able to adapt, reach its objectives, and serve its mission. Viewing the organization as a system is essential in this endeavor, as is choosing the correct production system for the particular needs or characteristics of the operation. Systems management is discussed first, followed by a section on production systems.

THE SYSTEMS CONCEPT AND APPROACH

■ **KEY CONCEPT:** Systems theory evolved from earlier management theories such as scientific management, the human relations movement, operations research, and general science theory.

Before discussing foodservice organizations as "systems," this section reviews the systems concept and systems approach and how systems theory has evolved from other theories of management. This review establishes a common basis of understanding and makes application of the systems concept to foodservice an easy transition.

A Brief History of Systems Theory. Organizations are systems. This concept has evolved gradually from earlier theories of management. Traditional views in prominence in the late nineteenth and early twentieth centuries included the scientific management theory, which puts emphasis on efficient work performance. Workers were trained to perform a task in what was perceived to be the one best way. If all performed efficiently, the goals could be reached. Often referred to as the classical approach to management, the principles developed from this theory are still believed by most managers to be important to the success of modern organizations.

In the late 1920s, research conducted by Elton Mayo and his associates at the Hawthorne Plant of the Western Electric Company led to the findings that social and psychological factors were critically important determinants of worker satisfaction and productivity. Thus, the human relations movement in industry began.

After World War II, quantitative methods began to be employed for the purposes of decision making. The application of computer technology and mathematical models was collectively called operations research or management science.

All of these early theories of management were internally focused despite the work of several management theorists who described organizations as systems interrelated with their environments. During the 1960s and 1970s, as organizations faced ever more turbulent social, economic, and technological environments, a broadly strategic orientation to organizational management began to emerge: systems theory. This new approach placed a greater emphasis on the organization's relationship with its environment and is based on the assumption that performance can be improved by aligning the mission and design of an organization with environmental constraints and demands.

This evolutionary process is graphically depicted in the triangular management model (Figure 4). As shown in this model, current concerns for efficiency and productivity come from the classical management perspective; current concerns for organizational

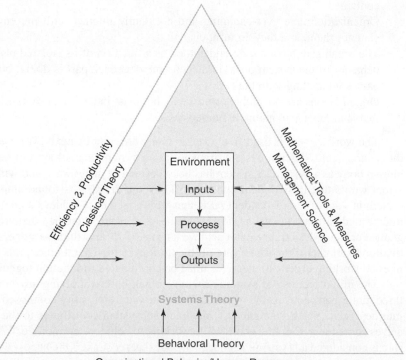

Figure 4 The triangular management model.

45

behavior and the importance of human resources come from the behavioral management perspective; and current concerns for mathematical tools and measures come from the management science perspective.

At times called the open systems theory, it is based on a 1949 work by Ludwig von Bertalanffy in which he described the nature of biological and physical systems. Katz and Kahn's groundbreaking classic, *The Social Psychology of Organizations*, published in 1966, paved the way for applying Bertalanffy's general science systems approach to the management of organizations. Contributions of this work include the concepts of organizational "inputs" and "outputs," which encouraged managers to pay attention to economic, psychological, and sociological factors in their analysis of an organization; discouraging the "one best way" approach; and recommending a contingency model in which factors in the environment help to determine organizational design. In 1968, Churchman suggested that the systems approach is imperative for strategic management and should involve five key essential processes: identification of the organization's fundamental values and goals and the objectives that arise from them (desired outputs); assessment of the organization's environment—forces outside the organization that may be opportunities or threats (environment); assessment of the organization's resources and capabilities (inputs); identification of the organization's structure (operations); and development of the management structure (management).

> ■ **KEY CONCEPT:** **A system is a set of interdependent parts that work together to achieve a common goal. A foodservice organization is a system.**

Some Basics of Systems Theory. Some foundational concepts underpin systems theory. They are as follows:

- Organizations are "collections of parts" united by prescribed interactions and are designed for accomplishing specified objectives and goals.
- Organizations are highly complex entities in which attention must be paid to myriad inputs, processes, outputs, feedback loops, and the general environment under which the organization functions.
- Organizations operate within a society and, as such, are interdependent, not self-contained.
- Organizations are ever-changing and constantly interact with the environment that changes them, and they, in turn, change it.
- The organization cannot be understood as a function of its isolated parts because the behavior of the system does not depend on what each part is doing, but on how each part is interacting with the rest.
- Organizations are not stable or unstable, but exist in a state of **dynamic equilibrium** that is necessary to maintain homeostasis.

The word **system** is used freely and in many different contexts. We read and speak of the solar system, defense system, transportation system, school system, and even of the human body as a system. A system has been defined in many ways and with so many different words that it may seem confusing. This commonality is found among systems: A system is a set of interdependent parts that work together to achieve a common goal. The interrelated parts are known as **subsystems**, each dependent on the others for achieving its goals. For example, a train cannot achieve its goal of transporting passengers from one destination to another if the wheels are off the track even though all other parts of the train are in good working order. All elements must be coordinated to function together for success.

The initial premise of **systems theory** is that, before applying any concept from the three major perspectives, the organization is viewed as an entity composed or made up of interdependent parts—the subsystems. Each subsystem contributes to the whole and receives something from the whole while working to achieve common goals. Management's role is considered a "systematic endeavor," one that recognizes the needs of all of the parts. Decisions are made in light of the overall effect of management on the organization as a

Dynamic equilibrium

Reacting to changes and forces, both internal and external, in ways that often create a new state of equilibrium and balance

System

A set of interdependent parts that work together to achieve a common goal

Subsystems

The interdependent parts of a system, the parts of a system

Systems theory

Viewing the organization as a whole made up of interdependent parts

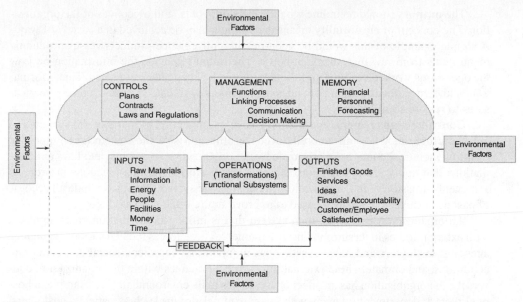

Figure 5 The systems model.

whole and its objectives. This type of leadership is the systems approach—that is, an acceptance of the systems theory of management and its use as a style of managing. The recognition that a change made in one part of the system has an impact on all other parts of the system is an example of the use of the systems approach. Three areas of common use of this approach are as follows:

- **Systems philosophy or thinking** is a way of thinking about phenomena in terms of the whole, including parts, components, or subsystems, with emphasis on their inter-relationships.
- **Systems analysis** is a method for problem solving or decision making.
- **Systems management** is the application of systems theory to managing organizational systems or subsystems.

■ **KEY CONCEPT:** **The systems model and some key systems definitions are important for developing an understanding of systems thinking.**

A Systems Model. Various diagrams can be used to illustrate an organization as a system with its inputs, the subsystems that perform the operations, and the outputs, together with their interactions with the environment. One diagram that is clear, simple, and easily adaptable to specific organizations is shown in Figure 5.

Some Key Systems Definitions. Money, raw materials, time, equipment, energy (utilities), facilities, and personnel, together with the necessary information, are the **inputs** into the system. The work that is performed, known as **operations**, transforms the inputs (such as raw material) into outputs (such as finished products or services). **Transformation** of these inputs into outputs takes place in the functional subsystems shown in Figure 6. Inputs, transformations, and outputs may be thought of as the Main Street of the foodservice system.

Systems philosophy or thinking

A way of thinking about phenomena in terms of the whole, the parts, and their interrelationships

Systems analysis

A method of problem solving or decision making

Systems management

Application of systems theory to managing organizations

Inputs

Resources such as money, material, time, and information required by a system

Operations

The work performed to transform inputs into outputs

Transformation

The processes required to change inputs into outputs

Figure 6 The functional subsystems of a traditional foodservice operation.

Outputs

Finished products and services of an organization

Equifinality

The same outputs may be achieved from different inputs or transformational processes

Feedback

Information on how operations worked or failed, or how they should be changed or modified to restore equilibrium

Controls

The self-imposed plans and legal documents that affect the organization's function

Management

The integration and coordination of resources to achieve the desired objectives of the organization

Memory

Records of past performance that assist in improving future effectiveness

Open system

A system that interacts with external forces in the environment

Linking processes

Methods used to unify a system

Entropy

The amount of disorder, uncertainty, or randomness in a system

Homeostasis

Proper balance of the internal environment

Hierarchy of systems

Characteristic of organizational structure ranging from subsystems to systems to suprasystems

Suprasystems

Larger entities, each made up of a number of systems

Interdependency

The parts of the system interact and are dependent on one another

The **outputs** should be in line with the mission, goals, and objectives of the organization. The concept of **equifinality** means that outputs may be achieved in a variety of ways. A simple example of this would be good-quality convenience products versus producing menu items from raw ingredients in-house. The outputs provide the information on how the operations worked or failed, or how they should be changed or modified. This information is known as **feedback** and provides management with data to initiate corrective measures to restore equilibrium.

Controls, **management**, and **memory** have an impact on all parts of the system and are, therefore, shown as an umbrella over the other parts of the system (see Figure 5). Controls include the internal plans made by the organization, contracts, and laws and regulations that apply to the operation. Management performs various functions in order to achieve the mission of the organization. *Memory* is the systems term to include all records of past performance that may be used to improve future effectiveness.

An organization is also an **open system** that is influenced by and interacts regularly with external forces in its surrounding environment. These forces include various regulatory agencies, customers and other constituents, competitors, suppliers, social and economic conditions, and climate. These external forces affect practices within the organization; conversely, the organization has an effect on the forces in its environment. (For example, a hospital dietary department interacts with many external groups such as patients, customers, medical staff, hospital administration, and some regulatory agencies. The department, in turn, affects the external groups with which it interacts.) In contrast, a closed system does not interact with its environment. Most examples of closed systems would be mechanical in nature. All organizations are open systems, but some make the mistake of ignoring their environment or behaving as though it were not important.

The resulting outputs are ready-to-serve foods, clientele and personnel satisfaction, and financial accountability. Ideas generated from the results of operations are the feedback for use in improving the operation as necessary. All parts of the system are linked by management functions, such as planning, organizing, and staffing. To accomplish unification of the system, managers use various **linking processes**, such as communication and decision making. Surrounding the system are environmental factors, such as regulatory agencies, the economy, social and cultural aspects, and the various constituents of the operation, such as customers and suppliers.

Change is constant and multidimensional. Change causes uncertainty and creates disorder or **entropy** in the organization. The organization must react to every change, force, or random disturbance, both internal and external, in ways that often create a new state of equilibrium and balance. These reactions are a series of modifications of equal size and opposite direction to those that created the disturbance—a dynamic or moving equilibrium. The goal of these modifications is to maintain the internal balances, or **homeostasis**. Systems must have homeostasis in order to have stability and survive. Homeostatic systems are ultrastable in that everything in their internal, structural, and functional organization contributes to the maintenance of the organization.

Feedback of information from a point of operation and from the environment to a control center or centers can provide the data necessary to initiate corrective measures to restore equilibrium. Organizations and the world of which they are a part consist of a **hierarchy of systems**. Thus, a corporation is composed of divisions, departments, sections, and groups of individual employees. Also, the corporation is part of larger systems or **suprasystems**, such as all the firms in its industry, firms in its metropolitan area, and perhaps an association of many industries such as the National Restaurant Association (NRA) or the American Hospital Association. **Interdependency** is a key concept in systems theory. The elements of a system interact with one another and are interdependent. Generally, a change in one part of an organization affects other parts of that organization. Sometimes the interdependencies are not fully appreciated when changes are made. A change in organizational structure and workflow in one department may unexpectedly induce changes in departments that relate to the first department. Systems theory contains the doctrine that the whole of a structure or entity is more than the sum of its parts. This is called **wholism**. The cooperative, synergistic working together of members of a department or team often yields a total product that exceeds the sum of their individual contributions. **Synergy** is achieved when the various units of an organization share common goals.

Wholism
The whole of the organization is more than the sum of the parts

Benefits of Systems Thinking.   Research in management sciences has shown that organizations should be seen as systems much like people, plants, and animals. There are many benefits for managers who adopt a systems view of their organization. Systems theory helps organize a large body of information that might otherwise make little sense. The use of systems thinking aids in diagnosing the interactive relationships among task, technology, environment, and organizational members. In contrast to the classical models of organization, the systems approach has shown that managers operate in fluid, dynamic, and often ambiguous situations. The manager generally is not in full control of these situations. Managers must learn to shape actions and to make progress toward goals, keeping in mind that the results achieved will be affected by many factors and forces.

Synergy
The working together of parts of a system such that the outcomes are greater than individual effort would achieve

Among specific benefits of the systems approach are the following:

- **More effective problem solving.** To effectively solve problems, it is imperative that the real causes of the problems be identified and addressed. Without an understanding of the "big picture" of the organization, the focus on problem solving will tend to be only on the behavior or event, not on the system or structure that caused the problem to occur.
- **More effective communication.** Ongoing communication among all parts of the organization is critical for the success of any system. A clear understanding of the parts of the organization and how they relate to each other is required in order to know what to communicate and to whom.
- **More effective planning.** The planning process requires starting with the mission statement, objectives, and goals of the organization and determining what outputs will indicate that the desired results have been achieved, what processes will achieve these results, and what inputs are required to conduct these processes in the system.
- **More effective organizational development.** Effective organizational development requires a knowledge and application of the principles of strategic planning, leadership development, team building, change, and personnel management. A manager must have a good understanding of the overall systems in their organization including its major functions, departments, processes, teams, and individual employees in order to employ these various strategies in an effective manner.

TYPES OF FOODSERVICE SYSTEMS

> **KEY CONCEPT:** **The four major types of foodservice operations in existence today are conventional, ready-prepared, commissary, and assembly/serve. These classifications are based on differences in location of preparation, amount of holding time and method of holding cooked food, the purchase form of the food, and labor and equipment required.**

Foodservices that operate in a similar manner, or with common elements, give the basis for grouping them into specific types of systems. Four major types of foodservice systems are in operation in the United States today.

The systems differ in where the food is prepared in relation to where it is served, the time span between preparation and service, the forms of foods purchased, methods of holding prepared foods, and the amount and kind of labor and equipment required. These four types of foodservice systems are conventional, ready-prepared (cook/chill or cook/freeze), commissary (central production kitchen), and assembly/serve.

Conventional.   As the name implies, the **conventional system** has been used traditionally throughout the years. Menu items are prepared in a kitchen in the same facility where the

Conventional system
Raw foods are purchased, prepared on-site, and served soon after preparation

meals are served and held a short time, either hot or cold, until serving time. In earlier years, all preparation, as well as cooking, took place on the premises, and foods were prepared from basic ingredients. Kitchens included a butcher shop, a bakery, and vegetable preparation units.

Over the years, a modified conventional system has evolved because of labor shortages, high labor costs, and the availability of new forms of food. To reduce time and labor costs, foodservice managers began to purchase some foods with "built-in" labor. Foods from butcher shops, in which meats were cut from prime cuts, and bakeshops are gone from most "conventional" kitchens today. Meats are now purchased ready to cook or portion controlled; bread and many bakery items are purchased from a commercial bakery or prepared from mixes; and produce is available in prewashed, pretrimmed, prepeeled, cut, frozen, or canned forms, all of which reduce the amount of production and labor required on the premises. Foods with varying degrees of processing are now used in conventional foodservice systems.

This system is most effective in situations and locales where the labor supply is adequate and of relatively low cost; where sources of food supplies, especially raw foods, are readily available; and when adequate space is allocated for foodservice equipment and activities.

Typical users of the conventional system are smaller foodservice operations such as independent restaurants, schools, colleges, hospital and health care facilities, homes for specialized groups, and in-plant employee feeding.

> ### ■ KEY CONCEPT: Each of the four major types of foodservice operations has distinct advantages and disadvantages.

Advantages of the Conventional System.   The conventional system has many advantages. Quality control is considered of primary importance. Through the menus, recipes, and quality of ingredients selected by the manager, the foodservice achieves its individuality and standard of quality desired. It is not dependent on the availability and variety of frozen entrées and other menu items commercially prepared. This system is more adaptable to the regional, ethnic, and individual preferences of its customers than is possible with other systems. From an economic standpoint, greater flexibility is possible in making menu changes to take advantage of good market buys and seasonal fluctuations. Also, less freezer storage space is required than with the other systems, and distribution costs are minimal, both of which save on energy use and costs.

Disadvantages of the Conventional System.   The conventional system produces an uneven, somewhat stressful workday caused by meal period demands. Because the menu differs each day, the workloads vary, making it difficult for workers to achieve high productivity. Skilled workers may be assigned tasks that could be completed by nonskilled employees just to fill their time between meal periods. When three meals a day are served, two shifts of employees are required to cover the 12- to 15-hour or longer workday. Scheduling workers may be difficult with overlapping shifts.

Rationale for Conventional Foodservice Systems.   Traditionally, effective foodservice administrators with conventional foodservice systems have utilized a skilled labor force for food production 13 to 14 hours per day. Given adequate food production equipment and available skilled labor, foods may be procured with limited amounts of processing. However, with constantly rising labor costs within the foodservice industry, the current trend in conventional foodservice systems is to procure more extensively processed foods.

Ready-prepared system

Also known as cook/chill or cook/freeze systems; foods are prepared on-site, then chilled or frozen, and stored for reheating at a later time

Ready-Prepared (Cook/Chill or Cook/Freeze).   In the **ready-prepared system**, foods are prepared on the premises, then chilled or frozen and stored for use at some later time. Thus, foods are "ready," prepared well in advance of the time needed. This is the distinct feature of ready-prepared foodservice systems—the separation between time of preparation and service. Unlike the commissary system, foods are prepared on-site; however, the place of preparation is not the place of service. In addition, the food is not for immediate use as in the conventional system.

Figure 7 A blast chiller used to bring bulk food from cooking temperature to 37°F in 90 minutes or less.
Source: Courtesy of Burlodge USA, Inc.

The **cook/chill method** can be accomplished in a variety of ways, but basically the food is prepared and cooked by conventional or other methods, then its temperature is brought down to 37°F in 90 minutes or less, and it is refrigerated for use at a later time. In one variation, prepared food is either pre-plated or put into bulk containers such as hotel pans, chilled in a blast chiller (Figure 7), stored in a refrigerator for up to five days, **rethermalized** (sometimes in carts such as that shown in Figure 8), and served. In another method, food items are prepared in kettles, pumped into special air- and water-tight plastic packages that hold 1.5 to 3 gallons, given an ice-water bath in a tumbler-chiller

Cook/chill method

Food production method in which food is prepared and cooked by a conventional or other method, then quickly chilled for use at a later time

Rethermalized

Chilled or frozen foods are returned to eating temperature

Figure 8 Carts that use convection heating to rethermalize one side of the tray while the other side remains cold.
Source: Courtesy of Burlodge USA, Inc.

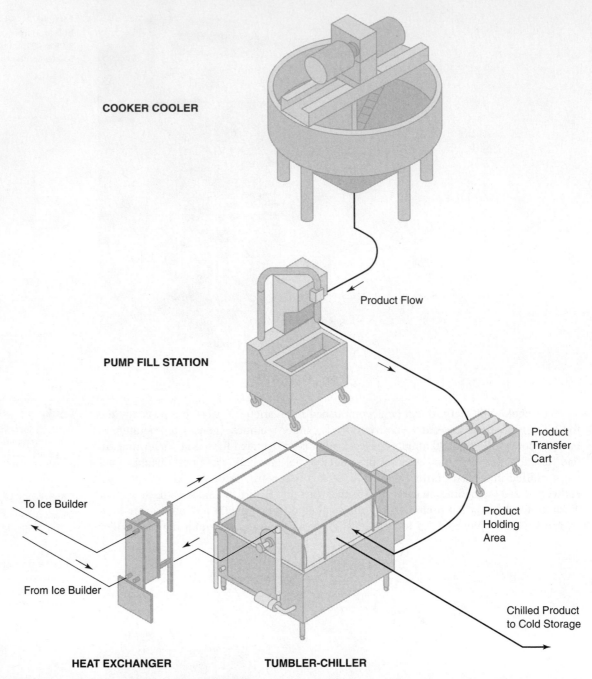

COOKER COOLER

Product Flow

PUMP FILL STATION

Product
Transfer
Cart

To Ice Builder

Product
Holding
Area

From Ice Builder

Chilled Product
to Cold Storage

HEAT EXCHANGER   **TUMBLER-CHILLER**

Figure 9   One method of cook/chill food preparation using a pump fill station, tumbler-chiller, and cook-chill tank.
Source: Courtesy of Chester-Jensen Co., Chester, P A.

(Figure 9), and stored in the refrigerator. Food items prepared by this method may be held for up to 45 days. Meat is prepared in this method by putting it in a large tank that automatically cooks the meat and then chills it in ice water as soon as the cooking cycle is over. Meats can then be refrigerated for up to 60 days.

In the **cook/freeze method**, a blast freezer or cryogenic freezing system must be available to freeze foods quickly and thus prevent cell damage. Foods for freezing may be pre-plated, but more often they are stored in bulk, which requires less freezer storage space.

Note that the ready-prepared entrées and vegetables undergo two heating periods: first, when foods are prepared and, second, after storage to reheat them for service to the consumer. Ready-prepared systems were developed to offset the critical shortage and high cost of skilled foodservice employees. Such systems were also seen as a way to even out

Cook/freeze method

Food production method in which food is prepared and cooked by conventional or other methods, then frozen for use at a later time

the workload from day to day and during each day because only certain menu items are prepared on any given day to build up an inventory for future use.

Advantages of the Ready-Prepared System. The advantages of the ready-prepared system are related to reducing the "peaks and valleys" of workloads that may be found in the conventional system. Production scheduling to build up the menu item inventory can be on a 40-hour week, eight-hour day, without early morning and late evening shifts. Employee turnover is decreased, and recruitment of new employees is enhanced by offering staff a more normal work week and reasonable hours.

Other advantages are reductions in production labor costs, improved quality and quantity control by decreasing job stress related to production deadlines, and improved nutrient retention by decreasing time food is held within the serving temperature range. Use of equipment is more balanced when preparation is spread over eight hours, rather than at mealtime only.

In this system, management has close control over menu selections, the quality of ingredients, and portion size and quantity. This is not always true in other systems, especially with the assembly/serve system. Menu variety is potentially greater with this system, because many items can be prepared and stored for future use.

One advantage that the ready-prepared system has over the commissary system is the lack of worry about delivery from the central production kitchen. When foods are prepared and stored on the premises, menu items are available on call, and no waiting is involved.

Disadvantages of the Ready-Prepared System. One disadvantage is the need for large cold storage and freezer units, which take space and add to energy costs. Depending on the method, a blast chiller or blast freezer is required, which is expensive to purchase and operate. Control for food safety is especially essential with the cook/freeze method. As Longree and Armbruster warn, "the production of precooked frozen foods must not ever be handled in a haphazard fashion; unless the freezing operation can be a continuous, streamlined, bacteriologically controlled, short-time process, the bacteriological hazards could be formidable" (Longree, K., and Armbruster, G.: *Quantity Food Sanitation*. 5th ed. New York: Wiley, 1996).

Because frozen foods are prone to structural and textural changes, extensive modifications in the recipe and ingredients are usually necessary to offset cell damage and to ensure high-quality products.

Appropriate and adequate equipment for the rethermalization of foods prior to service is essential and can be costly. Microwave and convection ovens are the equipment usually used in service units located near the consumers.

Although ready-prepared systems have been used primarily by large-volume institutions and centralized commissary chain setups, such as health care units, employee feeding facilities, airlines, and correctional institutions, lower volume applications have begun to appear. Schools, supermarkets, fast-food companies, and large restaurants are now utilizing this technology.

Rationale for Ready-Prepared Foodservice Systems. Mass-producing and freezing food may reduce labor expenditures by more effective use of labor in selected situations. Peak demands for labor may be removed because production is designed to meet future rather than daily needs. Furthermore, less-skilled employees can be trained to heat and serve menu items, thus reducing the number of highly skilled workers required by the system. Food procurement in volume may decrease food costs for the system. A foodservice system based on ready-prepared products is contraindicated if additional expenditures for storage facilities, equipment, and food inventory cannot be absorbed by the organization.

Commissary (Central Production Kitchen). The **commissary system** is described as a large, central production kitchen with centralized food purchasing and delivery of prepared foods to service (satellite) units located in separate, remote areas for final preparation and service. This system was made possible by the development of large, sophisticated equipment for preparing and cooking large quantities of food from the raw, unprocessed state. Foodservice organizations with many serving units, sometimes widely separated as in a large city school system, sought ways to consolidate operations and reduce costs. The commissary system is the result.

Commissary system
A central production kitchen or food factory with centralized food purchasing and delivery to off-site facilities for final preparation

Prepared foods may be stored frozen, chilled, or hot-held. Menu items may be distributed in any one of several forms: bulk hot, bulk cold, or frozen for reheating and portioning at the satellite serving units; or pre-portioned and pre-plated for service and chilled or frozen before delivery.

Typical users of this system are airline caterers, large city school systems, and franchised or chain restaurant organizations that provide food for their various outlets and vending companies.

Advantages of the Commissary System. The commissary foodservice system can realize cost savings due to large-volume purchasing and reduced duplication of the labor and equipment that would be required if each serving unit prepared its own food. Some facilities where food is served may not have adequate space for a production kitchen, or the space can be better utilized for some other purpose. Quality control may be more effective and consistent with only one unit to supervise.

Disadvantages of the Commissary System. Food safety and distribution of prepared foods may be concerns. There are many critical points in mass food production where contamination could occur. Employing a food microbiologist or someone knowledgeable about safe techniques in mass food handling with specialized equipment is highly desirable, yet often costly.

Food must be loaded and transported in such a manner that it is maintained at the correct temperature for safety and is of good quality and appearance when received for service. This requires specialized equipment and trucks for delivery. Poor weather conditions, delivery truck breakdowns, or other such catastrophes can result in food arriving late, causing irritating delays in meal service.

Another disadvantage is the high cost of purchase, maintenance, and repair of the sophisticated and specialized equipment needed for this type of production and distribution.

Rationale for Commissary Foodservice Systems. The commissary foodservice principles have been adopted in systems where service areas are remote from, yet accessible to, the production center. This concept can be applied to reduce the duplication of production labor and equipment that occurs if production centers are located at each foodservice site. Space requirements at the service sites are minimized because limited production equipment is required. By centralizing food procurement and production, the economies of volume purchasing may be realized. Commissary foodservice concepts are employed to meet various operational objectives related to effective use of resources.

Assembly/serve system

Also known as the "kitchenless kitchen," fully prepared foods are purchased, stored, assembled, heated, and served

Assembly/Serve. The **assembly/serve system** requires no on-site food production. This has led to the use of the term *kitchenless kitchen*. Fully prepared foods are purchased and require only storage, final assembling, heating, and serving. Assembly/serve systems evolved with the development of a variety of high-quality frozen entrées and other food products that have appeared on the market in recent years. Also, foodservice managers confronted with high labor costs and few skilled employees turned to this system to relieve the labor situation. Often with this system, "single-use" disposable tableware is used, thus eliminating the need for a dishwashing unit.

With the availability of frozen entrées with a starch that are low in fat and sodium, some hospitals have begun to purchase these retail-size commercially prepared frozen entrées for their patient foodservice. They are then "popped out" onto the service plate and rethermalized with individually quick frozen (IQF) vegetables and served. These pop-out food items have resulted in the system being characterized as "pick, pack, pop, and pitch!" In addition to the regular production line items, some companies are willing to produce items according to an individual purchaser's recipes and specifications. In addition to frozen foods, assembly/serve systems are also beginning to use sous vide, which is a method of food production in which foods are precooked and vacuum packed. Rethermalization is accomplished by boiling the food in the vacuum packages in which they are stored.

The primary users of the assembly/serve system are hospitals, yet some health care institutions and restaurants also use it. Although foodservices of all classifications can use prepared entrée items, few have adopted them exclusively. Hotels and restaurants that employ unionized chefs can be prohibited from using frozen entrées.

Advantages of the Assembly/Serve System. The foremost advantage of the assembly/serve system is the built-in labor savings. Fewer personnel are required, and they do not have to be highly skilled or experienced. Procurement costs are lower because of better portion control, less waste, reductions in purchasing time, and less pilferage. Equipment and space requirements are minimal, as are operating costs for gas, electricity, and water.

Disadvantages of the Assembly/Serve System. The availability in some markets of a good selection of desired menu items or those that have regional appeal is limited. However, more and better-quality frozen entrées are becoming available. The higher cost of these prepared foods may not be offset by the labor savings realized. Managers must carefully weigh the overall cost of this system.

Another disadvantage may be the quality of available prepared products and customer acceptability. The proportion of protein food (meat, fish, seafood, etc.) to sauce or gravy in some menu items may not be adequate to meet the nutritional requirements of the clientele. For example, two ounces of protein are required in the school meal pattern in school foodservice programs. Many frozen entrées may contain much less than that. Evaluation of products under consideration for use in the assembly/serve system is essential.

A manager considering a change from another system to the assembly/serve system should carefully evaluate the change in amount and kind of equipment needed. It may be excessively high in cost and in energy consumption to operate the duplicate pieces of heating equipment. Additional freezer space required for storage of the inventory of frozen entrées may not be available or may be too costly to install. Recycling or disposal of the large quantities of packaging materials and single-use tableware, if used, must be part of the total concern.

Rationale for Assembly/Serve Foodservice Systems. Assuming a lack of skilled food production employees and an available supply of highly processed, quality food products, an assembly/serve foodservice operation may achieve operational objectives to provide client satisfaction. Managerial decisions to adopt this form of foodservice system should consider the availability of these resources to the foodservice operation.

Each type of foodservice system has proved successful in providing acceptable quality food in specific organizations with the conditions described for each. However, foodservice managers attempting to decide on one system over another should undertake an extensive investigation and study before making any decisions. Among the factors to consider are cost comparisons, availability of foods in all forms, quality, and nutritional value of fully prepared items, customer needs and acceptability, equipment and space requirements, energy use as estimated by the amount and kinds of equipment needed for each system, and availability and cost of labor.

SUMMARY

The vast and ever-changing foodservice industry continues to be shaped by socioeconomic changes, demographic shifts, and the varying food habits and desires of the American people. Foodservice managers must keep abreast of these conditions and adapt their operations to the changing times in order to be competitive and successful. For a complex system to endure is not enough. It must adapt itself to modifications of the environment and evolve. Otherwise, outside forces will disorganize and destroy it. The difficult, paradoxical question that confronts those in the foodservice industry is, "How can a stable organization whose goal is to maintain itself and endure be able to change and evolve?"

Today's foodservice manager should view his/her organization as a system composed of various elements or subsystems that are united by a common goal and that are interdependent and interact so that the processes or functions involved produce outcomes to meet stated objectives. A foodservice system is an integrated program in which the procurement, storage, preparation and service of foods and beverages and the equipment, methods, and personnel required to accomplish these objectives are fully coordinated for minimum labor, optimum customer satisfaction, quality, and cost control.

Table 1 Summary of the characteristics of the four types of foodservice systems.

	CONVENTIONAL	COOK/CHILL	COOK/FREEZE	COMMISSARY	ASSEMBLY/SERVE
		READY PREPARED			
Location of food preparation kitchen in relation to where served:	On premises where food is served	On premises where food is served		Central production kitchen in building separate from service units. Food transported to satellite serving units.	Off premises (commercially prepared foods are purchased)
Form of food purchased:	Raw; some convenience foods	Raw; some convenience foods		Primarily raw ingredients	All convenience and prepared foods—frozen, canned, dehydrated, or prepeeled fresh
Food procurement:	Purchase for its own unit	Purchase for its own unit		Centralized purchasing for all service units	Purchase for own use
Time span between preparation and service, and method of holding:	Food prepared for immediate service (may be held hot, or chilled for a few hours)	Food prepared and cooked, then chilled and held for 1–3 days, or 45–60 days depending on the system	Food prepared and fast frozen; held for later use up to 3–4 months	Food prepared and may be (a) distributed to satellite units for immediate service, (b) chilled and either pre-plated or put into bulk, (c) chilled and frozen and pre-plated or in bulk	No on-premises preparation. Foods purchased pre-prepared are stored and ready for reheating and service at any time needed
Amount and kind of equipment required:	All pre-preparation, cooking, and serving equipment needed. Both skilled and unskilled employees needed	All pre-preparation and cooking and serving equipment. One or more blast chillers—large amounts of refrigerated storage space, or cook tank, water bath, and pumping equipment	A "blast" or cryogenic freezer—large amounts of freezer holding space	Large, sophisticated equipment for pre-preparation and cooking. Some robots may be used—can be reprogrammed for various tasks. Suitable containers for packaging and delivery; trucks to deliver prepared foods to service units; reheating equipment if foods frozen or chilled	Equipment for reheating such as steamers, steam jacketed kettles, convection or microwave ovens. Equipment for setting up and serving. Reheating equipment such as convection or microwave ovens and kettles for immersion heating
Labor needs:	Skilled cooks and preparation workers as well as less skilled for pre-preparation and serving	Fewer highly skilled cooks needed compared with conventional because of "production line" type of work and only one or two items prepared per day; workers needed to reheat foods, operate that equipment, and assemble and serve meals		Highly trained in technological aspects of food production in mass quantities. Food microbiologists to ensure food safety. Employees must be able to operate highly specialized equipment used for food production	No skilled cooks or other pre-preparation employees needed. Workers for assembling salads and desserts, etc. Workers for reheating and serving foods must be able to operate equipment

Table 1 **(Continued)**

| | READY PREPARED | | | | |
	CONVENTIONAL	COOK/CHILL	COOK/FREEZE	COMMISSARY	ASSEMBLY/SERVE
Typical foodservices using this:	Independent restaurants and cafeterias; hospitals and health care for specialized groups; in-plant foodservices; colleges and universities; schools	Large hospitals, some large colleges and universities		Airlines; chain restaurants; large school districts; commercial caterers and vending companies	Hospitals and nursing homes; some commercial foodservices and colleges; facilities; homes

The defining characteristic of a system is that it cannot be understood as a function of its isolated parts. The behavior of the system does not depend on what each part is doing but rather on how each part is interacting with the other parts. To understand a system, one must first understand how it fits into the larger system of which it is a part.

The arrangement of subsystems, procurement, food preparation, delivery and service, and sanitation in varying ways is the basis for grouping foodservices into types of production systems, each with common elements and procedures. Four major types of foodservice production systems found in the United States are conventional, ready-prepared, commissary, and assembly/serve. An evaluation of the merits of each system based on its characteristics, advantages, and disadvantages should be made before any one is adopted for use in a specific foodservice organization. A summary of the major characteristics of each system is given in Table 1. A flowchart of the step-by-step processes of the four foodservice systems is shown in Figure 10.

Recent research studies on foodservice systems in relation to time and temperature effects on food quality have been summarized and reported in another North Central Research bulletin. These microbiological safety, nutrient retention, and sensory quality studies provide specific data useful when deciding on a system to install or contemplating a change in systems. Further investigations are needed to advance understanding of the interrelationships among food products, resources, processes, and management in foodservices and so improve food quality in foodservice establishments.

APPLICATION OF CHAPTER CONCEPTS

The scope of services for the University of Wisconsin–Madison dining and culinary services department is outlined below:

Customer Base

- College students—6,900 residents
- Campus catering clients
- Cash—Small percentage of revenue in units less than 5 percent (campus community—faculty, staff, students)
- Summer conference operations—meals and catering
- Eagle's Wing Day Care

Self-Operated Food Program

- Food sold to customers via Housing Food Account Debit Card—they are not captive customers
- "Membership fee" paid in room and board fees $1,355/year
- Average Housing Food Account expenditure $1,076/year

Conventional	Commissary	Ready-Prepared	Assembly/Serve
Purchase raw basic foods and limited convenience items	Purchase raw basic foods for all units	Purchase raw basic foods and limited convenience items	Purchase fully prepared foods in frozen, canned, dehydrated form; salad ingredients pre-prepared
↓	↓	↓	↓
Receive goods	Receive goods	Receive goods	Receive goods
↓	↓	↓	↓
Store foods: refrigerator at 40° or lower Drystores 65–70°F	Store foods: refrigerator at 40° or lower Drystores 65–70°F	Store foods: refrigerator at 40° or lower Drystores 65–70°F	Store in freezer, 0°F or refrigerator 40°F or lower until serving time.
↓	↓	↓	↓
Prepreparation: washing, sorting, peeling, cutting, etc.	Prepreparation: washing, sorting, peeling, cutting, etc.	Prepreparation: washing, sorting, peeling, cutting, etc.	(none required)
↓	↓	↓	↓
Preparation and cooking: small to large batch and short order	Large batch cookery	Large batch cookery	(none required)
	↓	↓	
	Portion and freeze or chill & store OR bulk freeze or chill & store OR hold hot Transport in appropriate temperature-controlled equipment to satellite serving units	Portion & freeze or chill & store OR bulk freeze or chill & store OR hold hot. Transport in appropriate temperature controlled equipment to satellite serving units	
↓	↓	↓	↓
	Receive by units where foods are to be served	Store in freezer or refrigerator as appropriate for later use	
	↓	↓	
Short-time holding in refrigerated or heated cabinets (or serve at once)	Hold as appropriate until serving time	Hold as appropriate until serving time	Hold as appropriate until serving time
	↓	↓	↓
	Temper (thaw) frozen foods in refrigerator	Temper (thaw) frozen foods in refrigerator	Temper (thaw) frozen foods in refrigerator
	↓		
	Reheat as necessary and distribute OR distribute and reheat		
↓	↓	↓	↓
Distribute for service	Assemble and serve	Reheat as necessary & distribute OR distribute & reheat.	Reheat as necessary & distribute OR distribute & reheat

Figure 10 The step-by-step processes of the four foodservice systems.

- Cash customers charged 60 percent above Food Account item prices for "prepared" food items, and 15 percent above Housing Food Account pricing in carryout stores for "grocery" items

Operating Units

- 3 dining rooms—Pop's, Frank's, Elizabeth Waters
- 1 marketplace—Rheta's
- 2 carryout stores—Ed's Express & Carson's Carryout
- 1 hybrid unit—Newell's Deli
- 3 coffeehouses—Espress Yourself, Common Grounds, Now or Later
- Campus Catering

Support Units

- Large cook/chill commissary operation
- Large off-premise warehouse providing trucking and U.S. Mail service for residence halls

What we strive to have customers think of our program

- Serving quality food, we buy on quality, not price
- Having choice of options and variety
- Being flexible
- Being responsive and market driven

The dining and culinary services department at the University of Wisconsin–Madison falls most cleanly into the classification of noncommercial, on-site because its primary purpose is to serve the students, faculty and staff. However, one could argue that this department is, at least in part, a commercial operation given that a number of its units have the potential to generate revenue.

Just as there is a mix of business units, there is also is a mix of types of foodservice operations used to accommodate the various programs.

Collectively these business units represent a surprisingly high volume of meals and revenue:

- Annual Food Purchases—$8,600,000
- Revenue
  - Debit Card $8,750,000
  - Cash $435,000
  - Catering $795,000
  - Summer Conference $1,839,000

This department is a system within a system. The foodservice department is a system because it has inputs (food, labor, space, etc.) that are transformed into outputs such as food items, meals, catered events, etc. This transformation occurs through functional operations of purchasing, production, and service. At the same time, the department is part of the Division of University Housing system and interacts with other parts such as residence halls to achieve the goals and strategies, which are:

- Maintain high quality programs and services
- Provide space for all first-year students who want to live on campus
- Improve residence hall and foodservice facilities
- Keep room rates as low as possible

The mission statement for the Division of University Housing is, "Be the Place Where Everyone Wants to Live."

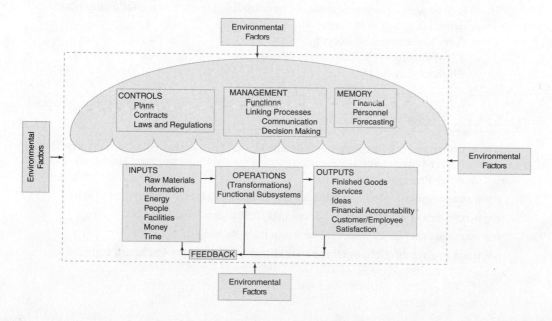

CRITICAL-THINKING QUESTIONS

1. Which of the socioeconomic trends and demographic changes discussed at the beginning of this chapter have the most influence on this particular foodservice operation?
2. Why does the University Dining and Culinary Services department offer such a broad scope of services?
3. In what way does this department serve as a commissary?
4. What challenges does a commissary using a cook/chill production system present when the goal is to provide quality food?
5. Which business unit do you think has the biggest impact on the larger system of the university? Why?
6. Based on the Division of Housing's mission statement, write a mission statement for the Dining and Culinary Services department.
7. How does the mission for the Division of Housing reflect that of the larger organization of the university?
8. What particular challenges does the housing mission statement present for the Dining and Culinary Services department?
9. One of the goals of the housing division is to provide high-quality services. In terms of the foodservice, what does this mean?
10. What political and economic conditions and governmental regulations do you think are currently influencing the department of Dining and Culinary Services?

CHAPTER REVIEW QUESTIONS

1. Name three or four major socioeconomic trends that are impacting the foodservice industry today.
2. Write a mission statement for a hypothetical foodservice operation.
3. What challenges face the foodservice industry today? How would you creatively overcome one of these challenges?
4. Compare and contrast commercial and on-site foodservice operations. Give examples of each.
5. Diagram the functional subsystems of a typical foodservice.
6. What is systems theory, and why is it an important concept for a foodservice manager to understand?
7. Compare and contrast the systems theory with the scientific management theory.
8. Diagram a foodservice organization as a system.
9. Compare and contrast the four major types of foodservice systems described.
10. Which foodservice system(s) should be considered in each of the following situations?
    a. High labor cost in the area
    b. Very low equipment budget
    c. Close quality control desired
    d. High food cost in the area

SELECTED WEB SITES

www.auburn.edu/~johnspm/gloss/index.html   (A Glossary of Political Economy Terms)

www.chester-jensen.com   (Chester-Jensen Co.—Manufacturers of Heat Exchange & other Process Equipment)

www.managementhelp.org/systems/systems.htm   (Free Management Library)

www.restaurant.org/research   (National Restaurant Association)

www.restaurantreport.com   (The Restaurant Report)

www.soi.org/reading/change/branches.shtml   (Symphony Orchestra Institute)

Food Safety

Bork/Shutterstock

GUESTS OF ANY EATING ESTABLISHMENT HAVE CERTAIN

expectations regarding the food that is prepared for and served to them. Minimally they expect it to be pleasing to the eye, flavorful, satisfying, and priced at a fair value. Patrons select dining establishments based on these and other aspects of quality.

One aspect of quality that is simply assumed is that of food safety. Customers take it for granted that food has been purchased from a safe source and handled properly from delivery to the dock until the final menu item is presented to the customer. It is the responsibility of the foodservice manager to ensure that these expectations are met every time food is served. To accomplish this, the manager needs the knowledge and skills to build, implement, and maintain a program of food safety that is consistent with the unique features of a given foodservice operation.

The manager must have an understanding of what foodborne illness is, the likelihood that it can occur, and the causes underlying outbreaks. In addition, the manager needs to develop the skills necessary to build an integrated program of food protection that includes prerequisite programs and **HACCP** plans. These programs and plans need to accommodate unique aspects of the foodservice and be in compliance with federal, state, and local regulations. Addressing the food safety program from the perspective of the system can ensure that all aspects of the operation are considered and that the program is indeed effective in preventing outbreaks of foodborne illness. The purpose of this chapter is to provide the reader with the foundation knowledge needed to build a comprehensive program of food safety. Details on food hazards and proper food handling in each functional operation set the stage for food safety planning. Guidance on how to design an integrated food safety program for a specific foodservice is offered along with valuable resources to ensure that the foodservice manager embraces a career-long commitment to learning principles and practices of food safety.

KEY CONCEPTS

1. Foodborne illness is a serious threat to public health.

2. The foodservice manager plays a leadership role in the prevention of foodborne illness.

3. Pathological hazards are inherent to some foods and can cause disease if allowed to grow.

4. Physical and chemical hazards, including allergens, pose threats to food safety.

5. Failures in operations and food handling practices contribute to outbreaks of foodborne illness

6. A matrix of food laws, regulations, codes, and standards provide the legal framework for food safety programming.

7. Well-designed and quantifiable prerequisite programs serve as the foundation of an integrated food safety program.

8. The single most important prerequisite program for an effective food safety program is personal hygiene.

9. Prerequisite programs that establish standard operating procedures for purchasing, production, and service maximize safety as food flows through a facility.

10. Hazard analysis and critical control point (HACCP) is a systematic approach to controlling identified hazards specific to foods or processes.

FOODBORNE ILLNESS

KEY CONCEPT: Foodborne illness is a serious threat to public health.

The incidence of foodborne illness is expressed in **outbreaks**. According to the **Centers for Disease Control and Prevention (CDC)** in Atlanta, an outbreak of foodborne illness is an incident where two or more people experience the same illness after eating the same food. An outbreak is confirmed when laboratory analysis shows that a specific food is the source of the illness. A **case** in a specific outbreak represents one individual in an outbreak. Number of cases per outbreak can vary widely from as few as two to hundreds of thousands. Table 1 represents a sampling of outbreaks reported to the CDC between 1999 and 2007.

Scope of the Problem: Incidence of Foodborne Illness

One of the most challenging aspects of managing a food safety program and the employees who handle the food is presenting a convincing argument that foodborne illness does indeed occur. Relative to the daily problems that foodservices encounter, the **risk** of an actual outbreak is low. In addition, there tends to be a lack of appreciation for the realities of the scope of the problem, given that the reported and confirmed outbreaks represent

Table 1 Examples of Confirmed Outbreaks: 1999–2007

BACTERIAL	NUMBER	LOCATION	VEHICLE
Bacillus cereus	23	School	Spanish rice; refried beans
Campylobacter jejuni	11	Restaurant	Chicken
Escherichia coli O157:H7	10 (5 deaths)	Day care center; private home	Ground beef
Salmonella enteritidis	27	Long-term care	Eggs

Source: www.cdc.gov/outbreaknet

only a fraction of how many people actually get sick from food. The CDC estimates that there are 48 million cases of foodborne illness in the United States each year. It is further estimated that there are 128,000 hospitalizations and 3000 deaths related to foodborne illness on an annual basis. Underreporting and underestimating the true incidence is a reflection of the complexity of foodborne illness.

Keeping track, or surveillance, of foodborne illness is complicated. Symptoms among victims vary widely. Some experience only mild symptoms, and their discomfort is temporary and short-lived. Others, especially those in highly susceptible populations, can experience much more severe, extended, and potentially life-threatening reactions. These populations include the elderly, very young children, pregnant women, and those with compromised immune systems. Chances that the less afflicted will go through the effort of reporting an illness, even if they suspect that it is foodborne, are quite small.

Another complicating factor is that agents of foodborne illness can be transmitted through water and through contact with infected farm animals and pets. Person-to-person contact is another means by which an individual can become infected with the very same causative agents that are attributed to foodborne illness. Surveillance has, however, greatly improved following a concerted effort on the part of the federal government to better track and document the incidence of foodborne illness.

During the mid- to late 1990s, there was a recognition on the part of the Clinton administration that oversight of food safety in the United States needed to be overhauled. This included better tracking of foodborne illness outbreaks to determine more accurately how widespread the problem is. A better program would also provide the framework to assess whether interventions were actually working. In 1997, the National Food Safety Initiative (NFSI) was launched. This initiative included a number of goals and triggered tracking programs for foodborne illness. One such program is the CDC's Emerging Infections program, Foodborne Diseases Active Surveillance Network (FoodNet). The surveillance program collects data on foodborne diseases at 10 U.S. sites. Each year the CDC releases a report that describes preliminary surveillance data and compares them to previous data. These reports can be accessed from the CDC Web site (see the URL at the end of this chapter).

Although accuracy and timeliness have improved as a result of the NFSI, a number of social, economic, and political issues present new challenges to ensuring that the U.S. food supply is indeed safe. These issues include:

- Advances in trade and transportation that have brought more food variety but new pathogens
- People eating a greater variety of food including raw seafood and more fresh produce
- An increase in the "at-risk" or "highly susceptible" populations comprising the elderly, children, and people with compromised immune systems such as individuals with acquired immunodeficiency syndrome (AIDS)
- More meals prepared and eaten outside of the home
- Changes in food preparation and handling practices

- Newly recognized microorganisms that cause foodborne illness
- Centralized food processing
- The globalization of the food market

In recognition of these challenges, the Obama administration has reinvigorated the federal government's commitment to ensuring a safe food supply for Americans. Newly introduced legislation addresses administrative and structural issues with our current system of laws and regulations. Issues include outdated laws, inadequate resources for inspection, suboptimal management structures, and inadequate coordination across agencies at the federal, state, and local levels. These issues are further complicated by the complexities of our existing laws and their enforcement. For example, at least 12 federal agencies are charged with some oversight responsibility for at least 30 laws.

On March 14, 2009, President Obama announced the formation of the Food Safety Working Group, a group specially charged with advising the president on issues in food safety and how to correct them. Details of this group's activities can be found at www .foodsafetyworkinggroup.gov. Two federal bills have been introduced as a result of the work of this group and are currently making their way through Congress. The bills are The Food Safety Modernization Act of 2010 (S. 510) and The Food Safety Enhancement Act of 2009 (HR 2749). Collectively these bills have far-reaching implications for all aspects of the food industry (including foodservice). Key provisions include stepped-up inspections for foods regulated by the U.S. Food and Drug Administration (FDA) and new standards for traceability of food products. The House and Senate of the 111th Congress put the finishing touches on the Food Safety Modernization Act as the session came to a close in December of 2010. The bill awaited President Obama's signature at the start of the 112th Congress.

Costs Associated with Outbreaks of Foodborne Illness

It is difficult to account for the total and true costs of foodborne illness, but the economic loss associated with foodborne disease outbreaks can be devastating and more broad than most foodservice directors realize. Medical care, lost business, and lawsuits against the foodservice contribute most to the cost, but loss of income for victims and infected food handlers is also considerable. The social costs of pain and suffering are impossible to measure, not to mention the embarrassment and damage to the reputation of the foodservice. The Economic Research Service is the division of the U.S. Department of Agriculture (USDA) that calculates the economic costs of foodborne illnesses outbreaks and estimates the loss at billions of dollars per year. To put this in perspective, the service estimates that salmonellosis alone accounted for an economic loss of $2,646,750,437 in 2008.

THE ROLE OF THE FOOD MANAGER

■ KEY CONCEPT: The foodservice manager plays a leadership role in the prevention of foodborne illness.

Food managers, especially those responsible for providing food to highly susceptible or at-risk populations, have a critical role in the prevention of foodborne illness. In effect, food managers and the employees they oversee are public health providers. It is their job to protect their customers from food that could become unsafe through mishandling. Foodservice managers need to instill a sense of urgency about the potential for foodborne illness and provide the training and education needed to ensure that food handlers know proper procedures and controls. Foodservice managers themselves must be well educated on the related topics of food microbiology, food law, risk analysis, HACCP, and standard operating procedures. These are a few of the knowledge and skill requirements needed on the part of the manager to design, implement, and manage an integrated food safety program effectively. Figure 1 provides a more comprehensive list of the knowledge expectations for the foodservice manager or person in charge.

Areas of knowledge for the Foodservice Manager:

- Federal, state, and local laws and regulations that pertain to a specific foodservice operation
- Relationship between the prevention of foodborne disease and the personal hygiene of a foodservice worker
- Means to prevent transmission of foodborne disease by a food worker who has a disease or medical condition that may cause foodborne disease
- Symptoms associated with the diseases that are transmitted through food
- Relationship between maintaining the time and temperature of potentially hazardous food and the prevention of foodborne illness
- Inherent hazards associated with potentially hazardous foods
- Minimum end-point temperatures for the safe cooking of potentially hazardous foods
- Required temperatures and times for safe and proper storage, hot holding, cooling, and reheating of potentially hazardous foods
- Relationship between the prevention of foodborne illness and good personal hygiene
- Procedures for proper care, cleaning, and sanitation of equipment and facilities in the prevention of foodborne illness

Figure 1 Foundation knowledge on food safety for the foodservice manager. Source: Adapted from the 2009 Food Code.

CAUSES OF FOODBORNE ILLNESS

Investigations of foodborne illness outbreaks indicate that contaminated food in itself does not explain why people get sick. In fact, the CDC identifies the following as the five most common risk factors that cause foodborne illness:

- Purchasing food from unsafe sources
- Failing to cook food properly
- Holding food at incorrect temperatures
- Using contaminated equipment
- Practicing poor personal hygiene

The food manager needs to understand the contaminants and the operational failures that result in foodborne illness in order to design and implement effective preventive measures in the foodservice facility.

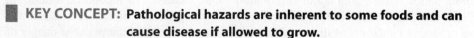 **KEY CONCEPT:** **Pathological hazards are inherent to some foods and can cause disease if allowed to grow.**

Hazards Inherent to Food

Any biological, chemical, or physical property that affects a person's health is called a **hazard**. The biological **pathogens** or disease-causing pathogens include bacteria, viruses, parasites, and fungi (molds). Illness resulting from live disease-causing or pathogenic microorganisms is called infection. Illness caused by eating toxins produced by microorganisms is called intoxication. Growth of pathogenic microorganisms in foods or on food contact surfaces increases the likelihood of either of these types of illness. Certain conditions support the survival and growth of harmful microorganisms. It is the responsibility of the foodservice manager to recognize these hazards and conditions, then implement procedures that will prevent them from becoming a food safety threat. This is challenging because microorganisms differ among food items and how they behave under various environmental conditions.

Most bacteria grow best in low-acid food; a few grow in acid food. Some grow best if sugar is present in the food, others if proteins are present. Some need oxygen for growth, and others thrive in its absence. The temperature most favorable for growth of pathogenic bacteria is body temperature, about 98°F; temperatures below 41°F inhibit their growth either totally or markedly, and temperatures above 130°F for a period of time are lethal to vegetative cells of pathogenic microorganisms. The federal government defines the tempera-

Hazard

A biological, chemical, or physical property that may cause an unacceptable consumer health risk

Pathogen

A disease-causing microorganism

65

ture range of 41°F to 135°F as the temperature danger zone, and all food handling in this range should be minimized.

The time required for growth and multiplication depends on the other environmental conditions present and the type of food being processed. Fungi require nutrients, oxygen, and time to grow. They are usually the dominant microorganisms only in foods that are too dry, acidic, or sugary for optimal growth by bacteria. Viruses and protozoa do not reproduce in foods and thus only cause infections.

Any food can be a vehicle for foodborne illness, but some are more likely to be involved than others. These foods are termed **potentially hazardous foods (PHF)**. According to the FDA Food **Code**:

1. "Potentially hazardous food (time/temperature control for safety food)" means a food that requires time/temperature control for safety (TCS) to limit pathogenic microorganism growth or toxin formation.
2. "Potentially hazardous food (time/temperature control for safety food)" includes:
   An animal food that is raw or heat-treated; a plant food that is heat-treated or consists of raw seed spouts, cut melons, cut leafy greens, cut tomatoes or mixtures of cut tomatoes that are not modified in a way so that they are unable to support pathogenic microorganism growth or toxin formation, or garlic-in-oil mixtures that are not modified in a way so that they are unable to support pathogenic micro–organism growth or toxin formation.

Simply put, potentially hazardous foods are those foods that favor rapid growth of microorganisms. The conditions that favor rapid growth can be remembered by the acronym FAT-TOM: food, acid, time, temperature, oxygen, and moisture.

The routes of transmission for **pathogens** are diagrammed in Figure 2. It should be noted that human wastes, particularly fecal material, are especially hazardous. An individual who has used the toilet is certain to have contaminated hands. If careful and thorough hand washing is ignored, the worker's hands can be a dangerous "tool" in the kitchen. Standards of personal hygiene are presented later in this chapter.

Carriers are an important source of infection or intoxication-causing microorganisms in foods. A *carrier* is a person who, without symptoms of a **communicable disease**, harbors and gives off from his or her body the specific pathogen of a disease, usually without being aware of it. Hepatitis A and Norovirus are examples of viruses that can be "carried" without notice and are both major contributors to the incidence of foodborne illness. An *infected* person is one in whose body the specific pathogens of a disease are lodged and have produced symptoms of illness. Thus, others may be aware of the possible danger of

Potentially hazardous foods (PHF)

Foods that are more likely than others to be implicated in an outbreak of foodborne illness

Code

A collection of regulations

Communicable disease

An illness that is transmitted from one person to another through direct or indirect means

Figure 2 Food handlers as a source of foodborne pathogens.

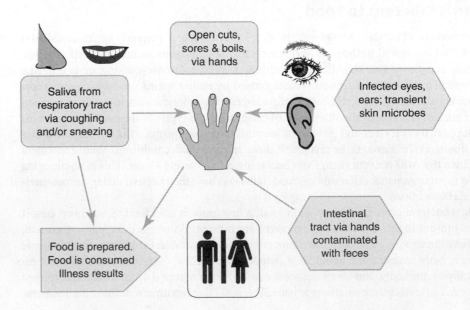

contamination. Consumers can become infected by ingesting water, milk, or other food products that have been contaminated with the fecal material of an infected person, animal, or carrier. Still another path of infection is drinking raw milk drawn from cows with infected udders.

An infectious disorder of the respiratory system such as a common cold can be spread by the droplet spray of infected discharges of coughing and sneezing without safeguard. An *indirect route* of infection spread through respiratory discharges is the used handkerchief, or the contaminated hand, and the subsequent handling of food or plates and cups in serving a patron. The following is a summary of some of the major pathogens that can cause foodborne illness. For a complete source of microorganisms and their relationship to foodborne illness, the reader is encouraged to visit the FDA's *Bad Bug Book* (see Web site at the end of this chapter).

Infectious Microorganisms. Primary organisms that cause **foodborne infections** include, but are not limited to, salmonella, *Campylobacter jejuni*, pathogenic *Escherichia coli*, and *Listeria monocytogenes*. The first two are especially prevalent and require special care in food handling.

Foodborne infection
Illness that results from ingesting foods containing live microorganisms

Salmonella infections account for numerous cases of gastrointestinal disorders called salmonellosis. Salmonellosis may be caused by any of the 2,300 known salmonella serotypes, each of which is primarily found in the intestinal tract of animals and humans. They are excreted in the feces and can contaminate food and water if personal hygiene and proper food handling are not practiced. Foods most often associated with salmonellosis are poultry, poultry products, beef, pork, and eggs and egg-containing foods. Proper cooking will kill salmonella, but cross-contamination of cooked foods with raw foods must be avoided as well.

Campylobacter jejuni, long known as an animal pathogen, has only recently been recognized as a very common cause of human gastroenteritis. *C. jejuni* is most often linked with consumption of raw milk, contaminated water, undercooked chicken, beef, pork, and raw clams. Poultry has an especially high carriage rate of this pathogen. Cross-contamination from raw animal foods to ready-to-eat foods via knives or cutting boards may be another transmission route. Evidence of the seriousness of *C. jejuni* is that it is now isolated from human diarrheal stools more frequently in the United States than are *Salmonella* spp. and *Shigella* spp. *C. jejuni* is readily killed by heat and is highly sensitive to chlorine-containing sanitizers.

Various types of pathogenic *Escherichia coli* have been responsible for a number of foodborne illness outbreaks in this country. Imported soft cheese was the cause of the first identified outbreak, which occurred in 1971. The most serious and highly publicized outbreak of *E. coli* O157:H7 occurred in 1993 when four children died after eating undercooked hamburgers. *E. coli* O157:H7 is found in the feces of humans and other animals and so may contaminate soil, water, and food plants. Illnesses caused by *E. coli* O157:H7 range from "traveler's diarrhea" to the life-threatening hemolytic uremic syndrome. The organism is easily killed by heat, but foods that have been heat-processed may be recontaminated after heating; improper temperature control can result in the organism increasing in numbers. In addition to cheese, both raw and processed shellfish, raw ground beef, inadequately cooked ground beef, and, more recently, some fresh produce items such as spinach, lettuce, and alfalfa sprouts have been associated with outbreaks of gastrointestinal illness caused by pathogenic *E. coli* O157:H7.

Intoxicating Microorganisms. Organisms that cause foodborne intoxication include *Staphylococcus aureus*, *Clostridium botulinum*, and *Clostridium perfringens*.

Staphylococcal food intoxication, the most frequent type of foodborne intoxication, results from toxin production by *Staphylococcus aureus* in high-protein menu items such as cooked meats, eggs, and milk, as well as cream pie. This organism is commonly found on healthy human skin, especially the nose, and is abundantly present in pimples and suppurating wounds. The toxin produced by *S. aureus* is not destroyed by cooking techniques commonly employed in food preparation, so refrigerated temperature control is critical.

General estimates are that most of the cases of food intoxication are caused by staphylococcal organisms. The illness is generally not fatal, but causes severe diarrhea and nausea in its victims for several hours. Usually the symptoms are evident within 0.5 to 6 hours after ingestion of the toxic food, which may have shown no visible indications of the contamination at the time of consumption.

Clostridium botulinum is a spore-forming organism that causes a far more serious food intoxication known as botulism. The organism can grow and produce toxin in various low-acid foods under anaerobic conditions. The toxin is often fatal. Food supporting growth of *C. botulinum* does not always show noticeable changes from normal. Certainly food that appears abnormal should not be "taste tested," because just a small amount of ingested toxin will cause illness. The toxin can be destroyed by boiling vigorously for 20 minutes, although this step is not recommended as the sole method of preventing botulism. There have been some outbreaks associated with baked potatoes, onion rings, and possibly other foods. Fortunately, botulism is an uncommon occurrence in foodservice operations. Commercially canned foods are heated to sterility with steam under pressure.

Clostridium perfringens, which is an anaerobic, spore-forming bacterium, is often placed in the group of organisms causing foodborne intoxication. Although the toxin may be present in food, it is believed to be usually produced in the intestinal tract, and thus the illness is actually most often an infection. The incubation period varies from between 8 and 20 hours, after which illness occurs. Symptoms are relatively mild, and the duration of the illness is usually about one day.

C. perfringens is found widely distributed in soil, water, dust, sewage, and manure and is also found in the intestinal tracts of humans and healthy animals. Many foods purchased by foodservices, especially meats and some spices, are probably contaminated with this organism. Foodservice workers may also carry this organism into the kitchen on their hands. Extreme care must be taken to keep hands clean and equipment clean and sanitized, especially meat slicers. Meats to be sliced should never be left to be "cut as needed" over a long serving period, and slicers must be thoroughly cleaned after each use. Meat slicers in continuous use should be cleaned and sanitized every 4 hours. Table 2 summarizes some of the major pathogens associated with outbreaks of foodborne illness.

Norovirus is a major and particularly serious virus typically linked with ready-to-eat food and shellfish from contaminated water. Illnesses attributed to a virus are best controlled through good practices of personal hygiene. Good hand washing and keeping ill employees out of the operation are particularly important.

KEY CONCEPT: Physical and chemical hazards, including allergens, pose threats to food safety.

Allergens: A Growing Concern.   Food allergies are a concern for 6 to 7 million Americans and need to be seriously considered as part of a comprehensive food safety program. An estimated 30,000 people visit hospital emergency rooms each year seeking treatment for food allergies. Up to 200 deaths per year are attributed to severe reactions, according to the Food Allergy and Anaphylaxis Network (FAAN).

Ninety percent of all food allergies are caused by what is referred to as the "big eight": milk, eggs, fish, wheat, tree nuts, peanuts, soybeans, and crustaceans. Other food ingredients that may cause an adverse, but nonallergic, reaction in some consumers include sulfites and monosodium glutamate (MSG). The food manager must work closely with suppliers and employees to ensure that composition of all foods is known and clearly communicated to customers.

The Food Allergen Labeling and Consumer Protection Act of 2004 went into effect on January 1, 2006. This law requires food manufacturers to clearly, and in plain English, identify any ingredients that contain protein derived from any one of the big eight. This labeling requirement does extend to retail and foodservice establishments that offer packaged, labeled food for human consumption. Managers should check with local and state agencies, because they may enforce more restrictive requirements.

Table 2	**Major foodborne pathogenic microorganisms.**			
Pathogen	*Salmonella* spp.	*Staphylococcus aureus*	*Clostridium perfringens*	*Bacillus cereus*	*Clostridium botulinum*
Disease	Salmonellosis infection	Staphylococcal intoxication	*Clostridium perfringens* infection/intoxication	*Bacillus cereus* intoxication	Botulism intoxication
Foods implicated	Poultry, poultry salads, meat and meat products, milk, shell eggs, egg custards and sauces, other protein foods, fresh fruits and vegetables	Foods that are cooked and then require considerable handling are ham and other cooked meats, dairy products, custards, potato salad, cream-filled pastries, and other protein foods	Meat, meat products, and gravy coupled with temperature abuse	A wide variety, including rice and rice dishes, custards, seasonings, dry food mixes, puddings, cereal products, sauces, vegetable dishes, meat, milk, and fish	Improperly processed canned low-acid foods
Incubation	6 to 48 hours	1/2 to 6 hours	8 to 22 hours	6 to 15 hours	18 to 36 hours
Symptoms	Abdominal pain, headache, nausea, vomiting, fever, diarrhea	Nausea, vomiting, diarrhea, dehydration, abdominal cramping	Abdominal pain, diarrhea	Diarrhea, abdominal cramps, vomiting, and pain	Lassitude, weakness, vertigo, double vision, difficulty in speaking, swallowing, and breathing
Duration	1 to 2 days	24 to 48 hours	24 hours	Up to 24 hours	Several days to a year
Pathogen	*Campylobacter jejuni*	*E. coli* O157:H7	*Listeria monocytogenes*	*Shigella* spp.	*Vibrio vulnificus*
Disease	Campylobacteriosis infection	Hemorrhagic colitis; hemolytic uremic syndrome	Listeriosis infection	Shigellosis	Wound infections, gastroenteritis, primary septicemia
Foods implicated	Raw poultry, raw vegetables, unpasteurized milk, untreated water	Raw and undercooked beef and other red meats, raw milk, cheese, unpasteurized milk, fresh fruits and vegetables	Unpasteurized milk and cheese, vegetables, poultry and meats, seafood, and prepared, ready-to-eat foods, including cold cuts and fermented raw meat sausages	Salads (potato, tuna, shrimp, macaroni, and chicken), raw vegetables, milk and dairy products, and poultry	Oysters, clams, and crab
Incubation	3 to 5 days	12 to 72 hours	12 hours to several days	1 to 7 days	3 to 76 hours
Symptoms	Diarrhea, fever, nausea, abdominal pain, headache, muscle pain	Bloody diarrhea, severe abdominal pain and cramping, nausea, vomiting, and occasionally fever, hemolytic uremic syndrome (kidney failure may result)	Nausea, vomiting, diarrhea, headache, fever, chills, backache, meningitis, spontaneous abortion, septicemia, encephalitis	Abdominal pain; cramps; diarrhea; fever; vomiting; blood, pus, or mucus in stools; tenesmus	Diarrhea, cramps, weakness, nausea, chills, headache, and vomiting
Duration	1 to 4 days	Up to 8 days	Depends on treatment—high mortality in highly susceptible populations	Varies	1 to 8 days

Source: The *Bad Bug Book*. U.S. Food and Drug Administration. Center for Food Safety and Applied Nutrition. Foodborne Pathogenic Microorganisms and Natural Toxins handbook. *www.fda.gov/Food/FoodSafety*.

Hazards Introduced to Food by People and Practices

Accidental Chemical Contamination. Microbial causes of foodborne illness are common, but disease and illness can also be caused by chemical contaminants in food. This type of foodborne illness results from eating food to which toxic chemicals have been added, usually by **accident**.

Chemical poisoning may result from contamination of food with foodservice chemicals such as cleaning and sanitizing compounds, excessive use of additives and preservatives, or contamination of food with toxic metals. The foodservice manager is responsible for implementing the necessary precautions to ensure that food is protected from these hazards. Minimum precautions include proper labeling and storage of all chemicals and frequent in-service training for employees on the hazards associated with the improper use of chemicals.

Physical Hazards. Physical hazards account for the third category of causes that contribute to outbreaks of foodborne illness. These, as the name suggests, include material or foreign contaminants that are accidentally or intentionally introduced into foods. Examples include metal shavings from cans, glass from service ware, and staples from packing materials. Compared to pathogenic microbes, physical hazards are rarely a cause of foodborne illness or injury.

> ■ **KEY CONCEPT:** **Failures in operations and food handling practices contribute to outbreaks of foodborne illness.**

A SYSTEMS APPROACH TO FOOD SAFETY

Ensuring food safety entails identifying every potential hazard within a foodservice operation that could, if left uncontrolled, lead to an outbreak of foodborne illness. Ultimately, it is the responsibility of the foodservice manager to design and implement a program of food safety that addresses each one of the identified hazards and includes procedures that prevent any and all potential hazards from becoming a threat to the well-being of diners. The challenge of designing such a program can be overwhelming, especially in high-volume, multiunit operations that handle hundreds, if not thousands, of menu items every day. A systems approach to food safety allows the manager to assess the entire operation, identify the good food safety practices already in place, and address those that need attention. Emphasis for food safety on inputs, operations, and outputs should be self-evident as the reader proceeds through the rest of this chapter and those that follow.

Controls and Food Safety

The food safety plan itself serves as an operational control, but there are other common controls in a foodservice that can be used to establish sound food safety practices for the operation. Menus, for example, are the formal documents of what will be served from the foodservice operation. Food safety can start at the menu planning process. It is during menu planning when the manager decides whether a potential menu item, regardless of its popularity, can be prepared and served safely. If there is any doubt, it may be wise to eliminate that item as part of the menu offerings. Some managers in long-term care facilities, for example, have eliminated poached eggs out of concern for the risk of salmonella from unpasteurized shell eggs. Other organizations will not place sprouts on menus because of the FDA warning for the risk of *E. coli* O157:H7.

Another control that can be used to reduce the risk of foodborne hazards is the purchasing contract for foodservices that buy through the competitive bid process. Under the terms and conditions of the contract, the manager can specify, for example, that delivery trucks be refrigerated. Forms of food can be specified such that food safety is "bought" as part of the product.

Precooked meat, for example, significantly reduces, if not eliminates, the risk of *E. coli* O157:H7 as compared to bringing raw product in.

Menus and purchasing contacts are examples of internal controls that can establish standards for food safety. External controls influence food safety programs as well. The most obvious example is the laws and regulations that pertain to the safety of food.

■ **KEY CONCEPT:** **A matrix of food laws, regulations, codes, and standards provide the legal framework for food safety programming.**

Laws, Regulations, and Codes. There are myriad laws and regulations that apply to foodservices, and several are specific to food safety. For example, the Pure Food Act of 1906 mandates that food be wholesome and safe for human consumption. Laws in themselves, however, are not particularly useful in establishing policies and procedures for a food safety program. The details and parameters of laws are found in regulations and codes.

A **regulation**, by definition, is a legal restriction set forth, or promulgated, by a government agency. Several levels of government mandate regulations including federal, state, and local, but the most direct enforcement comes from the local level. Enforcement is typically done through local branches or agencies. For example, the food and nutrition service within the USDA establishes food safety rules and regulations on food safety for schools that participate in child nutrition programs. State, county, or city agencies, however, enforce these regulations for the individual school districts. Similarly, the Center for Medicare and Medicaid Services within the Department of Health and Human Services is the federal agency that establishes food safety regulations for skilled care facilities. Enforcement is typically done by a state agency such as the Division of Health. In addition, foodservices may be regulated by a third-party organization specific to the type of industry in which the on-site foodservice is housed. For example, The Joint Commission for Healthcare organizations sets and oversees high standards of patient care for health care organizations in the United States. It establishes its own standards for food safety, which carry the same force as regulation once a facility is accredited. Regulations and standards established through laws and enforced by various agencies must serve as the *minimum* standards for food safety practices.

Regulation
An authoritative directive. A legal restriction set forth, or promulgated, by a government group

The Food Code. The Food Code was first developed in 1993 by the FDA in cooperation with the USDA as a guide for setting standards of food safety. The code is neither law nor regulation but is provided for guidance and consideration for adoption by jurisdictions that have regulatory responsibility for food service, retail, and vending operations. According to the FDA, the code provides the latest and best scientifically based advice about preventing foodborne illness. Highlights include the importance of time, temperature control, and safe hand washing. A most important and useful feature of the code is the framework it provides for designing a food safety program. The code promotes HACCP as the best available system for assurance of food safety. It is updated every four years, and supplements are released every two years as guidelines are revised to reflect the latest science. More than 30 states use the code as such, and many more are likely to follow suit as it is recognized as the best science-based source for standards of food safety.

FOOD SAFETY: AN INTEGRATED PROGRAM OF HACCP AND PREREQUISITE PROGRAMS

HACCP is not, and was never intended to be, a stand-alone food safety program. Rather HACCP is intended to be a part of a larger system of control procedures. These procedures must be in place for HACCP to function effectively. To understand these control procedures, one needs to understand the nature of hazards. As explained earlier, hazards can be categorized by type such as microbiological, chemical, and physical. These categories can be further subdivided relative to how they are introduced into a foodservice operation. As described earlier, there are hazards that are naturally occurring components of food. There are also those hazards that are introduced into or onto the food materials in the foodservice itself. The first classification of hazards is referred to as *inherent* hazards (e.g., a hazard specific to the food item) and would include, for example, salmonella on eggs. The second group of hazards represents environmental hazards and includes procedural failures such as cross-contamination from equipment that has not been properly cleaned and sanitized. HACCP addresses the first category. More detail on HACCP is provided later in this chapter. Methods to control the second grouping of hazards requires prerequisite programs and standard operating procedures (SOPs).

█ **KEY CONCEPT: Well-designed and quantifiable prerequisite programs serve as the foundation of an integrated food safety program.**

Prerequisite Programs: The Foundation of an Integrated Food Safety Program

Prerequisite programs are groupings of procedures that address operational conditions. By definition, the term *prerequisite* implies that something is required as a precondition to something else. In this case, prerequisite programs serve as the foundation for the development and implementation of HACCP. Prerequisite programs are not part of the formal HACCP plan, which is focused on the inherent hazards specific to individual menu items. Rather, prerequisite programs define interventions relative to people, facilities, and the work environment that are practiced routinely regardless of the nature of the food being prepared. If consistently and properly followed, prerequisite programs create an environment in which the food can safely flow from receiving to service with a minimum risk of being contaminated by environmental conditions.

In other words, prerequisite programs define the practices that the foodservice operation should be following regardless of the food item passing through. For example, clean utensils should always be used regardless of what food item is being prepared. Each foodservice operation must provide the conditions necessary to protect the food under its control. Once these programs are in place, HACCP can be more effective because it can concentrate on hazards specific and inherent to the food and its preparation rather than on the food preparation environment.

Prerequisite Programs and Standard Operating Procedures (SOPs)

Prerequisite programs are documented procedures that address the operational conditions necessary for the production and service of safe food. Individual prerequisite programs focus on one aspect of the foodservice operation such as personnel, a specific functional operation, or a physical aspect of the facility. Each of these programs includes defined procedures relative to its area of emphasis. Table 3 is a listing of the prerequisite programs and topics for SOPs that would likely be included in the food safety program of a typical foodservice. Many of the standard conditions and practices used to quantitatively define the SOPs are specified in federal, state, and/or local regulations and guidelines. The Food Code can serve as a basis for defining the standard operating procedures within each prerequisite program and the parameters by which compliance will be measured. For example, an SOP for receiving would be that any refrigerated meat or dairy products arriving at a temperature above 41°F shall be rejected at the dock. From there, individual foodservice operations can expand their prerequisite programs as necessary by adopting policies and procedures based on the unique needs of their operation and/or industry "best" practices. The following sections of this chapter provide detail for common prerequisite programs.

Table 3 Suggested prerequisite program topics for foodservice operations.

PERSONNEL	STORAGE	EQUIPMENT AND UTENSILS
Training and education	Temperature control	Preventive maintenance
Employee health and illness	Cleaning	Repair
Hygienic practices • Hand washing • Gloves • Attire and jewelry	Inventory rotation	Temperature measuring devices
MEAL PLANNING	**PREPARATION**	**PHYSICAL PLANT**
Recipe development for potentially hazardous foods	Thawing	Floors
	Time/temperature abuse (4-hour rule)	Walls
	Prevention of cross-contamination	Hoods
	Cooling (two-stage method)	Culinary steam
PURCHASING	**SERVICE**	**CHEMICAL CONTROL**
Vendor relations	Meal assembly	MSDS
Specifications	Hot holding	Storage
	Self-serve units	Disposal
	Time span and temperature maintenance	
	Handling leftovers	
RECEIVING	**CLEANING, SANITATION, WAREWASHING**	**PEST CONTROL**
Temperatures	Waste disposal	Prevention
Quality standards	Manual washing	Service contracts
Inspection	Machine washing	
	CIP equipment (clean in place)	**Miscellaneous**
	Food contact surfaces	Ice handling

EMPLOYEE HEALTH AND PERSONAL HYGIENE

■ KEY CONCEPT: The single most important prerequisite program for an effective food safety program is personal hygiene.

A wise foodservice manager instills the importance of food safety during the hiring process. As discussed earlier in this chapter, many cases of foodborne illness can be linked directly to lack of attention to personal hygiene, cleanliness, and food-handling procedures. In fact, the CDC issues a list of infectious and communicable diseases that are often transmitted through food contaminated by infected food handlers.

Some of the pathogens that can cause diseases after an infected person handles that food include:

- Hepatitis A
- Norwalk and Norwalk-like viruses
- *Salmonella typhi*
- *Shigella* species
- *Staphylococcus aureus*
- *Streptococcus pyogenes*

Contamination

The unintended presence of harmful substances such as microorganisms in food and water

There are preventive measures that the manager can implement beginning at the hiring stage to minimize the risk of food **contamination** and mishandling. This is accomplished though health screening and careful training of foodservice employees after they have been hired.

Individuals being considered for positions that involve food handling should undergo a health examination before being hired and at routine intervals thereafter. The exam should include a tuberculin test, and many foodservice operations, especially those in health care organizations, require screening for hepatitis A. Many state and local regulatory agencies require specific health tests before hiring. The manager should consult the local health department for specific requirements.

The successful hiring process should be followed by a thorough orientation and training on the standards of personal hygiene established for the foodservice operation. Personal hygiene is simply the application of principles for maintaining health and personal cleanliness. Policies should be designed, implemented, and monitored that cover proper attire, personal hygiene habits, and employee illness. The specific methods designed to fulfill the intent of these policies are frequently referred to as **infection control** procedures. Policy on infection control minimally should address the following:

Infection control

Specific procedures to prevent the entrance of pathogenic organisms into the body

Proper Attire

- Employees should wear clean, washable clothing. Uniforms are recommended, but, if not feasible, clean aprons are essential.
- Effective hair restraints must be worn to cover head and facial hair. Commonly used restraints include nets, bonnets, and caps. The purpose of hair restraints is to prevent hair from falling into the food and to discourage the food handler from touching his or her hair.
- Jewelry is discouraged because bacteria can lodge in settings and contaminate food.

Personal Hygiene Habits

The single most important practice in preventing the spread of foodborne illness is proper and frequent hand washing. Foodservice employees should wash their hands using the procedure illustrated in Figure 3. This technique is referred to as the double hand-washing technique and is recommended under the following circumstances:

- After defecating, contacting body fluids and discharges, or handling waste containing fecal matter, body fluids, or other bodily discharges (e.g., personal care attendants in day care centers and nursing homes may be responsible for changing diapers and serving food)
- Before beginning work or before returning to work following a break
- After coughing, sneezing, or using a handkerchief or disposable tissue
- After smoking, using tobacco, eating, or drinking
- After handling soiled equipment or utensils
- Immediately before food preparation, such as working with food, clean equipment, utensils, and supplies
- When switching from working with raw to cooked food

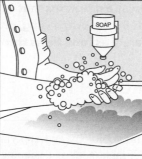
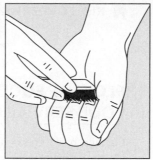

1. Use water as hot as the hands can comfortably stand.

2. Moisten hands, soap thoroughly, and lather to elbow.

3. Scrub thoroughly, using brush for nails. Rinse (this step is not included in the 2009 Food Code).

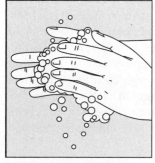

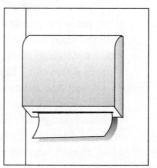

4. Resoap and lather, using friction for 20 seconds.

5. Rinse thoroughly under running water.

6. Dry hands, using single-service towels or hot-air dryer.

Figure 3 Proper hand-washing technique.
Source: Adapted from *Applied Foodservice Sanitation*, 4th ed. Copyright © 1992 by the Educational Foundation of the National Restaurant Association.

It is important to note that the hand-washing procedure in the Food Code does not require the nailbrush step. This is a somewhat controversial issue that is undergoing further study and consideration for future editions of the code.

Other Personal Hygiene Habits. Other personal hygiene habits to be addressed by policy include:

- Foodservice personnel should keep their fingernails trimmed and clean.
- Hands should be kept away from face, hair, and mouth.
- Disposable gloves should be encouraged for direct food contact and are required by law in some areas of the country. Employees should be trained to change gloves frequently to prevent **cross-contamination**.
- Smoking should be permitted in designated areas only and away from food preparation and service areas (preferably outdoors).
- Only authorized personnel should be allowed in production areas.

Cross-contamination

The transfer of harmful microorganisms from one item of food to another via a nonfood surface such as human hands, equipment, or utensils.

Cuts, Abrasions, and Employee Illness
- All cuts and abrasions, such as burns and boils, should be covered with a waterproof bandage.
- Cuts on hands should be covered with a waterproof bandage and a watertight disposable glove.
- Employees with symptoms of vomiting, diarrhea, fever, respiratory infection, or sore throat should not work as food handlers.
- Any employee suspected of having a communicable disease as listed by the CDC should be referred to employee health or their personal physician for clearance before returning to work.

■ **KEY CONCEPT:** **Prerequisite programs that establish standard operations procedures for purchasing, production, and service maximize safety as food flows through a facility.**

FLOW OF FOOD THROUGH THE FOODSERVICE OPERATION

Gaining basic knowledge of microbiology and applying it to personal hygiene practices are preliminary steps to the ultimate goal of designing an effective food safety program for the foodservice operation. A well-designed food safety program will address the entire foodservice operation. It is therefore essential that the manager understand how food moves through the operation.

The movement of food through a foodservice operation is referred to as the **flow of food**. It begins at the point where a decision is made to include a food item on the menu and ends with the final service to the customer. The functions basic to food flow in any operation include receiving, storage, preparation, holding, service, cooling leftovers, and reheating. Figures 4 through 7 illustrate how these functions relate to one another in the various types of foodservice systems and how food items typically flow through each type of system. The foodservice manager must be able to identify potential hazards at each step in the food flow and design a food safety program that will prevent the potential hazards from being realized. Part of the program design will include procedures for safe and proper food handling at each stage of the food preparation process.

Flow of Food

The route or path food follows through a foodservice or food processing operation

Figure 4 Flow of food for a conventional foodservice operation.

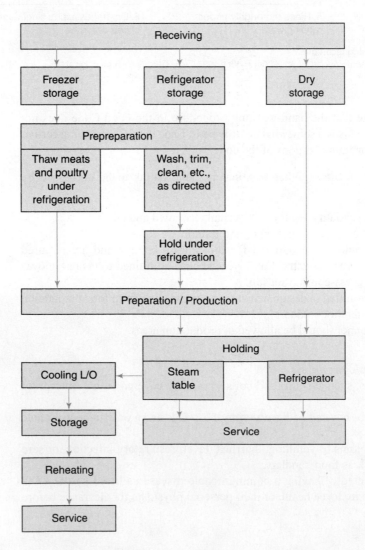

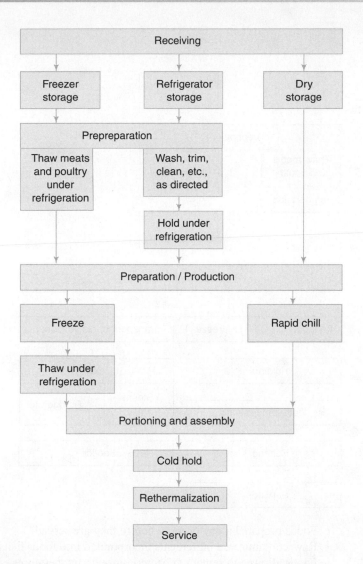

Figure 5 Flow of food for a ready-prepared foodservice operation.

Proper Food Handling

Hiring healthy employees and providing thorough, ongoing training in personal hygiene are important aspects of food safety but by no means guarantees against outbreaks of foodborne illness. Proper food handling techniques must be used to avoid conditions suitable for microbial growth and cross-contamination. Cross-contamination is the transfer of harmful microorganisms from one item of food to another via a nonfood surface such as human hands, equipment, or utensils. It may also refer to a direct transfer from a raw to a cooked food product.

Precautions for Safe Food Production. Proper food handling throughout the purchasing, storage, production, and service of food is critical in safeguarding the food against contamination. Legal safeguards are provided by federal, state, and local regulatory agencies, which are responsible for setting and enforcing standards for raw and processed foods. Minimum standards for sanitation in foodservice establishments are monitored by city and state agencies, but managers are responsible for the maintenance of sanitation standards in their respective foodservices.

Numerous factors can contribute to the outbreak of foodborne illness, but errors in food handling are often implicated in outbreaks of foodborne illness. The National Sanitation Foundation International lists the following as frequently cited factors in outbreaks of foodborne illness:

- Failure to cool food properly
- Failure to thoroughly heat or cook food
- Infected employees who practice poor personal hygiene at home and at the workplace

Figure 6 Flow of food for a commissary foodservice operation.

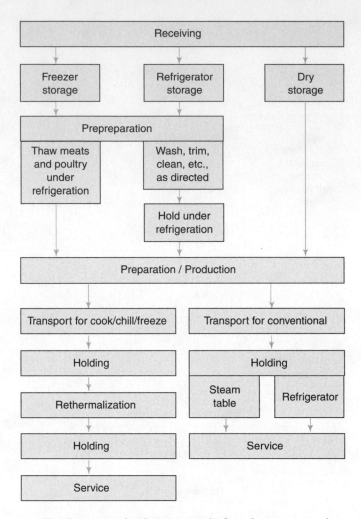

- Foods prepared a day or more before they are served
- Raw, contaminated ingredients incorporated into foods that receive no further cooking
- Foods allowed to remain at bacteria-growth temperatures
- Cross-contamination of cooked foods with raw food, or by employees who mishandle foods, or through improperly cleaned equipment

These errors can be avoided through thorough, ongoing training. Employees should understand time-temperature relationships and be able to practice proper food handling tech-

Figure 7 Flow of food for an assembly/serve foodservice operation.

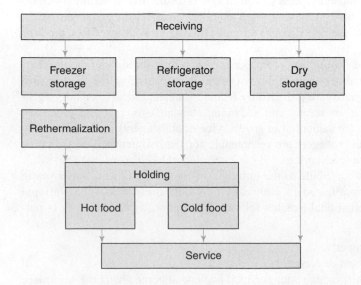

niques. Food managers can best integrate these techniques by established SOPs for each function along the flow of food.

Time-Temperature Relationships. Temperature has long been recognized as a particularly important factor in the control of harmful organisms. Time is an equally important factor in minimizing microbial growth during food storage, production, holding, transportation, and service. An important rule in food protection, then, is the time-temperature principle, which is based on three tenets regarding the handling of potentially hazardous foods:

1. Food items must be rapidly cooled to 41°F or less.
2. Cold food should be held at an internal temperature of 41°F or less.
3. Hot foods should be held at 135°F or higher.

According to the Food Code, the temperature range of 41° to 135°F is referred to as the **danger zone** because disease-causing bacteria are capable of rapid multiplication in this temperature range. Figure 8 is a temperature guide for food safety and highlights the danger zone. The time that food is allowed to remain in this critical temperature zone largely determines the rate and extent of bacterial growth. Most food handling techniques are designed to keep food items, especially potentially hazardous foods, out of this temperature range. Various stages of food preparation require that foods be in the danger zone at various times. For example, cooked meat will be at room temperature while it is being sliced and again while it is being used to make sandwiches. The Food Code recommends that the total time in the danger zone should be limited to 4 hours for any given food product.

The food manager must be aware of time-temperature relationships throughout the entire food production process. This concept is explained fully later in this chapter. It is imperative that the internal temperature of potentially hazardous food be kept *below* 41°F or *above* 135°F to ensure safety. This means that the temperature of the refrigerator should be

Danger zone

The temperature range between 41°F and 135°F in which most bacteria grow and multiply

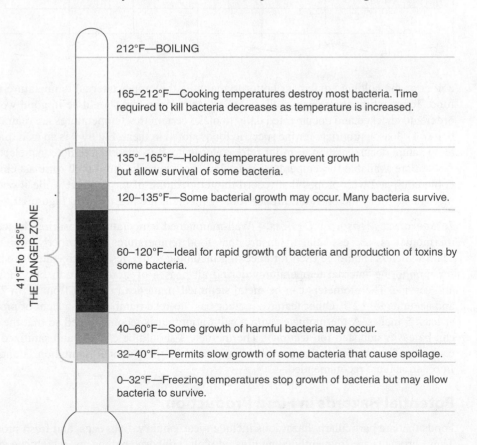

Figure 8 Temperatures and bacterial growth.
Source: Adapted from *Applied Foodservice Sanitation,* 4th ed. Copyright © 1992 by the Educational Foundation of the National Restaurant Association.

Day	Walk-in Freezer		Walk-in Refrigerator		Cook's Holding Refrigerator	
	AM Temp	PM Temp	AM Temp	PM Temp	AM Temp	PM Temp
1						
2						
3						
4						
5						
6						
7						
8						
9						
10						
11						
12						
13						

Refrigerator/Freezer Temperatures
Month of: _____

colder or the holding equipment hotter to maintain the proper internal temperature in the food. Temperature controls on walk-in and other refrigerators should be in good working order and checked and documented daily to make certain that temperatures are maintained below 41°F as appropriate for the specific foods stored in them. Figure 9 is an example of a temperature documentation form for refrigerator units. It is important to note that electronic devices are available for temperature recording. For example, rapid-chill (or blast chillers) come equipped with probes that record the temperature of the product while it cools in increments set by the operator. Proper cooling methods are illustrated in Figure 10

Temperature Measuring Devices. Well-maintained temperature measuring devices, or thermometers, are essential to ensure that food temperatures are properly monitored. Thermometers should be used for checking incoming deliveries of refrigerated foods and for monitoring internal temperatures during all phases of storage, production, holding, and service. Thermometers can be metal stemmed, numerically scaled from 0° to 220°F, and accurate to ±2°F. Other features include easy-to-read numbers and a stem or probe of at least 5 inches. A thermometer with a calibration nut is recommended so that the scale can be easily adjusted for accuracy. Thermometers should be cleaned and sanitized after each use. Thermometers that have been approved by the National Sanitation Foundation International are recommended.

Potential Hazards in Food Production

Foods that are particularly hazardous include meat, poultry, fish, eggs, and fresh produce. These products are frequently contaminated with foodborne pathogens, which can spread to surfaces of equipment, to the hands of workers, and to other foods. If frozen turkeys,

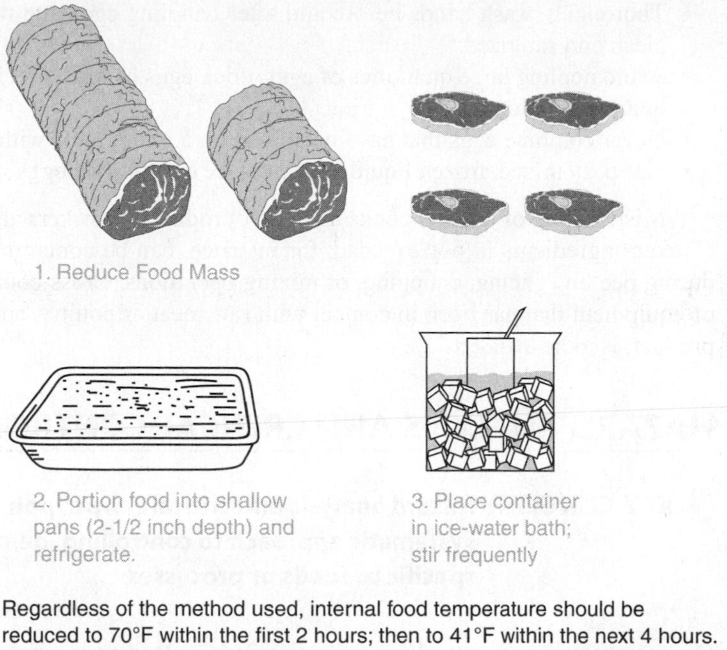

Figure 10 Safe methods for cooling hot food.

1. Reduce Food Mass

2. Portion food into shallow pans (2-1/2 inch depth) and refrigerate.

3. Place container in ice-water bath; stir frequently

Regardless of the method used, internal food temperature should be reduced to 70°F within the first 2 hours; then to 41°F within the next 4 hours.

for example, are to be cooked whole, they should be thawed completely in the refrigerator before being cooked, and if cooked the day before service, they should not be cooled without first reducing their bulk. The practice of cooking, chilling, and then reheating beef roasts is also potentially hazardous because reheating may not produce a temperature high enough to destroy any bacteria that may have survived in the meat. In these and other situations of thawing, cooking, cooling, reheating, and holding, the operator should refer to the Food Code for food-specific guidelines.

Food requiring preliminary preparation, which may include cooking prior to the final preparation, should be refrigerated following the preliminary steps. This includes items such as sandwich and salad mixtures; sliced, chopped, cut, and boned poultry and meats; ground, mixed, and shaped cooked meats; cream pie fillings and puddings; and sliced ham and similar items.

Attempting to cool any food item at room temperature to save refrigeration is a practice to be eliminated. Masses of hot food cool slowly, even in large walk-in refrigerators. To be cooled quickly, the food should be divided into shallow containers to a depth of no more than two inches and refrigerated, as shown in Figure 10. Other suggestions for cooling large amounts of food quickly include stirring the food and placing the pan of food in an ice bath or vat of cold running water. The FDA Food Code recommends that potentially hazardous cooked foods be cooled from 135° to 70°F within 2 hours, and from 70° to 41°F or below within 4 hours.

As mentioned earlier, the incidence of foodborne illness resulting from salmonella contamination is particularly challenging. This problem has been associated with raw or undercooked shell eggs. In the past, contamination was thought to result from dirty or cracked shells. The more recent outbreaks, however, suggest that *Salmonella enteritidis* is, in some instances, transmitted directly from the laying hen to the *inside* of the egg (generally the yolk). This means that more stringent guidelines must be implemented to handle eggs safely.

The following are general egg handling recommendations:

- Purchase **Grade** A or better eggs from a reliable source.
- Check eggs upon delivery to ensure that they have been kept refrigerated during transport.
- Keep eggs refrigerated, removing eggs from such storage only as needed; never store eggs at room temperature.
- Raw eggs should not be used as an ingredient to prepare food that will not be thoroughly cooked.
- Rotate eggs in inventory using the first-in/first-out (FIFO) method.
- Use only clean, crack-free eggs.

- Thoroughly wash hands before and after handling eggs and make sure equipment is clean and sanitized.
- Avoid pooling large quantities of eggs; cook eggs in small batches; no more than three quarts per batch.
- Never combine eggs that have been held on a steam table with a fresh batch of eggs.
- Use pasteurized, frozen liquid eggs in place of raw shell eggs when possible.

Mishandling of food by cooks and other production workers also constitutes a hazard. Cooked ingredients in potato salad, for instance, can be contaminated by food handlers during peeling, slicing, chopping, or mixing operations. Cross-contamination by a worker or equipment that has been in contact with raw meat or poultry, and then with the cooked product, is to be avoided.

HAZARD ANALYSIS AND CRITICAL CONTROL POINT

> **KEY CONCEPT:** Hazard analysis and critical control point (HACCP) is a systematic approach to controlling identified hazards specific to foods or processes.

Hazard analysis and critical control point (HACCP) is a proactive process of consecutive actions to ensure food safety to the highest degree through the identification and control of any point or procedure in a specific food system, from receiving through service, where loss of control may result in an unacceptable health risk. HACCP differs from traditional end-point food safety programs in that it is preventive in nature and focuses on the entire process of food preparation and service. In this sense, it is a self-inspection process sometimes described as a self-control safety assurance program. HACCP plans are designed to prevent the occurrence of potential food safety problems.

HACCP is not new; the concept originated more than 40 years ago. The Pillsbury Company is frequently credited with pioneering the application of HACCP to the food processing industry when, in 1971, they worked in cooperation with the National Aeronautics and Space Administration (NASA) to create food for the U.S. space program that approached 100 percent assurance against contamination by bacterial and viral pathogens, toxins, and chemical hazards or physical hazards that could cause illness or injury to the astronauts. HACCP has been used extensively in the food processing industry for many years.

Since the mid-1980s, HACCP has been recognized as a best-practice means of monitoring food safety in all segments of the food industry, including foodservice operations. On March 20, 1992, the National Advisory Committee on Microbiological Criteria for Foods (NACMCF) adopted a revised document on HACCP that included seven principles that provide guidance on the development of an effective HACCP plan. HACCP, as defined by NACMCF, emphasizes the concept of prevention and universal application and incorporates a decision tree for use in identifying critical control points (see Figure 11).

Unique to HACCP is that, by definition, it must be a documented system that delineates the formal procedures for complying with the seven principles. HACCP continues to evolve, especially for the foodservice segment of the food industry. Further refinements will evolve as new food products and systems are developed and as hazards and their control measures are more clearly understood.

Several issues have been raised specific to the foodservice segment as perceived barriers to the effective implementation of HACCP. These issues include:

- Lack of resources including time and personnel
- Complexity of foodservice operations
- High turnover of personnel
- Burden of required documentation procedures

Barriers are inherent to any new concept or procedure. It is also important to note that HACCP does not replace programs for personal hygiene or cleaning and sanitation. These

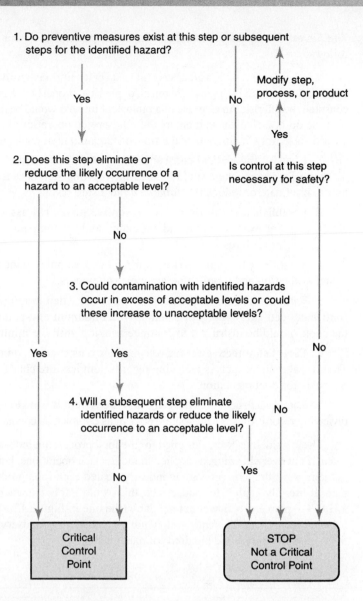

1. Do preventive measures exist at this step or subsequent steps for the identified hazard?

Yes → (down to step 2)

No → Is control at this step necessary for safety?

Yes → Modify step, process, or product

2. Does this step eliminate or reduce the likely occurrence of a hazard to an acceptable level?

No → (down to step 3)

3. Could contamination with identified hazards occur in excess of acceptable levels or could these increase to unacceptable levels?

Yes / Yes

No → STOP / Not a Critical Control Point

4. Will a subsequent step eliminate identified hazards or reduce the likely occurrence to an acceptable level?

No → Critical Control Point

Yes → STOP / Not a Critical Control Point

Is control at this step necessary for safety? No → STOP Not a Critical Control Point

Critical Control Point

STOP Not a Critical Control Point

Figure 11 Critical Control Point decision tree.
Source: From 2009 Food Code.

are important components of a comprehensive food safety program and are addressed through well-defined SOPs. Finally, HACCP is not a panacea; it does not address every conceivable or plausible hazard in a foodservice operation. The professional manager, however, accepts barriers and limitations as part of the challenge of implementing a system in the spirit that advantages far outweigh the perceived disadvantages.

HACCP is the best food safety system available to foodservice operators at this time. The primary benefit of HACCP is that it emphasizes control of hazards inherent to food at all stages of the processing continuum. Another advantage is that it clearly identifies the food establishment as the final party responsible for ensuring the safety of the food and handling procedures. HACCP is a rational, scientific approach and monitors both current and past conditions under which food is processed.

Because of its many advantages, HACCP is often a recommended, if not required, approach to food safety in all segments of the food industry. The seafood industry was the first processing segment to be required to implement HACCP, followed by the meat and poultry industries. Since the early 1990s, the foodservice industry has been under increasing pressure to adopt the principles of HACCP. The USDA, for example recently mandated that schools receiving federal reimbursement implement HACCP plans for child nutrition programs.

Some state regulatory agencies have already adopted the HACCP principles for use in survey processes. The Joint Commission has integrated HACCP into its standards for health care organizations.

The Seven Principles of HACCP. The seven principles of the HACCP program are as follows:

1. Identify hazards and assess their severity and risks: A hazard, as defined in the Food Code, means a biological, chemical, or physical property that may cause an unacceptable consumer health risk. An example of a **biological hazard** would be the presence of *Salmonella* bacteria on raw chicken as it enters the foodservice operation. The best means to evaluate hazards is to draw a diagram of the flow of food and then analyze each specific step.

2. Identify the critical control points (CCP) in food preparation: A critical control point for raw chicken would be the final cooking step because this is the last opportunity to eliminate or reduce the *Salmonella* to a safe level.

3. Establish critical limits for preventive measures associated with each identified CCP: For example, time and end-point cooking temperatures should be established for cooking procedures.

4. Establish procedures to monitor CCPs: Examples of these procedures may include visual evaluation and time-temperature measurements.

5. Establish the corrective action to be taken when monitoring shows that a critical limit has been exceeded: For example, if a minimum end-point temperature is not met, the cook should be instructed to continue cooking until the minimum is met.

6. Establish effective record-keeping systems that document the HACCP system: Traditional records such as receiving records, temperature charts, and recipes can serve as the basis for documentation.

7. Establish procedures to verify that the system is working: This may be as simple as reviewing records on a timely, routine basis or as complex as conducting microbiological tests.

These guidelines were designed for the food processing industry and may seem complicated, if not overwhelming, as applied to foodservice operations. For example, initial HACCP guidelines for the food processing industry treated each food product as a separate HACCP plan. If literally applied to foodservice, this would imply that each menu item be treated as a HACCP plan and a **flowchart** similar to the one in Figure 12 would need to be designed for *each* menu item. This may simply not be realistic for foodservice operations, especially those of high volume and hundreds of menu items.

Biological hazard
The threat to food safety caused by contamination of food with pathogenic microorganisms

Critical control point (CCP)
Any point or procedure in a specific food system where loss of control may result in an unacceptable health risk

Critical Limit
A specific criterion that must be met for each preventive measure identified for a critical control point

Flowchart
A written sketch of movement of people and/or materials from one step or process to the next

Steps	Hazard	Preventive Measure SOP	Corrective Action
Receiving			
• Ground beef frozen	• Contamination and spoilage	• Check for evidence of thawing	Reject delivery
• Fresh vegetables		• Packaging intact • No signs of insects or rodents	Reject delivery
• Dry and/or nonperishable ingredients		• No dented, bulging, or rusted cans	Reject delivery
• Cheeses		• No molds, off-odors • Accept cheese at 45°F or less	Reject delivery
Storing			
• Frozen beef	• Cross-contamination from other foods	• Check freezer storage; 0 to −10°F	• Discard ingredients if evidence of time, temperature abuse, or spoilage is noted
• Vegetables • Dry ingredients • Cheese	• Bacterial growth and spoilage	• Label, date, use FIFO • Keep raw food stored above cooked in refrigerators	

Figure 12 Flow of food and hazard analysis for lasagna recipe; receiving through service.

Steps	Hazard	Preventive Measure SOP	Corrective Action
Thawing Ground beef	• Cross-contamination from other foods	• Thaw under refrigeration at 41°F or less	• Discard if evidence of time, temperature, abuse is noted
Preparation Trim and chop/mince vegetables	• Contamination and cross-contamination • Bacterial growth	• Wash hands • Clean and sanitize utensils, knives, cutting boards • Wash vegetables before chopping and mincing	• Wash hands • Wash, rinse, sanitize utensils, knives, cutting boards

Cooking
Beef with vegetables
 	
   Add tomatoes
   & seasonings
 	
Simmering
 	
Assembling
Lasagna
 	
Baking
 	
Holding
	• Bacterial survival
	• Contamination from food handler
	• Contamination from seasonings
	
	• Contamination and cross-contamination from noodles, cheeses
	• Contamination from food handler
	• Bacterial survival growth
	• Bacterial survival and growth
	
	• Bacterial growth on serving utensils
		• Use clean and sanitized utensils and equipment
		
		• Add seasoning only in cooking process (allow 1/2 hour)
		
		• Cook/simmer all ingredients to 165°F
		
		• Use gloves, tongs, ladles to handle cooked ingredients
		• Bake to internal temperature of 165°F
		
		• Hot hold at 135°F or higher for 2 hours or less
		• Keep covered
		• Use clean and sanitized utensils
		• Keep serving utensils stored in lasagna during serving time
			• Wash, rinse, sanitize utensils and equipment
			
			• Continue cooking until 165°F is achieved
			
			• Continue baking until internal temperature reaches 165°F

Cooling	• Bacterial survival and growth • Cross-contamination	• Cool to 41°F within 6 hours • Cover and store above raw foods • Label with "use-by" date	Discard Discard
Reheating	• Bacterial growth and survival	• Reheat to 165°F within 2 hours	

Figure 12 *(Continued)*

Figure 13 Record for documenting end-point cooking temperatures.

HACCP Plan

Cooking Temperature

Date: _____

Menu Item	Cook Time Start	Cook Time Stop	Final Temp	Comments	Cook Initial

The previous model is one example of how HACCP might be adapted and applied from receiving to point of service (POS) in a small facility. The intent is that each phase of this model is supported with sound policies on food handling that include critical limits rather than starting at receiving for each menu item. Documentation requirements are achieved through existing records, including receiving records, storage temperature charts, standardized recipes, and service records (see, e.g., the time-temperature documentation sheet shown in Figure 13).

Figure 14 represents the flow of food from the time the ingredients are received to the point of service. Receiving, storage, and preparation are seen as individual HACCP plans because identified hazards, CCPs, critical limits, and monitoring procedures are similar for all ingredients regardless of the recipes in which they are used (see, e.g., the HACCP plan for receiving shown in Figure 15). Each recipe then is also an individual HACCP plan (see the sample recipe in Figure 16). Each recipe form includes identified hazards, CCPs, and critical limits (time and temperatures).

This process is cumbersome indeed! As mentioned earlier in this text, high-volume foodservices can have hundreds if not thousands of recipes. Applying the seven-step HACCP process to each recipe is simply not manageable or necessary. In April 2006, the FDA released a manual on HACCP specifically for foodservice and retail operations. The title of this practical guide is *Managing Food Safety: A Manual for the Voluntary Use of HACCP Principles for Operators of Food Service and Retail Establishments*. Rather than build HACCP plans one recipe at a time, this manual recommends categorizing recipes by preparation processes and building HACCP plans based on these processes. The three preparation processes are:

1. Food Preparation with No Cook Step
2. Preparation for Same Day Service
3. Complex Food Preparation

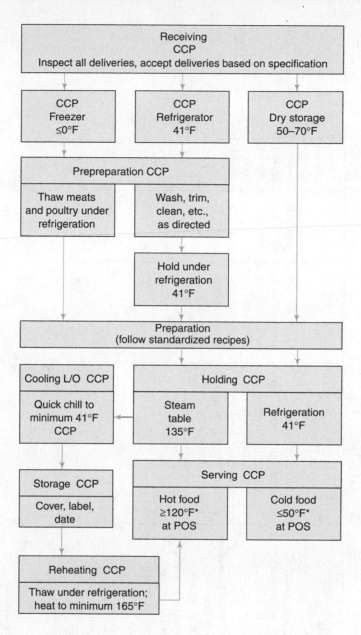

Figure 14 HACCP flowchart for a conventional foodservice system.

The manual can be accessed at www.fda.gov/Food/FoodSafety/RetailFoodProtection/ManagingFoodSafetyHACCPPrinciples/Operators/default.htm

MANAGING AN INTEGRATED FOOD SAFETY PROGRAM

The existence and effectiveness of prerequisite programs should be assessed before initiating an HACCP plan. Discrepancies and deficiencies need to be addressed to ensure that there is in fact a solid foundation of food safety procedures in place on which the HACCP plan can be built. Then, recipe by recipe, HACCP plans can be designed and implemented. These plans will focus on the hazards inherent with individual food items as they flow through the foodservice operation.

Given that HACCP and prerequisite programs are distinct but integrated components of a food safety program, they need to be managed as such. Prerequisite programs are established and can be managed separately from the HACCP plan as part of an organization's quality management program. For example, refrigerator temperature charts need to be audited regularly to ensure temperature maintenance. HACCP, on the other hand, has by definition

HACCP Plan

Process Step	Hazards	Preventive Measures and Critical Limits	Monitoring Process	Corrective Action	Records	Verification
Receiving CCP	Bacterial contamination, physical contamination	1. Frozen foods must be received at a product temperature of no higher than 0°F. 2. All refrigerated product, including fresh meat, produce, dairy, and eggs, must be received at a product temperature of no more than 40°F. 3. No off odor. 4. Packing intact.	All deliveries will be checked against specifications immediately upon arrival. Check temperatures of refrigerated items and conduct visual analysis for physical damage (bulging cans, open containers, etc.)	Reject all product that does not meet standards established by specification.	Standard receiving records.	Supervisor to review receiving records on weekly basis.

Figure 15 HACCP for receiving.

Heartland Country Village

Recipe Title   *Scrambled Eggs*

Yield Information			Cooking Temperature	350°F (conventional oven)
Portions	50		Cooking Time	1 hour
Pan Size	4 1/2" pan		Portion Size	1/4 c
Number of Pans	1		Portion Utensil	# 16 scoop

Ingredient	Amount	Procedures
Vegetable spray		– Spray pan with vegetable spray; set aside.
Eggs	5 dozen	– Remove eggs from refrigerator, check shells for cracks and soil; discard cracked eggs, remove soil.
		– Break clean eggs into mixer bowl.
		– Beat slightly on medium speed, using wire attachment.
1% Milk	4 cups	– Add milk, salt, and pepper Beat until well blended (3 to 5 minutes).
Salt	1 Tbsp.	– Pour mixture into prepared pan.
Pepper	1/4 tsp.	– (CCP) Bake for 1 hour at 350°F to minimal internal temperature of 165°F and until product is firm in center (do not overbake).
		– Transfer to steam table just prior to service.

Critical Control Point

Measure internal temperature of scrambled eggs.

If internal temperature of scrambled eggs is less than 165°F, continue to bake until internal temperature is at least 165°F and maintained for 15 seconds.

Figure 16   Sample recipe including HACCP.

a series of management procedures. These include the establishment and implementation of monitoring procedures, corrective actions, verification procedures, and record keeping specific to the HACCP plan.

ENFORCEMENT: THE REGULATORY INSPECTION

As described earlier in this chapter, many regulatory agencies at the federal, state, and local levels mandate minimum standards of food safety. These standards are documented in regulatory codes. Periodic inspections by agency representatives are required as part of the regulatory standards. Each agency specifies the frequency of these inspections, and the site visits are often staggered so that accurately predicting the arrival of unannounced inspectors is less likely. A food safety program designed simply to "get through" the inspection is certainly not in the spirit of the intent, much less a professional approach to protecting customers from unsafe food.

The professional manager approaches food safety as a way of life within the foodservice. In that respect, inspections will simply be a way of doing business and not a dreaded obligation. In fact, the inspection process can be viewed as a partnership in which the manager and inspector can work together to ensure the safest approach to food service possible.

When an inspector arrives, the manager should ask for identification. Managers are encouraged to accompany the inspector, but some inspectors prefer to conduct the inspection alone. After the inspection, the representative often presents a verbal report with the understanding that a formal report will be provided and submitted to the representative agency. Managers are typically free to appeal violations with which they do not agree, and there is usually a formal process by which such appeals can be made. The report will also categorize any violations by severity and explain corrective actions that must take place within a specific period of time. Figure 17 is an example of an inspection report form.

DEPARTMENT OF HEALTH & FAMILY SERVICES DPH 45002A (Rev. 07/06)
DEPARTMENT OF AGRICULTURE, TRADE AND CONSUMER PROTECTION FFD-111

STATE OF WISCONSIN
s. 97.30, s. 254.61, Subchapter VII, Wis. Stats.
Page_____ of _____

RESTAURANT / RETAIL FOOD SERVICE INSPECTION REPORT

Business Name	Business Address	County	License ID Number

Name of Legal Licensee	Mailing Address of Legal Licensee	Telephone Number ( )

Current Date	Date of Last Inspection	Release Date	Type of Establishment ☐ Restaurant ☐ Retail	Is operator certified? ☐ Yes ☐ No ☐ N/A

INSPECTION TYPE (check one) ☐ Pre-inspection ☐ Routine ☐ Reinspection   **ACTION TAKEN** (check one) ☐ Operational ☐ Conditional ☐ Withhold
☐ Complaint ☐ Downtime ☐ Visit/No Action ☐ Onsite Visit ☐ Other   ☐ License Suspended ☐ Revoke ☐ Other

Reinspection Fee Charged ☐ Yes ☐ No   Name of Certified Food Manager

---

FOODBORNE ILLNESS RISK FACTORS AND PUBLIC HEALTH INTERVENTIONS

Circle designed compliance status (IN, OUT, N/O, N/A) for each numbered item
IN=in compliance **OUT**=not in compliance **N/O**=not observed **N/A**=not applicable

Mark "X" in appropriate box for COS and/or R
COS=corrected on site during inspection **R**=repeat violation

Compliance Status

			COS	R
Demonstration of Knowledge				
1 A	IN OUT NA	Certified food manager; duties		
1 B	IN OUT	Person in Charge (PIC) id knowledgeable; duties and responsibilites		
Employee Health				
2	IN OUT	Management Awareness; Policy present		
3	IN OUT	Proper use of reporting, restriction & exclusion		
Good Hygienic Practices				
4	IN OUT N/O	Proper eating, tasting, drinking,		
5	IN OUT N/O	No discharge from eyes, nose, and mouth		
Preventing Contamination by Hands				
6	IN OUT N/O	Hands cleaned and properly washed		
7	IN OUT N/O N/A	No bare hand contact or using approved plan		
8	IN OUT	Adequate handwashing facilities supplied and accessible		
Approved Source				
9	IN OUT	Food obtained from approved source		
10	IN OUT N/O N/A	Food received at proper temperature		
11	IN OUT	Food in good condition, safe, & unadulterated		
12	IN OUT N/O N/A	Required records available: Shellstock tags, parasite destruction		
Protection from Contamination				
13	IN OUT N/A	Food separated and protected		
14	IN OUT N/A	Food contact surfaces: cleaned and sanitized		
15	IN OUT	Proper disposition of returned, previously served, reconditioned, & unsafe food		

Compliance Status

			COS	R
Potentially Hazardous Food Time/Temperature				
16	IN OUT N/O N/A	Proper cooking time and temperature		
17	IN OUT N/O N/A	Proper reheating procedures for hot holding		
18	IN OUT N/O N/A	Proper cooling time and temperature		
19	IN OUT N/O N/A	Proper hot holding temperatures		
20	IN OUT N/O N/A	Proper cold holding temperatures		
21	IN OUT N/O N/A	Proper date marking and disposition		
22	IN OUT N/O N/A	Time as a public health control: procedures and record		
Consumer Advisory				
23	IN OUT N/A	Consumer Advisory provided		
Highly Susceptible Populations				
24	IN OUT N/A	Pasteurized foods used; prohibited foods not offered		
Chemical				
25	IN OUT N/A	Food additives: approved and properly used		
26	IN OUT	Toxic substances properly identified, stored and used		
Conformance with Approved Procedures				
27	IN OUT N/A	Compliance with variance, specialized process, or HACCP plan		

Risk factors are improper practices or procedures identified as the most prevalent contributing factors of foodborne illness or injury. Public health interventions are control measures to prevent foodborne illness of injury

---

GOOD RETAIL PRACTICES

Good Retail Practices are preventative measures to control the addition of pathogens, chemicals, and physical objects into food
Mark "X" in box if item is not in compliance   Mark "X" in appropriate box for COS and/or R   **COS**=corrected onsite during inspection **R**=repeat violation

	Safe Food and Water		
28	Pasteurized eggs used where required		
29	Water and ice from approved source		
30	Variance obtained for specialized processing methods		
	Food Temperature Control		
31	Proper cooling methods used; adequate equipment for temperature control		
32	Plant food properly cooked for hot holding		
33	Approved thawing methods used		
34	Thermometers provided and accurate		
	Food Protection		
35	Food properly labeled; original container		
36	Pests and animals not present; no unauthorized persons		
37	Contamination prevented during food preparation, storage and display		
38	Personal Cleanliness		
39	Wiping cloths: properly used and stored		
40	Washing fruits and vegetables		

	Proper Use of Utensils		
41	In-use utensils: properly stored		
42	Utensils, equipment, and linens: properly stored, dried and handled		
43	Single-use and single-service articles: properly stored and used		
44	Gloves properly used		
	Utensils and Equipment		
45	Food and non0food contact surfaces: cleanable, properly designed, constructed and used		
46	Warewash facilities: installed, maintained, and used		
47	Non-food contact surfaces clean		
	Physical Facilities		
48	Hot and cold water available; adequate pressure		
49	Plumbing installed; proper backflow devices		
50	Sewage and waste water properly disposed		
51	Toilet Facilities: properly constructed, supplied, and clean		
52	Garbage and refuse properly disposed; facilities maintained		
53	Physical facilities installed, maintained, and clean		
54	Adequate ventilation and lighting; designated and used		

I understand and agree to comply with the corrections ordered on this report. I understand that failure to comply could result in legal action or loss of license.

SIGNATURE - Person in Charge	Date Signed
SIGNATURE - Inspector ID No.	Reinspection Needed ☐ Yes ☐ No Reinspection Date:

Figure 17 Example of a foodservice inspection report.
Source: Courtesy State of Wisconsin, Department of Health Services. Used with permission.

RESTAURANT / RETAIL FOOD INSPECTION REPORT
DPH 45002B (Rev. 07/06) or FFD-111

Page _____ of _____

Business Name

Date of Inspection

TEMPERATURES

Item / Location	Temp	Item / Location	Temp	Item / Location	Temp

WAREWASHING INFORMATION

Machine Name	Sanitization Method	Thermo Label	PPM	Sanitizer Name	Sanitizer Type

CDC Risk Code Factor Abbreviations and Violation by Category Numbers Table
(Use this table to group CDC risk factor listed below with violation from page 1)

Unsafe Sources (US)	Inadequate Cooking (IC)	Improper Hold (IH)	Cross Contamination (CC)	Personal Hygiene (PH)	Other CDC Factors (O)
9	16	18	13	3	1A
10	17	19	14	4	1B
11		20	15	5	2
12		21		6	23
		22		7	24
				8	25
					26

For each violation sited, use above table and record CDC Risk Code Factor abbreviation (such as "US" or "IH"), violation number, list from the Wisconsin Food Code (WFC) the reference number that refers to the area in violation.

CDC Code Factor Abbreviation	Violation Number	WFC Reference Number
Violation Description:		
Code Requirement:		
Corrective Action Required:		
Comply By:		

CDC Code Factor Abbreviation	Violation Number	WFC Reference Number
Violation Description:		
Code Requirement:		
Corrective Action Required:		
Comply By:		

CDC Code Factor Abbreviation	Violation Number	WFC Reference Number
Violation Description:		
Code Requirement:		
Corrective Action Required		
Comply By		

I understand and agree to comply with the corrections ordered on this report. I understand that failure to comply could result in legal action or loss of license.

SIGNATURE - Person In Charge   Date Signed

SIGNATURE - Inspector   ID No.

Figure 17 (Continued)

91

SUMMARY

Millions of people become ill each year as a result of consuming a food that was microbially, chemically, or physically contaminated. A single error in food handling in a foodservice operation can cause a major outbreak. It is the responsibility of the food manager to have the necessary knowledge base and an understanding of food handling principles to design, implement, and monitor a successful food safety program.

APPLICATION OF CHAPTER CONTENTS

The Dining and Culinary Services unit for the University of Wisconsin–Madison is complex in that food is produced in a high-volume commissary, using cook/chill production and transported across the 800-acre campus at least twice a day. In addition to its four main residential units, food is prepared and transported to a campus day care center and numerous catering events. One can well imagine the challenges these complexities pose for development, implementation, and maintenance of a comprehensive, integrated food safety program.

Despite these challenges, foodservice administration is committed to food safety, has made it a priority, and integrates principles of food safety in all aspects of its programming starting with menu planning. Food items are not placed on the menu unless administration has the utmost confidence that the item can be purchased, stored, produced, and served safely. Administration also recognizes that its food safety programming needs to be adapted to change, big and small, that may influence how food safety is practiced where and whenever food is handled.

At present, foodservice administration is assessing its food safety programming relative to its goal of increasing the percent of produce purchased fresh from local, organic producers. Given the high-volume of production (upwards of 15,000 meals per day), it is necessary to purchase most produce in a "foodservice ready" form. For example, on an annual basis, the dining unit uses in excess of 10,000 pounds of diced onions. Most of these onions are purchased through the prime vendor and are delivered diced, frozen ready-to-use. Products such as this are relatively low risk from a food safety perspective as they are fully processed and require little to no handling.

Fresh produce, on the other hand, needs to be trimmed, washed, and processed: activities that integrate handling and opportunity for contamination.

CRITICAL-THINKING QUESTIONS

1. Go to the CDC Web site and review confirmed outbreaks of foodborne illness. Have any outbreaks occurred in college and university settings? Compare the frequency to other types of on-site foodservices. What might explain any discrepancy?
2. Does the Dining and Culinary Services unit for UW-Madison serve any highly susceptible populations? Explain your answer.
3. What items might be left off of the menus at UW-Madison out of concern for food safety?
4. The 2009 Food Code states that all food must be purchased from "an approved source." What does this mean when purchasing fresh produce from a local farmer compared to a national distributor?
5. Describe how the prerequisite programs for receiving and storage might need to be revised to account for the increase of fresh produce.
6. Describe how a HACCP plan for vegetable soup may need to be altered when using fresh rather "foodservice ready" vegetables.
7. UW-Madison buys apples, onions, tomatoes, and melons from local producers. For the purposes of HACCP plans, identify the inherent biological hazards for each product.
8. Describe the role of administration in maintaining a comprehensive, integrated food safety program at UW-Madison. What are some of the unique challenges?

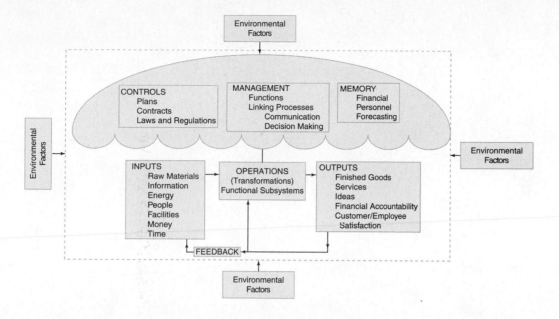

9. What regulatory authorities at the federal, state, and local levels might serve as good resources when questions arise relative to compliance?
10. What might a sanitarian look for during an inspection once he/she is aware that more local, fresh, and organic produce is being integrated into the menu?

CHAPTER REVIEW QUESTIONS

1. What is the definition of a foodborne illness?
2. Identify the federal agencies that oversee food safety in the United States.
3. What is the role of the food manager in food safety?
4. Identify at least three "at-risk" populations as defined by the U.S. Public Health Service.
5. What conditions contribute to the growth of bacteria?
6. Define *intoxication* and *infection* as related to foodborne disease.
7. Cite examples of chemical, physical, and biological hazards.
8. What is cross-contamination?
9. Describe how *Salmonella* and *Staphylococcus aureus* contamination can occur. How can they be controlled?
10. What is HACCP, and how can it be applied in the foodservice setting?

SELECTED WEB SITES

www.foodsafety.gov (U.S. government's "gateway" to food safety)
www.fsis.usda.gov (USDA Food Safety and Inspection Service)
www.fda.gov/Food/FoodSafety (Center for Food Safety and Nutrition; FDA)
www.cdc.gov (Centers for Disease Control and Prevention)
www.nraef.org (National Restaurant Association Educational Foundation)
www.foodallergy.org (Food Allergy and Anaphylaxis Network)
www.nsf.org (National Sanitation Foundation International)
www.osha.gov (Occupational Safety and Health Administration)

Facility Sanitation and Worker Safety

From Chapter 4 of *Foodservice Management: Principles and Practices*, Twelfth Edition, June Payne-Palacio, Monica Theis.
Copyright © 2012 by Pearson Education, Inc. Published by Pearson Prentice Hall. All rights reserved.

Facility Sanitation and Worker Safety

Scott David Patterson/Shutterstock

PROVIDING A CLEAN, SAFE FOODSERVICE FACILITY IS basic to achieving a successful operation and ensuring the health and well-being of both employees and customers. In addition, a clean, safe environment contributes to the aesthetic satisfaction that guests expect from dining and gives a feeling of personal security to all. Sanitation and safety are closely related environmental factors to be considered when planning a facility and followed in its daily operations. Maintaining high standards of cleanliness and making sure that the workplace is free from hazards are management responsibilities.

Regulations pertaining to cleaning, sanitation, and safety are established through city, state, and federal law. Agencies such as the **Occupational Safety and Health Administration (OSHA)**, U.S. Public Health Service (USPHS), and state and city health departments enforce these regulations. Organizations such as the National Sanitation Foundation International (NSF) and the National Safety Council recommend standards. Results of research conducted at universities, hospitals, and food, chemical, and equipment manufacturing companies provide data for recommending or setting industry standards. These groups, individually or cooperatively, work with the foodservice industry to prepare, distribute, and interpret pertinent information in publications, exhibits, and through the Internet. Some groups present seminars, classes, and programs for various foodservice groups and the public. All are aimed at informing those responsible for foodservice operations of the rules, regulations, and standards to be met and how to achieve them.

Standards of cleanliness and sanitation will be only as high as those established and enforced by the foodservice director. That person, *the person in charge*, must instill a philosophy of good sanitation and impart a sense of urgency about the matter to the employees. This is best accomplished through an ongoing training program for the foodservice workers. This assumes that foodservice directors themselves have had some training and are knowledgeable about cleaning and sanitation principles and practices that are either mandated by government regulation or accepted as best practice for the foodservice industry. In many states, a formal training program in food protection and safety is mandatory before foodservice operators can obtain a required food sanitation certificate. In other states and local jurisdictions, voluntary or mandatory certification programs for managers, as well as workers, have been initiated by state restaurant associations or by the local health department.

The purpose of this chapter is to review the principles of cleaning and sanitation as they relate to warewashing and maintenance of facilities. Worker safety is also included in this chapter because it closely relates to the care and maintenance of an operation. The chapter concludes with guidelines on how to design, implement, and monitor a prerequisite program on cleaning and sanitation.

Occupational Safety and Health Administration
the main federal agency charged with the enforcement of worker safety and health legislation

KEY CONCEPTS

1. Cleaning and sanitizing are distinct but related procedures.

2. Foodservice managers invest in a formulary of cleaners and sanitizers that best meets the needs of the operation.

3. Food contact surfaces can be sanitized using either the heat or the chemical method.

4. Type and use are indicators of how and when a piece of equipment should be cleaned.

5. Machine and manual methods of dishwashing are used to clean and sanitize production and service ware.

6. A carefully designed program of facility cleaning and maintenance protects food and workers.

7. Preventive maintenance extends the life cycle of equipment.

8. Pest control is logically a component of a cleaning and sanitation program.

9. Cleaning and sanitation inspections are typically conducted by local regulatory authorities.

10. The health of employees is protected through worker safety programs.

CLEANING AND SANITATION

■ **KEY CONCEPT: Cleaning and sanitizing are distinct but related procedures. Food contact surfaces must be cleaned and sanitized.**

The terms *cleaning* and *sanitizing* (or sanitation) are sometimes erroneously assumed to be one and the same, when in fact there are important differences. Cleaning is the physical removal of visible soil and food from a surface. Sanitizing is a procedure that reduces the number of potentially harmful microorganisms to safe levels on **food contact surfaces** such as china, tableware, equipment, and work surfaces. Sanitized surfaces are not necessarily *sterile*, which means to be free of microorganisms.

Cleaning and sanitizing are resource-intensive procedures in any foodservice operation. They require time, labor, chemicals, equipment, and energy. Careful design and monitoring of the cleaning and sanitizing procedures result in optimal protection of employees and customers. Mismanagement of these two functions can result in:

Ineffective cleaning and sanitation

- Injury or illness to employees or customers
- Waste of chemicals
- Damage to equipment and facilities

Typically the foodservice manager works closely with a representative of a chemical company to select cleaning and sanitation compounds appropriate to the needs of the operation. It is therefore essential that managers understand the principles of cleaning and sanitizing and the many factors that influence these procedures.

Principles of Cleaning

Cleaning is a two-step task that occurs when a cleaning compound (or agent) such as a detergent is put in contact with a soiled surface. Pressure is applied using a brush, cloth, scrub pad, or water spray for a long enough period of time to penetrate the soil so it can be easily removed during the second step of rinsing. Many factors influence the effectiveness of this cleaning process. Table 1 is a summary of these factors. Each of these factors must be considered when making a cost-effective selection of detergents and other cleaning compounds such as solvents, acids, and abrasives.

Food Contact Surface
a surface of equipment or a utensil with which food comes into contact

Table 1	Factors that influence the cleaning process.
FACTOR	**INFLUENCE ON CLEANING PROCESS**
1. Type of water	Minerals in hard water can reduce the effectiveness of some detergents. Hard water can cause lime deposits or leave a scale, especially on equipment where hot water is used, such as in dish machines and steam tables.
2. Water temperature	Generally, the higher the temperature of the water used for cleaning, the faster and more efficient the action of the detergent; however, $\leqslant 120°F$ is recommended (and in some cases mandated), as higher temperatures can result in burns.
3. Surface	Different surfaces, especially metals, vary in the ease with which they can be cleaned.
4. Type of cleaning compound	Soap can leave a greasy film. Abrasives such as scouring powders can scratch soft surfaces. Many cleaning agents are formulated for specific cleaning problems; lime removal products are an example.
5. Type of soil to be removed	Soils tend to fall into one of three categories: protein (eggs), grease or oils (butter), or water soluble (sugar). Stains tend to be acid or alkaline (tea, fruit juice). Ease of cleaning depends on which category the soil is from and the condition of the soil (e.g., fresh, baked-on, dried, or ground-in).

■ **KEY CONCEPT:** **Foodservice managers invest in a formulary of cleaners and sanitizers that best meets the needs of the operation.**

Detergents. The selection of a compound to aid in cleaning the many types of soil and food residues is complex because so many compounds are available from which to choose. An understanding of the basic principles involved in cleaning will assist the foodservice manager in making this decision.

Detergents are defined as cleaning agents, solvents, or any substance that will remove foreign or soiling material from surfaces. Specifically listed are soap, soap powders, cleansers, acids, volatile solvents, and abrasives. Water alone has some detergency value, but more often it serves as the carrier of the cleansing agent to the soiled surface. Its efficiency for removing soil is increased when combined with certain chemical cleaning agents.

The three basic phases of detergency are penetration, suspension, and rinsing. The following actions and agents are required for each phase:

1. **Penetration:** The cleaning agent must penetrate between the particles of soil and between the layers of soil and the surface to which it adheres. This action, known as **wetting**, reduces surface tension and makes penetration possible.

2. **Suspension:** An agent holds the loosened soil in the washing solution so it can be flushed away and not redeposited. Agents, which vary according to the type of soil, include the following: *For sugars and salts*, water is the agent because sugars and salts are water soluble and are easily converted into solutions. *For fat particles*, an emulsifying action is required to **saponify** the fat and carry it away. Soap, highly alkaline salts, and nonionic synthetics may be used. *For protein particles*, colloidal solutions must be formed by *peptizing* (known also as **sequestering** or deflocculating). This action prevents curd formation in hard water; otherwise, solvents or abrasives may be needed.

3. **Rinsing agent:** This agent flushes away soils and cleaners so they are not redeposited on the surfaces being washed. Clean, clear hot water is usually effective alone. With some types of water, a *drying* agent may be needed to speed drying by helping the rinse water drain off surfaces quickly. This eliminates alkaline and hard water spotting, films, and streaks on the tableware or other items being cleaned.

In foodservice, the cleaning function focuses mainly on food contact surfaces, including china, glass, and metal surfaces. Common soils to be removed are grease and carbohydrate and protein food particles that may adhere to dishes, glassware, silverware, cooking utensils, worktable tops, floors, or other surfaces. Some types of food soils such as sugars, starches, and certain salts are water soluble. The addition of a wetting agent to hot water will readily remove most of these simple soils. The soils that are insoluble in water, such as animal and vegetable fats and proteins, organic fiber, and oils, are more difficult to remove. Abrasives or solvents may be necessary in some cases to effect complete cleanliness.

The use of a "balanced" detergent or one with a carefully adjusted formula of ingredients suitable for the hardness of the water and the characteristics of the soil is advised in order to produce the best results. The properties of the detergent must cause complete removal of the soil without deposition of any substance or deleterious effect on surfaces washed.

Detergents for *dishwashing machines* are complex combinations of chemicals that completely remove soil in a single pass through the machine. The selected detergent works to soften the water, solubilize and emulsify greases, break down proteins, suspend soils, protect the metal of the machine, increase wetting action, and counteract minerals in the wash water. Other characteristics desired in some situations are defoaming action where excess sudsing is a problem and chlorination action where a chlorine-type detergent is used to remove stains and discolorations.

Solvent Cleaners. Solvent cleaners, commonly referred to as degreasers, are necessary to clean equipment and surface areas that get soiled with grease. Ovens and grills are examples of areas that need frequent degreasing. These products are alkaline based and are formulated to dissolve grease.

Detergent
cleaning agents, solvents, or any substances that will remove foreign or soiling material from a surface

Wetting
The action of a cleaning agent to penetrate between particles of soil and between the layers of soil and a surface to which the soil adheres

Suspension
The action of a cleaning agent required to hold the loosened soil in the washing solution so it can be flushed away and not redeposited

Saponify
To turn fats into soap by reaction with an alkali

Sequestering
The isolating of substances such as chemical ions so they cannot react. In foodservice this is a desired characteristic of polyphosphate detergents to bind lime and magnesium of hard water

Rinsing agent
A compound designed to remove and flush away soils and cleaners so they are not redeposited on surfaces being washed

Acid Cleaners.   Tough cleaning problems such as lime buildup on dishwashing machines and rust on shelving are treated with acid cleaners. There are a number of these products from which to choose, and they vary depending on the specific purpose of the product.

Abrasives.   Abrasive cleaners are generally used for particularly tough soils that do not respond to solvents or acids. These products must be used carefully to avoid damage to the surface that is being cleaned.

Principles of Sanitation

KEY CONCEPT: Food contact surfaces can be sanitized using either the heat or the chemical method.

Immediately after cleaning, all food contact surfaces must be sanitized. Heat and chemical sanitizing are the two methods for sanitizing surfaces effectively.

Heat Sanitizing.   The objective of heat sanitizing is to expose the clean surface to high heat for a long enough time to kill harmful organisms. Heat sanitizing can be done manually or by a high-temperature machine. The minimum temperature range necessary to kill most harmful microorganisms is 162°F to 165°F. Table 2 summarizes minimum washing and sanitizing temperatures for manual and machine methods.

Chemical Sanitizing.   A second method for effective sanitizing is through the use of chemicals. One of the reasons for choosing this method over heat sanitizing is the savings that are realized in energy usage, as lower water temperatures are used with chemical sanitizers, eliminating the need for booster heaters.

Chemical sanitizing is achieved in two ways. The first is by immersing the clean object in a sanitizing solution of appropriate concentration and for a specific length of time, usually one minute. The second method is by rinsing, swabbing, or spraying the object with the sanitizing solution. The rinsing and spraying methods can be done manually or by machine. Careful management of sanitizers is important for several reasons:

- The sanitizer becomes depleted over time and must be tested frequently to ensure that the strength of the solution is maintained for effective sanitizing. Test kits are available from the manufacturer.
- The sanitation solution can get bound up by food particles and detergent residues if surfaces are inadequately rinsed, leaving the sanitizer ineffective.

Table 2 Minimum washing and sanitizing temperatures for heat sanitation.		
	WASH	**SANITIZE**
Manual	110°F	171°F
Machine (spray types)		
1. Stationary rack, single-temperature machine	165°F	165°F
2. Conveyor, dual-temperature machine	160°F	180°F
3. Stationary rack, dual-temperature machine	150°F	180°F
4. Multitank, conveyor, multitemperature machine	150°F	180°F

(1) Some local regulations may mandate stricter standards.

(2) Minimum time for exposure to heat is 1 minute.

(3) 194°F is the maximum upper limit for heat sanitation for manual or machine methods, as higher temperatures cause rapid evaporation and therefore inadequate time for effective sanitation.

Source: From the 2009 Food Code, U.S. Public Health Service.

Table 3   Properties of commonly used chemical sanitizers.

	CHLORINE	IODINE	QUATERNARY AMMONIUM
Minimum Concentration			
• For immersion	50 parts per million (PPM)	12.5–25.0 ppm	220 ppm
• For spray cleaning	50 PPM	12.5–25.0 ppm	220 ppm
Temperature of Solution	Above 75°F (24°C) Below 115°F (46°C)	75°F (29°C) Iodine will leave solution at 120°F (49°C)	Above 75°F (24°C)
Contact Time			
• For immersion	7 seconds	30 seconds	30 seconds—some products require longer contact time—read label
• For spray cleaning	Follow manufacturer's directions	Follow manufacturer's directions	
pH (detergent residue raises pH, so rinse completely)	Must be below 8.0	Must be below 5.0	Most effective at 7.0, but varies with compound
Corrosiveness	Corrosive to some substances	Noncorrosive	Noncorrosive
Reaction to Organic Contaminants in Water	Quickly inactivated	Made less effective	Not easily affected
Reaction to Hard Water	Not affected	Not affected	Some compounds inactivated—read label; hardness over 500 ppm is undesirable
Indication of Proper Strength	Test kit required	Amber color indicates presence. Use test kit to determine concentration	Test kit required. Follow label instructions closely

The three types of commonly used chemical sanitizers in foodservice operations are chlorine, iodine, and quaternary ammonium compounds (quarts). The properties of these sanitizers are summarized in Table 3.

Methods of Cleaning Equipment

■ KEY CONCEPT: **Type and use are indicators of how and when a piece of equipment should be cleaned.**

Ease of cleaning is a factor considered during the purchase of equipment. This is made easier by organizations such as the National Sanitation Foundation International (NSF) and Underwriter's Laboratory. The NSF, for example, establishes standards for sanitary design and certifies equipment which is evident by its seal of approval (Figure 1) Methods by which equipment can be cleaned are categorized into three groups. **Clean-in-place (CIP)** or mechanical cleaning requires no disassembly or only partial disassembly. These pieces of equipment are cleaned and sanitized by the circulation of the chemical compounds through a piping system. This method of cleaning is most often applied to stationary or built-in

Figure 1   NSF seal of approval.

Clean-in-place (CIP)
A method of cleaning that requires no disassembly

Clean-out-of-place (COP)

A method of cleaning whereby equipment can be partially disassembled for cleaning

Manual cleaning

Complete disassembly of equipment can be partially dissembled for cleaning

equipment. **Clean-out-of-place (COP)** means that the equipment is partially disassembled for cleaning. Some removable parts may be run through a dish machine. The third category is **manual cleaning** that requires the complete disassembly for cleaning and functional inspection.

DISHWASHING

■ **KEY CONCEPT:** Machine and manual methods of dishwashing are used to clean and sanitize production and service ware.

Dishwashing (sometimes referred to as warewashing) requires a two-part operation, that is, the cleaning procedure to free dishes and utensils of visible soil by scraping or a water flow method, and the sanitizing or bactericidal treatment to minimize microbiological hazards. Dishwashing for public eating places is subject to rigid regulations.

The two groups of equipment and utensils that are commonly considered for discussion under dishwashing are production utensils, such as pots, pans, strainers, skillets, and kettles soiled in the process of food preparation, and service ware, such as dishes, glassware, spoons, forks, and knives.

Production Utensils

Mechanical pot and pan washing equipment is relatively expensive; therefore, in many foodservices this activity remains a manual operation. A three-compartment sink is recommended for any manual dishwashing setup (see Figure 2).

Soil is loosened from the utensils by scraping and then soaking them in hot water in one compartment of the sink. After the surface soil has been removed from the utensils, the sink is drained and refilled with hot water to which a washing compound is added. This step can be eliminated with a four-compartment sink that has a presoak compartment. The utensils are washed in the hot detergent solution in the first compartment; rinsed in the second compartment, and sanitized in the third compartment.

Figure 2 Three compartment sink for manual wash, rinse, and sanitation.
Source: Courtesy ITW Food Equipment Group, Troy, OH. Used with permission.

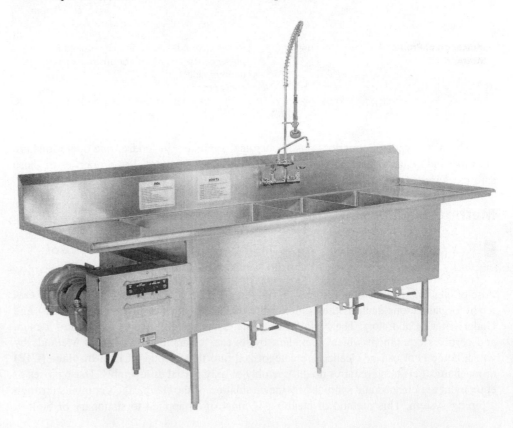

There are several methods for sanitizing both dishes and utensils. One recommended method is by immersing them for at least one minute in a lukewarm (at least 75°F) chlorine bath containing a minimum of fifty parts per million (ppm) available chlorine. Dishes and utensils must be thoroughly clean for a chlorine rinse to be an effective germicidal treatment. Another method of sanitizing hand-washed dishes or utensils is immersion in clean soft water of at least 170° for one minute. The hot, clean utensils should be air dried before being stacked upside down on racks or hung for storage.

Dishes, Glassware, and Silverware

Items used for eating and drinking can be washed by hand or by mechanical dishwashers. *Prewashing* or *preflushing*, which applies to any type of water scraping of dishes before washing, is recommended to minimize food soil in the wash water. The usual types of water scraping equipment include (1) a combination forced water stream and food waste collection unit built into the scraping table, by use of which dishes are rinsed under the stream of water before racking, (2) a hose and nozzle arrangement over a sink for spraying the dishes after they are in racks, and (3) a prewash cabinet through which the racks of soiled dishes pass and are jet sprayed to remove food particles before they enter the wash section of the dishwashing machine. The prewash cabinet can be built in as part of the larger model machines or, in small installations, may be a separate unit attached to the wash machine in such a way that the water used is the overflow from the wash tank. The prewash water should be at a temperature of 110°F to 140°F to provide for the liquefying of fat and the noncoagulation of protein food particles adhering to dish surfaces. The installation and use of a prewash system lessens the amount of organic waste and the number of microorganisms entering the wash tank, removes fat that might otherwise result in suds formation, reduces the number of wash water changes, cuts the costs for detergents, and results in cleaner dishes. Figure 3 is an example of a job breakdown for the mechanical washing of tableware.

After the prerinse, the dishes are loaded into racks or on conveyor belts in such a way that food-contact surfaces will be exposed to direct application of the wash water with detergent and to the clean rinse waters. Figures 4 and 5 are two examples of dishwashing machines. Cups, bowls, and glasses must be inverted and overcrowding or nesting of pieces avoided if dishwashing is to be effective. Wash water shall not be less than 120°F, and if hot water is the sanitizing agent, the rinse water shall be 180°F. Figure 6 is an example of a dish machine temperature documentation form for quality control. The pressure of the rinse water must be maintained at a minimum of 15 pounds per square inch (psi) but not more than 25 psi to make the sanitizing effective.

China, glassware, and silver can be washed in a multipurpose machine, but it is preferred wherever possible to subject glasses to friction by brushes so that all parts of the glass are

Figure 3 Job breakdown for washing tableware in a dish machine.

Tableware Cleaning and Sanitizing Procedure

1. Fill the soak tub with hot water.
2. Dispense soaking agent into the soak tub after water reaches proper depth as indicated by a line etched into the tub.
3. Place rack into the bottom of the soak tub.
4. Fill with soiled tableware to cover the bottom of the rack.
5. Send the rack through the dish machine.
6. Retrieve the rack and carry back to the loading end.
7. Place tableware in brown plastic cylinders with the food-contact end facing up (limit to 10 pieces per cylinder—do not overfill).
8. Place cylinders on the rack and run through the machine two more times.
9. Wash hands.
10. Shake excess water from cylinders and place on a clean cart; transport to the sorting area.

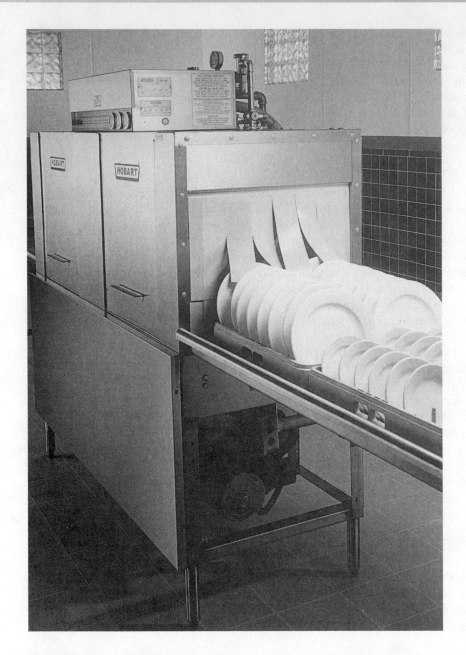

Figure 4 Double-tank automated dish machine.
Source: Courtesy ITW Food Equipment Group, Troy, OH. Used with permission.

thoroughly cleaned, which means the use of a special machine designed for that purpose (Figure 7). This is especially important in bars and similar establishments where glasses are the primary utensils used. To prevent water spotting, it is advisable to use a suitable detergent for the washing of silver and also a drying agent with high wetting property in the final rinse water to facilitate air drying. The introduction of a drying agent with low foam characteristics into the sanitizing rinse promotes rapid drying of all types of tableware. Provision for the storage of clean glasses and cups in the racks or containers in which they have been washed reduces the possibility of hand contamination.

Some machines are designed for a chemical solution rinse rather than the high-energy use of the 180°F temperature water. In this case, the rinse water used with the chemical sanitizer shall not be less than 75°F or less than that specified by the manufacturer. Chemicals used for sanitizing should be dispensed automatically to make certain that the proper amount and concentration are used. Dishes can be dried by hot air blast within the machine or allowed to air dry.

All steps require energy except air drying. For this reason, the low-temperature models are preferred by some operators. To minimize energy use, only fully loaded racks or conveyors should be put through the machine.

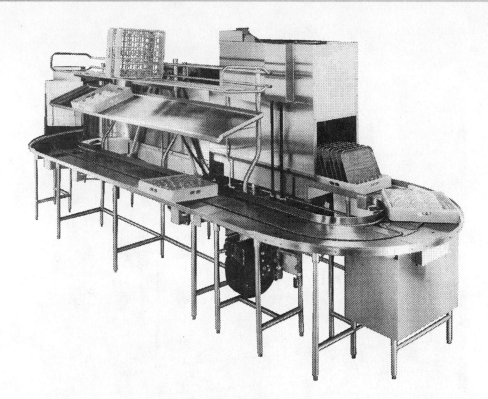

Figure 5 Automated dish machine; circular design.
Source: Courtesy ITW Food Equipment Group. Troy, OH. Used with permission.

The NSF International establishes standards for wash and rinse cycles of three types of dishwashing machines: (1) single-tank, stationary rack, hood, and door types; (2) single-tank, conveyor type; and (3) multiple-tank conveyor type with dishes in inclined position on conveyor or in rack. These standards can be obtained and used as a check on specifications of various makes of dishwashers and by managers for ensuring that specified conditions such as water temperature and pressure are met. Employees, too, should be trained to

Figure 6 Temperature documentation form.

Heartland Country Village	Dishwasher Temperatures					
Month	Breakfast		Lunch		Dinner	
	Wash	Rinse	Wash	Rinse	Wash	Rinse
1						
2						
3						
4						
5						
6						
7						
8						
9						
10						
11						

Figure 7 Glasswasher.
Source: Courtesy of ITW Food Equipment Group. Troy, OH. Used with permission.

follow proper procedures in the use and care of the dishwashing machine, or hand washing of dishes if no machine is available.

Any machine can fail in its function if it is not kept clean and properly maintained, and dishwashing equipment is no exception. Corrosion or lime deposits in nozzles can alter the jet or spray functionality. Also, detergent sanitizers can be inactivated by contact with soiled surfaces and lose their power of penetration. The removal of microbial contamination is necessary; otherwise the washed surfaces of dishes will have bacterial populations and soil deposited on them proportionate to that in the washing solution.

Good maintenance includes frequent examination and lubrication where needed by a qualified maintenance person to ensure the continuing satisfactory operation of motors, nozzles, pumps, thermostats, thermometers, and all moving parts of a dishwashing machine. This maintenance is often provided by a representative from the chemical company under a service contract.

The installation of elaborate equipment, however, offers no real insurance for good sanitation, because the efficiency of the machines depends almost entirely on the operator, the availability of an adequate supply of hot water at the proper temperature and pressure, the selection and concentration of the detergent used for the hardness of the water, and the length of time the dishes are subjected to treatment. In the small, hand-operated, single-tank machines, the process and length of washing time are under the control of the operator and are followed by the rinsing process, also under manual control. Other machines have automatic controls that regulate the length of times for washing and rinsing. Thermometers that record the temperatures of both wash and rinse waters and thermostatic controls are included as standard parts of dishwashing machines. Booster heaters with temperature controls are available and necessary to provide the sanitizing rinse temperature, because the water at 180°F in the pipe lines of a building would be a hazard to personal safety. The installation of electronic detergent dispensers makes it possible to maintain optimum detergent concentration in the wash water and sanitizing chemical rinse in low-temperature machines. Each of these mechanical aids is most helpful in reducing variability due to the human element and ensures clean, properly sanitized dishes and pots and pans.

FACILITIES CLEANING AND MAINTENANCE

■ **KEY CONCEPT:** A carefully designed program of facility cleaning and maintenance protects food and workers.

The total facility cleaning and maintenance program of a foodservice department must be planned to reflect concern for sanitation as "a way of life." Facility sanitation results can be obtained through establishing high standards, rigid scheduling of assignments that are clearly understood by the workers, ongoing training, proper use of cleaning supplies, provision of proper materials and equipment to accomplish tasks, and frequent meaningful inspections and performance reviews.

Organization and Scheduling

The organization of a plan for facility cleaning and maintenance begins with a list of duties to be performed daily, weekly, and monthly. In most organizations there is a philosophy of "sanitation is a part of every person's job," and the daily cleaning of the equipment and utensils used by each person is that person's responsibility.

Regular cleaning, for example, of counter tops, floors, and so on, needs to be done daily and is usually assigned as part of an employee's regular daily duties. Other cleaning tasks that need to be done less frequently must be scheduled and assigned as needed—for instance, daily, weekly, monthly. Examples include washing walls and cleaning hoods and filters. Some large operations have cleaning crews that are responsible for these tasks. In smaller operations, however, the manager must decide on a way to distribute these tasks fairly among the employees. All these tasks must be written as a master cleaning schedule that at a minimum includes what each task is, when it should be done, and who should do it. Master schedules must be supplemented with specific cleaning tasks, and employees must be trained on the proper cleaning procedures.

General cleaning of floors, windows, walls, lighting fixtures, and certain equipment should be assigned to personnel as needed, because it is often done in cooperation with the housekeeping and maintenance departments of organizations. Tasks can be scheduled in rotation so a few of them are performed each day; at the end of the week or month, all will have been completed and the workers then repeat the schedule. Figure 8 gives an example of such a schedule. Each of the duties on the assignment list must be explained in detail on a written work sheet or "job breakdown" for the employee to follow. This description is the procedure that management requires to be used in performing each task. The job breakdown includes the name of the task, tools, equipment, and materials to be used, and the step-by-step list of *what to do* and *how to do it*. Figure 9 is an example of such a job breakdown for cleaning and sanitizing a specific piece of equipment.

In addition to establishing procedures, a time standard for accomplishing each task is important. Based on studies of the actual time required for performing the same tasks by several different workers, an average time standard can be set. This is used to determine labor-hour requirements for each department within the foodservice and also provides management with data to establish a realistic daily workload.

Figure 8 Example of cleaning schedule for tasks that need to be done on a weekly or monthly basis.

Typical Job Assignments for Heavy-duty Cleaning

Monday	Filter grease in snack bar
	Clean left side of cafeteria hot-food pass-through
	Clean all kitchen windows
	Clean all kitchen table legs
	Vacuum air-conditioner filters; wipe exterior of air conditioner
	Wash all walls around garbage cans
	Complete high dusting around cooking areas
	Clean outside of steam kettles
	Wash kitchen carts
	Clean cart-washing area
Tuesday	Snack bar: Wash inside of hood exhaust
	Clean all corners, walls, and behind refrigerator
	Empty and clean grease can
	Wash garbage cans
	Main range area: Clean sides of ovens, deep-fat fryers, grills, drip pans, and hood over ovens
Wednesday	Clean two refrigerators in cooks' area
	Clean right side of cafeteria hot-food pass-through
	Clean kettles, backs of steamers, and behind steamers
	Clean walls around assembly line and pot room
Thursday	Clean all ovens in cooks' area, bottoms of ovens, and between ovens and stoves
	Clean long tables in cooks' area, including legs and underneath
	Clean and mop storage area
Friday	Clean stainless steel behind kettles and steamers
	Clean main range and tops of ovens
	Clean legs of assembly line tables
	Clean vents in all refrigeration equipment
	Clean cart-washing area

Equipment. Heavy-duty power equipment is available to foodservice managers to aid in keeping the facility clean and properly maintained. Mechanical food waste disposals are indispensable in most foodservices. Disposals are located where food waste originates in quantities such as in vegetable and salad preparation units, the main cooking area, and the dishwashing room. In the last, a disposal can be incorporated as a part of the scraping and prewash units of the dishwashing machine.

Figure 9 Example of a job breakdown for cleaning and sanitizing a piece of equipment.

Cheese Slicer
Cleaning Procedure

Tools and supplies needed:
Wash cloths
Red bucket for cleaning solution
Spray bottle for sanitizer

Cleaning products needed:
Detergent
Sanitizer

Cleaning and Sanitizing Procedure
1. Mix cleaning and sanitizing solutions per instructions on labels; place in appropriate containers. Label as appropriate.
2. Remove the slicing tray by turning the red knob that connects the bottom of the tray to the base of the machine.
3. Remove the circular guard on top of the blade by turning the black knob at the back of the machine until the guard comes loose
4. Wash the tray and the guard using the cleaning solution; rinse
5. Spray with sanitizer and allow to dry
6. While the tray and guard dry wipe down the rest of the machine with clean wash cloth, then sanitize

Compactors, pulpers, and can and bottle crushers (Figure 10) reduce appreciably the volume of trash, including items such as disposable dishes and tableware, food cartons, bags, and crates.

Care of equipment used in food preparation, storage, and service is an essential part of the maintenance program to ensure good sanitation. All food contact equipment, containers, and utensils must be cleaned thoroughly after *each* use. This is especially true of meat grinders and slicers, cutting boards, and knives in order to prevent any cross-contamination. Color-coded cutting boards, knives, and other food preparation utensils are available with the intent to keep different types of food separate.

The thorough cleaning and sanitizing of stationary equipment are more difficult but quite as necessary as the cleaning of dishes and small portable equipment. No piece of large equipment should be purchased unless the operating parts can be disassembled easily for cleaning purposes. Dishwashing machines, mixers, peelers, slicing machines, and stationary can openers are also examples of equipment that should be cleaned after each use. The standard practices for hand dishwashing should be followed in the routine cleaning of such equipment.

Preventive Maintenance

■ **KEY CONCEPT:** **Preventive maintenance extends the life cycle of equipment.**

Preventive maintenance is a documented program of routine checks or inspections of facilities and equipment to ensure the sanitary, safe, and efficient operation of a foodservice department. It includes regular cleaning and maintenance such as oiling motors on mixers, and any needed repairs that may become evident during the inspection process. This program is usually done in cooperation with the maintenance or plant engineering department.

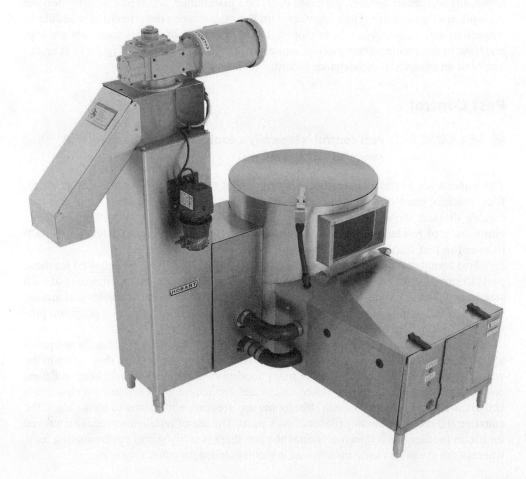

Figure 10   Equipment for waste management.
Source: Courtesy ITW Food Equipment Group, Troy, OH. Used with permission.

Figure 11 Equipment record for preventive maintenance.

EQUIPMENT RECORD CARD

Equipment: _____

Manufacturer: _____

Model No.: _____ Serial No.: _____

Capacity: _____ Attachments: _____

Operation: Electric [ ]   Gas [ ]   Steam [ ]   Hand [ ]

Purchased from: _____ [ ] New [ ] Used Cost: $ _____

Purchase date: _____ Guarantee: _____ Warranty: _____

Routine maintenance: _____ (daily weekly, monthly)

_____

Date	Description of Repairs	Cost
_____	_____	_____
_____	_____	_____
_____	_____	_____

Each piece of equipment is inspected by a representative from the department on a routine basis. The foodservice manager develops a list or file of all equipment including name, identification number, purchase date, and installation and repair information for each piece of equipment. Then, together with the maintenance department, a schedule of inspection and routine repair is developed. Detailed records of repairs and costs are kept and used to determine when a piece of equipment needs to be replaced. Figure 11 is an example of an equipment maintenance record.

Pest Control

■ **KEY CONCEPT:** **Pest control is logically a component of a cleaning and sanitation program.**

The importance of rodent and insect control cannot be emphasized enough. Rats, mice, flies, roaches, grain insects, fruit flies, and gnats all facilitate the transmission of communicable disease; therefore, it is essential for any foodservice to try to effect complete elimination of resident pest infestations and then to correct conditions within the establishment so that such pests cannot gain entrance in the future.

Two conditions—food and a place to "harbor" or hide and live—are required for these pests to survive. Adherence to strict rules for proper food storage and maintenance of high standards for cleaning the nooks and corners, such as drawers in cooks' tables and around sink pipes and drains, as well as the general overall sanitation and cleaning program, provide good preventive maintenance against pests.

Many roaches and insects gain entrance to a building on incoming foodstuffs and packages, which makes their control difficult. Their reproduction is rapid, and they thrive in the warm, damp hiding places afforded in many foodservices. Screens to help keep out flies, covered trash and garbage cans, closed cracks and crevices in walls and around equipment and areas around pipes, and clean storerooms are preventive measures to try to block the entrance and reduce the hiding places of such pests. The use of certain insecticides approved for use in foodservice is effective treatment when there is no danger of contaminating food, whereas the use of less toxic insecticides is recommended for contact spraying.

Ratproofing the building to make it impossible for rodents to gain entrance is the best preventive measure for ensuring that it will be free of rodents. This means closing openings as small as one-half inch in diameter, placing rat guards on all wires both inside and outside of pipes leading into the building, and careful joining of the cement walls and foundations of the building. Trapping and the use of rodenticides are part of a rodent-control program and are used either inside or outside the building. However, the most effective rodenticides are also the most dangerous to humans and pets; therefore, they must be used with care and caution.

Constant attention and alertness to signs of pests and an effective program for their destruction by a trained person within the organization or an outside agency are usually required. Specialized entomological services can be scheduled as often as once a month. The effectiveness of such an effort depends on its scope, regularity, and intelligent administration of a cleaning program and proper care of foodstuffs to eliminate the environmental factors conducive to the harboring of pests.

Checks and Inspections

KEY CONCEPT: **Cleaning and sanitation inspections are typically conducted by local regulatory authorities.**

Maintaining high standards of sanitation is essential in *all* foodservice establishments regardless of type or size. Consumers expect and demand a clean facility. In fact, it is one of the first criteria they use for judging an eating establishment. The best way to ensure that proper sanitation procedures and high standards of sanitation are followed and achieved is to develop a departmental cleaning sanitation program. A cooperative effort is necessary to carry out an effective program. By setting high departmental standards and conducting routine self-inspections, management can be assured that sanitation regulations are met. It is critical that management take corrective action on sanitation deficiencies in order for the program to be fully effective.

All foodservice operations are regulated by local, state, or federal agencies. The purpose of these agencies is to administer and enforce regulations and standards for food protection. The major federal agency involved in setting and enforcing standards is the Food and Drug Administration (FDA). The FDA has the responsibility for developing model codes to be adopted by state and local health departments. The FDA Food Code is increasingly recognized as the best source for guidelines and standards on food safety. Official inspections are conducted on a periodic, monthly, or annual basis depending on the type of foodservice and the government agencies to which it is held accountable.

WORKER SAFETY

KEY CONCEPT: **The health of employees is protected through worker safety programs.**

Physical safety of workers and customers alike is a major concern of foodservice administrators. A work environment free of hazards that cause accidents and a dining facility in which customers are safe and secure should be aims of all managers.

The Occupational Safety and Health Act, which became effective April 28, 1971, makes it illegal *not* to have a safe establishment. It is administered by the U.S. Department of Labor. The act mandates action on the part of management to ensure safe and healthful working conditions for all of the nation's wage earners. It states, among other things, that each employer has a duty to furnish the employees with a place of employment that is safe and free from any hazards that can cause serious physical harm or death. The organization set up to enforce this act has the authority to inspect any place of business and to penalize those who do not comply with the provisions of the law. Managers must strictly comply to correct specific potential hazards and furnish written records of any accidents that have occurred.

Two OSHA standards of particular concern to foodservice operators are the Hazard Communication Standard (HCS) and the bloodborne pathogens standard. The HCS, also recognized as the "right to know," requires that employers develop and implement a program to communicate chemical hazards to all employees. An inventory of all chemicals used by the operation must be maintained, and they must be properly labeled. The manufacturer must supply, for each chemical, a material safety data sheet (MSDS) that identifies the chemical and includes a hazard warning. Figure 12 is a sample of an MSDS form. The bloodborne pathogen standard requires that all employees be made aware of potentially infectious materials that they may be exposed to while on duty. Examples of pathogens include the hepatitis B virus and the human immunodeficiency virus (HIV). For the foodservice manager, this means educating employees on the risks of, and proper procedures for, entering patient rooms or cleaning food trays in the dishroom that may be contaminated with hazardous matter.

Figure 12 Example of a material safety data sheet (MSDS).

Material Safety Data Sheet
May be used to comply with
OSHA's Hazard Communication Standard,
29 CFR 1910.1200. Standard must be
consulted for specific requirements.

U.S. Department of Labor
Occupational Safety and Health Administration
(Non-Mandatory Form)
Form Approved
OMB No. 1218-0072

IDENTITY (As Used on Label and List)	Note: Blank spaces are not permitted. If any item is not applicable, or no information is available, the space must be marked to indicate that.

Section I

Manufacturer's Name	Emergency Telephone Number
Address (Number, Street, City, State, and ZIP Code)	Telephone Number for Information
	Date Prepared
	Signature of Preparer (optional)

Section II — Hazardous Ingredients/Identity Information

Hazardous Components (Specific Chemical Identity; Common Name(s))	OSHA PEL	ACGIH TLV	Other Limits Recommended	% (optional)

Section III — Physical/Chemical Characteristics

Boiling Point		Specific Gravity (H$_2$O = 1)	
Vapor Pressure (mm Hg.)		Melting Point	
Vapor Density (AIR = 1)		Evaporation Rate (Butyl Acetate = 1)	
Solubility in Water			
Appearance and Odor			

Section IV — Fire and Explosion Hazard Data

Flash Point (Method Used)		Flammable Limits	LEL	UEL
Extinguishing Media				
Special Fire Fighting Procedures				
Unusual Fire and Explosion Hazards				

(Reproduce locally)

OSHA 174, Sept. 1985

The National Safety Council, although not a regulatory agency but a nonprofit service organization, is devoted to safety education. Through its research, reports, and printed materials available to the public, the council provides valuable assistance to managers of numerous types of businesses, including foodservice.

Worker Safety

The provision of a safe workplace through a well-designed facility with equipment facilities that meet federal, state, and local standards is a first step toward ensuring worker safety. However, safety is more than a building with built-in safety features. Safety can never be *assumed*, because accidents can and do occur. Managers and employees must work together on a safety awareness program to attain a good safety record.

"Accidents don't happen; they are caused"—and they can be prevented. The National Safety Council has defined an accident as any suddenly occurring, unintentional event that causes injury or property damage. An accident has become a symbol of inefficiency, either human or mechanical, and usually represents a monetary loss to the organization. The company not only loses the productivity of the injured individual but also incurs indirect costs such as medical and insurance expenses, cost of training new workers, waste produced by inexperienced substitute workers, administrative costs for investigating and taking care of accidents, and cost of repair or replacement of broken or damaged equipment. Not only from the humanitarian standpoint, but also from the economic, foodservice managers should be aware of the advantages of good safety measures. All should seek ways to improve working conditions and employee performance that will reduce accidents, with their resulting waste, and maintain low accident frequency and severity rates. *Severity rate* is computed by the number of working days lost because of accidents, and *frequency rate* by the number of lost-time accidents during any selected period, each multiplied by 1,000,000 and the result divided by the total number of hours worked during the same period. National Safety Council statistics rank the food industry about midway among all industry classifications in terms of severity rates. However, in terms of frequency rate, it is nearly twice as high as the average for all industries reporting.

Foodservice managers must organize for safety and develop a wholesome regard for safe procedures among the entire staff.

Safety Program

Specific topics for a safety campaign may be centered around the "three Es" of safety: engineering, education, and enforcement.

The *engineering* aspect refers to the built-in safety features of the building and equipment, and the manner in which the equipment is installed to make it safe to use. Encased motors, safety valves on pressure steamers, easily manipulated spigots on urns, and guards on slicing and chopping machines are examples of safety features. A maintenance program to keep equipment in good working order is the responsibility of management, as are all other phases of providing a safe environment.

A study of traffic patterns in kitchen and dining areas and the placement of equipment and supplies in locations to avoid as much cross traffic as possible and the arrangement of equipment within a work unit to provide for logical sequence of movement without backtracking are a part of the engineering phase of the safety program.

Education for safety is a never-ending process. It begins with the establishment of firm policies regarding safety, which then should be discussed with each new employee during the orientation period. "Safety from the first day" is an appropriate slogan for any organization.

Because safety is an integrated part of every activity, it should be taught as a component of all skills and procedures. Written procedures for tasks to be performed by each employee must include the safe way of doing each task, and the written outline then used to train the employee in the correct steps to follow. These written, step-by-step procedures provide a follow-up, on-the-job reference for the employee and can be used by managers as a check against employee performance.

Safety education, however, is more than training each employee in the procedures for a particular job. An ongoing group program based on *facts* about safe and unsafe practices keeps employees aware of safety. The National Safety Council, the Bureau of Vital Statistics, various community safety councils, and trade and professional organizations can provide statistics and materials for planning such a program. Data obtained from records kept on accidents *within* the organization are invaluable and more meaningful than general statistics.

A form for reporting accidents should be completed for each accident, regardless of how minor it may seem (Figure 13 shows an example). These written records should include the type of accident, kind of injury that has occurred and to whom, when it occurred, the day and hour, and where it took place. In foodservices, most accidents occur at rush times, when it is especially difficult to take care of the injured, find replacement help, and continue efficient customer service. This fact alone should provide incentive enough for the manager to do all that is possible to promote safety.

An analysis of the causes of accidents provides further data for preventing them. Causes may be classified into "unsafe acts" and "unsafe conditions." Usually it is found that unsafe acts outnumber unsafe conditions three to one. From this, there is an immediate indication of the need for proper training to reduce accidents.

In the foodservice industry, falls cause the largest number of food-handling accidents, usually due to greasy or wet floors, with cuts second, and burns and strains from lifting next in order (Figure 14 illustrates the proper lifting technique). Falls and strains result in the greatest loss of time from the job and monetary loss to the institution.

It is management's responsibility to ferret out the reasons, remove the hazards, and then train the employees to prevent recurrence of the same accident. Good housekeeping procedures, such as storing tools and materials in proper places and keeping aisles and pathways clear, optimum lighting of work areas, prompt repair of broken tools and equipment, replacement of worn electrical cords, and proper care and removal of broken china and glassware, are only a few of the things that can be done to correct unsafe conditions. Employees should be encouraged to report to the manager any unsafe conditions they may notice. A simple form can be developed and made available to the employees for such reporting. Having the information in writing is helpful to the manager, who must then follow up to correct the situation.

The possibility of fires is an ever-present threat in foodservice establishments, making it essential that all employees follow proper procedures in use of equipment and cooking techniques. Further, they should know the location of fire extinguishing equipment and how to use it. Directions for and practice in the use of fire extinguishers, fire blankets, and other first aid equipment, necessities in every institutional kitchen, are included in training meetings, for supervisory personnel particularly. Information about the various types of fire extinguishers and which should be used for grease, paper, wood, and other types of fires is important. Tables 4 and 5 list the common classifications of fires and extinguishers. Group training in precautionary procedures to be followed in everyday work and instructions on what to do in case of an accident should be part of the overall safety program.

Many aids are available to foodservice managers to use in setting up a training program. The National Restaurant Association's *Safety Operations Manual* is an excellent resource. The National Safety Council has posters, pamphlets, and other materials available for use in training sessions. These are invaluable sources of information and illustration for foodservice managers. Clear, eye-catching posters that create favorable impressions and serve as reminders of good, safe practices are effective supplements to other types of training. The safety rules given in Figure 15 may be used as topics for training sessions. However, each foodservice organization should establish its own similar list of safety rules to be adhered to in its own department.

The third "E" in the overall safety campaign is *enforcement*. This represents the follow-up or constant vigilance required to prevent carelessness and to make certain that the rules and prescribed procedures are observed. Enforcement can be accomplished in many ways. In some organizations, safety committees are set up among the employees, who observe and report unsafe conditions and practices. Membership on this committee may be rotated

UWHCA
Worker's Compensation Coordinator
H4/860
600 Highland Avenue
Madison, WI 53792-0001

EMPLOYEE OCCUPATIONAL INJURY AND ILLNESS REPORT

INSTRUCTIONS:
1. Employee complete this entire side and top section of reverse side within 24 hours of accident.
2. Submit to supervisor to complete reverse side.
3. Submit completed form to Worker's Compensation Coordinator.
4. Direct questions to Worker's Compensation Coordinator, 263-9206.

Social Security Number			
Name Last	First	Middle	Position

Agency/Institution	Work Unit (Division, Department)		Date of Accident (Mo/Day/Yr)	Time of Accident	☐ AM ☐ PM
UWHCA					

		Name of Doctor/Hospital/Clinic
Were you treated at a clinic or hospital?	☐ Yes ☐ No	
Were you treated at the work site?	☐ Yes ☐ No	
Were you off work 4 days or more?	☐ Yes ☐ No	Address of Doctor/Clinic
If so, last day worked (Mo/Day/Yr):		

Nature of Injury/Illness/Accident

Part of body injured (Check ALL that apply and circle appropriate position)   (Thumb = Finger 1, Great Toe = Toe 1)

Abdomen	Back U M L	Finger R L 1 2 3 4 5	Head	Mouth	Shoulder R L
Ankle R L	Eye R L	Foot R L	Knee R L	Neck	Toe R L 1 2 3 4 5
Arm R L	Elbow R L	Hand R L	Leg R L	Nose	Wrist R L
Other (please specify)					

Exact location of accident (inside, outside, building name, room, vehicle, etc.)

Describe the activity you were engaged in at the time of the accident (explain in detail)

Witnesses (names, addresses, work telephone numbers)

In your opinion, what could be done to prevent other accidents of this nature?

Have you ever been treated for a similiar injury or condition? ☐ Yes ☐ No	Date(s) of treatment (Mo/Day/Yr)

Name of Doctor, Hospital, Clinic where you were treated for similiar injury or condition

The signature below authorizes medical, mental health and chiropractic provider's to release all medical, mental health and chiropractic records of treatment to the State of Wisconsin, Department of Administration, Worker's Compensation or its designated representative.

Date (Mo/Day/Yr)	Employee Signature	Work Phone ( )	Home Phone ( )

(REV. 6/96)

SUBMIT TO SUPERVISOR TO COMPLETE REVERSE SIDE

Figure 13   Example of a typical accident report form.

Figure 14 Proper lifting techniques.

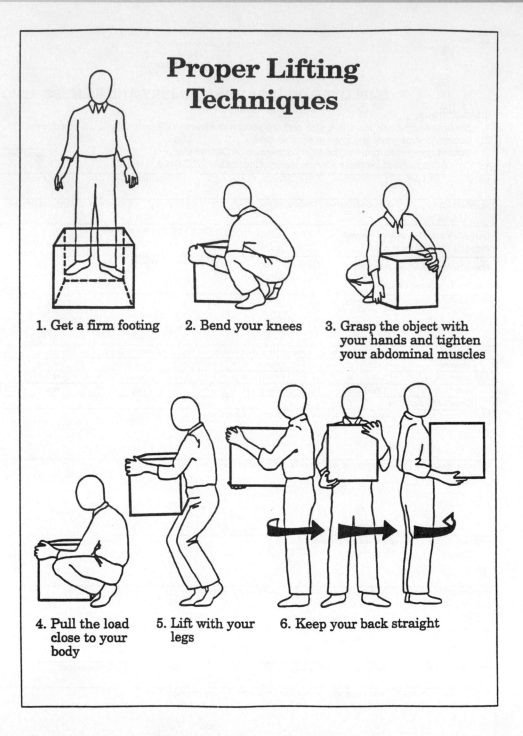

Proper Lifting Techniques

1. Get a firm footing

2. Bend your knees

3. Grasp the object with your hands and tighten your abdominal muscles

4. Pull the load close to your body

5. Lift with your legs

6. Keep your back straight

Table 4	Classification of fires.
CLASS	DESCRIPTION
A	Normal combustibles or fibrous material such as wood, paper, cloth, trash
B	Flammable liquids or gases such as gasoline or kerosene
C	Electrical: appliances, switches, or panel boxes
D	Combustible metals
K	Cooking oils

Table 5 Types of fire extinguishers and their uses.

TYPE	FEATURES
ABC Dry Chemical	Particularly effective on class A, B, and C fires but extremely messy. Operation is simple. Range is about 15 feet.
Carbon Dioxide	Used only on flammable liquid or electrical fires. Very limited range of 4 to 6 feet.
Halon	Halon is an exceptionally clean agent and leaves no residue. Good for use around computers and other sensitive equipment.
Dry Powder	For use on metal fires. Isolates and smothers the fire with either copper- or sodium chloride–based powder. Range is 3 to 6 feet.
Class K	Specifically designed for commercial kitchens that use cooking appliances and oils that operate at much higher temperatures than the previous appliances and oils. Range is 10 to 12 feet.

General Safety Rules
(please post)

- Report *every* injury at once, regardless of severity, to your Supervisor for first aid. *Avoid delay.*
- Report all *unsafe conditions,* broken or splintered chairs or tables, defective equipment, leaking radiators, torn carpeting, uneven floors, loose rails, unsafe tools or knives, broken china and glass, etc.
- Understand the *safe way* to perform any task assigned to you. If in doubt, see your Supervisor. Never take unnecessary chances.
- If you have to move over-heavy objects, ask for help. *Do not overlift.* When lifting any heavy object, keep your back straight, bend your knees, and *use your leg muscles.* Your back has weak muscles and can easily be strained.
- Aisles, passageways, stairways must be kept clean and free from obstructions. Do not permit brooms, pails, mops, cans, boxes, etc., to remain where someone can fall over them. Wipe up any grease or wet spots from stairs or floors or ramps *at once.* These are serious falling hazards.
- Walk, do not run, in halls, down ramps or stairs, or around work areas. Be careful when passing through swinging doors.
- Keep your locker clean and the locker top free from all loose or discarded materials, such as newspapers, old boxes, bottles, broken equipment, etc.
- Wear safe, sensible clothes for your work. Wear safe, comfortable shoes, with good soles. Never wear thin-soled or broken-down shoes. *Do not wear high-heeled shoes for work.* Ragged or over-long sleeves or ragged clothing may result in an injury.
- If you have to reach for a high object, use a ladder, not a chair or table or a makeshift. There is no substitute for a good ladder. *Never overreach.* Be careful when you have to reach high to fill coffee urns, milk tanks, etc.
- Horseplay or practical jokes on the job are forbidden.
- Do not argue or fight with fellow employees. The results are usually unpleasant and dangerous.
- Keep floors clean and dry. Pick up any loose object from the floor immediately to prevent someone from falling.
- Do not overload trays. Trays should be loaded so as to give good balance. An improperly loaded tray can become dangerous.
- Dispose of all broken glass and china immediately. Never serve a guest with a cracked or chipped glass or piece of china. Check all silverware for water spots, etc.
- Take sufficient time to serve your guests properly. Too much haste is may cause accidents to your guests and to yourself. *Haste makes waste.*
- Remove from service any chair, table, or other equipment that is loose, broken, or splintered so as to prevent injury.
- *Cashiers.* Close cash registers with back of hand. Do not permit fingers to hang over edge of drawer.
- Place "wet floor" sign as appropriate before and after mopping.
- Help *new employees* work safely on the job. Show them the right way to do the job—the safe way.

Figure 15 Examples of rules for safety.

so that everyone will be personally involved in a campaign against accidents. If possible, one person in each organization should have the overall responsibility for developing and supervising the safety program, after being specifically trained for the task.

Probably the most effective overall enforcement plan, however, is a periodic inspection of the department by someone on the supervisory staff. The use of a checklist as a reminder of all points to be observed is helpful. Any foodservice manager could develop a form for use in a specific operation. The comprehensive checklist illustrated in Figure 16 includes both food safety and sanitation and may serve as a model for developing a checklist for a specific department.

Check Sheet
Safety in the Kitchen

Rating Scale: 5–1; 5 points is highest and 1 point the lowest.

Burns
1. Are handles of pans on the stove turned so the pans cannot be knocked off?　_____
2. Are flames turned off when removing pans from stove?　_____
3. Are dry pot holders used for lifting hot pans?　_____
4. Are fellow workers warned when pans are hot? When pans of hot food are to be moved?　_____
5. Is steam equipment in proper working order to avoid burns from leaks?　_____
6. Is hot water regulated at proper temperature so it will not scald?　_____
7. Are lids lifted cautiously and steamer doors opened slowly to avoid steam burns?　_____

Cuts
1. Are broken dishes and glasses promptly cleaned up and disposed of in a special container provided?　_____
2. Are knives stored in the slotted case provided for them?　_____
3. Are knives left on the drain board to be washed, and not dropped into the sink?　_____
4. Is the safety hood put over the slicer after each use and cleaning?　_____
5. Is the can opener in good repair so it cuts sharply and leaves no ragged edges?　_____
6. Are safety devices provided on slicers and choppers?　_____

Electricity
1. Are electric cords in good repair?　_____
2. Are sufficient outlets provided for the equipment in use?　_____
3. Are hands always dry before touching electrical equipment?　_____
4. Are there extra fuses in the fuse box?　_____

Falls
1. Are spilled foods cleaned up immediately?　_____
2. Are corridors and stairways free from debris?　_____
3. Are articles placed on shelves securely so they will not jar off?　_____
4. Are stepladders sturdy and in good repair?　_____
5. Are brooms and mops put away properly after use and not left out against a wall or table to trip someone?　_____
6. Are hallways well lighted and steps well marked so no one will trip?　_____

Fires and Explosions
1. Are gas pipes free from leaks? Have they been checked by the gas company?　_____
2. Are matches kept in a covered metal container?　_____
3. Are fire blankets and extinguishers provided?　_____
4. Has the fire extinguisher been checked in the last month?　_____
5. Is the first-aid box fully supplied?　_____
6. Is hot fat watched carefully, and is cold fat stored away from flame?　_____

Please Report Immediately Any Fires or Accidents to the Food Manager
or Dial _____ to Report a Fire

Figure 16　Example of safety checklist.

Customer Protection

Customers of foodservices deserve the same careful concern given employees in regard to safety. They expect and should have assurance that the food served will be safe for consumption and that the facility for dining is also safe. This includes everything from a safe parking area that is well lighted and free of any stumbling blocks to furniture that is in good condition and will not cause snags or splinters. The flooring must be kept in good repair to prevent tripping and falls, and any spillage should be wiped up at once so that no one will slip or fall. Dining rooms should be adequately lighted and ample aisle space provided between tables so that diners can see to make their way through the room without tripping.

Servers must be well trained in correct serving procedures so they will not spill any hot food on the customers or anything on the floor that could cause accidents. Any spillage must be cleaned up at once. It is also recommended that employees, especially those working the "front of the house," be trained to initiate and do abdominal thrusts to provide assistance in the event that a customer chokes while dining.

Managers are liable for accidents that occur on the premises. Lawsuits could result that are costly and detrimental to the reputation of the establishment.

SUMMARY

It is the responsibility of the foodservice manager to design, implement, and monitor a program of cleaning and sanitation for his or her operation. Program design begins with an understanding of principles and factors that influence the cleaning and sanitation tasks. These principles and factors must be considered when managing the major cleaning and sanitation functions, which include dishwashing and facilities maintenance.

The steps to safety in any foodservice include awareness, involvement, and control. The first step is *awareness* on the part of managers for the need to provide a safe environment for employees and patrons, and to assume the responsibility for and positive attitude toward accident prevention. *Involvement* includes initiating a safety education program or campaign that keeps employees safety conscious. A training program that indoctrinates employees with the philosophy of working safely and instructs them in how to do so is a major part of being involved. Seeking employee suggestions about safe procedures and forming safety committees in which employees participate are other forms of involvement. *Control* is the process of insisting on safety, checking on safety codes and meeting them, analyzing accident records as a basis for improvement, and, above all, good consistent supervision of employee work. This assumes that the institution has established safety policies, written procedures for job performance, and adopted a procedure for reporting and handling accidents that are known to all in the organization.

Benefits of a safety program include a reduction in accidents; improvement in employee morale, patron satisfaction, and feeling of security; and fewer workers' compensation claims, resulting in reduced costs and better financial performance for the foodservice. The objective is to keep injuries to a minimum and the workforce at maximum efficiency.

APPLICATION OF CHAPTER CONCEPTS

The Dining and Culinary Services unit at the University of Wisconsin–Madison is diligent about enforcing its program of cleaning, sanitation, and safety in all work areas of all units. The receiving area at the commissary is no exception. Here every aspect and principle of cleaning, sanitation, and worker safety applies and is enforced without exception. The dock and staging area are kept clean and free of obstacles at all times. Floors, carts, and shelving are cleaned regularly, and all storage areas are straightened each day to keep areas clear of clutter that can pose safety risks.

Worker safety for the receiving staff is of particular concern. Employees in this area are particularly susceptible to injuries due to the nature of the work, which requires frequent lifting and pushing of very heavy loads. On the dock, for example, one delivery can include as many as eight pallets of product weighing up to 1,000 lb each! Cases of #10 cans vary in weight from 30 to 50 lb. Obviously, the receiving staff needs to be well trained and mindful of the risks that can occur if proper precautions are not taken to prevent injury.

CRITICAL-THINKING QUESTIONS

1. Why is it important to establish a cleaning program for the receiving area?
2. What are some of the unique factors that must be considered when developing a cleaning program for the receiving area?
3. Does anything in the receiving area need to be sanitized? If so, what and why?
4. How can a program of preventive maintenance enhance safety in the receiving area?
5. What should be included in a training program on safety for the employees who work in the receiving area?
6. Go to the Web site for the National Safety Council. What materials are available that might be of benefit for training employees who work in the receiving area?
7. Why is it important to train employees who work in the receiving area on OSHA's Hazard Communication Standard?
8. An employee in the receiving area "throws his back out" while lifting cases of canned vegetables. What should the manager do?
9. Should the employees who work in the receiving area wear weight belts? Why or why not?
10. Relative to safety, should the dress code for employees who work in receiving be different as compared to other employees? Why or why not?

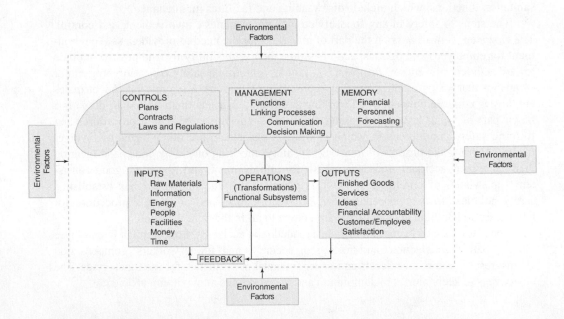

CHAPTER REVIEW QUESTIONS

1. Which organizations establish and enforce sanitation and safety standards?
2. What is OSHA? What is its influence on foodservice operation?
3. Compare and contrast the terms *clean* and *sanitized*.
4. What are the advantages of developing and implementing a cleaning program?
5. What are the most frequent causes of accidents in foodservice operations? How can they be prevented?
6. What is meant by the term *preventive maintenance?* Why is it important in a foodservice operation?

7. What factors should be considered when deciding between a high-temperature or chemical dishwashing machine system?
8. What is a material safety data sheet?
9. What is meant by the term *food contact surface*, and why is it important to determine this relative to a cleaning and sanitation program?
10. List some of the practices that keep pests from entering foodservices and harboring in work areas.

SELECTED WEB SITES

www.nsf.org   (The National Sanitation Foundation International)
www.ul.com   (Underwriters Laboratories)
www.osha.gov   (The Occupational Safety and Health Administration)
www.redcross.org   (The Red Cross)
www.nsc.org   (The National Safety Council)

The Menu

From Chapter 5 of *Foodservice Management: Principles and Practices*, Twelfth Edition, June Payne-Palacio, Monica Theis.
Copyright © 2012 by Pearson Education, Inc. Published by Pearson Prentice Hall. All rights reserved.

The Menu

Neffalis/Shutterstock

THE MENU IS THE SINGLE MOST INFLUENTIAL PLAN IN A foodservice operation. A well-planned menu serves as a catalyst that drives all operational functions: purchasing, production, and service. It is also a management control that influences resource acquisition and utilization. These resources include food, labor, equipment, time, money, and facilities.

A menu is a detailed list of food items that may be ordered (as in a restaurant) or served (as in a hospital, school, or corrections facility). A menu is a reflection of an operation's mission and, therefore, will vary greatly from one organization to the next. In the retail setting, the menu is designed to attract customers and generate sales, whereas noncommercial, on-site operations plan menus to meet the needs and wants of a known population. Regardless of the type of foodservice organization, careful planning, implementation, and evaluation of the menu are essential to the success of meeting customer needs and preferences within available resources.

The purpose of this chapter is to review the many factors that influence menu planning and to describe the process of planning, writing, and evaluating menus. One of the most important factors to consider is the customer profile. This review is followed by specific guidelines on how to write menus and includes step-by-step procedures to ensure that the menu process is completed in a timely fashion. The menu development section is followed by a discussion on menu design and layout. Strategies for menu evaluation are also included in this chapter.

KEY CONCEPTS

1. The menu is the single most impactful management tool in a foodservice operation.

2. A systems approach to menu planning will ensure that all aspects of an operation are considered for maximum efficiency and effectiveness.

3. The type of menu selected for a business unit within a foodservice is influenced by the unit's food and dining concept.

4. A successful menu planning process begins with clear objectives that reflect desired outcomes.

5. The savvy menu planner is attuned to and accounts for political, social, and economic trends and issues internal and external to the foodservice.

6. Development of and consideration for a comprehensive customer profile is essential to ensure that customer needs and wants are met.

7. Consideration for inputs is critical to ensure that planned menus can be produced and served within available resources.

8. Analysis of a new menu's impact on operations is essential to ensure a seamless transition from one menu to another.

9. Staff and customer acceptance of a new menu can be enhanced through active solicitation of input during the menu planning process.

10. Application of menu design principles for the posted menu maximizes its value as a marketing and education tool.

THE MENU

KEY CONCEPT: The menu is the single most impactful management tool in a foodservice operation.

Most of us think of a menu as a printed list of entrées, side dishes, and beverages offered in a restaurant. This is the front-of-the-house concept for a menu. For the foodservice manager, the concept of *menu* is much more broad. It refers to a plan, if not an entire program of several functional menus, that influences every aspect of the foodservice operation and the greater organization. It also relates to the comprehensive and, sometimes, arduous process of deciding what to offer and how to get the menu "into the system." The primary role of the manager relative to the menu is to plan and implement menus for each business unit, then manage the menu program to ensure that food is prepared and served to meet standards of quality every time an item or meal is ordered or served. The collection of all menus for a specific foodservice operation is referred to as the master menu and is used to manage the entire foodservice: front and back of the house.

THE SYSTEMS APPROACH TO MENU PLANNING AND MAINTENANCE

KEY CONCEPT: A systems approach to menu planning will ensure that all aspects of an operation are considered for maximum efficiency and effectiveness.

An appreciation for the impact of the menu on an entire system will become evident with a review of the systems model. Working from the outside in, one can see that environmental factors influence a system. Social issues such as dining trends and food preferences are examples of external influence. Today, a highly influential trend is the desire for locally grown and produced foods for health and sustainability. Second, a number of controls such as regulations and contracts establish nonnegotiable parameters for menu planning. Memory in the form of meal counts and sales data provides valuable information in understanding menu item popularity and purchasing behaviors. Moving down the model: consideration for availability of inputs and impact on operations is an obvious focus of good menu planning. Outcomes that meet customer expectations are the ultimate goal of menu planning. These expectations are determined through continuous and objective feedback mechanisms. Each of these components of the systems model is addressed in this chapter.

TYPES OF MENUS

KEY CONCEPT: The type of menu selected for a business unit within a foodservice is influenced by the unit's food and dining concept.

There are many types of menus from which to choose. The decision is primarily influenced by the type of foodservice operation and the needs of the customers to be served. All types of menus are defined, at least in part, by the degree of choice offered. For on-site foodservices, each business unit may have a specific type of menu. For example, in a hospital the patient menu may be a select cycle menu or a static menu. Single-use menus may be most appropriate for catered events. Foundation knowledge on types of menus and the degree of selection within each will allow the manager to select the best menu for the unit and to plan accordingly.

A **static menu**, or *set menu*, means that the same menu is used each day. This type of menu is found in restaurants and other foodservices where the clientele changes daily or where there are enough items listed on the menu to offer sufficient variety. Many hospitals are now experimenting with static or hotel-style menus because of shorter patient stays and implementation of the room-service concept. Some flexibility can be built into the static menu by changing an item or two daily or offering daily specials. On the other hand, the static menu may be quite limited in choice, as in many quick-serve restaurants. Changes in these menus are made only after careful development of a new product and extensive market research and testing. Figure 1 is an example of a static menu for a patient dining unit in a hospital.

A **single-use menu** is a menu that is planned for a certain day or event and is not repeated in exactly the same form. This type of menu is often used for special functions, holidays, or catering events. Figure 2 is an example of a single-use menu.

Static menu

A set menu with the same offerings every day, such as a restaurant or room-service menu

Single-use menu

A menu planned for a specific event and typically used only once; usually for a holiday or other special occasion

Lunch and Dinner

DELI DELIGHTS

- •Tuna Salad (2 carb)
- ♥Fat Free Tuna Salad (2 carb)
  Egg Salad (2 carb)
- ♥Peanut Butter and Jelly (3 carb)
  *These sandwiches are served on wheat bread or white bread.
- * ♥*Sub Sandwich*: Turkey, roast beef, American cheese, lettuce,
  tomato on french bread. (2 carb)
- •*BLT*: Bacon, lettuce, tomato sandwich served on wheatberry,
  white bread or toasted bread (2 carb)

FROM THE GRILL

- • ♥Grilled Chicken Fillet on a Bun (2 carb)
  - •Fried Chicken Fillet on a Bun (3 carb)
  - ♥Grilled Hamburger (2 carb)
  - •Grilled Cheeseburger (2 carb)
- • ♥Grilled Garden Burger (3 carb)
  - •Fish Sandwich on a Split Top Bun (3 carb)
  - •Hot Dog (2 carb)
  *Grilled Cheese (2 carb)

ENTREE SALADS

- • ♥Fresh Fruit Plate with Cottage Cheese (2 carb)
- • ♥Canned Fruit Plate with Cottage Cheese (2 carb)

- •*Chicken Caesar Salad*: Blend of fresh romaine lettuce, sliced
  chicken breast, seasoned croutons, shredded parmesan cheese,
  sliced cherry tomatoes in a tangy Caesar dressing (1 carb)

- * ♥*Chef Salad*: Fancy cheese, sliced egg, green pepper, cucumber, tomato,
  julienne ham and turkey with crackers (0.5 carb)

  Chef salad dressing choices served on the side are:
  Creamy Ranch, • ♥Catalina French, Thousand Island,
  • ♥Fat-Free Raspberry Vinaigrette (1 carb),
  • ♥Fat Free Golden Italian

Number listed behind food item represents carbohydrate choices.

♥Lower in saturated fat.

•Contains 400 mg sodium or more per serving.

*Available in low calorie, reduced fat/cholesterol, or sodium as applicable.

Figure 1 An example of a static menu.
Courtesy Mercy Health System, Janesville, Wisconsin. Used with permission.

Another variation on menu type is the **cycle menu**, a planned set of menus that rotate at definite intervals of a few days to several weeks. The length of the cycle depends on the type of foodservice operation. For example, many health care facilities, especially hospitals, are experimenting with shorter cycles as a result of a reduction in the average length of stay for patients. On the other hand, long-term care facilities such as nursing homes and corrections continue to work with longer intervals, ranging from three to eight weeks.

Cycle menus have several advantages. After the initial planning has been completed, time is freed for the planner to review and revise the menus to meet changing needs such as holidays, vacations, changes in personnel, or availability of a food item. Repetition of the same menu aids in standardizing preparation procedures and in efficient use of equipment.

Cycle menu

A carefully planned set of menus that is rotated at definite time intervals

Annual Meeting of the Members of Beloit Memorial Hospital, Inc.

May 27, 2009

"An Irish Evening on the Coast"

*The Hospitality Services Department is proud to present
the following for your dining enjoyment.*

Your wine selections this evening are:

Plungerhead 2007—California Zinfandel

Allendorf 2006—German Riesling

_____   _____   _____ _____

Salad Course
Butter Lettuce Salad with Shanagarry Cream Dressing

Entrée Selections

Tenderloin of Beef in Guinness Reduction
Colcannon
Carrot-Parsnip Julienne

Crab Cakes & Smoked Salmon with Roasted Red Pepper Sauce
Pomodoro Tomato Confit

Curried Nut Roast*
Colcannon
Baby Carrot & Onion Cream
*Vegan Selection

Homemade Breads

This Evening's Dessert Selection
Strawberry Flummery
Rice Pudding with Celtic Caramel Sauce

Forecasting and purchasing are simplified and, with repeated use of the menus, employee workloads can be balanced and distributed fairly.

Cycle menus do, however, have some potential disadvantages. They may become monotonous if the cycle is too short or if the same food is offered on the same day each week. The cycle menu may not include well-liked foods often enough, or it may include unpopular items too frequently. The cycle menu may not allow for foods that come into the market at varying times of the year, but many foodservices solve this problem by developing summer, fall, winter, and spring cycles; others note the seasonal alternatives on the menu. If these disadvantages can be resolved and the menu properly developed to meet the needs of a particular foodservice system, the cycle menu can become an effective management tool.

Whatever the length of the cycle, the menus must be carefully planned and evaluated after each use. A cycle menu should be flexible enough to handle emergencies and to accommodate new ideas and seasonal variations. Figure 3 is an example of a school menu that is based on a cycle concept.

MCPASD Elementary School Menu – October, 2010

Monday	Tuesday	Wednesday	Thursday	Friday
4 Chicken Nuggets & Dipping Sauce Our Own Cheesy Broccoli Rice Fresh Green Salad Cup Chilled Peaches Whole Wheat Bread Slice *Alternate:* *Turkey or PB&J Sack Lunch*	5 Pizza Dippers with Warm Marinara Sauce for dipping (V) Fresh Veggie Tray & Dip Fresh Lapacek Apple*** *Alternate:* *Turkey or PB&J Sack Lunch*	6 French Toast Sticks & Maple Syrup (V) Our Own Oven Hash Browns Turkey Sausage Links Orange Juice Cup *Alternate:* *Ham or PB&J Sack Lunch*	7 Our Own Rotini & Marinara (V) (Sauce on the side, of course!) Two Mozzarella Cheese Sticks Fresh Green Salad Cup Frozen 100% Fruit Juice Bar *Alternate:* *Turkey or PB&J Sack Lunch*	8 Grilled Cheese Sandwich (V) Our Own Chicken Noodle Soup Celery Sticks with Dip Mixed Fruit Cup *Alternate:* *Turkey or PB&J Sack Lunch*
11 Chicken Drummie Mashed Potatoes & Gravy on the side Seasoned Peas Chilled Peaches Petite Dinner Roll *Alternate:* *Turkey or PB&J Sack Lunch*	12 Individual 4-5" Cheese Pizza (V) Fresh Veggie Tray and Dip Fresh Lapacek Apple*** Our Own Butterscotch Pudding *Alternate:* *Turkey or PB&J Sack Lunch*	13 Turkey Sandwiches on Mini Buns Lettuce, Tomato Slices & Pickles Green Beans Cheez-It Scrabble Crackers Chilled Pears *Alternate:* *Ham or PB&J Sack Lunch*	14 Our Own Beef Taco Meat served on your choice of Hard or Soft Shells with all the Veggie Trimmings Seasoned Pinto & Black Beans Mixed Fruit Cup *Alternate:* *Turkey or PB&J Sack Lunch*	15 **Cardinal Homecoming** Mini Cheeseburgers on a Bun Lettuce, Tomato & Pickles Baked Chips Whole Kernel Corn Orange Smiles Our Own Cardinal Cake *Alternate:* *Turkey or PB&J Sack Lunch*
18 Chicken Strips Baked French Fries Steamed Broccoli Chilled Pears Petite Dinner Roll *Alternate:* *Turkey or PB&J Sack Lunch*	19 Our Own Italian Dunkers with Marinara Sauce for Dipping (V) (Melted Mozzarella Cheese over Garlic Bread) Fresh Veggie Tray with Dip Fresh Lapacek Apple*** Our Own Chocolate Pudding *Alternate:* *Turkey or PB&J Sack Lunch*	20 *Farm To School Taste Testing Today!!* *WI Ugly Duckling Pears* Chicken Patty on a Bun Lettuce, Tomato and Pickles Potato Smiles Cucumber Slices *Alternate:* *Ham or PB&J Sack Lunch*	21 Mini Turkey Corn Dogs Macaroni & Cheese Fresh Green Salad Cup Chilled Peaches *Alternate:* *Turkey or PB&J Sack Lunch*	22 Hot Dog on a Bun** Baked Chips Whole Kernel Corn Mixed Fruit Cup *Alternate:* *Turkey or PB&J Sack Lunch*
25 Popcorn Chicken Baked Sweet Potato Fries Green Beans Petite Dinner Roll Fresh Lapacek Apple*** *Alternate:* *Turkey or PB&J Sack Lunch*	26 Individual 4-5" Pepperoni Pizza** Fresh Veggie Tray & Dip Fresh WI Ugly Duckling Pears*** Our Own Snickerdoodle Cookie *Alternate:* *Turkey or PB&J Sack Lunch*	27 **Early Release Today** Scrambled Egg with Cheese Garnish (V) Turkey Sausage Links Our Own Hash Browns Applesauce Cup Our Own Petite Cinnamon Roll *Alternate:* *Ham or PB&J Sack Lunch* *Sauk Trail Harvest Day Sack Lunches Only*	28 No School Today *Alternate:* *Turkey or PB&J Sack Lunch*	29 No School Today
** May contain pork as an ingredient. (V) signifies vegetarian product. **All products offered on the elementary menu are peanut and tree nut free unless highlighted.**	***We are happy to feature fresh, locally grown Wisconsin produce when possible. Enjoy whole apples, grown locally by Lapacek's Orchard in Poynette, WI and our new locally grown pears from Future Fruit Farms in Ridgeway, WI.	*Farm To School:* Taste testing of locally grown produce sponsored & hosted by the PTO at each participating school.	**8 oz of fluid milk is offered with each school meal. We serve skim & 1% white plus skim chocolate daily.**	**While we strive for all choices available to each student each school day, this menu may change due to product availability. Thank you for understanding.** ???? Questions about your Lunch Express account – please call Kathy at 829-2343 or email at kschultz@mcpasd.k12.wi.us ???? Questions about allergies or health concerns – please call Susan at 829-2346 or email at speterman@mcpasd.k12.wi.us

Our sack lunch option: Sandwich on whole wheat or PB&J Uncrustable, baked chips, veggies, fruit and a small treat like zoo animals or teddy grahams.

Figure 3 An example of a school menu that illustrates the cycle concept.
Courtesy Middleton Cross Plains Area School District. Used with permission.

Table d'hôte menu
Menu that offers a complete meal at a fixed price

Du jour menu
Menu of the day

Selective menu
A menu that includes two or more food choices in each menu category such as appetizers, entrées, vegetables, salads, and desserts

Semiselective menu
A menu that includes one or more food choices in at least one menu category

Nonselective menu
A menu that offers only one item per menu category; no choice

Menu pattern
An outline of food to be included in each meal and the extent of choice at each meal

Meal plan
The number of dining options offered within a specific time period

Menus may also be categorized by the method of pricing. In the à la carte menu, food items are priced separately. This type of menu allows the patron to select only the foods wanted. The **table d'hôte menu** offers a complete meal at a fixed price, whereas the **du jour menu** refers to the menu of the day. It must be planned and written daily.

Extent of Selection. A **selective menu** includes two or more choices in some or all menu categories. Categories represent the groups of foods offered and usually include appetizers, entrées, side dishes, desserts, and beverages. The exact number of options within each category will vary among different types of foodservices. The menu mix, or the selection of food items to be offered in each food category, must be carefully planned to meet the needs of the customer and to ensure even workloads and balanced use of equipment.

A *full-selective menu* offers at least two choices in every category. The advantage of this approach is that it allows maximum choice to the customer. The primary disadvantage of full-selective menus is the obvious demand on operational resources. Ingredients and food products must be available in inventory to meet menu demand, and the production staff must have the skills and flexibility to respond to the variety of choices. In response to these demands and as a result of shorter hospital stays for patients, many health care facilities are implementing limited or semiselective menus.

A limited or **semiselective menu** allows one or more selections in some of the menu categories. For example, a long-term care facility may offer two entrées and two dessert selections at lunch and dinner, but no choice in the vegetable and salad categories. Restaurants, on the other hand, may offer a choice of entrées accompanied by standard side dishes.

A **nonselective menu** (also referred to as a preselective or a *house* menu) offers no choice in any category. Organizations using the nonselective menu usually have a list of alternatives to offer in the event that a customer does not want any of the menu items offered. These are frequently referred to as "write-ins" in the health care industry because they are handwritten directly onto the patient menu. Figure 4 illustrates the different types of selective menus. Figure 5 is an example of a nonselective menu for a long-term care facility.

Meal Plans and Menu Patterns

The **menu pattern** is an outline of the menu item categories offered at each meal and the depth of choice within each category. A **meal plan** refers to the number of meal opportunities offered over a specified period of time, usually 24 hours. For example, a small cafe may offer only breakfast and lunch; a day care center may offer two snacks and lunch; and a long-term care facility may offer breakfast, lunch, dinner, and an hour of sleep (HS) snack.

The following is an example of a three-meal plan with corresponding meal patterns:

Breakfast

> Fruit or juice
> Cereal, hot or cold
> Eggs and breakfast meats
> Toast or hot bread
> Choice of beverages

Lunch

> Soup (optional)
> Entrée or sandwich
> Salad or vegetable
> Bread with margarine or butter
> Fruit or light dessert
> Choice of beverages

Dinner

> Soup (optional)
> Entrée (meat, fish, poultry, or vegetarian)
> Two vegetables (one may be potato or pasta)

Full Selective	Limited Selective	Nonselective
Appetizers Chilled tomato juice Cream of mushroom soup	*Appetizers* Chilled tomato juice	
Entrées Roast beef with gravy Grilled tuna steak with dill sauce Chicken salad on croissant Fresh fruit and cottage cheese plate with muffin	*Entrées* Roast beef with gravy Chicken salad on croissant with relishes	*Entrée* Roast beef with gravy
Vegetables Mashed potatoes with gravy Boiled red potatoes Steamed broccoli spears Creamed carrots	*Vegetables* Mashed potatoes with gravy Steamed broccoli spears Fresh vegetable plate	*Vegetables* Mashed potatoes with gravy Steamed broccoli spears
Salads Garden salad with French dressing Mandarin orange gelatin salad	*Salads* Garden salad with French dressing	*Salads* Garden salad with French dressing
Desserts Pecan pie with whipped topping German chocolate cake with coconut icing Butter brickle ice cream Fresh fruit	*Desserts* Pecan pie with whipped topping Butter brickle ice cream Fresh fruit	*Desserts* Pecan pie with whipped topping
Breads Dinner roll White bread Whole wheat bread Bread sticks	*Breads* Dinner rolls Whole wheat bread	*Breads* Dinner roll
Beverages Coffee 2% milk Tea Skim milk Hot cocoa Chocolate milk	*Beverages* Coffee Tea 2% milk	*Beverages* Coffee 2% milk

Figure 4   Sample menus for various degrees of selection.

Salad
Bread with margarine or butter
Dessert
Choice of beverages

For years, a traditional meal plan has been three meals a day, including breakfast, lunch, and dinner, served within a certain time span. In some cases, the larger meal has been served at noon, resulting in a pattern of breakfast, dinner, and supper. In foodservice, the trend is moving away from this traditionally structured plan because of the desire of many patrons to eat what they want and when they want it. To accommodate these dining preferences, cafeterias and other retail units now offer a wide variety of selections during all hours of operation.

Inspiration

Ideas for new menu items can come from a wide array of sources. Most foodservice managers subscribe to a number of industry trade journals. Common trade journals for on-site foodservices are *Food Management* and *The Foodservice Director*. There are also trade journals that target specific segments of the industry. Managers affiliated with foodservices on college campuses, for example, peruse publications such as *On-Campus* and *Hospitality* for menu ideas. Food magazines are another source of menu ideas for most any type of foodservice. Foodservice managers who are searching for new and innovative

WEEKLY OVERVIEW SIMPLIFIED MENUS

	Sunday	Monday	Tuesday	Wednesday	Thursday	Friday	Saturday
B R E A K F A S T	Orange juice Malto Meal or asst. cold cereal Egg sausage bake WW toast w/m & j 2% milk	Grapefruit juice Oatmeal or asst. cold cereal Scrambled eggs Bran muffin w/m & j 2% milk	Apple juice (Vit C) Asst. hot cereal or asst. cold cereal Biscuit 2% milk	Orange juice Cream of wheat or asst. cold cereal Pancakes w/marg Pancake syrup 2% milk	Pineapple jc (Vit C) Asst. hot cereal or asst. cold cereal Scrambled eggs WW toast w/m & j 2% milk	Grapefruit Sections Cream of rice or asst. cold cereal Coffee cake Ham slice 2% milk	Blended citrus juice Asst. hot cereal or asst. cold cereal Scrambled eggs WW toast w/m & j 2% milk
L U N C H	Sliced turkey Gravy Mashed potatoes Bu Brussels sprouts Cranberry sauce Coconut cream pie Roll w/marg 2% milk	Baked ham Sw potato soufflé Orange wedge Bu peas/mushrooms Strawberry short cake/top Bread w/marg 2% milk	Crispy baked chicken Gravy Rice pilaf Buttered spinach Blondie Roll w/marg 2% milk	Roast pork Gravy Mashed potatoes Bu carrots Bread w/marg Choc pudding cake 2% milk	Lasagna But ltln Grn Beans Cottage cheese Pear half Apricot half Pineapple ring Garlic bread w/marg 2% milk	Lemon baked fish w/tartar sauce Au gratin potatoes Bu broccoli spears Fresh fruit cup Roll w/marg 2% milk	Swedish meat balls Buttered noodles Scand mixed veg Shr lettuce salad w/dressing Chilled peaches Roll w/marg 2% milk
D I N N E R	Hamburger on bun Mustard/mayo Melon wedge Macaroni salad Carrot raisin salad Cookies 2% milk	Cream broccoli soup Tuna melt w/cheese on bun Lettuce/tomato slice Crackers 3 bean salad Fruit cocktail 2% milk	Vegetable soup Roast beef on bread Mayo & mustard Cucumber salad Crackers Baked apples 2% milk	Beef cubes w/gravy Buttered noodles Buttered mixed vegs. Peach crisp Roll w/marg 2% milk	Potato soup w/chives Reuben grill sand corn beef/cheese sauerkraut Spinach salad w/ drsg Mand. orange whip 2% milk	Tomato soup Grilled cheese on bread/marg Relish tray Potato chips Crackers Ice cream	Chicken salad on croissant Tomato wedges Melon salad Pineapple upside down cake 2% milk
A L L	Beverage of choice Salt, pepper, sugar	Beverage of choice Salt, pepper, sugar	Beverage of choice Salt, pepper, sugar	Beverage of choice Salt, pepper, sugar	Beverage of choice Beverage of choice	Beverage of choice Salt, pepper, sugar	Beverage of choice Salt, pepper, sugar

Figure 5 Example of a menu for a long-term care facility.
Courtesy Becky Donner and Associates. Used with permission.

menu items commonly refer to *Bon Appetit, Vegetarian Times, Cooks Illustrated, A Taste of Home*, and *Cooking Light*. Other common sources of inspiration include the customers, employees, menus at local restaurants, cooking shows, and culinary Web sites. It is important for the menu planner to understand that great menu ideas can come from a variety of places. A creative open approach to new menu ideas and concepts will keep current and potential customers interested in the dining program.

THE MENU PLANNING PROCESS

■ **KEY CONCEPT:** **A successful menu planning process begins with clear objectives that reflect desired outcomes.**

As stated earlier, menu planning can be an arduous process, absorbing a great deal of time and energy. The wise planner, then, begins the process with thoughtful reflection on the purpose of the menu planning process. It is important to recognize that the menu planning process is the same regardless of the nature, depth, and degree of the task. The intent of one menu planning process may be to develop and launch a new menu for a business unit that is being added to the scope of services for a foodservice. For example, a health care system could open a memory care or rehab unit. These units would necessitate the development of completely new menus. On the other extreme, an existing menu for a unit such as patient dining services may simply need a bit of an upgrade due to seasonal change or perhaps simply to add a new item. Sometimes a menu revision has nothing to do with the food. Feedback from patients may indicate that font size is too small or the posted menu is too "busy" to read. The objectives of these three processes are quite different but important nonetheless to ensure that the planning process is focused and results in the desired menu outcomes.

■ **KEY CONCEPT:** **The savvy menu planner is attuned to and accounts for political, social, and economic trends and issues internal and external to the foodservice.**

A primary goal of a foodservice is to serve food that is pleasing to the clientele. However, numerous factors both external and internal to the foodservice need to be taken into consideration when planning menus. External influences are often political, social, and economic in nature and reflect trends that can influence the menu planning process. For example, government entities at the federal, state, and local levels can set mandates on what must be included in a meal to justify reimbursement. Many local entities are now requiring that multiunit restaurants post nutrition information, a mandate that will be expanded nationally under recent legislation relative to health care reform. Social trends in food and dining preferences significantly influence menu planning, as do economic challenges such as employment rates and spending habits.

Internal factors tend to fall into four categories of influence, including *the organizational mission, the customer, inputs*, and *operations*. Organizational influences include components of the organization's business plan such as its mission, vision, and philosophy. Customer characteristics such as age, ethnicity, and health status play a huge role in menu planning. Significant inputs are money for food and allocations of labor. Operational functions including purchasing, production, and service need to be carefully considered along with managerial controls such as the budget to ensure that the menus can be implemented and served within available resources. The following is a more detailed description of some of the important menu planning considerations.

Organizational Mission and Goals

The planned menu must be appropriate for the foodservice and consistent with its organizational mission and goals. Whether the major goal is to provide nutritionally adequate meals at a reasonable cost, as in school foodservice, or to generate profit, as in a restaurant, the menus must reflect the organization's stated purpose as defined in the mission statement. This can sometimes present a challenge for the menu planner, especially when there is a conflict between what customers want and the mission of the organization. For example, it may be the mission of a school foodservice to provide nutritious meals that promote health. However, customers, especially those in the middle and high schools, may prefer items that are not consistent with nutrition guidelines (soda over low-fat milk, for example) or that are perceived as unhealthful even if the items are prepared within nutrition guidelines . This conflict can be further aggravated if the foodservice is required to generate enough revenue to stay in operation. It is not uncommon for cafeterias in schools and hospitals to be required by their host organizations to generate enough revenue to cover all costs incurred, including food, labor, equipment, supplies, and overhead. The food service manager must plan menus that somehow satisfy these conflicting goals. Whatever the facility-specific goals, all foodservices strive to offer menus that meet the **quality** expectations of the customers. Variety and familiarity of menu items are two quality attributes highly desired and valued by clients.

Quality
The aspects and degree of excellence in a thing

> **KEY CONCEPT:** **Development of and consideration for a comprehensive customer profile is essential to ensure that customer needs and wants are met.**

The Customer

The menu planner should carefully study the population to be served regardless of whether menus are being planned for a commercial or noncommercial operation. Data and information on demographics, sociocultural influences, spending, and eating habits will generate a composite profile of the customer, thus improving the likelihood that menus will satisfy their expectations.

Demographics. The term *demographics* refers to the statistics of populations. Specific indicators include but are not limited to age, gender, health status, ethnicity, and level of education. Economic information such as personal income may also be included in this definition. Trends in this information are important to the menu planner because eating habits vary among population groups and change frequently.

It is well known, for example, that the American population is getting older. Persons 65 years or older currently represent nearly 13 percent of the U.S. population. This number is expected to increase to 30 percent by the year 2030. The eating habits and preferences of this population are very different compared with those of younger populations.

Along with demographic information, the geographic distribution of populations may be of interest to the menu planner. Certain states including Florida, West Virginia, and Pennsylvania, for example, have a particularly high percentage of individuals over the age of 65.

Sociocultural Influences. The term *sociocultural* refers to the combining of the social and cultural factors of a population. These factors include marital status, lifestyle, ethnic background, values, and religious practices. These issues have a greater impact on menu planning than ever before, given the increase in the cultural diversity and rapidly changing lifestyles within the United States.

Race and ethnicity of the target consumer markets to be served will influence the menu offerings as well. The U.S. population continues to diversify as once-minority populations continue to increase. According to the 2004 census, the Hispanic population is one of the largest minority groups in the country, at roughly 13 percent of the total population. This population is concentrated primarily in the West and South. The African-American population is also roughly 13 percent of the total, whereas Asian populations account for approximately 4 percent. Population growth and geographic location are not, however, the only factors that influence interest in ethnic cuisine. World travel, the media, and the proliferation of ethnic restaurants have broadened the appeal of ethnic foods beyond Italian, Mexican, and Chinese. Interest in other Asian fare (Thai, Vietnamese, and Korean) and Indian cuisine is on the rise. Diners are looking for greater authenticity and variety in the ethnic selections.

Food plays an important role in our social lives. The wise menu planner becomes knowledgeable about social influences and respects the personal preferences of the customer. Closely related to sociocultural influences are psychological needs. Many diners turn to food for comfort and familiarity.

Nutritional Requirements. The degree to which nutrition influences the menu planning process depends on the type of foodservice and the market it serves. Retail operations, for example, integrate nutrition to the extent that customers demand it and are willing to pay for it. On-site operations, on the other hand, may be under a much greater obligation to meet the nutritional needs of their customers. This is especially true in facilities that are responsible for providing all meals to a resident population, such as in a long-term care facility, hospital, or corrections facility. Schools that participate in the federal Child Nutrition Program for breakfast and lunch need to comply with one of several plans for the nutrition composition of meals in order to qualify for federal reimbursement. The traditional food-based models are presented in Figures 6 and 7. Details on meal requirements for schools can be found on the Web site of the USDA.

Current regulations for on-site facilities often mandate that the *RDAs (recommended daily allowances)*, as defined by the Food and Nutrition Board of the National Academies' Institute of Medicine, be used as a guide for ensuring that menus are nutritionally sound. The RDAs specify nutrient levels for various age groups by gender. The RDAs were initially developed as a guide to evaluate and plan for the nutritional adequacy of groups, including the military and children participating in school lunch programs. They were never intended to be used to assess individual needs—a situation that has resulted in confusion and misuse for more than 50 years. It was for this reason that a process was initiated in 1993 to replace the RDAs with a set of four nutrient-based reference values that are intended for use in assessing and planning diets. This set is referred to as the Dietary Reference Intakes (DRIs).

Dietary Reference Intakes. The Food and Nutrition Board first considered redefining the RDAs in 1993. In 1995, a subcommittee, referred to as "The Dietary Reference Intake Committee," announced that a panel of experts would review major nutrient and other important food components. Reports with recommendations were first released in 1997 and continued through 2004. The intent was to redefine nutrient requirements and establish specific nutrient recommendations for groups *and* individuals.

The results of the committee's work is a comprehensive package of four guidelines, including the RDAs, which account for various needs among individuals and groups. Figure 8 provides the definitions of the four components of the DRIs. Specific information on nutrient values, uses, and interpretations of the DRIs is available through the Food and Nutrition Board IOM of the National Academies. Table 1 is an example of recommended intakes.

Other guidelines are available, including the U.S. Dietary Guidelines and the Food Guide Pyramid, to assist menu planners in translating nutrient requirements to food items and portion sizes. Each of these guides is depicted in Figures 9 and 10. The Food Guide Pyramid is a graphic depiction of the dietary guidelines and was developed to offer a visual outline of what healthy Americans should eat each day. These guidelines, with adaptations for specific ethnic and age groups, are available through the USDA. The menu planner needs to consider carefully the nutrient needs of individuals and groups to be served in order to select the most appropriate menu planning guide. The reader should be aware that new Dietary Guidelines are due to be released in August 2010.

Food Consumption, Trends, Habits, and Preferences. As stated earlier, the clientele of a foodservice operation is generally composed of individuals from different cultural, ethnic, and economic backgrounds, many of whom have definite food preferences. The menu planner must keep this in mind when selecting foods to satisfy this diverse group.

MEAL PATTERN FOR LUNCH—TRADITIONAL FOOD-BASED MENU PLANNING

• MEAT OR MEAT ALTERNATE
Per day serve one of the following food items or a combination of these items to provide at least the quantity listed. The quantities shown are the *edible* portion as served.

	Ages 1–2 yrs	Ages 3–4 yrs	Grades K–3	Grades 4–12	Grades 7–12*
Lean meat, poultry, or fish	1 oz	1-1/2 oz	1-1/2 oz	2 oz	3 oz
Cheese	1 oz	1-1/2 oz	1-1/2 oz	2 oz	3 oz
Large egg	1/2	3/4	3/4	1	1–1/2
Cooked dry beans or peas	1/4 cup	3/8 cup	3/8 cup	1/2 cup	3/4 cup
Peanut butter or other nut or seed butters	2 Tbsp	3 Tbsp	3 Tbsp	4 Tbsp	6 Tbsp
Yogurt	4 oz or 1/2 cup	6 oz or 3/4 cup	6 oz or 3/4 cup	8 oz or 1 cup	12 oz or 1-1/2 cup

The following foods may be used to meet *part* of the Meat/Meat Alternate as explained below.

	Ages 1–2 yrs	Ages 3–4 yrs	Grades K–3	Grades 4–12	Grades 7–12*
Peanuts, soy nuts, tree nuts, or seeds**	1/2 oz= 50%	3/4 oz= 50%	3/4 oz= 50%	1 oz= 50%	1-1/2 oz= 50%

• GRAINS/BREADS:
Must be enriched or whole grain or contain germ or bran.

A serving is . . .
   A slice of bread or an equivalent serving of biscuits, rolls, etc.,
   OR 1/2 cup of cooked rice, macaroni, noodles, other pasta products, or cereal grains.

	Ages 1–2 yrs	Ages 3–4 yrs	Grades K–3	Grades 4–12	Grades 7–12*
Minimum per WEEK:	5 serv	8 serv	8 serv	8 serv	10 serv
Minimum per DAY:	1/2 serv	1 serv	1 serv	1 serv	1 serv

• VEGETABLES/FRUITS
At least two different vegetables and/or fruits must be offered. Minimum requirements per day . . .

	Ages 1–2 yrs	Ages 3–4 yrs	Grades K–3	Grades 4–12	Grades 7–12*
	1/2 c	1/2 c	1/2 c	3/4 c	3/4 c

MILK (Fluid):
Must be served as a beverage.

	Ages 1–2 yrs	Ages 3–4 yrs	Grades K–3	Grades 4–12	Grades 7–12*
Per day:	6 fl oz	6 fl oz	8 fl oz	8 fl oz	8 fl oz

*Grades 7–12: This is an optional age/grade group. USDA recommends using it along with the others.
**These foods may be used to meet *no more than* 50 percent of this requirement. In addition, they must be used *in combination* with one or more of the other meat/meat alternates listed above.

Figure 6 National School Lunch Pattern.

MEAL PATTERN FOR BREAKFAST—TRADITIONAL OR ENHANCED FOOD-BASED MENU PLANNING

- **GRAINS/BREADS and/or MEAT/ALTERNATES:**

Select ONE serving from EACH of these components to equal:

> one **GRAINS/BREADS**
> -and-
> one **MEAT/MEAT ALTERNATE**

OR select TWO servings from ONE of the these components to equal:

> two **GRAINS/BREADS**
> -and-
> two **MEAT/MEAT ALTERNATES**

- **If you are using the optional extra age/grade group for the Enhanced system (Grades 7–12), serve one additional serving of Grains/Breads.**

GRAINS/BREADS:
You can serve one of the following food items or combine them to meet the requirements.

	Ages 1–2 yrs	Pre-school	Grades K–12	Grades 7–12*
(a) Whole-grain or enriched bread	1/2 serv	1/2 serv	1 serv	1 serv
(b) Whole-grain or enriched biscuit, roll, muffin, etc.	1/2 serv	1/2 serv	1 serv	1 serv
(c) Whole-grain, enriched, or fortified cereal	1/4 c or 1/3 oz	1/3 c or 1/2 oz	3/4 c or 1 oz	3/4 c or 1 oz

MEAT/MEAT ALTERNATE
You can serve one of the following food items or combine them to meet the requirements.

	Ages 1–2 yrs	Pre-school	Grades K–12	Grades 7–12*
Meat, poultry, or fish	1/2 oz	1/2 oz	1 oz	1 oz
Cheese	1/2 oz	1/2 oz	1 oz	1 oz
Egg (large)	1/2 egg	1/2 egg	1/2 egg	1/2 egg
Peanut butter or other nut or seed butters	1 Tbsp	1 Tbsp	2 Tbsp	2 Tbsp
Cooked dry beans or peas	2 Tbsp	2 Tbsp	4 Tbsp	4Tbsp
Yogurt	2 oz or 1/4 cup	2 oz or 1/4 cup	4 oz or 1/2 cup	4 oz or 1/2 cup
Nuts and/or seeds**	1/2 oz	1/2 oz	1 oz	1 oz

- **MILK (Fluid):**
As a beverage or on cereal or both.

	Ages 1–2 yrs	Pre-school	Grades K–12	Grades 7–12*
	1/2 cup	3/4 cup	8 fl oz	8 fl oz

Figure 7 National School Breakfast Pattern.

- **JUICE/FRUIT/VEGETABLE:**

Include a minimum of one serving. You can serve a fruit or vegetable or both; or full-strength fruit or vegetable juice.

	Ages 1–2 yrs	Pre-school	Grades K–12	Grades 7–12*
	1/4 cup	1/2 cup	1/2 cup	1/2 cup

*Optional extra age/grade group for the Enhanced system. Recommended but not required.
**No more than 1 oz of nuts and/or seeds may be served in any one meal.

Figure 7 (*Continued*)

Food habits are based on many factors, one of the most direct being the approach to food and dining at home. A household's ethnic and cultural background, lifestyle, and economic level combine to determine the foods served and enjoyed. These habits are sometimes passed down from generation to generation. When several different cultural or ethnic backgrounds are represented in the clients of a single foodservice for which a menu is to be planned, the task of satisfying everyone can be challenging indeed.

In today's mobile society, people are becoming more knowledgeable about ethnic and regional foods. Interest in Thai, Ethiopian, Vietnamese, and other international cuisine is evident from the growth of ethnic restaurants. Many health care facilities, schools, colleges, and similar foodservices include these foods on their menus to add variety and to contribute to the cultural education of their clientele. The menu planner should be aware of local and regional food customs and religious restrictions. For example, a menu planner should be well aware of Kosher and Muslim dietary laws.

In addition, the traditional three-meals-a-day pattern, with the entire family eating together, has changed. People eat fewer meals at home. They are eating more frequently and at less regular hours. To accommodate this change in eating habits, a more flexible meal schedule is evident in most on-site foodservices, and continuous service is available in many restaurants. For example, many hospitals today are converting their patient tray service to hotel-style room service. This is in response to patient demand to eat what they want, when they want it. The person planning menus for any type of foodservice should monitor such trends to ensure that choices reflect the food preferences of customers. Careful study of local populations and the community is essential for effective menu planning.

Figure 8 Definitions relative to Dietary Reference Intakes.

DEFINITIONS

Dietary Reference Intakes (DRIs): The new standards for nutrient recommendations that can be used to plan and assess diets for healthy people. Think of Dietary Reference Intakes as the umbrella term that includes the following values:

- **Estimated Average Requirement (EAR):** A nutrient intake value that is estimated to meet the requirement of half the healthy individuals in a group. It is used to assess nutritional adequacy of intakes of population groups. In addition, EARs are used to calculate RDAs.
- **Recommended Dietary Allowance (RDA):** This value is a goal for individuals, and is based upon the EAR. It is the daily dietary intake level that is sufficient to meet the nutrient requirement of 97% to 98% of all healthy individuals in a group. If an EAR cannot be set, no RDA value can be proposed.
- **Adequate Intake (AI):** This is used when an RDA cannot be determined. A recommended daily intake level based on an observed or experimentally determined approximation of nutrient intake for a group (or groups) of healthy people.
- **Tolerable Upper Intake Level (UL):** The highest level of daily nutrient intake that is likely to pose no risks of adverse health effects to almost all individuals in the general population. As intake increases above the UL, the risk of adverse effects increases.

Table 1 Dietary Reference Intakes (DRIs): Recommended Intakes for Individuals, Vitamins.

Food and Nutrition Board, Institute of Medicine, National Academies

LIFE STAGE GROUP	VIT A (µg/d)[a]	VIT C (mg/d)	VIT D (µg/d)[b,c]	VIT E (mg/d)[d]	VIT K (µg/d)	THIAMIN (mg/d)	RIBOFLAVIN (mg/d)	NIACIN (mg/d)[e]	VIT B_6 (mg/d)	FOLATE (µg/d)[f]	VIT B_{12} (µg/d)	PANTOTHENIC ACID (mg/d)	BIOTIN (µg/d)	CHOLINE[g] (mg/d)
Infants														
0–6 mo	400*	40*	5*	4*	2.0*	0.2*	0.3*	2*	0.1*	65*	0.4*	1.7*	5*	125*
7–12 mo	500*	50*	5*	5*	2.5*	0.3*	0.4*	4*	0.3*	80*	0.5*	1.8*	6*	150*
Children														
1–3 y	300	15	5*	6	30*	0.5	0.5	6	0.5	150	0.9	2*	8*	200*
4–8 y	400	25	5*	7	55*	0.6	0.6	8	0.6	200	1.2	3*	12*	250*
Males														
9–13 y	600	45	5*	11	60*	0.9	0.9	12	1.0	300	1.8	4*	20*	375*
14–18 y	900	75	5*	15	75*	1.2	1.3	16	1.3	400	2.4	5*	25*	550*
19–30 y	900	90	5*	15	120*	1.2	1.3	16	1.3	400	2.4	5*	30*	550*
31–50 y	900	90	5*	15	120*	1.2	1.3	16	1.3	400	2.4	5*	30*	550*
51–70 y	900	90	10*	15	120*	1.2	1.3	16	1.7	400	2.4[i]	5*	30*	550*
>70 y	900	90	15*	15	120*	1.2	1.3	16	1.7	400	2.4[i]	5*	30*	550*
Females														
9–13 y	600	45	5*	11	60*	0.9	0.9	12	1.0	300	1.8	4*	20*	375*
14–18 y	700	65	5*	15	75*	1.0	1.0	14	1.2	400[i]	2.4	5*	25*	400*
19–30 y	700	75	5*	15	90*	1.1	1.1	14	1.3	400[i]	2.4	5*	30*	425*
31–50 y	700	75	5*	15	90*	1.1	1.1	14	1.3	400[i]	2.4	5*	30*	425*
51–70 y	700	75	10*	15	90*	1.1	1.1	14	1.5	400	2.4[h]	5*	30*	425*
>70 y	700	75	15*	15	90*	1.1	1.1	14	1.5	400	2.4[h]	5*	30*	425*

(continued)

Table 1 (Continued)

LIFE STAGE GROUP	VIT A (µg/d)[a]	VIT C (mg/d)	VIT D (µg/d)[b,c]	VIT E (mg/d)[d]	VIT K (µg/d)	THIAMIN (mg/d)	RIBOFLAVIN (mg/d)	NIACIN (mg/d)[e]	VIT B_6 (mg/d)	FOLATE (µg/d)[f]	VIT B_{12} (µg/d)	PANTOTHENIC ACID (mg/d)	BIOTIN (µg/d)	CHOLINE[g] (mg/d)
Pregnancy														
14–18 y	**750**	**80**	5*	**15**	75*	**1.4**	**1.4**	**18**	**1.9**	**600**[j]	**2.6**	6*	30*	450*
19–30 y	**770**	**85**	5*	**15**	90*	**1.4**	**1.4**	**18**	**1.9**	**600**[j]	**2.6**	6*	30*	450*
31–50 y	**770**	**85**	5*	**15**	90*	**1.4**	**1.4**	**18**	**1.9**	**600**[j]	**2.6**	6*	30*	450*
Lactation														
14–18 y	**1,200**	**115**	5*	**19**	75*	**1.4**	**1.6**	**17**	**2.0**	**500**	**2.8**	7*	35*	550*
19–30 y	**1,300**	**120**	5*	**19**	90*	**1.4**	**1.6**	**17**	**2.0**	**500**	**2.8**	7*	35*	550*
31–50 y	**1,300**	**120**	5*	**19**	90*	**1.4**	**1.6**	**17**	**2.0**	**500**	**2.8**	7*	35*	550*

NOTE: This table (taken from the Food and Nutrition Information Center of the USDA, see http://fnic.nal.usda.gov) presents Recommended Dietary Allowances (RDAs) in **bold type** and Adequate Intakes (AIs) in ordinary type followed by an asterisk (*). RDAs and AIs may both be used as goals for individual intake. RDAs are set to meet the needs of almost all (97 to 98 percent) of the individuals in a group. For healthy breastfed infants, the AI is the mean intake. The AI for other life-stage and gender groups is believed to cover needs of all individuals in the group, but lack of data or uncertainty in the data prevent being able to specify with confidence the percentage of individuals covered by this intake.

[a] As retinol activity equivalents (RAEs). 1 RAE = 1 µg retinol, 12 µg β-carotene, 24 µg α-carotene, or 24 µg β-cryptoxanthin. The RAE for dietary provitamin A carotenoids is twofold greater than retinol equivalents (RE), whereas the RAE for preformed vitamin A is the same as RE.

[b] As cholecalciferol. 1 µg cholecalciferol = 40 IU vitamin D.

[c] In the absence of adequate exposure to sunlight.

[d] As α-tocopherol. α-Tocopherol includes *RRR*-α-tocopherol, the only form of α-tocopherol that occurs naturally in foods, and the *2R*-stereoisomeric forms of α-tocopherol (*RRR*-, *RSR*-, *RRS*-, and *RSS*-α-tocopherol) that occur in fortified foods and supplements. It does not include the *2S*-stereoisomeric forms of α-tocopherol (*SRR*-, *SSR*-, *SRS*-, and *SSS*-α-tocopherol), also found in fortified foods and supplements.

[e] As niacin equivalents (NEs). 1 mg of niacin = 60 mg of tryptophan; 0–6 months = preformed niacin (not NE).

[f] As dietary folate equivalents (DFEs). 1 DFE = 1 µg food folate = 0.6 µg of folic acid from fortified food or as a supplement consumed with food = 0.5 µg of a supplement taken on an empty stomach.

[g] Although AIs have been set for choline, there are few data to assess whether a dietary supply of choline is needed at all stages of the life cycle, and it may be that the choline requirement can be met by endogenous synthesis at some of these stages.

[h] Because 10 to 30 percent of older people may malabsorb food-bound B_{12}, it is advisable for those older than 50 years to meet their RDA mainly by consuming foods fortified with B_{12} or a supplement containing B_{12}.

[i] In view of evidence linking folate intake with neural tube defects in the fetus, it is recommended that all women capable of becoming pregnant consume 400 µg from supplements or fortified foods in addition to intake of food folate from a varied diet.

[j] It is assumed that women will continue consuming 400 µg from supplements or fortified food until their pregnancy is confirmed and they enter prenatal care, which ordinarily occurs after the end of the periconceptional period—the critical time for formation of the neural tube.

Source: Copyright 2004 by the National Academy of Sciences. All rights reserved.

DIETARY GUIDELINES FOR AMERICANS

FOOD GROUPS TO ENCOURAGE

- Consume a sufficient amount of fruits and vegetables while staying within energy needs. Two cups of fruit and 2½ cups of vegetables per day are recommended for a reference 2,000-calorie intake, with higher or lower amounts depending on the calorie level.
- Choose a variety of fruits and vegetables each day. In particular, select from all five vegetable subgroups (dark green, orange, legumes, starchy vegetables, and other vegetables) several times a week.
- Consume 3 or more ounce-equivalents of whole-grain products. In general, at least half the grains should come from whole grains.
- Consume 3 cups per day of fat-free or low-fat milk or equivalent milk products.

FATS

- Consume less than 10 percent of calories from saturated fatty acids and less than 300 mg/day of cholesterol, and keep *trans* fatty acid consumption as low as possible.
- Keep total fat intake between 20 to 35 percent of calories, with most fats coming from sources of polyunsaturated and monounsaturated fatty acids, such as fish, nuts, and vegetable oils.
- When selecting and preparing meat, poultry, dry beans, and milk or milk products, make choices that are lean, low-fat, or fat-free.
- Limit intake of fats and oils high in saturated and/or *trans* fatty acids, and choose products low in such fats and oils.

CARBOHYDRATES

- Choose fiber-rich fruits, vegetables, and whole grains often.
- Choose and prepare foods and beverages with little added sugars or caloric sweeteners, such as amounts suggested by the USDA Food Guide and the DASH Eating Plan.
- Reduce the incidence of dental caries by practicing good oral hygiene and consuming sugar- and starch-containing foods and beverages less frequently.

SODIUM AND POTASSIUM

- Consume less than 2,300 mg (approximately 1 teaspoon of salt) of sodium per day.
- Choose and prepare food with little salt. At the same time, consume potassium-rich foods, such as fruits and vegetables.

ALCOHOLIC BEVERAGES

- Those who choose to drink alcoholic beverages should do so sensibly and in moderation—defined as the consumption of up to one drink per day for women and up to two drinks per day for men.
- Alcoholic beverages should not be consumed by some individuals, including those who cannot restrict their alcohol intake, women of childbearing age who may become pregnant, pregnant and lactating women, children and adolescents, individuals taking medication that can interact with alcohol, and those with specific medical conditions.
- Alcoholic beverages should be avoided by individuals engaging in activities that require attention, skill, or coordination, such as driving or operating machinery.

Figure 9 Dietary Guidelines for Americans.
Source: U.S. Department of Agriculture/U.S. Department of Health and Human Services, 2005.

KEY CONCEPT: **Consideration for inputs is critical to ensure that planned menus can be produced and served within available resources.**

Budget Guidelines

Before any menu is planned, the amount of money that can be spent on food must be known. In retail operations, the amount to be budgeted is based on projected income from the sale of food. This income must generate adequate revenue to cover the cost of the raw food, labor, and operating expenses and allow for desired profit. Management determines these financial objectives through strategic menu pricing.

Figure 10 My Pyramid. Graphic presentation of dietary guidelines for Americans.
Source: U.S. Department of Agriculture.

In a school, health care facility, or other noncommercial organization, a raw-food-cost allowance per volume unit such as a person, meal, or day may be determined. For example, a private, long-term care facility may set a dollar target of $6 to $8 per resident per day to cover food costs of meals, snacks, and nutritional supplements. On the other hand, long-term care facilities with a high percentage of residents on Medicare funding will likely have a much lower per day allocation, perhaps as little as $3 per resident per day. Schools, too, are greatly challenged with very limited funding for raw food costs. Allocations can be as little at $0.70 per meal to cover the costs of the food. This does not mean that the cost of every item must fall below the budgeted figure. Rather, the planner needs to look at the total weekly or monthly food cost and calculate an average cost per unit.

By balancing more costly items with less expensive foods, a more interesting variety can be offered, and the budget can still be maintained. For example, the relatively high raw-food cost of fresh fish may be offset by low-cost ground beef items. On selective menus that offer a choice of two or more entrées, a well-liked lower-cost item could be offered with a more expensive food. Tacos and burritos are popular and relatively low-cost entrées that could be offered to offset more costly items. Costs, then, may determine the choices, but it is important to remember that variety in the menu may be enhanced by balancing the use of high-cost and low-cost items.

Another aspect of cost that needs to be considered is the labor intensity of each item. Baked chicken breasts, for example, are expensive in raw food cost but require little preparation time or skill compared to from-scratch lasagna, which requires a great deal of preparation time.

Personnel. Availability and skill of employees are factors to consider when determining the variety and complexity of a menu. Understanding the relationship between menu and personnel helps the planner to develop menus that can be prepared with the available staff. Work schedules must be considered for all days because some foods require advance preparation, whereas others are prepared just prior to service. Menu items should be planned that enable employees' workloads to be spread evenly throughout the day and that do not result in too much last-minute preparation.

KEY CONCEPT: **Analysis of a new menu's impact on operations is essential to ensure a seamless transition from one menu to another.**

Production and Service Capabilities

Equipment and Physical Facilities. The menu planned for any given day must be one that can be produced in the available work space and with the available equipment. Care should be taken to distribute the workload evenly for ovens, ranges, mixers, and other large pieces of equipment. The ovens are especially vulnerable to overuse. The inclusion of too many foods at one meal that require oven use can cause an overload or complicate production schedules. For example, it may not be possible to bake chicken, baked potatoes, and roasted potatoes, if scheduled for the same meal. If equipment must be shared among production units, the menu should not include items that will cause conflict. For example, unless a baking unit has its own ovens, it may not be possible to bake fresh breads if other menu items must be baked just prior to service. Equipment usage errors can be alleviated by involving the production staff in the menu planning process.

The planner should be aware of restrictions on equipment and space and be familiar with the methods of preparation, equipment capacity, and the pans or other utensils needed before choosing the menu items. Refrigerator and freezer space must also be considered. Chilled desserts, side salads, fresh vegetable plates, and portioned juices may be difficult to refrigerate if all are planned for the same day's menu.

The amount of china, glassware, or tableware available may influence the serving of certain menu items at the same meal. For example, some desserts and sides of hot vegetables may both require sauce dishes.

Purchasing and Availability of Food. The dynamics of the markets or sources of food may have a limiting effect on the menu, although this is less of an issue in today's global market economy. Global trade and mass transportation ensure an ample and ready supply of most foods. However, there are some trends in food preferences that can pose challenges. One such trend is the demand for fresh, organic, and locally grown produce. Depending on the geographic location of the foodservice, a source with adequate supply may be difficult to secure. Knowledge of fruits and vegetables and their seasons enables a planner to include them on the menu while they are at their peak of quality and at an affordable price. Regardless of whether the menu planner is responsible for purchasing the food, he or she should keep abreast of new items on the market and be alert to foods that could add interest to the menu or improve the variety and quality of menu items offered.

Style of Service. Style of service influences food item selection and the number of choices on the menu. Some foods are more adaptable to seated service than to cafeteria service. Tray design may limit the number or form of foods offered in a health care system. For example, a layered cake with whipped topping may not work if a covered, insulated tray is used for meal delivery.

Distance between the point of preparation and the point of service should be considered, along with the elapsed time between the completion of preparation and service. If the food is prepared in a central kitchen and sent to service areas in remote locations, the menu planner must consider what the quality of the product will be by the time it reaches the final point of service. Foods transported in bulk to a service unit must be of a type that will hold well, maintain palatable temperatures, and be appetizing when served.

MENU DEVELOPMENT

KEY CONCEPT: **Staff and customer acceptance of a new menu can be enhanced through active solicitation of input during the menu planning process.**

An inherent appreciation of good food, a lack of prejudice, a flair for planning based on creativity and imagination, and the ability to merchandise food attractively are traits that aid the menu planner. If one person is responsible for menu planning, it is helpful to get input from purchasing, production, and service personnel. Many foodservices assign the menu planning responsibility to a team rather than to an individual, a practice that is especially appropriate for a multiple-unit foodservice. Input from the actual and potential customers through marketing research, food preference studies, test marketing, and participation on food or menu committees can be of assistance. The planner should be alert to new products and to trends in consumer preferences and also be aware of menu items that are offered successfully by the competition, whether it is a nonprofit or commercial situation. Menu planning should be ongoing, current, and flexible enough to respond to changing conditions.

Timetable for Planning, Development, and Implementation

How far in advance of actual production and service should menus be planned? The answer depends greatly on the type of menu used, the extent of selections offered, and the size and complexity of the foodservice system. For example, a single-use menu for a holiday meal in a restaurant may require as little as a week of planning time, assuming the recipes are tested and standardized. A selective, cycle menu with several selections and never-before-tried items for a large hospital can take several months of advance planning to ensure proper implementation.

Steps in Menu Development

Examples of menu planning worksheets are shown in Figures 11 and 12. For a selective menu offering certain items daily, time is saved by having the names of these foods printed on the worksheet. A suggested step-by-step procedure for planning menus follows.

1. **Entrées:** Plan the meats and other entrées (i.e., center of the plate) for the entire period or cycle because entrées are generally the most expensive items on the menu. Costs can be controlled to a great extent through careful planning by balancing the frequency of high-cost versus low-cost entrées. If the menu pattern provides entrée choices, it is recommended that the selection include at least one vegetarian option.

2. **Soups and sandwiches:** If a soup and sandwich combination is to be an entrée choice, it should be planned with the other entrées. In a cafeteria, a variety of sandwiches may be offered, and these may not change from day to day. If more than one soup is included, one should be a cream or hearty soup and one a lighter, stock-based soup.

3. **Vegetables and "sides":** Decide on the vegetables and side dishes appropriate to complement the entrées. Potatoes, rice, pasta, or other grains may be included as one choice. On a selective menu, pair a less popular vegetable with one that is well accepted.

		Menus		
Week of _____				
	Monday	Tuesday	Wednesday	Thursday
Breakfast				
Fruit	1.			
Fruit juice	1.			
	2.			
Cereal	1.			
	2. Assorted dry	Assorted dry	Assorted dry	Assorted dry
Entrée	1.			
Bread	1. Toast	Toast	Toast	Toast
	2.			
Beverages	1. C.T.M.	C.T.M.	C.T.M.	C.T.M.
Lunch				
Soup	1.			
Entrées	1.			
	2.			
Vegetable	1.			
Bread	1. Assorted	Assorted	Assorted	Assorted
Salads	1. Salad bar	Salad bar	Salad bar	Salad bar
	2.			
Desserts	1.			
	2.			
Beverages	1. C.T.M.	C.T.M.	C.T.M.	C.T.M.
	2.			
Dinner				
Soup	1.			
Entrées	1.			
	2.			
Potato or pasta	1.			
Vegetables	1.			
	2.			
Salads	1. Salad bar	Salad bar	Salad bar	Salad bar
	2.			
Desserts	1.			
	2.			
	3.			
Beverages	1. C.T.M.	C.T.M.	C.T.M.	C.T.M.

Figure 11 Worksheet for menu planning.

Weekly Meal Planner

WEEK 1	Entrees	Veggies and Fruits	Starches	Dessert	Extras
Sunday	1		Pasta:		
	2		Potato:		
	3		Alternate:		
			Bread:		

Menu 1	**Entrees**	**Veggies and Fruits**	**Starches**	**Dessert**	**Extras**
Monday	Deli platter	Steamed carrots	Pasta #3	Chocolate chip cookies	Crackers
	Italian beef	Snow peas	Steak fries		Shredded cheese
	BBQ drumsticks	Assorted whole fruit	Hamburger buns		Sour cream
	Chili	Cantaloupe and Honeydew	Hoagies		Dice onion

Menu 2	**Entrees**	**Veggies and Fruits**	**Starches**	**Dessert**	**Extras**
Tuesday	Rotisserie Chicken	Fruit salad		Peach cobbler with vanilla	Cocktail sauce
	Steamed shrimp	Assorted whole fruit	Potato: Roasted Red		Tartar sauce, lemons
	Carved Round steak	Green beans	Alternate: Rice pilaf		Horseradish sauce
		Corn niblets	Bread: Dinner rolls		Au Jus
					Sauteed mushroom/onions
					Crackers

Menu 3	**Entrees**	**Veggies and Fruits**	**Starches**	**Dessert**	**Extras**
Wednesday	Calzones-saus and pep	Zuchinni saute	Pasta #18 with cavatappi	Snickerdoodles	Extra marinara sauce for dipping
	Lemon pepp-Orange roughly	California blend	Fried potatoes w/onions		Tartar sauce
	Chicken Madiera	Assorted whole fruit	Breadsticks		Lemons
		Watermelon			

Menu 4	**Entrees**	**Veggies and Fruits**	**Starches**	**Dessert**	**Extras**
Thursday	BBQ Ribs	Sliced Pineapple	Pasta #1 with Spaghetti	Chocolate toffee cookies	Tartar sauce
	Sliced Cajun Turkey Breast	Assorted whole fruit	Potato: Mashed with gravy		Lemons
	Baked cod	Glazed carrots	Bead: Corn muffins		Moist Towelettes
		Peas			

Menu 5	**Entrees**	**Veggies and Fruits**	**Starches**	**Dessert**	**Extras**
Friday	Italian Chicken Breast	Broccoli		Peanut butter choc chip	Cocktail sauce
	Fried Shrimp	Asparagus	Pasta #25		Tartar sauce
	French dip	Assorted whole fruit	Tomato basil rice		Lemons
		Red grapes	Hoagies		Lettuce and tomato
		Strawberries	Sandwich rolls		Sliced cheese

Menu 6	**Entrees**	**Veggies and Fruits**	**Starches**	**Dessert**	**Extras**
Saturday	Sloppy Joes	Sunshine blend	Pasta #21 with Farfalle	Chocolate cake	
	Turkey and Gravy	Assorted whole fruit	Mashed potatoes		Lettuce and tomato
	BBQ Chicken breasts	Sliced pears	Sandwich buns		Sliced cheese
		Mandarin oranges			

Figure 12 Menu planning guide for the training table of an athletic department.
Source: Courtesy of the University of Wisconsin–Madison Athletic Department. Used with permission.

4. **Salads:** Select salads that are compatible with the entrées and vegetables. If a protein-type salad, such as chicken, tuna, or deviled egg, is planned as an entrée choice, it should be coordinated with the other entrée selections. If only one salad is offered, choose one that complements or is a contrast in texture to the other menu items.

   On a selective menu, include a green salad plus fruit, vegetable, and gelatin salads to complete the desired number. Some salads, such as tossed salad, cottage cheese, or cabbage slaw, can be offered daily as popularity indicates.

5. **Desserts:** For nonselective menus, plan a light dessert with a hearty meal and a richer dessert when the rest of the meal is not too filling. On a selective menu, the number of choices may be limited to two or three plus a daily offering of fruit, ice cream or sherbet, and yogurt. For a commercial cafeteria, the dessert selection may be quite extensive and include a two-crust pie, a creme pie, cake or cookies, pudding, fruit, ice cream or sherbet, and gelatin dessert.

6. **Garnishes:** To maximize plate appearance, it is recommended that a planned garnish be considered for each meal. The garnishes should be part of the master menu or a separate cycle. The planned garnishes eliminate last-minute decision making and allow adequate time to ensure that proper ingredients are available to assemble garnishes for each meal. Menu planning books and trade publications are excellent resources for garnish ideas.

7. **Breads:** Vary the kinds of breads offered or provide a choice of white or whole-grain bread and a hot bread. Many foodservices use homemade breads as one of their specialties. Vary the shape and ingredients of bread selections to maximize variety.

8. **Breakfast items:** Certain breakfast foods are standard and generally include fruit juices, hot and cold cereals, and toast. It is customary to offer eggs in some form and to introduce variety through the addition of other entrées, hot breads, and fresh fruits.

9. **Beverages:** A choice of beverages that includes coffee, tea, and a variety of milk is offered in most foodservices. Decaffeinated coffee and tea are generally provided, and soft drinks and a variety of juices also may be included. Some hospitals offer wine selections to their patients when approved by the attending physician.

Food Characteristics and Combinations

When planning menus, one must make an attempt to visualize how the food will look on the plate or tray. This is referred to as *presentation* and is based on the sensory and aesthetic appeal of food. One must also consider how the flavors will combine and whether there is contrast in texture, shape, and consistency.

Color gives eye appeal and helps to merchandise the food. At least one or two colorful foods should be included on each menu. A green vegetable adds color to an otherwise colorless combination of broiled fish and creamed potatoes. Other green vegetables, tomatoes, and beets also add color, as do garnishes of fruit, watercress, or radishes.

Texture refers to the structure of food and is experienced by mouth-feel. Crisp, soft, smooth, and chewy are adjectives describing food texture. A variety of textures should be included in a meal. A crisp vegetable salad accompanying a chicken and rice casserole, along with a fruit dessert, would offer a pleasing contrast in textures.

Consistency is the way foods adhere—their degree of firmness, density, or viscosity—and may be described as firm, thin, thick, or gelatinous. Again, the menu planner should work toward a balance of consistencies and be aware of consumer preferences and expectations.

Shape of food plays a big part in eye appeal, and interest can be created through variety in the form in which foods are presented. One way to add interest to the menu is to vary the way in which vegetables are cut; for example, carrots can be cut into julienne strips or circles, cubed, or shredded; green beans can be served whole, cut, or French cut. Dicing and cutting machines provide an easy method for obtaining different forms and sizes. Variation in height of food as presented on a plate also contributes to eye appeal for the customer.

Flavor combinations and profiles are important in menu planning. In addition to the basic flavors of sweet, sour, bitter, and salty, vegetables are often perceived as strong or mild flavored, chili as spicy or highly seasoned. A variety of flavors in the meal is more enjoyable than duplication of any one flavor. Foods with the same basic flavors, such as spaghetti with tomato sauce and sliced tomato salad, should be avoided in the same meal.

Certain food combinations complement each other, such as turkey and cranberries. The planner should avoid exclusive use of stereotyped combinations, however, and explore other accompaniments to make menus more interesting.

Variety in preparation should be considered in menu planning. For example, a meal of baked chicken, baked potatoes, and baked squash obviously relies on only one preparation technique. Variety may be introduced by marinating or stir-frying foods in addition to the traditional fried, broiled, baked, braised, or steamed methods. Foods can be varied further by serving them creamed, buttered, or scalloped, or by adding a variety of herbs.

Menu Evaluation

Menu evaluation is an important part of menu planning and should be an ongoing process. The menu as planned should be reviewed prior to its use and again after it has been served. A food-service manager can best evaluate menus by looking at the entire planned menu and responding to the following questions. The use of a checklist helps to make certain that all factors of good menu planning have been met. (Figure 13 is an example of a menu evaluation tool.)

Menu Evaluation Form

Cycle _____   Dates _____   Evaluator _____

Place a check mark on days when a problem is noted for any characteristic. Comment on the problem.

CHARACTERISTICS	DAYS							COMMENTS
	S	M	T	W	T	F	S	
Menu Pattern—Nutritional Adequacy Each meal is consistent with the menu pattern. All food components specified met the nutritional needs of the clientele.								
Color and Eye Appeal A variety of colors is used in each meal. Color combinations do not clash. Colorless or one-color meals are avoided. Attractive garnishes are used.								
Texture and Consistency A contrast of soft, creamy, crisp, chewy, and firm-textured foods is included in each meal, as much as possible, for clientele served.								
Flavor Combinations Foods with compatible, varied flavors are offered. Two or more foods with strong flavors are avoided in the same meal. For example, onions, broccoli, turnips, cabbage, or cauliflower; tomato juice and tomato-base casserole; and macaroni and cheese and pineapple-cheese salad, are not served together.								
Sizes and Shapes Pleasing contrasts of food sizes and shapes appear in each meal. Many chopped or mixed items are avoided in the same meal. For example, cubed meat, diced potatoes, mixed vegetables, and fruit cocktail are not served together.								

Figure 13   Example of a menu evaluation form.

Checklist for Menu Evaluation

1. Does the menu meet nutritional guidelines and organizational objectives?
2. Are the in-season foods that are offered available and within an acceptable price range?
3. Do foods on each menu offer contrasts of color? texture? flavor? consistency? shape or form? type of preparation? temperature?
4. Can these foods be prepared with the personnel and equipment available?
5. Are the workloads balanced for personnel and equipment?
6. Is any one food item or flavor repeated too frequently during this menu period?
7. Are the meals made attractive with suitable garnishes and accompaniments?
8. Do the combinations make a pleasing whole, and will they be acceptable to the clientele?

Testing the Potential. Once a menu item has been identified as having the potential to appeal to a customer base, it is wise to test the item before adding it to the menu and implementing it into the system. Foodservice operations have a number of strategies for testing menu items. One way to test an item that is being considered is to offer it as a daily special or as part of a special event. This gives the manager an opportunity to test the item with customers before formally adding it to the menus.

Some organizations have a very formal process for menu item testing. The foodservice division at the University of Wisconsin–Madison, for example, conducts new menu item testing two times per month. Usually, 13 to 15 items are tested at each session. A group of administrators and students participate in the tastings. Figure 14 is an example of the form used to document participant response. Menu items are added or rejected based on the collective response of all participants.

Writing Menus for Modified Diets

In many foodservice operations, especially those affiliated with health care, the foodservice department is responsible for ensuring that physician-ordered diets are provided accurately. A qualified dietetics professional, such as a registered dietitian or dietetic technician, works with the foodservice manager to implement these special menus. Modified menu extensions are an excellent management tool for monitoring this responsibility. The modified menu extensions are generated from the master menu and a diet manual that defines the modified diets for a particular facility. Many dietetic associations and hospitals have written diet manuals that are available for sale. It is important to select a diet manual that best represents the diets needed in a given situation. For example, a manual developed for a hospital may not be the best choice for a long-term care facility.

Once diets are defined, the foodservice administrator should meet with a dietetics professional knowledgeable in modified diets and develop the menu extensions (Figure 15). A menu extension should be planned for each day. The extended portion of the menu illustrates how the modified diet, as defined in the manual, can be adapted from the master.

Extended menus have several advantages. These menus serve as a tool for menu analysis to ensure that modified diets are prepared and served according to physicians' written diet orders. The extensions also serve as a reference for the foodservice employees so they can be certain that diets are prepared and served accurately. Finally, the extensions are a useful purchasing tool, clearly identifying the need for special dietary foods (i.e., low-sodium items).

Menus as Documents. Printed master menus for both general and modified diets are excellent documents for department evaluation and budget planning functions. Any menu changes made should be noted on the master menu for future evaluation. Master menus are sometimes signed and dated by the person responsible for menu content.

RECIPE TESTING

Student _____
Staff _____
6/2/2006

FOOD ITEM	On a scale of 1–5 with 5 being the highest, please rank the following:			COMMENTS	Add to Menu	
	Flavor	Texture	Appearance		Yes	No
1. Tofu and Spinach Samosas						
2. Tandoori Chicken Breast Sandwich						
3. Cilantro Slaw						
4. Mango Salsa						
5. Mushroom Curry						
6. Coconut Vegetable Stew						
7. Bombay Beef Curry						
8. Grilled Tandoori Marinated Shrimp w/Basmati Rice						
9. Indian Mango Ice Cream						
10. Steve's Dessert						

Figure 14 Example of a recipe testing form.
Courtesy of the University of Wisconsin–Madison, Division of Housing and Dining and Culinary Services. Used with permission.

General Menu		Portion	Modified Diets				
			Mechan	Puree	2 gm Na+	1500 ADA	1200 ADA
	Orange Jc.	1/2c	✓	✓	✓	✓	✓
	Scr. Egg	1/4c (#16)	✓	✓	SF	✓	✓
B	WW Toast	2 sl.	✓	Hot Cereal	✓	✓	1
	Margarine	2 pats	✓	—	✓	✓	1
	Jelly	2 pkt.	✓	—	✓	diet	diet
	Milk—2%	8 oz	✓	Whole	✓	✓	skim
	Baked Chic.	3 oz	ground	puree	✓	2 oz	2 oz
	Mashed pota.	1/2c (#8)	✓	✓	✓	✓	✓
	Gravy	2 T (1 oz)	✓	✓	SF	FF	FF
	Broccoli	1/2c	✓	puree	✓	✓	✓
L	Orange Garnish	1 slice	✓	—	✓	✓	✓
	WW Roll	1	✓	—	✓	✓	—
	Margarine	1 pat	✓	—	✓	✓	—
	S.B. Shortcake	1	✓	puree	✓	1/2c Berries	1/2c Berries
	Milk 2%	8 oz	✓	whole	✓	✓	skim
	Veg. Soup	3/4c (6 oz)	✓	puree	SF	✓	✓
	Crackers	3	✓	puree	SF	—	—
	Ham Sand.	1	w/ground meat	puree	Beef	1/2	1/2
D	Sweet Pickle	2	—	—	✓	✓	✓
	Mixed Melon	1 cup	✓	puree	✓	✓	✓
	Milk 2%	8 oz	✓	whole	✓	✓	skim
H	Gr. Crax	1	✓	✓	✓	✓	✓
S	Milk 2%	4 oz	✓	✓	✓	✓	skim

Walnut Grove Health Care Center — General and Modified Diets — Cycle 1 — Day Wednesday — Dietitian

Figure 15 Example of a menu extension for a modified menu.

THE POSTED MENU

KEY CONCEPT: Application of menu design principles for the posted menu maximizes its value as a marketing and education tool.

As indicated at the beginning of this chapter, the menu is an itemized list of foods served at a meal. From it, a working menu and production schedules evolve. The term also refers to the medium on which the menu is printed, which presents the food selection to the restaurant customer, the hospital patient, or other clientele. The menu may also be posted on a menu board, as is the custom in most cafeterias and fast-food restaurants.

Menu Design and Format

A menu card must be designed and worded to appeal to the guest, to stimulate sales, and often to influence clientele to select items that the foodservice wants to sell. The menu card should be of a size that can be easily handled. It should also be spotlessly clean, simple in format with appropriate print size and type, and have ample margin space. The menu should be highly legible and interesting in color and design, harmonizing with the decor of the foodservice. The printed menu is a form of merchandising and an important marketing tool. It should not be thought of as a price sheet alone, but as a selling and public relations device.

Descriptive Wording. Menu items are usually listed in the sequence in which they are served and should present an accurate word picture of the foods available so that the patron can properly visualize the menu items. It is disappointing for the customer to imagine one thing and be served something entirely different.

Truth-in-Menu Legislation. Giving misleading names to menu items is unfair to the customer and is illegal where truth-in-menu legislation has been enacted. In general, these laws require that the menu accurately describes the foods to be served. If baked Idaho potatoes are listed on the menu, they must indeed be Idaho potatoes. The same is true when listing Maine lobster, or the point of origin for other foods. "Fresh" foods listed on the menu must be fresh, not frozen or canned. If the word "homemade" is used on the menu, it means that the food was made on the premises. If a menu lists a grade such as USDA Choice beef and indicates portion size, the meat must be of that grade and size.

Descriptive words do enhance the menu and, if accurate, may influence the customers' selections. Examples of descriptive wording include sliced, red tomatoes on Bibb lettuce, fresh spinach salad with bacon-mayonnaise dressing, old-fashioned beef stew with fresh vegetables, chilled melon wedge, and warm peach cobbler with whipped topping. The menu should not include recipe names that are unknown to the customer or that do not indicate the contents. Even where truth-in-menu legislation is not in effect, accuracy in menu wording helps to ensure customer satisfaction.

SUMMARY

The menu is the focal point from which many functions and activities in a foodservice organization begin. It determines the foods to be purchased, it is the basis for planning production and employee schedules, and it is an important factor in controlling costs.

In planning foodservice menus, many factors must be considered: (1) the nutritional requirements, food habits, and preferences of the individuals in the group for which menus are being planned; (2) the goals of the organization; (3) the amount of money available; (4) limitations on equipment and physical facilities; (5) the number and skill of employees; and (6) the type of service. The menu must offer a selection of foods that is satisfying to the clientele, but it must be one that can be produced within the constraints of the physical facility and limitations dictated by management policies.

The menu can take different forms, each written for the needs of a particular type of foodservice. The static or set menu, in which the same menu items are offered each day, is found mainly in commercial foodservices. A selective menu offers two or more choices in each menu category and is widely used in various types of foodservices. A nonselective menu offers no choice, but in schools and health care facilities where this type of menu is often used, choices in some categories may be limited. A cycle menu is a carefully planned set of menus that are rotated at definite intervals. The single-use menu is planned for a certain day and is not repeated in the same form.

Systematic planning procedures that include continuous evaluation of the menus as served should be followed. The menu planner should keep abreast of new products on the market and should be alert to the preferences of the clientele and the need for changes in the menu. Innovation is a key word in today's menu planning. New menu ideas and marketing techniques must be developed if the foodservice is to satisfy a clientele that is becoming increasingly sophisticated about food.

APPLICATION OF CHAPTER CONCEPTS

Menu planning is a ongoing process at University of Wisconsin Housing and includes frequent recipe testing throughout the academic year. The process begins with a list of recipes, usually 6 to 10, that management wants to test or retest. The list is sent to the manager at the commissary, who reviews the recipes with the production staff and ensures that ingredients are on hand.

On the day of testing, one chef is assigned to prepare all the recipes for a 1:00 p.m. testing session. Administrators, managers, production staff, and students are invited to participate. Each item is tested, and participants complete a form ranking the quality aspects of each item: flavor, texture, and appearance. The form also asks the participants to indicate whether they would buy the item and whether they think it should be added to the menu.

A recent testing included three items with variations. The first item, tuna casserole, was a favorite comfort food for some students, and the purpose of the testing was to determine if a base of cream of chicken or cream of mushroom was more appealing. The second item was a buffalo pot pie. This was in acknowledgement of interest in local and native foods. Local buffalo and seasonal vegetables will be used if this item is added to the menu. The final item was a precooked beef: one an eye of round, the other a pot roast. These last two items were tested primarily for their value as an item to use for high-volume catering events.

CRITICAL-THINKING QUESTIONS

1. For which business units are recipes being tested?
2. How would type of menu per business unit influence how these items are presented on the posted menus?
3. Which of these recipes would be most challenging for the production staff relative to culinary skills? Why?
4. Which of these recipes would have the most impact on equipment use?
5. Does the testing team fully represent the customer profile? Why or why not? Who would you include?
6. Tuna casserole isn't terribly popular compared to some other menu items, yet Housing chooses to continue to work on its formulation and keep it on the menu. How would you decide if a menu item is popular enough to keep on the menu?
7. During the testing process, what might the team discuss relative to service of each item? What needs to be taken into consideration that is unique to UW Housing?
8. What is the value of asking testing participants both whether they would buy an item and whether the item should be placed on the menu? Are both questions necessary? Why or why not?

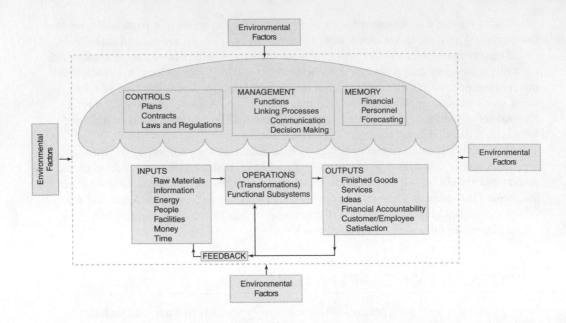

9. How might each of these items influence the purchasing function?
10. How might the season of the year influence when each of these items is placed on the menu?

CHAPTER REVIEW QUESTIONS

1. Compare and contrast what the term *menu* means in the front versus the back of the house.
2. Refer to the examples of Scope of Services presented in Figure A (Fig. 3). What would be the most appropriate type of menu for each business unit in each of these examples?
3. What is the difference between a menu plan and a meal pattern? In what contexts are these concepts used?
4. Describe some strategies by which a director of for school nutrition could keep her fingers on the pulse of food trends and school children.
5. Why is it important to define a clear objective for any menu planning or revision process?
6. What strategies do you think menu planners for colleges and universities should use to generate inspiration for menu planning?
7. Should front-of-the-house staff be involved with menu planning? Why or why not?
8. It is said on occasion that food safety begins at menu planning. Explain and give an example.
9. Plan a one-week, limited, select menu for a psychiatric facility; age range is 18 to 85 years. What factors did you consider in planning this menu?
10. Obtain a menu from a local organization (i.e., hospital, restaurant, school, or nursing home). Evaluate the menu on food characteristics and combinations. What changes would you recommend?

SELECTED WEB SITES

www.cms.hhs.gov/manuals/downloads/som107c07.pdf   (Center for Medicare and Medicaid Services)

http://fns.usda.gov/cnd/menu/menuplanning.NSLP.htm   (USDA Food and Nutrition Services)

www.census.gov   (U.S. Census Bureau)

www.nfsmi.org   (National Food Service Management Institute)

Purchasing

Eldad Yitzhak/Shutterstock

PURCHASING IS AN ESSENTIAL FUNCTION IN A FOOD-service system. Although the purchasing process for both noncommercial and commercial foodservice operations involves food, supplies, and capital equipment, major emphasis in this chapter is given to the buying of food.

From Chapter 6 of *Foodservice Management: Principles and Practices*, Twelfth Edition, June Payne-Palacio, Monica Theis.

Today's market offers a large variety of products from which well-informed selections must be made in order to meet the needs of a particular foodservice operation. Whether the buying decisions are made by the manager, a chef, a purchasing agent, or other qualified personnel, they must be based on quality standards, the economic structure of the organization, and a thorough understanding of the markets that encompass the purchasing environment.

The primary purpose of this chapter is to provide the reader with basic information about purchasing in foodservice operations. In this chapter, approaches to selecting vendors, determining food needs, and writing specifications are discussed, as are the methods of purchasing. From this information, the reader will be able to build a framework for making facility-specific buying decisions.

KEY CONCEPTS

1. Purchasing is a management function focused on securing resources needed to operate a foodservice.

2. In the context of purchasing, the term *market* has several meanings.

3. Products are distributed through a series of channels and transfer of ownership.

4. Markets and the function of purchasing are regulated at the federal, state, and local levels.

5. A buyer is a member of the professional administrative team and is held to high standards of work performance and ethical behavior.

6. The structure of purchasing varies depending on the size and type of organization.

7. A foodservice can purchase food and products from a wide variety of vendors.

8. Formal and informal methods of purchasing are used by foodservice operations.

9. Numerous factors need to be considered when selecting products for a foodservice operation.

10. Procedures used to purchase products vary depending on the formality of the purchasing function.

WHAT IS PURCHASING?

■ **KEY CONCEPT: Purchasing is a management function focused on securing resources needed to operate a foodservice.**

Purchasing
is the function of acquiring desired products and services

Purchasing or procurement is the *process* of securing the right product for a facility at the right time and in a form that meets preestablished standards for quantity, quality, and price. In practice, purchasing is a complex and dynamic process; it is a sequence of consecutive actions with a goal of securing food, supplies, and equipment to meet the needs of the foodservice operation. From beginning to end, an exchange of ownership occurs between the buyer and the seller; that is, usually goods in exchange for money. Figure 1 shows the basic flow of purchasing activities. It is important to recognize that the flow varies in sequence and content depending on the needs and structure of a specific foodservice.

Influential factors include the formality of the purchasing program and regulatory mandates. The steps specific to various methods of purchasing are discussed later in this chapter.

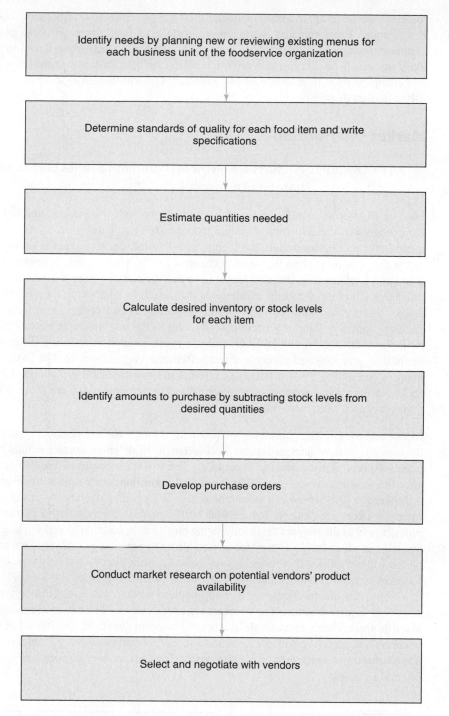

Figure 1 The basic flow of purchasing activities.

Identify needs by planning new or reviewing existing menus for each business unit of the foodservice organization

Determine standards of quality for each food item and write specifications

Estimate quantities needed

Calculate desired inventory or stock levels for each item

Identify amounts to purchase by subtracting stock levels from desired quantities

Develop purchase orders

Conduct market research on potential vendors' product availability

Select and negotiate with vendors

THE MARKET

■ KEY CONCEPT: **In the context of purchasing, the term** *market* **has several meanings.**

The term **market** in the context of purchasing is actually a reflection of several concepts related to the products available for purchase and the processes involved in moving them from the original source of supply to the point of service, or from *field to fork*. Sometimes the term is used in reference to **commodities** or the raw agricultural products used to produce foods. These include the meat, grain, and milk markets, to name a few. Another use

Market

The medium through which a change of ownership occurs

Commodities

Raw agricultural products used to produce food

157

refers to the geographic locations of the growing or production regions of food sources. For example, California and Florida are referred to as the markets for fresh produce. The commodities and regions in which they are grown are collectively referred to as the primary market. A market can also refer to a collection of activities that results in transfer of ownership of food from producer to consumer. This continuum of exchange activities is called market distribution.

Market Distribution

■ KEY CONCEPT: **Products are distributed through a series of channels and transfer of ownership.**

Market channels

The food processing and distribution system, beginning with the grower of raw food products and ending at the final customer or point of consumption

Middlemen

Conduits between manufacturers, distributors, and consumers

Brokers and manufacturer's representatives

Wholesalers who do not assume ownership of goods, but whose responsibility it is to bring buyers and sellers together

Broker

Serves as a sales representative for a manufacturer or group of manufacturers

Manufacturer's representative

Serves as a sales representative for a single manufacturer

Food is distributed from sources to consumers through a series of **market channels**. Components of the distribution system include growing, harvesting, storage, processing, manufacturing, transportation, packaging, and distribution. A channel is simply a segment of the distribution process where an exchange of ownership occurs. For example, a farmer who grows wheat sells the post-harvest product to a mill where the wheat is processed into flour. The farmer-to-mill exchange is a channel. In addition to the exchange of ownership, there is a change in form and consequently added costs. Costs increase at each exchange point and are ultimately passed along to the consumers at the end of the distribution system (see Figure 2). Today there is much interest in reducing if not eliminating the middle channels and purchase directly from the original source. The local food movement is certainly a case in point. As interest in environmental protection, fresh product and support of local economies increases, foodservice operations are seeking to increase their purchases from local producers.

Intermediaries. The movement of products through the distribution system is guided through the work of intermediaries or **middlemen**. Middlemen act as conduits between the manufacturers, distributors, and consumers. The two most common middlemen who influence the foodservice segment are **brokers and manufacturer's representatives**. A **broker** or brokerage firm serves as a sales representative for a manufacturer or group of manufacturers. Brokers are paid on commission by the manufacturers, often a percentage of the product sold to distributors or directly to the end user. In addition to serving as a conduit on available product, brokers introduce new products to potential buyers. Brokers make money on the volume of food they move, so they typically work directly and only with large-volume foodservices and distribution companies such as U.S. Food Service and Sysco.

Some manufacturers use another approach to product movement through *direct representation*. Rather than invest in a broker, a manufacturer will hire its own product representative or agent. Heinz, for example, might send its agent directly to distributors or foodservice operations to introduce new products and address product or delivery problems. In practice, a **manufacturer's representative** may visit a foodservice to introduce a new product and provide samples.

Figure 2 Market channels and transfer of ownership.

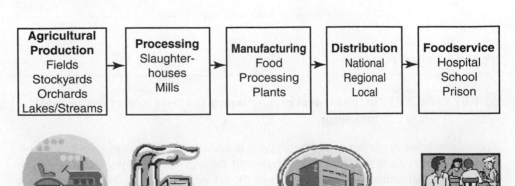

Understanding the Market

The market is dynamic and ever changing, and the food buyer must be alert to trends and conditions that affect it. Government policy, economic trends, and adverse weather conditions are but a few of the factors that demand the attention of the buyer. For example, global trade agreements, including the North America Free Trade Agreement (NAFTA), have had a significant influence on the availability and price of commodities.

Exchange of information between seller and buyer is an important function of the market and is made possible through various media, such as the Internet, trade association newsletters, local and federal market reports, and the press. Other sources of market information are technical and trade association meetings and magazines, research reports, communication with sales representatives, and visits to the markets and wholesale distributors.

Adverse growing conditions can affect food prices, as can unusual consumer demands and seasonal variations. Some foods are relatively stable in price and follow general economic conditions; others are more perishable and have greater price fluctuations during the year. Most fresh fruits and vegetables are considered best at the height of the production season, particularly those grown within a given market area. However, processing of fresh produce and changes in transportation, refrigeration, and storage facilities have greatly expanded the availability of these products year round. Stocks of processed foods may be high or depleted at times, which will affect both price and availability.

Technology has brought the global and domestic markets into the buyer's office. The Internet, fax machines, and e-mail allow for easy access and communication with all segments of the market without leaving the office.

Market Regulation: U.S. Food and Inspection Programs

█ **KEY CONCEPT:** **Markets and the function of purchasing are regulated at the federal, state, and local levels.**

The safety and wholesomeness of the U.S. food supply are ensured through government safety and inspection programs. Quality is defined and ensured through grading services, which are not to be confused with the inspection programs. Grading is discussed later in this chapter.

Government safety and inspection programs are used to evaluate foods for signs of disease, bacteria, chemicals, infestation, filth, or any other factor that may render the food item unfit for human consumption. All foods shipped in **interstate commerce** must meet the requirements of federal laws and regulations. Foods sold in **intrastate commerce** must meet state and local regulations that are *at least equal to* the federal requirements.

The major responsibility for ensuring safe, wholesome food lies with the U.S. Department of Agriculture (USDA) and the Food and Drug Administration (FDA), an agency of the Department of Health and Human Services. Numerous other government departments and agencies are also involved in specific aspects of food safety regulation. The following is a summary, by both government department and enforcement agency, of food safety programs in the United States.

U.S. Department of Agriculture. Within the USDA, the Food Safety and Inspection Service is responsible for enforcing the Meat Inspection Act, the Poultry Products Inspection Act, and the Egg Inspection Act. Inspection of commodities for wholesomeness is *mandatory* for meats, poultry, and other processed foods. An official stamp affixed to the product indicates that it is a high-quality product and processed under sanitary conditions. Figure 3 shows examples of federal food inspection stamps.

Food and Drug Administration. The FDA is an enforcement agency within the Department of Health and Human Services. It is responsible for the enforcement of the federal Food, Drug, and Cosmetic Act; the Fair Packaging and Labeling Act; and the Nutritional Labeling and Education Act. The FDA covers the production, manufacture, and distribution of all food involved in interstate commerce except meat, poultry, and eggs.

Interstate commerce

Financial transactions (buying and selling of goods) carried on between states

Intrastate commerce

Financial transactions (buying and selling of goods) carried on within state boundaries

Figure 3 Federal inspection stamps for meat, poultry, seafood, and eggs.

Federal Inspection Stamp for Meat

Federal Inspection Stamp for Fish

USDA Poultry Inspection Mark

USDA Egg Products Inspection Mark

Under the Food, Drug, and Cosmetic Act, no food may enter interstate commerce that is deemed adulterated or misbranded. A food is adulterated under the following conditions:

- It contains substances that are injurious to health.
- Any part of it is filthy or decomposed.
- It has been prepared or held under unsanitary conditions.
- It contains portions of diseased animals.

A food is **misbranded** if the label does not include the information mandated by law or if it gives misleading information.

The FDA also determines and enforces standards of identity, quality, and fill. **Standards of identity** define what a food product must contain to be called by a certain name. For example, percent butterfat is defined for the different types of fluid milk (i.e., whole, reduced fat, fat free). **Standards of quality** apply primarily to canned fruits and vegetables. These standards limit and define the number and kinds of defects permitted. They do not provide a basis for comparing foods as do grades, but they do establish minimum quality requirements. **Standards of fill** regulate the quantity of food in a container. They tell the packer how full the container must be to avoid deceiving the consumer. All these standards are mandatory for foods in interstate commerce and may be used voluntarily for others.

The FDA is responsible for enforcing federal labeling requirements. Such requirements were first made mandatory with the passage of the Fair Packaging and Labeling Act of 1966. Since then, several laws have been passed by Congress to define these labeling requirements in more detail. Table 1 provides a historical review of major food law legislation.

National Marine and Fisheries Service. A voluntary inspection system for fish, fish products, and grade standards for some products is controlled by the National Marine and Fisheries Service, an agency of the Department of Commerce. If the product carries a U.S. grade designation, the purchaser is ensured of continuous in-plant inspection during processing by federal inspectors.

U.S. Public Health Service. The U.S. Public Health Service (PHS) is concerned primarily with control of infections and contagious disease but is also responsible for the safety of some foods. This agency is responsible for the inspection of some shellfish, and they advise state and local governments on sanitation standards for the production, processing, and distribution of milk. The PHS standard for Grade A fresh milk is a standard of wholesomeness, which means that it has met state or local requirements that equal or exceed federal requirements.

Misbranded

A food product whose label either does not include information mandated by law or includes misleading information

---

Standards of identity

Defines what a food product must contain to be called a certain name

---

Standards of quality

Set minimum standards for features such as aesthetics of a product before it can enter interstate commerce

---

Standards of fill

Regulate the quantity of food in a container

Table 1 Major food laws.

LEGISLATION	PURE FOOD AND DRUG ACT, 1906	FOOD, DRUG, AND COSMETIC ACT (FDCA), 1938	FAIR PACKAGING AND LABELING ACT (FPLA), 1966	NUTRITION LABELING REGULATIONS, 1973	NUTRITIONAL LABELING AND EDUCATION ACT (NLEA), 1990
Intent	Protects the public. Defines misbranding and adulteration. Prohibits foods that *are* injurious to a person's health.	Establishes standards of identity. States specific labeling requirements. Prohibits foods that *may be* injurious to a person's health.	Provides consumer with accurate information for value comparison. Prevents use of unfair or deceptive methods of packaging or labeling of consumer products.	Educates the consumer about the nutrient content of foods.	Provides extensive nutrient information on packaged foods. Improves nutritional content of packaged foods.
Key requirements	Authorized food processing plant inspections to ensure sanitary conditions.	Name and address of manufacturer or distributor. Name of the food. Quantity of content. Statement of ingredients listed by common or usual name in decreasing predominance.	Same information as the FDCA. Defines a food label in terms of format and information. Name of food/net quantity must appear on "principal display panel." Net content must be in legible type and in distinct color contrast. Defines type size and location.	*Voluntary* except for foods fortified with vitamins, minerals, or protein, or in situations where a nutritional claim is made.	*Mandatory* for all packaged food. Includes provisions for the nutritional labeling of the 20 most common produce and seafood items. Serving sizes are stated in household units. Regulates nutrient content and health claims including those made by restaurants on signs and placards.

Environmental Protection Agency.   The Environmental Protection Agency (EPA) regulates pesticides. Responsibilities include setting tolerance levels for pesticide residues in foods, establishing the safety of new pesticides, and providing educational materials on the safe use of pesticides. The EPA also determines quality standards for water.

Department of the Treasury.   The Bureau of Alcohol, Tobacco, Firearms and Explosives (ATF) in the Department of the Treasury is responsible for monitoring the production, distribution, and labeling of alcoholic beverages. This includes all alcoholic beverages except those that contain less than 7 percent alcohol, which are monitored by the FDA.

THE BUYER

▌ **KEY CONCEPT:** **A buyer is a member of the professional administrative team and is held to high standards of work performance and ethical behavior.**

Food and supplies for a foodservice organization may be purchased by an individual, by a purchasing department, or through a cooperative arrangement with other institutions, depending on the size and ownership of the organization and its procurement policies. In a small operation, the buying may be done by the manager as part of his or her responsibilities.

Whatever the arrangement, it is the responsibility of the foodservice department or the individual functional units within a foodservice to communicate its needs to the buyer to ensure delivery of the needed amount of food and supplies at an appropriate time and of the desired quality. This requires cooperation on the part of the buyer, as well as the foodservice personnel, and a willingness to honor the quality standards set by the foodservice.

Purchasing the amount and quality of food required for the foodservice within the limitations imposed by the budget and financial policies of the organization requires knowledge of internal and external factors. Internal factors include the customers, the menus, recipes, labor availability and skills, equipment, storage facilities, and quantities of foods needed. External factors include the marketing system, food standards and quality, product availability, and purchasing methods.

The buyer represents the institution in negotiations with market representatives and should have extensive knowledge and understanding of legal requirements, especially as they relate to orders and contracts. There should be a clear understanding of the buyer's decision-making authority and of the institutional policies within which the buyer must operate.

The Art of Negotiation

Negotiation
The communication skill used by individuals to confer with others to reach an agreement or compromise

Excellence in a number of communication skills is essential for the successful buyer. The ability to establish professional working partnerships through sound interpersonal skills and listening and technical writing skills are key to the development of effective specifications and contracts. Buyers must be diligent in seeing that the products of best value for the organization are secured. Therefore, a communication skill that is of particular importance to the function of purchasing is that of **negotiation**.

The ability to negotiate is essential to successful purchasing. It is a skill that can be learned and perfected over time. The buyer needs to negotiate informal and/or contract purchases that are fair to the foodservice and the vendor. The first step in successful negotiations with a potential vendor is for the buyer to be well prepared with knowledge and information about the products needed and the foodservice operation in which they will be used. As stated earlier, there are a number of means by which the buyer can stay current on food and supply trends. In addition, the buyer needs to work closely with the production and service staffs to ensure that operational needs and limitations are well understood. For example, the buyer needs to be familiar with the amounts and types of storage space available for products in all forms. An appreciation for the types and capacities of production equipment will help the buyer to better understand the forms and volumes of product that are feasible for a specific foodservice operation.

Ethics in Purchasing

Ethics
The science of morals in human behavior

Buying demands integrity, maturity, negotiation skills, and commitment to a high standard of **ethics**. Acting as an agent for the institution, the buyer is entrusted with making decisions concerning quality, price, and amounts to purchase and cannot afford to compromise either money or position. Buyers may be subjected to bribes and other kinds of inducements to influence buying decisions. *Collusion* refers to a secret arrangement or understanding between the buyer and the seller for fraudulent purposes. The most common example of this comes in the form of "kickbacks" where the buyer accepts something of value (money or merchandise) from the vendor in exchange for a sale. Less obvious conflicts may come in the form of free lunches, holiday gifts, and free samples. Violations of professionalism in purchasing should be clearly identified in the organization's policy on ethics (frequently referred to as a code of ethics). No gifts or other favors should be accepted that could compromise the buyer's ability to make objective purchasing decisions.

A buyer must be able to deal successfully with sales representatives, brokers, and other marketing agents. Courtesy and fair treatment contribute to establishing a satisfactory working relationship with these agents, who can be valuable sources of information on new products and the availability of foods on the market. The buyer must take caution to avoid compromising a professional relationship.

Products should be evaluated objectively and buying decisions made on the basis of quality, price, and service. Information received in confidence from one company should not be used to obtain an unfair advantage in competitive negotiations.

Structure of Purchasing

■ **KEY CONCEPT:** The structure of purchasing varies depending on the size and type of organization.

Foodservice operations work under different types of purchasing arrangements depending on a number of factors, including organizational size, ownership, and geographic location. Centralized and group purchasing are common types of purchasing and are described on the following pages. It is important for the reader to realize that many single-unit operations conduct their purchasing functions as part of the departmental operations. For example, a chef in a single-unit restaurant may have full responsibility for purchasing, independent of a purchasing department or group contract.

Centralized Purchasing. Centralized buying, in which a purchasing department rather than a department manager is responsible for obtaining needed supplies and equipment for all units in the organization, is used in many large organizations, including universities, schools, multiple-unit restaurants, and hospitals. By relieving the individual units of the responsibility for interviewing sales representatives, negotiating contracts, and placing orders, this system has proven to be cost effective and time saving for the foodservice. Where centralized purchasing is used, the authority to buy some product, such as fresh produce or other perishables, may be delegated to the foodservice, or in multiple-unit organizations to the individual units. Sometimes a unit manager has purchasing authority up to a specific dollar amount. For example, a chef in a large hospital may have authority to initiate purchases up to $500. Needs costing more than $500 would have to be handled through the central purchasing office.

One potential disadvantage of centralized purchasing is that friction can develop between the purchasing department and the foodservice unit if there is not a clear understanding of decision-making authority, especially on quality standards. The possibility for friction exists in all large-scale purchasing unless the limits of authority are well defined and the lines of communication are kept clear and open.

Group and Cooperative Purchasing. It is beneficial for buyers to increase volume and lower service requirements to improve leverage with suppliers and, thus, buy at lower prices. Efforts to increase volume have led some foodservice directors to consolidate their buying power with that of other organizations in cooperative purchasing arrangements. For example, several hospitals in a metropolitan area may combine their purchases to obtain lower prices and possibly more favorable service arrangements; or in smaller communities, two or more dissimilar foodservices, such as a school, hospital, and nursing home, may join in a cooperative purchasing agreement. Central warehousing may be part of this type of plan, but if the volume is large enough, vendors may agree to deliver merchandise directly to the individual units.

Group buying differs from central purchasing in that members of the group are independent organizations and are not under the same management or within one organization. In cooperative purchasing, the members are usually units of a larger system, such as schools in a citywide or countywide school system. Obviously, the main advantage of cooperative buying is the price advantage gained by increased volume, which in turn may attract more prospective vendors. Other advantages of cooperative purchasing for the foodservice managers include freedom from having to meet with sales representatives and time savings through streamlined paperwork and administration of the purchasing function.

The buyer is selected by the members and maintains an office independent of the participating organizations. The purchasing service generally is supported by a fee paid by each institution that is based on the percentage of its orders. To be effective, all members of the cooperative must commit their time and the majority of their purchase orders to the group's efforts. Participating organizations must agree on common specifications and establish a bid schedule. Food preferences may vary among organizations, so members must occasionally be willing to compromise their requirements for the benefit of the group.

Centralized purchasing

A structure of purchasing in which a department within an organization assumes the main responsibility for the purchasing function

---

Group and cooperative purchasing

An organization that represents member organizations and oversees their purchasing function

State of Wisconsin Department of Administration
    Oversees contracts for some products used in all state-run facilities
    Example: garbage bags
    Mandates that all state facilities use prime vending concept	

University of Wisconsin–Madison: Purchasing Services
    Manages contracts that are shared with other campus
    divisions including the student union and the athletic
    department. Example: bagels
 	
University of Wisconsin–Madison: Division of Housing
    Oversees competitive bid contracts
    Example: meat, bread, cheese and produce contracts are
    managed at division level	

Housing Food Service
    Has authority to purchase some food items directly from
    vendors without approval from division, campus, system, or
    state levels assuming the vendors meet campus requirements.
    Example: Organic foods but vendors must meet campus
    requirements for insurance and submit certifications	

Figure 4 Purchasing structure for a state-run university dining service.

Group purchasing organizations (GPOs), sometimes referred to as purchasing alliances or consortiums, are a relatively new twist in the group purchasing concept. A GPO is an organization that represents member organizations and oversees the purchasing function for the entire organization. For example, today there are a number of national and regional GPOs that represent various segments of the health care industry such as university hospitals, community hospitals, nursing homes, and clinics. The GPO negotiates with and selects a list of vendors for all categories of needs for the member institutions, including not only food, but linens, surgical supplies, pharmaceuticals, and x-ray film, to name a few. Depending on the nature of the GPO, purchasing managers are committed to securing needs from these vendors' unit managers, including those in foodservice, and do not have the freedom to negotiate or purchase from other vendors.

The advantage of these alliances is an overall cost savings for the organization rather than the individual units. Because foodservice generally represents only a fraction of a health care facility's budget, it rarely has much negotiating leverage in these programs.

The structure of purchasing within an organization can be further complicated if it is a public entity such as a federal prison or state-run hospital. Policy on purchasing at the government level must be honored throughout all purchasing processes. Figure 4 illustrates the complexity of purchasing in a state university.

VENDORS AND FOOD DISTRIBUTORS

■ **KEY CONCEPT: A foodservice can purchase food and products from a wide variety of vendors.**

Vendors

Sellers. Sources of supply

The selection of suppliers, or **vendors**, is one of the most important decisions that must be made in a purchasing program. Management and those with purchasing authority need to work together to establish quality standards for food and supplies to be purchased, and to conduct a market search for reliable vendors that are able to furnish the desired products.

In practice there are actually several categories of vendors or food distributors. The two most common categories used in foodservice are *broadline* and *specialty* vendors. A specialty vendor typically carries a limited product line. For example, a specialty vendor may limit its line to only groceries or carry a single commodity such as meat, fish, or produce.

A broadline food distributor carries large inventories of food and supplies, representing numerous specialty vendors, in an attempt to meet nearly every need that a single foodservice may have. In addition to food, these broad- or full-line vendors are likely to carry chemicals, paper products, and equipment. Sysco and U.S. Foodservice are the two most recognized food distributors at the national level. Other regional distributors include Reinhart Foodservice and Gordon Food Service. A key advantage is the convenience of streamlining the administrative tasks such as placing orders and processing invoices. Buyers also enjoy discounts through volume purchasing, especially if the distributor is the *prime vendor*. The concept of prime vending is addressed later in this chapter. Foodservice operations often work through at least one broadline distributor and several specialty vendors to meet their full range of food and supply needs.

A buyer new to a foodservice operation can locate vendors through numerous resources, including:

- The Internet
- Other foodservice operators
- Trade journals and publications
- Trade shows

A key responsibility of the buyer in initiating a professional working relationship with a vendor is to evaluate carefully the vendor's scope of products and services. To accomplish this, the buyer must make the necessary inquiries into the vendor's product line, available services, and reliability in meeting contract specifications.

The buyer should carefully evaluate the product line of the potential vendor to assess availability of needed products and to ensure that the products meet the quality standards of the organization. Details of delivery schedules, payment policies, and contingency plans for situations in which standards are not met should be known by the buyer. For example, a buyer would want to know the vendor's policy regarding credit when a damaged or spoiled product is delivered. Policies on emergency deliveries should also be reviewed. Some vendors have policies on how to deliver food supplies in the event of a disaster such as a tornado, snowstorm, or earthquake. It is very important to review discount policies on early payments, rebates, and volume purchasing discounts. Visits to the vendor's local headquarters and talks with other foodservice operators can supply much of this information.

Many vendors provide support equipment or service programs with the purchase of certain food products. These are sometimes referred to as *value-added* services, or services included with the purchase of a product at no additional cost. For example, a vendor may offer to supply coffeemaking equipment at no extra cost with the purchase of its coffee products or a popcorn popper with the purchase of the vendor's popcorn line. It is important for the buyer to inquire about the technical assistance provided by the vendor for service and maintenance of these programs. Necessary information would include service availability in the event of equipment failure and scheduling of routine maintenance on the equipment.

Location and size of the foodservice are important factors in the selection of a supplier. If the operation is located in or near a large metropolitan area, there may be several suppliers that could meet quantity and quality needs and whose delivery schedules are satisfactory for the foodservice.

For an operation in a small or remote location, part or all of its supplies may be purchased locally. In this situation, the buyer should be sure that the vendors carry adequate stocks and are able to replenish products quickly. If there are not enough local suppliers to offer competitive prices, the buyer may prefer to purchase only certain products locally, such as dairy products, bakery items, and fresh produce, and place less frequent orders for canned foods and groceries with a larger wholesaler that will break, or split, cases of food or supplies into quantities more appropriate for the foodservice operation.

In some situations, large-volume operators may be able to purchase canned foods or other nonperishable items directly from the processor and work out satisfactory arrangements for delivery of their products. Because the quantity of foods purchased would be large, the amount and kind of storage space and the financial resources can be determining factors in whether direct buying is possible.

METHODS OF PURCHASING

■ **KEY CONCEPT:** Formal and informal methods of purchasing are used by foodservice operations.

The two principal methods of buying are *informal* or *open-market buying* and *formal competitive-bid buying*. Both may be used at various times for different commodities. Variations of these methods or alternative buying arrangements may be preferred by some foodservices or may be used during uncertain market conditions.

Purchasing is a management function, and, as such, the foodservice administrator will have policies and procedures to guide him or her in setting up a course of action. The selected methods of buying depend on these institutional policies, the size of the organization, the amount of money available, location of the vendors, and the frequency of deliveries.

Informal or Open-Market Buying

Quotation
An amount stated as the current price for a desired product or service

Informal purchasing is a commonly used method of buying, especially in smaller foodservice operations. The system involves ordering needed food and supplies from a selected list of vendors based on a daily, weekly, or monthly price **quotation**. Prices are based on a set of specifications furnished to interested vendors. The buyer may request daily prices for fresh fruits and vegetables but may use a monthly quotation list for grocery items. The order is placed after consideration of price in relation to quality, delivery, and other services offered.

Contact between the buyer and vendor is made by fax, computer, telephone, or through sales representatives who call on the buyer. The use of price quotation and order forms on which to record the prices submitted by each vendor (Figure 5) is an aid to the buyer. If the quotations are provided via the telephone, the prices should be recorded. For large orders of canned goods or groceries, or where the time lapse between quotations and ordering is not important, requests for written quotations can be made by mail or fax, as shown in Figure 6. Today, however, much if not most of purchasing communication is done by computer.

Considering new vendors from time to time and visiting the market when possible enables the buyer to examine what is available from other vendors and to note the current prices. When using informal purchasing, the buyer and vendor must agree on quantities and prices before delivery. Only vendors who give reliable service and competitive prices should be considered for open-market buying.

Formal Competitive-Bid Buying

In formal competitive-bid buying, written specifications and estimated quantities needed are submitted to vendors with an invitation for them to quote prices, within a stated time, for the items listed. The request for bids can be quite formal and advertised in the newspaper, and copies can be printed and widely distributed, or the request can be less formal, with single copies supplied to interested vendors. Bids are opened on a designated date, and the contract generally is awarded to the vendor that offers the best price and meets product and service specifications.

Purchasing agents for local, state, or federal government-controlled institutions are usually required to submit bids to all qualified vendors, especially those bids over a certain dollar amount. Buyers for private organizations, however, may select the companies whom they wish to invite to bid, and the buyer may include only those vendors whose performance and reliability are known. The procedure for competitive bid buying is discussed in more detail later in this chapter in the section on "Purchasing Procedures."

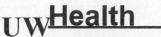
Purchase Order

University of Wisconsin
Hospital and Clinics

Ship To: Food Service Receiving
600 N Highland Ave.
F4/150
Madison WI 53792

OPEN

Purchase Order	Date	Revision	Page
FS10800868	10/25/2010		1

Payment Terms	Freight Terms		Ship Via
Net 30	FOB Destination		BEST WAY

Buyer	PHONE:	Fax:
Bruce A Carlson	608/263-1525	608/263-0343

Vendor: 001547   (800/366-8711 X2)

SYSCO INC
910 SOUTH BLVD
61
Baraboo WI 53913-0090
PHONE: (800)366-8711   FAX: (608)355-8401

Bill To: DEPT OF ACCOUNTS PAYABLE
P.O. BOX 5448
MADISON WI 53705-5448

Tax Exempt? Y   **Tax Exempt ID:** 39-1835630

Line	Description	Mfg ID	Quantity	UOM	PO Price	Extended Amt	Due Date
1	1516236 APPLES RED DEL. FCY 72 COUNT	MISC	1	CS	31.65	31.65	10/25/2010
	UWH Item ID: 3272884						
2	8337842 AVOCADO 100% FRESH PULP, 4/4# BAGS/CS		1	CS	37.79	37.79	10/25/2010
	UWH Item ID: 4009009						
3	2004513 HERB BASIL FRESH 4 OZ BAG		1	BG	5.40	5.40	10/25/2010
	UWH Item ID: 4006118						
4	7700404 CARROTS,PRECLEANED,WHOLE,PEELED,5 #BAG..	MISC	1	CS	18.48	18.48	10/25/2010
	UWH Item ID: 3273691						
5	1750041 CAULIFLOWER FLORETS 2/3 LB BAG/CS		9	CS	18.41	165.69	10/25/2010
	UWH Item ID: 4002786						
6	6524086 Celery Diced 3/8		2	EA	26.00	52.00	10/25/2010
7	1739846 CUCUMBERS,50# BOX,USFANCY,NOT<6"LONG	MISC	1	CS	30.12	30.12	10/25/2010
	UWH Item ID: 3270205						
8	1821537 GARLIC FRESH PEELED 5 LB JAR		1	JAR	42.44	42.44	10/25/2010
	UWH Item ID: 4002534						

DEPARTMENT OF PURCHASING
8501 EXCELSIOR DRIVE #328
MADISON WI 53717

Unauthorized

NOTE: Material safety data sheets must be provided for any shipment containing a hazardous chemical as defined under 29 CFR 1910 1200.
The central MSDS depository for UWHC is currently located at the 3E Company at 1905 Aston Avenue, Carlsbad, CA 92009
NOTE: UWHC Standard Terms and Conditions will apply to this purchase order.

Figure 5   Purchase Order Form.
Courtesy of the University of Wisconsin–Madison, Division of Housing Dining and Culinary Services.

Figure 6 Sample form for requesting price quotations by fax.

_____ University
Food Stores Department

_____
(Date)

To:

INQUIRY NO.

Quote on this sheet your net price f.o.b. for the items specified below.
We reserve the right to accept or reject all or part of this proposal.

Quotations received
until 4:00 P.M. _____

Important: Read instructions on reverse side before preparing bid.

Quantity	Unit	REQUEST FOR QUOTATIONS —This is NOT an order	Price Unit	Total Price
		Return—TWO COPIES—To: Food Stores Department		

We quote you f.o.b. _____

_____

Sign Firm Name Here

_____ Per _____
Date

Delivery can be made { immediately
                      { _____ days.

Cash Discount: _____

Advantages and Disadvantages. Bid buying is often required by government procurement systems, such as those found in corrections facilities, and is found to be advantageous by large foodservices or multiple-unit organizations. The formal bid, if written clearly, minimizes the possibility of misunderstandings occurring with regard to quality, price, and delivery. The bid system is satisfactory for canned goods, frozen products, staples, and other nonperishable foods. Food that is purchased by standing order, such as milk and bread, is also appropriate for this type of buying, but it may not be practical for perishable items because of the day-to-day fluctuation in market prices.

There are two main disadvantages to formal competitive bidding. The system is time consuming, and the planning and requests for bids must be made well in advance so that the buyer has time to distribute the bid forms and the suppliers have time to check availability of supplies and determine a fair price. Although this type of buying was designed to ensure honesty, it does lend itself to manipulation when large amounts of money are involved, especially if the buyers and the purchasing department are open to political pressure.

Competitive Bidding Variations. Many variations and techniques are found in formal competitive bidding, depending on the type of institution, financial resources of both vendor and buyer, and storage facilities of the foodservice and delivery capabilities of the vendor. Bids can be written for a supply of merchandise over a period of time at prices that fluctuate with the market; for example, a six-month supply of flour may be required, with 500 pounds delivered each month, at a price compatible with current market conditions.

In a firm fixed price (FFP) contract, the price is not subject to adjustment during the period of the contract, which places maximum risk on the vendor and is used when definite specifications are available and when fair and reasonable prices can be established at the outset. A buyer may request bids for a month's supply of dairy products, to be delivered daily as needed. Another variation involves the purchase of a specific quantity of merchandise, such as a year's supply of canned goods, but because of inadequate storage, the foodservice may arrange to draw on the contract throughout the duration of the contract period.

Many different forms are used in the written bidding system, and the terms may differ in various parts of the country, but all of them basically are invitations to bid with the conditions of the bid clearly specified. Attached to the invitation is a listing of the merchandise needed, specifications and quantities involved, and any conditions related to supply and fluctuations in the market. (An example of a bid request is given later in this chapter in Figure 14.)

Variations on Methods of Purchasing

Cost-Plus Purchasing. In *cost-plus purchasing*, a buyer agrees to buy certain items from a purveyor for an agreed-on period of time based on a fixed markup over the vendor's cost. The time period may vary and could be open for bid among different vendors. Such a plan is most effective with large-volume buying.

The vendor's cost generally is based on the cost of material to the buyer plus any costs incurred in changes to packaging, fabrication of products, loss of required trim, or shrinkage from aging. The markup, which must cover overhead, cost of billing or deliveries, or other expenses that are borne by the vendor, may vary with the type of food being purchased. When negotiating a cost-plus purchasing agreement, a clear understanding should be reached on what is included in the cost and what is considered part of the vendor's markup. Some way of verifying the vendor's cost should also be part of the agreement.

Prime Vending. Prime vending is a method of purchasing that has gained popularity and acceptance among restaurant and noncommercial buyers during the past several years. The method involves a formal agreement (secured through a bid or informally) with a single vendor to supply the majority of product needs. Needs are generally specified in percent of total use by category. Categories may include fresh meat and poultry, frozen, dairy, dry, produce, beverages, and nonfood categories such as disposables, supplies, equipment, and chemicals. The percents can range 60 to 95, with the mid to high levels being the most common. The agreement is based on a commitment to purchase the specified amount for a specified period of time.

The primary advantages of this method are reduced prices, which are realized through high volume and time savings. The time savings result from not having to fulfill administrative and accounting requirements for numerous vendors. Additional advantages include the development of a strong, professional partnership with the vendor and the potential for value-added services such as computer software for submitting and tracking orders.

The buyer must be alert to potential problems with prime vendor contracts. For example, prices may increase over time; therefore, procedures for periodically auditing prices should be clearly defined as part of the agreement.

Blanket Purchase Agreement. The *blanket purchase agreement* (BPA) is sometimes used when a wide variety of items are purchased from local suppliers, but the exact items, quantities, and delivery requirements are not known in advance and may vary. Vendors agree to furnish—on a "charge account" basis—such supplies as may be ordered during a stated period of time. BPAs should be established with more than one vendor so that delivery orders can be placed with the firm offering the best price. Use of more than one vendor also allows the buyer to identify a "price creep," which can occur when only one vendor is involved.

Just-in-Time Purchasing. Just-in-time purchasing, or JIT, is yet another variation of purchasing. It is in fact an inventory and production planning strategy where the product is purchased in the exact quantities required for a specific production run and delivered "just in time" to meet the production demand. The goal is to have as little product in inventory for as little time as possible in an effort to maximize cash flow. Some products such as milk, bread, and possibly fresh meat can go directly into production and avoid inventory costs altogether. Other benefits include better space management and fresher product. This method has an impact on all functional units, the most obvious being production. This arrangement must be carefully planned and orchestrated to ensure that shortages do not occur.

PRODUCT SELECTION

■ **KEY CONCEPT:** **Numerous factors need to be considered when selecting products for a foodservice operation.**

Market Forms of Foods

Deciding on the form in which food is to be purchased is a major decision that requires careful study. Form refers to the physical shape (whole, sections, diced, etc.) and temperature (dry, frozen, or refrigerated). Costs involved in the purchase and use of fresh or natural forms of food versus partially prepared or ready-to-eat foods and the acceptability of such items by the consumer are major factors to consider. Several options may be available to prepare the same menu item. Fruit pies, for example, can be made from scratch, or by using partially prepared ingredients such as ready-to-bake crusts and ready-to-pour fillings. Other options include ready-to-bake pies and fully baked, ready-to-serve pies.

Because of a lack of space, equipment, or personnel, a foodservice manager may wish to consider purchasing partially or fully processed convenience items. Before making this decision, the cost, quality, and acceptability to patrons of the purchased prepared food should be compared with the same menu item made on the premises. Table 2 lists the factors to consider in a make-or-buy decision. If the decision is to

Table 2 Make-or-buy decisions.	
FACTOR	**CONSIDERATIONS**
Quality	Evaluate whether quality standard, as defined by and for the organization, can be achieved.
Equipment	Assess availability, capacity, and batch turnover time to ensure that product demand can be met.
Labor	Evaluate availability, current skills, and training needs.
Time	Evaluate product setup, production, and service time based on forecasted demand for the product.
Inventory	Gauge needed storage and holding space.
Total cost	Conduct complete cost analysis of all resources expended to make or buy product. Use cost as decision basis after other factors have been carefully analyzed.

buy the prepared product, the manager and the buyer must establish quality standards for these foods.

For foodservices preferring the preparation of product in their own kitchens, there are alternatives in purchasing that can save preparation time. The market offers a variety of processed ingredients from which to choose. Frozen chopped onions, precut melons, shredded cheese, frozen lemon juice, cooked chicken and turkey, and various baking, soup, sauce, and pudding mixes are examples.

Choosing fresh, frozen, or canned foods depends on the amount of labor available for preparation, comparative portion costs, and acceptability by patrons. The high cost of labor has caused many foodservices to limit the use of fresh fruits and vegetables except for salads or during times of plentiful supply when costs are lower. There may be times when a menu change must be made because of the price differential among fresh, frozen, and canned food items.

Keeping in mind the quality standard established for the finished product, the manager must find the right combination of available foods in a form that will keep preparation to a minimum yet yield a product of the desired quality. Figure 7 shows a make-or-buy calculation.

Food Quality

Before food can be purchased, the quality of foods most appropriate to the foodservice operation and their use on the menu must be decided. The top grade may not always be necessary for all purposes. Foods sold under the lower grades are wholesome and have essentially the same nutritional value, but they differ mainly in appearance and, to a lesser degree, in flavor.

Figure 7 Make-or-buy calculations.

Scenario: Need lettuce for a salad bar. Which is the best buy, whole head lettuce or chopped ready-to-serve?

Information	Whole Fresh Head Lettuce	Chopped Ready-to-Serve Lettuce
Pack	24 count per case	4/5# bags
Weight A.P.	36#	20#
Yield	76%	100%
Price/unit	$17.35	$15.56
Labor time to process unit	0.317 hours (19 minutes)	0
Labor cost/hour	$12.00	$12.00

Calculations for whole fresh head lettuce

1. As purchased (A.P.) 36# × 0.76 = 27.36# edible (usable) portion (E.P.)
2. Labor cost per case: $12.00 × 0.317 = $3.80
3. Labor cost per usable pound: $3.80/27.36 = $0.138
4. Food cost per usable pound: $17.35/27.36 = $0.63
5. Total cost per usable pound: $0.138 + $0.63 = $0.77

Calculations for chopped ready-to-serve lettuce

1. As purchased (A.P.) 20# @ 100% yield = 20# edible (usable) portion (E.P.)
2. No labor needed for preparation
3. Total costs per usable pound: $15.56/20# = $0.78

Factors beyond cost that need to be considered

1. Quality and shelf life
2. Availability of refrigerated versus freezer space
3. Food safety

Foods that have been downgraded because of lack of uniformity in size or that have broken or irregular pieces can be used in soups, casseroles, fruit gelatin, or fruit cobblers. Also, more than one style or pack in some food items may be needed. Unsweetened or pie pack canned peaches can be satisfactory for making pies, but peaches in heavy syrup would be preferable for serving in a dish as a dessert.

Quality Standards.   Quality may refer to wholesomeness, cleanliness, or freedom from undesirable substances. It may denote a degree of perfection in shape, uniformity of size, or freedom from blemishes. It may also describe the extent of desirable characteristics such as color, flavor, aroma, texture, tenderness, and maturity. Assessment of quality may be denoted by grade, brand, or condition.

Grades.   Grades are market classifications of quality. They reflect the relationship of quality to the standard established for the product, and they indicate the degree of variation from that standard. Grades have been established by the USDA for most agricultural products, but their use is voluntary.

Grading and Acceptance Services.   The USDA Agricultural Marketing Service, in cooperation with state agencies, offers official grading or inspection for quality of meat and meat products, fresh and processed fruits and vegetables, poultry and eggs, and manufactured dairy products. Grading is based on U.S. grade standards developed by the USDA for these products.

Included in the grading and inspection programs is a USDA *Acceptance Service* available to institutional food buyers on request. This service provides verification of the quality specified in a purchase contract. The product is examined at the processing or packing plant or at the supplier's warehouse by an official of the Agricultural Marketing Service or a cooperating state agency. If the product meets the specifications as stated in the contract, the grader stamps it with an official stamp and issues a certificate indicating compliance. If the purchases are to be certified, this provision should be specified in contracts with vendors. The inspection fee is then the responsibility of the supplier.

USDA grades are based on scoring factors, with the total score determining the grade. See the USDA Web site for details on grade standards and guidelines on how to buy various commodities (*http://www.ams.usda.gov/*). The grades vary with different categories of food as noted in the following list:

- **Meats:** U.S. Prime, U.S. Choice, U.S. Select, and U.S. Standard. Quality grades are assigned according to marbling, maturity of the animal, and color, firmness, and texture of the muscle. Yield grades of 1, 2, 3, 4, or 5 are used for beef and lamb to indicate the proportion of usable meat to fat and bone, with a rating of 1 having the lowest fat content. Veal and pork are not graded separately for yield and quality.
- **Poultry:** Consumer grades are U.S. Grades A, B, and C, based on conformation, fleshing, fat covering, and freedom from defects. Grades often used in institutional purchasing are U.S. Procurement Grades 1 and 2. The procurement grades place more emphasis on meat yield than on appearance.
- **Eggs:** U.S. Grades AA, A, and B. Quality in shell eggs is based on exterior factors (cleanliness, soundness, shape of shell, and texture) and interior factors (condition of the yolk and white and the size of the air cell, as determined by candling). Shell eggs are classified according to size as extra large, large, medium, and small.
- **Cheddar cheese:** U.S. Grades AA, A, B, and C. Scores are on the basis of flavor, aroma, body and texture, finish and appearance, and color.
- **Fresh produce:** U.S. Fancy, U.S. Extra No. 1, U.S. No. 1, U.S. Combination, and U.S. No. 2. Fresh fruits and vegetables are graded according to the qualities deemed desirable for the individual type of commodity but may include uniformity of size, cleanliness, color, or lack of damage or defects. Grades are designated by name or by number. Because of the wide variation in quality and the perishable nature of fresh fruits and vegetables, visual inspection may be as important as grade; or a buyer might specify that the condition of the product at the time of delivery should equal the grade requested.

Figure 8 Standards for USDA grades of canned fruits and vegetables.

Standards for Canned Foods

Fruits

Grade	Quality of Fruit	Syrup
U.S. Grade A or Fancy	Excellent quality, high color, ripe, firm, free from blemishes, uniform in size, and very symmetrical.	Heavy, about 55%. May vary from 40% to 70%, depending on acidity of fruit.
U.S. Grade B or Choice or Extra-Standard	Fine quality, high color, ripe, firm, free from serious blemishes, uniform in size, and symmetrical.	About 40%. Usually contains 10% to 15% less sugar than Fancy grade.
U.S. Grade C or Standard	Good quality, reasonably good color, reasonably free from blemishes, reasonably uniform in size, color, and degree of ripeness, and reasonably symmetrical.	About 25%. Contains 10% to 15% less sugar than Choice grades.
Substandard	Lower than the minimum grade for Standard.	Often water-packed. If packed in syrup, it is not over 10%.

Vegetables

Grade	Quality of Vegetable
U.S. Grade A or Fancy	Best flavored, most tender and succulent, uniform in size, shape, color, tenderness; represents choice of crop.
U.S. Grade B or Extra-Standard (sometimes called Choice)	Flavor fine; tender and succulent; may be slightly more mature, more firm in texture, and sometimes less uniform than Fancy grade.
U.S. Grade C or Standard	Flavor less delicate; more firm in texture, often less uniform in size, shape, color; more mature.
Substandard	Lower than the minimum grade for Standard.

- **Canned fruits and vegetables:** U.S. Grade A (or Fancy), U.S. Grade B (or choice for fruits and extra standard for vegetables), U.S. Grade C (or standard), and U.S. Grade D (or substandard). The factors for canned fruits and vegetables include color, uniformity of size, absence of defects, character, flavor, consistency, finish, size, symmetry, clearness of liquor, maturity, texture, wholeness, and cut. In addition to these factors, general requirements must be met, such as fill of container, drained weight, and syrup density. The grading factors vary with individual canned fruits and vegetables, but the scoring range is the same. Figure 8 shows standards for canned foods.
- **Frozen fruits and vegetables:** U.S. grade standards are available for many frozen fruits and vegetables, but not standards of identity, quality, or fill of container. Fruit can be packed with sugar in varying proportions such as four or five parts of fruit to one part of sugar by weight or without sugar. Fruits or vegetables can be individually quick frozen or frozen in solid blocks.

Designation of U.S. grades and marking in the form of a shield are permitted only on foods officially graded under the supervision of the Agricultural Marketing Service of the USDA. Figure 9 shows examples of grade stamps.

Brands. A **brand** is assigned by a private organization. Producers, processors, or distributors attempt to establish a commodity as a standard product and to develop demand specifically for their own brands. The reliability of these trade names depends on the reliability of the company. Brand names may represent products that are higher or lower in quality than the corresponding government grade. However, some brand-name products

Brand
A particular make of a good or product usually identified by a trademark or label

Figure 9 Federal grade stamps for meat, poultry and eggs.

Federal grade
stamp for meat

USDA poultry
grade mark

USDA shell egg
grade mark

are not consistent in quality. Private companies may set up their own grading system, but such ranking may show variation from season to season.

Some knowledge of brand names is essential in today's marketing system. USDA grades are used for most fresh meats and for fresh fruits and vegetables, but very few canners use them, preferring instead to develop their own brands. If USDA grades are specified and bidders submit prices on brand products, the buyer should be familiar with USDA grades and scores in order to evaluate the products. The buyer may wish to request samples or, if the order is large enough to justify it, request a USDA grading certificate.

PURCHASING PROCEDURES

■ **KEY CONCEPT:** **Procedures used to purchase products vary depending on the formality of the purchasing function.**

The complexity of the purchasing system depends on the size and type of an organization, whether the buying is centralized or decentralized, and established management policies. Procedures should be as simple as possible, with record keeping and paperwork limited to those essential for control and communication.

Good purchasing practices include the use of appropriate buying methods, a systematic ordering schedule, maintenance of an adequate flow of goods to meet production requirements, and a systematic receiving procedure and inventory control.

The process of purchasing, using the informal and formal methods of buying, is shown in Figure 10 and discussed in the following sections.

Figure 10 The process of purchasing using informal and formal methods of buying.

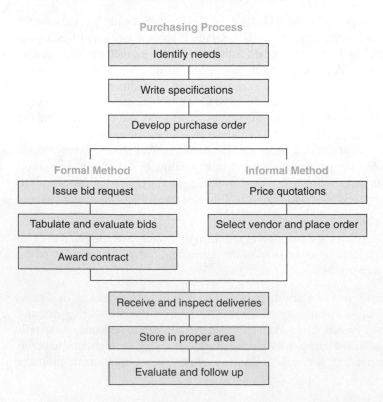

Identifying Needs

Quantities of food needed for production of the planned menus are identified from the menus and from recipes used to prepare them. Added to this are staples and other supplies needed in the various departments or production and service areas.

The submission of a request to purchase, or **requisition**, is the action that triggers the purchasing process, especially when formal methods are used. Figure 11 is an example of a requisition form.

Requisition

An interdepartmental form used to request desired products including food and supplies

UNIVERSITY OF WISCONSIN-MADISON
Division of University Housing

REQUEST TO PURCHASE

QTY.	ITEM	MODEL #	UNIT PRICE	TOTAL PRICE

Give complete information as to Model No., Catalog No., Dimensions, Colors etc.

Freight: prepaid = vendor pays   collect = housing pays
prepaid   collect   (check one)

Total $ amount of order _____
Quote or Estimate (list one)

Special Instructions (date needed, special shipping, other funding source, etc.)

Charge to General ledger # _____ **or Capital budget #** _____

DELIVER TO:

Vendor Number   # _____
Company _____
Address _____
_____

_____ Raywood Warehouse
_____ Haight Road Warehouse
_____ Other-specify location _____
Vendor should contact you
_____ hours prior to delivery (write 0 if prior notice is not needed).

Vendor Contact _____
Phone # _____
Fax # _____

Person ordering: _____
Phone:

Check here if requesting signature approval for the following blanket orders:
Regular blanket or Open vendor blanket $1,500.00 to $5,000.00—Contract blanket over $1,500.00

BLANKET ORDER NUMBER:

Signed   Date

Supervisor (Required for purchases under $1,500.00)

Approved   Date

Assoc./ Asst. Director (Required for purchases over $1,500.00)

Purchasing Use Only

Commodity Code _____   FOB _____   Reference _____

Class Code _____   Terms _____   Bid/Bulletin No. _____

Figure 11 Example of a requisition form.
Courtesy of the University of Wisconsin–Madison, Division of Housing Dining and Culinary Service.

Figure 12 Comparison of par stock and mini-max inventory systems with reorder points.

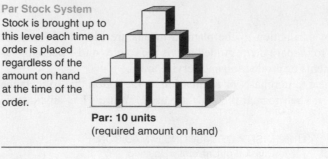

Par Stock System

Stock is brought up to this level each time an order is placed regardless of the amount on hand at the time of the order.

Par: 10 units
(required amount on hand)

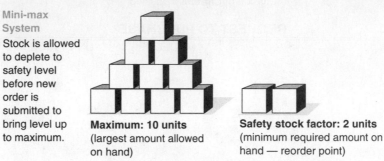

Mini-max System

Stock is allowed to deplete to safety level before new order is submitted to bring level up to maximum.

Maximum: 10 units
(largest amount allowed on hand)

Safety stock factor: 2 units
(minimum required amount on hand — reorder point)

Inventory

A detailed and complete list of goods in stock

Inventory Stock Level. A system of communicating needs from the production areas and the storeroom to the buyer is essential. Establishment of a minimum and maximum stock level provides a means of alerting the buyer to needs. The minimum level is the point, established for each item, below which the **inventory** should not fall. This amount depends on the usage and time required for ordering and delivery. If canned fruits and vegetables, for example, are purchased every three months through the formal bidding procedure, the time lapse would be longer than for fresh produce that is ordered daily or weekly through informal buying.

The *minimum stock level*, then, includes a safety factor for replenishing the stock. The *maximum inventory level* is equal to the safety stock plus the estimated usage, which is determined by past usage and forecasts. From this information, a reorder point is established. Figure 12 compares the mini-max and par stock systems for establishing reorder points.

Another factor to be considered in the amount to reorder is the quantity that is most feasible economically. For example, if five cases of a food are needed to bring the stock to the desired level, but a price advantage can be gained by buying ten cases, the buyer may consider purchasing the larger quantity. The buyer is encouraged to weigh carefully the true economic advantages of these price incentives. Stored food ties up cash, and unused food that spoils is literally money down the drain.

Quantity to Buy. The amount of food and supplies purchased at one time and the frequency of ordering depend on finance and accounting procedures, the method of buying, the frequency of deliveries, and storage space. With adequate and suitable storage, the purchase of staples may vary from a two- to a six-month supply, with perishables being ordered weekly and/or daily.

Meat, poultry, fish, fresh fruits and vegetables, and other perishable foods may be purchased for immediate use on the day's menu or more likely are calculated for two or more days, depending on delivery schedules, storage facilities, and preparation requirements. Quantities are based on the portion size and projected number of servings needed, taking into consideration the preparation and cooking losses. If the recipes are stored in a computer, it is a simple task to calculate the amount needed for the desired number of servings.

Some products, such as milk and bread, are delivered daily or several times a week, and the orders are based on the amount needed to keep the inventory up to a desired level. The price can be determined by a contract to furnish certain items as needed for a period of

Daily Purchase Order

Date _____

ON HAND	ORDER	ON HAND	ORDER	ON HAND	ORDER

Dairy:
- _____ gal whole milk _____
- _____ cs ½ pt whole _____
- _____ cs ½ pt choc _____
- _____ cs ½ pt B. milk _____
- _____ cs ½ pt skim _____
- _____ lb cot. cheese _____
- _____ Ice cream _____

Bread:
- _____ White bread _____
- _____ Wheat bread _____
- _____ Rye _____
- _____ Sandwich white _____
- _____ Sandwich wheat _____
- _____ Sandwich rye _____
- _____ Crumbs _____

Sweet Rolls:
- _____ Raisin bread _____
- _____ Cinnamon _____
- _____ Butterscotch _____
- _____ Raised donuts _____
- _____ Bismark _____
- _____ Twist _____
- _____ Pecan strip _____
- _____ Stick donuts _____
- _____ Jelly donuts _____

Potato Chips:
- _____ ____
- _____ ____
- _____ ____
- _____ ____
- _____ ____

Meats:
- _____
- _____
- _____
- _____
- _____
- _____
- _____

Fish:
- _____
- _____
- _____

Poultry:
- _____ Chicken
- _____ Turkey _____
- _____ Eggs _____

Fresh Vegetables:
- _____ Cabbage _____
- _____ Carrots _____
- _____ Cauliflower _____
- _____ Celery _____
- _____ Celery cabbage _____
- _____ Cucumbers _____
- _____ Egg plant _____
- _____ Head lettuce _____
- _____ Leaf lettuce _____
- _____ Onions _____
- _____ Parsley _____
- _____ Peppers _____
- _____ Potatoes _____
- _____ Spinach _____
- _____ Squash _____
- _____ Tomatoes _____

Frozen Vegetables:
- _____ Asparagus _____
- _____ Green beans _____
- _____ Lima beans _____
- _____ Broccoli _____
- _____ Brussels sprouts _____
- _____ Cauliflower _____
- _____ Peas _____

Fresh Fruits:
- _____ Apples _____
- _____ Bananas _____
- _____ Berries _____
- _____ Cantaloupe _____
- _____ Grapefruit _____
- _____ Grapes _____
- _____ Lemons _____
- _____ Oranges _____
- _____ Peaches _____
- _____ Pineapple _____
- _____ Plums _____
- _____ Watermelon _____

Frozen Fruits and Juices:
- _____ Apples _____
- _____ Cherries _____
- _____ G. fruit sections _____
- _____ Lemon juice _____
- _____ Orange juice _____
- _____ Peaches _____
- _____ Rhubarb _____
- _____ Strawberries _____

Miscellaneous:
- _____
- _____
- _____

Figure 13 Daily purchase order form.

a month or longer. A stock level of butter and margarine, cheese, eggs, lettuce, celery, onions, and certain other fruits and vegetables can be established and maintained, whereas other produce is ordered as needed from the menu. Figure 13 is a suggested form for recording supplies on hand and the amounts to order.

Canned foods and groceries are generally purchased less often than are perishable foods, the frequency depending on storage space and money available. Assuming that adequate storage is available, a year's supply of canned goods can be purchased at one time if bought on competitive bid or if growing conditions indicate a possible shortage or a rise in prices. In some cases, an arrangement can be made for the supplier to store the food and deliver it as needed. A projection is made of the quantity that will be needed for the designated period, based on past purchases. That amount less the inventory is the quantity to purchase.

Specifications

A **specification** is a detailed description of a product, stated in terms that are clearly understood by both buyer and seller. Specifications should be brief and concise but contain

Specification

A detailed description of a product, stated in terms that are clearly understood by both the buyer and the seller

enough information so that there can be no misunderstanding. Certain information is included in all specifications for food products:

- **Name of the product:** This is the common or trade name of an item.
- **Federal grade or brand:** As already noted, the USDA has established federal grades for most agricultural products, but many packers or food processors have developed their own brands or trade names for canned, frozen, or other processed foods. If a bidder submits a quotation on a brand name product in lieu of a federal grade, buyers may request verification of quality by the USDA Acceptance Service; see "Grading and Acceptance Services" earlier in this chapter under "Food Quality."
- **Unit on which price is quoted:** This refers to the size and type of unit, such as case, pound, gallon, can, bunch, or other unit in common use.
- **Name and size of container:** Examples of container size include a case holding six No. 10 cans, a 30-pound pail of frozen cherries, or a crate of fresh shell eggs.
- **Count per container or approximate number per pound:** Examples include 30/35 count canned peach halves per No. 10 can; eight-per-pound frankfurters; or size 36 grapefruit, which indicates the number of fruit in a bushel box. Oranges and apples also are sized according to the number in a box. Apples 80 to 100 are large; 113 to 138, medium; and 150 to 175, small.

Additional information may be included for various categories of food:

- **Fresh fruits and vegetables:** Variety, degree of maturity, geographic location; for example, Jonathan apples, Indian River grapefruit, or bananas turning ripe, pale yellow with green tips. If needed immediately, specify fully ripe, bright yellow flecked with brown, and no green.
- **Canned foods:** Type or style, pack, size, syrup type, drained weight, specific gravity. Examples include cream style corn; whole vertical pack green beans; No. 4 sieve peas; apricot halves in heavy syrup or 21 to 25 degrees **brix** (syrup density); diced beets, drained weight 72 ounces (per No. 10 can); or tomato catsup with total solids content of at least 33 percent.
- **Frozen foods:** Variety, sugar ratio, temperature during delivery and on receipt; for example, sliced strawberries, sugar ratio of 4:1, or delivered frozen, 0°F or less.
- **Meats and meat products:** Age, market class, cut of meat, exact cutting instructions, weight range, fat content, condition on receipt.
- **Dairy products:** Milk fat content, milk solids, bacteria count, temperature during delivery and on receipt.

Brix

The percent of sugar by weight in a sugar solution. Expressed as degrees brix and usually applied to canned fruits packed in syrup

A well-written specification includes all of the information needed to identify the food item and to ensure that the buyer is getting exactly the quality desired. It should be identifiable with products or grades currently on the market and capable of being checked by label statements or USDA grades. Resources and guidelines for writing specifications are available from the USDA and from material published by industry trade groups such as the National Association of Meat Purveyors and the Produce Marketing Association. The USDA, for example, publishes the Institutional Meat Purchasing Specification (IMPS). IMPS are a series of meat specifications used primarily by large-volume buyers. See their Web site at the end of the chapter.

Issuing Bid Requests

An invitation to bid provides vendors an opportunity to submit bids for specific items needed by a buyer. Bid requests originate in the office of the purchasing agent or the person authorized to purchase for the foodservice. A bid request includes quantities required and specifications for each item. In addition, the general conditions of acceptance are outlined, including the date and method of delivery, terms of payment, willingness to accept all or part of the bid, discounts, the date of closing bids, and other terms of the negotiations. Figure 14 is a sample bid request that includes general requirements.

RETURN TO: University of Wisconsin-Madison
Purchasing Services
750 University Ave, 2nd Floor Reception
Madison, WI. 53706-1490

REQUEST FOR BID   THIS IS NOT AN ORDER

OFFICIAL SEALED
BID NUMBER: 02-5472

ISSUE DATE:

DUE DATE: 2:00 PM CDST

Bid prices and terms shall be firm for sixty (60) days from the date of bid opening, unless otherwise specified in this Request for Bid by the UW-Madison Purchasing Services.

DO NOT use any type of felt tip marker when filling out the Request for Bid form.

AGENT: Gail Movrich at (608) 262-1323

DESCRIPTION	DELIVERY DAYS ARO
The University of Wisconsin-Madison request bids for **MEAT, FRESH AND FROZEN FOR THE RESIDENCE HALLS** for the period July 1, 2001, through June 30, 2002, or one year after date of award, with options to renew for two additional one-year terms, in accordance with the attached in this order: Special Conditions of Bid, Bidder Response Sheet, Specifications, Itemized Bid List, MBE Plan of Action, and Standard Terms and Conditions. The University reserves the right to extend beyond the Contract Term if deemed to be in the best interest of the University.	_____

In signing this bid, we have read and fully understand and agree to all terms, conditions and specifications and acknowledge that the UW-Madison Purchasing Services bid document on file shall be controlling. We certify that we have not, either directly or indirectly, entered into any agreement or participated in any collusion or otherwise taken any action in restraint of free competition; that no attempt has been made to induce any other person or firm to submit or not to submit a bid; that this bid has been independently arrived at without collusion with any other bidder, competitor or potential competitor; that this bid has not been knowingly disclosed prior to the opening of bids to any other bidder or competitor; that the above stated statement is accurate under penalty of perjury.

SIGNATURE: _____ DATE _____

TYPE OR PRINT NAME: _____

TITLE: _____ TELEPHONE NUMBER: (_____) _____

FEIN NUMBER: _____ FAX NUMBER: (_____) _____

EMAIL ADDRESS: _____

REVERSE SIDE OF THIS FORM (VENDOR NOTE) MUST BE COMPLETED.

Figure 14   Sample bid request.
Courtesy of the University of Wisconsin–Madison, Division of Housing Dining and Culinary Services.

The bid request may also ask for samples to be tested. This is especially important when large quantities are involved and often is requested when purchasing canned foods. Testing of canned foods is done by "can cutting," which involves opening the sample cans and evaluating the products according to USDA scoring factors. If samples from more than one company are being tested, the labels on the cans should be covered so the test will be impartial.

Score Sheet for Canned Tomatoes

Number, Size, and Kind of Container

Label

Container Mark or Identification	Cans/Glass		
	Cases		

Net Weight (oz)

Vacuum (in.)

Drained Weight (oz)

Factors		Score Points			
I. Drained weight	20	(A) (B) (C) (SStd)	18–20 15–17 12–14 0–11		
II. Wholeness	20	(A) (B) (C)	18–20 15–17 12–14		
III. Color	30	(A) (B) (C) (SStd)	27–30 23–36 19–22 0–18		
IV. Absence of defects	30	(A) (B) (C) (SStd)	27–30 22–26 17–21 0–16		
Total Score	100				

Normal flavor and odor

Grade

Figure 15 Government score sheet for grading canned tomatoes.

Copies of USDA specifications and score sheets are available from the Government Printing Office. An example of a score sheet for canned foods is shown in Figure 15. Scores from different samples would be summarized on a form similar to that in Figure 16. Product evaluation forms may be developed for testing of other foods and should include specific qualities to be judged. A panel composed of persons who are involved in foodservice quality control should participate.

A bid schedule outlining the bid periods and delivery frequency should be established and, when possible, planned so that new packs of processed fruits and vegetables, usually available in October and January, can be used. This step is omitted in informal buying. Quotations are requested from two or more vendors, usually by telephone or from price sheets.

Developing Purchase Orders

The procedure for authorizing purchases differs in various foodservices. The process may begin with a purchase request, to be used along with quality specifications, as the basis for a **purchase order** and bid request to be issued by an authorized purchasing agent. A foodservice director, who is also the buyer, may develop a purchase order that has been

Purchase order

Written request to a vendor to sell goods or services to a facility

Kind	Code	Label Net Weight	Actual Weight	Sp. Gr. or Drained Weight	Brix	Count	Remarks and Ratings (Defects, Color, etc.)	Price Per Dozen	Price Per Can	Price Per Piece
.										

Figure 16 Sample form for recording data on samples of canned products.

compiled from requisitions from the various production and service units or from individual units in a school system or multiple-unit organization. In central purchasing for these operations, the requisitions originating in individual units do not necessarily need to include specifications, because the quality is determined at a central point and is uniform throughout the system.

Regardless of the method used, there should be a clear understanding of who is authorized to issue purchase requests or orders, and the vendors should be aware of the name, or names, of authorized purchasing personnel. Authorization to sign for goods received and to requisition supplies from the storage areas should also be understood.

The purchase order specifies the quantity of each item needed for the bid period, quality specifications, and required date of delivery. The order must include the name of the organization, the individual making the request, and the signature of the person officially authorized to sign the order. Purchase order forms can be prenumbered, or the number can be added at the time of final approval, but a number, as well as the date of issue, is essential for identification. Figure 17 shows a suggested purchase order form.

Tabulating and Evaluating Bids

Bids should be kept sealed and confidential until the designated time for opening. Sealed envelopes containing the bids should be stamped to indicate the date, time, and place of receipt. Bids received after the time and date specified for bid opening must be rejected and returned unopened to the bidder.

The opening and tabulation of bids should be under the control of an appropriate official. When schools and other public institutions are involved, the quotations and contents of bids should be open to the public. The bids and low bids should be carefully examined. In most instances, public purchasing laws specify that the award be made to the lowest responsible bidder. The following points should be considered before accepting bids:

1. Ability and capacity of the bidder to perform the contract and provide the service
2. Ability of the bidder to provide the service promptly and within the time specified
3. Integrity and reputation of the bidder
4. Quality of bidder's performance on previous contracts or services
5. Bidder's compliance with laws and with specifications relating to contracts or service
6. Bidder's financial resources

Before the bid is awarded to a vendor, the buyer may request test samples of the product from each qualified bidder to compare the actual product against the predetermined specifications. Can cutting, as mentioned earlier, is a formal process for evaluating the actual quality of canned goods against those identified in the bid specification. This process is recommended to ensure that the products meet or exceed the standards as specified. If specifications are not met and the contract award is not awarded to the lowest bidder, a full and complete statement of the reasons should be prepared and filed with other papers relating to the transaction.

Figure 17 Sample purchase order form.

Purchase Order

Name of Institution _____ Date _____

Address _____ Purchase Order # _____
(Please refer to above number on all invoices)

Address _____

Requisition No. _____

Department _____ Date Required _____

To _____

_____

_____

_____

Instruction for Completing Order. Prepare in triplicate for the vendor, business office, and the manager.

Shipped to: _____ FOB _____ Via _____ Terms _____

Unit	Total quantity	Specification	Price per unit	Total cost

Approved by _____

Awarding Contracts

The contract should be awarded to the most responsive and responsible bidder with the price most advantageous to the purchaser. Buying on the basis of price alone can result in the delivery of products that are below the expectations of the foodservice. Purchasing should be on the basis of price, quality, and service.

The general conditions of the contract should include services to be rendered, dates and method of deliveries, inspection requests, grade certificates required, procedure for substitutions, and conditions for payment. The following information should also be provided: name and address of the foodservice, a contract number, type of items the contract covers, contract period, date of contract issue, point of delivery, quantities to be purchased, and the signature of an authorized representative of the firm submitting the bid. The terms of sale must be clearly stated in the contract. Table 3 is a summary of the various FOB

Table 3   Terms of sale and freight charges.

	RESPONSIBILITIES			
TERMS OF SALE	PAYS FREIGHT CHARGES	BEARS FREIGHT CHARGES	OWNS PRODUCT DURING TRANSIT	FILES DAMAGE CLAIMS (IF NECESSARY)
FOB origin—freight collect	Buyer	Buyer	Buyer	Buyer
FOB origin—freight prepaid	Seller	Seller	Buyer	Buyer
FOB origin—freight prepaid and charged back	Seller	Buyer	Buyer	Buyer
FOB destination—freight collect	Buyer	Buyer	Seller	Seller
FOB destination—freight prepaid	Seller	Seller	Seller	Seller
FOB destination—freight collect and allowed	Buyer	Seller	Seller	Seller

FOB = Free on Board

(free on board) terms of sale methods used in formal purchasing. Point of origin is defined as the manufacturer's loading dock.

An issued contract represents the legal acceptance of the offer made by the successful bidder, and it is binding. All bidders, both successful and unsuccessful, should be notified of the action. When the contract is made by a purchasing agent, the foodservice should receive a copy of the contract award and specifications.

Legal and Regulatory Aspects of Purchasing

Numerous laws and regulations at the federal, state, and local levels influence the function of purchasing. In some situations, the buyer is responsible for understanding and complying with the law, regulation, or policy. For example, a buyer would be held accountable for local policy on special consideration for minority-owned vendors. Accountability for other laws, especially those that relate to contract specifications, competition, and pricing structures, may fall into the domain of the organization's legal team. The buyer for an organization often works in tandem with the legal department to ensure that contracts and buyer/supplier interactions are in compliance with applicable legislation.

Regardless of accountability, the wise buyer keeps abreast of legislation and litigation as it pertains to the purchasing function to ensure that purchasing practices and contracts honor all legal parameters set forth and enforced by various levels of government.

Legislation that applies to purchasing generally falls into three categories. In one category are laws that focus on contract content and language. A second category of legislation relates to the topics of fair competition and pricing. The final category targets the market and specifically addresses issues of fraud and food safety. The following is a summary of some of the key pieces of legislation in the first two categories. This summary is followed by an in-depth review of laws that pertain to market regulation.

Laws and Contract Management.   The purchase/sale exchange between buyer and seller is a legal and binding commitment even if made in good faith. The legal aspects of this exchange are covered in the *Uniform Commercial Code* (UCC). The purpose of the UCC is to provide uniformity of law pertaining to business interactions. The code includes nine articles that emphasize different areas of business transactions. The entire code can be accessed at http://www.law.cornell.edu/ucc/ucc.table.html.

Of the areas covered in the code, Article 2 is of particular importance because it addresses purchase and sales transactions. The primary intent is to protect the buyer from deceptive practices on the part of the supplier. This protection is addressed in three major components referred to as the laws of agency, warranty, and contracts.

The *law of agency* defines the buyer's authority to act for the organization. It also defines the obligation that each of these two parties owes each other and the degree to which either party is held liable for the actions of the other. From a practical perspective, this law outlines the extent to which a buyer is bound by the promises of a sales representative if those promises are not documented in a contract that has been approved by an authorized person with the supplier's organization. The *law of warranty* defines warranty as a supplier's promise that a product will in fact perform as specified.

The third major law within this category is the *law of contract*. This defines a contract as an agreement between two or more parties. A legal contract includes at least five components: (1) an offer, (2) an acceptance, (3) consideration, (4) competent parties, and (5) legality. A contract must include evidence of each one of these requirements in order to be legally recognized as valid, enforceable, and binding.

Laws Relating to Competition and Pricing. A second and major category of laws that can influence the purchasing function relates to the issues of fair competition and pricing. Again, the buyer for a foodservice is likely not the person within the organization who is responsible for complying with this set of legislation but will most certainly be working closely with the legal team that is granted this authority. The four major laws that encompass this category are the (1) Sherman Act, (2) the Federal Trade Commission Act, (3) the Clayton Act, and (4) the Robinson-Patman Act. The *Sherman Antitrust Act* prohibits conspiracy and/or collusion where the intention is to restrict trade in interstate commerce. The *Federal Trade Commission Act* enables the Federal Trade Commission to challenge companies that promote unfair competition through deception in advertising and promotions. The *Clayton Act* is closely related to the Sherman Act and makes it unlawful for a supplier to require a purchase of one product before allowing the purchase of another. Finally, the *Robinson-Patman Act* protects buyers from unfair pricing strategies.

SUMMARY

Purchasing is an essential function in the operation of a foodservice organization and is vital to maintaining an adequate flow of food and supplies to meet production and service requirements.

Informal or formal methods of buying may be used, sometimes varying for different commodities. The buyer should be knowledgeable about the market and should understand the legal implications of contracts and bid buying. Purchasing may be the responsibility of the foodservice administrator or may be done centrally through a purchasing department. Group buying, in which several organizations combine their purchasing volume, has been successful in many cases.

The safety of food products is protected by several federal agencies, and quality grades have been established for many products. Detailed specifications should be used to ensure the purchase and delivery of products of the desired quality. Decisions must be made by the foodservice on the market form preferred, the quality to buy, and whether to make or buy prepared foods.

Good purchasing procedures include the use of appropriate buying methods, establishment of ordering schedules, and a system of communicating needs from production and service areas to the buyer. Foods and supplies should be received and checked by trained personnel and properly stored at appropriate temperatures. A storeroom control system that includes authorized issuing of supplies and complete inventory records is essential, but the procedures and paperwork should be limited to those necessary for control and communications.

APPLICATION OF CHAPTER CONCEPTS

Interest in and pressure to buy local is particularly intense on college campuses across the country. Students are seeking local options for a number of reasons including the desire for fresh food, to support the local economy and to protect the environment. The Dining and Culinary Services department at the University of Wisconsin–Madison is committed to doing its part to honor these interests and has in fact been building its local purchasing program for well over a decade.

There are of course challenges with purchasing locally grown products, especially in the Midwest where the growing season is very short; also, the demand at UW–Madison is huge. Some of the challenges include finding a source of supply that can meet demand, ensuring that suppliers meet regulatory standards for safety, and developing billing systems that work with accounting systems. In addition, it may be difficult for local vendors to provide the insurance coverage required for doing business with the state of Wisconsin. And, of course, competitive pricing is always an issue. Despite these challenges, UW–Madison has made a commitment to continually add local product to its menus and to increase the annual expenditures on local product.

Another particularly interesting challenge is that the term *local* is not legally defined. It is up to the buyer to decide what *local* means in the context of his or her operation.

CRITICAL-THINKING QUESTIONS

1. Do you think there should be a legal definition of *local*? Why or why not?
2. Given that there is no legal definition, what would you recommend for a definition at UW–Madison?
3. What geographic factors need to be considered when defining the term local at UW–Madison? In other areas of the United States?
4. Search the Web. How are various on-site foodservice operations defining the term *local*?
5. UW–Madison is under a prime vendor contract as mandated by the state of Wisconsin. Under these mandates, how do you think they can buy from a local supplier?
6. The Food Code states that an operation must buy from "an approved source." How would a buyer determine whether a local grower is "approved"?
7. What method of purchasing do you think would be used if buying from a local vendor?
8. What does the concept of "market form" mean when buying local, fresh vegetables?
9. Would the concept of ethics be any different when working with local vendors? Explain.
10. Use the Web to learn about co-ops and local food distribution. Do you think a co-op would be of value to a high-volume on-site foodservice? Why or why not?

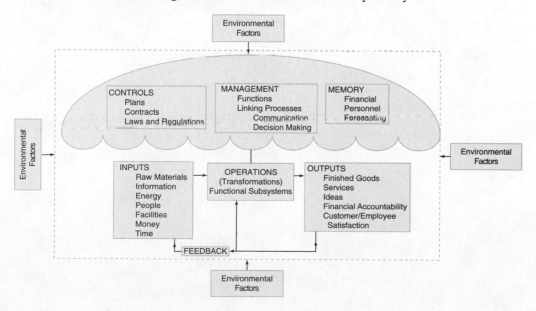

CHAPTER REVIEW QUESTIONS

1. What are the most recent trends and changes in the food market? How have these changes influenced the purchasing function of the foodservice organization?
2. Follow the local and national news for several consecutive days. What events (economic, political, environmental, social) might have an impact on purchasing decisions made in a foodservice department? How could a buyer or food manager plan ahead for the impact?
3. How does the marketing channel have an impact on the price paid for a food product by the consumer?
4. Identify the major federal agencies that oversee the food supply.
5. What are the advantages and disadvantages of department, group, and centralized purchasing?
6. What are the advantages and disadvantages of the two principal methods of buying? What are some alternative methods of purchasing?
7. Explain the following recommendation: "Level of quality purchased should match intended use."
8. Ethical behavior is important in any professional position. What is unique about the application of ethics to purchasing and the buyer?
9. What should a buyer look for when selecting a full-line vendor?
10. Why is it important to write clear specifications when entering into a competitive bid process?

SELECTED WEB SITES

www.theproducehunter.com   (The Produce Hunter)
www.usda.gov   (U.S. Department of Agriculture)
www.foodbuy.com   (FoodBuy Purchasing Service)
www.nfsmi.org   (National Food Service Management Institute)
www.foodsafety.gov   (USDA food safety: gateway)
www.pma.com   (Produce Marketing Association)

Receiving, Storage, and Inventory

Kevin Norris/Shutterstock

A SUCCESSFUL PURCHASING FUNCTION IN A FOOD-
service operation is integrated with a series of receiving, storage, and inventory
procedures for food and supplies. Standard operating procedures for these activities
are of particular importance to ensure that delivered products meet predetermined
standards of quality and are held under conditions to preserve this quality until the

From Chapter 7 of *Foodservice Management: Principles and Practices*, Twelfth Edition, June Payne-Palacio, Monica Theis.

item is issued to production. A review of specific receiving practices is included in this chapter. Requirements for storage facilities and records for inventory control are also included.

KEY CONCEPTS

1. Receiving is the point at which an organization takes legal ownership and physical possession of items ordered.

2. Receiving is an interdepartmental activity.

3. Personnel specifically allocated to and trained in receiving contribute to an efficient and effective program.

4. Physical arrangement and availability of supplies in the receiving area influence the efficiency of the product inspection process.

5. Clearly defined and consistently enforced security measures prevent theft and deliberate contamination of food and supplies.

6. Receiving is a process of consecutive steps from receipt of product to proper storage.

7. There are three basic types of storage that must be maintained and managed for maximum shelf life of products.

8. A program of regular inventory contributes to product protection and cost containment.

9. Perpetual inventory is a method of continuous tracking of product held in storage.

10. Physical inventory is an exact count of product held in storage.

RECEIVING

KEY CONCEPT: Receiving is the point at which an organization takes legal ownership and physical possession of items ordered.

Receiving is the point at which foodservice operations inspect the products and take legal ownership and physical possession of the items ordered. The purpose of receiving is to ensure that the food and supplies delivered match preestablished specifications for quality and quantity. It is also a goal of the receiving process to prevent product loss by mishandling and theft. The process of receiving includes inspection of product, completion of documents, and prompt transfer to appropriate storage. Inputs include trained personnel, physical space, supplies, and equipment.

A well-designed receiving process is important to cost and quality control and therefore warrants careful planning and monitoring. Minimally, a good receiving program should include clearly written policies and procedures on each of the following components:

- Coordination with other departments (e.g., production and accounting)
- Training for receiving personnel
- Parameters of authority and supervision
- Scheduled receiving hours
- Security measures
- Documentation procedures

Potential consequences of a poorly planned receiving program include the following:

- Short weights
- Substandard quality
- Double billing
- Inflated prices

- Mislabeled merchandise
- Inappropriate substitutions
- Spoiled or damaged merchandise
- **Pilferage** or theft

Pilferage
is the act of stealing, usually in small quantities

In simple terms, a poorly planned and executed receiving program results in financial loss for the operation.

Coordination with Other Departments

> **KEY CONCEPT:** Receiving is an interdepartmental activity.

The receiving function needs to be coordinated with other functions and departments in the foodservice organization. Purchasing, production, and accounting are three key areas that need a well-coordinated working relationship with receiving personnel. In middle-sized to large foodservice operations, the purchasing department, in cooperation with the food manager, defines standards of quality that the receiving personnel use to analyze product at the point of receiving. The purchasing department typically is also responsible for scheduling deliveries through contractual agreement. The production department depends on the receiving unit to get needed food and supplies in the storage areas in time for scheduled production. Receiving sometimes transfers product directly to production, a JIT practice that is increasingly popular as demand for fresh and made-to-order (MTO) grows.

In many organizations, the accounting department is responsible for processing the billing of food and supply purchases. Receiving records must be completed and submitted to accounting in a timely fashion so that payments are made on time. Prompt payment allows the organization to take advantage of discounts and avoid late payment penalties. Discrepancies between what was ordered and what was delivered are also handled by the accounting department.

Personnel

> **KEY CONCEPT:** Personnel specifically allocated to and trained in proper receiving contribute to an efficient and effective program.

In an ideal world, responsibility for receiving would be assigned to a specific, competent, well-trained employee. However, in reality this job is often not specifically assigned at all, but simply handled by any employee scheduled when a delivery arrives. Regardless of who performs the receiving function, principles of proper inspection and record keeping must be clearly understood.

Desirable qualifications for a receiving or storeroom clerk include knowledge of food quality standards as established through specifications, the ability to evaluate product quality and recognize unacceptable product, and an understanding of the proper documentation procedures. The receiver's degree of authority must be well defined by policy to ensure that decisions made at the dock are consistent with standards and in the best interest of the foodservice. Even though the receiver may be well trained and trustworthy, consistent and routine supervision of the receiving area is recommended to ensure that procedures are followed and that the area is kept secure.

Facilities, Equipment, and Sanitation

> **KEY CONCEPT:** Physical arrangement and availability of supplies in the receiving area influence the efficiency of the product inspection process.

A well-designed receiving area should be as close to the delivery docks as possible, with easy access to the storage facilities of the operation. This arrangement helps to minimize cross traffic through the production area and reinforces good security measures.

Figure 1 A lift used to transport pallets from the dock to appropriate storage.
Courtesy University of Wisconsin–Madison Babcock Dairy Plant.

Figure 1 A lift used to transport pallets from the dock to appropriate storage.
Courtesy University of Wisconsin–Madison Babcock Dairy Plant.

The area itself should be large enough to accommodate an entire delivery at one time. If a receiving office is in the area, it should have large glass windows so that receiving personnel can easily monitor the activities of the area.

The amount and capacity of receiving equipment depends on the size and frequency of deliveries. Large deliveries may require a forklift for pallet deliveries. A hand truck may be adequate in medium-to-small operations. Figure 1 is a picture of a lift used to transport pallets from the dock to the appropriate storage area.

Scales, ranging from platform models to countertop designs, are needed to weigh goods as they arrive. A policy should be in place such that the scales are calibrated on a regular basis to ensure accuracy.

A supply of small equipment is also needed, including thermometers for checking refrigerated food temperatures and various opening devices, such as shortblade knives and crate hammers. Specifications, purchase orders, and documentation records need to be readily available.

Cleaning and sanitation procedures for the receiving area should be defined by policy. Plans for pest control need to be determined, and some cleaning supplies should be readily available to keep the area clean during all hours of operation.

Scheduled Hours for Receiving

Hours of receiving should be defined by policy or contract, and vendors should be instructed to deliver within a specific time range. The purpose of defined receiving times is to avoid the busiest production times in the operation and the arrival of too many deliveries at the same time. Dedicated hours also ensure that receiving areas are accessible and personnel are on hand. Thus, many operations instruct vendors to deliver midmorning or midafternoon to avoid high food production and service times.

Security

■ **KEY CONCEPT:** **Clearly defined and consistently enforced security measures prevent theft and deliberate contamination of food and supplies.**

The receiving components already discussed contribute to the security of the receiving process. A few additional practices, however, can contribute to an even more secure receiving area. Deliveries should be checked immediately on arrival. After the receiving personnel have confirmed that the order meets specifications, the invoice can be signed, and the delivery should be moved immediately to the proper storage. This practice minimizes quality deterioration and opportunity for theft.

Doors to the receiving area should be kept locked. Some facilities keep doors locked at all times, with a doorbell or buzzer system for delivery personnel to use when they arrive. Finally, only authorized personnel should have access to the receiving area. This is particularly difficult in facilities where the area is used for other purposes, but the policy must be strictly enforced. Security measures in receiving areas are under close scrutiny today following relatively recent terrorist attacks and cases of deliberate product tampering.

The Receiving Process

KEY CONCEPT: **Receiving is a process of consecutive steps from receipt of product to proper storage.**

Once the components of a receiving program are planned and implemented, an organization is ready to receive goods. The receiving process involves five key steps:

1. Physically inspect the delivery and check it against the purchase order.
2. Inspect the delivery against the **invoice**.
3. Accept an order only if all quantities and quality specifications are met.
4. Complete receiving records.
5. Transfer goods to appropriate storage.

Invoice
A list of goods shipped or delivered. Includes price and quantities

Methods. The two main methods of receiving are the blind and the invoice receiving methods. The *blind method* involves providing an invoice or purchase order, one in which the quantities have been erased or blacked out, to the receiving clerk. The clerk must then quantify each item by weighing, measuring, or counting and recording it on the blind purchase order. The blind document is then compared with the original order. This method offers an unbiased approach by the receiving clerk but is time consuming and, therefore, more labor intensive.

A frequently used and more traditional method is *invoice receiving.* Using this method, the receiving clerk checks the delivered items against the original purchase order and notes any deviations. This method is efficient but requires careful evaluation by the clerk to ensure that the delivery is accurate and quality standards are met. Figure 2 is an example of an invoice.

Tips for Inspecting Deliveries. The following are some additional tips that the receiver should keep in mind when evaluating food and supply deliveries:

• Anticipate arrival and be prepared.
• Have purchase orders and specifications ready.
• Inspect food immediately on arrival.
• Check temperatures of refrigerated items on arrival.
• Check frozen items for evidence of thawing or burn.
• Randomly open cases or crates for large deliveries to determine that the container includes the entire order.

This traditional process meant that the driver bringing the delivery had to wait while the receiving clerk conducted the inspection and signed the invoice. This was in part to discuss and account for discrepancies before the invoice was signed. Relatively recently, foodservices and vendors have reached agreement, often under contract, that the driver can leave once the delivery is dropped and discrepancies can be reported to the vendor if and when they are found. This of course requires a certain amount of trust on behalf of both parties, but it does get the driver back on the road, which is highly valuable to the vendor.

Evaluation and Follow-Up. Evaluation of products should be continued as they are issued for use because some discrepancies may not be detected until the item is in use. When products are found to be defective, some type of adjustment should be made with the vendor. The purchasing agent or other proper official should be notified of deficiencies in quality, service, or delivery. This is typically accomplished by issuing a discrepancy report to the

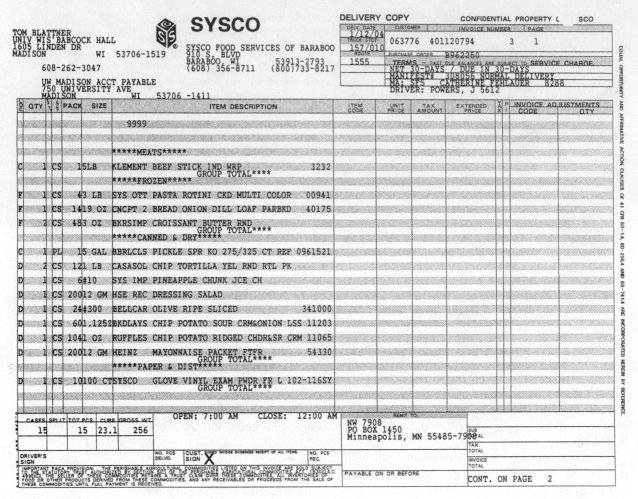

Figure 2   An example of an invoice.
Source: Courtesy Sysco of Baraboo. Used with permission.

vendor and a corresponding credit memo to the accounting office. Figure 3 is a example of a discrepancy report form. All discrepancies must be noted, whether compensated or not, because this collective information will be of value when the foodservice begins to prepare for the next bid period if using formal purchasing methods.

STORAGE

■ **KEY CONCEPT:** There are three basic types of storage that must be maintained and managed for maximum shelf life of products.

The flow of material through a foodservice operation begins in the receiving and storage areas. Careful consideration should be given to procedures for receiving and storage, as well as to the construction and physical needs of both areas. In planning, there should be a straight line from the receiving dock to the storeroom and refrigerators, and, preferably, the dock should be on the same level as the kitchen. A short distance between receiving and storage reduces the amount of labor required, reduces pilferage, and causes the least amount of deterioration in food products.

The proper storage of food immediately after it has been received and checked is an important factor in the prevention and control of loss or waste. When food is left unguarded in the receiving area or exposed to the elements or extremes of temperature for even a short time, its safekeeping and quality are jeopardized.

UW Health
University of Wisconsin
Hospital and Clinics

UNIVERSITY OF WISCONSIN HOSPITAL AND CLINICS
DISCREPANCY REPORT

VENDOR		RECEIPT DATE		PREPARATION DATE	
		RECEIVED BY			

PURCHASE ORDER #		REC.REPT #	PACKING SLIP	FREIGHT BILL		CARRIER	

ITEM #	DESCRIPTION	ORDERED	SHIPPED	REC-DOCK	REC-P.O.

COMMENTS

PURCHASING AGENT	DATE

ACTION TO BE TAKEN

Figure 3 Example of a discrepancy report form.
Source: Courtesy of the University of Wisconsin Hospital and Clinics. Used with permission.

Adequate space for dry, refrigerator, and freezer storage should be provided in locations that are convenient to receiving and preparation areas. Temperature and humidity controls and provision for circulation of air are necessary to retain the various quality factors of the stored foods. The length of time foods can be held satisfactorily and without appreciable deterioration depends on the product and its quality when stored, as well as the conditions of storage. Suggested maximum temperatures and storage times for a some common foods are given in Figure 4. The condition of stored food and the temperature of the storage units should be checked frequently.

Dry Storage

The main requisites of a food dry-storage area are that it be dry, cool, and properly ventilated. If possible, it should be in a location convenient to the receiving and preparation areas.

Food	Suggested Maximum Temperature (°F)	Recommended Maximum Storage	
Canned products	70	12 months	
Cooked dishes with eggs, meat, milk, fish, poultry	36	Serve day prepared	
Cream filled pastries	36	Serve day prepared	
Dairy products			
Milk (fluid)	40	3 days	In original container, tightly covered
Milk (dried)	70	3 months	In original container
Butter	40	2 weeks	In waxed cartons
Cheese (hard)	40	6 months	Tightly wrapped
Cheese (soft)	40	7 days	In tightly covered container
Ice cream and ices	10	3 months	In original container, covered
Eggs			
Shell, fresh	40	3 weeks	Unwashed, not in cardboard
Pasteurized liquid	40	3 days (once container is open)	Loosely wrapped
Hardcooked	40	7 days	In covered container
Fish (fresh)	36	2 days	
Shellfish	36	5 days	
Frozen products			
Fruits and vegetables	0 (to −20)	1 growing season to another	Original container
Beef, poultry, eggs		6–12 months	Original container
Fresh pork (not ground)		3–6 months	Original container
Lamb and veal		6–9 months	Original container
Sausage, ground meat, fish		1–3 months	Original container
Fruits			
Peaches, plums, berries	50	7 days	Unwashed
Apples, pears, citrus	50 (to 70)	2 weeks	Original container
Leftovers	36	2 days	In covered container
Poultry	36	1–2 days	Loosely wrapped
Meat			
Ground	38	2 days	Loosely wrapped
Fresh meat cuts	38	3–5 days	Loosely wrapped
Liver and variety meats	38	2 days	Loosely wrapped
Cold cuts (sliced)	38	3–5 days	Wrapped in semimoisture-proof paper
Cured bacon	38	7 days	May wrap tightly
Ham (tender cured)	38	1–6 weeks	May wrap tightly
Ham (canned)	38	6 weeks	Original container, unopened
Dried beef	38	6 weeks	May wrap tightly
Vegetables			
Leafy	45	7 days	Unwashed
Potatoes, onions, root vegetables	70	7–30 days	Dry in ventilated container or bags
Mayonnaise (commercial)	40	2 months after opening	
Salad mixtures: egg, chicken, tuna, ham, macaroni	40	3–5 days	
Soups and stews, fresh	40	3–4 days	
Soups and stews, frozen	0 (to −20)	2–3 months	
Sausage, raw from pork, beef, turkey	40	1–2 days	
Sausage, frozen	0 (to −20)	1–2 months	

Figure 4 Suggested maximum storage temperatures and times.

Dry storage is intended for nonperishable foods that do not require refrigeration. Paper supplies often are stored with foods, but a separate room must be provided for cleaning supplies, as required in many health codes. The separation of food and cleaning materials that could be toxic prevents a possible error in identification or a mixup in filling requisitions.

Temperature and Ventilation. The storage area should be dry and the temperature not over 70°F. A dark, damp atmosphere is conducive to the growth of certain organisms, such as molds. Dry staples such as flour, sugar, rice, condiments, and canned foods are more apt to deteriorate in a damp storage area. The storeroom is more easily kept dry if located at or above ground level, although it need not have outside windows unless required by code. All plumbing pipes should be insulated and well protected to prevent condensation and leakage onto food stores. If the storage area does have windows, they should be equipped with security-type sashes and screens and painted opaque to protect foods from direct sunlight.

Ventilation is one of the most important factors in dry storage. The use of wall vents, as shown in Figure 5, is the most efficient method of obtaining circulation of air, but other methods are possible. The circulation of air around bags and cartons of food is necessary to aid in the removal of moisture, reduction of temperature, and elimination of odors. For this reason, it is recommended that containers of food be cross-stacked for better air circulation.

Storeroom Arrangement. Foods and supplies should be stored in an orderly and systematic arrangement. A designated place should be assigned to each item, with similar products grouped together. The containers are dated and usually left in the original package or placed in tightly covered containers if the lots are broken. All items should be stored on racks or shelves instead of directly on the floor or against walls.

Cases and bags of food can be stacked on slatted floor racks, pallets, or wheeled metal platforms. Hand or power lifts are useful for moving loaded pallets from one location to another, but the aisles between shelves and platforms should be wide enough for the use of such mobile equipment.

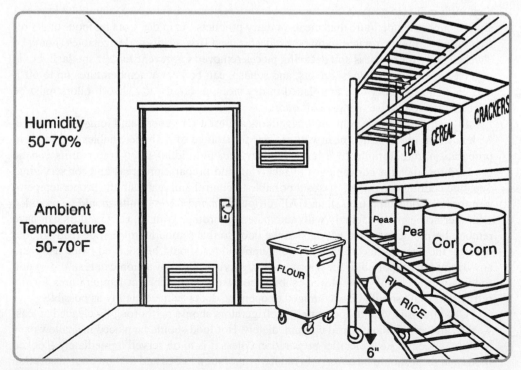

Figure 5 Example of arrangement in dry storage for good ventilation.

Shelving, preferably metal and adjustable, is recommended for canned foods or other items that have been removed from cases. Shelves should be far enough off the floor and away from the wall to permit a free flow of air. Some state regulations may have specific measures. For example, some codes will specify that shelving be at least six inches above the floor. Broken lots of dry foods, such as sugar and flour, should be stored in metal or plastic containers with tightly fitted lids. The items can be arranged according to groups, and foods in each group can be placed on the shelves in alphabetical order—for example, canned fruits would be shelved as follows: apples, apricots, and so on. Food should also be stored using the **FIFO (first-in/first-out)** method. New shipments should be placed in back to ensure use of the oldest stock first. Alphabetical arrangement facilitates counting when the physical inventory is taken and locating items when filling storeroom requisitions. A chart showing the arrangement of supplies is helpful to storeroom personnel. It should be posted near the door or some other place where it can be easily seen.

Sanitation.   Food in dry storage must be protected from insects and rodents by means of preventive measures, such as the use of proper insecticides and rodenticides, the latter under the direction of pest management personnel. Many operators contract with a pest control service to provide routine monitoring. Floors in the dry storage area should be slip resistant and easily cleaned. A regular cleaning schedule designed according to the volume of traffic and other activity in this area is vital to the maintenance of clean and orderly storage rooms. No trash should be left on the shelves or floor, and spilled food should be wiped up immediately.

Refrigerated and Freezer Storage

The storage of perishable foods is an important factor in their safety and retention of quality. Fresh and frozen foods should be placed in refrigerated or frozen storage immediately after delivery and kept at these temperatures until ready to use. Recommended holding temperatures for fresh fruits and vegetables are 40°F to 45°F, and 32°F to 40°F for meat, poultry, dairy products, and eggs. Frozen products should be stored at 0° to −10°F.

In some foodservices, separate refrigerators are available for fruits and vegetables, for dairy products and eggs, and for meats, fish, and poultry. Fruits and vegetables, because of their high moisture content, are susceptible to freezing and, therefore, should be kept at a slightly higher temperature than meats or dairy products. As in dry storage, foods under refrigeration should be rotated so that the oldest is used first. Fruits and vegetables should be checked daily for ripeness and decaying pieces removed to prevent further spoilage. Some vegetables, such as potatoes, onions, and squash, can be kept at temperatures up to 60°F and, in some foodservices, are placed in dry storage. Foods that absorb odors must be stored away from those that give off odors.

In many operations, walk-in refrigerators are used for general and long-term storage, with reach-in units located near workstations for storage of daily perishables and foods in preparation and storage. In a large foodservice, individual refrigerator units can be grouped together for convenience to receiving and preparation areas and for servicing. Separate cooling equipment makes it possible to control and maintain the proper temperature for the food stored in each unit. All refrigeration and freezer units should be provided with thermometers, preferably with automated recording. Walk-in refrigerators can have remote thermometers mounted outside the door so that temperatures can be read without opening the door, as shown in Figure 6. Temperatures should be checked twice daily and any irregularity reported to the appropriate supervisor. Prompt action can result in saving food as well as money. Employees should be aware of the correct temperatures for the refrigerators and should be encouraged to open the doors as infrequently as possible.

Cleanliness is vital to food safety. Refrigerators should be thoroughly cleaned at least weekly, and any spillage wiped up immediately. Hot food should be placed in shallow pans to chill as soon as possible after preparation unless it is to be served immediately. Cooked foods and meat should be covered to reduce evaporation losses and to limit odor absorption and damage from possible overhead leakage or dripping. Cooked meats should be stored

FIFO (first-in/first-out)

An inventory method in which stock is rotated to ensure that items in storage are used (or issued) in the order in which they were received

Figure 6 Walk-in refrigerator.
Source: Courtesy Kolpak and Clark, Malone and Associates. Used with permission.

above raw meats in the refrigerator to ensure that cooked foods are protected from raw meat drippings. Daily checks on the contents of refrigerators are advisable so that leftover and broken package foods are incorporated into the menu without delay.

Self-contained refrigeration units are used for ice makers, water dispensers, counter sections for display of salads, and storage for individual milk cartons. Each is adjusted to maintain the temperature needed. Freezer storage generally is in walk-in units, which may open from a walk-in refrigerator to conserve energy. Ice cream and other frozen desserts may be kept in separate freezer cabinets to eliminate odor transfer.

The maintenance of refrigeration equipment requires regular inspection and service by a competent engineer to keep the equipment in good working order. However, the manager and other employees must be able to detect and report any noticeable irregularities, because a breakdown in the system could result in heavy loss of food and damage to equipment. In most installations, the refrigerator system is divided into several units so that failure in one will not disrupt the operation of the others.

INVENTORY RECORDS AND CONTROL

KEY CONCEPT: A program of regular inventory contributes to product protection and cost containment.

Accurate records are essential to inventory control and provide a basis for purchasing and for cost analysis. The exact procedure and forms used will vary according to policies of the institution and the degree of computerization, but an adequate control system requires that a record be made of all food products and supplies as they are received and stored, and again as they are issued for use in production or other areas of the foodservice.

Receiving

All incoming supplies should be inspected, as explained earlier, and recorded on a receiving record form such as the one shown in Figure 7. A journal in which to list the items received, with date of receipt, can also be used as a receiving record. Whatever form is used, the information should be checked against the purchase order, the delivery slip, and the invoice to be sure that the merchandise has been received as ordered and that the price is correct.

Receiving Record							Date_____	
							Distribution	
Quantity	Unit	Description of item	Name of vendor	Inspected and quantity verified by	Unit price	Total cost	To kitchen	To store room

Figure 7 Sample of receiving record form.

Storeroom Issues

Control of goods received cannot be effective unless storerooms are kept locked and authority and control over the merchandise are delegated to one person. Even if the foodservice is too small to justify the employment of a full-time storeroom clerk, an employee may be made responsible for receiving, putting away, and issuing goods from the storeroom in addition to other assigned duties.

No food or other supplies should be removed from the storeroom without authorization, usually in the form of a written requisition. An exception may be perishable foods that are to be used the same day they are received and are sent directly to the production units. In that case, they are treated as direct issues and are charged to the food cost for that day. All foods that are stored after delivery are considered storeroom purchases and in most operations can be removed only by requisition.

A list of supplies needed for production and service of the day's menu is compiled by the cook or other person responsible for assembling ingredients. If the foodservice uses an ingredient room for weighing and measuring ingredients for all recipes, the personnel in this unit are responsible for requesting supplies. The list of needed supplies is then submitted to the storeroom clerk, who completes the requisition. The order is filled and delivered to the appropriate department or workstation. The exact procedure for issuing supplies varies with the size of the operation and whether there is a full-time storeroom clerk.

Requisitions should be numbered and made out in duplicate or triplicate as the situation requires. Prenumbering of the requisitions makes it possible to trace missing or duplicate requisitions. An example of a storeroom requisition is shown in Figure 8. Columns

Figure 8 Requisition form for storeroom issues.

		Storeroom Requisition				

Issue following items to   Date:

_____ Department   Signed:

Item	Description	Quantity Ordered	Quantity Received	Unit Price	Total Cost	Authorized Signature

should be included for unit price and total cost unless a computer-assisted program is used, in which case the data will be available from the stored information in the computer. An inventory number is needed for each item on the requisition if a computer is used in calculating costs.

The requisition should be signed by a person authorized to request supplies and should be signed or initialed by the individual who fills the order. The requisitioning of food and supplies is an important factor in controlling costs and in preventing loss from pilferage, and it should be practiced in some form even in a small foodservice.

Perpetual Inventory

■ **KEY CONCEPT:** **Perpetual inventory is a method of continuous tracking of product held in storage.**

The **perpetual inventory** is a running record of the balance on hand for each item in the storeroom. Computers have simplified the process of maintaining the perpetual inventory and are used for that purpose by many foodservices.

The perpetual inventory provides a continuing record of food and supplies purchased, in storage, and used. Items received are recorded from the invoices, and the amounts are added to the previous balance on hand. Storeroom issues are recorded from the requisitions and subtracted from the balance. Additional information usually includes the date of purchase, the vendor, the brand purchased, and the price paid.

If minimum and maximum stock levels have been established, these figures should be indicated on the inventory.

These inventory records are recommended for all items except perishable foods that are delivered and stored in the production area. A physical inventory taken at the time perishable foods are ordered is more realistic. However, if there is a need for purchasing information on prices or total amounts of these foods used during a certain period of time, a purchase record, as illustrated in Figure 9, may be used to record the date of purchase, amounts, prices, and vendors.

Perpetual inventory

A running record of the balance of product in stock

UWHealth

University of Wisconsin
Hospital and Clinics

DEPARTMENT OF PURCHASING
610 N WHITNEY WAY, #4400
MADISON WI 53705

VENDOR:

DUPLICATE Purchase Order

Purchase Order FS10054443	Date 12/13/1999	Revision	Page 1
Payment Terms Net 30	Freight Terms FOB Destination		Ship Via TRUCK
Buyer Norris,Ron		PHONE: FAX:	(608)263-1525 (608)263-0343

Ship To: 600 N Highland Ave.
F4/150
Madison WI 53792
Drop - F4/150A, CSC

Bill To: DEPT OF ACCOUNTS PAYABLE
P.O. BOX 5448
MADISON WI 53705-5448
PHONE: (608)263-4945

Tax Exempt?   Tax Exempt ID:

Line Item	Description	UWH Item#	Quantity	UOM	Unit Price	Line Amt	Due Date
1	CHEESE CHEDDAR BACON 5# LOAF	3278073	2	LF	9.12	18.24	12/14/1999 10889
2	CHEESE CHEDDAR CARAWAY 5# LOAF	3278072	2	LF	8.62	17.24	12/14/1999 10889
3	CHEESE CHEDDAR LOW-FAT,LOW-SALT 5# LOAF	3270201	16	LF	19.00	304.00	12/14/1999 10889
4	CHEESE LOW FAT,LOW SALT,COLBY,5# LOAF	3275042	2	LF	7.85	15.70	12/14/1999 10889
5	CHEESE FARMER LOW-FAT,LOW SALT, 5# LOAF	3270195	2	LF	7.10	14.20	12/14/1999 10889
6	CHEESE MONTOREY JACK,LOW-FAT-L/S 5#LOAF	3270194	6	LF	7.80	46.80	12/14/1999 10889
7	CHEESE MOZZARELLA SHREDDED 6/5# BOX.....	3271021	12	LF	9.31	111.66	12/14/1999 10889
8	CHEESE SWISS LOW SODIUM 10 # LOAF......	3272811	2	LF	17.18	34.35	12/14/1999 10889

Total PO Amount   562.19

Figure 9 Example of purchase order.
Courtesy of the University of Wisconsin Hospital and Clinics, Department of Foodservice, Madison, Wisconsin. Used with permission.

Time and strict supervision are required if the perpetual inventory is to be an effective tool, but it is a useful guide for purchasing and serves as a check on irregularities, such as pilferage or displacement of stock. It also provides useful information on fast-moving, slow-moving, or unusable items.

Physical Inventory

■ **KEY CONCEPT:** Physical inventory is an exact count of product held in storage.

Physical inventory

An actual count of items in stock

An actual count of items in all storage areas should be taken periodically, usually to coincide with an accounting period. In some organizations, a **physical inventory** is taken at the end of each month, in others two or three times a year. The inventory is simplified if two people work together, one in a supervisory position or not directly involved with the storeroom operation. As one person counts the number of each item on hand, the other enters it on the inventory.

The procedure for taking a physical inventory is simplified by developing a printed form on which are listed the items normally carried in stock and their unit sizes, as shown in Figure 10. For convenience and efficiency in recording, the items on the inventory form can be classified and then arranged alphabetically within the group or listed in the same order as they are arranged in the storeroom and in the perpetual inventory. Space should be left on the form between each grouping to allow for new items to be added.

	The Student Union Food Division				Page 1	

Physical Inventory _____ 20 _____

Classification	Item	Unit	Quantity	Unit Price		Total Cost	
Beverages:							
	Coffee	14 oz pkg					
	Tea, iced	1 gal					
	Tea, individual	100/Box					
Cereals:							
	Assorted individual	50/carton					
	Corn Flakes	100/cs					
	Cream of Wheat	1# 12 oz box					
	Hominy grits	1# 8 oz box					
	Oats, rolled	3# box					
	Ralstons	1# 6 oz box					
	Rice, white	1# box					
Cereal Products and Flour:							
	Cornmeal	Bulk/lb					

TOTAL PAGE 1 _____

Figure 10   A sample page from a physical inventory form.

After the physical inventory is completed, the value of each item is calculated, and the total value of the inventory determined. Inventory figures are used to calculate food costs by adding the total food purchases to the beginning inventory and subtracting the ending inventory. The physical count also serves as a check against perpetual inventory records. Minor differences are expected, but major discrepancies should be investigated. Carelessness in filling requisitions or in record keeping is the most common reason for these errors, which may indicate a need for tighter storeroom controls or more accurate record keeping.

Both perpetual and physical inventories should be kept of china, glassware, and silverware. These items should be revalued at least once a year on the basis of physical inventory, although it may be desirable to revalue them at more frequent intervals. An inventory of other kitchen and dining room equipment and furniture normally is taken once a year.

Management of inventory is practiced both to determine quantities to keep on hand and to determine the security methods used to control how the stock influences overall foodservice costs. Each organization should decide on maximum and minimum quantities desirable to maintain in the storeroom. This decision is based on storage facilities and capacities, delivery patterns, and the volume of business. Established standards for quantities desirable to keep on hand aid in purchasing—for determining both the quantity to order and when to order.

SUMMARY

Receiving, storage, and inventory are important foodservice activities that are closely tied to the purchasing function. The primary purpose of these activities is to ensure that, beginning with the point of delivery, food and supply items meet predetermined quality standards and are held under conditions that preserve quality before they are issued to production or service.

Clearly written and strictly enforced policies and procedures are essential to ensure that incoming goods are carefully checked to confirm desired quality and quantities. Failure to abide by such policies can result in consequences that are costly to the operation. A sound receiving process is coordinated with other departments, executed by well-trained personnel, supported with well-maintained and adequate amounts of space and equipment, and managed through a series of accurate, current records.

Once received, food and supply items must be promptly transferred to appropriate storage. Storage facilities include refrigerators, freezers, and dry storage areas. Each type of storage has specific environment requirements of organization, temperature, and humidity. These conditions need to be monitored frequently, if not continually, to ensure that quality standards are maintained during storage.

Inventory control contributes to the safe and appropriate storage of food and supplies. By various methods, stock levels are set high enough to make sure that items are on hand when needed, but not so high as to create a cash flow problem for the operation. Perpetual and physical inventories are taken into account for product on hand and to calculate costs. As with receiving and storage, a system of records is essential for managing inventories.

APPLICATION OF CHAPTER CONCEPTS

The Dining and Culinary Service unit of University of Wisconsin Housing is a high-volume and complex foodservice. Obviously, the receiving, storage, and inventory system and processes need to be highly organized and orchestrated to ensure that food and supplies are where they need to be, when needed. Receiving is actually done in three places: at an off-campus warehouse, at the commissary, and at individual units. The warehouse is used to store supplies and food products that have a relatively long shelf life: canned products, for example. The most active area of receiving is at the dock of the commissary.

Each day multiple deliveries are made to the commissary from a variety of vendors. These include 53-foot semitrucks from the main food distribution companies such as Sysco and U.S. Foodservice as well as small vans from local bakeries. Numbers of deliveries vary greatly by day of the week. Monday and Fridays are big reception days with as many as 40 deliveries, whereas Tuesdays and Thursdays may see as few as five. Complicating matters is the fact that trucks for catering and garbage removal use the same dock. Obviously it takes a great deal of planning and coordinating to prevent backups at the dock and on the local streets.

This function is managed by the commissary's Inventory Control Coordinator, who in turn supervises three employees, two of whom transport product from the dock to the appropriate storage areas. The third employee is responsible for inventory.

CRITICAL-THINKING QUESTIONS

1. How does the Inventory Control Coordinator likely interface with the purchasing department to keep the receiving operation running smoothly?
2. What formal or informal arrangements can be made with the vendors to prevent backups and limit the amount of time any one truck sits in the dock?
3. The Inventory Control Coordinator explains that once a delivery is "dropped," it is "staged" for transport to storage. What do you think this means?
4. There is a huge difference in volume of delivery on Tuesdays and Thursdays compared to Mondays and Fridays. What do you think the receiving employees do during their "down" time?
5. What type of equipment needs to be in the receiving area to ensure prompt transport from the dock to the storage areas?
6. Of the four employees in receiving, which one or ones should have the authority to sign off on invoices? Why?

7. Currently inventory is done "by hand" using the physical method. How might technology be used to increase the speed and accuracy of inventory?
8. This dock is used for garbage removal. How might this influence management of the receiving area?
9. During the course of an active contract, what information could the Inventory Control Coordinator collect and provide to the purchasing department that would be useful during the next bid period for each vendor?
10. Are there any unique security measures that need to be implemented in the receiving function at the commissary?

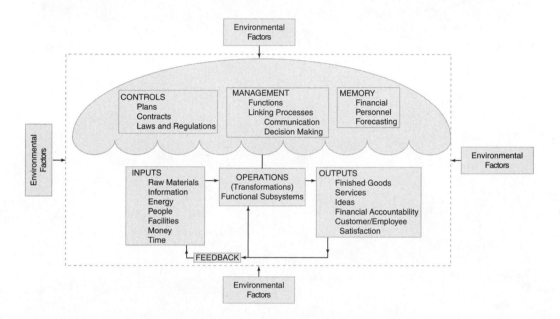

CHAPTER REVIEW QUESTIONS

1. How does a well-planned receiving program contribute to cost and quality control?
2. What are some potential consequences of a poorly planned and monitored receiving process?
3. Identify food items where the mini-max stock level would be most appropriate. Do the same for the par stock method.
4. Most organizations today use a computer to track inventory (perpetual). What value then might a periodic physical inventory offer?
5. With what foodservice and organizational departments would the receiving function be coordinated?
6. What are the pros and cons of a structured process for issuing product from storage?
7. Why are tight security measures important in receiving, storage, and inventory?
8. What skills and qualities would be desirable when hiring an employee to work in receiving?
9. Why is it particularly important to keep the receiving area clean and in good repair?
10. What are the limitations to enforcing strict hours of delivery for all vendors?

SELECTED WEB SITES

http://www.foodsafety.gov (U.S. government portal to food safety information)
http://www.nfsmi.org (National Food Service Management Institute)

Production

Production

John Wollwerth/Shutterstock

THE TRANSFORMATION OF RAW OR PROCESSED INGRE-

dients into a menu item, ready for service, is an essential function in any food-service system and involves a number of interrelated steps. It requires transfer of ingredients to the production unit, pre-preparation, cooking, and holding.

Traditionally, these procedures have been carried out in the individual food-service, and menu items were prepared "from scratch." Today, however, there are alternatives to this conventional system. Foodservice organizations composed of several individual units may centralize all or part of their food production in a commissary or central production kitchen. Preparation in these facilities can range from complete cooking of menu items to pre-assembly of ingredients that will be used for made-to-order concepts at service or satellite units.

Many foodservices prepare either all or part of the food for immediate service or hot-holding. In some, however, food is cooked, then chilled or frozen for later service. Others purchase certain menu items in ready-to-cook or ready-to-serve forms, and most use some type of convenience ingredients or components. These foodservice systems include conventional, commissary (central production kitchen), ready-prepared (cook/chill or cook/freeze), and assembly/serve.

Regardless of the system used, production planning and control are vital to the successful production of high-quality food. Recipe formulation, forecasting and scheduling of production are discussed in this chapter. Various elements of production and quality control are included to illustrate the importance of management to ensure that established standards are consistently met.

KEY CONCEPTS

1. Production, especially in high-volume operations, is a complex transformation of ingredients to final product.

2. An objective approach to production contributes to conservative use of inputs and desired product outputs.

3. Recipe formulation is used to develop standard recipes that serve as production controls.

4. The factor and percentage methods are commonly used approaches for recipe formulation.

5. Estimates of production demand can be determined through forecasting.

6. Consistent and comprehensive collection of data is essential for accurate and reliable forecasting.

7. Numerous factors, internal and external to the foodservice, influence production demand.

8. Clear communication between management and the production staff is essential for successful production.

9. Ingredient assembly, as a distinct and separate function, is a common control in high-volume foodservice operations.

10. Portion control is used to contain costs and ensure nutrient composition of menu items.

FOOD PRODUCTION

KEY CONCEPT: Production, especially in high-volume operations, is a complex transformation of ingredients to final product.

Production planning and scheduling are vital to the production of high-quality food and are important management responsibilities. The true test of the planning, however, is the production of food that is appealing to the clientele, prepared in the appropriate quantity, microbiologically safe, and within budgetary constraints. Knowledge of basic food preparation techniques and equipment will assist the foodservice manager in planning and achieving these goals.

The extent of actual preparation and cooking done on the premises depends on the type of foodservice system (conventional, commissary, ready-prepared, or assembly/serve). Even in the conventional system, in which all or most of the food is prepared, the production methods and equipment needs vary with the type and size of the foodservice. For example, in some retirement homes in which all residents are served at the same set time, it is necessary to prepare larger amounts of food at one time and with different equipment than in a restaurant where much of the food is prepared "to order" during an extended service period.

Quantity is the element that introduces complexity to food preparation in the foodservice system. Therefore, the foodservice manager not only should be knowledgeable about basic cooking methods but also needs to understand the time-temperature relationships and quality control challenges inherent in quantity food production. Mechanized equipment is essential for large batch sizes and for time-consuming procedures, especially in larger operations. Steam-jacketed kettles with stirring paddles, timers on steam-cooking equipment, metering devices for measuring water, and high-speed vegetable cutters are examples of equipment used in quantity food production. Convection ovens and compartment steamers used in many foodservices reduce the time required for cooking.

Nontransfer cooking, in which foods are cooked in the same pans used for serving, saves time and maximizes quality by minimizing handling.

As discussed previously, a list of steps required in the transformation of raw food into acceptable finished products includes storage, thaw time, pre-preparation, preparation, assembly, and holding before serving. The extent of ingredient assembly, pre-preparations, and preparation of the food before being delivered to the production area depends on the size, physical layout, and organization of the foodservice operation. Some foods, such as fresh fruit and certain salads and sandwiches, require no cooking. However, most foods do require cooking, and at this point, quality control becomes critically important. Constant vigilance is required to make certain that food is cooked properly and not held too long before service.

Objectives of Cooking in Food Production

KEY CONCEPT: **An objective approach to production contributes to conservative use of inputs and desired product outputs.**

The vast majority of food production involves at least some cooking. The basic objectives of cooking are to:

- Enhance the *aesthetic* appeal of the raw food product by maximizing the sensory qualities of color, texture, and flavor.
- Destroy harmful organisms to ensure that the food is microbiologically safe for human consumption.
- Improve digestibility and maximize nutrient retention.

It is the responsibility of the food manager, through planning and control, to ensure that these objectives are met each time a menu item is produced.

It is essential, then, that the food manager be knowledgeable about the physical and chemical properties of food and about the basic principles and techniques of food preparation. Appendix: Principles of Basic Cooking provides basic information on culinary techniques and terminology.

Computers in Production

The computer has simplified every aspect of the production function. Beginning with recipe formulation, the computer makes it easier to adjust recipes once the base recipe has been entered. For example, a recipe can easily be batched up (exploded) or reduced to the forecasted demand. This is a far more accurate and cost-effective production control compared to the traditional methods of expanding recipes in 25- or 50-serving increments.

Another advantage of computers in production is management of recipe files. It is not uncommon for large, multiunit foodservices to have thousands of recipes. The foodservice unit within the Housing Division at the University of Wisconsin–Madison, for example, has a minimum of 8,000 recipes in its computerized recipe file. Even small operations can have hundreds of recipes in their recipe banks. A file of hard copies for this volume of recipes would be difficult, if not impossible, to manage with a manual system.

RECIPE FORMULATION

KEY CONCEPT: **Recipe formulation is used to develop standard recipes that serve as production controls.**

Standardized Recipes

Numerous production controls are needed in a foodservice operation to ensure that preestablished standards for quality are consistently achieved. In food production, the most important control tool is the *standardized recipe*, sometimes referred to as a recipe formulation. By definition, a recipe is a statement of ingredients and procedures required to prepare a food item. A recipe is standardized when it has been tested and adapted to the requirements of a specific foodservice operation. These requirements include customer expectations and efficient, effective use of available resources, including personnel, equipment, and money.

There are numerous advantages in developing and using standardized recipes, the most important of which is consistency. Customers in all types of foodservice operations often expect and sometimes need to be able to depend on a food item being the same each time it is selected or served. This consistency is expected for a number of quality aspects, including flavor, texture, and portion size. In some operations, including schools and health care facilities, consistency in nutrient composition is essential to ensure that the nutritional needs of customers are met. The purpose of the standardized recipes is to ensure consistency of each aspect of quality every time a menu item is prepared.

Use of standardized recipes also simplifies other functions of a foodservice operation, including planning, purchasing, forecasting, recipe costing, and pricing. Costing and pricing, for example, can easily be calculated because ingredients and amounts are the same each time a recipe is used.

Standardized recipes minimize the effects of employee turnover on food quality and simplify the training of new staff by serving as a form of communication between the food manager and the production staff. Standardized recipes are essential for computerized foodservice operations because individually coded recipes trigger other functions, such as purchasing and forecasting. Standardized recipes are also the key to the success of centralized ingredient assembly where accuracy in weights and measures is essential.

Format. A recipe format that provides all information needed for production of a menu item should be selected. An orderly arrangement of this information should be developed and the same general pattern followed for all recipes on file. Each foodservice should decide on the format best suited to its operation and use this format consistently. Employees who work in production can be a valuable source on best design as they are most experienced in recipe use.

Most recipes list the ingredients in the order in which they are used. A block arrangement, in which ingredients that are to be combined are grouped, is helpful. Separating these groups with space or lines makes following recipes easier and faster. Listing the procedures directly across from the ingredients involved simplifies preparation and enables clear directions to be written in a minimum number of words. Figure 1 illustrates this suggested format.

Certain information is essential, regardless of the form in which the recipe is written. The following are suggestions for recipe content:

Recipe Title. The title should be printed in large type and either centered on the page or placed to the left of the top of the page as shown in Figure 1. The recipe identification code for computerized systems may also be placed here.

Yield and Portion Size. The total recipe yield may be provided in measure, weight, number of pans, or number of portions. The portion size may be in weight, measure, or count. It is also important to define the serving utensil for portioning so service staff can portion accurately at the front of the house.

Cooking Time and Temperature. This information is often listed at the top of the page so preheating of equipment and scheduling of cooking can be determined without reading the entire recipe. Some recipe writers repeat the cooking times and temperatures in the instructions so the cooks can see them while working with the ingredients. It is important to identify the piece of production equipment in some cases. Conventional and convection ovens cook at different times and temperatures, for example. This needs to be made clear to the production staff.

Ingredients and Quantities. Names of ingredients are generally listed on the left side of the recipe with the quantities arranged in one or more columns to accommodate different yields (Figure 2), although this need is eliminated in computerized systems. For the sake

CHICKEN AND BROCCOLI STIR-FRY

Yield 50 portions   *Portion* 4 oz chicken and broccoli + 4 oz rice

Ingredient	Amount	Procedure
Water (cold)	4½ qt	Prepare sauce by blending together the liquids, spices, and
Soy sauce	2⅔ cup	cornstarch. Stir with a wire whip until well blended.
Chicken base	1½ oz	Cook over medium heat until thick and translucent.
Garlic, minced fresh	2 oz	Stir often during cooking.
Ginger, ground	1 Tbsp	Keep hot (above 165°F). Save for later step.
Red pepper, crushed	¼ tsp	
Sesame seed oil	4 oz	
Cornstarch	7 oz	
Vegetable oil	½ cup	Saute ginger and garlic in hot oil for 2–3 minutes, until softened.
Ginger, fresh, thinly sliced	1 tsp	Add chicken and cook until done, 165°F, stirring often
Garlic, minced	1 tsp	during cooking.
Chicken, raw, cut in strips	6 lb	
Water chestnuts, sliced, drained	2 lb (EP)	Add water chestnuts and mushrooms to the cooked chicken.
Mushrooms, sliced fresh	1 lb (EP)	Stir-fry until mushrooms are softened.
Chinese cabbage, 1-inch slices	2 lb (EP)	Add Chinese cabbage, broccoli, and onions. Stir-fry for an
Broccoli florets	1 lb 8 oz (EP)	additional 2–3 minutes, until vegetables are barely tender.
Green onions, 1-inch slices	6 oz (EP)	Pour hot sauce reserved from earlier step over
		chicken-vegetable mixture.
Rice, converted	3 lb 8 oz	Cook rice according to directions on p. 594.
Water, boiling	4¼ qt	Serve 4 oz chicken-vegetable mixture over 4 oz rice.
Salt	2 Tbsp	
Vegetable oil	2 Tbsp	

Approximate nutritive values per portion   **Calories** 275

Amount/portion	%DV	Amount/portion	%DV	Amount/portion	%DV		%DV		%DV
Total Fat 7g	11%	**Cholest.** 38 mg	13%	**Total Carb.** 35 g	12%	Vitamin A	5%	Calcium	6%
Sat. Fat 1g	6%	**Sodium** 1300 mg	56%	Fiber 2 g	9%	Vitamin C	31%	Iron	10%
Protein 16 g				Sugars 2 g					

Percent Daily Values (%DV) are based on a 2,000-calorie diet.

Notes
- Potentially hazardous food. *Food Safety Standards:* Hold food for service at an internal temperature above 140°F. Do not mix old product with new. Cool leftover product quickly (within 4 hours) to below 41°F. See p. 105 for cooling procedures. Reheat leftover product quickly (within 2 hours) to 165°F. Reheat product only once; discard if not used.
- Always wash hands and wash and sanitize countertops, utensils, and containers between production steps when preparing raw poultry.

Variations
- **Beef and Broccoli Stir-Fry.** Substitute beef strips for chicken, and beef base for chicken base. Reduce water chestnuts to 1 lb 8 oz and Chinese cabbage to 1 lb 6 oz. Increase broccoli to 3 lb and mushrooms to 1 lb.
- **Chicken and Vegetable Stir-Fry.** Follow recipe for Chicken and Broccoli Stir-Fry. Use a total of 7 lb assorted vegetables. Select from broccoli florets, carrots, Chinese cabbage, mushrooms, water chestnuts, onions (green or mature), snow peas, or sugar snap peas.

Figure 1 Recipe format showing block arrangement. Nutrient composition, notes, and variations are given at the bottom of the recipe. Reprinted with permission from *Food for Fifty*, 12th ed., by Mary Molt. Copyright 2006 by Pearson Prentice Hall.

of accuracy, however, there should be no more than three ingredient amount columns on one recipe. Too many columns increase the chance of error by crowding the space needed to give complete directions for preparation.

Names of ingredients should be consistent. Descriptive terms are used to clearly define the style and form of each ingredient. In some recipes, the term *before* the name of the ingredient designates the form **as purchased** or that the ingredient has been cooked or

As purchased

Refers to weight before trimming

Applesauce Cake			
Desserts No. Ck–3		Oven temperature: 350°F	
Portion: 2 × 2¾ in.		Time: 30–35 minutes	
Cut 6 × 8			

Ingredients	2 pans	3 pans	Procedure
Shortening	1 lb 7 oz	2 lb 3 oz	Cream 5 min. on medium speed, with
Sugar	2 lb 14 oz	4 lb 5 oz	paddle.
Eggs	2 cups	3 cups	Add and beat 5 min. on medium speed.
Applesauce	2 qt + ½ c	3¼ qt	Add gradually on low speed. Beat 1 min. on medium speed after last addition. Scrape down.
Cake flour	2 lb 14 oz	4 lb 5 oz	Sift dry ingredients together and mix
Salt	4 tsp	2 Tbsp	with raisins.
Soda	1 oz	1½ oz	Add to creamed mixture gradually on
Cinnamon	1 Tbsp	4½ tsp	low speed.
Nutmeg	1½ tsp	2¼ tsp	Beat 2 min., medium speed, after last
Cloves	1½ tsp	2½ tsp	addition. Scrape down once.
Raisins	12 oz	1 lb 2 oz	Weigh into greased baking pans,
Total wt	13 lb 6 oz	20 lb 2 oz	12 × 22 × 2 in., 6 lb 8 oz / pan.

Figure 2 Recipe format with columns for two quantities.

heated before using in it the product. Examples are *canned* tomatoes, *frozen chopped* broccoli, *hot* milk, *boiling* water, and *cooked* turkey. The descriptive term is placed *after* the ingredient to indicate processing after the ingredient is weighed or measured—onions, *chopped*; eggs, *beaten*; or raw potato, *grated*. It is important in some recipes to designate AP (as purchased) or EP (edible portion) to account for trim loss. For example, 15 pounds (AP) of fresh broccoli would be 12 pounds (EP) or less assuming an 81 percent yield. Whatever approach is used, it should be consistent and understood by those using the recipes. Abbreviations should be consistent and easily understood, such as "qt" for quart or "lb" for pound. Tables 1 and 2 provide information on product yield and common abbreviations, respectively.

Procedures.   Directions for preparation of the product should be divided into logical steps and are most effective when placed directly across from the ingredients to be combined. Procedures should be clear and concise so that employees can easily read and understand them. It is helpful if basic procedures are uniform in all recipes for similar products. For example, roux is basic to sauces and in many recipes. The procedures on the recipe should be worded the same in each recipe. Likewise, there are several basic procedures in baked products, such as those for creaming fat and sugar or for combining dry and liquid ingredients, that should be the same on all recipes using them.

Timing should be provided for procedures in which mixers, steamers, or other mechanical equipment is used. For example, "cream shortening and sugar on medium speed for 10 minutes" or "cook on low heat until rice is tender and all water is absorbed, about 15 to 20 minutes."

Panning instructions should include the weight of product per pan to help in dividing the product equally into the required number of pans. For example, "Scale batter into two prepared 12 × 18 × 2-inch full pans, 4 lb 10 oz per pan." When layering ingredients in full pans for a casserole-type entrée, it is helpful if the weight or measure of each layer is given. For example, "Place dressing, sauce, and chicken in two 12 × 20 × 2-inch full pans, layered in each pan as follows: 4 lb 8 oz dressing, 1 ½ qt sauce, 3 lb chicken, 1 ¼ qt sauce."

Additional information that is not essential to the recipe but may be helpful (e.g., substitution of ingredients, alternate methods of preparation, or comments about the appearance of the product, such as "These cookies puff up at first, then flatten out with crinkled tops") can be added as footnotes. Variations on a basic recipe usually are included at the end of the recipe and may include tips on how to plate or garnish the product.

Table 1   Approximate yields expressed by weight of selected fruits and vegetables.

FOOD ITEM	YIELD
Apple, fresh	.78
Asparagus	.60
Bananas	.65
Beans, green or wax	.88
Beets, with tops	.45
Blueberries	.95
Broccoli	.70
Cantaloupe, peeled	.52
Carrots	.70
Celery	.75
Corn on the cob	.48
Grapes, seedless	.94
Lettuce, head	.76
Mushrooms	.90
Peaches	.76
Potatoes, white	.81
Squash, acorn	.80
Tomatoes	.80

Source: Adapted from *Food for Fifty*, 12th ed., by Mary Molt. Copyright © 2006 by Pearson Prentice Hall.

For manual systems, decisions regarding the size and form of the recipe card or sheet, the format to be followed, and the manner of filing the recipes are contingent on the needs of the operation. Cards 4 × 6 inches and 5 × 8 inches are popular sizes, and heavy typing paper, 8 ½ × 11 inches, is used in some operations. In deciding on a size and format, keep in mind that the recipes will be used by cooks and other employees who will be busy weighing and mixing ingredients and may not be able to read a small, crowded card easily.

Table 2   Common abbreviations used in food production.

AP	As purchased	oz	Ounce
AS	As served	pkg	Package
c	Cup	psi	Pounds per square inch
EP	Edible portion	pt	Pint
°F	Degrees Fahrenheit	qt	Quart
fl oz	Fluid ounce	tsp	Teaspoon
gal	Gallon	Tbsp	Tablespoon
lb	Pound		

Recipes should be typed or printed and should be readable at a distance of 18 to 20 inches. Recipes that are used in the production or ingredient assembly areas should be placed in clear plastic covers to keep the copy clean.

In foodservices using a computer-assisted system, recipes are printed as needed and in the quantities required for the day's production. Because the printout is generated each time the recipe is used, it is considered a working copy and does not need a protective covering. An example of a computer-generated recipe is shown in Figure 3. The format for

```
                                                        PAGE:   2
               KITCHEN PRODUCTION RECIPE

Production Unit : 1  FOOD PRODUCTION CENTER    Prod Date : FRIDAY    01/30/04
Preparation Area: HOT FOOD PRODUCTION          Cust Count:  1900

================================================================
 0585  CHILI                              Yield   :    5.35 QUARTS

Prepare Main Batch  1 TIME(S)          Cooking Time : 1'35"
Ptn Desc :7 OZL                        Cooking Temp
Prep Time:                             Cooking Equip:
Portions :  23.0    7.44 OZ
----------------------------------------------------------------
     Ingredient        |------ Main Batch -------||----- Partial Batch -----|
                                    Quantity                  Quantity
----------------------------------------------------------------
SOAKED KIDNEY BEANS/SUB     1 LBS    4 1/2 OZS
MT GROUND BEEF W/TVP,3%      3 LBS    2     OZS
ONIONS DICED 1/4"/SUB                8 1/2 OZS
CELERY DICED 1/4"/SUB                13 1/2 OZS
TOMATOES DICED              1 LBS   12     OZS
TOMATO PASTE  6/#10/CS               1 2/3 CUP
WATER                       1 QT     3     CUP
SPICE CHILI PWDR DRK 18OZ   3 TBSP   1 1/2 TSP
SPICE BAY LEAVES 10OZ TUB            - TO TASTE -
SPICE OREGANO GRND PURE              1 3/4 TSP
SPICE CELERY SALT 30 OZ              1 3/4 TSP
VINEGAR WHITE 6GAL/CS       1 TBSP     1/2 TSP
SUGAR WHITE 50# BAG         1 TBSP     1/2 TSP
SPICE GARLIC GRANULATED              1     TSP
SALT IODIZED SHAKE SPOUT    1 TBSP   2 1/4 TSP
SPICE PEPPER CAYENN GRND             1     TSP
SPICE CUMIN GRND 14 OZ      1 TBSP   2 1/2 TSP
SAUCE TABASCO 24/2 OZ                  1/2 TSP
================================================================
                   METHOD OF PREPARATION
 1.  COOK KIDNEY BEANS IN STEAMER FOR 45 MIN. DRAIN 1/2 LIQUID.
 2.  BROWN GROUND BEEF.  DRAIN OFF FAT.
 3.  ADD REMAINING INGREDIENTS AND SIMMER 1 HOUR AND 30 MINUTES.
 4.  REMOVE BAY LEAVES.
 5.  PAN 8 QTS. PER 4 IN. FULL SIZED PAN.  RAPID CHILL.  COVER AND
     DATE.
DOUBLE AMOUNT OF KIDNEY BEANS AS OF 4/1/85  ANG.
INCREASED AMOUNT OF WATER AS OF 8/23/85.  CKS.
**NOTE.  2 LBS DRIED BEANS AFTER SOAKED AND COOKED EQUALS 1 #10 CAN.
11/6/88  INCREASED RECIPE. INCREASED CHILI POWDER.  ADDED CUMIN AND
     TABASCO SAUCE.
12/23/88 INCREASED SPICES.  DJS
9/96 CUT AMOUNT OF KIDNEY BEANS IN HALF BAC.

253 KCAL, 12 G FAT, 906 MG SODIUM PER SERVING (7/94)
```

```
               KITCHEN PRODUCTION RECIPE       PAGE:   3
                     CONTINUED
Production Unit : 1  FOOD PRODUCTION CENTER    Prod Date : FRIDAY    01/30/04
Preparation Area: HOT FOOD PRODUCTION          Cust Count:  1900

================================================================
 0585  CHILI                              Yield   :    5.35 QUARTS
----------------------------------------------------------------
                   RECIPE DISTRIBUTION
================================================================
     Unit           Date          Meal      Yield       Portions    Service Pan/Utensil/or Main Recipe
----------------------------------------------------------------
CAFETERIA        WEDNESDAY 02/04/04   LUNCH   5.35 QUARTS  23  7.44 OZ   FULL PAN 4"
                 Actual Distribution           <_____><      >
----------------------------------------------------------------
NOTES: 1. '*' FOLLOWING PORTION INFORMATION INDICATES ROUNDED QUANTITY
       2. '-' IN FRONT OF QUANTITY INDICATES RECIPE BY-PRODUCT
```

Figure 3 Example of computer-generated recipe.
Courtesy of the University of Wisconsin Hospital and Clinics, Food and Nutrition Services Department.

recipes in this type of system depends on the software purchased, so the format should be considered when comparing different software packages.

A recipe is considered standardized only when it has been tried and adapted for use in a given foodservice operation. Quantity recipes are available from many sources, such as cookbooks, trade journals, and materials distributed by commercial food companies from their own test kitchens, as well as from other foodservice managers. Regardless of the source, each recipe should be tested and evaluated, then standardized and adjusted for use in a particular situation.

The first step in standardizing a new recipe is to analyze the proportion of ingredients and clarity of instructions and to determine whether the recipe can be produced with the equipment and personnel available.

It is also important to assess the portion size defined for the original recipe to determine whether it is appropriate for the customer and financial objectives of the operation. For example, a recipe obtained from a restaurant would likely define portions in excess of what would be appropriate for a school or nursing home.

The recipe should then be tested. When doing so, make certain ingredients are weighed and measured accurately and that procedures are followed exactly. The yield, number, and size of portions as well as problems with preparation should be recorded.

Recipe Yield. Recipe yield is simply a measure of the total amount produced by a recipe. Recipe yield can be expressed in weight, measure, or count. For example, the yield of a soup recipe would be measured and expressed in quarts; a cake recipe would be measured and expressed in size and number of sheet pans; and the yield of a cookie recipe is measured and expressed by count. Figure 4 is an example of a recipe evaluation form that may be used to document actual recipe yield. Along with yield analysis, the finished products should be evaluated for acceptability based on predetermined quality standards. Some foodservices request that cooks note problems or inconsistencies directly on the working copies while the recipes are being used. These marked copies are then sent to the manager who in turn assesses the issues and adjusts the recipe as needed for the next production run.

Quality Standards. Quality standards are measurable statements of the aesthetic characteristics of food items, and they serve as the basis for sensory analysis of the prepared product. Quality aspects include appearance, color, flavor, texture, consistency, and temperature.

Figure 4 Recipe evaluation form.

Recipe Yield Evaluation

Menu Item: _____

Unit: _____

Date: _____

Total yield specified on recipe: _____

Did the recipe yield this amount? Yes: _____   No: _____

If no, what was the actual yield?

Explain any factors that may have contributed to the discrepancy.

Please provide any suggestion you have to improve this recipe. Consider ease of use, readability, format, layout, etc.

_____
Signature of employee

Score Card for Cake

Date _____

Factor	Qualities	Standard	1	2	3	Comments
I. External appearance	Shape, symmetrical, slightly rounded top, free from cracks or peaks	10				
	Volume, light in weight in proportion to size	10				
	Crust, smooth uniform golden brown	10				
II. Internal appearance	Texture tender, slightly moist, velvety feel to tongue and finger	10				
	Grain, fine, round, evenly distributed cells with thin cell walls, free from tunnels	10				
	Color, crumb even and rich looking	10				
III. Flavor	Delicate, well-blended flavor of ingredients. Free from unpleasant odors or taste	10				

Directions for use of score card for plain cake:

Standard	10	No detectable fault, highest possible score
Excellent	8–9	Of unusual excellence but not perfect
Good	6–7	Average good quality
Fair	4–5	Below average, slightly objectionable
Poor	2–3	Objectionable, but edible
Bad	0–1	Highly objectionable, inedible

Signature of evaluator

Figure 5 Suggested score card for evaluating cakes or muffins.

Figure 5 is an example of a score card for evaluating cakes and muffins and includes quality standards for shape, volume, color, texture, and flavor.

If the tested product is deemed suitable, the recipe is then adjusted to the quantities needed to meet production demand.

Recipe Adjustment

KEY CONCEPT: The factor and percentage methods are commonly used approaches for recipe formulation.

Two methods commonly used to adjust recipes are the factor method and the percentage method.

Factor Method. In the factor method, the quantities of ingredients in the original (or source) recipe are multiplied by a conversion factor, as explained in the following steps:

Step 1 Divide the desired yield by the known yield of the source recipe to obtain the conversion factor. For example, if the source recipe has a yield of 12 and the

Table 3 Adjusting a recipe from a yield of 12 to 75: African vegetable stew.

	STEP 1	STEP 2	STEP 3	STEP 4
INGREDIENTS	ORIGINAL RECIPE YIELD = 12	CONVERTED VOLUME MEASURES TO WEIGHTS	MULTIPLIED BY FACTOR	ROUNDED WEIGHTS
Onion, diced	3 c	1# (16 oz)	6.25#	6.25#
Swiss chard	3 bunches*	2.25# (36 oz)	14.063#	14#
Garbanzo beans	4.5 c	1.8# (28.8 oz)	11.25#	11.25#
Raisins	1.5 c	8 oz	3.125#	3#, 2 oz
Rice, raw	1.5 c	10 oz	3.9#	4#
Sweet potatoes	6 c	2#	12.5#	12.5#
Tomatoes	6 c	2.66# (43 oz)	16.23#	16.25#
Garlic	3 cloves	.5 oz	3.125 oz	3 oz

Factor: 75/12 = 6.25.

*Assume one bunch equals 12 oz.

desired yield is 75, then the factor is 6.25 (75 ÷ 12 = 6.25). Table 3 is an example of how a source recipe is adjusted using the factor method.

Step 2 Convert all volume measurements to weights, when possible. For example, 3 cups of water weighs 1 pound 8 ounces. For ease in figuring, weights should be expressed in pounds and decimal components of pounds; 1 pound 8 ounces is 1.5 pounds.

Step 3 Multiply the amount of each ingredient in the original recipe by the factor.

Step 4 Round off unnecessary or awkward fractions. Table 4 is a guide for rounding off weights and measures.

Percentage Method. In the percentage method, the percentage of the total weight of the product is calculated for each ingredient. Once this percentage has been established, it remains constant for all future adjustments. Recipe increases and decreases are made by multiplying the total weight desired by the percentage of each ingredient.

The percentage method is based on weights expressed in pounds and decimal parts of a pound. The total quantity to be prepared is based on the weight of each portion multiplied by the number of servings needed. The constant number used in calculating a recipe is the weight of each individual serving. A step-by-step procedure, as used at Kansas State University and reported by McManis and Molt (NACUFS J. 35, 1978), follows for adjusting a recipe by the percentage method:

Step 1 Convert all ingredients in the original recipe from measure or pounds and ounces to pounds and tenths of a pound. Make desired equivalent ingredient substitutions, such as fresh eggs for frozen whole eggs and powdered milk for liquid milk.

Step 2 Total the weight of ingredients in the recipe. Use EP weights when a difference exists between EP and AP weights. For example, the weight of onions or celery should be the weight after the foods have been cleaned, peeled, and are ready for use. The recipe may show both AP and EP weights, but the edible portion is used in determining the total weight.

Step 3 Calculate the percentage of each ingredient in relation to the total weight. Repeat for each ingredient. Use this formula:

Sum of percentages should total 100%

Table 4   Guide for rounding off weights and measures.

IF THE TOTAL AMOUNT OF AN INGREDIENT IS	ROUND IT TO
Weights	
Less than 2 oz	Measure unless weight is $\frac{1}{4}$-, $\frac{1}{2}$-, or $\frac{3}{4}$-oz amounts
2–10 oz	Closest $\frac{1}{4}$ or convert to measure
More than 10 oz but less than 2 lb 8 oz	Closest $\frac{1}{2}$ oz
2 lb 8 oz–5 lb	Closest full ounce
More than 5 lb	Closest $\frac{1}{4}$ lb
Measures	
Less than 1 Tbsp	Closest $\frac{1}{8}$ tsp
More than 1 Tbsp but less than 3 Tbsp	Closest $\frac{1}{4}$ tsp
3 Tbsp–$\frac{1}{2}$ cup	Closest full tsp or convert to weight
More than $\frac{1}{2}$ cup but less than $\frac{3}{4}$ cup	Closest full tsp or convert to weight
More than $\frac{3}{4}$ cup but less than 2 cups	Closest full Tbsp or convert to weight
2 cups–2 qt	Nearest $\frac{1}{4}$ cup
More than 2 qt but less than 4 qt	Nearest $\frac{1}{2}$ cup
1–2 gal	Nearest full cup or $\frac{1}{4}$ qt
More than 2 gal but less than 10 gal[a]	Nearest full quart
More than 10 gal but less than 20 gal[a]	Closest $\frac{1}{2}$ gal
More than 20 gal[a]	Closest full gallon

[a]For baked goods or products in which accurate ratios are critical, always round to the nearest full cup or $\frac{1}{4}$ qt.

NOTE: This table is intended to aid in rounding fractions and complex measurements into amounts that are as simple as possible to weigh or measure while maintaining the accuracy needed for quality control.

Source: Mary Molt, *Food for Fifty*, 12th ed. Copyright © 2006 by Pearson Prentice Hall. Used with permission.

Step 4 Check the ratio of ingredients, which should be in proper balance before going further. Standards have been established for ingredient proportions of many items.

Step 5 Determine the total weight of the product needed by multiplying the portion weight expressed in decimal parts of a pound by the number of servings to be prepared. To convert a portion weight to a decimal part of a pound, divide the number of ounces by 16 or refer to a decimal equivalent table (Table 5). For example, a 2-ounce portion would be 0.125 pound. This figure multiplied by the number of portions desired gives the total weight of product needed. The weight is then adjusted, as necessary, to pan size and equipment capacity. For example, the total weight must be divisible by the optimum weight for each pan. The capacity of mixing bowls, steam-jacketed kettles, and other equipment must be considered in determining the total weight. Use the established portion, modular pan charts, or known capacity equipment guides to determine batch sizes to include on recipes.

Step 6 Add estimated handling loss to the weight needed. An example of handling loss is the batter left in bowls or on equipment. This loss will vary according to the product being made and preparation techniques of the worker. Similar recipes, however, produce predictable losses, which with some experimentation can be accurately assigned. The formula for adding handling loss to a recipe follows.

Table 5 Ounces and decimal equivalents of a pound.

OUNCES	DECIMAL PART OF A POUND	OUNCES	DECIMAL PART OF A POUND
1/4	0.016	8 1/4	0.516
1/2	0.031	8 1/2	0.531
3/4	0.047	8 3/4	0.547
1	0.063	9	0.563
1 1/4	0.078	9 1/4	0.578
1 1/2	0.094	9 1/2	0.594
1 3/4	0.109	9 3/4	0.609
2	0.125	10	0.625
2 1/4	0.141	10 1/4	0.641
2 1/2	0.156	10 1/2	0.656
2 3/4	0.172	10 3/4	0.672
3	0.188	11	0.688
3 1/4	0.203	11 1/4	0.703
3 1/2	0.219	11 1/2	0.719
3 3/4	0.234	11 3/4	0.734
4	0.250	12	0.750
4 1/4	0.266	12 1/4	0.766
4 1/2	0.281	12 1/2	0.781
4 3/4	0.297	12 3/4	0.797
5	0.313	13	0.813
5 1/4	0.328	13 1/4	0.828
5 1/2	0.344	13 1/2	0.844
5 3/4	0.359	13 3/4	0.859
6	0.375	14	0.875
6 1/4	0.391	14 1/4	0.891
6 1/2	0.406	14 1/2	0.906
6 3/4	0.422	14 3/4	0.922
7	0.438	15	0.938
7 1/4	0.453	15 1/4	0.953
7 1/2	0.469	15 1/2	0.969
7 3/4	0.484	15 3/4	0.984
8	0.500	16	1.000

NOTE: This table is useful when increasing or decreasing recipes. The multiplication or division of pounds and ounces is simplified if the ounces are converted to decimal parts of a pound. For example, when multiplying 1 lb 9 oz by 3, first change the 9 oz to 0.563, by using the table. Thus, the 1 lb 9 oz becomes 1.563 lb, which multiplied by 3 is 4.683 lb or 4 lb 11 oz.

Table 6   Original recipe for muffins (yield: 60 muffins).

INGREDIENTS	AMOUNT
Flour, all-purpose	2 lb 8 oz
Baking powder	2 oz
Salt	1 Tbsp
Sugar	6 oz
Eggs, beaten	4
Milk	1½ qt
Shortening	8 oz

Step 7   Multiply each percentage number by the total weight to give the exact amount of each ingredient needed. Once the percentages of a recipe have been established, any number of servings can be calculated and the ratio of ingredients to the total will be the same. One decimal place on a recipe is shown (e.g., 8.3 lb) unless it is less than one pound; then two places are shown (e.g., 0.15 lb).

Tables 6 to 8 illustrate the expansion of a recipe for muffins from 60 to 340 servings.

Adapting Small-Quantity Recipes.   Many quantity recipes can be successfully expanded from home-size recipes, but their development involves a number of carefully planned steps. Before attempting to enlarge a small recipe, be sure that it is appropriate to the food-service and that the same quality can be achieved when prepared in large quantity and held for a time before serving. Procedures should be checked because many home recipes lack detailed directions for their preparation. Before preparing the product, the extent of mixing, the time and temperature used in cooking or baking, and special precautions that should be observed and any other details that may have been omitted should be determined.

If using pounds and ounces, change decimal part of pounds to ounces by using Table 5. If using measures for some ingredients, adjust to measurable amounts.

Enlarging the recipe in steps is more likely to be successful than increasing from a small quantity to a large quantity without the intermediate steps.

Table 7   Percentage calculated on original recipe (yield: 60 muffins).

PERCENTAGE	INGREDIENTS	MEASURE	POUNDS
35.79	Flour	2 lb 8 oz	2.500
1.79	Baking powder	2 oz	0.125
0.67	Salt	1 T	0.047
5.37	Sugar	6 oz	0.375
6.27	Eggs	4	0.438
42.95	Milk	1½ qt	3.000
7.16	Shortening	8 oz	0.500
100.00	Total		6.985

6.985 lb divided by 60 = 0.116 lb per muffin.

Table 8	Expanded recipe for muffins (yield: 340 muffins).	
POUNDS	**PERCENTAGE**	**INGREDIENTS**
14.260	35.79	Flour
0.713	1.79	Baking powder
0.267	0.67	Salt
2.140	5.37	Sugar
2.500	6.27	Eggs
17.110	42.95	Milk
2.850	7.16	Shortening
39.840	100.00	Total

.116 lb per muffin $\times$ 340 = 39.44 lb with 1% handling loss, 39.84 lb batter needed, 39.84 lb $\times$ % each ingredient = weight of ingredient.

Suggestions follow for a step-by-step approach for expanding home-size recipes.

Step 1 Prepare the product in the amount of the original recipe, following exactly the quantities and procedures, noting any procedures that are unclear or any problems with the preparation.

Step 2 Evaluate the product, using a written form such as that shown in Figure 4, and decide if it has potential for the foodservice. If adjustments are necessary, revise the recipe and make the product again. Work with the original amount until the product is satisfactory.

Step 3 Double the recipe or expand to the appropriate amount for the pan size that will be used and prepare the product, making notations on the recipe of any changes you make. For example, additional cooking time may be needed for the larger amount. Evaluate the product and record the yield, portion size, and acceptability.

Step 4 Double the recipe again, or if the product is to be baked, calculate the quantities needed to prepare one baking pan that will be used by the foodservice. If ingredients are to be weighed, home-size measures should be converted to pounds and ounces or to pounds and tenths of a pound before proceeding further. Prepare and evaluate the product as before.

Step 5 If the product is satisfactory, continue to enlarge by increments of 25 portions or by pans. When the recipe has been expanded to 100 or some other specific amount that would be used in the foodservice, adjustments should be made for handling or cooking losses. Handling loss refers to losses that occur in making and panning batters. About 3 percent to 5 percent more of batter, sauces, and puddings is required to compensate for the handling loss. Cooking losses result from evaporation of water from the food during cooking. Soups, stews, and casseroles can lose from 10 percent to 30 percent of their water in cooking. The actual yield of the recipe should be checked carefully. Mixing, preparation, and cooking times should be noted because these may increase when the product is prepared in large quantities. Preparation methods should be checked to see if they are consistent with methods used for similar products. An evaluation of the product should be made and its acceptance by the clientele determined before it becomes a part of the permanent recipe file.

FORECASTING DEMAND

■ **KEY CONCEPT: Estimates of production demand can be determined through forecasting.**

The goal of forecasting is to estimate future demand using past data. Applied to foodservice, **forecasting** is a prediction of food needs for a day or other specific time period. Forecasting differs from tallying, which is a simple count of menu items actually requested or selected by the customers. Production planning begins with the menu and the production forecast. Other foodservice functions, such as purchasing, are triggered by the forecast. Sound forecasting is vital to financial management; it facilitates efficient scheduling of labor, use of equipment, and space.

Forecasting
A prediction of food needs for a day or other specific period of time

Reasons for Forecasting

Some lead time is needed to complete all phases of menu item preparation: purchasing, storage, thawing, pre-preparation, production, distribution, and final service. Forecasting serves as a means of communication with purchasing and food production staff to ensure that all of these stages are completed in a timely manner and that the final product meets standards of quality.

The purchasing representative needs to know how much food to order and when it needs to be available for use in the foodservice production area. The hot and cold food production staff(s) need to know how many servings of each menu item are needed, in what form, and for which service unit (e.g., cafeteria, vending, patients, or catering).

Accurate forecasting minimizes the chance of overproduction or underproduction—both of which have serious consequences. Without proper guidelines, production employees have a tendency to overproduce food for fear of running short of actual need. This can be a costly comfort measure. Leftover food is often held for later service or redirected to an alternate service unit such as the cafeteria or vending or catering services. Each choice is risky in that the food may not meet quality standards at point-of-service, thereby risking customer dissatisfaction.

Underproduction can be costly as well and result in customer dissatisfaction. To compensate for shortages, managers often substitute expensive heat-and-serve items, such as ready-prepared chicken cordon bleu. More serious than increased raw food costs, however, is the risk of upsetting a customer by providing him or her with a substitute menu item that was not ordered. Foodservice employees may get frustrated if food shortages occur too frequently, resulting in rushed, last-minute food preparation or delayed service.

In small health care organizations, such as long-term care facilities or hospitals, amounts to be produced can be determined by simple tally, especially if the patient census is stable and a nonselective menu is used. In large organizations with multiple service units, more sophisticated forecasting may be beneficial, especially if there is wide variation in menu item demand. A tally system would be far too time-consuming for these larger, more complex organizations. Regardless of the size and complexity of the foodservice organization, a good forecasting system is based on sound historical data that reflect the pattern of actual menu item demand in the foodservice operation.

■ KEY CONCEPT: **Consistent and comprehensive collection of data is essential for accurate and reliable forecasting.**

Historical Data

Historical or past data are used to determine needs and to establish trends in all forecasting methods. To be of value, these data must be consistently and accurately recorded. Categories of data to collect vary depending on the type of foodservice organization, scope of services provided, and whether customers are allowed to select menu items. The following are a few examples of data categories for various organizations:

Restaurants/Cafeterias

- Customers served per meal
- Menu items sold per meal period
- Beverage sales (types and amounts)

Schools

- Student enrollment
- Students purchasing full USDA meal
- À la carte items sold per lunch period
- Teachers and staff purchasing meals

Hospitals

- Daily patient census
- Patients on therapeutic diets
- Daily patient admissions and discharges

Vending Services

- Product placed in machine at each fill
- Total cash removed
- Food remaining in machine at each refill

Records designed for individual service units are used to document and collect data. Figure 6 is an example of a form designed to document meal participation in a school lunch program. All service records should include a space to document total meals served per unit and whether there were leftovers or shortages. Over time, a pattern of menu item demand or total meals served will emerge from the recorded data. This pattern, along with knowledge of pattern variance, will assist the production planner in making a valid estimate of future menu item demand. Factors influencing pattern variance include holidays, weather conditions, and special events.

Criteria for Selecting a Forecasting Method

Careful planning and evaluation are essential in selecting the best forecasting method for a given foodservice operation. Numerous computer forecasting models have been developed during the past several years, which are a great aid to the foodservice manager. However, regardless of whether a manual or computer-assisted method is chosen, several factors should be considered before deciding on a forecasting system. These factors include cost, accuracy, relevancy, lead time, pattern of food selection, ease of use, level of detail, and responsiveness to changes. Table 9 is a summary of the considerations related to each of these factors.

Forecast Models

Types of forecasting models include moving average, exponential smoothing, regression, and autoregressive moving average (Box-Jenkins). These models are mathematical descriptions of meals served or of menu item selection behavior. The information for the mathematical models is based on historical data and is expressed as an average of past service or selection behavior.

The moving average and exponential smoothing models are commonly used in foodservices for production forecasting. Figure 7 illustrates the calculations for the moving average model and gives an example of how this method is used with past data from a small hospital. The number of customers served from a foodservice is generally different on each day of the week. For this reason, forecasts are calculated for intervals of seven days. For example, in a hospital, data collected on Mondays are used to forecast needs for future Mondays.

The *moving average* model is referred to as a time series method of forecasting and is easy to use. Using records from the past, a group of data is averaged and used as the first forecast. The next forecast is calculated by dropping the first number and adding the next. This process continues for all data available.

The *exponential smoothing* model is another time series model, similar to the moving average technique except that it accounts for seasonality of data and adjusts for forecast

DAILY PARTICIPATION RECORD
LUNCH PROGRAM

School _____   Month _____

Days of Operation	Students				Adults		Second Lunches	Field Trips
	Paid (1)	Reduced (3)	Free (2)	Total	*Program	**Non Program		
1								
2								
3								
4								
5								
6								
7								
8								
9								
10								
11								
12								
13								
14								
15								
16								
17								
18								
19								
20								
21								
22								
23								
24								
25								
26								
27								
28								
29								
30								
31								
Monthly Total								

* Program Adults: all food service workers. Adult meals are not reimbursable.

** Nonprogram Adults: Teachers, administrators, office workers, janitors, and any occasional visitors. Adult meals are not reimbursable.

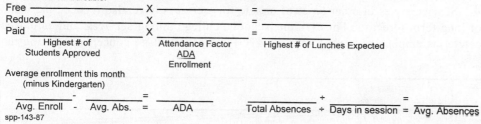

Free _____ X _____ = _____

Reduced _____ X _____ = _____

Paid _____ X _____ = _____

Highest # of Students Approved   Attendance Factor ADA Enrollment   Highest # of Lunches Expected

Average enrollment this month (minus Kindergarten)

_____ - _____ = _____   _____ ÷ _____ = _____
Avg. Enroll - Avg. Abs. = ADA   Total Absences ÷ Days in session = Avg. Absences

spp-143-87

Figure 6 Sample form for lunch participation in a school lunch program. Courtesy Sun Prairie Area School District, Wisconsin.

error. This results in a higher level of forecast accuracy. The simple exponential smoothing model predicts the next demand by weighting the data; more recent data are weighted more heavily than older data. The factor used to weight the data is referred to as *alpha*. Alpha is determined statistically and, in foodservice forecasting, is generally valued at 0.3. The purpose of alpha is to adjust for any errors in previous forecasts.

Regression and *autoregressive moving average* models are sophisticated statistical methods in which past data are analyzed to determine the best mathematical approach to forecasting. These methods generally require the assistance of a statistician and are used with computer-assisted forecasting systems.

Table 9   Criteria for selecting a forecasting system.

FACTOR	CONSIDERATIONS
Costs	Development, implementation, and system operational costs (e.g., data collection, analysis) are reasonable; that is, within budgetary guidelines Training and education for staff
Accuracy/relevancy	Past data and food selection patterns are relevant and accurately reflect current demand
Lead time	System allows adequate time for purchasing, delivery, and production Accounts for perishability of food items
Pattern of behavior	System can be adjusted for changes in menu item demand as a result of seasonality and consumer preference
Ease of use	Use of system is easily understood What knowledge and skills are required to operate system?
Level of detail	System can generate desired forecasts What is to be forecasted?
Responsiveness	System generates accurate information on a timely basis

Trends in Predicting Production Demand

█ **KEY CONCEPT:** **Numerous factors, internal and external to the foodservice, influence production demand.**

Trends in food preferences and service styles have greatly influenced the use of formal forecasting methods, especially in on-site foodservice operations. Some hospitals, for example, rely less on formal forecasting for patient meals today, compared to the recent past, for the following reasons:

- Huge day-to-day fluctuations in patient census
- Short length of stay/high patient turnover
- Rapidly changing and increasingly complicated diet orders
- Implementation of room service/meals-on-demand service concepts

Service styles in other types of on-site foodservices have also reduced the value of long-term forecasts. For example, schools, college dining services, and employee cafeterias emphasize made-to-order (MTO) and grab-and-go concepts, reducing the

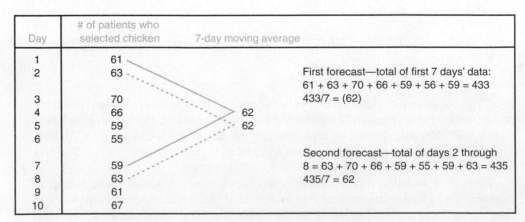

Figure 7   Moving average model applied to one item on selective menu.

need to predict demand in advance. More and more, these operations are predicting demand based simply on past demand and establishing par levels that are adjusted as needed on day of service. The very simple approach is to ask the following questions: How many did we serve last time? Do we have any stock? Has anything changed since last time?

QUANTITIES TO PRODUCE

The forecast is the basis for estimating in advance the quantities of menu items to be prepared and foods to be purchased or requisitioned from the storerooms. Forecasts are often adjusted at the time of actual production because of influences that were unforeseen at the time the forecasts were calculated. For example, forecasts in schools often need to be reduced during the cold and flu seasons to account for children who are ill and at home. The weather can have a profound impact; for example, participation in lunch programs increases as the weather gets colder in fall and more students prefer to eat indoors. Conversely, a sudden snowstorm can cause customer volume to plummet for retail operations, including restaurants and cafeterias. It is during these periods that the food manager uses his or her intuition to make last-minute adjustments to the forecast. The actual amount of food prepared is based on the number of persons to be served, portion size, and the amount of waste and shrinkage loss in the preparation of foods.

Recipes adjusted to the predicted number of portions needed provide much of this information. Most quantity recipes for noncomputerized systems are calculated in modules of 50 or 100 or, in foods such as cakes or casserole-type entrées, to pan sizes and equipment capacity. For example, if a recipe produces 2 sheet cakes, which can be cut into 30 or 32 servings each, 3 cakes (or one and one-half times the recipe) would be required for 75 portions. When very large quantities are produced, the amount to prepare in one batch is limited to the capacity of the production equipment.

In foodservices that are computerized, recipes are printed daily and provide amounts for the exact number of individual portions, or are adjusted to the number of pans or other modules required to serve the predicted numbers. To be effective, computer-assisted programs include recipes for all menu items offered, including fresh vegetables and fruits, salads, relishes, and meats, such as roast beef or baked pork chops. Quantities to purchase or requisition are readily available from these computer-generated recipes. In foodservices without a computer-assisted system, standardizing and calculating recipes for more than one amount lessens the need for refiguring the quantities for each forecast.

A general procedure for determining amounts of meats, poultry, fruits, and vegetables follows:

Step 1 Determine the portion size in ounces.

Step 2 Multiply portion size by the estimated number to be served and convert to pounds. This is the EP required.

$$\frac{\text{ounces} \times \text{number of portions}}{16 \text{ oz}} = \frac{\text{number of pounds EP}}{\text{required}}$$

Step 3 To determine the amount to order, divide the EP weight by the yield percentage (or the weight in decimal parts of a pound of ready-to-eat or ready-to-cook product from ONE pound of the commodity as purchased). A yield guide is included in Appendix: Principles of Basic Cooking.

$$\frac{\text{EP weight}}{\text{yield}} = \text{amount of order}$$

Step 4 For foods to be purchased, convert the amount needed to the most appropriate purchase unit (e.g., case, crate, or roast). If the food is to be used for other menu items, combine the amounts and then convert to purchase units.

As an example, if 3-ounce portions of fresh asparagus are needed for 50 people, one would calculate the amount to purchase in the following way:

1. $3 \text{ oz} \times 50 \text{ portions} = \dfrac{150 \text{ oz}}{16 \text{ oz}} = 9.375 \text{ lbs of EP needed}$

2. $\dfrac{9.375 \text{ lbs needed}}{0.53 \text{ lb yield from 1 lb as purchased}} = 17.68 \text{ lbs to purchase}$

3. Convert to purchase unit, 18 lb to 20 lb

In a computer system, these figures would be calculated automatically from the forecast, portion size, and yield data.

PRODUCTION SCHEDULING

> **KEY CONCEPT:** **Clear communication between management and the production staff is essential for successful production.**

Formulating recipes, forecasting demand, and calculating quantities to produce are all part of the planning phase of production. The next and last phase of this planning process is the scheduling of actual cooking of the menu items. *Production scheduling* is a decision-making and communication process whereby the production staff is informed of how the actual activity of food preparation is to take place over a specified unit of time. This unit of time may be a day or a specific work shift for a production team; 5 A.M. to 1:30 P.M., for example. The purpose of production scheduling is to ensure efficient use of time, equipment, and space by identifying:

1. What menu items to prepare
2. What quantities to produce
3. When individual items are to be produced
4. Who is to prepare each item

Thoughtful production planning minimizes production problems and maximizes product quality. This aspect of the production planning phase is particularly important in large, multiunit foodservice operations where hundreds of menu items may be produced over the course of a day.

Foods prepared too far in advance are at increased risk for quality deterioration, low yield, and microbial contamination. On the other hand, the manager who schedules production too close to service runs the risk of delaying service or creating chaos in the production.

Production scheduling requires a knowledge of the steps through which a menu item must go from the time ingredients are assembled to the point of service. This sequence is referred to as the flow of food. Each step must be carefully monitored to ensure that each of the cooking objectives is achieved and maintained, and that products are ready for service units on time for distribution.

Depending on the type of foodservice system in operation, the sequence of food flow may include some or all of the following phases of production:

- Preparation of ingredients, including thaw time for frozen meats, cleaning and peeling vegetables, retrieving and assembling dry ingredients
- Production of menu items, including combining ingredients and cooking
- Holding under appropriate conditions: frozen, refrigerated, hot-hold
- Transport and service to customers

When planning for production, the food manager accounts for the time required for each one of these steps for each recipe and then schedules the activity of production accordingly.

```
                                                              PAGE:
                    PRODUCTION RECIPE

FUNCTION NAME:
        UNIT:
        DATE: FRIDAY     06/18/99
================================================================================
4675  BEEF BURGUNDY PATIENTS                 YIELD   :    21.84 QTS

-----------------------------------------------------------------------
PORTIONS :     174.72      6.00 OZ    COOKING TIME :
PORTION DESC : 4 OZL                  COOKING TEMP :
PREP TIME:                            COOKING EQUIP:
                                      SERVING PAN  :
PREPARE MAIN BATCH   1 TIME(S)        SERVING UTEN : #8 SCOOP (4-5 OZ)
-----------------------------------------------------------------------
     INGREDIENT          -------- MAIN BATCH --------   ------ PARTIAL BATCH ------
                                  QUANTITY                      QUANTITY

-----------------------------------------------------------------------
BEEF STEW MEAT SUB BROWN     33 LBS   4      OZS
ONIONS DICED 1/4"/SUB         1 LBS   5      OZS
ROSE WINE GAL INGLENOOK       1 QT    3      CUP
BEEF SF STOCK/SUB             3 GAL   1      QT
CELERY DICED 1/4"/SUB         1 LBS   5      OZS
SALT IODIZED SHAKE SPOUT      1 CUP   1      TBSP
SAUCE WORCESTERSHIRE 4/GL            1/2 CUP
SPICE CELERY SALT 30 OZ       1 TBSP   1/2 TSP
SPICE THYME GROUND 11 OZ      1 TBSP  2 1/4 TSP
SPICE PEPPR WHTE GRND 160     1 TBSP   1/2 TSP
VEGI MUSHROOMS FRESH 10LB     5 LBS   4      OZS
CARAMEL COLOR 32 OZ BT               1/2 CUP
WAXIE MAIZE WASH/SUB               49 OZL
================================================================================
                    METHOD OF PREPARATION
****BEFORE PREPARATION SEE HACCP NOTES BELOW****
1. BROWN BEEF TIPS UNTIL THEY'RE BROWN. ADD ONIONS AND CELERY. SAUTE
UNTIL THE ONIONS ARE TRANPARENTS, ADD THE BEEF STOCK AND SIMMER UNTIL
MEAT IS TENDER.
2. ADD THE SEASONINGS AND WHIP IN THE STARCHES TO THICKEN THE SAUCE.
3. SIMMER THE MIXTURE FOR 20 MINUTES.
4. PAN 6 QTS PER 4 IN FULL SIZE PAN.
11/08/96 CHEF JERRY
```

Figure 8 Example of a complex recipe.
Courtesy of the University of Wisconsin Hospital and Clinics, Department of Food and Nutrition Services, Madison, Wisconsin.

The recipe for Beef Burgundy in Figure 8 offers a perfect example of why a complex recipe necessitates advance planning and careful scheduling. The sequence of production planning and cooking of this product in a cook/chill system for a patient meal service in a hospital would unfold as follows:

Monday: Beef stew meat is pulled from the freezer and placed in the tempering refrigerator for a controlled thaw.

Tuesday: Dry ingredients are weighed, measured, and packaged for the production unit in the central ingredient assembly area.

Wednesday: Cooks prepare the recipe, pan it, and transfer it to a blast chiller for holding.

Friday: Product is transferred to a refrigerated entrée station on a trayline for final assembly and distribution to patient units, where it is held under refrigeration until it is heated for service.

Production of entire recipes as described in this example is appropriate for menu items that hold well and will be portioned and served quickly. Other recipes and situations, however, may call for variations on production methods and scheduling of production. Cooked fresh vegetables, for example, lose their nutritional and aesthetic qualities if prepared by the "bath" method (boiling in water) and do not hold well for any length of time. For menu items such as this, a method called batch cooking is used. Batch cooking is a variation of production scheduling whereby the total quantity of a recipe is divided into smaller batch sizes and cooked as needed rather than all at once. For example, fresh, steamed broccoli spears are on the cafeteria menu, and 257 servings have been forecasted. The cleaned and trimmed spears could be placed in 2-inch steam pans of 25 servings each and held in a refrigerator. Individual pans would be cooked in a high-speed piece of equipment such as a compartment or jet steamer and transferred to the cafeteria just in time for service. Rice and pastas are often produced using batch cooking.

Production Schedules

A production schedule is a detailed document used to communicate with/to the production staff the work that needs to be done for a specific period of time. An individual production schedule or sheet may represent an entire day or a specific work shift (e.g., 5 P.M. to 1:30 A.M. each shift). Well-designed production sheets will include:

- Work to be done, usually expressed as the specific menu items to be produced within the defined period of time
- Who is to perform the specific tasks
- Amounts of individual menu items to produce
- Source recipe, identified by name and code number
- Standard portion sizes and variations for specific service units and for modified diets
- Target completion times

Other information may be included to meet the needs of the operation and ensure clear, concise communication with the staff. Figure 9 is an example of a production schedule for a multiunit health care system that serves patient units, cafeterias, vending locations, a food court, and a catering division.

Production Meetings

A meeting with the production staff to discuss the menu and production plans heightens the effectiveness of the written production schedule. Such meetings generally do not need to be long, but they should be held regularly and at a time when activity in the production area is at a minimum. At meeting time, the menu can be explained and special instructions given for the items as needed. Employees also have an opportunity to discuss the schedule and any production problems they may anticipate.

No amount of paperwork can replace the human element in food production. Food must be prepared by people, and no matter how carefully plans are made and how many instructions are written, a manager must monitor and be involved in the production process to be certain that the menu as served measures up to the menu as planned.

PRODUCTION CONTROL

Ingredient Assembly

KEY CONCEPT: Ingredient assembly, as a distinct and separate function, is a common control in high-volume foodservice operations.

Central assembly of ingredients for food production has been found to be cost-effective in many operations. In this system, the ingredients needed for recipes for the day's production

RES HALLS COMM P
Print Date: 4/16/2010 14:05:57

Unit Distribution Spreadsheet
Report Period: 4/15/2010–4/15/2010
Page 4 of 4

Meal: PM   **Prep Area: PM**

Thursday, April 15, 2010

Keyname	Item Name	Issue Unit	CARS	CCAT	FRAN	LIZ	Newell's	POPS	Rheta's M PI
0343502518	Beef Hamburger Noodle-rhc	HPN				9.00		10.00	7.00
BeefHli-RHC	Beef Hard Salami-RHC	Pound	8.00						3.00
0690605990	Coffeecake Blueberry Homemade(24)-rhc	PN-24						1.00	
0690405988	Coffeecake Cherry(24)-rhc	PN-24			2.00	1.00		2.00	1.00
Crustd-rhc	Crust Pie Unbaked-rhc	PPN				1.00			
0000000481	c-Taco Plate/chips-rhc	PLATE/20					2.00		
0131405593	C-veg/French Onion Dip Platter-rhc	3# PLATE					1.00		
0138305765	Ee Burrito Bean & Cheese	HPN-12		3.00					
0081705797	Ee Juice Orange Tropicana - 64oz	64 oz. bottle		4.00					
EeParfait	Ee Parfait	4.3 oz portion		40.00					
0054400633	Pork Sausage In Country Gravy-rhc	HPN-12			6.00	2.00		3.00	2.00
0151200154	Salad Tabbculeh-rhc	2 LB CTN							1.00
Sauce Ancho Base	Sauce Ancho Base-RHC	Pound						2.00	
sauce Tequila Li	Sauce Tequila Lime-RHC	Quart				2.00			
Snackw-RHC	Snack Mix Puppy Chow-RHC	Pound					3.00		
TOGOCe-rhc	TO GO Cantaloupe - rhc	7.5 oz Cup	5.00		3.00		3.00	8.00	2.00
TOGOCp-rhc	TO GO Carrots w/Dip - rhc	8 oz Cup	10.00		4.00	1.00	2.00	8.00	2.00
TOGOCr-rhc	TO GO Celery w/Peanut Butter- rhc	6.5 oz Cup	10.00		2.00		2.00	10.00	2.00
TOGOGs-rhc	TO GO Grapes - rhc	6.4 oz. bag			3.00	1.00	3.00	16.00	2.00
ToGoPapple	TO GO Pineapple -rhc	7.5 oz Cup	5.00		4.00	1.00	5.00	25.00	2.00
TOGOTd-rhE	TO GO Tuna Macaroni Salad - rhc	5 oz portion	10.00		4.00		8.00	16.00	2.00
Dveggies-rhc	TO GO Veggies and Dip - RHC	7.73 oz. portion					4.00		
0313306131	Torte Blueberry-rhc	HPN-12			2.00	1.00		1.00	2.00

Figure 9a Examples of a production schedule.
Courtesy of UW Housing, Dining and Culinary Services.

MCPASD Central Kitchen Food Service—Daily Menu Production Plan

Program: USDA CN   Traditional OVS

Date:

Initials:

Number of Meals Planned, Forecasted & Shipped:

KMS	
MHS	
Adults	
Total:	

USDA Credit ***	Menu Product	Recipe # or Product Description	Process 1, 2, 3	Temp (°F)	Time	Quantity Prepared	Serving Utensil	Grades 6–12 Portion	Grades 6–12 Planned Servings	Adult Portion	Adult Planned Servings	&& Leftover
All	Turkey Sack		1	n/a	n/a			1 ea		1 ea		
All	PBJ Sack		1	n/a	n/a			1 ea		1 ea		

*** B/G = Bread/Grain   M/MA = Meat or Meat Alternate   F/V = Fruit or Vegetable

&& Returned Product recorded by pans or fractions of pans and product destination denoted as: W = waste R = refrigerated or F = frozen for later use

Figure 9b   (Continued)

Courtesy of Middleton Cross Plains Area School District. Used with permission.

and for advance preparation are weighed, measured, and assembled in a central ingredient room or area. If pre-preparation equipment and low-temperature storage are available, certain other procedures such as peeling, dicing, and chopping of vegetables; breading and panning of meats; opening of canned goods; and thawing of frozen foods can be completed in the ingredient area. The extent of responsibilities depends on the space, equipment, and personnel available.

After ingredients have been weighed or measured and the pre-preparation completed, each ingredient is packaged in a plastic bag or other container and labeled. The ingredients for each recipe are assembled and delivered, with a copy of the recipe, to the appropriate production unit. In some operations, the assembled ingredients are distributed when needed according to a predetermined schedule.

There are many advantages to centralized ingredient assembly. Increased production control, improved security, consistent quality control, and efficient use of equipment, especially if pre-preparation is included in this area, are possible with central ingredient assembly. Because cooks are not involved in the time-consuming job of weighing and measuring ingredients, their time and skills can be used more effectively in production.

There are some potential disadvantages, the main one being the lack of flexibility. For example, the ingredients must be weighed the day before, or earlier in some cases, which does not provide for last-minute changes in menus or quantities needed. Cooks may feel restricted by not being able to add their own touches to the food they are preparing. This concern is usually alleviated when cooks are allowed to adjust seasonings at the point of production.

Personnel and Equipment. Accuracy in measuring ingredients contributes to the acceptability of the finished product, so it is important that the ingredient room personnel be well qualified and that they be provided with adequate equipment.

Personnel assigned to the ingredient room must be able to read, write, and perform simple arithmetic. Safety precautions and sanitation standards should be stressed in their training.

Weighing is the quickest, easiest, and most accurate means of measure, so good scales are essential. A scale that accurately weighs up to 25 pounds is usually adequate, but if larger quantities are needed, the ingredients are divided in two or three lots for easier handling. Some foodservices have separate scales for ingredients needed in small amounts. If scales for measuring small amounts are not available, volume measures are an acceptable alternative for ingredients such as herbs and spices.

A list of other equipment to be included in a centralized ingredient area follows:

- Worktable, 6 to 8 feet long, with one or two drawers
- Counter scales, with gradations of 1 ounce minimum to 25 pounds
- Mobile storage bins for sugar, flour, and other large-volume staples
- Shelving for bulk staples and spices
- Mobile racks for delivery of foods to production areas
- Refrigeration (and freezer if frozen foods are distributed)
- Sink and water supply
- Can opener
- Trash receptacles
- Counter pans with lids if canned foods are opened
- Trays for assembling ingredients
- Rubber spatulas
- Measuring utensils (gallon, quart, pint, cup measures; measuring spoons)
- Scoops for dipping flour and sugar
- Packaging materials (paper and plastic bags, paper cups)
- Masking tape and marking pens to label ingredients

If vegetable preparation is also done in the ingredient room, the following additional equipment is needed:

- Double or triple sink
- Waste disposal

- Peeling, slicing, and dicing equipment
- Cutting boards
- Assorted knives and sharpening equipment
- Plastic tubs or bags for cleaned products

Portion Control

KEY CONCEPT: **Portion control is used to contain costs and ensure nutrient composition of menu items.**

Compliance with previously established portion sizes for individual menu items is an important part of the production function. Standardized portions are important not only for cost control, but also in creating and maintaining consumer satisfaction and goodwill. No one likes to receive a smaller serving than another customer for the same price.

Food is portioned by weight, measure, or count. Some portion control can be integrated into the purchasing function. Portioned meats, fish, and poultry; fresh fruits ordered by size (count per shipping box); canned peaches, pears, pineapple slices, and other foods in which the number of pieces is specified are examples. Other examples include the purchase of individual butter and margarine pats and individually packaged crackers, cereals, and condiments.

A knowledge of common can sizes is also helpful in portion control. For example, No. 10 cans are common in large-volume operations. They generally come packed six to a case, and each can contains approximately 12 cups of product.

Table 10	Dipper (or scoop) equivalents.		
DIPPER NO.*	**APPROXIMATE MEASURE**	**APPROXIMATE WEIGHT**	**SUGGESTED USE**
6	10 T (⅔ c)	6 oz	Entrée salads
8	8 T (½ c)	4–5 oz	Entrées
10	6 T (⅜ c)	3–4 oz	Desserts
12	5 T (⅓ c)	2½–3 oz	Muffins, salads, desserts
16	4 T (¼ c)	2–2¼ oz	Muffins, desserts
20	3⅕ T	1¾–2 oz	Sandwich fillings, muffins, cupcakes
24	2⅔ T	1½–1¾ oz	Cream puffs
30	2⅕ T	1–1½ oz	Large drop cookies
40	1½ T	¾ oz	Drop cookies
60	1 T	½ oz	Small drop cookies, garnishes
Ladles	⅛ c	1 oz	Sauces, salad dressings
	¼ c	2 oz	Gravies, sauces
	½ c	4 oz	Stews, creamed foods
	⅔ c	6 oz	Stews, creamed foods
	1 c	8 oz	Soup

These measurements are based on level dippers and ladles.

*Portions per quart.

Menu Item	Portion	Utensil
Meats		
Bacon	2 strips	Tongs
Canadian bacon	2 oz. slice	Tongs
Sausage, links (16 per lb.)	2 each	Tongs
Mixed fruit	½ c. (4 oz)	Spoodle, slotted
Juices, pre-portioned	4 oz.	N.A.
Breads		
Toast	2 slices	Tongs
Sweet rolls	1 each	Tongs
Coffee cakes, 18 × 26″ pan	6 × 10 cut	Spatula
Biscuits	1, 2 oz.	Tongs
Muffins	1, 2½ oz.	Tongs
Pancakes	3, 1 oz. each	Spatula
Hot cereal	¾ c. (6 oz)	Ladle
Dry cereal, pre-portioned boxes	1 each	N.A.
Eggs		
Scrambled	¼ cup	#16 scoop
Omelette	3 oz. each	Spatula

Figure 10 Example of portion guide for breakfast items.

During food production, portions are measured by scoop or dipper or are weighed on portion scales. For example, the recipe for meatballs may call for dipping the mixture before cooking with a size 16 dipper (or scoop), which results in a ¼-cup or 2-ounce portion. The numbering system for scoop sizes is based on the number of scoops per quart. Table 10 shows approximate dipper and ladle sizes. Dippers range from size 6 (10 tablespoons/6 ounces) to size 100, which holds a scant 2 teaspoons.

Ladles, used for serving sauces, soups, and other liquids, are sized according to capacity (1 ounce/⅛ cup to 8 ounces/1 cup). Although spoons are used for serving some foods, they are not particularly accurate. Spoodles are the utensil of choice for vegetables. Cakes and pies can be portioned accurately using scoring aids.

Employees should know the number of servings expected from a certain batch size and should be familiar with the size of the portion. In addition to the information included on recipes, a list of portion sizes for all foods should be made available to employees either in an employees' manual or posted in a convenient location (see Figure 10).

PRODUCT EVALUATION

As mentioned earlier in this chapter, product evaluation is part of the initial testing phase of a new recipe and is important for quality control. Product evaluation or sensory analysis is actually an ongoing process to ensure that the yield expectations and quality standards established during the recipe standardization process are met each time a menu item is produced.

Many foodservice organizations conduct sensory analysis just prior to meal service. This analysis is best done by a team or panel of persons knowledgeable about product standards and trained to judge quality characteristics in the interest of the customers. Figure 11 is an example of a sensory analysis form.

	RECIPE TESTING Date: _____ Place: _____ Time: _____							
Item	On a scale of 1 to 5, with 5 being the highest, please rank the following:			Comments	Would you buy?		Add to menu?	
	Flavor	Texture	Appearance		Yes	No	Yes	No

Figure 11 Sensory analysis form.

SUMMARY

Management's responsibility to serve high-quality food starts with setting standards and ensuring that employees are aware of them. The use of standardized recipes, good-quality ingredients, and proper supervision of food production are vital to quality control.

Basic to production planning and scheduling is the forecast, which is a prediction of the menu item demand for a meal or a day. Quantities of food to prepare are based on the predicted number of servings needed and the portion size to be offered. This information, plus special instructions for preparation and work assignments, is documented on a production schedule.

Once standardized recipes are implemented, the manager must design, monitor, and control procedures to ensure that preestablished quality standards are met. Centralized ingredient assembly, portion control, and sensory analysis are examples of quality control methods.

APPLICATION OF CHAPTER CONCEPTS

The food production unit of the Dining and Culinary Services for UW Housing is truly a high-volume and complex system. The main production kitchen sits on the southeast side of the 800-acre campus and produces, on average, 15,000 meals per day. A cook/chill concept is used, and food is shipped to the four main dining units twice per day. As with its other operational units, the leaders who oversee production work diligently to keep abreast of and integrate trends and change, especially those that are of most interest to the students. One such trend is that of increasing the purchase and use of locally produced foods. This is in fact not a new concept at UW Housing. Administration has been working with local growers and producers for roughly 15 years. There has, however, been a recent effort to increase local purchase for production of fresh and sustainably produced foods. Although UW Housing is fully committed to this effort, it does come with some unique challenges when it comes to production.

Not so long ago, an early frost threatened to destroy a crop of basil. The farmer called UW Housing and explained that if he did not sell off the basil that very day, it would freeze and he would incur a complete loss of the crop. He was calling to inquire if the Dining and Culinary unit could use that crop and could there be a negotiation of a fair price. After several phone calls that included University purchasing, administration and, of course, the basil managers, a deal was reached and 120 lb of fresh basil was delivered. The production was cleaned, trimmed, chopped, and frozen within 24 hours, then used throughout the fall season for products such as organic pasta sauce.

CRITICAL-THINKING QUESTIONS

1. What operational factors did administration need to take into account during this decision-making process?
2. What impact did this decision have on operational inputs?
3. For the sake of discussion, let us say that UW Housing paid $3.00 per pound for the basil. What was the aggregate cost of getting it "foodservice ready"?
4. Do you think UW Housing made the right decision? Why or why not?
5. Identify any risks that administration assumed in approving this rather unusual decision.
6. How do you think the production staff felt about this decision? Would you have sought their input before making the decision? Why or why not?
7. Why do you think the administration agreed to purchase the basil on such short notice?
8. Do you think the recipe for organic pasta sauce had to be altered at all given that fresh basil was used? Explain your answer.
9. Were any unique food safety risks incurred?
10. What can administration do to prevent a last-minute situation like this during the next growing season?

CHAPTER REVIEW QUESTIONS

1. List the objectives of cooking. How might these be prioritized in a school? Patient dining unit? For-profit cafeteria?
2. What is the value of a standardized recipe? What are its limitations?
3. Why is it important to define recipe yield in total volume as well as expected portions?
4. What quality standards would you establish for muffins? How would you instruct the production staff to use quality standards in recipe testing?
5. What data would you collect for predicting production demand for an à la carte program in a high school? How would you collect the data?
6. What is the purpose and value of production scheduling?
7. What are the advantages and disadvantages of centralized ingredient assembly?

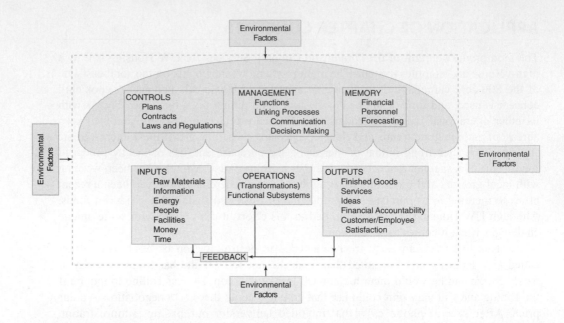

8. Describe how portion control can contribute to cost containment.
9. Why is portion control particularly important in health care settings?
10. How is technology changing the function of production in high-volume foodservice?

SELECTED WEB SITES

www.researchchef.org   (Research Chefs Association)
www.ciachef.edu   (Culinary Institute of America)
www.acfchefs.org   (American Culinary Federation)

Service

Hans Slegers/Shutterstock

FOODSERVICE MANAGERS HAVE THE RESPONSIBILITY OF

making certain that after food is prepared, it is safely held, delivered, and served to consumers. Therefore, the goals of a delivery and service system should include the following:

- Maintain the aesthetic quality of the food
- Ensure microbial safety of food
- Serve food that is attractive and satisfying to the consumer

In addition, the system should be designed and selected for optimal use of available resources: labor, time, money, energy, and space. It is equally important for the food manager to recognize and nurture the guest or customer relations aspect of service. Customers have high expectations for personalized and attentive service. A comprehensive service program includes a guest relations component.

This chapter explores concepts of service so that the foodservice manager can make good decisions regarding the delivery and service of food. The information is appropriate whether the manager is evaluating a currently existing system or preparing to select a new system for a particular situation. Chapter content includes factors that affect selection of a system, equipment needs for delivery-service functions, and a review of various styles of service. The chapter concludes with a section on customer service.

OUTLINE

KEY CONCEPTS

1. Numerous options and alternatives exist to assemble, distribute, and serve meals.

2. The service function can be designed using a centralized or decentralized structure.

3. Methods of meal assembly vary depending on the service objectives of the foodservice.

4. System selection for assembly, distribution, and service is contingent on many organizational and operational factors.

5. Economic factors often serve as the "bottom line" in system selection.

6. Service systems require investment in capital and small equipment.

7. Specialized equipment may be required for some service systems.

8. Style of service refers to the method by which a customer accesses and receives prepared food.

9. Off-site or portable meal service necessitates special attention to food quality during transport.

10. Customer service (or guest relations) refers to the interactions between customers and service staff.

METHODS OF ASSEMBLY, DELIVERY, AND SERVICE

KEY CONCEPT: Numerous options and alternatives exist to assemble, distribute, and serve meals.

Modern technological research and development related to foodservice have brought many advances in methods of delivery and service of food and in the equipment used for these processes. These developments resulted in part from the production systems and from the complexity of modern-day foodservice operations. With the increased time and distance between production and service, the potential for loss of food quality has also increased. Newer delivery and service methods have been designed to protect against such loss.

Most menu items are at peak quality immediately on completion of the cooking process. It is not possible to serve food at that precise time in many foodservice systems because of the need to assemble, transport, and deliver meals for service. Equipment is needed that can maintain food at proper temperatures for best quality and ensure safety of the food in transit. Methods of delivery and service that involve the shortest possible time and distance are best able to help achieve the desired goal.

Methods—Delivery and Service as Subsystems

KEY CONCEPT: The service function can be designed using a centralized or decentralized structure.

The term *distribution* or *delivery* refers to the transportation of prepared foods from production to place of service; *service* involves assembling prepared menu items and distributing them to the consumer. The equipment required for both delivery and service is an essential part of these subsystems. Whereas delivery and service *are* subsystems in the overall foodservice system, they are small systems within themselves and are therefore referred to here as "systems." Basically, there are two major *on-premise* delivery systems: centralized and decentralized.

Centralized Delivery-Service System. In the centralized method, prepared foods are portioned and assembled for individual meals at a central area in or adjacent to the main kitchen. The completed orders are then transported and distributed to the customer. This is typical of over-the-counter service in quick-service restaurants, of table or counter service in restaurants, and of banquet service where food is plated in a central location and transported to the dining areas for service. This method is also used in many on-site facilities, including hospitals and long-term care facilities. Foods are portioned and plated, and trays for individual patients are assembled in the central kitchen. Completed trays are then transported by various means to the patients throughout the facility using various types of transport carts. Soiled trays and dishes are returned to the central area for washing.

Centralized delivery-service systems are prevalent today because of the close supervision and control of food quality and portion size, assurance of correct menu items on each tray or order, and correct food temperatures at point of service that this system affords. Also, it requires less equipment and labor time than does the decentralized method. If the number of people to be served is large, however, the total time span required for service may be excessively long.

Decentralized Delivery-Service System. In the decentralized system, bulk quantities of hot and/or cold prepared foods are sent to serving galleys or ward kitchens located throughout the facility, where reheating, portioning, and meal assembly take place. Thus, instead of one central serving area, there are several smaller ones close to the consumers. Often these galleys may have equipment for limited short-order cooking of eggs and toast and for coffeemaking. Refrigerators, ovens for reheating, temperature-holding cabinets, and a counter or conveyor belt for tray assembly may also be included in these service galleys. Dishwashers may be provided for warewashing in the ward kitchens, or soiled dishes and trays can be returned to the central area for washing, which eliminates the need for duplication of dishwashing equipment in each galley. If dishes are washed in the central area, the clean dishes must be returned to the galleys for use for the next meal. It is time and energy consuming to transport dishes twice each meal, soiled and clean, to and from the service units. Over a period of time, this may be more expensive than installing dishwashing facilities in each serving unit.

Decentralized service is considered most desirable for use in facilities that are on one level and spread out in design or in any facility where there are great distances from the main kitchen to the consumers. It is expected that foods will be of better quality and retain desired temperatures more effectively if served near the consumer rather than plated in a central location and transported to distant locations within the facility.

Types of foodservices that use the decentralized system include large hospitals and medical centers; school districts that transport prepared food from a commissary to individual schools; hotels that provide room service from service units on various floors; and banquets from a serving kitchen within the facility.

Costs and values of centralized versus decentralized methods should be studied and carefully considered before deciding on which one to adopt. Both can be successfully used if factors and conditions unique to the foodservice operation are carefully considered and accounted for.

ASSEMBLY

KEY CONCEPT: Methods of meal assembly vary depending on the service objectives of the foodservice.

Assembly is the piecing together of prepared menu items to complete an entire meal. Assembly can occur at a number of points along the sequence of process steps, depending on the type of foodservice operation and the production system used. Restaurants, for example,

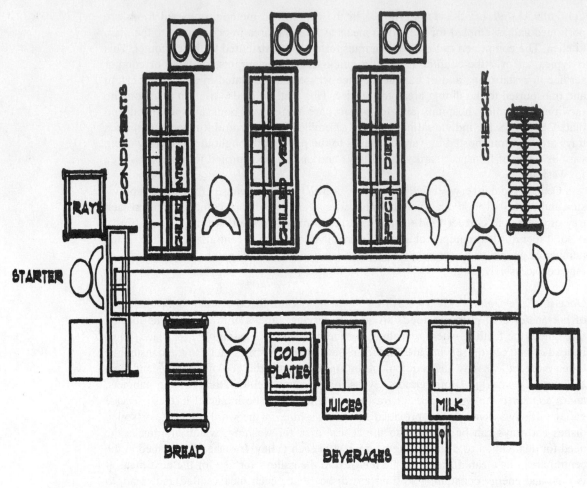

COOK-CHILL STRAIGHT POWERED CONVEYOR WITH PERPENDICULAR EQUIPMENT:

This is the ideal layout for cook-chill when space is available. Speed is not a problem when traying up for a cook chill system, as the tray is going back into a refrigerated space, before delivery to retherm. The system shown was for a restaurant style menu and a Crimsco convection retherm in a floor pantry.

Figure 1 Cook/chill trayline.
Source: Courtesy of Crimsco, Inc., Kansas City, MO.

assemble hot meals at the centralized production point and serve the meal immediately and directly to the waiting customer. Institutions, on the other hand, use tray assembly systems for speed and efficiency. This method of assembly is common in organizations such as health care facilities, schools, and airlines where large numbers of meals must be served at specific times.

Tray Assembly

Two major systems are used to assemble meal trays. In one, food is assembled at a central location, usually the production kitchen, using a trayline, and then various distribution methods are used to deliver the trays to units. Figures 1, 2, and 3 illustrate various traditional trayline configurations. Figure 4 is unique to the hotel or room service concept and is referred to as the pod concept. The second system transports food in bulk to units where it is assembled or plated as individual meals. This is referred to as decentralized assembly and service.

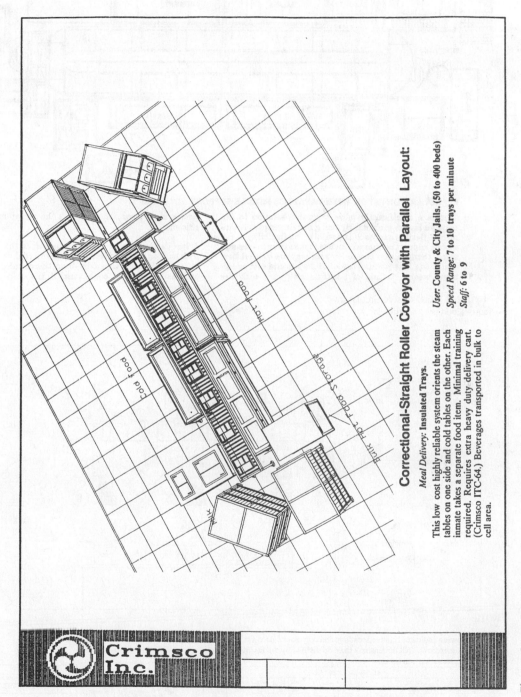

Correctional-Straight Roller Coveyor with Parallel Layout:

Meal Delivery: Insulated Trays.

This low cost highly reliable system orients the steam tables on one side and cold tables on the other. Each inmate takes a separate food item. Minimal training required. Requires extra heavy duty delivery cart. (Crimsco ITC-64.) Beverages transported in bulk to cell area.

User: County & City Jails. (50 to 400 beds)
Speed Range: 7 to 10 trays per minute
Staff: 6 to 9

Figure 2 Parallel cook/serve trayline.
Source: Courtesy of Crimsco, Inc., Kansas City, MO.

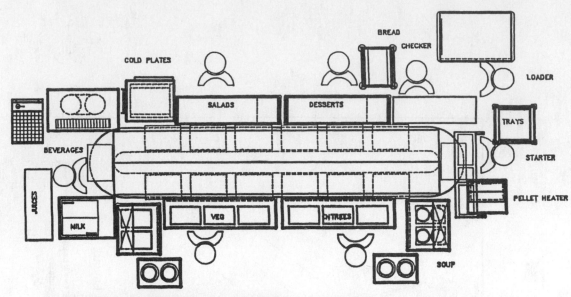

CIRCULAR CONVEYOR WITH PARALLEL MOBILE SUPPORT EQUIPMENT:

This is a significantly more expensive solution to the trayline layout problem. By using mobile support equipment a flexible approach is possible. The flexibility of the mobile support equipment means that as your census and menu changes, you can re-lay your trayline to meet new conditions. The parallel layout of the hot and cold equipment means staffing of positions also vary with the census, up or down. This layout is the second most space efficient.

A less desirable type circular conveyor is the giant one with built-in work stations both hot and cold. It is approximately 25% more expensive than the circular conveyor with mobile support equipment. It is totally inflexible.

Figure 3 Cook/serve circular trayline.
Source: Courtesy of Crimsco, Inc., Kansas City, MO.

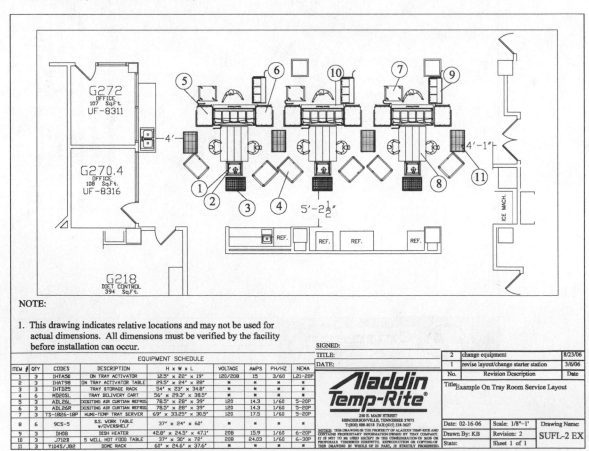

Figure 4 Floor plan for POD tray assembly system.
Source: Courtesy of Aladdin Temp-Rite, Hendersonville, TN. Used with permission.

FACTORS AFFECTING CHOICE OF DISTRIBUTION SYSTEMS

■ **KEY CONCEPT: System selection for assembly, distribution, and service is contingent on many organizational and operational factors.**

Every organization has its own requirements for delivery and service based on the type of foodservice system, the kind of foodservice, the size and physical layout of the facility, the style of service used, the skill level of available personnel, economic factors related to labor and equipment costs, quality standards for food and microbial safety, the timing of meal service, space requirements versus space available for foodservice activities, and the energy use involved.

No one factor can be considered alone when deciding on a delivery-service system, because most of the factors interact with, and have an influence on, the others. They must be regarded as a whole when a choice is made.

Type of Foodservice System

The type of foodservice system used determines to some extent its own needs for delivery and service. Of the four types of foodservice systems, the commissary system is the only one requiring delivery trucks to take prepared foods to satellite serving units.

As noted previously, menu items processed in the commissary are either held in bulk or portioned, then held in temperature-control inventory until time of service. Three alternatives for this holding are frozen, chilled, or hot-held. Each method requires different equipment.

Bulk foods may be placed in 12-inch × 20-inch counter-size pans for freezer storage so that the food can be reheated and served from the same pan. Or, if the pans are to be transferred to serving units in the chilled or hot state instead of frozen, they are placed in heavy containers with lids that clamp on securely. Otherwise, spillage may result during transport to the foodservice facility.

Insulated carriers (Figure 5, for example) to hold the portioned food in its containers are filled at the commissary. At scheduled times each day, carriers are loaded onto a truck for transfer to the service unit. In many cases, the driver is responsible for unloading the truck

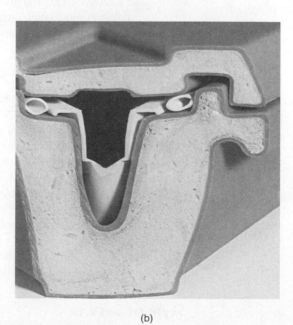

(a)   (b)

Figure 5 (a) Example of carrier for transporting prepared hot food. (b) Cutaway of same carrier exposes insulation.
Source: Courtesy of Cambro Manufacturing Company, Huntington Beach, CA. Used with permission.

and taking the food carriers to the storage or service area as required. Empty carriers from the previous delivery are collected and returned to the commissary on the delivery truck.

The fleet of trucks required by the commissary depends on the geographic distances to be traveled and number of deliveries to be made by each truck driver. Timing can be crucial, especially in those situations where the food is delivered hot just-in-time for service. Ideally, distances for hot foods to be transported should be short.

Delivery of frozen foods requires well-insulated carriers to maintain food in the frozen state during the time it is being transported. If the service facility has adequate space for holding frozen food, there is little problem with delivery time, because meals can be sent a day or two ahead. If there is no such storage space, delivery timing must be correlated with meal periods and time for rethermalizing and assembling the menu items.

At this point, foods are on the premises, and the procedures for delivery and service within the facility may be the same for all four systems.

Kind of Foodservice Organization

The type of organization determines to a large extent the delivery and service system requirements. Those where large numbers of people must be served quickly, such as schools, colleges, and industrial plants, usually provide cafeterias for meal service. Fast-food restaurants serve foods as quickly as possible, too, but with over-the-counter or drive-up service.

Hospitals and nursing homes cater to the foodservice needs not only of their patients but also of the employees, professional staff, and visitors. This calls for tray service for patients who are bedfast; perhaps dining room service for ambulatory patients in some care centers; cafeteria service for staff, employees, and visitors; and vending machines as a supplemental service for between-meal hours.

Table service restaurants may use different styles of service (see later section titled "Style of Service"), but all employ servers to carry meals from the kitchen to the guests. In restaurants in which customers serve themselves, *cafeteria* or *buffet service*, employees replenish the food and may serve beverages to the guests' tables.

Large hotels may have several types of service within the facility, including a counter or coffee shop for fast meals and table service dining rooms. Some may be more "exclusive" and expensive than others, so more formal types of service may be offered. Because many hotels cater to conventions and group meetings, banquet service is also offered. Room service is available in most hotels, which calls for a different means of delivery and service, such as servers using trays or tables on wheels to take meals to guests in their rooms.

Size and Physical Layout of Facility

The size and building arrangement of the facility are additional factors to consider when selecting a delivery system. Some restaurants, for example, may be in a high-cost downtown location and, thus, are generally narrow and several stories in height in order to utilize valuable land to its best advantage. In this case, the bakery may be on one level, preparation and cooking units on another, and dishwashing on still another—all on different levels from the dining room. This calls for a well-coordinated system of mechanized conveyors, subveyors, and elevators to deliver food quickly to the place of service.

Hospitals and health care facilities can be constructed as high-rise buildings or low, rambling facilities with miles of corridors. Different systems are required for each to ensure tray delivery to the patient within a reasonable time. The distance and the routing from production to service areas are points for consideration.

Style of Service

Whether the style is *self-service* such as cafeteria, buffet, vended, or pickup by the consumer; *tray service*, either centralized or decentralized; *wait service* for table, counter, or drive-up facilities; or *portable service* with meals delivered to home or office throughout an industrial plant, each has different equipment and delivery needs (see later section on "Equipment Needs").

Skill Level of Available Personnel

Labor needs and required skills vary for different types of delivery systems and for the equipment used in each type of system. When planning to alter the current delivery system or select a new one, the foodservice manager must assess the current skills and availability of the foodservice employees. Judgment must be made on the skills needed to operate a new system and on the learning ability of the employees. A training program should then be designed to ensure that employees are well trained in the use, care, and safety features of all equipment and delivery procedures.

Economic Factors

> ■ KEY CONCEPT: **Economic factors often serve as the "bottom line" in system selection.**

Labor and equipment required for the various delivery-service systems must be calculated and evaluated in relation to budget allocations. Unless adequate funding is available, the foodservice would not, for example, be able to install automated electronic delivery equipment. Economic factors play a part in deciding where and how frozen or chilled foods should be reheated, assembled, and served. Decentralized service requires duplication of assembling and serving and, sometimes, dishwashing equipment, as well as personnel for the many service units throughout the facility, and so may be more expensive to install and operate than the centralized service. Cost comparisons of the numerous types of carts and trucks for transporting food should precede the selection of a specific delivery and serving system.

Quality Standards for Food and Microbial Safety

Management establishes standards for food quality and safety, then selects equipment for heating, holding, and transporting food to achieve those standards. How hot should the food be when served to the consumer? How can that temperature be maintained through delivery and service? How hot must foods be at the time of portioning and serving to aid in achieving the desired standards?

Considerable research has been conducted to find answers for these questions. Studies relate to the four foodservice systems, microbial safety, nutrient retention, and sensory qualities. Microbial quality of menu items is dependent on the type of food, quality of raw ingredients, batch size, type of equipment used for cooking, and position of menu items in foodservice equipment. The management of time and temperature relationships throughout all stages of product flow in every foodservice system is considered of major importance. Time and temperature relationships are also important in nutrient retention and for sensory qualities of food products. Standards for end-point and service temperatures are mandated by many regulatory agencies. Managers should be knowledgeable about these factors to comply with standards of expectations of quality.

Timing Required for Meal Service

The time of day desired or established for meals is another factor influencing the choice of a delivery-service system. For example, if 1,200 people are to be served at a 7 P.M. seated banquet, all food must be ready at once and served within a few minutes to all of the guests. Many serving stations and adequate personnel for each station are prerequisites for achieving the time objective. Preheated electric carts can be loaded with the preplated meals a short time before service and then taken to various locations in the dining room for service from the carts to guests. An alternate method is to place the plates as they are served on trays and carried by servers to the dining room. This will require several trips from serving area to dining room, thus taking more time than when carts are used.

If only a few people need to be served at one time, as in a restaurant where customer orders come to the kitchen over a period of a few hours, food is cooked to order, or in small batches, and held for short periods of time.

In school foodservice, many children are ready for lunch at the same time. To avoid long waits in a cafeteria line, however, a staggered meal period can be scheduled, which allows various grades to be dismissed for lunch at 5- or 10-minute intervals. Another option, if space allows, would be multiple serving lines.

Large hospitals have the challenge of serving their many patients within a reasonable meal period time span. Should all be served at approximately the same time, as may be possible with decentralized service? Or is a one- to two-hour time span acceptable as provided through centralized service? Various systems meet specific needs. The food manager or dietitian must work with the nursing staff to ensure that patient care is not disrupted and that quality food and service are provided.

Space Requirements or Space Available

Allocation of space for departments and their activities is determined at the time of building construction. The delivery-service system preferred should be stated early in the facility planning process so adequate space will be available for those foodservice activities. Any later remodeling to change to a different system can be disruptive and expensive, if it is possible at all.

Decentralized systems require less space in the main kitchen area but more throughout the facility for the serving units than do centralized systems. In hospitals with centralized service, tray assembly equipment, as well as trucks or carts, takes up considerable space. Based on the number and size of the transport carts or trucks, the space needed for their storage when not in use can be calculated. Added space must be allocated for moving the carts through the facility with ease.

Energy Usage

A concern for energy use and its conservation plays a role in deciding on a delivery-service system. Systems that use a large number of pieces of electrically powered or "active" equipment are more costly to operate than those that use the "passive" temperature retention equipment, such as insulated trays or **pellet**-heated plates.

Today, energy awareness is on the increase again, and energy savings are an important consideration in delivery system and equipment selection.

Pellet

A preheated metal disk used to maintain the temperature of an individual portion of plated hot food

EQUIPMENT NEEDS

■ **KEY CONCEPT:** Service systems require investment in capital and small equipment.

Delivery and service of food in institutions necessitates the use of specialized equipment for each step of the procedure: reheat if necessary, assemble, transport, distribute, and serve. Every foodservice system has its own requirements. Manufacturers work closely with foodservice directors to design pieces of equipment that best fill those specific needs. Equipment for delivery and service may be classified in several ways:

- In general: fixed or built in, mobile, and portable
- For a specific use: reheating, assembling, temperature maintenance, transporting, and serving
- For each of the four foodservice systems: conventional, commissary, ready-prepared, and assembly/serve

A brief description of general and specific classification follows for an understanding of the various delivery-service systems in their entirety.

General Classification of Delivery-Service Equipment

Fixed or Built-In Equipment. Equipment that is fixed or built in should be planned as an integral part of the structure at the time a facility is being built.

One such system is the automated cart transport or monorail. This has its own specially built corridor for rapid transit, out of the way of other traffic in the building. It is intended for use by all departments because it is so expensive to install. It can transport items in a few seconds from one part of the building to another and is desirable because of its speed. An alternate plan for tray delivery may be needed if a power failure should occur, which could incapacitate the automated tray delivery system.

Other fixed equipment includes elevators, manual or power-driven conveyors for horizontal movement such as for tray assembly, and subveyors and lifts (dumbwaiters) to move trays, food, or soiled and clean dishes to another level within the facility.

Mobile Equipment. Mobile equipment is equipment that is moved on wheels or casters. This includes *delivery trucks* for off-premise use to transport food from a commissary or central kitchen to the meal sites, and for Meals-on-Wheels delivery to home or offices.

Another type is *movable carts and trucks*, either hand-pushed or mechanized, for on-premise transport of either bulk food for decentralized service or preplated meals for centralized service. Such carts are available in many models, open or closed, insulated or not, temperature controlled for heated or refrigerated units, or combinations of both (Figure 6 shows an example). Some movable carts are designed to accommodate the plates of hot food for banquet service, others are designed for entire meals assembled on trays for service in hospitals, and still others for bulk quantities of food. Assembly equipment and galley units can be mobile, instead of built in, which permits flexibility of arrangement. An example of a galley is shown in Figure 7.

Portable Equipment. Included in this category are items that can be *carried*, as opposed to mobile equipment that is moved on wheels or casters. For delivery and service, equipment such as pans of all sizes and shapes, many with clamp-on lids to prevent spillage in transit, and hand carriers (also called totes) are commonly used. Totes are usually insulated to retain temperature of foods for short-time transport or delivery (Figure 8).

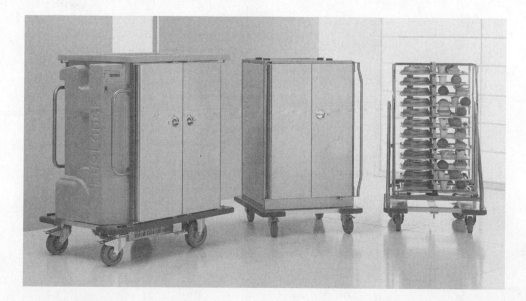

Figure 6 Examples of meal distribution carts.
Source: Courtesy of Burlodge USA. Used with permission.

Figure 7   Galley Station.
Source: Courtesy of Crimsco, Inc., Kansas City, MO. Used with permission.

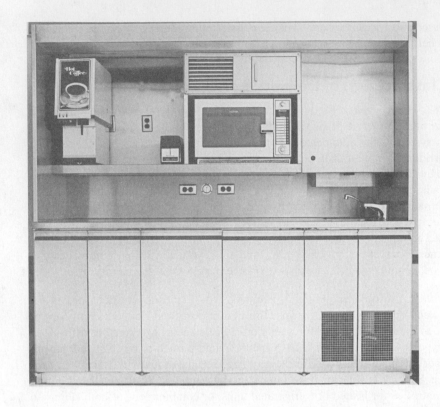

Also, a variety of plates and trays can keep pre-plated foods at proper temperatures for service. When these are used, unheated carts can be employed for transporting meals to consumers. Common types of plates and trays include pellet disc and insulated trays.

Pellet Disc.   A metal disc (pellet) is preheated and at mealtime is placed in a metal base. Individual portions of hot food are plated and placed over the base and then covered. Either china or disposable dishes can be used. This hot metal pellet radiates heat and keeps the meal at serving temperature for approximately 40 to 45 minutes.

Figure 8   Portable totes are insulted for temperature maintenance.
Source: Courtesy of Cambro Manufacturing Co., Huntington Beach, CA. Used with permission.

Insulated Trays with Insulated Covers. Insulated trays are designed with a variety of configurations for the different types of dishes used for the menu of the day. Thermal, china, or disposable dishes can be used. After the food is portioned, the dishes are placed on the tray and covered with the insulated cover. No special carts are needed to transport these trays because they are nesting and stackable, and, of course, no temperature-controlled units are necessary. Some insulated tray systems are designed to create **synergism**; that is, when stacked properly, the cold and hot sections of each tray work together in a column to maintain proper temperatures. The combined temperatures of the individual sections exceed the sum of the individual temperatures. Meals in these insulated trays retain heat quite well for short periods of time, such as during transport and distribution.

Synergism
The combined effects of individual units exceeds the sum of the individual effects

Equipment for Specific Uses

KEY CONCEPT: Specialized equipment may be required for some service systems.

Reheating Frozen or Chilled Foods. Foods prepared, cooked, and then frozen or chilled for later service must be reheated at serving time. This may be done in the central serving area or in service units throughout the facility. Equipment used for reheating in either case is the same and includes convection ovens, conduction (conventional) ovens, microwave ovens, and infrared ovens. Also used are immersion equipment (for food in pouches) such as steam-jacketed kettles or tilting frypans. Microwave ovens are the fastest for single portions, but unless a fleet of these ovens or a tunnel-type microwave is available, reheating a large number of meals can take a long time. Convection ovens with forced-air heat can reheat many meals at one time, depending on the oven size. Frozen foods usually are tempered in the refrigerator before reheating to reduce time for bringing foods to serving temperature. With any rethermalization system, the objective is to heat the food product to service temperature and to retain nutrient content, microbial safety, and sensory quality.

Meal Assembly. Assembling of meals for service is an important step in the delivery-service system. Methods vary for different types of establishments, and the activities involved must be suited to the specific needs of each.

Meal assembly requires that the various menu items that make up a meal be collected and put in one place. This may require equipment as simple as a convenient table or counter for bagging or plating the foods cooked behind the counter in a fast-food restaurant. In a table service restaurant, servers may pick up the cold foods at one or more stations and hot foods from the chef's station and assemble them all on a tray for service.

The most complex type of assembly is that of tray service for many patients or other consumers. Trays, dishes, silverware, and food are pre-positioned along a conveyor belt. Employees are stationed to place a specific item or items on the tray as it passes along. A patient menu or diet card precedes the tray and indicates which menu items should be placed on the tray. Conveyors of various types are commonly used for this purpose. All must be sized to the width of the trays used. The simplest is a manual or self-propelling conveyor with rollers that move trays when they are pushed from one station to the next. Others are motor driven. Power-operated conveyors can be set at varying speeds for moving trays along the belt automatically (Figure 9). Conveyors may be mobile or built in.

Temperature Maintenance and Holding. Foods prepared and ready for service often must be held for short periods until needed, while being transported to another area for service, or during the serving period itself. Equipment for this short-time holding includes refrigerated and heated storage units of many types. Note that heated storage cabinets will *not* heat the food, but, when preheated, will maintain the temperature of the food for short periods as it was when it was placed in them.

Heated or refrigerated cabinets may be built in, pass through from kitchen to serving area, or may be on mobile carts and trucks of all types, some designed with both refrigerated and heated sections. Movable refrigerated units are often used for banquet service.

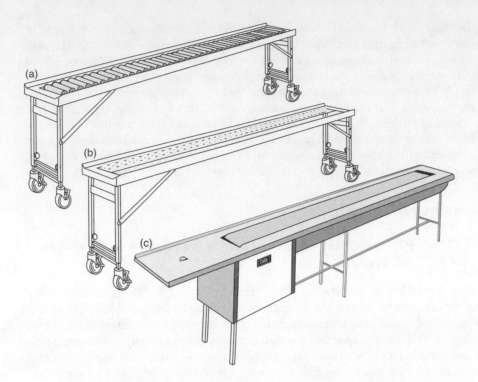

Salads and desserts can be preportioned, placed in the production area, and held until moved to the banquet hall at service time. Likewise, hot foods for large groups can be portioned and placed in preheated carts close to serving time but held until all plates are ready to be served at the same time.

Infrared lamps are also used to keep foods hot on a serving counter during the serving period.

Transportation and Delivery. Equipment for transportation and delivery is described earlier in this chapter under "Mobile Equipment" and "Portable Equipment." Open or closed noninsulated carts, including the monorail, are used to transport meals served on pellet- or capsule-heated dishes, or placed on insulated trays with covers. Temperature maintenance carts with heated and refrigerated sections or insulated nonheated carts are used to transport meals preplated on regular dishes and placed on noninsulated trays. Other carts are designed with heated wells and compartments for bulk amounts of soup, vegetables, meats, and so forth, as well as for cold ingredients and other food items for meal assembly in another location.

Roll-in refrigerator units serve as transport equipment also, with pre-plated salads and desserts set up in the production area and moved later to the dining areas. Similarly, other mobile serving equipment, such as banquet carts and buffet or catering tables, can serve the dual functions of transporting and serving. Some catering carts for snack items, soups, sandwiches, and beverages are used to take food to workers in plants or office buildings. Insulated totes are an inexpensive yet effective means for home delivery of meals.

Many methods and pieces of equipment are available for transporting food from the kitchen to the consumer. The manager must identify the specific needs of the organization when choosing among them. Consideration must be given to the total number to be served; the distance to be traveled between production and service areas; layout of the building with routes including doors, ramps, and elevators involved; and the form of food to be transported: hot, cold, bulk, or pre-plated.

Serving. Cafeteria counters of varying configurations and with sections for hot and cold foods, buffet tables with temperature-controlled sections and sneeze guards, and vending machines all provide a means for self-service. Various methods for tray service have been described.

For dining room table service, trays or carts are used to carry the assembled menu items to the guests. Serving stations, small cabinets often located in or near the dining room, are equipped with table setup items such as silverware, napkins, and perhaps water, ice, glasses, coffee, and cups. This speeds service and reduces the distance traveled to serve guests. Other specialized serving equipment is noted under "Styles of Service."

STYLES OF SERVICE

KEY CONCEPT: **Style of service refers to the method by which a customer accesses and receives prepared food.**

There are many styles of service used within organizations. All have the common objective of satisfying the consumer with food of good quality, at the correct temperature for palatability and microbial safety, and attractively served.

The style of service selected, appropriate for a particular type of foodservice operation, should contribute to reaching these objectives. Also, the style must be economically compatible with the goals and standards of the organization. The basic types or styles of service include:

1. **Self-service:** cafeteria—traditional, free flow, or scramble; machine vended; buffet, smorgasbord, salad bar; and drive-up
2. **Tray service:** centralized or decentralized
3. **Wait service:** counter, table—American, French, Russian, family, banquet
4. **Portable meals:** off-premise or on-premise delivery

Self-Service

The simplest provisions for foodservices involve guests or customers carrying their own food selection from place of display or assembly to a dining area. The best known example of self-service, or grab-and-go, is the cafeteria, although buffet service with its variations, smorgasbord and salad bars, and vending are also popular.

Cafeteria.   Cafeterias are of two types. The *traditional* cafeteria is one in which employees are stationed behind the counter to serve the guests and encourage them with selections as they move along a counter displaying the food choices. There are many configurations for counter arrangement, from the straight line to parallel or double line, zigzag, and U-shaped. In each case, however, the patrons follow each other in line to make their selections.

The traditional self-service is used in colleges and other residences, cafeterias open to the public, school lunchrooms, in-plant foodservices, and commercial operations. The emphasis is on standardized portions and speedy yet courteous service. The rate of flow of people through the cafeteria line varies according to the number of choices offered and patron familiarity with the setup.

The second type of cafeteria is known variously as the *hollow square, free flow,* or *scramble system*. In this, separate sections of counter are provided for various menu groups, such as hot foods, sandwiches and salads, and desserts. The sections are usually placed along three sides of the serving room, and customers flow from the center to any section desired. This may seem confusing for the first-timer, but it does provide speed and flexibility by eliminating the need to wait in line for customers ahead to be served. Also, it relieves the pressure on those who do not wish to hurry in making decisions. To be successful, it is necessary to have repeat business and a mechanism for controlling the number of people who enter at one time.

A relatively new concept in cafeteria design is that of the *marche* or *food court* configuration. These cafeterias offer a number of theme-based stations where customers can have menu offerings made-to-order (MTOs). The intent is to provide a variety of fresh, made-to-order menu offerings to satisfy a wide variety of food and dining preferences.

Typical station concepts include deli, sandwich shop, comfort food, pizza, grill, and one or more stations that emphasize ethnic cuisine.

Machine Vended. The history of vending dates back as far as 215 B.C. in Greece, but *food* vending began in this country centuries later with penny candy and gum machines. Other items such as cold drinks and coffee soon were dispensed from vending machines. Today, a complexity of menu items, including complete meals, is available through vending machines. Some machines contain heating elements to cook or reheat foods before dispensing them; others are refrigerated or low-temperature controlled for holding frozen foods, such as ice cream.

Machine-vending foodservice skyrocketed in use and popularity in the 1950s and 1960s as it met a demand for speedy service and allowed foodservice to be available 24 hours a day, 7 days a week. Its popularity continues, and today vending is accepted as an important component of the foodservice industry, especially as a means for supplementing other styles of service. Schools, residence halls, hospitals, industrial plants, office buildings, and transportation terminals in particular have used this mode of service for coffee breaks, after-meal-hour snacks, and, in some, as the sole means of providing meals.

Food for the vending machines can be prepared by the institutions using them or by an outside vending company that delivers fresh foods at frequent intervals and keeps the machines supplied and in good working order. Fast turnover of the food and good supply service are requisites for the safety and success of vended foods. Also, the foods offered must be fresh and displayed attractively. Cleanliness and adherence to city health and sanitation codes are essential. Cooperative efforts by those concerned with packaging, production, merchandising, transportation, storage, and sanitation have brought about improvements in the quality and variety of the food offered and will continue to do so in the future.

Buffet. Buffet service, such as the smorgasbord and the popular salad bar, provides a means for dramatically displaying foods on a large serving table. Guests move around the table to help themselves to foods of their choice. Selections usually are numerous, and eye appeal is an important factor in the foods offered. Foods that hold up during the meal hour and the proper equipment to keep this food hot or cold as desired are essential to the success of this type of service. For aesthetic appeal and to comply with health regulations, displayed food must be protected against patron contamination. Portable sneeze guards placed around the foods give some protection as customers serve themselves.

Drive-Thru Pick-up. This type of service, popular with fast-food establishments to speed customer service, is a variation of the drive-in service. Customers drive through the restaurant grounds in a specially designated lane, make their food selection from a large menu board posted outside, and call their order in through a speaker box (usually next to the menu board). By the time they reach the dispensing window, their order has been assembled and packaged for pick-up.

Tray Service

Meals or snacks that are assembled and carried on a tray to individual consumers by an employee is a type of service provided for those unable to utilize other dining facilities. Hospitals, nursing homes, and other health care facilities use this method. For persons who are ill or infirm, attractively appointed trays served by pleasant-mannered employees do much to tempt their appetites and help restore health.

The two types of tray delivery service in hospitals, centralized and decentralized, are described earlier in this chapter. After trays have been transported to serving pantries, they are carried to patients by an employee of either the nursing or dietary department. Good cooperation between the two departments is a prerequisite to coordinate timing for prompt delivery. Delays in getting trays to patients can cause loss of temperature and quality of the food, and thus a major objective of foodservice is not attained. Many hospitals are integrating room service concepts for patient meals to improve satisfaction and reduce food waste.

Wait Service

Counter.   Lunch counter and fountain service are perhaps the next thing to self-service in informality. Guests sit at a counter table that makes for ease and speed of service and permits one or two attendants to handle a sizable volume of trade. Place settings are laid and cleared by the waiter or waitress from the back of the counter, and the proximity of the location of food preparation to the serving unit facilitates easy handling of food. The U-shaped counter design utilizes space to the maximum, and personnel can serve many customers with few steps to travel.

Table Service.   Most restaurants and hotel or motel dining rooms use more formal patterns of service in addition to the counter service, although both employ service personnel. Many degrees of formality (or informality) can be observed as one dines in commercial foodservice establishments around the world. Generally, the four major styles of service classified under table service are American, French, Russian, and banquet.

American service is the one generally used in the United States, although all styles are employed to some degree. A maître d', host, or hostess greets and seats the guests and provides them with a menu card for the meal. Waitresses or waiters place fresh table covers, take the orders, bring in food from the kitchen serving area, serve the guests, and may also remove soiled dishes from the tables. Busers may be employed to set up tables, fill water glasses, serve bread and butter, and remove soiled dishes from the dining room. Checkers see that the food taken to the dining room corresponds with the order and also verify prices on the bill before it is presented to the guest. Characteristic of this type of service is that food is portioned and served onto dinner plates in the kitchen.

For American style, dinner plates filled in the kitchen are transported to the guests in one of several different ways. For example, preheated carts are filled with numerous plates and taken to the dining room before guests arrive. Service personnel remove plates from these carts to serve their guests. Another way is for each server to obtain two dinner plates from the serving station, and with one in each hand, go, as a group, to the dining room and serve one table completely. Several trips back and forth are required to finish this service. Still another method is to use busers to carry trays of dinner plates to the dining room, place them on tray stands, and return for another load. Service personnel, working as a team in the dining room, serve the plates as busers bring them in. The head table is served first; then the table farthest from the serving area is served next, so that each succeeding trip is shorter. All guests at one table are served before proceeding to the next table.

French service (synonymous with "fine dining") is often used in exclusive, elegant restaurants. In this style, portions of food are brought to the dining room on serving platters and placed on a small heater (*rechaud*) that is on a small portable table (*gueridon*). This table is wheeled up beside the guests' table, and here the chief waiter (*chef de rang*) completes preparation, for example, boning, carving, flaming, or making a sauce. The chief waiter then serves the plates, which are carried by an assistant waiter (*commis de rang*) to each guest in turn. This style is expensive, because two professionally trained waiters are needed to serve properly, and service is paced slowly. The atmosphere is gracious, leisurely, and much enjoyed by patrons because of the individual attention they receive.

Russian service is the most popular style used in all of the better restaurants and motel dining rooms of the world. Because of its simplicity, it has replaced, to a high degree, the French style, which seems cumbersome to many. In Russian service, the food is completely prepared and portioned in the kitchen. An adequate number of portions for the number of guests at the table are arranged on serving platters by the chef. A waiter or waitress brings the platters, usually silver, with food to the dining room along with heated dinner plates and places them on a tray stand near the guests' table. A dinner plate is placed in front of each guest. The waiter then carries the platter of food to each guest in turn and serves each a portion, using a spoon and a fork as tongs in the right hand and serving from the left side. This is repeated until all items on the menu have been served. Although this service is speedy, requires only one waiter, and needs little space in the dining room, it has the possible disadvantage that the last person served may see a disarrayed, unappetizing serving platter. Also, if every guest ordered a different entrée, many serving platters would be required.

Rechaud

A small heater placed on a small table. Used for table-side temperature maintenance of hot foods

---

Chef de rang

The principal food server in French-style table service. Responsible for all table-side preparation

---

Commis de rang

An assistant in French-style table service. Carries the food to the table and removes dishes when guests complete the courses

Banquet

An elaborate, intensive feast where the service and menu are preset for a given number of people and specific time of day

The Russian style is used at banquets as described for restaurant service. Sixteen to twenty guests per server is a good estimate for banquet service.

Banquet service, unlike other types discussed, is a preset service and menu for a given number of people for a specific time of day. Some items, such as salads, salad dressings, butter, or appetizers, may be on the table before guests are seated. Either the American style or the Russian style of service is used.

Family style is often used in restaurants or residences of various types. Quantities of the various menu items, appropriate for the number of guests at the table, are served in bowls or platters and placed on the dining table. Guests serve themselves and pass the serving dishes to the others. This is an informal method that is popular for Sunday "fried chicken dinner specials" and in Chinese restaurants for foods that are to be shared, family style. Family-style service is used in some long-term care facilities in an effort to create a homelike atmosphere.

Portable Meals

KEY CONCEPT: Off-site or portable meal service necessitates special attention to food quality during transport.

Off-Premise Delivery. One example of off-premise service is delivering meals to the homes of elderly, chronically ill, or infirm individuals not requiring hospitalization. This plan, sometimes called Meals-on-Wheels, attempts to meet the need for nutritious meals for persons who are temporarily disabled, or for the elderly who may live alone and are unable to cook for themselves. In communities where such a plan is in operation, meals are contracted and paid for by the individual in need of the service or by some federal or community agency or volunteer organization for persons unable to pay. Desirably, the menus are planned by a dietitian working cooperatively with the organization providing the meals. Food may be prepared by restaurants, hospitals, colleges, or other foodservices and delivered by volunteer workers. Pre-plated meals are covered and loaded into some type of insulated carrier to ensure food safety while in transit and to maintain desired temperatures until delivered to the home.

A similar service is provided by caterers for workers in office buildings or to customers in their homes by pizza restaurants or others, but on a profit-making basis.

On-Premise Delivery. Another example of portable meals often used in some industrial plants is the distribution of foods to workers at their workplace by mobile carts that move throughout the plant. Carts are equipped with heated and refrigerated sections for simple menu items such as soup, hot beverages, sandwiches, snack items, fruits, and pastries. Workers pay the cart attendant as selections are made. This provides a time-saving service for employees who might have long distances to go to a central cafeteria in a large plant during a short meal period.

An alternative type of portable service is utilized by some companies not having foodservice facilities: A mobile canteen is provided by a catering firm and driven each day to the yard of the plant. Workers go outside to buy their meals from the canteen truck.

Although variations of these basic styles of service can be found in today's innovative foodservice systems, the types discussed here should provide understanding of the most commonly used service systems.

Room Service

Hotel-style room service is one of the hottest trends for patient meal service in the health care industry. This is in response to a customer no longer willing to eat at the convenience of the organization. Patients want to eat what they want, when they want. To accommodate this customer demand, hospitals across the country have implemented the room service concept to varying degrees. Some facilities have invested in major kitchen renovations, including the removal of centralized traylines. Time of service varies among facilities, with some operations offering the service 24 hours a day, 7 days a week. In addition to kitchen renovation, the concept requires major changes in staffing and communication systems.

CUSTOMER SERVICE

> **KEY CONCEPT:** **Customer service (or guest relations) refers to the interactions between customers and service staff.**

Service is more than the physical act of getting food to the customer wherever or whoever he or she may be. It is also the act, if not the art, of helping others. The focus of this text is foodservice, and, as the name implies, the nature of the business includes a commitment to service. Some on-site foodservice operations have actually changed their name to *hospitality services* to reflect their commitment to satisfying customers as the main mission of their operation. Good service is about listening to and observing customers to identify what they really want or need rather than imposing ideas on them that may not be of value. This is most certainly true in today's foodservice.

Why care about and invest in a customer service program? From a philosophical perspective, simply because it is the right thing to do. But, from another view, commitment to customer service makes good business sense. We are living in a customer-driven society. Customers whose needs and demands are not met will simply take their business elsewhere; foodservice is no exception. Consumers today have choices. In many settings, especially those in urban area, they can choose from myriad eateries, or they can "brown bag it." So to maintain or grow a business, foodservice managers need to build a guest relations program to keep guests coming back.

First and foremost, the manager needs to create a customer-focused environment and then motivate the staff to adapt the same philosophy and attitude. Second, the manager needs to set standards of customer service based on the needs and wants of the clients. The next phase of the program is to train the staff. The final piece of the program is to monitor it and assess its success.

Program standards should reflect the needs of the customer base. They must be measurable in order to assess the effectiveness of the program. Aspects of program standards can focus on a number of things, including staff attitude, appearance, and response time to customer requests or complaints. The following is a sampling of some standards for a guest relations program.

- Anticipate needs.
- Be observant of customers' behavior and environment.
- Never say "I don't know" to a customer. Challenge yourself to find the answer to the inquiry or find someone who can.
- Be positive. Choose to adopt a positive attitude and use language that reflects it. Use words and phrases such as "Certainly," "I would be happy to," and "What can I do for you?" and be pleasant and reassuring.
- Be specific. Say, "I'll be back in 10 minutes." Avoid vague promises such as, "I'll be back soon."
- Admit mistakes and take action to satisfy the customer. This is referred to as a service recovery. Figure 10 is an example of a coupon used to compensate for a customer service error.

Standards such as these can be presented as part of a training program in guest relations along with strategies on how to handle customer complaints and angry customers.

Some organizations have developed very formal and sophisticated programs of guest relations. It is not uncommon in hospitals, for example, for administration to establish a committee or task force to work specifically on improving customer satisfaction through guest relations.

Figure 10 Examples of coupons used to compensate for food quality or service errors.
Source: Courtesy of the University of Wisconsin, Division of Housing, Dining and Culinary Services. Used with permission.

SUMMARY

The delivery and service of food after it has been prepared are important aspects of the total foodservice system. Consumer satisfaction in every type of foodservice operation depends in large part on the pleasing presentation of carefully prepared, assembled, and transported food.

Foodservice managers should be cognizant of the major goals of delivery and service systems. These goals are to maintain quality food characteristics including desirable temperatures, ensure microbial safety, and present food attractively. In addition, the system selected should save steps and energy, reduce labor time and costs, and lessen worker fatigue.

Factors affecting the selection of a particular delivery system, either centralized or decentralized, as well as the appropriate equipment needed include the type of foodservice system (conventional, commissary, ready-prepared, or assembly/serve); the type of organization, such as school, hospital, commercial, or other; the size of physical facilities and amount of space available; the style of service to be used; the skill level of personnel; the labor and equipment costs involved; the quality standards required and desired; the timing for meal service; and the energy usage involved.

The style of service used—whether self-serve, tray, or waiter-waitress service—must be appropriate for the type of operation and for attaining its goals. Training the workers to use correct serving procedures and to present the food to the consumers in a pleasing and courteous manner is also an essential element in achieving a successful foodservice operation.

APPLICATION OF CHAPTER CONCEPTS

The Dining and Culinary Services (DCs) unit of UW Housing is undergoing massive renovation, much of which will be complete in 2012. Two of the biggest projects are a new commissary and redesigned dining units where service style will switch from traditional cafeteria tray service to food count and MTO. Items such as pastas, stir-frys, and omelets will be made per customer request at the point-of-service. In addition, the DCS will continue to expand its grab-and-go concepts of premade sandwiches, salads, and fruit cups.

The MTO concept has had a particularly drastic influence on all aspects of service. It needs to be understood that traditionally, most food has been prepared in the commissary, transported to the units, and held until it is reheated for service. All of the production employees worked in the back of the house. The MTO concept requires at least some of the production staff to move to the front of the house and have direct customer contact. Even though the newly renovated units will not open until 2012, the DCS has been working to retrain staff in preparation for this new concept.

CRITICAL-THINKING QUESTIONS

1. Review the systems model. What inputs are influenced as the DCS units move from commissary production to MTO concepts?
2. What does the fact that the DCS will offer both MTO and grab-and-go suggest about the diversity of service expectations from the customers?
3. Compare and contrast the influence that MTO and grab-and-go concepts will have on production.
4. What equipment needs to be available at the front of the house to accommodate MTO concepts?
5. What needs to be considered relative to guest relations as MTO and grab-and-go concepts expand?
6. Review your local regulations on take-out food. What needs to be on the labels of grab-and-go foods relative to quantity/container, ingredients, nutrition, and safety?
7. UW Housing uses a "secret shopper" to assess the quality of service. What should the shopper look for when assessing MTO service?
8. What aspects of "going green" could be integrated into MTO and grab-and-go concepts?
9. There is much that the staff needs to learn in order to successfully launch MTO concepts. What topics should the training plan include?
10. What impact does MTO have on the scheduling of other functions such as purchasing and production?

CHAPTER REVIEW QUESTIONS

1. Define the terms *delivery* and *service* as they relate to foodservice in institutions.
2. Discuss the advantages and disadvantages of centralized and decentralized delivery-service systems.
3. Describe the impact of the skill level of available personnel on the choice of delivery-service systems.

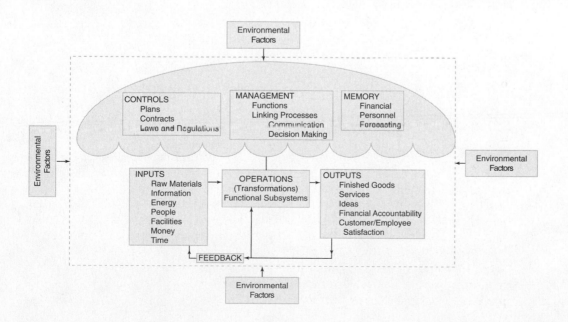

4. What is the difference between energy usage of "passive" and "active" temperature retention equipment?

5. Describe the various equipment options that can be employed for heat retention in a centralized hospital delivery system.

6. How does the design of a foodservice influence the choice of trayline configuration?

7. What factors would need to be taken into consideration when purchasing tray delivery carts for a hospital?

8. Why is it important to know the maximum temperature holding capacity of delivery systems when selecting them for a specific foodservice?

9. Why is the establishment of a guest relations program important?

10. How would you determine what your guests value when it comes to service?

SELECTED WEB SITES

www.crimsco.com   (Crimsco Corporation)

www.aladdintemprite.com   (Aladdin Temp-Rite Corporation)

www.burlodgeca.com   (Burlodge Corporation)

www.cambro.com   (Cambro Corporation)

www.dinex.com   (Dinex Corporation)

Facilities Planning and Design

Yuri Arcurs/Shutterstock

FOODSERVICE FACILITY DESIGN IS A CRITICAL FUNCTION for foodservice managers in all types of operations. Tight budgets and small footprints are increasingly the constraints within which on-site and commercial foodservices must operate. A sound design plan can improve the entire foodservice operation. It has been estimated that 50 percent of a foodservice employee's time is spent walking, talking, watching, and waiting. If the design can reduce any of these four, then efficiency has been improved. A good design can also improve productivity, quality of food and service, employee comfort and safety, and customer appeal. A poor design can increase operating costs and/or decrease revenue. The foodservice industry becomes increasingly competitive each day. Because there is documented evidence that the design and layout of an operation is a key factor in determining the success or failure of the business, the initial planning or renovation of a facility takes on added importance.

Facility planning and design are among the responsibilities of foodservice managers. Their involvement can range from planning a new foodservice facility to renovating or making minor changes within an existing facility.

The concepts presented in this chapter apply to all planning projects regardless of size or scope. However, managers must identify their own goals and needs,

From Chapter 10 of *Foodservice Management: Principles and Practices*, Twelfth Edition, June Payne-Palacio, Monica Theis.
Copyright © 2012 by Pearson Education, Inc. Published by Pearson Prentice Hall. All rights reserved.

work to maximize the project's attributes, and plan for, and around, any constraints that exist. Providing an appropriate, efficient facility for the production and service of high-quality, attractive food with an ambiance that will attract more customers and retain employees is the desired outcome of all foodservices.

KEY CONCEPTS

1. Preliminary planning for a foodservice design project should include study of the current trends in foodservice design, innovations in equipment and design, regulatory codes and operating licenses required, and specific needs for various types of foodservices.

2. The first step in a facility design project is to prepare a prospectus, which is a written description of all aspects of the project under consideration.

3. The planning team may include any or all of the following members: the owner or administrator, foodservice manager, architect, foodservice design consultant, equipment representative, business manager, builder/contractor, and maintenance/mechanical engineer.

4. The menu is the key to equipment needs, which in turn determines space requirements for the equipment.

5. Decisions made on architectural features are important for determining project cost, ease of cleaning, good sanitation, safety, adequate type and amount of lighting and temperature control for high productivity, and noise reduction for a more pleasant work environment.

6. All initial expenditures must take into consideration the project budget and also such factors as operating costs, life expectancy, conformance to sanitary standards, and provision of comfort for employees and customers.

7. The first step in design development is to determine optimum space allowances and draw a flow diagram showing the location of the work units.

8. In the schematic drawing, equipment is drawn to scale in each work unit with required traffic aisles and work spaces included.

9. The Americans with Disabilities Act mandates some general guidelines for implementing reasonable accommodations in the workplace and dining areas for persons with disabilities.

10. The seven major work areas in foodservice departments are receiving, storage and issuing, pre-preparation, preparation, serving, warewashing, and support services.

DEFINITIONS AND GOALS

To understand the planning process thoroughly, foodservice managers and others involved in a design project need to know certain definitions of words and examples of terminology, as used in this chapter, and also the goals to be achieved. Definitions include the following:

- **Physical:** Pertains to material existence measured by weight, motion, and resistance. Thus anything taking up space in a facility must be accounted for and fit the available space.
- **Design:** Refers to the broad function of developing the facility, including site selection, menu, equipment requirements, and other planning functions that will guide the project into reality.

- **Layout:** Refers to the process of arranging the physical facilities, including equipment, such that operational efficiency is achieved. This involves a design drawn on paper to show walls, windows, doors, and other structural components. After this outline drawing is complete, required work areas are designated on the plan. The equipment and other facilities are then arranged and drawn onto the plan.

Foodservice managers must be involved with the development of all aspects of the design plan to ensure that the facility is properly coordinated and functional. Although other professionals will design the electrical, water, and plumbing systems, as well as the lighting, heating, ventilation, and structural components of the building, the foodservice manager must provide input on the specific needs of the foodservice facility. The finished project plan results in either success or failure for the organization involved!

PRELIMINARY PREPARATION FOR FACILITY PLANNING

KEY CONCEPT: **Preliminary planning for a foodservice design project should include study of the current trends in foodservice design, innovations in equipment and design, regulatory codes and operating licenses required, and specific needs for various types of foodservices.**

Trends Affecting Foodservice Design

Changes in Patterns of Dining Out.   More people are eating meals away from home than ever before. Depending on the economy, however, the types of foodservices patronized will be affected. The foodservice industry is responding to this trend by making changes in the style of foodservices, types of food served, and prices charged. All of these factors, in turn, influence a facility's design.

Change in Desired Menu Items.   Continuing changes in customer preferences for types of foods and meals eaten away from home also affect the design requirements of a foodservice facility. A concern for physical fitness and well-being, for example, has changed the menus of most foodservices. Menus now offer lighter, healthier food selections and limited desserts. This changes the equipment needed and the space requirements and thus affects the renovation or new construction to accommodate preparation of foods that customers prefer. For example, today's customers are seeking just-prepped freshness, or at least the perception of it. This has led to an increase of display or exhibition cooking where customers can see and smell food being prepared at the last minute and to smaller kitchens using value-added convenience products that do not require multiple cooking steps and equipment.

Concern for Employees.   Shortages of both skilled and unskilled labor and the desire to retain trained employees has led designers to consider making foodservice facilities both functional and attractive places in which to work. Some of the ways that this is being implemented include specifying quality equipment and flooring that is easy to clean and safer to use; proper lighting especially chosen for each work area, color and patterns on walls, floors, and painted surfaces; and curves replacing squares and rectangles where possible.

Concern for the Environment.   The slogan "Lean Is Green" as it applies to the design of foodservice facilities means shrinking the kitchen space. Meeting volume demands with less space has been the goal of many businesses. Many chains, such as Denny's, IHOP, Einstein Bros. Bagels, Chili's, and Ruby Tuesday, have developed new store prototypes with significant reductions in both production and dining square footage. This has resulted in an overall reduction in energy and gas use, labor costs, rent, and building costs. LEED (Leadership in Energy and Environmental Design) standards have become an industry norm in recent years, with architects and construction firms competing to market their buildings as green.

Economic Factors. Costs of wages, food, and utilities can influence selection of a type of foodservice and its design. For example, as employees' wages increase, automation of equipment (e.g., robots) and the purchase of convenience foods become more common. In addition, as costs for food and the energy to prepare it continue to rise, the foodservice design must provide for efficient operation. The basic considerations to ensure that a renovation or new construction will result in the most efficient operation possible are work flow, traffic flow, energy use, and resource maximization.

Work flow is essential for the efficient use of labor. This requires that workers have as little difficulty as possible moving from task to task and that the tools, supplies, storage, and equipment that they need to do each task are close at hand.

Traffic flow refers to the ease with which customers can move around the facility. The more people who can be served in a given amount of time and the more who are attracted by the ease and convenience of dining in the operation, the greater the potential sales volume. Figure 1 shows an attractive and efficiently designed college cafeteria serving area with a dish drop for the return of soiled dishes to the warewashing area.

Energy use involves considering both the type of energy to be used (gas, electricity, or steam) and how efficiently it is used. Because energy is cheaper than labor, energy-saving decisions should not make more work for employees. With the current ever-rising energy costs, the trend is to design and equip foodservice facilities to save energy to the greatest extent possible. Equipment manufacturers are producing equipment that gives a high yield of energy for the work accomplished. The energy used by specific pieces of equipment is stated in the specifications. The foodservice manager should make comparisons before selecting a particular make or model.

Other energy conservation trends are toward better insulation, heat recapture for other uses, and recirculation of heat. Solar heat designs are used in some areas, especially for restaurants, and may be a future trend of other types of foodservices.

Resource maximization often requires negotiating the best balance among finite resources such as space, labor, and money. For example, should a bakeshop be included when it will take up valuable space but potentially increase customer satisfaction and revenue?

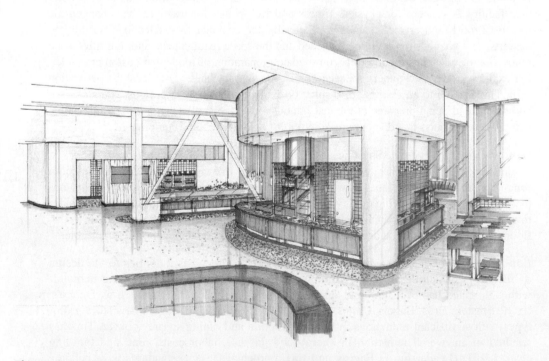

Figure 1 An attractive and efficiently designed college cafeteria serving area with a dish drop for the return of soiled dishes to the warewashing area.

Source: Webb Design, Tustin, CA (James Webb, Principal, Linda Midden, Director of Design).

One trend in facility design is to make the existing space adaptable either to multiple uses or to meeting future demands. With money for design projects so scarce and the environment in the foodservice industry so dynamic, making it difficult to predict what will happen in the future, the challenge is to design a facility that will last at least 30 to 40 years. This may be accomplished in part by selecting wheel-mounted and modular equipment or by using portable units. The key is to choose equipment that is uniform in size, movable, and adaptable for numerous work activities. Another option being implemented in at least one recent 17,000-square-foot, $8 million health care facility kitchen is to incorporate a blend of three different production systems—conventional, cook/chill, and assembly/serve.

Built-In Safety, Sanitation, and Noise Reduction. In planning the total facility, the safety of the employees, safety of food, and overall sanitary conditions are considerations in new designs. These may be achieved by the type of floor covering, ventilation, building materials, lighting, and equipment selected, and by the method of their installation. Ease of cleaning reduces labor costs, and materials and designs chosen for their safety features help reduce accidents. All make for an attractive, safe working environment for the employees. Many of these features reduce noise and worker fatigue, and hence result in greater productivity.

Information on Developments in Design and Equipment

Visits to new or renovated facilities of the same type you are planning and talks with managers of those facilities may garner new ideas and serve as a means to obtain first-hand information. Those with recent building experience usually are pleased to share workable ideas, mistakes that were made, and suggestions for improvement.

Obtaining catalogs and specification sheets from various equipment companies for comparative purposes and determining equipment space needs is essential. A file of such reference materials will be invaluable during work on the project. Equipment company representatives can be excellent sources of information for learning what is new and workable in various situations. Design consultants can also be contacted with any specific questions that arise. Figures 2, 3, 4, and 5 show a college foodservice floor plan and interior renderings of three service areas drawn by a design consultant.

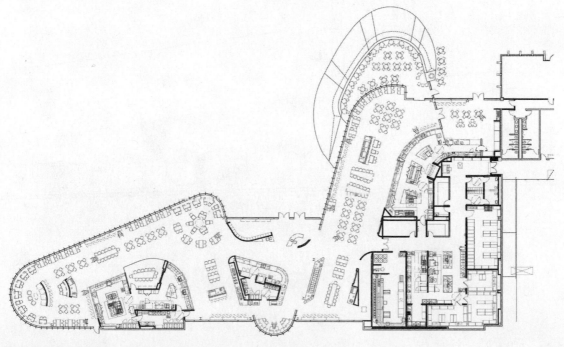

Figure 2 A college foodservice floor plan drawn by a design consultant.
Source: Webb Design, Tustin, CA (James Webb, Principal, Linda Midden, Director of Design).

Figure 3 A rendering of the exhibition cooking, chef's portico, and Euro areas of a college cafeteria.
Source: Webb Design, Tustin, CA (James Webb, Principal, Linda Midden, Director of Design).

Trade journals should be reviewed for articles on planning and design. Information gained can contribute new ideas and helpful suggestions to the planner. If the project is to renovate a facility, existing staff and employees may have excellent suggestions resulting from their own work experience. Giving them an opportunity to express opinions is a valuable resource and should be mutually beneficial.

Regulatory Considerations

Foodservice managers need to know which federal, state, and local laws, codes, and regulations will affect their building or renovation project. These regulations concern zoning

Figure 4 The pizza and grill areas of a college cafeteria.
Source: Webb Design, Tustin, CA (James Webb, Principal, Linda Midden, Director of Design).

Figure 5 The late night/retail operation offered by a college foodservice.
Source: Webb Design, Tustin, CA (James Webb, Principal, Linda Midden, Director of Design).

restrictions; building standards, including those to accommodate persons with disabilities; electrical wiring and outlets; gas outlets and installations; health, fire, and safety codes; sanitation standards that govern water pollution and waste disposal systems; and installation of heavy-duty equipment.

Regulations have been established by agencies and organizations such as state, county, and local health and engineering departments, the American Gas Association, Underwriters Laboratories, and the National Sanitation Foundation International, and by federal legislation such as the Occupational Safety and Health Act and the **Americans with Disabilities Act**. Copies of these codes may be obtained by writing to or by visiting the appropriate agency or by visiting the Web site (www.ada.gov/). Large libraries also usually have copies of the codes and regulations.

Other professionals can assist in the identification and application of regulatory codes and standards. These individuals are part of the planning team discussed later in this chapter.

Building permits are required, but in most instances, permits will not be issued for foodservice projects until health department officials have reviewed and approved the plans. It is expedient, therefore, to contact a local health department official and work closely with that person as plans are developed, so that approval is ensured.

Americans with Disabilities Act (ADA)
Prohibits discrimination against qualified persons with disabilities in all aspects of employment

Special Considerations for Specific Types of Foodservices

A brief review follows of some special considerations to keep in mind when planning a specific type of foodservice.

Commercial Facilities.   Restaurants catering to downtown shoppers and businesspeople prefer a location near a busy intersection. Their customers, who often have a limited lunch period, may be those within a 10-minute walk of the restaurant. Because rents for prime downtown sites are likely to be high, effective use of every square inch of space is a top planning priority. Many such restaurants are built vertically, with several levels for their various functions. Coordinating these activities with a good transport system between floors is a unique planning challenge. Suburban restaurants typically draw patrons from a larger area, making adequate parking the first essential. In addition, the location should be easily accessible and highly visible to approaching motorists. Shopping centers, which not only attract large numbers of customers but also provide ample parking, are considered desirable locations for commercial foodservices.

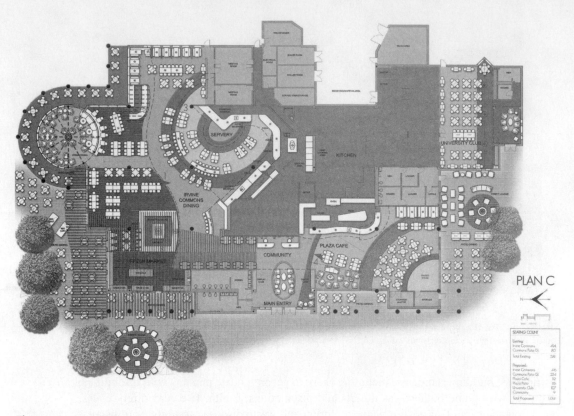

Figure 6 A plot plan for a college foodservice operation showing various dining choices available including a cafeteria, café, deli, market, and fine dining, all clustered around a central kitchen.
Source: Webb Design, Tustin, CA (James Webb, Principal, Linda Midden, Director of Design).

Hotels and motels usually have coffee shops located in visible locations, with entrances from both the street and the lobby. However, the main dining, party, and banquet rooms are frequently less visible, with access only through the lobby. For these facilities, basic food items are often prepared in a central kitchen. Finishing or banquet kitchens should be located adjacent to the various serving areas.

Schools and Universities. School foodservices are preferably located on the first floor, convenient to the central hallway. The area should be well ventilated to allow cooking odors to dissipate rather than to permeate classrooms. Dining areas in some schools may have to double as study halls or gymnasiums, which presents a different planning situation.

Many large city school systems utilize a central production kitchen, or commissary, for food production for all schools in the system. Often, these are cook/chill or cook/freeze systems, which require specialized cooking equipment and good transportation systems and schedules. With this system, individual schools need only limited equipment for completing baking, reheating certain items, and serving the food.

Colleges and universities provide many and varied types of foodservices to accommodate the needs of the entire campus community. Residence halls may have their own kitchen and dining rooms or, if there are several halls on campus, may have a central production unit for certain items, such as baked goods, or for pre-preparation of produce or meats. The trend is to have a choice of menu items, usually served cafeteria style (Figures 6 through 8).

Peak workloads at the three meal periods may necessitate duplicate pieces of large equipment and adequate work space for personnel. Student unions usually offer a variety of types of foodservices, including large banquet halls for seated service, short-order units, cafeterias/food courts, and possibly small dining rooms for special meals. Some colleges and universities have invited various fast-food companies to operate one of their units on campus to satisfy student requests for that type of food. Each type of foodservice requires different space and equipment, making planning for these facilities a challenge (Figures 9 through 11).

Figure 7 A rendering of the plaza café area of Figure 6.
Source: Webb Design, Tustin, CA (James Webb, Principal, Linda Midden, Director of Design).

Figure 8 A rendering of the salad bar/exhibition area of the fresh market shown in Figure 6.
Source: Webb Design, Tustin, CA (James Webb, Principal, Linda Midden, Director of Design).

UNIVERSITY CLUB

WEBB   HUNKSAKER UNIVERSITY CENTER DINING   BON APPÉTIT

Figure 9   A photo of the fine-dining area of the University Club shown in Figure 6.
Source: Webb Design, Tustin, CA (James Webb, Principal, Linda Midden, Director of Design).

In-Plant Facilities.   The in-plant or industrial foodservice area should be in a central location, allowing for ready access from as many places in the plant as possible. Every provision should be made to expedite service so that all workers can be accommodated quickly during a fairly short lunch break. Mobile units and vending operations can be used in remote areas of large plants or in those too small to justify the space and expenditure for kitchen equipment, management, and labor. Adequate passageways for such carts are essential.

Hospitals and Health Care Centers.   Facility planning for hospitals and other health care centers must provide for the needs of staff, employees, visitors, and guests, as well as the

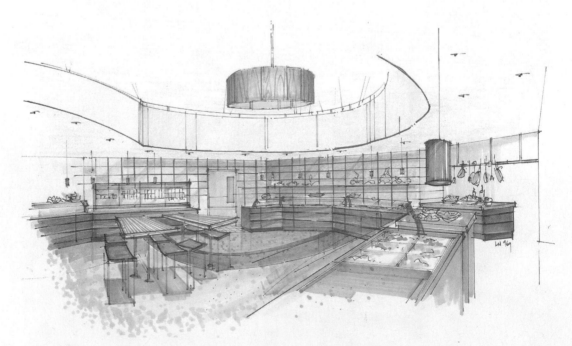

Figure 10   A rendering of the main servery of the college foodservice shown in Figure 6.
Source: Webb Design, Tustin, CA (James Webb, Principal, Linda Midden, Director of Design).

Figure 11   The deli area of the college foodservice shown in Figure 6.
Source: Webb Design, Tustin, CA (James Webb, Principal, Linda Midden, Director of Design).

patients. The type of service to use, centralized or decentralized, must be decided at the outset of planning, because space and equipment requirements differ greatly for each. A central kitchen ordinarily provides food for these groups with one dining room/cafeteria that serves everyone except bed patients. Sometimes small, private dining rooms can be planned for official catering functions. For after hours, vending machines can be installed to supplement regular meal service. Adequate passageways for transporting patients' meals on carts and trucks, as well as space for cart storage, are other special considerations. Elevators or lifts designated solely for foodservice use will expedite meal service to patients. Office space for clinical dietitians in large hospitals is another planning consideration. If off-premise catering, Meals-on-Wheels, or other services are to be provided, adequate space for them must also be included in the facility plan.

Correctional Facilities.   Kitchens and dining rooms for correctional facilities present a planning challenge different from those of most other types of foodservices. Because inmates often serve as foodservice workers, the basic design consideration is to provide for personal safety, security, and protection against sabotage. The foodservice manager should have a full view of all operations. Therefore, the office should be centrally located in the kitchen, raised above the floor level, and safety glass windows should be in place on all four sides. For security, all cabinets should be open with no drawers, and secure locks should be provided for all storage areas. A storage warehouse should be located outside but adjacent to the kitchen so deliveries for daily use can be made easily. This eliminates the need for large storage areas in the kitchen and reduces chances of theft. Serving areas designed to prevent face-to-face interaction between servers and inmate "customers" prevent confrontations. A partitioning wall from the ceiling down to within approximately 24 inches of the front of the serving counter achieves this objective while still allowing easy viewing for selection of foods. The dining area is best divided into small units seating 100 to 125 persons for control of potential riots.

Other planning considerations may include the delivery of food to some inmates in their cells. The planning team should choose either centralized service with food portioned and served onto trays in the kitchen for distribution or decentralized service with bulk food delivery to serving areas throughout the facility.

Generally, kitchens and dining areas in any type of foodservice facility should provide maximum convenience and accessibility for customers. For efficiency, locating dining rooms adjacent to kitchens is preferable. Foodservices are best located on the first floor to obtain the best lighting, ventilation, and outdoor views. Basement-level locations can have a poor psychological effect on both patrons and employees if the area is dark and unattractive. The disadvantages of foodservices located above the first floor are inaccessibility to patrons and problems related to bringing in supplies and removing trash and waste. The physical environment is very important to the success of any foodservice design.

STEPS IN THE PLANNING PROCEDURE

After preliminary study to prepare for the facility design project, completing the following developmental steps will lead to a finished layout design:

- Prepare a prospectus (a program or planning guide).
- Organize a planning team.
- Conduct a feasibility study.
- Make a menu analysis.
- Consider the desired architectural features: building materials, floors, walls, lighting, heating, cooling, ventilation, refrigeration, and plumbing.
- Consider (and adjust if necessary) the costs versus money available relationships.

On completion of these preliminaries, the design development process can proceed.

> **KEY CONCEPT:** The first step in a facility design project is to prepare a prospectus, which is a written description of all aspects of the project under consideration.

The Prospectus

Prospectus

A written plan for a building/designing project that details all elements of the situation being planned, used as a guide and communication tool to aid clear understanding by all who are involved in the planning

The **prospectus** is a written description that details all aspects of the situation under consideration and helps other professionals on the planning team understand the exact needs of the foodservice department. It should contain the elements that will affect and guide the proposed design and also present a clear picture of the physical and operational aspects of the proposed facility or renovation project. Usually it is based on questions such as these:

- What type of foodservice is planned?
- What is the foodservice to accomplish? What are its goals?
- Which major type of food production system will be used?
- How many people and what age groups are to be served? How many must be served at one time?
- What will be the hours of service? Style of service?
- What is the menu and the menu pattern? *The menu drives the layout.*
- In what form will food be purchased? How often?
- What storage facilities will be needed? Amount of refrigerated and amount of freezer space? *Storage is a critical aspect of the facility design. The menu drives the amount and location of each type of storage.*
- What equipment and what capacity for each piece will be required to prepare and serve the menu items?
- What are desirable space relationships?
- How will safety precautions be incorporated in the plan? Sanitary measures?
- What facilities must be planned for persons with disabilities?
- What energy sources are most economical? Available?
- What activities will be computerized?

The prospectus usually contains three major sections:

1. The *rationale* includes title, reason or need for project, and its goal, objectives, policies, and procedures.
2. *Physical and operational characteristics* include architectural designs and features, all details about the menu, food preparation and service, employee and customer profiles, and anticipated volume of business.
3. *Regulatory information* includes built-in sanitation, safety, and noise control features, and energy and type of utility usage desired.

Rationale. The title, goal, objectives, policies and procedures, and a statement of need for the project are, perhaps, the most difficult components to define. The following definitions and examples should help make the exercise easier:

- **Title:** Description of the plan. Narrow the title to reflect the actual scope of the design that is proposed.
  Example: Design for a warewashing area of the Coastal Restaurant Foodservice.
- **Goal:** State the single outcome of the project.
  Example: To develop a central warewashing area that will process all dishes, utensils, and pans of the foodservice.
- **Objective:** Specific statements that indicate what is necessary to achieve the goal.
  Example: The warewashing area will (1) utilize no more than 36 square feet of floor space, (2) be operated with no more than four persons, and (3) operate with minimum energy usage.
- **Policy:** A definite course or method of action selected from among alternatives and in light of given conditions to guide and determine present and future decisions.
  Example: All dishes, utensils, and pans will be washed and stored within 45 minutes of use.
- **Procedure:** A particular way of accomplishing something.
  Example: Conveyor belts will be used to carry dirty dishes to the warewashing area, or scraping, racking, and washing of dirty utensils and pans and storing clean ones should be accomplished with 80 percent automation.

The statement of need for the project may be simple or complex, depending on the project; for example, "The foodservice dry and refrigerated storage areas need to be expanded 60 percent to accommodate an increase in meal census from 500 per day to 1,200 per day as a result of a recent building addition."

Physical and Operational Characteristics. Physical characteristics relate to architectural or design features, such as building style appropriate to the type of food to be served. Mexican foods, for example, often call for Mexican or Spanish architecture. Color, both interior and exterior, is an important design feature (Figures 12 and 13). Existing design features to identify in a renovation project could be a support pillar, an elevator shaft that cannot be moved, or a desired solar heating system. These must be identified at this stage because they could affect other considerations, such as the style of the roof and types of windows.

Operational data refer to activities that take place in the foodservice department. The types of food on the menu are the key concern in the planning stage. Further, the form in which food will be purchased—fresh, canned, or frozen—and the approximate quantities of each must be estimated with some accuracy. This information helps planners determine the amount and kind of storage space required. Food preparation methods to be used, including on-premise pre-preparation, tell the planners what equipment is needed and the amount of space that is required to accommodate the equipment.

The major operational characteristic, or type of foodservice system, is basic to all design planning. Space requirements for an assembly/serve system are quite different from those of a conventional system. Other decisions to make in advance are whether to use centralized or decentralized service and the method of delivery and service to be employed.

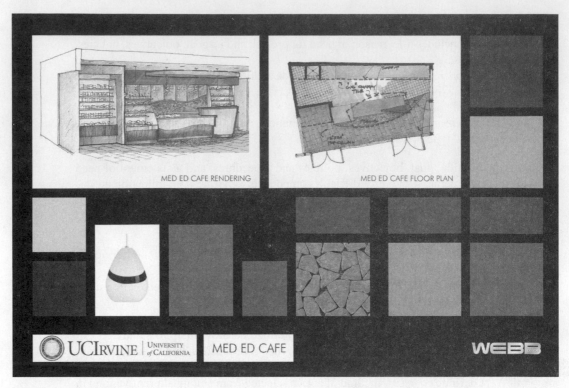

Figure 12 A color board prepared by a design consultant showing the palette of colors, textures, and lighting to be used in a college café.
Source: Webb Design, Tustin, CA (James Webb, Principal, Linda Midden, Director of Design).

Other operational characteristics are the hours of service, the anticipated volume of business (both total and per meal period), and the number of diners to be seated at any one time. These data help determine the required size for the dining area.

A customer profile, including age, size of group, and mobility, helps determine the probable dining space required per person. An employee profile includes the number of employees, the number of shifts and employees on duty per shift, the employees' sex (to plan locker and rest room space), and each work position as it relates to standing, sitting, walking, pushing carts, and so forth. Special considerations to meet the needs of persons with disabilities are included as well. This information is essential so that adequate space for work and movement of people and equipment will be allocated.

Regulatory Information. This section identifies the standards of safety, sanitation and cleanliness, noise control, and waste disposal that the design must meet. Also included are standards established by the Americans with Disabilities Act to provide for employees

Figure 13 A color rendering showing the use of the colors on the color board in Figure 12.
Source: Webb Design, Tustin, CA (James Webb, Principal, Linda Midden, Director of Design).

and patrons with disabilities. Guidelines for selection of the type of utilities to be used and energy constraints are also stated.

Because every project is unique, the various sections of a prospectus will not always include all of the same data, just those that pertain to the situation. For example, a dry and refrigerated storage design does not need a customer profile. Instead, employee and equipment characteristics would be the focus, in addition to information regarding the menu, food items, and safety and sanitation regulations.

The key in writing the plan is to include all pertinent technical data and how the data presented will affect the proposed design. The seating space in a cocktail lounge, for example, will depend on the size of the tables and chairs selected. The person who writes the prospectus and later helps develop the design should be a professional foodservice manager with the knowledge and authority to make decisions about the anticipated menu, space, and equipment needs. That person must also be able to provide other operational data required by planning team members.

When the project plan is complete, it is time to organize a team to develop the design plan. The expertise required of those on the team will vary depending on the extent of the project, its objectives, and its size.

The Planning Team

KEY CONCEPT: **The planning team may include any or all of the following members: the owner or administrator, foodservice manager, architect, foodservice design consultant, equipment representative, business manager, builder/contractor, and maintenance/ mechanical engineer.**

All team members need to have a clear understanding of the project plan. An important part of each team member's role is to educate the others on his or her own area of expertise and to prevent them from making mistakes that might harm the project. Communication is critical from the very beginning. Each member of the team should know how decisions will be made and communicated and what his or her role will be in the decision-making process. A checklist for every stage should be created and responsibilities assigned.

Not all team members are involved in all planning stages. Certain members are included at intervals throughout design development. Generally, the owner or administrator and foodservice manager will co-plan the initial design and bring in other team members for planning meetings at appropriate times during the project's development.

The planning team chooses a floor plan, selects materials, and writes specifications cooperatively. However, team members need to check the plans many times before submitting final proposals to builders and to equipment vendors for bids. It is essential to include every detail and be so specific that no part of the architectural features, equipment layout, and specifications is left to chance or misinterpretation.

Feasibility Study

A feasibility study—the collection of data about the market and other factors relating to the operation of the proposed facility—justifies the proposed project, helping to ensure that the project is worth pursuing. This study follows the prospectus outline, with data being collected for each major category. Because each project is unique, categories vary according to need. For instance, the feasibility study for a new restaurant would include research on the proposed site, potential customer profiles and community growth, building trends, competition in the area, and possible revenue-generating sources, such as catering. For a small renovation project in an existing building, the feasibility study would focus more on operational details than on community and competitive information.

Because the financial commitment for most projects is so large, cost information for construction, renovation, and equipment is an essential part of the feasibility study.

Many people can assist in this effort, but one person should be the coordinator. This person may be the business or financial manager who also interprets the cost data for the planning team.

Data sources for the feasibility study may include the following:

1. Payroll, production, cash register, and inventory records
2. City, county, state, and national regulations, obtained from the respective agencies involved or from library copies of those documents
3. Statistics regarding trends, average costs, and customer information obtained from trade journals and independent studies

The feasibility study is a critical component of a project plan. If the study is done well, funds are more likely to be made available, allowing the project to proceed. Resources for a restaurant feasibility study are shown in Table 1.

Table 1 Restaurant feasibility study resources.

SOURCES	AVAILABLE INFORMATION
Chamber of Commerce, economic development authority, or city planning office	Population trends (historical and projected). Age, occupation, income level, ethnic origin, and marital status by census tract
	Retail sales, food and beverage sales
	Maps
	Consumer shopping habits and patterns
	Employment and unemployment statistics
	Major employers and industries
	Planned commercial, residential, and industrial developments
	Demographic and socioeconomic trends
	Area master plan
Housing and community development	Residential occupancy and housing
	Urban renewal projects
	Property values
Building commission	Building permits data
	Planned construction developments
Zoning commission	Planned uses for zoned areas
	Building height, signage, parking, and construction restrictions
Transportation department	Road traffic patterns and counts
	Proposed traffic developments
	Types of public transportation and routes
Department of revenue	Income and other related sales taxes
	Real estate assessments
Convention and visitors' bureau	Number of visitors by month and spending habits/statistics
	Conventions—size, type, frequency, and duration
	Recurring festivals and fairs
Utility companies	Estimates of gas and electric expenses for the proposed restaurant
Local newspapers	Restaurant critiques and magazines
	Dining guides
	Planned commercial developments

Source: Courtesy of National Restaurant Association.

Menu Analysis

KEY CONCEPT: The menu is the key to equipment needs, which in turn determines space requirements for the equipment.

The Menu Drives the Layout. An important step in preliminary planning is identifying the type of menu to be served and the various food preparation methods required for that menu type. This is the key to equipment needs, which in turn determines the space requirements for the equipment.

Menu, foodservice-system, and style-of-service decisions are the major foodservice planning components. The menu affects equipment design and layout, as well as personnel skills and staffing levels required. For example, if the menu and menu pattern contain no fried foods, frying equipment need not be included in the design, and no cooks will be needed to perform this task.

The prospectus should include a sample of several days' menus and a menu pattern. The pattern specifies meal categories or courses, whereas the menu identifies the respective preparation methods required. From this sample menu, the foodservice manager analyzes the variables involved in producing menu items, such as type of storage needed, portion size, total number of portions, batch size, processing required, utensils needed, necessary work surfaces, and type of equipment required (Table 2). The estimated time when a batch is needed and when preparation is complete is also helpful in deciding whether equipment could be shared or whether duplication is necessary. The manager also evaluates the menu for production, service, acceptability, and feasibility. At this point, menu changes can be made to balance equipment use, workload, and acceptability.

Architectural Features

KEY CONCEPT: Decisions made on architectural features are important for determining project cost, ease of cleaning, good sanitation, safety, adequate type and amount of lighting and temperature control for high productivity, and noise reduction for a more pleasant work environment.

During a project's planning phase, the planning team considers certain architectural features such as building style and materials; types of floors, walls, ceilings, and noise reduction components; lighting; heating and cooling; ventilation; built-in refrigeration; and plumbing. Making a decision on these features is essential not only for determining project cost, but also for ensuring ease of cleaning, good sanitation, safety, adequate type and amount of lighting and temperature control for high productivity, and noise reduction methods for a more pleasant work environment. Because certain refrigeration units are usually built in, the number and location of such units must be determined before construction or renovation begins.

Some of the components previously mentioned are included here as a basic information review.

Table 2 Menu analysis.

MENU ITEM	STORAGE TYPE	PORTION SIZE	TABLE PORTIONS	BATCH SIZE	PROCESS REQUIRED	UTENSILS	WORK SURFACE	LARGE EQUIPMENT	HOLDING EQUIPMENT
Spinach salad	Refrigerated	1 ounce	350	100	Wash, trim, drain	Knife Drain pan	Sink Counter	Sink Counter	Refrigerator
Beef patty	Freezer	4 ounces	300	50	Grill	Spatula	Counter Utility cart	Grill	Warming oven

Building Style and Materials. The type of foodservice operation, its geographic location, and its menu markedly influence the type of architecture and materials used. Material selection for any building depends on the type of architecture planned, the permanence desired, the location, and the effect of local weather conditions on the materials. The building engineer and the architect will know the characteristics of the various building materials and help select the most suitable in relation to cost.

Location is increasingly important to the success of a restaurant operation. Dining rooms with floor-to-ceiling windows can take full advantage of panoramic views. Al fresco, or outdoor, dining is also popular.

A sample of a menu analysis should be made for all menu categories. When similar menu items are used, such as several salad dressings that require the same production and service treatment, only one analysis is needed. This information is the basis for determining equipment and space needs for designing a foodservice facility.

Floors. Floors have to meet certain utility, durability, and resiliency requirements. They should be impervious to moisture, grease, and food stains, as well as be nonslippery and resistant to scratches and acids, alkalis, and organic solvents. Floors should be durable enough to withstand the wear from heavy traffic characteristic of large food units and, in kitchens, to support the weight of heavy-duty equipment. The various floor finishes chosen for one facility are shown in Figure 14.

What is the best flooring material for a foodservice unit? Opinions vary. Hard surfaces tire employees and may cause accidents by causing persons to slip or fall when the floor is wet. However, this type of flooring is highly resistant to wear and soil, comparatively easy to maintain, and permanent. Rough or abrasive slip-resistant tile is safer but more difficult to clean and, therefore, less hygienic. Abrasive, slip-resistant, thickset **quarry tile** (unglazed red clay tile) seems to be the preferred flooring in most on-site foodservice kitchens today. Any floor surface that is to comply with health department requirements must be **coved** six inches up at all walls and equipment bases. In addition, floors must be installed so that they are sloped to drain at various parts of the kitchen for ease in cleaning.

Quarry Tile

Unglazed red clay tile

Coved

A curved rather than an angled joining, such as at a floor and wall joining

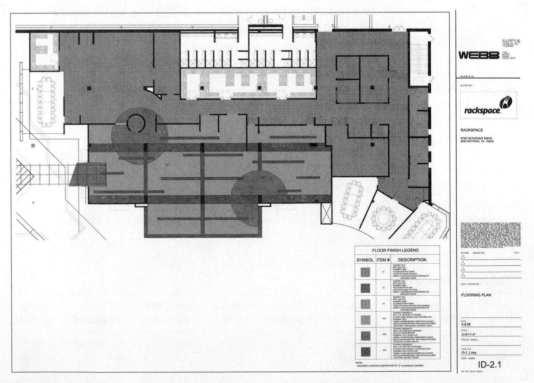

Figure 14   A flooring plan showing the floor finishes to be used in an in-plant cafeteria.
Source: Webb Design, Tustin, CA (James Webb, Principal, Linda Midden, Director of Design).

Walls, Ceilings, and Noise Reduction. The type of wall and ceiling materials selected for kitchen and dining areas can contribute to the overall aesthetic value and sanitary conditions, as well as help to reduce the noise level. As with floors, wall and ceiling materials that are durable and easily cleaned will meet health department regulations and reduce labor time required for cleaning. In addition to wall and floor joinings being coved, all other corners and angles used in installations should be rounded to make cleaning easier and prevent chipping. All pipes and wiring conduits should be concealed in walls.

The amount of natural and artificial light available helps determine the wall finish for a given room. Various colors and textures of materials reflect and absorb different amounts of light. Consider this aspect in relation to the amount of light desired.

Several materials are suitable for walls in foodservice kitchens. Ceramic tile is probably the most suitable material because it lasts for years and is easy to maintain, although it is expensive to install. However, over its expected life span, the cost of ceramic tile is comparable with other materials such as stainless steel.

Fiberglass reinforced panel (FRP), a plastic-like paneling, is quite durable, available in several colors, and less expensive to install than ceramic tile. A minimum-quality material for kitchen wall surfaces is wallboard painted with washable enamel. Because it lacks durability, it is not suitable for use in wet areas, such as around sinks and in warewashing rooms.

A desirable arrangement is to cover walls with ceramic or other glazed tile to a height of five to eight feet where food and water splashes occur. The remainder of the wall may be smooth-finished washable enamel or semigloss paint.

Stainless steel is another material highly suited for kitchen walls; however, because of its very high cost, its use is often limited to cooking areas. It is also quite reflective and may cause glares from the lighting.

Ceiling heights vary widely, with kitchens typically averaging 14 to 18 feet. Kitchen and dining room ceilings should be acoustically treated and lighter in color than the walls. The use of sound-absorbing materials, such as draperies and carpeting, tends to minimize local noises in dining rooms. There are many acoustical ceiling materials to choose from for kitchen use. They must resist deterioration from rapid temperature and humidity changes and from corrosive cooking fumes. In addition, those that have a low reflectance value, are resistant to fire, and are washable are most suited for new or renovated foodservice kitchens.

Sound-absorbing materials are used not only as surface finishes in construction but also as insulators. Vents, radiator pipes, and water pipes may act as carriers of sound, and the most effective means of noise prevention is careful and thorough insulation with sound-absorbing material. Because of later inaccessibility and prohibitive costs, it is most important that this precaution be taken in the original construction.

Features such as automatic lubrication of the so-called noiseless power equipment that keeps it in quiet working condition, rubber-tired carts, rubber collars on openings in dish-scraping tables, and ball-bearing glide table drawers help to minimize noise in the kitchen.

Lighting. The amount and kind of lighting required for a foodservice represent a long-term investment and merit the assistance of technical experts in the field. However, the lighting's adequacy, efficiency, and suitability are far more important concerns than its installation cost.

The design should allow for as much natural light as possible. Natural light not only makes food look more appealing, but can also reduce operating expenses. In addition, natural light exerts a positive psychological effect on workers and guests. Because it is not possible to rely totally on natural light, it is desirable for foodservice managers to have some knowledge of lighting and its requirements when working with lighting experts.

The amount or intensity of light, the kind and color of light, and type of fixtures and their placement combine to create good lighting. Figure 15 shows the effective use of lighting and color to create a warm, inviting look. Recessed, covered, daylight fluorescent is recommended in all back-of-the-house areas, whereas incandescent or halogen, never fluorescent, is recommended in serveries and display kitchens. The reflective values of walls, ceiling, and other surfaces also affect lighting. Light intensity is measured in foot

Figure 15 The use of lighting to enhance the food presentation and the ambiance of the serving area.
Source: Webb Design, Tustin, CA (James Webb, Principal, Linda Midden, Director of Design).

candles obtained from light meter readings, and the number of required foot candles per square foot depends on the work to be done. The general guidelines shown in Table 3 are helpful for planning.

Planners should choose the light fixtures and their placement during the project's design phase so outlet and switch locations can be identified. Fixtures should harmonize with the architectural plan and be placed to provide the recommended illumination level and balance for dining areas as well as for food storage, preparation, and serving areas. Studies have shown that proper workplace lighting can increase employee productivity by 3 percent to 4 percent, a significant amount in terms of overall efficiency.

Lighting systems may be indirect, direct, or a combination of the two. In indirect systems, about 90 percent to 100 percent of the light is directed upward, whereas in direct systems, a corresponding amount is directed downward. Luminous ceiling lighting gives an evenly dispersed light that creates the effect of natural sunlight and is desirable in kitchen areas. Brightness, though, should be low enough to prevent glare or reflections on shiny surfaces that may affect workers' eyes. Light fixtures should be positioned to prevent employees

Table 3   Guidelines for achieving effective lighting.

LIGHT INTENSITY (IN FOOT CANDLES)	ACTIVITY
15 to 20	Fine dining
20	Walkways (halls and corridors), storerooms
30 to 40	Kitchens
40 to 50	Fast service/cafeterias
70 to 150	Reading recipes, weighing and measuring ingredients, inspecting, checking, and record keeping

from standing in their own shadows while working. Good lighting reduces eyestrain and general worker fatigue and is conducive to accuracy in work, as well as to good sanitation and safety in the workplace.

Heating, Ventilation, and Air Conditioning.

The heating, ventilation, and air conditioning (HVAC) system provides comfortable temperatures for employees and guests. An architect, working with an HVAC specialist, is best qualified to specify a system of sufficient capacity for the facility in question. Foodservice presents a somewhat different problem from other building uses because cooking processes generate heat, moisture, and food odors.

Air conditioning means more than air cooling. It includes heating, humidity control, and circulating, cleaning, and cooling of the air. Systems are available with controls for all features in one unit. The system may be set up to filter, warm, humidify, and circulate the air in winter and, by adding cooling coils and refrigeration, maintain a comfortable summer temperature. Dehumidification may be necessary in some climates.

The placement of air ducts is important to prevent direct blasts of cold air onto those in the room. Satisfactory kitchen ventilation typically consists of an exhaust fan system, built into a hood placed over cooking equipment, to eliminate cooking odors, fumes, moisture, and grease-laden vapors. In the absence of direct air conditioning, cool outdoor air may be drawn into the kitchen by fans to reduce the temperature and increase circulation of air, making body surfaces feel cooler.

Although air conditioning may be considered expensive to install and operate, employee productivity is estimated to increase 5 percent to 15 percent in such a controlled environment. As a result, planners should carefully consider what type of temperature control system is most appropriate for their climate and facility.

Built-In Refrigeration.

Storage is a critical aspect of the facility design. The menu drives the amount and location of each type of storage. The smooth, efficient operation of foodservice departments will be enhanced by planning for an adequate kind and amount of refrigeration. The foodservice manager should have some knowledge of the principles of refrigeration, types of systems used, and process for determining space needs for the facility being planned. Walk-in, built-in, and reach-in refrigerators and freezers are essential. At this stage of planning, however, only the permanent built-in types need to be considered.

Mechanical refrigeration is the removal of heat from food and other products stored in an enclosed area. The system includes the use of a refrigerant (chemical) that circulates through a series of coils known as the evaporator. It begins as a liquid in the coils and is then vaporized. Pressure builds up as the vapor absorbs heat from the food. This process starts a compressor, which pumps the heat-laden gas out of the evaporator and compresses it to a high pressure. The compressed gas flows to a condenser, which is air or water cooled; the heat is released, the gas is re-liquefied, and the cycle is ready to repeat when the temperature in the refrigerator or freezer becomes higher than desired.

It is desirable for a refrigerant to have a low boiling point, an inoffensive odor, high latent heat, and a reasonable cost, as well as to be nontoxic, nonexplosive, nonflammable, noncorrosive, stable, and not harmful to foods. With today's concerns over depletion of the ozone layer in our atmosphere, refrigerants used must be "ozone friendly." Less harmful than the formerly used Freon® are the hydrochlorofluorocarbons (HCFCs), which are now being used by manufacturers for refrigerants in their compressors. Thus, the foodservice industry is doing its share to help alleviate the worldwide concern over stress on the ozone layer.

Refrigeration systems may be central, multiple unit, or single unit. In a central system, one machine supplies refrigeration in an adequate amount for all cooling units throughout the building. This system is rarely used because of the problem of trying to maintain desirable refrigeration in all the different units and because, in case of a breakdown, all refrigeration is gone. A multiple or parallel system of refrigeration has a compressor for a series of coolers, the compressor being of proper capacity to carry the load required to maintain the desired temperature in the series of coolers. A single unit is the self-contained refrigerating system used in the reach-in types.

The location and space allocations for built-in units require careful planning. Generally, they are placed close to the delivery area to minimize distance to transport items received into refrigerated storage. They also need to be close to the preparation units that most frequently use the products stored in them. Three separate walk-in refrigerators are recommended as a minimum—one for fresh produce, one for dairy products and eggs, and one for meat and poultry. Each food group requires a different temperature for optimum storage. Walk-in freezers may also be planned.

Many factors influence the amount of refrigerated and freezer space needed:

1. **The size of the establishment:** Because permanent walk-in units that are smaller than about 8 × 10 feet are uneconomical to install, small facilities may use reach-in rather than walk-in units.
2. **The kind of foodservice system used:** Systems with cook/chill methods require a large amount of refrigerated space, whereas cook/freeze and assembly/serve systems require primarily freezer space.
3. **The frequency of deliveries:** Establishments that are close to markets and receive daily deliveries require less storage space than do foodservices located in remote areas where deliveries are infrequent.
4. **The form in which food is purchased:** If primarily frozen foods are purchased, more freezer space is required than if all fresh or canned goods are used.

The total space required may be estimated by measuring the size of units of purchase (e.g., cases, bags, or crates) and multiplying each by the number of units to be stored at one time. This will give the total cubic feet of space required, which will be divided into the separate food items to be stored together. Most walk-in units are seven or eight feet high. Aisle space in the refrigerator must be wide enough for trucks or carts to enter. Width of shelving is based on the items to be stored; two to three feet is the usual width. Space for the insulation of the walk-ins also has to be included, a minimum of three inches on all sides for built-in refrigerators and five to eight inches for built-in freezers.

Floors of walk-ins should be strong, durable, easily cleaned tile that is flush with the adjoining floor to permit easy entry and exit of food on trucks or carts. Wall surfaces should be washable and moisture resistant. Each unit should be equipped with an internal door-opening device and a bell as a safety measure. An exterior wall-mounted recorder to show the refrigerator's inside temperature saves energy by eliminating the need to open the door to check temperatures. (See the "Schematic Drawing" section in this chapter for more information on location of refrigerated storage space.)

Plumbing. Although architects and engineers plan the plumbing for a facility, foodservice managers must be aware of and able to describe the foodservice's need for kitchen and dishroom floor drains and proper drains around steam equipment; the desired location for water and steam inlets and for hand-washing sinks in work areas and rest rooms; the water and steam pressure needs for equipment to be installed; and adequate drains to sewer lines for waste disposal equipment.

Electricity. Food managers are responsible for providing information on the needed location of electrical outlets and the voltage requirements of all equipment to be used in the facility. Equipment manufacturers' specifications list power requirements for their equipment. These must be compatible with the building's power supply, or the equipment will not operate at peak efficiency or will overload the wiring.

The mechanical engineer on the planning team details the electrical specifications, based on the foodservice's requirements, including the wattage and horsepower of the facility's equipment. Hospitals and health care facilities may require special electrical receptacles for food carts used to deliver patients' meals. Because these carts will be moved to various locations, compatible receptacles must be installed at all points of use.

All pipes and wiring going into a kitchen should be enclosed and out of sight. A modular utility distribution and control system offers many advantages compared with fixed and permanent installations. The entrance of and controls for all utilities are centered in one end-support column or panel of the system. All pipes and wiring are enclosed, but controls for both operation and quick-disconnect are on the outside of the panel within easy reach. Water, steam, gas, and electrical outlets may be installed as desired in panels extending from the one-point control column along a wall, to a center room unit, directly behind equipment or from above. Utility distribution systems are usually custom designed. A wall-type unit may house electrical wiring, plumbing assemblies, and gas piping and contain controls for water-wash cleaning for the exhaust ventilator. A fire control system for protection of cooking equipment may be located in the exhaust ventilator, which is located above the utility distribution system.

Budget/Cost Relationship

> **KEY CONCEPT:** All initial expenditures must take into consideration the project budget and also such factors as operating costs, life expectancy, conformance to sanitary standards, and provision of comfort for employees and customers.

Because unlimited budgets are rare, studying the costs involved in any facility design project is inevitable. Planners usually establish a predetermined budget, which the project's total cost cannot exceed. Yet, the quality and features that foodservice managers select for a facility may well affect its operating costs. A detailed financial analysis may reveal that a higher initial expenditure for top-quality design and fixtures will result in lower operating costs during the project's anticipated life cycle than would be the case for a less expensive design.

An example of a renovation that was economical and still provided a significant boost in operational efficiency is the hospital cafeteria shown in Figure 16. A few simple, well-considered design touches were enough to achieve both goals for this hospital.

Building and construction costs are affected by many interrelated factors, including the prevailing prices for labor and materials, quality and quantity of items selected, and the building's overall design. It may be helpful to think of these three factors—cost, quality, and quantity—as a triangle. If the project's budget is a fixed amount, it may be necessary to restrict quantity, quality, or both. However, if a predetermined amount of space is the top priority for the facility, planners must anticipate financing a building or site large enough to accommodate the required size. Alternatively, if planners assign top priority to the quality of fixtures and equipment, they must be flexible regarding the project's cost and quantity factors.

The particular design selected for the building or foodservice department will impose certain operating costs, especially those for labor. A well-planned arrangement on one floor minimizes the distance that food and people must travel and permits good supervision. Compact work units, with the proper equipment easily accessible to workers, tend to reduce steps, motion, and fatigue, helping to minimize labor and operating costs. In poorly planned facilities, it is not uncommon for employees to spend at least 10 percent of their time locating and assembling utensils and supplies. Some assessments indicate that in an efficiently planned department, only the dietitian or foodservice supervisor, storeroom clerk, dishroom supervisor, pot and pan washer, and janitor would need to leave their work areas.

It is also important to include the total costs for cleaning materials, utilities, building and equipment depreciation, and the amount of equipment needed. Such costs will vary directly with the amount of space allocated to the foodservice department.

Furnishings and other equipment should contribute to efficient operation and reflect the best design, materials, and workmanship to conform to established sanitary standards. The degree of comfort for both guests and employees depends on the provisions made for them during the project's planning phase. Examples are such amenities as air conditioning, type of lighting, sound deadening, artistic incorporation of color and design, comfortable chair and work surface heights, and clean, well-ventilated rest rooms.

The facility's cost directly influences what can be done with a fixed budget. However, the material in the remainder of this chapter assumes that adequate funds are available for foodservice planning on a moderate scale.

Fine Tuning a Hospital Cafeteria

Original Layout

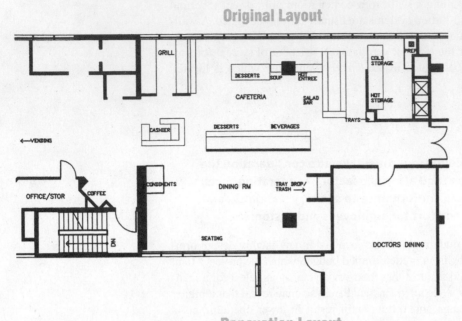

1) Beverage/dessert counter concaved to increase length and create better traffic circulation.
2) Soiled dish-drop relocated to existing cafe area.
3) Open grab-and-go refrigerated cases added to expedite customer throughput.
4) Soup station expanded to better accommodate customer volume.
5) Salad bar expanded and moved to create efficient traffic circulation.
6) Hot entree station expanded to feature "Daily Special" cooking podium.
7) Existing grill given facelift with new fascia, tray slide and sneeze guard.
8) Cashier counter expanded to two stations to assist better customer throughput at peak periods.
9) Vending area moved out of seating area into a more visible location for 24-hour accessibility.

Renovation Layout

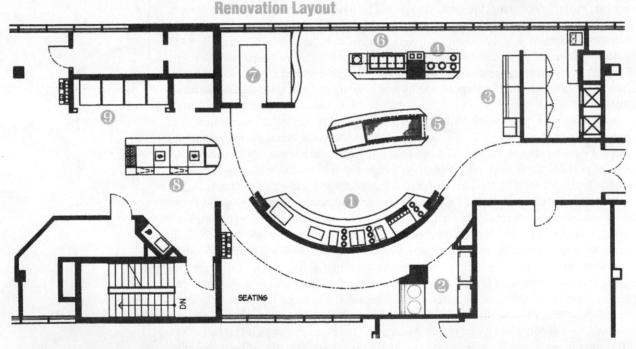

Figure 16 The renovation of a hospital staff cafeteria required a few simple changes to achieve improved operational efficiency at a reasonable cost.
Source: Courtesy Jim Webb, Webb Design.

DESIGN DEVELOPMENT

After completing preliminary preparations, the feasibility study, menu analysis, prospectus writing, and cost considerations, the foodservice manager or design consultant needs to develop a design and layout plan. Providing adequate facilities for all anticipated activities, incorporating the ideas that planning members generate, and considering the facility's future growth are important aspects of design development.

A logical sequence for developing a design and for completing a foodservice facility follows:

1. Determine space allowances. Draw a flow diagram showing the space relationships of the work units and routes for supplies and workers.

   KEY CONCEPT: **The first step in design development is to determine optimum space allowances and draw a flow diagram showing the location of the work units.**

2. Prepare a schematic design to scale, showing space allowances and relationships and placement of equipment, for consideration by the planning team before the architect begins preparing blueprints. Revise as needed.

   KEY CONCEPT: **In the schematic drawing, equipment is drawn to scale in each work unit with required traffic aisles and work spaces included.**

3. Prepare and submit the architect's complete set of blueprints and contract documents, including specifications, to reliable interested contractors, builders, engineers, and equipment representatives for competitive bids.
4. Formulate contracts with accepted bidders.
5. Inspect construction, wiring, plumbing, finishing, and the equipment and its installation, as specified in blueprints and contracts. This is the responsibility of the architect and contractor.

Space Allowances and Relationships

Determining the amount of floor space and how to divide it for foodservice activities varies with every operation. Each activity needs adequate space to prepare and serve the planned number of meals, yet allowing too much space can result in inefficiency and lost time and effort.

The prospectus and menu analysis specify the number and kind of activities to be performed. The required equipment is listed for each activity, such as vegetable preparation, cooking specific menu items, and service methods to be used. The manufacturers' equipment catalogs contain the size and space requirements for each model to be purchased. The space for equipment plus adequate aisle space represents a fair estimate of the total area required.

One commonly used procedure to determine kitchen space requirements begins with a calculation of the amount of space needed for the dining room. Fairly accurate estimates for dining areas can be calculated if the type of service and number of persons to be seated at one time are known. Likewise, seating capacity can be determined by using the generally accepted number of square feet per seat for different kinds of foodservices. Variations from the following suggestions will depend on the sizes of tables and chairs and whether a spacious arrangement is desired:

School cafeterias	10 to 14 sq ft per seat
Banquet dining	10 to 14 sq ft per seat
Counter/fast-service seating	10 to 14 sq ft per seat
Prison/jail dining	18 sq ft per seat
Commercial cafeterias	15 to 18 sq ft per seat
Industrial and university cafeterias	13 to 15 sq ft per seat
Cafés/bistros	17 to 20 sq ft per seat
Hotels, clubs, and fine dining	22 to 24 sq ft per seat
Wheelchair dining	20 to 24 sq ft per seat
Cocktail lounge	12 to 14 sq ft per seat, 20 sq ft per stool (includes the bar)

If 100 percent represents the total facility, on average 35 percent of the space is used by the serving/dining areas and 65 percent is used by the kitchen/storeroom/dishwashing

Table 4   Space allowance guidelines for specific kitchen areas.

AREAS	CAFETERIAS	RESTAURANTS	HOSPITALS
Receiving	1.0 sq. ft./seat	1.2 sq. ft./seat	2.0 sq. ft./bed
Dry Storage	2.0 sq. ft./seat	2.5 sq. ft./seat	4.3 sq. ft./bed
Refrigeration	1.0 sq. ft./seat	1.3 sq. ft./seat	2.5 sq. ft./bed
Preparation	4.4 sq. ft./seat	5.5 sq. ft./seat	6.5 sq. ft./bed
Dishwashing	1.2 sq. ft./seat	1.1 sq. ft./seat	1.8 sq. ft./bed
Sanitation	2.0 sq. ft./seat	1.8 sq. ft./seat	3.0 sq. ft./bed

areas. This is a rough estimate at best because so many variables are involved. For example, dining-room and kitchen space requirements are entirely different for a fast-food restaurant and a school cafeteria serving the same number of persons per meal period. The restaurant's turnover rate may be three customers per hour for each seat during a three-hour meal period; thus, the restaurant would need to prepare food in small batches. In the school cafeteria, one half of the group may be seated at one time with the total number served during a 50-minute period; therefore, larger quantities of food would be prepared and ready to serve the students. As a result, the restaurant kitchen would most likely be considerably smaller than the school kitchen with its larger-capacity equipment.

Hospital foodservices confront a unique situation for space determination because only one-third to one-half of the total number of meals served are eaten in the dining room; patients are usually served in bed. Consequently, hospital kitchen space requirements are large, relative to dining areas, so the quantity and variety of food needed for patient, staff, employees, and guests can be prepared and assembled. General guidelines for specific kitchen areas are shown in Table 4.

Flow Diagram of Space Relationships.   Designing the floor plan begins with a diagram showing the flow of work, food, and supplies for one procedure to the next in logical sequence. To find the shortest, most direct route is the goal. The assembly-line concept provides for efficient operations by creating a continuous workflow for the tasks of receiving, storing, issuing, preparing, cooking, and serving the food, while minimizing traffic lines, backtracking, and cross traffic. After food has been served and consumed, the direction reverses to remove soiled dishes and trash. Figure 17 shows a typical foodservice flow diagram with desirable work-area relationships. Only those work units required in a specific planning project need be shown. Because many foods are now purchased ready-to-cook, certain preparation units may be unnecessary in some kitchens. For example, because most foodservices no longer purchase carcass meat or wholesale cuts of meat, the meat pre-preparation unit has been eliminated entirely in those facilities.

The relationship of one work unit to another is also a consideration, that is, deciding on which work units need to be close to each other, which should be adjacent to other areas of the building, and which must be located near an outside door. Figure 18 shows the relationship of areas in a medium-sized facility using the conventional foodservice system. As can be noted, the main cooking unit is the central area of most kitchens, with supporting units feeding to or from it. Further discussion of desirable relationship of units is given in the "Work Areas" section later in this chapter.

Schematic Drawing

Translating a flow diagram into a preliminary floor plan schematic is the next step in design development. The floor plan is a sketch or sketches of possible arrangements of the work units, with equipment drawn to scale within the allocated space. The required traffic

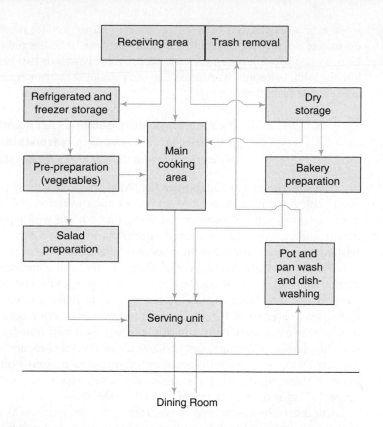

Figure 17 Flowchart diagram showing desirable work area relationships and progression of work from receiving goods to serving without backtracking and with little cross traffic.

aisles and work space also must be included. Some general guidelines and a brief description of various work areas and their basic equipment needs follow.

General Guidelines. Several considerations should be noted when planning a foodservice facility. The main traffic aisles should be a minimum of 5 feet wide, or wide enough to permit carts or hand trucks to pass without interfering with each other or with the

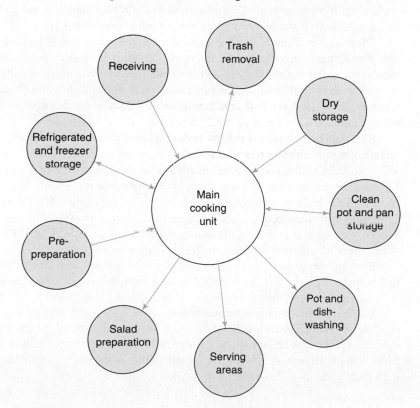

Figure 18 Relationship of main cooking unit to other work areas in a conventional foodservice system.

workers in a unit. Aisles between equipment and worktables must have at least a 3-foot clearance; 3.5 to 4 feet is required if oven doors are to be opened or contents from tilting kettles must be removed in the aisle space. Usually one or two main aisles go through a kitchen with aisles into work areas that are parallel or perpendicular to the main aisle but are separate from them.

KEY CONCEPT: The Americans with Disabilities Act mandates some general guidelines for implementing reasonable accommodations in the workplace and dining areas for persons with disabilities.

The Americans with Disabilities Act (ADA) protects the rights of those with disabilities to enjoy and have access to employment, transportation, public accommodation, and communications. It has two main sections, one dealing with employment and the other with public accommodation. The provisions detailed in the act are voluminous, and anyone wishing to ensure compliance must become familiar with them.

The ADA, which went into effect July 26, 1992, for companies with 25 or more employees (July 26, 1994, for companies with 15 or more), mandates some general guidelines for implementing "reasonable accommodation" to make the workplace and dining area accessible to persons with disabilities. The ADA applies to almost every public facility and to new construction and alterations in existing facilities. Accommodations may include installing ramps, widening doors, and lowering shelves and counters. Aisles must be at least 36 inches wide (preferably 42 inches) to accommodate persons with wheelchairs. Figure 19 gives dimensions of dining and serving room space requirements for wheelchair accommodation in order to comply with the ADA regulations.

Checklists for determining compliance with some of the ADA regulations are given in Figures 20 and 21. These lists serve as aids in assessing a facility for compliance and for future building programs. Taking the actions outlined in these checklists will not necessarily ensure compliance with the ADA; however, the lists can be used as tools to identify and eliminate potential problem areas. The diagrams of space requirements, shown in Figure 22, help interpret some of the requirements of this act. A minimum of 4 linear feet of worktable space is recommended for each preparation employee, but 6 feet is preferable. Work heights are generally 36 to 41 inches for standing and 28 to 30 inches for sitting positions. Refer to the act itself for complete regulations.

Tools and equipment require adequate storage space that is located at the place of use. Sinks, reach-in refrigerators, and space for short-term storage of supplies should be located in or near each of the work areas so employees at one location will have everything needed to perform their work. This includes space for racks to store clean pots and pans. Hand-washing facilities and drinking water should also be in a convenient location for all personnel.

Rectangular or square kitchens are considered the most convenient. The length of a rectangular kitchen should be no more than twice its width for best efficiency. Employees will save steps if the dining room entrance is on the longer side of a rectangular kitchen. Figure 23 shows another efficient arrangement for some restaurants, with a square dining space and the kitchen occupying a smaller space in one corner. The dining area is on two sides, and entrances to the kitchen can be located on each side. During slow periods of service, one section or side of the dining room can be closed off with a folding partition. When there is sufficient business, both sides can be used.

Routing servers counterclockwise through the kitchen or patrons through a cafeteria line is more efficient than a clockwise arrangement, at least for right-handed people. This way the right hand of the patron or employee is closest to the food to be selected.

Large kitchens usually have specialized work areas, each with its own equipment and short-term storage facilities. For efficiency in work and to reduce the noise level in the kitchen, these work areas may be divided with semi-partitions, walls 5 to 5.5 feet high. Thus, there is separation of work, but air circulation in the kitchen is not blocked by ceiling-high partitions.

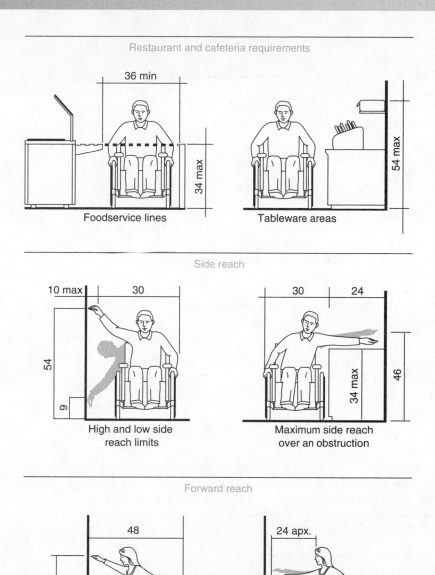

Figure 19 ADA requirements for space to accommodate wheelchair patrons in foodservice facilities.

Restaurant and cafeteria requirements

Foodservice lines

Tableware areas

Side reach

High and low side reach limits

Maximum side reach over an obstruction

Forward reach

High forward reach limit

Maximum forward reach over an obstruction

In smaller kitchens, the work areas may merge, and equipment can then be shared by employees. For example, the cook and the salad worker may share an electric mixer that could be located at the end of the cook's table but close to the salad preparation area. This requires careful planning of work schedules so both workers will not need the equipment at the same time.

WORK AREAS

▐ **KEY CONCEPT:** The seven major work areas in foodservice departments are receiving, storage and issuing, pre-preparation, preparation, serving, warewashing, and support services.

Storage includes issuing of dry and refrigerated foods. Support services are administration and janitorial work, employee/storage areas such as the locker and rest rooms, and storage for extra china, linens, paper goods, and supplies. The number of work areas to plan for a

287

(a) General. A public accommodation shall remove architectural barriers in existing facilities, including communication barriers that are structural in nature, where such removal is readily achievable (i.e., easily accomplishable and able to be carried out without much difficulty or expense).

(b) Examples. Examples of steps to remove barriers include, but are not limited to, the following:

1. Installing ramps
2. Making curb cuts in sidewalks and entrances
3. Lowering shelves
4. Rearranging tables, chairs, vending machines, and other furniture
5. Lowering telephones
6. Installing flashing alarm lights
7. Widening doors
8. Installing offset hinges to widen doorways
9. Eliminating a turnstile or providing an alternative accessible path
10. Installing accessible door hardware
11. Installing grab bars in toilet stalls
12. Rearranging toilet partitions to increase maneuvering space
13. Insulating lavatory pipes
14. Installing a raised toilet seat
15. Installing a full-length bathroom mirror
16. Lowering the paper towel dispenser in a bathroom
17. Creating a designated accessible parking space
18. Removing high-pile, low-density carpeting

BARRIERS CHECKLIST

Building Access
1. Are 96" wide parking spaces designated with a 60" access aisle?
2. Are parking spaces near main building entrance?
3. Is there a "drop off" zone? at building entrance?
4. Is the gradient from parking to building entrance 1:12 or less?
5. Is the entrance doorway at least 32 inches?
6. Is door handle easy to grasp?
7. Is door handle easy to open (less than 8 lbs pressure)?

Building Corridors
1. Is path of travel free of obstruction and wide enough for a wheelchair?
2. Is floor surface hard and not slippery?
3. Do obstacles (e.g., phones, fountains) protrude no more than 4 inches?

Rest Rooms
1. Are rest rooms near building entrance/personnel office?
2. Do doors have lever handles?
3. Are doors at least 32" wide?
4. Are rest rooms large enough for wheelchair turnaround (51" minimum)?
5. Are stall doors at least 32" wide?
6. Are grab bars provided in toilet stalls?
7. Are sinks at least 30" high with room for a wheelchair to roll under?
8. Are sink handles easily reached and used?
9. Are soap dispensers and towels no more than 48" from floor?

Figure 20 Compliance with the ADA barriers checklist.

specific foodservice depends on the type of operating system to be used, the volume of business, the types of menu items to be prepared, and the form in which food will be purchased.

1. Receiving: The *receiving area* includes an outside platform or loading dock, preferably covered, and adjacent floor space, large enough to check in, examine, weigh,

ADA Compliance Checklist

The following checklist will aid in assessing the current level of compliance and assist in future accessibility issues. Any changes in an establishment must be readily achievable. This means that the task must be easily accomplished and able to be carried out without much difficulty or expense.

Passenger Arrival
- ☐ Adequate space
- ☐ Ramp to entry
- ☐ Proper width of walk
- ☐ Door opening clearance
- ☐ No obstructions

Parking
- ☐ Special stalls
- ☐ Access to building by level path

Walks
- ☐ Minimum 48" wide
- ☐ Firm, nonslip surface
- ☐ Curb cuts at streets, driveways, parking lots
- ☐ 5% maximum grade
- ☐ Free of obstructions
- ☐ Level platforms at doors

Ramps
- ☐ Maximum 8½% grade
- ☐ Free of grates
- ☐ Landings at 32" high, extended 12" beyond ramp
- ☐ Well illuminated
- ☐ Firm, nonslip surface
- ☐ Level approaches
- ☐ Guardrails on walls

Entrances
- ☐ One major entrance for wheelchair
- ☐ Level approach platform

Doors
- ☐ 32" wide clear opening
- ☐ Thresholds flush with walk or floor
- ☐ Vestibules with 6'6" separation
- ☐ Handles maximum 42" high
- ☐ Closers with time delay
- ☐ Closers with 8 lbs maximum pressure
- ☐ Single effort with 8 lbs maximum pressure
- ☐ Kickplates 16" high
- ☐ Vision panels at 36" above floor maximum

Corridors, Public Spaces, Work Areas
- ☐ Corridors minimum 60" wide
- ☐ Floors on common level
- ☐ Nonslip floor materials
- ☐ Recessed doors when opening to corridor
- ☐ Noncarpeted circulation paths

Stairs
- ☐ Minimum 42" wide
- ☐ Nonprojecting nosings
- ☐ Level, differentiated approaches
- ☐ Handrails 18" beyond top/bottom
- ☐ Maximum 7" risers
- ☐ Nonslip treads
- ☐ Handrails 32" high
- ☐ Well illuminated

Figure 21 ADA Compliance Checklist.

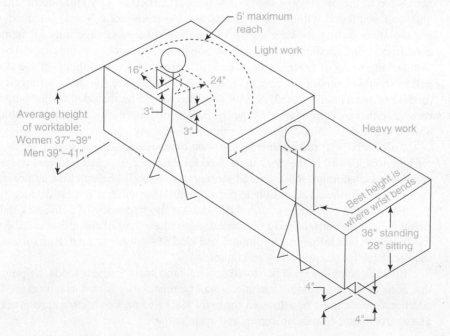

Figure 22 Optimum heights for a worktable and for a working area.

Figure 23 Efficient kitchen/dining room arrangement.

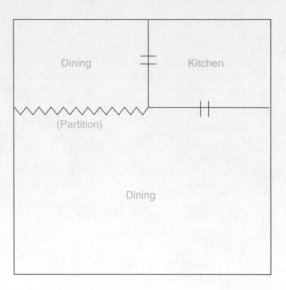

and count food, and to check invoices when they are delivered. The floor of the platform should be equal to the height of a standard delivery truck bed and on the same level as the building's entrance. The suggested minimum width is eight feet. The length is dictated by the number of trucks that are to be unloaded at any one time.

Space should also be allowed for hand trucks, platform scales, and a desk or work space for the receiving clerk for checking off items delivered. Large institutions that process their own meat need to include an overhead track with hooks for carcass meat. This track would extend from the loading platform through to the meat department's refrigerators.

The exterior door must be wide enough (six feet is common) to accommodate hand trucks, large cartons, and any large pieces of equipment that are to be installed in the kitchen. A glass-walled office facing the loading dock that is equipped with a double-faced platform scale is efficient for a clerk in the office to check weights of goods being delivered and received.

2. Storing and issuing food: The *storage areas* should be close to the delivery entrance so goods will not have to be moved far to be stored. Space needed for canned foods, staples, and grocery items is known as "dry stores." This area should be easily accessible to the bakery and the cook's units in particular. Dry storerooms must be cool and well ventilated. Other requirements are moisture-proof floors, screened windows, metal-slatted shelves for case goods, and tightly covered storage bins for items such as cereals, rice, and condiments. Wooden, or polypropylene, mobile pallets should be provided for stacking sacks of flour, sugar, and similar products to keep them off the floor. These pallets should be mobile for ease in cleaning the floor. Space should be arranged to accommodate carts and hand trucks. A desk and files should be included for keeping inventory records, either by computer or manually. Scales are a necessity. Lockable double doors or a wide single door should open to the preparation areas.

Walk-in refrigerators and freezers must be provided for perishable foods. Reach-in refrigerators located in the work units used for daily supplies and leftovers are usually not considered as storage. Refrigerated storage areas should be as close as possible to the receiving platform and accessible to the work unit that will use it most frequently.

The amount of storage required depends on the frequency of deliveries, daily or less frequent, and the form of food purchased. Also, the extent of the menu and the variety of foods offered will influence the amount and kind of storage required. Restaurants may also require space for storing wines and liquor.

Cleaning supplies must be stored separate and apart from all foods, helping to ensure that none of those poisonous chemicals will be mistakenly issued as a food product. Also, additional space must be allocated for extra stocks of paper goods and reserves of china, glassware, linens, towels, uniforms, and aprons.

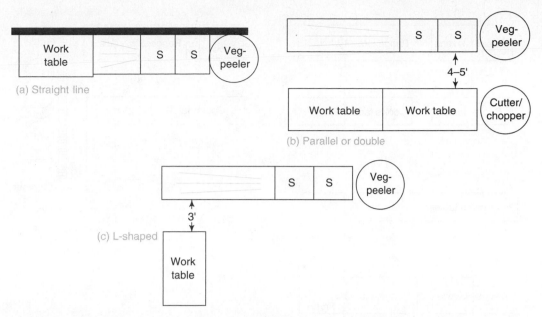

Figure 24 Three possible arrangements for vegetable preparation unit: (a) straight line, (b) parallel, and (c) L-shaped.

3. **Pre-preparation:** A *central ingredient room*, if used, will be located adjacent yet connected to the storage areas. Adequate table or counter space for weighing, measuring, and counting ingredients and ample aisle space for carts carrying assembled ingredients to the production units are basic requirements for this room.

The *vegetable preparation area* should be located near the refrigerated storage and the cooking and salad areas. The usual vegetable preparation area is equipped with a chopper, a cutter, a two-compartment sink, worktables, a cart, knives, and cutting boards. If a peeler is needed, it may be either a pedestal or a table model, placed to empty directly into a sink. Figure 24 shows three possible arrangements for this unit.

Two separate sinks should be provided to permit unhampered use. Food waste disposals are placed in the drain board to the sink or on a worktable near the end of the sink, or space for a garbage can may be provided, often under an opening cut into the worktable or drain board.

Because the vegetable preparation area is often responsible for pre-prepping some items for the salad unit, ample space for many workers may be needed.

Tables that are 30 to 36 inches wide and 6 to 8 feet long are adequate, permitting employees to work on either side for most types of preparation. Providing at least one table low enough for employees to sit comfortably to perform certain tasks is advisable.

4. **Preparation:** The *preparation area* for meat, fish, and poultry includes butcher blocks, an electric saw and grinder, sinks, storage trays, and refrigerators. The overhead tracks for bringing in carcass meat from the delivery area that were mentioned earlier would lead to this unit.

For many foodservices, however, this unit is almost a thing of the past except in very large facilities. The trend toward buying prefabricated and pan-ready meats, poultry, and fish decreases the need for this once-necessary work unit.

The main cooking area is the hub of the kitchen, which is usually located in or near the center of the kitchen. It is most efficient when adjacent to the vegetable preparation area, the storage rooms, and behind or near the serving area (Figure 25). The equipment needs are entirely dependent on the amount and type of foods to be cooked on the premises. The usual for a conventional type of production method would include ovens, broilers, fryers, steam equipment, mixers with attachments, and cook's tables with a sink, pot and pan storage racks, and overhead utensil racks. Ranges may also be used, although in many cases they have been replaced with specialized pieces of equipment such as pressure steam

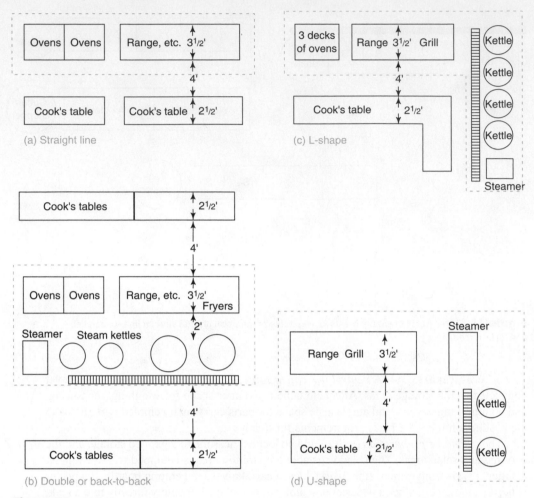

Figure 25 Four suggested arrangements for a main cooking area: (a) straight line, (b) back-to-back or double, (c) L-shape, and (d) U-shape. Note the amount of aisle space and total floor space required for each.

cookers for batch cookery, tilting fry pans, meat roasting ovens, convection ovens, and grills. These may be more energy efficient and generate less heat than the ranges.

The grouping of equipment varies according to the size and shape of the kitchen. However, steam equipment is usually installed together in a row with the appropriate floor drains in front. Grills and broilers for short-order cooking should be closest to the serving unit but not next to deep-fat fryers. Fire danger is great when the intense heat from grills and broilers is close to hot fat that may splatter. Figure 25 illustrates four possible arrangements for the cook's unit. Note the amount of space required for each arrangement, including a 12- to 18-inch cleaning space between back-to-back rows of cooking equipment.

Ceiling-mounted hoods with separately vented exhaust fans, which extend one foot down over all cooking equipment, help ventilate the kitchen by removing odors, smoke, moisture, and fumes. Hoods also facilitate the installation of direct lighting fixtures to illuminate cooking surfaces.

Water outlets at each point of use, such as a swing-arm faucet between each pair of steam-jacketed kettles, above or beside a tilting fry pan, or over the range area, are a great convenience and a timesaver for the cooks. A cook's table, located directly in front of the cooking equipment, may contain a small hand sink at one end and an overhead rack for small utensils. A rack for storing clean pots and pans should be easily accessible to the cook's unit, the pot and pan sink, and the power washer, if one is used. Much of the equipment in the cook's area can be wall or wheel mounted for ease in cleaning.

The *salad area* is generally located at one side or at the end of the kitchen, as close as possible to the serving unit and to the product walk-in refrigerators. The unit requires a

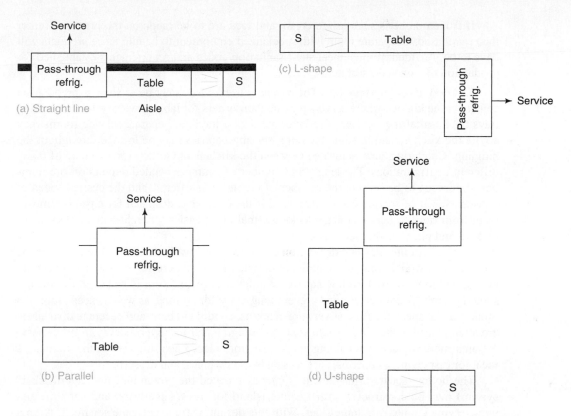

Figure 26 Four suggested arrangements for a salad unit: (a) straight line, (b) parallel, (c) L-shape, and (d) U-shape. Note that equipment is arranged so work progresses from right to left (preferred progression) in all except (c).

liberal amount of worktable space and refrigeration for set-up salads. In cafeterias, it is most efficient to have the salad preparation area located directly behind the salad counter on the cafeteria line. A pass-through refrigerator allows kitchen workers to place the trays of set-up salads in the refrigerator from their side and the counter workers to remove them as needed. Figure 26 shows four suggested arrangements for a salad unit.

Mobile refrigerated units are available for banquet or special party use so that set-up salads may be refrigerated until mealtime and then moved directly to the dining area for service. For short-order salad making, a refrigerated table is a convenience for storing salad ingredients between times of use. In a hospital, nursing home, or restaurant that is built on more than one floor, easy access to service elevators, subveyors, or dumbwaiters enables made-up salads to be delivered in good condition.

The *bakery and dessert preparation area* operates as a fairly independent unit. Having little direct association with the other preparation areas, it may be separated from them. Because the quality of the products from this unit is not as dependent on time and temperature as are meats, vegetables, and salads, the bakery need not be as close to the serving area as the other units.

Equipment for a typical bakeshop unit includes a baker's table with roll-out bins, ovens, pan storage and cooling racks, mixers, steam-jacketed kettle, dough divider and roller, pie crust roller, and reach-in or small walk-in refrigerator. Large bakery units may include dough mixer, proof box, dough troughs, and reel ovens. Small operations may not have a separate bakery unit, but placing a baker's table near the cooking unit allows the equipment to be shared.

Routing of work and placement of equipment should be in a counterclockwise arrangement for greatest efficiency. The finished product should be on the side closest to the serving unit for shortest transport distance. Performance of tasks should proceed in a direct line from one function to the next without any backtracking or crisscrossing of workers.

If frozen desserts such as ice cream and ices are to be made on the premises rather than purchased, a separate room with specialized equipment to handle these products will have to be provided. It must meet strict sanitation codes and requirements established for production of frozen dessert items.

5. Food assembly/serving: The *assembly/serve area* may be at various preparation centers in the kitchen where servers pick up their orders for table service or for assembling trays for hospital tray service. The latter requires a trayline. Separate serving rooms may adjoin the kitchen, and in some facilities, serving pantries may be located throughout the building. Cafeteria counters located between the kitchen and dining room can be of many different configurations. The length and number of counters needed depend on the number of persons to be served, the number of menu items offered, and the desired speed of service. Speed of service can be increased if the counter is designed for customer movement from right to left or counterclockwise, making it easier for right-handed persons to pick up and put food on their trays.

Serving-counter designs depend on the amount of available space. Counters can be arranged in a straight line, in a parallel or double line with a serving station in between, in zigzag sections, or in a hollow square. Whatever configuration is selected, the design should permit speedy service and prevent long waits for patrons, as well as keep labor at a minimum. To speed the flow, silverware, napkins, condiment bars, and beverage dispensers are often placed in the dining room area, encouraging patrons to move away from the serving area more rapidly. A revolving counter section, placed near the wall to the kitchen, is ideal for displaying cold items, such as salads, sandwiches, and desserts.

The hollow square arrangement (sometimes called the "scramble" or "supermarket" system) may be constructed with a center island for trays, silverware, and napkins, and with serving counters on three sides. With this design, patrons enter the square, pick up a tray and utensils, and move to any section of the counter that they desire without standing in line to wait for others to make their choices. A typical arrangement is illustrated in Figure 27.

Figure 27 An example of a hollow square cafeteria arrangement with revolving three-tiered salad display.

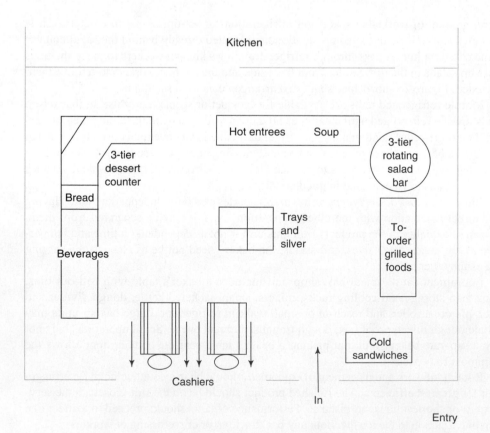

Cafeteria counters are usually custom made so that the desired length and design can be obtained. Sections for hot food, once heated with steam, are now mostly electrically heated and have thermostat-controlled units. Hot foods may be placed on the counter in the pans in which they were cooked, if the counter openings are the same size as the pans. This hot unit should be located as close as possible to the kitchen cooking area. Heated, pass-through holding cabinets can be installed into the wall between the kitchen and serving room close to the hot-food section to facilitate supplying foods to the counter.

The arrangement of food items on a cafeteria line may be in a logical sequence, that is, in the order that the food would be eaten. Schools usually prefer this arrangement so that students will choose the most nourishing items first and desserts last. For commercial cafeterias, however, a psychological arrangement might be more profitable; for example, the most eye-appealing items, such as salads and desserts, are placed first for greater selection, and hot foods placed near the end of the counter. Counter units can be mobile to provide flexibility in arrangement.

The size of serving pantries, such as those in hospitals, depends on whether centralized or decentralized service is used.

6. **Warewashing:** *Warewashing* includes dishes, silverware, glassware, trays, and pots and pans. Each of these is discussed individually. The pot and pan washing area should be located near the cooking and bakery units because most of the soiled pots and pans come from those units. The area should not be in a main aisle or traffic lane. It is often at the end or back of the cook's unit or in an alcove allocated for this purpose.

Equipment needs include a three-compartment sink: one for soaking and washing, one for rinsing, and one for sanitizing (with drain boards). Racks for clean pots and pans are also needed and, in some facilities, a mechanical pot and pan washer. Hand washing of pots and pans may be aided by a manually guided power scrubber or a pump-forced flow of water to loosen food from pans. After hand washing, pots and pans may be sanitized in a steam cabinet or run through the dish machine. Large foodservices, particularly hospitals with serving carts for meal delivery to patients, may need space for a room-sized cart and pan washer.

Dishwashing areas should be compact, well lit, and well ventilated. It is desirable to locate this unit away from the dining room because of the noise. If this is not possible, surrounding the area with acoustical material will help muffle the sounds. Mechanical conveyors save time and money by transporting soiled dishes from the dining area to the dishwashing room. The location of the dishwashing area should be such that the return of soiled dishes will not interfere with the routine of service or cross through work units.

The design of, and space for, the dishwashing area must allow for the smooth flow of dishes through the processes of sorting, scraping, washing, rinsing, drying, and storage. The overall arrangement of the area and the size and type of dishwashing machine to be selected depends on the number of pieces to be washed, the speed with which they must be returned for reuse, and the shape of the available space. Arrangements for a dishwashing area may be straight line, L-shaped, U-shaped, open-square, platform, or closed circle. The straight-line type is often installed near a sidewall in small operations. The U-shaped arrangement is compact and efficient for small spaces, whereas the open square might be preferable for a larger facility and could easily accommodate a glass washer. Machines are designed for either right- or left-hand operation, although the usual flow direction is from right to left. Figure 28 shows one layout plan for a small space. Figure 29 shows a closed-circle, or fast-rack conveyor, arrangement that mechanically moves racks continuously to the soiled-dish end of the machine. Although this arrangement requires about the same amount of floor space as a straight-line type, it is more compact and can be operated by fewer employees.

Any dishwashing layout should be arranged far enough away from the walls to permit workers to have easy access. At least a four-foot aisle is desirable on either side of the dishwasher.

Equipment for the dishwashing unit may include a prewash arrangement, the dish machine, possibly a glass washing machine, soiled and clean dish tables, waste disposals,

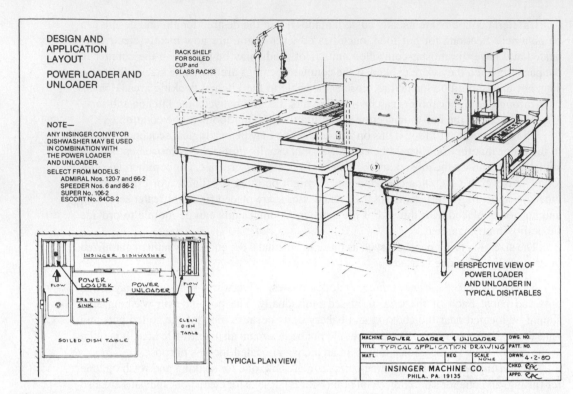

Figure 28 A dishroom layout plan for a small space. This company's power loader and unloader enables many facilities to use larger dish machines in a small area. The unloaders eject dish racks at a right angle to the machine, which is a space-saving feature.
Source: Courtesy of Insinger Machine Co., Philadelphia, PA.

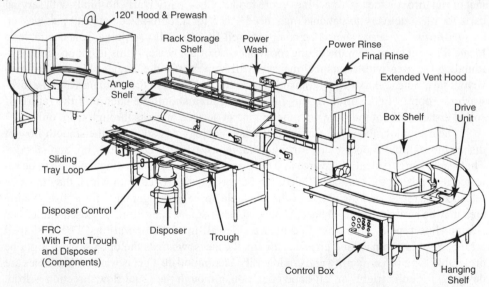

Figure 29 Fast-rack conveyor warewashing system can be custom designed to fit the space and needs of the situation.
Source: Reprinted courtesy of Hobart Corporation, Troy, OH.

storage carts, and carts or conveyors to transport dishes to and from this area. The usual division of space allocated to dish tables is 60 percent for soiled dishes and 40 percent for clean. (See Appendix: Foodservice Equipmemt for further details on dishwashers.)

Prewashing or preflushing equipment includes a unit built into the dish machine, a hose and nozzle, or a forced-water spray as illustrated in Figure 30. The forced-water spray method uses more water than the other methods; therefore, it is not a desirable choice if water conservation is a concern. The hose and nozzle can be near the machine, but the forced spray should be far enough away so that dishes can be easily racked following the

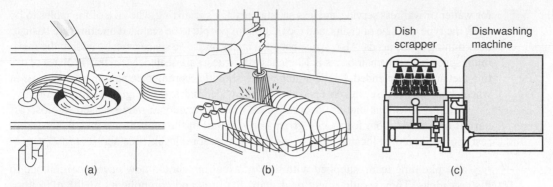

Figure 30 Three arrangements for preflushing soiled dishes: (a) forced water spray, (b) hose and nozzle, and (c) water scrapping unit on dish machine.

pre-flush. Food waste disposals can be installed with either type. A method for returning emptied racks to the soiled dish table for reuse should also be provided. (See the power-driven conveyor in Figure 29.)

A booster heater to increase the temperature of the usual 120°F to 140°F water used throughout the building to the 180°F required for the sanitizing rinse water for the dish machine should be installed near the machine. Some dishroom layouts may include an oversized sink for washing serving trays that are too large to go through the dish machine. If many trays are to be washed (as in hospitals serving patients in bed), a special machine designed for washing trays would be desirable. This type of machine is shown in Appendix: Foodservice Equipment.

Proper ventilation of the dishwashing area is essential. A hood-mounted exhaust fan should be installed over the unit, or rustproof, watertight exhaust ducts, which are vented directly to the outside. These may be attached directly to the machines to remove steam and hot air.

7. Supporting services: *Supporting/auxiliary services* must not be forgotten when planning a facility. Space for employees' rest rooms, lockers, showers, and hand-washing facilities are to be included. The number of toilets and other amenities is determined by the number of workers of each sex on duty at any one time and by the Health Department's standards and codes. Requirements of the ADA must be met when planning these facilities as well.

Office space for the foodservice management staff is preferably located so the staff has a view of the kitchen and the work going on. This may be accomplished in part by using glass walls or large windows for the office. The number of persons who will need desks, files, chairs for visitors, and aisle space will determine the size of the offices. Those staff members not directly supervising food production may have offices in an area adjacent to the kitchen.

Janitors' closets for storage of mops, brooms, and cleaning materials, as well as a large, low sink for washing mops, require consideration in planning a foodservice facility. An area equipped with a steam hose, often located near the back door, may be required for sanitizing food carts and trucks, especially in hospitals that have many such items to clean. This should be a separate area with curbing around it, and it should be equipped with floor drains.

Trash and food waste storage and removal space is necessary if disposal facilities are not available in the building. Many buildings have their own incinerator for burning trash, central compactors to compress trash and cans, and preparation unit waste disposals. When such facilities are not available, both garbage and trash must be collected and held for frequent removal. A cooled room near the back entrance may be provided for the daily storage of garbage, but when feasible, unit or central disposers incorporated into the system are more desirable and efficient.

The dining room is generally a part of the total foodservice design plan. For greatest efficiency, it is located adjacent to the kitchen or serving area, sometimes opening off the cafeteria. Dining rooms that are quiet, well lit, and well ventilated are conducive to the enjoyment of food and hospitality. The size of the dining room was discussed in the "Space Allowances and Relationships" section earlier in this chapter.

Equipment for dining areas includes the tables, chairs, and small serving stations. Two- and four-seat tables that can be combined to accommodate larger groups are typical of most public dining rooms. Tables in school foodservices are larger to conserve space, but difficult for waiter or waitress service and less satisfactory for socializing. The size of the tables to be used, the type and size of chairs, and the number of people to be seated at one time are basic to determining space needs. Also, space between tables and aisle space must be added; the minimum space between chair backs is 18 inches after guests are seated. Main traffic aisles of 4.5 to 5 feet are recommended. Public dining rooms should accommodate patrons who may be in wheelchairs or who use walkers and so may need wider aisles. (See Figure 21 for details.)

Folding partitions that are decorative as well as functional may be used to close off part of the dining room for special groups or when all of the room is not in use. Customer rest rooms should be located close to the dining area for convenience and security.

The planning team, supplied with this information, should now have a conference to discuss ideas. They should reject or discard features and components of the plan until agreement is reached on what should be included and the boundaries for the project. If it is a renovation project, the team decides how much can be done and, perhaps, what has to be left undone. Decisions on quantity and quality within the confines of the budget will be made. Agreement among all team members is critical so that each will be fully committed to the project and continue to devote work time and provide the expertise needed to bring the project to a successful conclusion—to bring the menu and customers together through a planned system of time and motion.

Mechanics of Drawing

The actual drawing of a plan to scale requires certain tools and techniques. Paper with a 1/4-inch grid is a convenient size with which to work (usual scale is 1/4 inch to 1 foot) and yet also provides a good scale for visually depicting the layout. (If a 1/8-inch scale is used, buy 1/8-inch squared paper, and so on.) A pen and India ink, or a heavy black ink pen; a good ruler, preferably an architect's ruler with various scales marked on it; and some tracing paper and masking tape are other needed supplies.

An outline of the size and shape of the space allocated is first drawn to scale with pencil on the squared paper. When the location of doors and windows has been decided on, these are marked off on the outline. Then, the outline of the space is inked in, using proper architectural symbols for walls, doors, and windows as illustrated in Figure 31.

The next step is to obtain a set of templates, to-scale model drawings, of each piece of equipment to be used. They must be to the same scale as the floor plan. Label each template with the name and dimensions of the piece of equipment it represents (Figure 32). Sometimes a different color is used for each work unit. Templates should include overall measurements of features that require space, such as the swing of door openings, control boxes or fittings, and any installation needs as specified in equipment catalogs. The templates are then cut out, placed on the floor plan, and moved about until a good arrangement is found. Templates may then be secured to the plan with a bit of rubber cement (for easy removal if changes are made).

A sheet of thin tracing paper is taped over the floor plan, and lines are drawn on it to show the route used in the preparation of several menu items. Drawing lines that trace the movements of food and workers from one key work point to the next within a unit, as well as from one work area or department to the next, is a good check on the efficiency of the arrangement. Actual measurement of the distances can be made by passing a string over pintacks at each key point during the preparation of a menu item, and then measuring the string. At this time, a check on width of aisles, work area space, location of hand-washing sinks for employees, storage space for carts and trucks, and similar details is made.

The foregoing procedures afford good checks of the adequacy of the tentative floor plan, necessary equipment, and work areas before the final plan is made. The space allowances for passageways between working areas, between tables, between ranges and the cook's table, and between other major pieces of equipment should also be checked for adequacy. Changes and adjustments should be made on paper instead of after construction has begun, because it is costly to make revisions at that time.

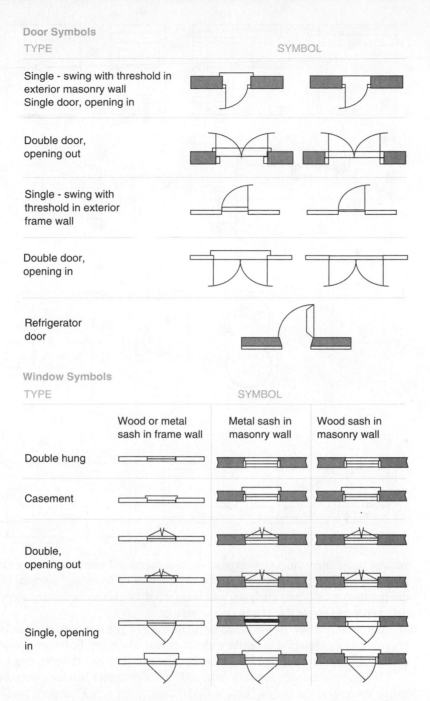

Separate drawings are made by the architect for plumbing, electrical, and gas installations in addition to those for the building construction. All must be coordinated and checked carefully to ensure that gas, water, and waste outlets and vents will be in the correct positions for the equipment planned. Also, the electrical wiring with convenient switch control boxes, power and regular outlets and turn-on switches, and locations and kinds of light fixtures must be noted. Telephone conduits and outlets, wiring for computers, and intercom, public address, or TV system as decided on are indicated.

Designing by Computer

Computer-aided design/computer-aided manufacturing (CAD/CAM) planning began in the early 1960s and has grown and expanded rapidly during the past four decades. Computer capability for graphically designing a floor plan and equipment layout and con-

Computer-aided design/ computer-aided manufacturing (CAD/CAM)

Software programs used to assist in the design and layout of a facility

Figure 32 Templates of sample pieces of equipment drawn to 1/4-inch scale. Cutout templates may be moved about on a floor plan of the same scale to determine floor space needs and to determine the most efficient arrangement of equipment.

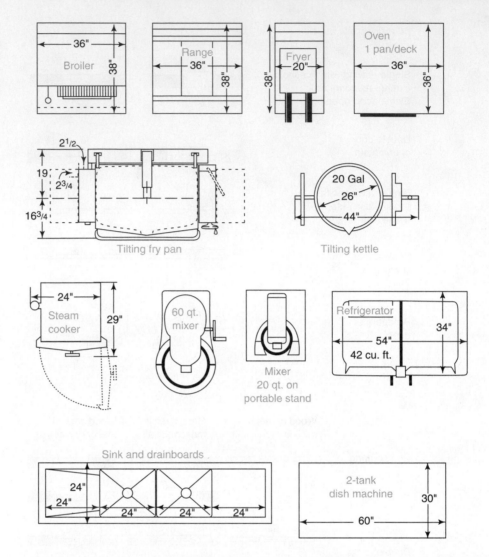

verting two-dimensional drawings to three-dimensional computerized renderings can replace the method just described in the "Mechanics of Drawing" section. However, all of the preliminary studies, analyses, and team input remain as necessary steps to obtain the data needed to create the design on a computer.

CAD for foodservices is based on an interactive graphic concept; that is, the software programs are developed to assist with schematic planning. Software programs use variables that must be identified by the foodservice manager and the planning team.

Today, programs are sophisticated, and the technologies that have been developed have led to the use of the terms "before CAD" and "after CAD." *Before CAD* is computer-modeling software meant to replace the use of "sketching on napkins and tissues" as the starting point for conceptual design. *After CAD* refers to computer-aided facilities management (CAFM), which provides a greater range of services for managing the building project beyond the designing function.

CAD software systems have been adapted and expanded by many companies. An update on the most recent systems is best obtained by reviewing trade journals and contacting companies that sell CAD systems. Many software programs can be used on personal computers, as well as on more powerful, networked workstations. CAD systems run on a variety of platforms, such as UNIX, DOS, Mac, and VAX.

Many add-on packages are available today to make floor plan design faster and easier. They have features such as instant viewing and zooming, display of several views simultaneously, cutting and pasting of drawings to create new ones, and marking drawings for modifications and easier version control. The output devices may include high-end digital plotters, interactive video displays, or virtual reality programs.

Foodservice managers or planning teams wishing to design facilities by computer will want to search the market carefully for appropriate software and add-ons. New developments appear almost daily, and any listing of components today may soon be outmoded or obsolete. Some resources for keeping abreast of developments are listed at the end of this chapter under "Selected Web Sites."

Architect's Blueprints

After the dietitian, foodservice manager, and others thoroughly check the preliminary plans, the architect prepares a complete set of drawings that are reproduced as blueprints. Blueprints always include the name and address of the facility, the scale used, and the date the plan was prepared. Details of construction, material, plumbing, and electrical wiring, connections, and fixtures are indicated and coded. Side elevation drawings are included for door and window finishings, stairways, and built-in or attached equipment.

When reading and checking blueprints, one must constantly consider the scale to which they are drawn. The scale should be sufficiently large to permit detailed study. The heavy, solid lines indicate walls; the space between lines indicates the wall thickness; and the markings in between denote the kind of materials, such as stone, brick, and concrete blocks. Three or four parallel lines at a break in the wall denote the position and size of windows. The direction in which doors will open appears in blueprints as an arc extending from the door hinge to the door's fully open position (see Figure 26). Steps are shown as parallel lines with an arrow and the words "up" or "down." Dimensions of all spaces are indicated, and rooms and equipment are labeled. Architects use a variety of symbols to identify special features; for example, some electrical symbols are shown in Figure 33. All of the symbols the architect uses are explained in a legend on the drawing.

Specifications and Contract Documents

The architect must also prepare a set of written documents to accompany the blueprints when presented to contractors for bid. These documents include a statement of general conditions and scope of the work to be done; a schedule of operation, which includes a timetable for contractors to complete their work and detail of penalties resulting from failure to meet deadlines; a list of those who are responsible for installations and inspections; and specifications for all aspects of the work and for the equipment required.

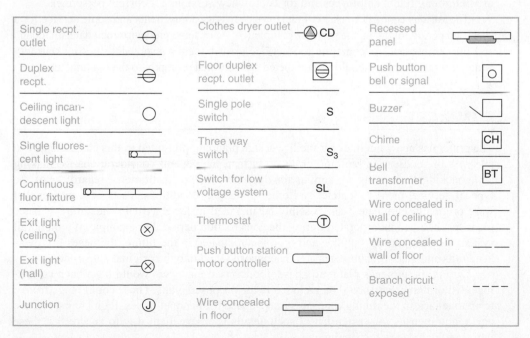

Figure 33 Electrical symbols used on blueprints to indicate type and location of wiring and outlets.

Specifications include details such as the location of the building; type of base construction; mix of cement; size and kinds of conduits, drains, and vents; type and installation of roofing and flooring; wall finishes and colors; hardware; doors and windows; and all other construction features. Equipment specifications generally include the brand name and model number, material to be used, size or capacity, and the number required. In large installations, separate contract documents may be prepared for bids on the electrical or HVAC system. All specifications must meet applicable building and installation codes, and all of the documents must be clearly worded to avoid misinterpretations.

Bids, Contracts, Construction, and Inspection

When the contract documents are completed, they are advertised and made available to interested bidders. Certain reputable contractors and equipment dealers may be notified that the plans are complete and be invited to bid on the project.

The contract is generally awarded to the low bidder, who then works closely with the architect until construction is complete. The foodservice manager closely monitors developments during the construction phase of the project, checking frequently with the architect. Conditions of the contract, as well as the individuals concerned, will determine what adjustments can be made after the contract is signed.

The actual construction time will vary, depending on the type and size of the building and the availability of labor, materials, and equipment. During construction, the architect will frequently check the progress and quality of work to be sure that both meet contract specifications. In addition, the architect must inspect and approve all construction, equipment, and installations before the sponsoring organization accepts the facility. At least two to three weeks before the scheduled opening, a **punch list** should be prepared. A punch list is a detailed checklist that would reveal any defective, substitute, or inferior equipment so that corrections could be made before the opening or training dates. A qualified professional who is neither supplying nor installing the kitchen should prepare the punch list. Each item of equipment is performance tested to see that it meets specifications and claims and that it has been installed correctly.

In addition, performance tests, usually conducted by the equipment vendor's representative to demonstrate proper operation, care, and maintenance of the equipment, should be attended by the dietitian, the foodservice manager and assistants, the kitchen supervisor, maintenance personnel, and the architect. The demonstrations may also be videotaped for use in training future employees and for later review sessions for current personnel.

The various contractors usually guarantee necessary adjustments and some service for a specified period following the project's completion. After some predetermined date, all repairs and full maintenance become the foodservice management's responsibility. Any warranty contract forms supplied should be completed and returned promptly to the manufacturer.

SUMMARY

The principles and guidelines for facility design planning presented in this chapter apply to all types of foodservice building projects. In fact, the general considerations for making and checking floor plans are similar for different kinds of institutions, regardless of the type of service, menu, clientele, and other governing conditions. Parts of a project that were originally eliminated can possibly be included at lower cost in the future if basic plans for them are incorporated during the construction period. For example, if a monorail system for transporting supplies and food is anticipated in the future, the necessary overhead rails and other requirements could be incorporated into the original construction.

During the project's planning phase, foodservice managers would have been collecting a list of items that should be included in the proposed plans. These could range from a telephone jack in the dining room to storage space for banquet tables, high chairs, reserve china, and utensils. A written list of such details is an excellent way to ensure that these items are included in the final plans.

Punch list

A detailed checklist that would reveal any defective, substitute, or inferior equipment so that corrections could be made before an opening or training date for a new or renovated facility

A balance of beauty and utility in the structure, furnishings, and equipment is helpful for successful foodservice planning. Colorful walls and floor coverings, modern lighting, streamlined modular kitchen equipment made of well-finished metals, machines with mechanical parts and motors enclosed, and the use of attractive woods and metals in dining-room furniture are but a few of the many features contributing to the functionality of modern foodservice areas. Sanitation, ease of maintenance, noise reduction, and controlled environmental temperatures for comfort are built-in features that contribute to making a facility successful and help to achieve the objectives outlined in the prospectus for the foodservice operation. A final consideration is that the design should always be flexible enough to allow for future alterations to meet new equipment needs and trends.

APPLICATION OF CHAPTER CONCEPTS

The recognition for renovation/rebuilding is often a "twinkle in someone's eye" long before the project comes to fruition. This is certainly true for on-site foodservices where there is much competition throughout the university system for limited resources.

Sustainability influenced the design of the new foodservice facilities at the University of Wisconsin–Madison in a number of ways. The goal of using local produce necessitated the incorporation of local produce storage and cleaning areas adjacent to the receiving dock. In addition, the new buildings will have "green roofs," dedicated dock areas for composting, pulpers, boilers for deep-fat-fryer oil conversion, focused use of locally derived exterior materials, furniture purchased locally, and intentional placement of windows and type of windows chosen.

The new buildings will be built to LEED certified standards, but the university chose to not go through the LEED certification process. Much of the old building will be recycled.

CRITICAL-THINKING QUESTIONS

1. What is meant by "intentional placement" and type of window chosen in terms of sustainability?
2. What does it mean to have a "green" roof?
3. Why does the use of local produce necessitate storage and cleaning of these products in the receiving dock area?
4. Why would the university choose not to go through the LEED certification process?
5. What impact does the use of locally manufactured furniture and building supplies have on the environment?
6. What items in a university foodservice might be put into a pulper?
7. What items from the foodservice will be composted? How could the university then make use of the compost?
8. How are recycled building materials used?
9. Who would be the logical members of the planning team for this particular project?
10. In your area of the country, what local products (food, building materials, etc.) could be used in a foodservice operation?

CHAPTER REVIEW QUESTIONS

1. What does facilities planning and design encompass?
2. What preliminary studies and data collection are essential to prepare for a facilities planning project, and why?
3. How can a foodservice manager keep abreast of new developments in foodservice design equipment?
4. What are some of the sources of information on the ADA regulatory considerations that must be observed in planning a new foodservice facility?

5. Generally, who are the members of the team who cooperatively plan a foodservice facility? What contributions does each make? What information must the foodservice manager be prepared to provide for the other team members?

6. Why is a prospectus an important document in a planning project? What are the three parts of a prospectus?

7. Point out some ways that sustainability, sanitation, safety, and noise control can be built in to a facility plan.

8. For greatest efficiency, what is the recommended flow of work and people, and the space relationships for a foodservice facility?

9. What determines the number and kind of work units that are to be included in any given floor plan design?

10. What are the mechanics of drawing a floor plan and arranging the equipment layout by hand? By computer-aided design/computer-aided manufacturing (CAD/CAM), or by Revit?

11. What contract agreements and specifications must be prepared and included in the documents sent out for bid for the facility construction?

12. After construction is complete, what inspections and performance tests should be made before the sponsoring organization formally and finally accepts the facility?

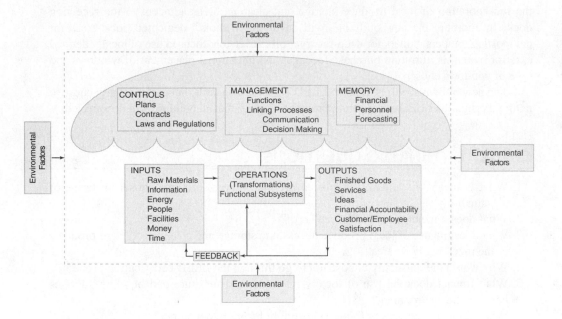

SELECTED WEB SITES

www.alibre.com   (Alibre, CAD/CAM software source)

www.autodesk.com   (Autodesk, design software)

www.caddepot.com   (CADdepot, CAD shareware)

www.cad-portal.com   (CAD industry news)

www.cadstd.com   (Computer-aided design software)

www.cfldesign.com   (Clevenger Frable LaVallee Foodservice & Laundry Consulting & Design)

www.dupagehealth.org/safefood/industry/construct/FS_Design.pdf   (Foodservice Design and Construction Manual)

www.fesmag.com   (*Foodservice Equipment & Supplies* magazine)

http://food-management.com   (*Food Management* magazine)

http://hightechinstitute.edu   (Career training)

www.hospitalityexpos.com   (Hospitality industry trade shows and events)

www.kclcad.com   (Kochman Consultants Ltd., a supplier of AutoCAD-based foodservice equipment symbol libraries)

www.ki-inc.com (Commercial furniture suppliers)

www.nacufs.org (National Association of College and University Food Services, for campus dining professionals)

www.nafem.org (North American Association of Food Equipment Manufacturers)

www.nal.usda.gov/fnic (USDA National Agricultural Library Food and Nutrition Information Center)

www.nemetschek.net/community/addons/symbols/food_service.php (Nemetschek 3D foodservice design equipment software)

www.nfsmi.org (National Food Service Management Institute, child nutrition)

www.ada.gov (Information and technical assistance on the Americans with Disabilities Act)

www.webbfoodservicedesign.com (Webb Food Service Design Consultants)

Equipment and Furnishings

From Chapter 11 of *Foodservice Management: Principles and Practices*, Twelfth Edition, June Payne-Palacio, Monica Theis.
Copyright © 2012 by Pearson Education, Inc. Published by Pearson Prentice Hall. All rights reserved.

Equipment and Furnishings

Ariadna De Readl/Shutterstock

THE CHOICE OF EQUIPMENT IS, LIKE DESIGN AND LAYOUT, a major factor in determining the success or failure of the business. Equipment choices are among the responsibilities of foodservice managers. A manager's involvement can range from planning equipment purchases for a new foodservice facility or for a renovation to making choices for replacement of equipment within an existing facility. This task is not an easy one because of the many factors in an operation that affect equipment needs and the myriad choices that are available.

The first step for managers is to identify their goals and needs in terms of equipment and furnishings. Some common goals/needs in today's economic environment are: (1) improve customer service and speed with the intent of increasing sales; (2) improve food quality and consistency with the intent of increasing sales; (3) increase labor efficiency with the intent of reducing labor cost and increasing sales; and (4) reduce impact on the environment.

Complete coverage of this broad subject area is impossible in a general textbook, but an effort is made here to include pertinent basic information that can be supplemented by current literature from the manufacturers and from observations of equipment in use. Attending foodservice equipment trade shows such as the North American Association of Food Equipment Manufacturers (NAFEM) where chefs and equipment representatives demonstrate the latest equipment is a good way to find out what is available.

The selection and purchase of furnishings and equipment for any foodservice are major responsibilities of the director and the staff, and the wisdom with which a selection is made determines in large measure whether lasting satisfaction will be attained. Employee and customer safety, the efficiency of work units, and the beauty of the environment may be marred by poor selection and placement of furnishings and equipment. The quality of service that an organization may render is influenced, if not limited, by these choices.

The wise selection of equipment for any foodservice can be made only after a thorough study of all factors affecting the particular situation. Items are available in many designs, materials, sizes, and within a wide cost range, but only those items that will help to meet the specific needs of the foodservice and contribute to its efficient operation should be purchased.

The problem of selection is so important and errors so costly that major characteristics to consider in the selection of certain basic pieces of equipment are included in Appendix: Foodservice Equipment.

A section devoted to dining room furnishings concludes this chapter. Basic information needed for the wise selection of dinnerware, tableware, glassware, and table covers is presented in Appendix: Foodservice Equipment.

KEY CONCEPTS

1. Specific characteristics of the foodservice operation must be carefully considered before making any equipment selection decisions.

2. The first consideration for any equipment decision is the menu. It is the menu that determines what equipment should be selected.

3. Equipment features such as design and function, size or capacity, material and construction, and initial and operating costs must be thoroughly studied and considered before choosing each piece of equipment.

4. Maintenance of high standards of sanitation in foodservice is aided by selecting equipment that meets the standards set by NSF International (NSF).

5. Stainless steel is widely used in foodservice equipment construction because of its permanence, resistance to stains and corrosion, lack of reaction with food, appearance, ease of cleaning and fabrication, and price.

6. Stainless steel may be chosen by gauge and finish. The gauge number is a measure of weight (pounds per square foot), which in turn determines the thickness of the steel.

7. A record of maintenance and repair performed on each piece of equipment should be maintained in order to provide data for appraising upkeep costs and depreciation of equipment.

8. Successful maintenance of equipment requires definite preventive maintenance plans to prolong its life and maintain its usefulness.

9. Well-written (specific and definite) specifications are an absolute necessity in any good equipment-purchasing program.

10. Dining-room furnishings and tabletop items should be pleasing, durable, serviceable, and easy to maintain.

FACTORS AFFECTING SELECTION OF EQUIPMENT

■ **KEY CONCEPT:** **Specific characteristics of the foodservice operation must be carefully considered before making any equipment selection decisions.**

1. The menu
2. Number and type of diners to be served

3. Form in which the food will be purchased
4. Style of service and length of serving period
5. Number of labor hours available
6. Ability of employees to do the work
7. Accessibility and cost of utilities
8. Budget and amount of money allotted for equipment
9. Floor plan and space allotments

Most foodservices include one or more of each of the following: oven, range, tilting frypan, fryer, broiler, steam-jacketed kettle, pressure steam cooker, coffeemaker, refrigerator, freezer, ice maker, mixer with attachments, food cutter, sinks, tables, or carts. A wide variety of additional equipment may be purchased as necessity demands and money permits.

Before final decisions are made, individual pieces of equipment should be considered according to design, ease of operation, materials in relation to suitability for the purpose, durability and cleanability, construction and safety, size and capacity, installation, performance, maintenance, and replacement of parts. Cost and method of purchase are also major considerations in the selection of equipment.

Sound generalizations concerning equipment needs are difficult to formulate because each foodservice presents an individual problem with an interplay of factors not exactly duplicated elsewhere. The determination of these needs, therefore, should be one of the first and most important considerations of the foodservice manager as a basis for deciding what equipment should be purchased. Each item selected must accomplish those definite tasks peculiar to the specific situation. If the installation is new, information concerning the demands to be made of the facility and the ways in which the furnishings and equipment may help to meet these demands is of primary importance in planning the layout and selecting the equipment. If the installation is already in operation and has been found to be inefficient, an analysis should be made of the layout and equipment as it exists. This study can be used as a basis to rearrange the floor plan and include any additional furnishings and equipment needed.

The Menu

> ■ KEY CONCEPT: The first consideration for any equipment decision is the menu. It is the menu that determines what equipment should be selected.

The menu pattern and typical foods to be served must first be decided before the extent and complexity of the required food preparation can be determined. Detailed analysis of the preparation requirements of several typical menus provides the best basis for estimating foodservice equipment needs for a particular situation.

Standardized recipes that include AP and EP (as purchased, and edible portion) weights of ingredients, yields, pan sizes, and portion size are invaluable aids to planning for efficient equipment. Batch size and how often a procedure is repeated are important considerations for determining equipment needs. A large mixer and both large-capacity and duplicate steam-jacketed kettles or tilting frypans might be advisable, because they are used in the preparation of many menu items. An increase in the amount of time needed to prepare 500 portions over that needed for 100 portions would be necessary but not always proportional to the increase in quantity. In general, little difference in time is required for chopping various amounts of food in less than machine-capacity quantities or for mixing or cooking an increased amount of food in larger equipment. Repetitive processes such as hand rolling of pastry or batch cooking of vegetables in a small pressure steamer require almost proportional quantity, time, and space increases.

Once the equipment has been installed, care must be taken that menus are planned with consideration for its balanced use. This means that the person responsible for planning menus must be familiar with the facilities at hand and know the capacities of the equipment and timing of processes for the amounts of food to be prepared. Demands for oven cooking beyond the capacity load may lead to much unhappiness between manager and cook and may also encourage the production of inferior food or too-early preparation. Preparation timetables, equipment capacity charts, and standardized recipes that indicate AP and EP weights of ingredients, yield, and pan size for the particular setup can contribute much to effective planning for the efficient use of equipment.

Number and Type of Patrons

The number and type of patrons are important factors in selecting the appropriate amount and kind of equipment for a foodservice. The equipment needs for the preparation and serving of a plate lunch to 500 children in a school dining room are quite different from those of a service restaurant offering a diversified menu to approximately the same number of people three times daily. A school foodservice probably would not offer more than two hot entrées on the menu for any one day, but all food would have to be ready to serve within a short period of time.

In a restaurant, a variety of items would be ready for final preparation over extended serving periods; also, some items would be cooked in small quantities at spaced intervals according to the peak hours of service. Obviously, smaller and more varied types of equipment would be needed in a restaurant than in a school dining room. Production schedules in a short-order operation would require duplicates of such items as griddles, broilers, and fryers, whereas a residence hall foodservice would need steam-jacketed kettles, steamers, and ovens to produce a large volume of food within a specified time period.

The number of people to be fed determines to a great extent the total volume of food that must be prepared, but numbers in themselves cannot be used to evaluate equipment needs. Estimates of number of persons to be served during each 15-minute interval of the serving period will provide a guide to food and equipment needs. Amount and capacity of equipment to select are based on the number served at the interval of greatest demand in relation to cooking time required for specific items.

Form of Food Purchased and Styles of Service

The form in which the food is to be purchased will greatly influence equipment needs. The selection of fabricated meats and poultry, frozen portioned fish, frozen juices and vegetables, juice concentrates, ready-to-bake pies, and some cooked entrées, chilled citrus fruit sections, washed spinach and other greens, and processed potatoes, carrots, and apples eliminates the need for space and equipment usually required for preparation and disposal of waste. Adequate facilities for short and long storage at the proper temperatures must be provided, but other equipment needs would be limited primarily to those pieces required in the final stages of production and the serving of the finished products.

Various styles of service, such as self-service in a cafeteria, table or buffet service in a public dining room, or vended service, require particular kinds of equipment for their efficient functioning. Length of serving period is another factor. A good example of a shift in equipment needs because of style of service is the trend in hospitals toward the room-service concept. In order to accommodate this style of service in a hospital, the facility will most likely need to include the following pieces of equipment: a flat-top grill, broiler, range top, fryer, hot/cold shelf stations, conveyor toaster, deli station, pizza station, fast-cook oven, under-the-counter refrigerator and freezer, induction-based heater, and delivery carts that can hold 10 trays.

Labor Hours and Worker Abilities

The labor hours available and the skill of the workers cannot be overlooked in considering the equipment needs of any foodservice. If the labor budget or local labor market is limited, usually the selection of as much labor-saving equipment as possible is warranted. Judgment must be exercised in deciding which equipment will provide the smoothest functioning of the organization and also give the best return on the investment. Will the increased productivity of employees with automated equipment compensate for the possible increased payroll costs, initial costs, and maintenance costs? With the rising pay rates for employees at all levels, managers must weigh values carefully when selecting equipment they can operate successfully, efficiently, and economically to accomplish the job to be done.

Utilities

The adequacy of utilities for the successful installation and performance of commercial cooking and warming or power-driven equipment must be checked before the final selection decision is made. Often the choice among gas, electric, or steam-heated cooking equipment demands considerable investigation of the continuing supply of the source of heat, the replaceability of parts, the relative costs of operation and maintenance, and the probable satisfaction received from use in the particular situation. High-pressure steam is not always available; thus, self-generating steam units would be a necessary choice. Power-driven equipment is equipped with motors of the proper size for the capacity of the machine, but cycle and current would have to be designated so that the machine would operate properly for the wiring and power in the building.

The Budget

The budgetary allowance must cover not only the initial cost of the equipment but also often the additional cost of installation. Available funds determine to a great extent the possible amount and quality of equipment that can be purchased at any given time. If the initial equipment budget is adequate, the choice among various pieces becomes mere determination of the superior and preferred qualities for each article desired. Sometimes the equipment budget is so limited that the food director is forced to decide between certain desirable articles and to weigh with serious thought the relative points in quality grades of the pieces believed to be essential. It is advisable then to list all of the needed equipment so that unbalanced expenditure will not result. Lack of such thought or insistence on the best may lead to disastrous spending.

Consensus is that equipment of good quality is the most economical. Generally, if the amount of money is limited, it is better to buy a few well-chosen pieces of equipment that will meet basic needs and make additions as funds are available than to purchase many pieces of inferior quality that will need to be replaced in a short time. In contrast, some consultants warn that because of the rapid change in the trend toward the use of prepared foods, it may be preferable in some installations to plan equipment for a short life span and early replacement until such developments are stabilized. The initial cost of equipment is influenced by the size; materials used; quality of workmanship; construction, including special mechanical features; and finish of the article. The limitation of funds may lead to having to choose which one or more of these points can be sacrificed with least jeopardy to the permanence of the article and satisfaction in its use.

Estimates of cost for foodservice equipment are difficult to ascertain because each operation must be considered individually. It is advisable to learn the costs of comparable situations before making tentative estimates for a new or remodeled setup.

The Floor Plan

Space allocation for the foodservice may restrict the amount and type of equipment and its placement, especially in old buildings where architectural changes are limited and in new ones where the original planning may have been ill advised regarding functions and needs. The size and shape of the space allotted to food preparation and its relation to receiving, storage, and dining areas greatly influence the efficiency of operation and, ultimately, customer satisfaction. Floor space either too small or too large to accommodate the equipment that is most suitable and desirable for the volume of food production anticipated creates an unsatisfactory situation. In the first instance, the overcrowding of work makes for confusion and frustration, limits the amount and type of preparation that can be done, and slows production. Time and effort can be wasted by workers transporting food long distances, when the space is too large. Also, there can be a tendency to overequip with needless items simply because ample space is available. In any case, a complete analysis of the real needs is necessary before an equipment investment is made.

FEATURES OF EQUIPMENT

■ **KEY CONCEPT:** Equipment features such as design and function, size or capacity, material and construction, and initial and operating costs must be thoroughly studied and considered before choosing each piece of equipment.

General objectives and trends in current equipment developments include an increase in the number and kind of specialized items, many of which are adaptable to multiple use; function and attractiveness in appearance; compactness and efficient utilization of space to reduce labor hours and time requirements to a minimum; speed output of quality products; **modular** planning of matched units as shown in Figures 1 and 2; mobility and flexibility of arrangement; exact engineering tolerances and effective insulation; computerized and solid-state controls (Figure 3) for even temperatures and operation; built-in sanitation; and fuel efficiency. With the change in the type and amount of food preparation in the individual units has come a corresponding change in equipment to meet the particular production needs.

Modular

A module is a standard or unit of measure. Modular is that size to which all units, such as pieces of equipment, are proportioned; compatible in size to fit together

Design and Function

The design of equipment and furnishings for the foodservice should be in close harmony with the general plan of the building, especially in the decorative features and items such as table appointments. This is particularly noticeable in summer resorts, children's hospitals, and certain types of restaurants, where not only has the modern trend of foodservice planning and interior decoration been followed, but also some specialized idea or theme has been

Figure 1 A bank of steam-jacketed kettles, steamers, and tilting braising pans in a large foodservice operation.
Source: Robert Norlander, VP of Marketing, Cleveland Range, Cleveland, OH.

NEW Heavy Duty Gas Ranges

Chef Series

Customized to meet your heavy duty kitchen specifications!

Design your kitchen to meet the most demanding requirements. Lang Chef Series™ Heavy Duty Gas Ranges are customized to a virtually endless variety of configurations of high performance, reliable and durable cooking platforms. From ranges with open burners, hot tops, griddles or charbroilers to fryer, cheesemelters, salamanders and refrigerated bases, Lang ChefSeries™ ranges are designed and built for demanding chefs in today's high volume kitchen. Lang Manufacturing is a world class manufacturer of heavy duty, high performance reliable cooking solutions since 1904. Our heavy duty line of hotel series ranges continue this tradition and extend Lang's range of chef focused cooking equipment with gas high performance, customizeable ranges, fryers, broilers and cheesemelters.

Figure 2 A compact arrangement of gas cooking equipment. This one includes three ovens, open-top range, hot-top range, broiler, underfired charbroiler, over-range shelving, and a salamander or cheese melter.
Source: Star/Lang Manufacturing International, Inc., St. Louis, MO.

Figure 3 This computerized convection oven utilizes solid-state temperature devices accurate to within one degree (±1°F). A digital control panel replaces conventional control knobs and allows entry of exact cooking temperatures and times.
Source: Star/Lang Manufacturing International, Inc., St. Louis, MO.

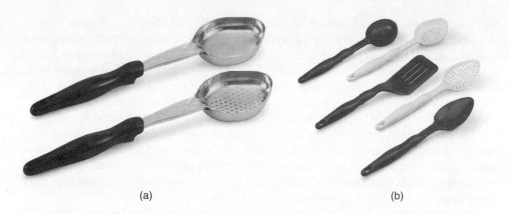

Figure 4 Spoodles are designed to give the portion control of a ladle with the ease and balance of a spoon. Made either (a) of stainless steel with plastic handles or (b) entirely of high-impact plastic in a variety of capacities with perforated or solid bowls.
Source: Courtesy of Volrath Company, Sheboygan, WI.

(a)   (b)

expressed through the design and type of furnishings selected. Sensitivity to the artistic design of foodservice furnishings and equipment is often more acute than for similar items in a home because of the larger size of items required and duplication in number, as in dining-room tables and chairs. Generally speaking, heavy-duty equipment is designed to give a streamlined effect.

Beauty and utility may be combined in foodservice equipment. The designer must combine art principles and consideration of function for the various pieces designed. The gadget or piece of equipment may be beautiful in line and design but of little value if it serves no real purpose or if an unreasonable amount of time is required for its operation or care. The design of cutlery such as a chef's knife with a heavy wide blade shaped for cutting on a board and a long-handled cook's fork are examples of how closely design is related to the use of an article. Also, the design may influence the timing, efficiency, and comfort of operation, as is the case with the utensils shown in Figure 4. These **spoodles,** or combination spoons and ladles, not only are color coded for portion control, but also feature a handle that is designed for control and comfort.

Although the foodservice equipment industry strives for modernization and automation, it must at the same time keep functions simple. A range that is so complicated that it must be taken apart to light the pilot light is not a functional design.

Spoodles

Serving utensils that are a combination of a spoon and a ladle

■ **KEY CONCEPT:** Maintenance of high standards of sanitation in foodservice is aided by selecting equipment that meets the standards set by NSF International (NSF).

Simplicity of design is pleasing and restful and usually results in a minimum amount of care. The maintenance of high sanitation standards in a foodservice is aided if the equipment selected is designed so that sharp corners, cracks, and crevices are eliminated, and all surfaces are within easy access for cleaning. The Joint Committee on Food Equipment Standards of NSF has stressed the sanitation aspect of kitchen equipment design and construction as exemplified in the following statement:

> Foodservice equipment and appurtenances shall be fabricated to exclude vermin, dust, dirt, splash, or spillage as may be encountered under normal use, and shall be easily cleaned, maintained, and serviced.

All equipment mounted on legs or casters should be designed to have a minimum clearance of 6 inches, but preferably 8 inches, between the floor and bottom surfaces of equipment, shelves, pipes, drains, or traps, to permit ease of cleaning. Heavy stationary equipment such as ranges and cabinets can be mounted successfully on a raised masonry, tile, or metal platform at least 2 inches high, sealed to the floor at all edges. Usually, this type of island base is recessed to allow for toe space beneath the equipment.

Specially designed mountings on wheels for specific purposes have become an important feature of foodservice planning for convenience, sanitation, and economical use of space and labor. Portable back-of-the-counter breakfast service units, including toasters, waffle irons, and egg cookers, can be transported out of the way during the remainder of the day. Dispenser units can be filled with clean trays in the dishwashing room and wheeled into position at the counter with minimum handling. Portable bins for flour and sugar are more convenient to use and easier to keep clean than built-in bins. Sections of shelves in walk-in refrigerators and dry storage rooms mounted on wheels are more convenient for cleaning and rearrangement of storage. The importance of designing general utility trucks and dollies to fit into the places in which they are to be used cannot be overestimated.

Heavy-duty wheeled equipment, such as range sections, tilting frypans, fryers, ovens, reach-in refrigerators, and the many mobile work and serving units, make rearrangement possible in order to adapt to changing needs at minimum cost. Often the conversion of certain spaces from limited- to multiple-use areas can be effected through the inclusion of mobile equipment. Also, thorough cleaning in back of and underneath equipment is made easier when it is movable and accessible from all sides.

One of the outstanding improvements in serving equipment has been made possible through a change in the design and construction of heated serving counters. This change from the old pattern of a given number of rectangular and round openings, far apart, in an elongated steam-table arrangement with limited fixed storage, to a condensed type with fractional size containers, has been estimated to permit up to 50 percent greater food capacity in the same amount of space. This arrangement also allows almost unlimited flexibility in service through the close arrangement of a few regular 18 × 12-inch rectangular top openings into which full-size or combinations of fractional-size pans of different depths may be fitted with or without the aid of adaptor bars. Hot food serving counters may be designed and constructed for two or more openings, moist or dry heat, gas or electricity, separate heat controls for individual sections or for the unit, and space below enclosed or fitted for dish storage.

The selection of inserts for this type of counter should be made to meet the demands at peak times for the best service of all of the usual types of hot foods included on a menu. The number of each size and depth of pans to purchase can be determined easily by careful analysis of several sample menus, the quantities of each type of food required, and the most satisfactory size and depth of pans for their preparation and service. In most instances, this will mean a relatively small number of sizes with ample duplication of those used most often.

Common depths of the counter pans are 2½, 4, and 6 inches, with some sizes available 1 inch and 8 inches deep. Capacities are listed for each size, for example, as shown in Table 1. All inserts fit flush with top openings, except the 8-inch-deep pans, which have a 2-inch shoulder extending above the opening. Pans of one size and depth are designed to nest together for convenient storage. Because these pans are made of noncorrosive well finished metal, certain types of menu items may be cooked in and served directly from them, whereas other foods will need to be transferred to them for serving. Recipes can be standardized for a specific number of pans of suitable size and depth for a product and with the exact number of portions predetermined. The pan shown in Figure 5 is designed with reinforced corners to add strength and prevent vacuum-sticking of stacked pans. As with most hotel pans, they are available in full, half, one-third, one-fourth, and one-sixth sizes.

Table 1 Sample capacities of hotel pans.

ONE-HALF SIZE DEPTH (in.)	ONE-FOURTH SIZE CAPACITY (qt)	DEPTH (in.)	CAPACITY (qt)
1	1¾		
2½	4½	2½	2⅛
4	7¼	4	3⅜
6	10⅞	6	4¾
8	15		

Figure 5 A hotel pan designed to last longer, not stick together when stacked, be more comfortable to carry, provide a better steam table seal, and be easier to clean.
Source: Courtesy of Volrath Company, Sheboygan, WI.

Size or Capacity

The size or capacity of equipment to select for a given situation is determined largely by the type of menu and service offered and the quantities of different types of foods to be prepared at one time. More pieces of heavy-duty equipment of larger capacities are required for the preparation of food for a college residence hall serving a nonselective menu at a set hour than for the preparation and service for a short-order lunch counter serving comparable or even greater numbers throughout an extended meal hour. Batch cooking, the cooking of vegetables in not more than 5-pound lots, timed at intervals to provide for a continuous supply to meet the demands of the service, is far preferable to cooking the entire amount at one time and holding the cooked product through the serving period. The latter would require one or two large steam-jacketed kettles instead of a battery of small ones and would mean less effort and time for the cook, but at the sacrifice of eye appeal, flavor, crispness, and nutritive value of the food served and satisfaction of the guests.

Large equipment, such as ranges, ovens, tilting frypans, mixers, and dishwashers, may be obtained in more or less standard sizes, with slight variations in the articles produced by different manufacturers. For example, range sections may vary a few inches in the overall measurements and the inside dimensions of ovens may differ, whereas the capacities of mixers made by most firms are comparable.

Charts are available from most manufacturers that show the capacity or output per hour for each size of machine. For example, the capacity of a dishwasher is measured by the number of dishes that can be washed in an hour. The size of mixer to purchase would be determined by the volume of a product to be prepared each mixing, the time required for mixing or mashing each batch, and the total quantity of the produce needed within a given period of time. Obviously, the size and number of pieces of each item of equipment required will depend on the needs of the particular institution.

The articles most often fabricated or built to individual specifications are those that must conform to a given size or are desired because of special material. Special orders make the equipment more expensive and often delay delivery; however, to most people, the satisfaction of having a piece of equipment that exactly fits usually more than compensates for the disadvantages.

Standards of uniformity in size of both large and small equipment have become fairly well established through the experience of users and their work with designers, manufacturers, and consultants. Many kitchens of the past have had a multiplicity of sizes of cooking utensils, baking pans, and trays that may not always have made economical use of range, oven, refrigerator, cabinet, or truck spaces in the particular situation. An example is the large oval serving tray that would never fit on a rack, shelf, or truck. Alert foodservice directors and planning experts have come to recognize some of these problems and the advantages that could be gained by simplifying the whole setup through improved planning for the efficient and interrelated use of the items selected.

The selection of certain modular items of equipment, or those of uniform size, has proven advantageous in quantity food operations. When a specified size pan, tray, or rack fits easily in the refrigerator, storage cabinet, serving counter, on racks, or in carts, great adaptability and economical utilization of space are possible. Also, worker efficiency is increased and labor hours are reduced; less floor area is required with improved use of vertical space; the use of pans and trays of the same size or in their multiple units reduces the total number and kind to buy, their cost, and the storage space needed; the number of shelves in refrigerators, cabinets, and carts can be reduced when trays and pans can be inserted at close intervals on angle runners or glides; the rehandling or transfer of foods or dishes is reduced, because the tray rack fits into any unit, either on a shelf, on glides, or in the counter; and sanitation is improved through reduced handling of food or dishes, low spillage, and machine washing of trays and pans.

Common modules are the 12 × 18-inch and 18 × 26-inch trays, which are easily accessible in several materials and convenient to use. The 12 × 18-inch trays fit into the standard dishwashing racks of conveyor-type machines. Cabinets, shelves, refrigerators, and carts are readily available to accommodate one or a combination of such trays. Some spaces could be sized so that either one 18 × 26-inch bun pan or two 12 × 18-inch trays could be used. Another common module is space into which 20 × 20-inch dishracks would fit, for storage of cups and glasses in the racks in which they were washed.

This system merits careful consideration in planning equipment for simplified operation with maximum efficiency and economy. Each unit will continue to need a certain amount of its equipment custom built according to specification, but certainly there should be uniformity within each operation.

Materials

Materials for the various pieces of foodservice equipment should be suitable for the purpose and give the best satisfaction possible. The materials used in the equipment influence price, wearing qualities, sanitation, satisfaction, and usefulness. The weight, finish, and quality of the materials are important factors in determining their suitability and durability.

The Joint Committee on Food Equipment Standards has established minimum requirements for materials and construction of certain foodservice equipment items as follows:

> Materials shall withstand normal wear, penetration of vermin, corrosive action of refrigerants, foods, cleaning and sanitizing compounds, and other elements in the intended end use environment.

The committee further specifies that surface materials in the food zone

> shall not impart toxic substances, odor, color, or taste to food. Exposed surfaces shall be smooth and easily cleanable.
>
> Non–food zone materials shall be smooth and corrosion resistant or rendered corrosion resistant. Coatings, if used, shall be noncracking and nonchipping.
>
> Solder in food zones shall be formulated to be nontoxic and corrosion resistant under use conditions. Lead based solder shall not be used.

Metal. Metals have become increasingly important in foodservice planning. Today, we depend on them for nearly everything, from structural features such as doors, flooring under steam units, and walk-in refrigerators to tables, sinks, dishwashers, and cooking equipment. A wide variety of old and well-known metals and alloys, such as copper, tin, chromium, iron, steel, and aluminum, were used in the foodservices of the past, but have been made obsolete by the chromium and chromium-nickel stainless steels. At one time, copper cooking utensils and dishwashers were commonly found in on-site foodservices. Their care and upkeep were high because they required frequent polishing and replacement of nickel or tin linings to prevent the reaction of foodstuffs with the copper. Such utensils were heavy to handle and were used mostly in hotels and the military, where male cooks were employed. Nickel was used considerably as plating for equipment trim, rails of cafeteria counters, and inexpensive tableware.

Aluminum lends itself to fabrication of numerous kinds and will take a satin, frosted, or chrome-plated finish. It can be painted, etched, or engraved. It is relatively light in weight, has high thermal and electrical conductivity, does not corrode readily, and if cold rolled, is relatively hard and durable. It is capable of withstanding pressure at high temperature, which makes it particularly well suited for cooking and baking utensils and steam-jacketed kettles. Aluminum cooking utensils often become discolored by food or water containing alkali, certain acids, and iron. Many items are manufactured from anodized aluminum that has been subjected to electrolytic action to coat and harden the surface and increase its resistance to oxidation, discoloration, marring, and scratching. Anodized aluminum is often used for items such as dry storage cabinets and service carts and trays. Its strength and light weight are factors in its favor for mobile equipment. Aluminum may be combined with other metals to produce alloys of higher tensile strength than aluminum alone.

Cast iron is used in commercial equipment as braces and castings for stands and supports, for pipes, and for large pieces of equipment such as ranges. Its use in small equipment is restricted to skillets, Dutch ovens, and griddles.

Galvanized steel and *iron* were long used for such equipment as sinks, dishwashers, and tables. In the process of galvanizing, a coating of zinc, deposited on the base metal, protects it to a certain extent from corrosion. The initial cost of equipment made of galvanized material is comparatively low, but the length of life is short, repair and replacement expenses are high, sanitation is low, contamination is likely, and the general appearance is undesirable and unattractive in comparison to equipment made of noncorrosive metal.

The use of *noncorrosive metals*, mainly the alloys of iron, nickel, and chromium, for equipment at food-processing plants such as bakeries, dairies, canneries, and in-home and institution-size kitchens has increased tremendously within recent years until at present all such units are planned with widespread usage of this material. These materials are available in forms suitable for fabrication into any desired type of equipment. If the sheets are too small for the particular item, they may be joined and welded most satisfactorily. The price is not prohibitive, so that this type of material functions in many and varied instances, from decorative effects in or on public buildings to heavy-duty equipment, cooking utensils, and tableware. Improved methods of fabrication and the unprecedented emphasis on sanitation have been important factors in the high utilization of noncorrosive metal in items of equipment.

The outstanding characteristics of noncorrosive metals for foodservice equipment include permanence, resistance to ordinary stains and corrosion, lack of chemical reaction with food, attractive appearance, ease of cleaning and fabrication, and nonprohibitive price. Tests show that with proper construction and care, noncorrosive metals wear indefinitely, and equipment made from them may be considered permanent investments. Strength and toughness are so great that even a comparatively lightweight metal may be used for heavy-duty items. These metals do not chip or crack. High ductility and weldability also make for permanence of the equipment made from them; thus, upkeep costs are reduced to a minimum.

Resistance to stains and corrosion is a major feature in foodservice equipment where cleanliness, appearance, and sanitation are of utmost importance. The freedom from chemical reactions of the noncorrosive metals with foodstuffs at any temperature makes their use safe in food preparation. Tests show few or no traces of metals or metallic salts present after different foods have been heated and chilled for varying periods of time in containers made of these metals.

The appearance of noncorrosive metal equipment when well made and carefully finished is satisfying and conducive to the maintenance of excellent standards of cleanliness and order. The smooth, hard surface is not easily scratched or marred, and the cleaning methods are simple. Special metal cleaners are available, but a good cleaner and water and the usual polishing should be enough to keep the equipment in good condition. Common steel wool, scouring pads, scrapers, or wire brushes may mar the surface or leave small particles of iron embedded in the stainless steel, which can cause rust stains. Darkened areas are caused usually by heat applied either in fabrication or in use and may be removed by vigorous rubbing with stainless steel wool, a stainless steel pad and powder, or a commercial heat-tint remover. To avoid heat tinting of cooking utensils, they should be subjected to no more heat than required to do the job effectively and should never be heated empty or with heat concentrated on a small area.

The noncorrosive alloys manufactured most often into commercial equipment are nickel-copper and the stainless steels. Monel metal is a natural alloy that contains approximately two-thirds nickel and one-third copper, with a small amount of iron. The supply is fairly limited so it is seldom selected for fabrication into foodservice equipment.

■ **KEY CONCEPT:** **Stainless steel is widely used in foodservice equipment construction because of its permanence, resistance to stains and corrosion, lack of reaction with food, appearance, ease of cleaning and fabrication, and price.**

Stainless steel

A low-carbon steel that contains the alloy chromium at 10 percent or more by weight

Each company producing **stainless steel** under its own trade name may use a slightly different formula, but the important elements are practically the same. Relatively low carbon content in stainless steels gives increased resistance to attack by corrosive agents. A chromium-nickel stainless steel alloy commonly called 18–8 (number 302) is a favorite material for foodservice equipment. As its name indicates, it contains approximately 18 percent chromium and 8 percent nickel, with no copper present. Heavy-duty equipment made of the noncorrosive alloys retains its appearance and sanitary qualities over long-term use. One manufacturer is now producing stainless steel with a special antimicrobial compound that will retard the growth of bacteria, mold, and mildew.

■ **KEY CONCEPT:** **Stainless steel may be chosen by gauge and finish. The gauge number is a measure of weight (pounds per square foot), which in turn determines the thickness of the steel.**

Standard Gauge. The gauge of thickness of metals is an important consideration in selecting materials for equipment. The adoption of the micrometer caliper scale to indicate the thickness of sheet metal in decimal parts of an inch and the abolition of gauge numbers are strongly recommended. However, the U.S. standard gauge is used by most manufacturers of iron and steel sheets. This system is a weight, not a thickness, gauge. For instance, number 20 U.S. gauge weighs 1.5 pounds per square foot, subject to the standard allowable variation. Weight always is the determining factor. That this gauge is 0.037 inch thick is secondary in the system. Numbers 10 to 14 gauge galvanized steel or 12 to 16 noncorrosive metals are most generally used for foodservice equipment. Metal lighter than 16 gauge is commonly used for sides or parts where the wear is light. Most saucepans are made from 18–20 gauge because heavier stainless steel does not conduct heat as well (Figure 6).

Finish of Metals. The surface or finish of metals may be dull or bright; the higher the polish, the more susceptible the surface is to scratches. The degree of metal finish is indicated

Figure 6 A diagram showing actual thickness of commonly used gauges of metals.

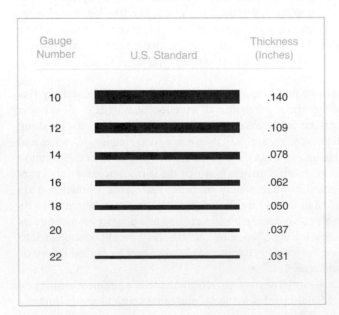

Gauge Number	U.S. Standard	Thickness (Inches)
10		.140
12		.109
14		.078
16		.062
18		.050
20		.037
22		.031

Table 2   Stainless steel finishes.

FINISH	DESCRIPTION
No. 1	Hot-rolled, annealed, and pickled
No. 2B	Full finish—bright cold-rolled
No. 2D	Full finish—dull cold-rolled
No. 4	Standard polish, one or both sides
No. 6	Standard polish, tampico brushed one or both sides
No. 7	High-luster polish on one or both sides

by a gradation in number. The larger numbers indicate a finer finish and a higher degree of polish. Standard finishes for the steels in sheet form are listed in Table 2. Numbers 4, 6, and 7, as described in the table, are produced by grinding and polishing the sheets of metal with different grades of abrasives. These original finishes are capable of being retained in the usual fabrication of equipment, which requires only local forming. Materials with a No. 4 grind surface are more often selected for such items as tabletops, sinks, and counters than are those with shiny or mirror-like finishes.

Glass.   Glass and ceramic-lined equipment, such as drip coffeepots, are most satisfactory for certain purposes. They protect against metallic contamination, corrosion, and absorption. Glass-lined equipment is highly acid resistant and will withstand heat shock. This last quality is because the coefficient of expansion of the glass enamel is similar to that of the steel shell. Most ceramics will break readily when exposed to extreme heat or mechanical shock.

Other Materials.   Items such as counter fronts and ends and food tray delivery carts made of mirror-finish fiberglass with stainless steel structural trim are available in many beautiful colors. The interior and exterior walls of the food delivery carts are molded in one piece, then insulated with polyurethane foam. The surfaces are strong, dent and scratch resistant, and lightweight. Porcelain (glass on steel) or vinyl-covered galvanized steel may be used satisfactorily on outside walls of refrigerators and on counter fronts at less cost than stainless steel. The materials just mentioned contribute to a colorful and pleasing decor, reduce reflected glare of light, and are easily maintained. Detached, well-laminated, and sealed hardwood cutting boards are permissible in some cities and states, although for purposes of sanitation, an increasing number of operators are choosing to use cutting boards made of reversible nontoxic, nonabsorbent polyethylene or hard rubber.

Carts, racks, stands, and dollies made of polycarbonate are lightweight, but capable of carrying heavy loads. They resist stains, dents, and scratches; will not rust or crack; and are easily disassembled for cleaning in a conveyor-type dishwashing machine. Side panels may be of a solid color or transparent, and most models are designed to accommodate 18 × 26-inch food boxes with fitted lids, trays, and bun pans (Figure 7). All items can be fitted with nonmarking neoprene brake wheels and ball bearings.

Construction

The construction and workmanship of equipment determine whether it is durable, attractive, and sanitary. High-quality material and a perfect design for the purpose do not ensure good construction, although they contribute to it. Accurate dimensions, careful and well-finished joinings, solidarity, pleasing appearance, and ease of cleaning are important factors. Sinks, drainboards, and dishtables sloped to drain; tables and chairs properly braced; hinges and fasteners of heavy-duty materials and drawers constructed to function properly; adequate insulation where needed; and safety features are a few of the points to consider under construction. In addition, all parts must be easily cleanable.

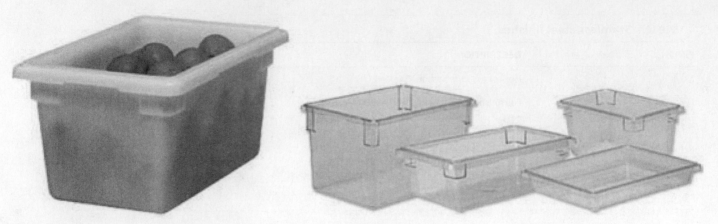

Figure 7 A selection of food storage containers that stack or nest easily and are available with snap-tight covers facilitates sanitary and efficient storage and transportation of food. Boxes made from (a) white high-density polyethylene and (b) clear polycarbonate are shown.
Source: Courtesy of Cambro Manufacturing Company, Huntington Beach, CA.

Welding has replaced riveting, bolting, and soldering of both surface and understructure joinings in metal foodservice equipment. Great emphasis is placed on the importance of grinding, polishing, and finishing of the surfaces and welded joints for smoothness and to ensure against possible progressive corrosion. Mitered corners (Figure 8) that are properly welded and finished smooth in items such as dishtables and sinks are superior to deep square corners or those filled with solder. The construction recommended for items of equipment used for unpackaged food is for rounded internal angles with a minimum continuous and smooth radius of 1/8 inch and internal rounded corners with a minimum continuous and a smooth radius of 1/4 inch for vertical and horizontal intersections and 1/8-inch radius for the alternate intersection.

The bull-nosed corner construction is used most often in finishing off the corners of horizontal surfaces such as worktables. The corner section of the top material is rounded off and made smooth both horizontally and vertically as an integral part of the horizontal surface. If the edge is flanged down and turned back, a minimum of 3/4 inch should be allowed between the top and the flange, and the same distance should be allowed between the sheared edge and the frame angle or cabinet body to provide easy access for cleaning (see Figure 9).

To simplify construction and eliminate some of the hazards to good sanitation, fittings and parts have been combined into single forgings and castings wherever possible, and tubular supports sealed off smooth or fitted with adjustable, screw-in, solid, pear-shaped feet have replaced open angular bracings with flange bases. In many instances, mobile, self-supporting, or wall-hung structures have replaced external framing. Several items welded or fitted together into a continuous unit may need to be brought into the facility and positioned before construction of the building is complete and while there is ample space for transporting the unit into the area.

The Joint Committee on Food Equipment Standards of NSF outlines in detail permissible methods for construction of such general parts as angles, seams, finishes of joinings, openings, rims, framing and reinforcement, and body construction. Specifically, they give construction features for special items such as hoods, water-cooling units, counter guards, doors, hardware, sinks, refrigerators, and power-driven machines, and their installation. Many health

Figure 8 A mitered corner, welded and finished smooth.
Courtesy of NSF International.

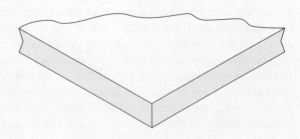

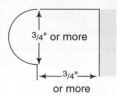

Figure 9 A bull-nosed corner, rounded off and finished smooth. Courtesy of NSF International.

departments use the recommended standards as a basis for approving equipment and its installation. An example of such a standard follows. Figure 10 shows the diagram.

Food Shields. Display stands for unpackaged foods are to be effectively shielded so as to intercept the direct line between the average customer's mouth and the food being displayed and shall be designed to minimize contamination by the customer.

Shields shall be mounted so as to intercept a direct line between the customer's mouth and the food display area at the customer-use position. The vertical distance from the average customer's mouth to the floor shall be considered to be 4 feet 6 inches (1.4 meters) to 5 feet (1.5 meters) for public eating establishments. Special consideration must be given to use location conditions such as tray rails and average customer's mouth height in educational institutions and other installations. Such shields are to be fabricated of easy-to-clean, sanitary materials conforming to materials specifications.

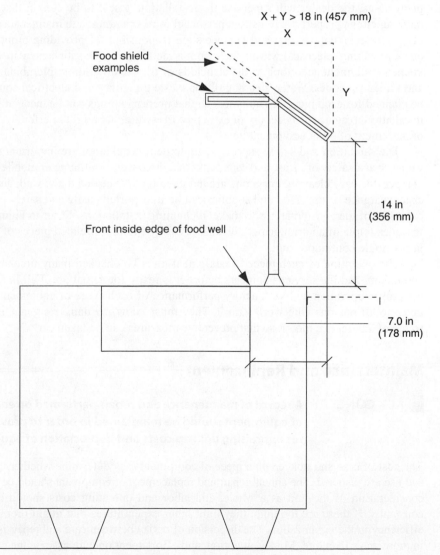

Figure 10 Standards for food shields. Source: Courtesy of NSF International.

Safety Features.   Safety features for the protection of workers in the use and care of equipment and for the production of safe food are important factors in the design, choice of materials, and construction of kitchen equipment. There is also a close relationship between these and the standards and controls for sanitation in a foodservice operation. Smooth, rounded corners on work surfaces; table drawers with stops and recessed pulls; automatic steam shut-off when cooker doors are opened; temperature controls; guards on slicers and chopping machines; brakes on mixers; recessed manifold control knobs on ranges and ovens; smooth, polished, welded seams; rounded corners; and knee-lever drain controls on sinks are a few examples of built-in safety in heavy-duty kitchen equipment. The incorporation of antimicrobial compounds in the manufacture of some equipment components is a relatively new innovation. These compounds are not a coating and do not wear off. Ice-makers, food slicers, and stainless steel are all available with the antimicrobial feature. However, their use is not a substitute for normal cleaning and sanitation.

Installation, Operation, and Performance

Proper installation is a necessity for the successful operation of all equipment. The best design and construction would be worthless if electrical, gas, or water connections were inadequate or poorly done. The dealer from whom the equipment was purchased may not be responsible for its installation by contract but will usually deliver, uncrate, assemble, and position the item ready for steam fitting or electrical and plumbing connections. In many cases, the dealer will supervise the installation, test it to be certain that the equipment functions properly, and instruct personnel in its operation and maintenance.

Architects, contractors, and engineers are responsible for providing proper and adequate plumbing, electrical wiring, and venting facilities for the satisfactory installation of kitchen equipment according to the standards of the local building, plumbing, electrical, and sanitation codes. Water, steam, gas, and waste pipe lines and electrical conduits must be planned for each piece of equipment so that proper joinings can be made at the time of installation to avoid the necessity of extra pipe or wiring that might interfere with cleaning or placement of other equipment items.

The sanitation and safety aspects of equipment installation are important to the convenience and safety of its use and care. Sinks that drain well, wall-hung or mobile equipment that permits easy cleaning under and around it, equipment sealed to the wall, and adequate aisle clearance so that food and supplies can be transported easily and safely on carts are but a few of the considerations to make in planning installations. Refer to Figures 1 and 2 for an example of an arrangement that successfully combines related pieces of equipment into a single continuous unit.

The operation of each piece of equipment must be checked many times by both the contractors and the service engineers before it is ready for actual use. Full instruction for the proper operation and satisfactory performance of each piece of equipment should be given to all persons who work with it. They must know the danger signals, such as the sound of a defective motor, so that preventive measures can be taken early.

Maintenance and Replacement

> ■ KEY CONCEPT: A record of maintenance and repair performed on each piece of equipment should be maintained in order to provide data for appraising upkeep costs and depreciation of equipment.

The cost of care and upkeep on a piece of equipment may determine whether its purchase and use are justified. The annual repair and replacement of equipment should be made with consideration of the unit as a whole, and labor and operating costs should be checked constantly. If these are too high, they limit other expenditures that might promote greater efficiency in the organization. The dispersion of outlay between care and repair is important in more ways than one. Money, attention, and effort spent on care assume the continuance of the necessary equipment in use; money and the effort spent on repair are often attended by a disrupted work schedule, unpleasant stresses and strains on personnel, and sometimes definite fire hazards.

Many questions arise in regard to care and upkeep costs when equipment is selected. Are parts readily available, easily replaced, and relatively inexpensive? Does the replacement require the services of a specialist, or can a regular employee be trained to do the work? Should some piece of equipment fail to operate when needed, has provision been made so that operations can continue? Are special cleaning materials needed in caring for the equipment?

The care and repair of electrical equipment represents a major item in the maintenance cost of many foodservices. The adequate care of electric motors requires expert attention by technically trained and responsible engineers. Arrangements for such care are commonly made with the maintenance department on a contract basis, covering weekly inspection and other checkups necessary for good maintenance. Competent maintenance personnel will have a record card for every motor in the plant. All repair work, with its cost, and every inspection can be entered on the record. If this system is used, excessive amounts of attention or expense will show up, and the causes can be determined and corrected. Inspection records will also serve as a guide to indicate when motors should be replaced because of the high cost of keeping them in operating condition.

To evaluate a piece of equipment in use, an analysis of the expenditures for care and upkeep is made, and the condition of the equipment is checked to determine if the deterioration has been more rapid than it should have been under normal usage, exposure, cleaning operation, and contacts with food and heat. A factual basis for appraising upkeep costs and depreciation of equipment can be obtained by keeping careful records on each major piece. Figure 11 is a suggested method for keeping such records.

■ KEY CONCEPT: Successful maintenance of equipment requires definite preventive maintenance plans to prolong its life and maintain its usefulness.

The reasons for **preventive maintenance** are to minimize down time, to extend equipment life, to provide a budgeted cost for service, to reduce energy costs, to provide operational safety, to ensure consistent product quality, to correct small problems before they become large and expensive problems, and to be able to offer the full menu at all times.

Preventive maintenance

Regular and systematic inspection, cleaning, lubrication, and replacement of worn parts, materials, and systems in order to prevent costly breakdowns and prolong equipment life

Preventive maintenance requires a few simple procedures: Keep the equipment clean; follow the manufacturer's printed directions for care and operation, including lubrication; keep the instruction card for each piece of equipment posted near it; stress careful handling as essential to continued use; and make needed repairs promptly. Some pieces of equipment, such as the dishwasher, may require a service contract.

Some pertinent suggestions for the care of machines and instructions for their use include the assignment of the care of each machine to a responsible person; daily inspection for cleanliness and constant supervision by the manager when in use; immediate completion of even minor repairs; thorough knowledge of operating directions; regular oiling and inspections; and repairs by a competent person. Printed instructions should be easily available. Directions for operation with a simple diagram should be posted by the machine, and any special warning should be printed in large or colored letters. When explaining its operation, the function and relationship of each part should be described in detail so that they can be understood by the operator. There should also be a demonstration of proper use of the machine and an explanation of its value and a cost of repairs. Similar directions should be formulated for each piece of equipment and incorporated into a manual for use by employees responsible for the care and cleanliness of the various items.

The operating cost is an important feature often overlooked in purchasing equipment. In some localities, electricity may be available for cooking purposes at a lower operating cost than gas, or vice versa. When all factors are considered, an electric range may be

Figure 11 Suggested form for recording information on each piece of (a) large equipment and (b) small equipment.

Name of Institution:			
Equipment or appliance item:		Purchase Date:	
Motor serial number	Motor make model	Equipment number	Location
Original cost	Estimated period of use: Months ☐ Years ☐	Make of equipment item:	Description: Type _____ Size _____ Capacity _____ Design _____
Appraisal Date | Value	Motor specification: W __ V __ Amp. __ H.P. __	Estimated depreciation per Month ___ Year ___	Date fully depreciated

	Repairs and replacements			
Date	Nature	By whom	Cost	Remarks

(A) Large equipment record

Name of Institution:			
Name of item:	Purchase date:	Purchased from:	Location
Style ___ Size ___	Amount of original purchase _____	Quality or grade _____	Uses

Appraisal		Repairs or replacement				Amount on hand
Date	Value	Date	Nature	By whom	Cost	

(B) Small equipment record

more economical in this particular instance, even though the initial cost may be more. Due consideration and investigation of the relative efficiency of various models and types are also necessary in selecting any piece of equipment.

According to the National Restaurant Association (NRA), energy management programs and the wise selection of equipment can result in savings of up to 20 percent on utility costs for the average foodservice establishment.

METHOD OF PURCHASE

◼ **KEY CONCEPT: Well-written (specific and definite) specifications are an absolute necessity in any good equipment-purchasing program.**

The method of purchase of equipment varies somewhat with the operation. However, regardless of whether the order is placed by the manager of the foodservice, the purchasing agent, or the owner, the preliminary procedures are much the same.

First, all available data on the needs and requirements of the foodservice operation should be collected. Representatives of various equipment firms are willing to demonstrate equipment and to give the prospective buyer information concerning the particular piece of equipment needed. Foodservice equipment shows are held annually throughout the country. Exhibits at these shows are a good place to see and compare various models and features. Gas and electric utility companies have set up facilities around the country where foodservice operators may go to test and evaluate a wide variety of equipment with their own customized menu items. Visits may be made to various institutions to see similar models in operation.

After such investigations are made, and a definite idea of what is wanted is established, specifications are written and submitted to reliable firms. Written bids are then received and tabulated, and a comparison is made, after which the order is placed.

The reliability of the firm from which the equipment is purchased is very important to any institution. A reputable company with a record of successful operation usually strives to sell dependable merchandise of good quality. The company can be counted on to honor the guarantee and to do everything possible to keep the goodwill and confidence of the customer. In their planning and engineering departments, equipment dealers employ experts whose services are always available to the prospective customer. Years of experience and constant contact with both the manufacturing and operating units in the field enable them to be of valuable assistance. Most companies keep records of the sale, service calls, and repairs of the various pieces of equipment. In return, they deserve fair treatment and consideration from the director of the foodservice or the purchasing agent for the institution.

To be of value, a specification for equipment must be specific and definite. It should cover every detail in relation to material, construction, size, color, finish, and cost, eliminating any question in the mind of either the buyer or the manufacturer as to what the finished product will be. When delivered, if the equipment does not measure up to the specified order, it need not be accepted. If the buyer is disappointed but has permitted loopholes in the specification, it must be accepted. However, most firms are so desirous of selling satisfaction that they check orders carefully with the buyer to see that everything is included before the equipment is made or delivered.

The following examples of a vague and a definite specification for a particular piece of equipment illustrate the difference between the two types. Specifications may be indefinite, and yet to the casual observer all points may seem to be included. After reading the second example, one can readily see the weak spots in the first.

Vague Specifications

- **Item number:** xx
- **Name of item:** Cook's table with sink
- **Dimensions:** 8 ft long, 2 ft 6 in. wide, 3 ft high
- **Material and construction:** Top of this table to be made of heavy-gauge stainless steel with semirolled edge and to be furnished with one sink, 18 in. long, 24 in. wide, 12 in. deep, fitted with drain. Sink to be located 3 in. from left end of table. The underside of this table to be reinforced with channel braces. Table to be supported by four stainless steel tubular standards with adjustable feet. Stainless slatted shelf to rest on cross rails 10 in. above floor. Table to be equipped with one drawer, 24 in. long, 22 in. wide, and 5 in. deep. Drawer to be made of heavy stainless steel, reinforced on front facing. All joints of this drawer to be welded, and drawer equipped with ball-bearing drawer slides. This drawer to be fitted with a white metal handle.
- **Price:** $......

Definite Specifications

- **Item number:** xx
- **Name of item:** Cook's table with sink

- **Dimensions:** 8 ft long, 2 ft 6 in. wide, 3 ft high
- **Material and construction:** Top of this table to be made of No. 14 gauge, No. 4 grind, No. 302 stainless steel with all edges turned down 1-1/2 inches, semirolled edge. All corners to be fully rounded bull-nose construction and integral with top. Top of this table to be fitted with one sink, 18 in. long, 24 in. wide, and 12 in. deep, with all corners and intersections fully rounded to a 1-in. radius. All joints to be welded, ground smooth, and polished. Bottom sloped to drain in center. Sink to be located 3 in. from left end of table, 3 in. from each side. Sink to be equipped with 2-in. white metal drain with plug and chain complete.

  The underside of this table top is to be properly reinforced and braced with 4-in. No. 14-gauge stainless steel channel braces welded on. Four tubular leg standards to be welded to these channel cross braces. Standards are to be made of seamless stainless steel tubing 1 5/8 in. outside diameter, cross rails and braces of the same material, fitted and welded together. Resting on these cross rails and braces will be a slatted bar shelf elevated 10 in. above floor. Slats to be made of No. 16 stainless steel, No. 4 grind, welded to 2-in. No. 16 stainless steel supports. Slats 2 in. wide and bent down at ends and formed to fit over cross rails. Slatted shelf are to be built in two removable parts of equal length. Leg standards are to be fitted with adjustable inside threaded, stainless-steel, tubular, closed, smooth-finish feet.

  Table to be equipped with one drawer, 24 in. long, 22 in. wide, and 5 in. deep. Drawer to be made of No. 16 gauge, No. 4 grind stainless steel throughout, reinforced on front facing with No. 14 gauge, No. 4 grind stainless steel. All joints of this drawer to be welded, ground, and polished. Each drawer to be equipped with nontilting, easy-glide roller-bearing drawer slides, and all metal tracks welded to underside of table top. This drawer to be fitted with a polished white metal pull handle.
- **Price:** F.O.B $........
- **Delivery date:** Not later than..............

When purchasing electrically operated equipment, it is essential that exact electrical specifications be given to the manufacturer at the time the order is placed. A motor is wound to operate on a certain voltage current, and when set up to operate on another, it may run more slowly or more rapidly than was intended, causing its output to be greater or less than its rated horsepower. There is danger of overheating and a breakdown of insulation, which will result in short circuits and the necessity for motor repairs or replacements. A three-phase motor is desirable because the absence of brushes lessens the maintenance problems. Motors of less than 1 horsepower may be used equally well on 110- or 220-volt currents, but motors of larger horsepower should be operated only on a 220-volt current. Manufacturers now use ball-bearing motors, fully enclosed and ventilated, which eliminate the need for frequent oiling. Most motors are built especially for the machines they operate. They must be adequate in power to easily carry the capacity loads of the machines.

SELECTION OF SOME BASIC ITEMS

An analysis of the basic considerations discussed thus far helps to determine whether the selection of certain items of kitchen equipment is justified and gives attention to the mechanics of buying. Standards for various types of equipment have been mentioned. The problem of selection is so important and errors are so costly that major characteristics to consider in the selection of certain types of items are given in Appendix: Foodservice Equipment. No attempt is made to evaluate or identify equipment by trade name. The buyer may need to make a selection between the products of several competitive manufacturers or jobbers, each of whom may have quality products but with a wide variance in some details. All equipment should be a sound investment for the operator, easily cleaned, and safe to operate, and it should accomplish the work for which it was designed. Wise selection can be made only after an exhaustive study of all available data and observation of similarly installed equipment has been accomplished.

Manufacturers' specification sheets, brochures, and catalogs, trade shows, current professional and trade journals and magazines, and the representatives of the manufacturing companies are the best sources of up-to-date information on specific items. Special features may be changed fairly often, so that detailed information on certain models is soon outdated in a publication like this one.

Some points for consideration when selecting foodservice equipment, other than price, cost of operation, and maintenance, are included in Appendix: Foodservice Equipment to help acquaint the reader with possible features and variations of certain items. The availability of utilities and other factors may predetermine some decisions; for example, the choice between an electric or gas range presents no problem if the advantages of one source of heat over the other are evident in the particular situation. Instead, the problem becomes one of a choice between various models manufactured by several different firms. Space permits only a limited amount of basic information on certain fundamental items. It is expected that supplementary material will be kept up to date and made available in library or office files for students and foodservice operators.

Cooking Equipment

This equipment must conform to requirements for material, construction, safety, and sanitation established by groups such as the American Standards Association, American Gas Association, National Board of Fire Underwriters, Underwriters Laboratories, Inc., American Society of Mechanical Engineers, and National Sanitation Foundation International. Buyers should be sure that parts are replaceable and service is available for all items selected, and should also give consideration to original and operating costs, effectiveness in accomplishing the task to be done, and the time and skill required for ordinary maintenance. The life expectancy requirement depends somewhat on the situation, but the selection of durable, high-quality equipment is usually economical.

Electric, Gas, and Steam Equipment. This includes electrically heated cooking equipment designed for alternating or direct current of specified voltage; rating required expressed in watts or kilowatts (1,000 watts = 1 kilowatt) per hour; wiring concealed and protected from moisture; switches plainly identified; thermostatic heat controls; flues not required for electric cooking equipment but the usual hood or built-in ventilating system necessary to remove cooking vapors and odors.

Gas-fired cooking equipment is designed for natural, manufactured, mixed, or liquefied petroleum fuel; adapted to given pressures; rating requirement expressed in British thermal units (Btus) per hour; individual shut-off valve for each piece of gas equipment; manifolds and cocks accessible but concealed; removable burners; automatic lighting with pilot light for each burner; thermostatic heat controls; gas equipment vented through hood or built-in ventilator instead of kitchen flue to exhaust combustible gases.

The most commonly used pieces of gas- and electric-heated cooking equipment are ranges, griddles, broilers, fryers, tilting frypans, and ovens.

Steam-heated cooking equipment includes steam-jacketed kettles, cabinet steamers, steam tables, and combination ovens, which combine steam with gas or electric heat. In a *steam cabinet,* steam is injected into a closed cavity where it comes into direct contact with the food. Under pressure, steam has a higher temperature than nonpressurized steam, thereby allowing quicker cooking times. A *low-pressure steamer* utilizes steam at 5 psi (pounds per square inch), which converts to approximately 227°F. The standard pressure in a high-pressure steamer is 15 psi or 250°F. A batch of peas cooked in the low-pressure steamer will take eight minutes; in the high-pressure steamer, one minute. A third type of steam cabinet is the *pressureless convection steamer,* in which steam enters at atmospheric pressure (0 psi) or 212°F but is convected or circulated continuously over the food. This constant movement of steam shortens cooking time to less than that of low-pressure static steamers. Specifics about these types of cooking equipment are included in Appendix: Foodservice Equipment.

Noncooking Equipment

Power-Operated Equipment. Modern foodservices depend on motor-driven machines for rapid and efficient performance of many tasks. Safety precautions are necessary. Capacity charts for all types of machines are available from manufacturers and distributors. Motors, built according to capacity of machine, must carry peak load easily; specify voltage, cycle, and phase; and have sealed-in motors and removable parts for ease of cleaning. A three-phase motor is usually used for 3/4 horsepower or larger.

Power-operated noncooking equipment includes mixers, choppers, cutters, slicers, vertical cutter mixers, refrigerators, freezers, dish and utensil cleaning equipment, waste disposals, and transport equipment. Among the more common pieces of nonmechanical kitchen equipment are tables, sinks, storage cabinets, racks, carts, scales, cooking utensils, and cutlery. More detailed information about each of these types of noncooking equipment is included in Appendix: Foodservice Equipment.

The most commonly used types of serving equipment are counters, utensils, dispensers, coffeemakers, and mobile serving carts. These are also discussed in Appendix: Foodservice Equipment.

Some New Equipment Designs

The latest innovations in foodservice equipment focus on efficiency, simplicity, cost effectiveness, use of technology, and sustainability. A few examples include:

- **Modular Mobile Cooking:** The popularity of display cooking in restaurants and the desire for flexibility has led to the development of self-venting, mobile, modular cooking units. Designed to be used anywhere a 400-volt electrical connection is available, this equipment features a filtration system that removes grease, moisture, and odors during cooking (www.blanco.de).
- **Heat Recovery in Washers:** Warm water vapor from the dishwasher or pot and utensil washer is recycled to heat the cold water supply, thereby reducing energy cost and exhaust air temperatures (www.winterhalter.de).
- **A Mixer That Cooks:** This piece of equipment allows cooking directly in the mixing bowl. Food may be gently warmed or fully cooked, and eight mixing speeds maintain the consistency of the product during the cooking process. A steam basket and food processor attachment give added flexibility for the use of this mixer/cooker (www .kenwoodworld.com/en/CookingChef/Home).
- **Wok-Range:** As part of an induction cooktop, this wok-range is safer and quicker than a gas unit (Figure 12).
- **Wet Waste to Compost:** First a disposer macerates waste into small particles, excess liquid is then pressed out, dry waste is expelled and collected, and finally heat is used to produce the compost (www.imco.co.uk).
- **A New Way to Handle FOG:** FOG (fat, oil, and grease) is normally prevented from entering and clogging sewer systems, in restaurant operations, by a grease trap. An innovative method of handling FOG automatically cleans kitchen waste water before it ever gets to the grease trap, without the use of chemicals or enzymes. First, food particles are removed from the waste water by use of a screen, dewatered by an auger, and discharged into a separate container for disposal. Using baffles and a reverse-direction flow, FOG is forced against a slow-rotating roller. As the roller becomes coated with FOG, a rubber blade scrapes it clean and deposits the FOG in an external container (www.epas-ltd.com).
- **Super-fast Sandwich Press:** Using a combination of microwave, infrared radiation, and contact plates, sandwiches are perfectly toasted with grill marks from 39°F to 140°F core temperature in less than 60 seconds. Additional benefits include self-adjusting upper plate, automatic holding and automatic lid opening when a sandwich is done, programmable electronic control panel, four automatic cooking programs, and a nonstick surface for ease of cleaning (www.electroluxusa.com/professional).

DINING ROOM FURNISHINGS

KEY CONCEPT: Dining-room furnishings and tabletop items should be pleasing, durable, serviceable, and easy to maintain.

Figure 12 A wok-range.

A dining area that is attractive and appealing does much to make patrons feel comfortable and adds to their enjoyment of the food they are served. The foodservice director may be responsible for the selection of some of the furnishings, especially for the dinnerware, tableware, and glassware. The services of an interior designer or decorator may be employed, however, to help create the desired atmosphere through selection of the appropriate style and type of tables and chairs, window treatment, and a color scheme that will coordinate all furnishings into a harmonious effect.

Basic information needed for the wise selection of dinnerware (dishes), tableware (knives, forks, and spoons), glassware, and table covers is presented in Appendix: Foodservice Equipment. Specialized assistance likely will be sought for the purchase of furniture, drapes, curtains, and other furnishings. All furnishings should be pleasing, durable, serviceable, and easy to maintain.

Dinnerware

Many types of material are used in making dishes for today's foodservice market, including china, glass, and melamine or other plastic ware or combinations of other materials kept secret by their manufacturers. Dinnerware suitable for foodservices varies with the type of service given. A club or fine-dining restaurant may wish to use fine china. In contrast, a school foodservice needs more durable ware. Fast-food establishments usually find disposable dinnerware best fills their needs. Other considerations in choosing dinnerware include durability, budget, heat resistance, color and design, intended uses, ambiance and/or theme desired, and amount needed. These are discussed in greater detail in Appendix: Foodservice Equipment.

Tableware

The most satisfactory type of eating utensil for institutions is that which has been designed and made especially for heavy-duty use. Such ware falls into two classes: flatware of the usual array of knives, forks, and spoons; and items such as teapots, sugar bowls, pitchers, and platters, known as hollow ware if made of metal. All must be durable and serviceable and, at the same time, attractive in line and design. Silver, stainless steel, and disposable tableware are the types used, and which type is chosen will depend largely on the type of foodservice, the tastes of the clientele served, and the amount of money available for the initial expenditure, replacement, and upkeep. Once the type is decided on, consideration must be given to the design, amount, storage, maintenance, and durability. Tableware is discussed in greater detail in Appendix: Foodservice Equipment.

Glassware

Glassware is a major item of purchase for dining room furnishings for foodservices, because it is easily broken and replacement is frequent. It is usually more economical to purchase good-quality glassware than inexpensive types.

Table Covers

One other furnishing to consider is the type of covering, if any, to be used on the dining tables, or trays if that type of service is used. Many tabletop surfaces are attractive, durable, and suitable for use without a cover. Simplicity and informality in dining have made this custom popular, and it does reduce laundry costs.

For many people, much of the charm of a foodservice is conditioned, if not determined, by the use of a clean tablecloth of good quality, freshly and carefully placed. Paper napkins and placemats and plastics have replaced cloth in many foodservices for convenience and economy. Whatever the choice, the cover should be of a type and color appropriate for the facility, contribute to the total atmosphere of the room, and be harmonious with the dishes to be used.

SUMMARY

Prospective foodservice managers, as well as those already employed in the field, should have a "working" knowledge of equipment and furnishings—construction, materials suitable for various uses, something of the sizes or capacities available, and how to relate that information to meeting the needs of the individual foodservice. Wise selection and proper care of the many items that must be provided for efficient operation of the foodservice should result in economies for the organization and a satisfied working crew because they have been supplied with the correct tools to accomplish their task.

APPLICATION OF CHAPTER CONCEPTS

The University of Wisconsin–Madison University Foodservice has a large commissary operation that uses cook/chill technology to produce food for the other operating units within the system. In this commissary there are currently two blast chillers. The university foodservice operation has one other blast chiller in Rheta's, a marketplace type of foodservice operation. Their goal is to have more blast chillers in several of the other individual operating units.

The use of blast chilling and shock freezing is not new but is becoming more and more popular in large-scale, high-volume, noncommercial foodservice operations such as schools, colleges, and hospitals. Its popularity stems from the numerous advantages blast chilling affords an operation. The most obvious benefit of this production method is food safety. The product being cooked is in the danger zone for a minimal period of time. However, some other very important benefits also make it a method of choice for many operations. These include better food quality, waste reduction, labor savings, menu flexibility/better purchasing, and sustainability. Food quality is better because the method preserves the integrity of the normal cell structure of the food. Waste is reduced because blast chilled or shock frozen food can be stored much longer and rethermalized only when needed. Labor savings is attained by having the ability to forecast and prepare food days in advance of when it is needed. This allows for an efficient workflow and flexibility in preparation time and pace. Blast chilling and shock freezing allow for menu flexibility and better purchasing by giving operators the opportunity to buy and store large quantities of foods when prices are lower. Of great importance to the UW–Madison foodservice is the sustainability benefit achieved with blast chilling/shock freezing. The desire to create seasonal menus incorporating local and regionally grown produce is possible with blast chilling/shock freezing. Operations located in colder winter areas, such as the Midwest and Northeast, can buy from local farmers in the summer, blast chill or freeze these products, and serve them on their menu in the winter. This not only cuts down on shipping costs but reduces the operation's carbon footprint by reducing the CO_2 emissions from cross-country shipping.

CRITICAL-THINKING QUESTIONS

1. What principles from food science explain why the processes of blast chilling or shock freezing maintain the cell integrity of food products?
2. Give an example of what would happen to a specific food product that was frozen by placing in an ordinary freezer.
3. How long would you estimate that a food product remains in the danger zone during the blast chilling process?
4. Food that has been blast chilled or shock frozen must be rethermalized. Give some examples of methods of rethermalization. What pieces of equipment would be needed for these methods?
5. When UW–Madison puts blast chillers in some of its other operations, what pieces of equipment will no longer be needed?
6. How would the incorporation of this technology affect needed storage space?
7. What challenges do you think management faces when blast chill equipment is first installed in an operation?
8. Why would an operation choose blast chilling rather than blast freezing?
9. Go to the Chester-Jensen Web site at www.chester-jensen.com and review the several types of Advanced Meal Preparation Systems the company manufactures. What products do they list that can be cooked via the cook/chill technology?
10. After reading the chapter case study, what disadvantages do you see to using blast chilling or shock freezing methods of food production?

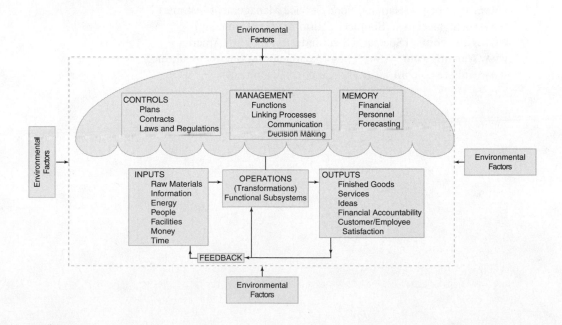

CHAPTER REVIEW QUESTIONS

1. List the many factors that affect decisions regarding equipment selection.
2. If labor cost is high in a particular area, what type of equipment should be given strong consideration?
3. In an assembly/serve foodservice system, what pieces of equipment are most warranted?
4. Discuss the advantages of modular equipment.
5. Discuss the factors that determine the size and capacity of equipment chosen.
6. What are the most common materials used in the manufacture of foodservice equipment? For what are they usually used?
7. List and briefly explain the desired characteristics of a metal chosen for foodservice equipment.
8. Describe how the gauge of metals is determined in the United States.
9. Identify what should be included in a specification for a piece of foodservice equipment.
10. What is the role of NSF International regarding foodservice equipment and furnishings?
11. List and briefly explain the various types of ovens now in use in foodservice operations.

SELECTED WEB SITES

www.americangriddle.com   (American Griddle Corp.—the Steam Shell Griddle)

www.amfab-inc.com   (American Metal Fabricators, Inc.)

www.burlodgeusa.com   (Burlodge, USA—meal delivery systems)

www.cfesa.com   (Commercial Food Equipment Service Association)

www.chester-jensen.com   (Chester-Jensen Co., Inc.—manufacturers of heat exchange and process equipment)

www.cmadishmachines.com   (CMA Dishmachines)

www.feda.com   (Foodservice Equipment Distributors Association)

www.fermag.com   (*Foodservice Equipment Reports* magazine)

www.fesmag.com   (*Foodservice Equipment & Supplies* magazine)

www.frymaster.com   (Frymaster Corp.)

www.hobartcorp.com   (Hobart Corp.—foodservice equipment)

www.montaguecompany.com   (Montague Co.—cooking equipment)

www.nafem.org   (North American Association of Food Equipment Manufacturers)

www.nal.usda.gov/fnic   (USDA National Agricultural Library, Food and Nutrition Information Center)

www.nemetschek.net   (Nemetschek—Vectorworks Architect Software)

www.nfsmi.org   (National Food Service Management Institute)

www.socalgas.com   (Southern California Gas Company)

www.ssina.com   (Specialty Steel Industry of North America)

www.star-mfg.com   (Star/Lang Manufacturing International, Inc.)

www.wolfstoves.com   (Wolf—Cooking Equipment)

Resource Conservation

Joe Sohm/Chromosohm/Stock Connection

RESTAURANTS AND FOODSERVICES ARE USUALLY THE

largest energy users and polluters among a commercial building's tenants on a square-foot basis. In addition, they are also the largest compromisers of air quality and consumers of fresh water and toxic chemicals. Foodservices are making efforts to conserve energy and water and control pollution. Because buildings are

From Chapter 12 of *Foodservice Management: Principles and Practices*, Twelfth Edition, June Payne-Palacio, Monica Theis.

now responsible for 40 percent of U.S. energy consumption, 25 percent of water use, and 35 percent of carbon dioxide emissions, green design practices are also being adopted in the new construction or renovation of existing foodservice operations.

Foodservice operations are among the major contributors to the amount of solid waste generated in the United States. We generate more than 210 million tons of solid waste a year in this country. Only 56 million tons of this solid waste is recovered through recycling or composting. The Environmental Protection Agency (EPA) estimates that each person is responsible for approximately 4.6 pounds per day. As the cost of disposing of this waste and consumer interest in protecting the environment and sustaining natural resources increase each year, foodservice operations seek ecologically and economically sound ways in which to dispose of, or minimize, the solid waste that they generate. This, along with efforts involving energy and water conservation and pollution control, can have a significant impact on more global efforts to protect the environment and to preserve natural resources.

The first Earth Day, celebrated on April 22, 1970, was marked by nationwide demonstrations and political speeches drawing attention to our heavy dependence on nonrenewable sources of energy and to the fact that the supplies of these sources were dwindling rapidly. *The Limits of Growth*, a book published by the Club of Rome in 1972, intensified the importance of the message by predicting the year in which resources would be completely depleted. The authors based their predictions on conservative estimates of known reserve growth rate, population, food production, available capital, and land use on a global scale for a closed system, "spaceship" Earth. The predicted depletion dates for resources included petroleum, 2020; natural gas, 2019; aluminum, 2025; zinc, 2020, copper, 2018; and iron, 2143. Although there is some disagreement about these dates, no one debates the fact that these resources will eventually run out and that strategies must be developed to cope with increasing scarcity as total depletion approaches.

Many advances have been made in our efforts to shift from oil, natural gas, coal, and nuclear to renewable sources of energy such as geothermal, hydroelectric, biomass, wind, and solar. With energy being one of the biggest overhead costs in a foodservice operation, these new sources of energy hold much hope. Utility rates have, in most cases, paralleled the general inflation rate, and foodservice operators have faced increasing energy usage during the past several years. One of the primary causes of this escalation of energy use is the demand from customers and employees for comfort. No matter what type of foodservice operation, air-conditioned dining rooms and kitchens have become the norm. In many areas, an air-conditioned working environment has become a union bargaining position.

In addition to the depletion of natural resources, the world faces other environmental issues such as soil, water, and air pollution; global warming; acid rain; deforestation; and the generation of ever-increasing amounts of waste.

As in all American businesses, the foodservice industry is constantly facing competitive challenges. In the 1960s, low cost was the competing challenge. Flexibility and quick response to customer demands were the challenges of the 1970s. Quality was the emphasis in the 1980s. And now, in the first decade of the twenty-first century, the entire world is entering an era of environmentalism, "zero discharge," and "total pollution management." This focus on the environment has been motivated by increasing public pressure, skyrocketing cleanup costs, rising criminal and civil liabilities, and stringent laws and regulations. Environmental excellence is becoming a number one priority of corporate management.

A staggering statistic is the conservative estimate that of the 20,000 pounds per person of active materials (food, fuel, forest products, and ores) extracted in the United States each year, only 6 percent becomes durable goods. The other 94 percent is wasted within a few months of extraction. Each person in this country creates 4.5 pounds of garbage per day, which adds up to more than 210 million tons of garbage being created each year ("Billionaires in the future will be created out of trash," *Financial News*, April 28, 1995).

Reductions in pollution and waste can lead to a healthier environment and a healthier economy. The Institute for Local Self-Reliance in Washington, D.C., estimates that nine jobs are created for every 15,000 tons of solid waste that are recycled into a new product, whereas only two jobs are created for every 15,000 tons incinerated, and only one job for every 15,000 tons sent to landfills. Each environmental issue, however, is complex because each has economic, sociological, political, and ecological ramifications that must be considered. Effective solutions will require the collaboration of those in agriculture, manufacturing, the packaging industry, foodservice operators, policy makers, and consumers.

Foodservices are actively engaged in solid waste management programs that include source reduction and recycling of virtually every waste product generated in the operation and waste stream analyses and audits. Some examples of these are discussed in this chapter.

KEY CONCEPTS

1. There are many ecological and economic benefits that derive from a foodservice's adoption of "green" design practices.

2. Development of an effective energy management program can begin with an analysis of utilities.

3. Proper use and maintenance of equipment contributes to energy conservation.

4. Additional steps, relative to equipment use, can be taken to maximize energy conservation.

5. Effective energy management requires commitment by organizational leaders and participation by every employee within the organization.

6. Solid waste management is an ethically, legally, and economically mandated priority of foodservice management today.

7. The first step in an integrated solid waste management program is source reduction.

8. Recycling reduces waste handling costs, dependence on scarce natural resources, manufacturing energy costs, amount of material sent to landfills, and the potential pollution of nature.

9. Composting is growing in popularity as a means to manage solid waste in foodservice operations

10. Waste assessment, audits, and analyses can be used to determine the amount and type of waste generated by a foodservice operation.

CONSERVATION OF NATURAL RESOURCES

KEY CONCEPT: There are many ecological and economic benefits that derive from a foodservice's adoption of "green" design practices.

Much attention has been focused on ways to cut energy costs. Foodservice operators have found that targeting unnecessary energy usage and incorporating techniques to reduce energy consumption result in a more efficient operation overall. Water conservation has received less attention. However, as more and more communities suffer from periodic water shortages, this precious resource will become the focus of more effort.

Green Design

Green design is the use of "sustainable" principles that minimize the use of nonrenewable resources and seek to prevent air, water, and ground contamination and other activities that degrade the environment. Commonly accepted standards for green design have been

Green design
The use of sustainable principles that minimize the use of nonrenewable resources and seek to prevent air, water, and ground contamination and other activities that degrade the environment

337

Figure 1 Award-winning "green" building at the Woods Hole Research Center, MA.
Source: Courtesy of Charles C. Benton, Professor of Architecture, UC Berkeley.

established by the U.S. Green Building Council (USGBC). These standards are known as the LEED (Leadership in Energy and Environmental Design) Green Building Rating System. The aerial view of the Ordway building at the Woods Hole Research Center (Figure 1) shows the two-part array of 88 photovoltaic panels that generate 34 percent of the building's total energy requirement. In addition, the building uses less total energy, has lower energy costs, and generates 28 percent fewer emissions due to operations.

The goals in a green foodservice design project most likely would be as follows:

- Reduce or eliminate the negative impact of the building on local ecosystems
- Develop a sustainable site plan
- Safeguard water supplies and ensure water-use efficiencies
- Determine optimum facility and equipment energy efficiency
- Make use of recyclable and recycled materials in construction and operations
- Preserve indoor environmental quality after the facility opens

The benefits that accrue from following green design principles include increased worker productivity, reduced long-term costs of daily operations, reduced negative environmental impacts, and healthy, sustainable communities.

Following the design of a green building, energy use and cost can be reduced with careful equipment selection. Choosing equipment that has received the Environmental Protection Agency's Energy Star ratings (Figure 2), which are based on the government's most stringent efficiency standards, can lower energy costs and usage from 25 percent to 60 percent. In addition, rebates and tax credits are available from water boards, utilities, and some state governments for operators who switch to Energy Star–rated equipment. Refrigerators, freezers, gas-powered fryers, steamers, hot-food holding cabinets, and ice machines all are among the pieces of equipment that have been rated.

Figure 2 The Energy Star logo.
Source: U.S. Environmental Protection Agency.

Energy Conservation

■ **KEY CONCEPT:** Development of an effective energy management program can begin with an analysis of utilities.

Utilities consume a large and ever-growing portion of operating costs for foodservice operations. Predictions indicate that natural gas supplies are tightening and energy prices are likely to increase in the coming years.

An energy management program requires the constant participation of every employee in the operation. In-service training and incentive programs should be set up to ensure the cooperation of all involved. Recent developments in equipment and technology are available to reduce energy consumption and to save money. Foodservice managers should carefully consider the cost and energy savings these may offer.

The Ventilation System. The single biggest controllable energy user in most commercial kitchens is the ventilation system. Every cubic foot of air exhausted from a kitchen must be replaced with fresh or make-up air, which, in most locations and at most times of the year, is either air conditioned or heated. Fundamental breakthroughs in understanding how ventilation works under real cooking conditions have occurred in the past few years. This knowledge has allowed fans and make-up air systems to be sized with lower airflows, reducing both motor size and energy usage.

Many electric utility companies now provide an analysis of air conditioning demand and special cooling control programs. These programs monitor temperatures and compressors, turn off units during off-peak periods, and keep temperatures in the comfort zone. Moving heat-producing equipment out of the air-conditioned or ventilated area is another energy-saving practice. Refrigerator condensing coils and compressors generate a surprising amount of heat, and they can be moved outside the building or into a basement. The heat generated from an ice machine can be eliminated from a service area by remotely locating the ice machine and pumping ice to each of the stations where it is needed.

Heat-pump water heaters use the heat generated by all of the cooking equipment in the kitchen to warm water and at the same time return cool, dehumidified air to the kitchen, lowering the air temperature and humidity. The cool air may be directed to the general kitchen area, to a specific area, or outside when cooling is not needed. This type of water heater is four to six times as efficient as conventional gas water heaters, is three times more efficient than conventional electric water heaters, and does not require a flue or fireproof enclosure because no combustion is involved.

Manufacturers of cooking equipment are adding more insulation in their equipment to keep the kitchen cooler and finding that an additional benefit is more efficient equipment. Additional examples of energy-efficient equipment are high-efficiency gas burners and infrared heating in fryers, both of which produce far more heat from the same amount of gas, and electrical induction heating in fryers and grills, which keeps the kitchen cooler and is more efficient than traditional heating methods.

Radiant heat barriers (RBs) are materials installed in the attics or on the undersides of roofs to reduce summer heat gain and winter heat loss and thus to reduce heating and cooling energy usage. Usually made of thin sheets of a highly reflective material such as aluminum, RBs radiate heat back into the building during the heating season and reduce air conditioning cooling loads in warm or hot climates.

The cost of heating or cooling the kitchen can be reduced by transferring air from the dining room rather than from the outdoors. Direct-drive, variable-speed fans can be connected to control systems that sense heat, smoke, and vapors and change fan speed accordingly.

Mixing Power Sources. Deregulation of electricity and gas has given rise to some new options. New compact cogeneration systems use gas, fuel oil, diesel fuel, or scrap wood to power an engine that turns an electrical generator. A by-product of cooling an engine in this way is hot water that may be used by the foodservice as a source of "free" hot water.

Two new alternative energy sources—wind power and fuel cells—have the potential to provide new opportunities for energy cost reductions. New regulations allow tie-ins to existing energy grids, as well as tax credits and government grants for those who use renewable energy sources.

Heating Water. Another major energy user in the kitchen is the hot water generated by dishwashers and booster heaters. Over the past five years, gas booster heaters have improved in efficiency and reliability. Many operators have switched from three- or six-gallon coffee urns to thermal pots and instant hot water dispensers.

Lighting. Turning off lights in areas not being used and using daylight for ambient illumination can reduce the lighting load during peak demand hours. To use "free" daylight, the task is to admit the sun's rays in a way that makes this "free" energy truly usable as light. It is possible to eliminate daytime lighting costs entirely by installing skylights in kitchens and dining rooms in single-story buildings. Large retailers such as Walmart, Target, and Home Depot have utilized this concept to save significant amounts on lighting costs.

Computerized lighting control and dimming systems are available and provide a low-cost solution to controlling lighting levels in all areas of a foodservice. Timers and motion detectors have also been used effectively to save on lighting costs.

> ### ■ KEY CONCEPT: Proper use and maintenance of equipment contributes to energy conservation.

Use Equipment at Full Capacity. Using large pieces of equipment at less than full capacity is one of the most common energy wasters. This includes, but is not limited to, dishwashers, ovens, griddles, fryers, ranges, and steam-jacketed kettles, which can be operated with partial loads or left on between loads.

Turn Equipment On Only When Needed. Standard operating procedure in the past has been that the first person in the kitchen in the morning turns everything on, from the salamanders to the broilers, and the last person to leave at night turns everything off. By shutting off equipment when it is not being used, utility costs can be dramatically reduced. The disadvantage of this procedure is that some pieces of equipment require a considerable amount of time to reach the desired cooking temperature. New technology is available to handle this problem.

Systems may be installed in the gas supply line that allow for the firing of gas cooking equipment on demand. One such system installed in a grill restricts gas flow to 20 percent—just enough to keep the burners warm. When the grill is needed, the cook hits a button to restore full gas flow, which takes 20 to 30 seconds. The system can be programmed to cook items from two to ten minutes. At the end of the timed cooking period, the grill automatically shuts down. This system not only saves on gas usage costs but also reduces the amount of heat released into the kitchen, which in turn saves on air conditioning costs. Employee safety is also improved by reducing the number of high-heat surface areas on which a worker can be inadvertently burned. In addition, food waste from overcooking is eliminated by the timing device.

Cash rebate programs are popular inducements for operators to install energy-saving equipment. Usually these rebates are a percentage of the equipment's installed cost. Most utilities have special rates for off-peak hours. Making use of those hours can lower utility costs.

Practice Preventive Maintenance. Routine maintenance and cleaning of equipment are essential components of an energy reduction program. Weak or broken door springs on ovens and refrigerators may reduce efficiency by 35 percent. Carbonized grease and cooking residue on griddle plates can reduce cooking efficiency by 40 percent.

Utility Company Energy-Saving Suggestions. Utility companies often offer free equipment service adjustment, energy audits, and assistance in establishing effective energy management programs. An example of information that may be obtained from a utility company follows:

> How Much Energy Does It Save . . . to use open burner ranges instead of hot tops?
>
> You are way ahead in conserving fuel and reducing operating costs when you use *open burner ranges*. Tests show dramatic savings in fuel consumption when *open burner ranges* are compared to hot top ranges:

- Similar quantities of water boil in up to one-third less time on the *open burner range*.
- Boiling similar quantities of water requires up to 55 percent less fuel on the *open burner range*.
- Hot tops must be preheated. Preheating takes 30 to 60 minutes. The gas flame on the *open burner range* comes on instantly when you need it. No preheating necessary! Tests show additional energy can be conserved no matter what kind of range top you have.
- Covering pans reduces energy consumption
  - on *open burner ranges* by up to 20 percent.
  - on hot tops by up to 35 percent.
- Heating larger quantities of food can be done more efficiently than heating smaller quantities of food.
  - On *open burner ranges*, Btu consumption per pound was reduced up to 19 percent when the quantity of water heated was doubled.
  - On hot top ranges, Btu consumption per pound was reduced up to 20 percent when the quantity of water heated was doubled.

KEY CONCEPT: Additional steps, relative to equipment use, can be taken to maximize energy conservation.

Other energy conservation suggestions for use of equipment in foodservice establishments follow:

- **Heating, ventilation, air conditioning systems (HVAC):** (HVAC systems account for up to half of an operation's energy use.)
  - Make-up air for hoods: use thermostatically controlled unheated and unrefrigerated air.
  - Use heat recovery systems in hoods: heat exchangers for hot water and/or comfort heating.
  - Use evaporative coolers (swamp coolers) to comfort-condition kitchen air (do not use refrigerated air).
  - Size air-conditioning units and comfort heaters accurately for climate area; limit size of heaters for kitchen area to take advantage of heat from cooking equipment.
  - Use economizer cycle systems (use of outside air when cool enough to eliminate need for refrigerated air).
  - Place air conditioning and furnace filters in an easily accessible location to ensure frequent scheduled cleaning or replacement.
  - Insulate heating and air conditioning ducts adequately and completely, using two inches of insulation.
  - Zone and wire air conditioning and furnace units to permit zone control of unoccupied areas.
  - Install covered and locked thermostats, 68°F for heating, 78°F for cooling.
  - Use time clocks to decrease utility consumption by mechanical equipment in off-peak periods.
  - Keep filters and extractors clean, changing air filters regularly.
- **Water heating:** (Heating water is one of the more energy-intensive aspects of an operation.)
  - Locate water heater in close proximity to major use.
  - Insulate all hot water lines.
  - Size water heating equipment accurately; do not undersize or oversize; use quality equipment.

- Install spring-loaded faucet valves or spring-loaded food controls to limit hot water waste.
- Use quality valves to minimize dripping faucets and repair all leaks promptly.
- Consider solar-assisted and/or waste heat exchanger water heating systems to preheat water.
- Use single-system, high-temperature water heating equipment and automatic mixing valves.
- Use water-softening equipment to soften water in areas where water is hard. Reduce water temperature where possible.
- **Dishwashing:**
  - Size dishwasher to handle average maximum requirements.
  - Install easily accessible switch to permit shutdown of equipment in slack periods.
  - Consider chemical dishwasher for small establishments.
- **Cooking equipment:**
  - Be selective in specification of equipment offering greatest efficiency and flexibility of use.
  - Careful planning can save on operating and initial equipment costs. Do not overestimate equipment requirements. Specify thermostatically controlled equipment whenever possible.
  - Preheat just before use and turn off when not in use.
  - Keep equipment clean for most efficient operation.
  - Use the correct size equipment at all times.
  - Establish equipment startup and shutdown schedules.
  - Make sure the most energy-efficient cooking techniques are used when options are available.
  - Keep equipment calibrated. Regular thermostat calibration saves energy and produces more consistent results.
- **Ranges:** Specify open-top burners—they require no preheat and offer maximum fuel efficiency as compared to center-fired and front-fired hot tops, or even heat tops. Open burners reduce the air cooling load because there is minimal heat radiation when cooking operation is completed.
- **Convection ovens:** Versatile and performs most baking/roasting operations in the shortest period of time.
- **Steamers:** Self-contained (boiler); high production at minimal operating cost.
- **Grooved griddle:** Replaces the underfired broiler; minimizes air pollution problems; operates much more efficiently than underfired broilers and places less of a load on air cooling systems; generally has greater cooking capacity.
- **Broilers:** Underfired—minimize specifying; reasons stated in grooved griddles. Overfired—preferred over underfired. More efficient, faster, no pollution problems. Compartment over broiler provides use for waste heat as plate warmer, finishing foods, browning, cheese melting (may be used for these purposes in lieu of salamander).
- **Salamanders/cheese melters:** Specify those that use infrared ray radiation; they reach full operating temperature within seconds, are efficient, can be turned off when not in use.
- **Braising pans/tilting skillets:** A versatile volume production piece of equipment that can serve many cooking operations—fry, boil, braise, roast, steam, food warmer. Consider caster-equipped pans and installation of additional gas outlets near serving lines, banquet facilities, and such to obtain maximum utilization of this equipment and reduce gas consumption.
- **Fryers:** Floor fryers provide maximum production capabilities and have self-contained power oil filter units for ease and speed of filtering, which prolongs oil life. Consider inclusion of multiproduct programmed computers; they are available built into the fryer and will provide consistently high-quality fried products by novice operators; lowers labor, food, and oil costs. Specify more than one size of fryers; full production capacity and standby or nonpeak-period smaller capacity fryers; save on initial equipment cost, fuel costs, and oil costs.

KEY CONCEPT: **Effective energy management requires commitment by organizational leaders and participation by every employee within the organization.**

All of the previously mentioned energy-saving suggestions will also require a commitment on the part of the management team to continuously develop, communicate, and monitor energy-saving strategies. The National Restaurant Association and the Federal Energy Administration recommend that foodservice operations organize energy management programs in the following manner:

1. Assign responsibility for energy conservation to a committee comprising members representing all areas of the company's operations and chaired by a manager committed to the program.
2. Conduct an energy audit to determine baseline data on current operating costs, energy consumption, and operating practices.
3. Develop an energy conservation plan based on the energy audit with specific goals and strategies, including the improvement of employee practices in all areas of energy use and the acquisition of energy-saving equipment.
4. Measure the results by comparing baseline to postimplementation results.
5. Maintain or modify the plan as needed based on feedback and results achieved.

Water Conservation

Water conservation programs in foodservice operations should be developed in the same manner as those for energy conservation. Simple practices such as turning off faucets completely, running dishwashers at full capacity, using low-flow toilets in rest rooms, recycling **gray water** for watering exterior landscaping, and serving water to customers only when requested can reduce water usage and result in cost savings for the operation.

Gray water
Wash water and other waste that goes down sink drains

SOLID WASTE MANAGEMENT

KEY CONCEPT: **Solid waste management is an ethically, legally, and economically mandated priority of foodservice management today.**

An urgent need exists to reduce the amount of **municipal solid waste (MSW)**, which are durable goods, nondurable goods, containers and packaging, food scraps, yard trimmings, and miscellaneous inorganic wastes produced at residences, commercial, institutional, and industrial establishments. Some examples of waste from these categories include appliances, automobile tires, newspapers, clothing, boxes, disposable tableware, office and classroom paper, wood pallets, and food wastes. MSW does not include waste from other sources such as construction and demolition debris, automobile bodies, municipal sludge, combustion ash, and industrial process wastes that might be disposed of in municipal landfills or incinerators. The issue of solid waste management has economic, political, ecological, and sociological ramifications.

Municipal solid waste (MSW)
The solid waste produced at residences and commercial and industrial establishments

The cost for hauling away solid waste continues to rise. For example, the Los Angeles Unified School District Foodservice generates approximately 60,000 tons of trash annually—70 percent is from the meal program, 29 percent is paper, and 1 percent is glass and metal. The cost of disposing of this trash in landfills is approximately $100 per ton, or $6 million per year.

Legislation has been passed in several states to reduce solid waste output. Mandatory recycling regulations, including landfill bans, are in place in an increasing number of communities across the country.

In foodservice operations, a number of factors affect the amount of waste generated. These are the type of foodservice system, the style of service, the type of serviceware

Integrated solid waste management system

The complementary use of a variety of waste management practices to safely and effectively handle the integrated solid waste stream with the least adverse impact on human health and the environment

Source reduction

The design and manufacture of products and packaging with minimum toxic content and minimum volume of material and/or a longer life

used, the market forms of foods purchased, the menu, and the use and effectiveness of forecasting.

An **integrated solid waste management system** should be employed by all foodservice operations. By definition, an integrated solid waste management system is the "complementary use of a variety of waste management practices to safely and effectively handle the municipal solid waste stream with the least adverse impact on human health and the environment" (U.S. EPA, 1989). The goals of such a system are to reduce air and groundwater pollution, to reduce the volume of waste, and to extract energy and materials safely before final disposal. The hierarchy of integrated solid waste management is:

- **Source reduction** including reuse of materials
- Recycling of materials including composting
- Waste combustion with energy recovery
- Use of landfills

Source Reduction

▌ KEY CONCEPT: **The first step in an integrated solid waste management program is source reduction.**

Source reduction is "the design and manufacture of products and packaging with minimum toxic content, minimum volume of material, and/or a longer useful life" (U.S. EPA, 1989). Source reduction has been identified as a priority by many. This includes the elimination of single-use containers and double packaging, phasing out of metal containers, banning of packaging that is not recyclable, sanitizing glass and plastic containers for storage purposes, and donating leftover food to programs for the homeless.

The closing of landfills and geometric increases in waste disposal costs have led to the need to reduce trash volume. A variety of equipment options are available to accomplish this goal. Most pay for themselves within a year of purchase with the savings they make possible. Among some commonly used waste management tools are the following:

- Cardboard crushers
- Garbage disposals in all sinks to keep trimmings out of the trash
- Pulper extractor systems, which shred and sanitize garbage (see Figure 49 in Appendix: Foodservice Equipment)
- Trash "crushers" including can compactors and glass "smashers"
- Polystyrene "melters"

Recycling

▌ KEY CONCEPT: **Recycling reduces waste handling costs, dependence on scarce natural resources, manufacturing energy costs, amount of material sent to landfills, and the potential pollution of nature.**

Recyclable symbols such as the one shown in Figure 3 indicate that the product, container, or packaging material can be recycled. This same symbol when enclosed in a circle indicates that the product, container, or package contains at least some recycled materials (Figure 4).

Figure 3   An example of a recycling symbol.

'Recyclable' symbols

The symbols to the left represent two variations of the original recycling symbol. The upper symbol in outline form is accepted as the traditional, or universal recycling symbol while the lower one was a modification. Paper products typically display the outline form, often with lettering such as- 'This product can be recycled' or 'Recyclable'. When identified with one of the symbols, products, containers or packaging materials are referred to as *recyclable* products, or products that are able to be recycled. A product marked with either symbol can be recycled *if the regulations and/or ordinances of the local community provide for its collection.* Although the symbols are used on products distributed nationwide, the laws governing collection of these products for the purpose of recycling are determined locally and vary widely from locality to locality.

'Recycled' symbols

A product, which may be a container or package, marked with this symbol was manufactured with at least some materials that have been *recycled.* Generally, additional information is conveyed with the symbol such as- 'Printed on recycled paper'.

When a percentage is indicated within the symbol, that percentage of the product has been made from recycled materials.

Figure 4 Recycling symbols.

Next to source reduction, **recycling** is critical for the following reasons:

- Conserves scarce natural resources for future generations
- Reduces the quantity of waste materials sent to landfills because landfill space in many locales will be exhausted shortly if present trends continue
- Reduces energy costs in manufacturing because using recycled materials often requires less energy and releases less air pollution than does the use of raw materials
- Reduces waste that is dumped in oceans, streams, forests, and deserts
- Prevents the contamination of groundwater sources caused by flushing hazardous materials down drains

Many companies have appointed recycling coordinators and formed recycling committees and teams. Their responsibilities include implementing the recycling program, training staff and customers, encouraging involvement, communicating regarding issues and concerns, and overseeing the program on a daily basis.

Nonprofit organizations, such as the Steel Recycling Institute, offer their services to the foodservice industry. Representatives work with public recycling officials, haulers, scrap dealers, and foodservice organizations to help raise awareness of and implement steel recycling programs.

Every foodservice setting produces some steel waste; the most common type is the No. 10 can. However, smaller cans and lids from plastic and glass containers are also found in the waste stream. All steel products can, and should be, recycled because the steel industry needs old steel to produce new steel. Approximately 66 percent of steel is now recycled in the United States. Recycling foodservice steel waste provides the steel industry with a much-needed resource, reduces material sent to a landfill, helps save energy, and conserves precious domestic natural resources.

Recycling

The series of activities by which discarded materials are collected, sorted, processed, and converted into raw materials and then used in the production of new products

The steps in recycling steel cans are as follows:

Step 1 Rinse the cans to remove most of the food particles. This is required for basic sanitation reasons because the cans usually sit for some time before being picked up. To reduce the amount of water consumed in this process, cans may be rinsed in leftover water that has been used to wash pots and pans, or they may be put through the dish machine in available empty spaces.

Step 2 Flatten the cans to reduce volume for efficient storage and economical transportation. This may be done manually by removing the bottom in the same manner as the lid and stepping on the body of the can. Mechanically, machines are available that will flatten all sizes of cans with the bottom intact. Steel lids and bottoms have sharp edges and should be stored in a can until it is full. The top of this full can may then be taped or crimped shut and transported to storage.

Step 3 Recycle the cans through local options. Dockside recycling may be accomplished by having the company's waste hauler provide a container for steel recyclables. A ferrous scrap processor or independent recyclers will also provide this service, or used steel cans may be delivered to a scrap yard or recycling facility.

Many large foodservices use a piece of equipment that rinses the unopened can, opens it, empties the contents into the desired container, rinses the empty can, flattens it, and delivers it to a dumpster.

Foodservice operations that use large quantities of glass bottles, such as bars, employ equipment designed to "disintegrate" glass containers. By crushing the bottles to a "gravelly" consistency that is not sharp and is ecologically correct, the volume of glass waste is reduced to 1/12 of its original size. The crushed glass may be recycled, and the operator has a cleaner, safer working environment. Additional advantages accrue from reductions in empty bottle storage space, waste removal costs, and number of required trips to the dumpster.

Polystyrene, commonly called foam or Styrofoam® (Figure 5), was the target of environmental activists in past years because it was manufactured from chlorofluorocarbons (CFCs), which reduce the earth's protective ozone layer. Currently, polystyrene is manufactured by an injection process using hydrocarbons, a by-product of the oil refining industry, which have no effect on the ozone layer. The manufacture of polystyrene from hydrocarbons does contribute to air pollution, as did the "burning off" of the by-product when it was not used.

The National Polystyrene Recycling Company's (NPRC) facilities accept used and baled polystyrene (Figure 6). The bales are broken apart and loaded onto a conveyor leading to a grinder. The little pieces of polystyrene are washed and ground. After drying,

Figure 5 Polystyrene (Styrofoam) products.

Figure 6 A pile of used polystyrene.

the polystyrene is sent to an extruder where it is melted, extruded into strands, and cut into pellets. NPRC sells the postconsumer polystyrene pellets to manufacturers who produce items such as school and office supplies, construction materials, protective foam packaging, video and audio products, egg cartons, and sandwich clamshells.

Other plastic compounds, such as polyethylene terephthalate (PETE), high-density polyethylene (HDPE), polyvinyl chloride (V), low-density polyethylene (LDPE), polypropylene (PP), and polystyrene (PS), are also used in foodservice products and all may be recycled. Figure 7 shows recyclable symbols on some of these products. The number shown in the center of the symbol indicates the ease of recycling; generally the lower the number the greater the ease for recycling (PETE—1, HDPE—2, V—3, LDPE—4, PP—5, PS—6).

Paper, plastic, and other dry fibrous materials are turned into building material for low-cost housing. The multipurpose product is cost effective, and construction time is minimal compared with other building alternatives.

A reusable, recyclable entrée dish made out of resin has recently been developed for United Airlines. The dish can be used up to 20 times before being reground into resin flakes to become part of new dishes.

The purchase of products made from recycled material whenever feasible should be practiced in order for recycling to be an effective method of waste management. Some governmental agencies require that a certain percentage of all paper products purchased be made from recycled materials.

Figure 7 Recyclability of various plastic compounds.

Figure 8 The composting cycle.

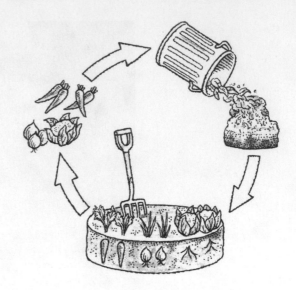

■ **KEY CONCEPT:** **Composting is growing in popularity as a means to manage solid waste in foodservice operations.**

Composting

The biological decomposition of organic materials by microorganisms under controlled, aerobic conditions to a relatively stable humus-like material called compost that is used as fertilizer

Composting.   Why compost? Reasons given for **composting** solid waste include to conserve resources, reduce pollution, reduce landfill costs, and produce healthy soil (Figure 8). Composting conserves resources by keeping valuable organic material from being landfilled, returning valuable nutrients to the soil, and saving fossil fuels that are otherwise used to transport organic waste to the landfill.

Composting reduces pollution because organics in landfills break down anaerobically, producing methane gas—a substance 20 times more powerful than carbon dioxide as a contributor to climate change. Transporting compostable wastes to landfills produces air pollution, which also fuels climate change. Buried organics can react with metals in landfills to produce toxic leachate that has to be removed and treated to eliminate a potential source of groundwater pollution. Compost is a pollution-free soil enhancer compared to chemical fertilizers whose residues leach nitrogen, phosphorus, and potassium into sewer systems.

Composting reduces landfill costs by reducing costs for waste collection and disposal because of the reduced waste volume. This in turn extends the life of current landfills and will postpone the need for costly new landfill sites.

Composting improves soil texture, air circulation, and water retention by breaking down heavy soils. It feeds the soil, providing the organic matter and nutrients necessary for plant growth and survival, and improves yields.

Compost is mild and will not burn plants. It is a natural, slow-release fertilizer.

The Hilton Hotels Corporation has found that putting food waste and by-products into the compost heap not only helps the environment but saves money as well. As part of a comprehensive focus on environmentalism, the hotel chain has implemented employee-driven environmental programs, including purchasing only recycled products where possible and recycling paper, glass, cardboard, aluminum, and food waste. One hotel in the chain converts 15 tons of wet garbage a day into 1 ton of fertilizer and a rich soil conditioner and then sells this compost to golf courses and horticulturists in the area. The compost heap generates temperatures of 160°F, which is adequate to destroy any pathogenic bacteria. The challenge is to control the odor. Using a combination of fans and biologically active filters, a 95 percent reduction in noxious odors has been attained. The final product looks like peat moss and smells like a rich, soil-like, humus peat moss. A nutrient analysis reveals a rich nitrogen, potassium, and phosphorus product.

A 500-bed New York hospital netted a total savings over a four-year period of close to $1 million by implementing a waste reduction program that includes two composting initiatives. For every patient tray, they found that there were 15 pounds of waste, including cans, glass, cardboard packaging, tray mats, and napkins. Cans and glass are separated into blue barrels and recycled. Every staff member was given a reusable mug to use in the cafeteria. Employees who come to the cafeteria without their mugs are charged 15¢ for a cup. Food waste is collected in plastic bags and placed in green barrels in an assigned area of the kitchen. The first composting initiative involves vermin-composting preconsumer residuals. Vegetable trimmings, coffee grounds, fruit rinds, and clean organics are composted in worm wigwams. The finished product is used for grounds-keeping or given away to staff members. The vermin-composting removes 15,600 pounds of clean organics from the waste stream.

The second composting initiative involves the composting of postconsumer residuals. Yellow cans are used to gather milk cartons, dairy and meat products, cereal boxes, shellfish, tray mats, napkins, postconsumer vegetable products, and shredded paper. Wood chips are used as a bulking agent. The compost is cured on site. This initiative diverted 41,600 pounds of organics in a one-year period from the waste stream.

Red River College undertook a composting project collecting 2.7 tons of compostable material from the foodservice during the first 10 weeks. Compostable materials include all vegetable/fruit scraps and peelings, coffee grounds and filters, cooked rice and pasta, tea bags, egg shells, beans, bread, oatmeal, buckwheat, peanut shells, and wheat bran. Noncompostable materials include all dairy products, fish and meat scraps, bones, peanut butter, and oily products (Figure 9).

Animal Feed.   Much research has been done on the feeding of food by-products and food wastes to cattle and sheep. The advantages of this idea are that the wastes are diverted from landfills, nutrient density of animal diets can be increased, ration costs can be reduced, and profits for farmers may be increased. The challenges of such a program are that the by-products or wastes must be carefully matched to the animals' requirements, transportation and processing must prevent spoilage without adding to costs, and moisture content must be reduced. In one operation, food wastes are processed through a pulper and packed in 30- to 40-gallon tubs. The food waste is mixed with ground waste paper, cracked corn, and a nonprotein nitrogen source. The mixture is then stored in a storage silo. The recycled newsprint lowers the moisture content; the corn and nitrogen provide energy for the fermentation process and raise the crude protein content to an acceptable level.

A simpler "food waste to animal fodder" recycling program is used by some communities and foodservice operations. By allowing pig farmers to pick up food waste dockside or curbside, everyone saves.

Fat to Fuel.   U.S. military engineers are testing a plan to recycle used restaurant oil into biodiesel, a cleaner-burning fuel. Several U.S. cities currently use biodiesel to fuel city

Figure 9   Food waste in a compost container.

Figure 10 An incinerating facility.

buses and cars. The four branches of the military use over 400 million gallons of diesel a year. Slightly more than 1 gallon of used cooking oil can be converted to 1 gallon of biodiesel in a relatively simple operation. The oil is warmed in a stainless steel reactor and then treated with methanol and lye. Glycerin produced by the process is poured off, and the remainder is ready-to-use biodiesel.

Incineration and Landfilling

The final alternatives in the integrated waste management system are incineration, which reduces the volume of solid waste and can produce energy, and landfilling, which is the least desirable option. An incinerator is shown in Figure 10 and a landfill site in Figure 11.

> **KEY CONCEPT:** Waste assessment, audits, and analyses can be used to determine the amount and type of waste generated by a foodservice operation.

Facility Waste Assessments

In order to develop an effective waste management plan, foodservice managers first need to determine the amount and type of waste being generated by the operation. A *waste assessment* is a systematic way to identify waste reduction opportunities in a specific operation.

Figure 11 A landfill site.

The method used may be as simple as a quick walk-through of a facility or as detailed as a complete review of all purchasing, materials use, and disposal practices. A waste assessment serves three main purposes: (1) it establishes a better understanding of current purchasing, waste generation, and waste disposal practices; (2) it identifies potential waste reduction options for evaluation; and (3) it establishes a baseline from which to measure the success of the waste reduction program. Simple waste reduction measures can be implemented without a waste assessment. For example, a foodservice operation may switch from disposables to reusables. However, an assessment helps to identify those actions that will have the greatest impact and cost savings and documents those savings that may be important in securing management support for the program.

At present, no standardized methods exist to conduct waste assessments. However, several studies have been undertaken to compare several possible techniques. *Waste stream analysis* involves (1) collecting all waste from the opening to the closing of the operation, (2) sorting by type of waste (paper, plastic, paper napkins, aluminum, non-aluminum metal, paperboard, plastic containers, production food waste, and service food waste), and (3) weighing each category of waste products. A *waste audit* is used to determine the amounts and types of waste produced by a specific location in a foodservice establishment. Rather than taking a complete inventory of waste generated in a day, random samples are obtained over at least a one-week time span.

The waste stream analysis has been found to give the most accurate and precise information but is time consuming and costly to perform. The waste audit method, although not as precise and accurate, has been found to be a cost-effective and efficient alternative. Visual methods used to estimate the volume of waste generated were found to be the easiest to perform of the three methods and yielded data that were not significantly different from the waste stream analysis.

SUMMARY

For both the foodservice operator and the environment, real savings may be obtained from better control of energy use. Cutting overhead costs in order to boost profits is a far better alternative to raising menu prices in this economic climate. The foodservice management team needs to develop strategies for their particular operation that will accomplish energy savings without compromising the quality of products and service provided to customers.

The deterioration of the global environment, which supports life, is accelerating. Human use of resources and energy is largely responsible. Using less need not mean a resulting decline in quality of life and may result in the creation of jobs.

As Margaret Mead so wisely put it, "Never doubt that a small group of thoughtful, committed people can change the world. Indeed, it is the only thing that ever has." It is now an ethical imperative that management makes the environment a corporate commitment that each employee understands. Implementing an integrated solid waste management system is a foodservice practice that both preserves natural resources and protects the environment. A waste assessment will provide the manager with the information necessary to make wise solid waste management system decisions.

APPLICATION OF CHAPTER CONCEPTS

The University of Wisconsin–Madison has an extensive program on sustainability entitled We Conserve. UW Housing, too, is doing its part to conserve resources and educate faculty, staff, and students on the virtues of conservation. Initiatives include opening a new residential learning community focused on the concept of sustainable living. The Dining and Culinary Services is working to increase the amount of food purchased from local sources and to reduce the use of disposables.

Specific to the foodservice, composting was introduced in the commissary during the summer of 2009. Compostable foods are disposed of in specially marked garbage containers that are located in each of the work stations. At the end of the workday, the contents of these containers are removed from the commissary and placed in specially labeled holding containers on the dock. Twice per week the compost is collected and hauled to the Westside Research Station, where it is placed on a compost heap and used in the fields and gardens at the station. Dining and Culinary Services does plan to expand the composting program by eventually placing compost containers at the tray return areas of the dining halls.

CRITICAL-THINKING QUESTIONS

1. Visit the Web site for UW Housing Dining and Culinary Services. Take a look at a menu and list the items that are compostable.
2. Why do you think leaders within Dining and Culinary Services chose to start the composting program in the commissary?
3. What are some of the challenges with expanding the composting program to the dining units?
4. What "value-added" learning opportunities arise for Dining and Culinary Services as they introduce composting in the commissary?
5. How might composting influence safety and pest management programs?
6. Describe how a composting program can have implications for space management and use in a foodservice operation.
7. Describe what the planning and implementation process might look like to expand the composting program to the tray return areas in the dining units.
8. How might Dining and Culinary Services use its composting program to participate in the campus-wide conservation programs?
9. Relative to the Systems Model, what inputs are needed to design, implement, and maintain a composting program?
10. What conservation program do you think Dining and Culinary Services should tackle next?

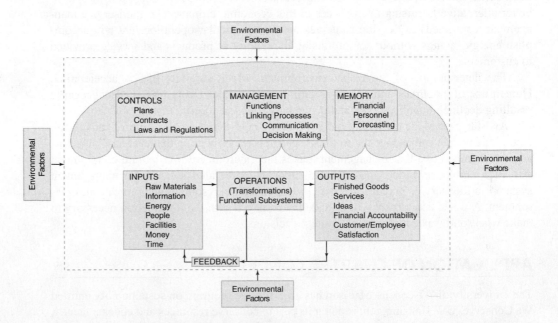

CHAPTER REVIEW QUESTIONS

1. Identify some of the most common energy "wasters" in a foodservice operation.
2. Describe how preventive maintenance and routine cleaning can reduce energy usage.
3. Compare and contrast energy use on an open-burner range versus a hot-top range.

4. In what ways do utility companies help foodservices to reduce energy use?

5. List and describe several ways in which air-conditioning costs can be controlled.

6. Why is solid waste management such a concern for today's foodservice manager?

7. Give several specific examples of source reduction to control foodservice waste.

8. List and describe several solid waste management "tools" employed in the foodservice industry.

9. Describe the steps in the recycling of polystyrene.

10. What is necessary to recycle No. 10 food cans? Why is it particularly important that foodservices recycle this product?

SELECTED WEB SITES

www.aia.org   (The American Institute of Architects)

www.earthodyssey.com   (EarthOdyssey, LLC)

www.epa.gov   (The Environmental Protection Agency)

www.gdrc.org   (The Global Development Research Center)

www.rff.org   (Resources for the Future)

www.tva.gov   (Tennessee Valley Authority)

www.usgbc.org   (U.S. Green Building Council)

www.whrc.org   (Woods Hole Research Center)

Organizational Design

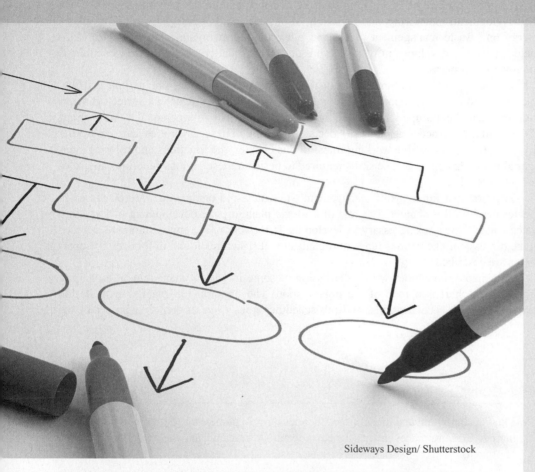

Sideways Design/ Shutterstock

BUSINESS VISIONARIES HAVE SAID THAT TODAY'S ORGA-nizations will need to have leaner staffs, empower their employees by sharing decisions, obtain commitment and innovation from employees, and create an organizational culture that is adaptive and responsive to change. Organizations will also need strong, competent management who are able to design properly and lead the organization to meet its goals and objectives efficiently and effectively. The return that organizations realize from human resources is determined, in large part, by the competence of their managers.

This chapter examines theories of management—from the classical to the modern, the importance of strategic management in today's environment, the functions performed by a manager, the requisite managerial skills, management activities and roles, the tools of management, and the principles of organizational structure.

Historical theories of management have contributed a great deal to modern management theories. The growing complexity of organizations today results in a greater need to examine them as a whole. Using the systems approach, a manager recognizes that the organization as a whole is greater than the sum of its parts.

From Chapter 13 of *Foodservice Management: Principles and Practices*, Twelfth Edition, June Payne-Palacio, Monica Theis. Copyright © 2012 by Pearson Education, Inc. Published by Pearson Prentice Hall. All rights reserved.

The systems manager sees the contributions of each part to the whole system and that a change in one part will have an impact on other parts of the system. This approach allows a manager to diagnose and identify reasons for the occurrence of a situation. The contingency approach leads management to apply different basic guidelines to leading, motivating, and organizing depending on the particular situation. Strategic management also requires the manager to formulate a forward-looking strategy to achieve the organization's goals and objectives.

Strategic management is the function of applying broad, systematic management planning for the organization. Included in strategic management are the activities involved with the development, monitoring, and reviewing of business plans, strategic plans, work plans, energy and waste management plans, and other long-term organization strategies. Also included are the development of a mission, objectives, quality assurance, and continuous improvement processes.

To accomplish the common managerial functions of planning, organizing, staffing, directing, coordinating, reporting, and budgeting, a manager engages in a variety of activities that can be grouped into three basic categories: (1) interpersonal relationships, (2) information processing, and (3) decision making. These categories can be further divided into ten observable working roles. In this chapter, the functions and roles of managerial work are explored. The skills required to perform these various functions and roles are also described.

The first two functions of management—planning and organizing—are discussed in greater detail in this chapter. The role of strategic planning, the development of a mission statement, and the steps necessary to develop the framework of the organization are included in the discussion. The various types of organizational structures found in foodservice operations are described.

The chapter concludes with a discussion of some important management tools. The organization chart is a map of the organization. The organization manual with its job descriptions, job specifications, and job schedules goes even further as a model of the organization.

KEY CONCEPTS

1. The four important and predominant theories of management are classical or traditional, human relations, management science or operations research, and the modern or systems approach.

2. Classical management theory contributed a number of principles to the successful division, coordination, and administration of work activities: the scalar principle, delegation, unity of command, the functional principle, and the line and staff principle, among others.

3. Important systems theory concepts are feedback, hierarchy of systems, interdependency, and wholism.

4. Strategic management requires that managers steer the organization through strategic change under conditions of complexity and uncertainty.

5. Important strategic management concepts are strategic planning, strategic thinking, strategy formulation, total value, strategic success, and systems framework.

6. The basic functions performed by managers are planning, organizing, staffing, directing, coordinating, reporting, and budgeting.

7. The planning function involves a sequence of steps, including writing a vision, philosophy, slogan, mission, strategic plans, intermediate plans, policies, procedures, schedules, and rules, and then implementing, following up, and controlling the plans.

8. The four basic steps necessary to develop the framework of an organization's structure are to (1) determine and define objectives, (2) analyze and classify work to be done, (3) describe in detail work to be done, and (4) determine and specify the relationship between and among workers and management.

9. Organizations may be structured on a line, line and staff, or functional basis.

10. Managers need varying degrees of three skills (technical, human, and conceptual skills), depending on the level in the hierarchy at which the manager is working.

11. Managerial roles may be classified as interpersonal (figurehead, leader, and liaison), informational (monitor, disseminator, and spokesperson), and decisional (entrepreneur or initiator, disturbance handler, resource allocator, and negotiator).

12. Useful mechanical or visual tools of management are organization charts, job descriptions, job specifications, and work schedules.

THEORIES OF MANAGEMENT

KEY CONCEPT: **The four important and predominant theories of management are classical or traditional, human relations, management science or operations research, and the modern or systems approach.**

Many of the challenges that managers faced many years ago are the same as those faced by today's managers. For example, increasing worker productivity, decreasing production costs, maintaining employee motivation and morale, and meeting the challenges of stiff competition are just some of the issues that have persisted through the years.

People have always been of prime importance in all thinking about management. However, the views on why people work and how they are best managed have changed through the years. In some cases, these changes have occurred because the historical conditions dictated the need for such changes in thinking.

Modern management theories are both a reflection of and a reaction to past management theories. There has never been, nor is there now, one best theory of management. Each theory has its own particular worthwhile applications as well as some limitations.

Classical

KEY CONCEPT: **Classical management theory contributed a number of principles to the successful division, coordination, and administration of work activities: the scalar principle, delegation, unity of command, the functional principle, and the line and staff principle, among others.**

Classical theory is a grouping of several similar ideas that evolved in the late 1800s and early 1900s. Pioneers in this theory were Frederick W. Taylor, who was known as the father of scientific management; Max Weber; Frank and Lillian Gilbreth; and Henri Fayol. The basic tenets of classical theory were that (1) there is one best way to do each job; (2) there is one best way to put an organization together; and (3) the organization should be arranged in a rational and impersonal manner. Fayol's (1949) principles encompass these tenets:

1. **Division of work:** This is essential for efficiency, and specialization is the most efficient way to use human effort.
2. **Authority and responsibility:** Authority is the right way to give orders and obtain obedience, and responsibility is the natural result of authority.

Classical theory

A historical theory of management that focuses on tasks, structure, and authority

3. **Discipline:** The judicious use of sanctions and penalties is the best way to obtain obedience to rules and work agreements.
4. **Unity of command:** This specifies that each person should be accountable to only one superior.
5. **Unity of direction:** This specifies that all units should be moving toward the same objectives through coordinated and focused effort.
6. **Subordination of individual interest to general interest:** The interests of the organization should take priority over the interests of individuals.
7. **Remuneration of employees:** Pay and compensation should be fair for both employee and organization.
8. **Centralization:** Subordinates' involvement through decentralization should be balanced with managers' final authority through centralization.
9. **Scalar chain:** In a scalar chain, authority and responsibility flow in a direct line vertically from the highest level of the organization to the lowest.
10. **Order:** People and materials must be in the appropriate places at the proper time for maximum efficiency.
11. **Equity:** All employees should be treated equally to ensure fairness.
12. **Stability of personnel:** Employee turnover should be minimized to maintain organizational efficiency.
13. **Initiative:** Workers should be encouraged to develop and carry out plans for improvements.
14. **Esprit de corps:** Managers should promote a team spirit of unity and harmony among employees.

Classical theory continues to have great relevance and application to basic managerial problems, but it has been criticized as being too mechanistic and not cognizant of the differences in people and organizations. Not all people are motivated by economic rewards, and not all organizations can take the same approach to managing their employees.

Human Relations

Unity of command
Each person should report to only one supervisor

Human relations theory evolved during the 1920s through the 1950s from the effort to compensate for some of the deficiencies of classical theory. Where classical organization advocated focus on tasks, structure, and authority, human relations theorists introduced the behavioral sciences as an integral part of organization theory. They view the organization as a social system and recognize the existence of the informal organization, in which workers align themselves into social groups within the framework of the formal organization. Many human relations theorists hold that employee participation in management planning and decision making yields positive effects in terms of morale and productivity.

Human relations theory
A historical theory of management that views the organization as a social system and recognizes the existence of the informal organization

Management Science/Operations Research

The *management science theory* of management combines some of the ideas from classical and human relations theories. It emphasizes research on operations and the use of quantitative techniques to help managers make decisions. Advances in computer technology have made possible the wide variety of mathematical models and quantitative tools that are integral to this approach to management.

One extension of this theory has been the development of **management information systems (MIS)**. MIS include such tools as linear programming, queuing models, and simulation models to facilitate decision making. The **program evaluation and review technique (PERT)** is another tool for the effective planning and control functions of management.

Management information systems (MIS)
Computerized data processing to facilitate management functions

Modern Management Theories

Program evaluation and review technique (PERT)
A management tool used for planning and controlling operations

Modern management theories have evolved because of the complex nature of today's organizations. Ideas from classical, human relations, and management science have been integrated into the modern theories. The understanding that organizations and people are complex entities with differing motives, needs, aspirations, and potentials has led to the widely held belief that there can be few static and universal management principles. This complex view is evident in the three modern management theories: (1) systems theory, (2) contingency theory, and (3) chaos theory.

> ■ **KEY CONCEPT:** Important systems theory concepts are feedback, hierarchy of systems, interdependency, and wholism.

Systems Approach. The systems approach has had a significant effect on management science and the understanding of organizations. A system is a collection of parts unified to accomplish common goals. If there is a change in one part of the system, it will affect all parts of the system. For example, the body is a system. Removal of one part of the body affects all of the other parts. A system has inputs, operations, outputs, controls, memory, and management functions and linking processes. Feedback between each of these aspects of a system is solicited and used.

In an organization, inputs include resources such as raw materials, information, energy, people, facilities, money, and time. These inputs are transformed by the functional subsystems to meet the organization's goals. Outputs are products, services, ideas, enhanced quality of life for customers and employees, and financial accountability. Feedback is information from internal and external sources such as customers, employees, society, and the government.

Understanding systems theory helps a manager to look at the organization from a broader perspective. Recognition of the various parts of the organization and the interrelationship of these parts is critical for systems thinking. In the past, managers have focused on one part or on one problem.

Another key aspect of systems theory is that being predominantly open systems, human organizations interact with various elements of their environment. (For example, a hospital dietary department interacts with many external groups such as patients, customers, medical staff, hospital administration, and some regulatory agencies. The department, in turn, affects the external groups with which it interacts.) Consideration of the opportunities and threats posed by the external environment is part of systems thinking.

Organizations tend toward a dynamic or moving equilibrium. Members seek to maintain the organization and ensure its survival. They react to changes and forces, both internal and external, in ways that often create a new state of equilibrium and balance. Feedback of information from a point of operation and from the environment to a control center or centers can provide the data necessary to initiate corrective measures to restore equilibrium.

Organizations and the world of which they are a part consist of a hierarchy of systems. Thus, a corporation is composed of divisions, departments, sections, and groups of individual employees. Also, the corporation is part of larger systems, such as all the firms in its industry, firms in its metropolitan area, and perhaps an association of many industries such as the National Restaurant Association (NRA) or the American Hospital Association.

Interdependency is a key concept in systems theory. The elements of a system interact with one another and are interdependent. Generally, a change in one part of an organization affects other parts of that organization. Sometimes the interdependencies are not fully appreciated when changes are made. A change in organizational structure and workflow in one department may unexpectedly induce changes in departments that relate to the first department.

Interdependency
A key concept in systems theory that the elements of a system interact with one another

Systems theory contains the doctrine that the whole of a structure or entity is more than the sum of its parts. This is called **wholism**. The cooperative, synergistic working together of members of a department or team often yields a total product that exceeds the sum of their individual contributions.

Wholism
The systems theory doctrine that the whole of an entity is more than the sum of its parts

Systems theory helps organize a large body of information that might otherwise make little sense. It has made major contributions to the study of organization and management in recent years. Systems theory aids in diagnosing the interactive relationships among task, technology, environment, and organization members.

In contrast to the classical models of organization, the systems approach has shown that managers operate in fluid, dynamic, and often ambiguous situations. The manager generally is not in full control of these situations. Managers must learn to shape actions, to make progress toward goals, and to keep in mind that results are affected by many factors and forces.

Systems theory has become popular because of its apparent ability to serve as a universal model of systems, including physical, biological, social, and behavioral phenomena.

Contingency approach

An approach to management based on the belief that activities should be adjusted to fit the situation

Contingency Approach. The **contingency approach** holds that managerial activities should be adjusted to suit situations. Factors within the situation, such as characteristics of the workforce, size and type of organization, and its goals, should determine the managerial approach that is used. The contingency approach is dependent on seeing the organization as a system and emphasizes the need for managers to strategize based on the relevant facts. Important principles of the contingency approach are as follows: Individual motivation may be influenced by factors in the environment; managers must adjust their leadership behavior to fit the particular situation; and the structure of the organization must be designed to fit the organization environment and the technology it uses.

Chaos theory

The complex and unpredictable dynamics of systems that recognizes that organizational events are rarely controlled

Chaos Theory. **Chaos theory**, second-order cybernetics, and complexity theory are all terms that attempt to describe the fact that things are not always neat and orderly and can indeed be messy. This messiness tends to disrupt the linearity seen in the systems model, and eventually both negative and positive feedback will actually cause the system to change and/or adapt. Chaos theory suggests that managers should work with, rather than against, the nonlinearity of the process. Chaos theorists suggest that as systems become more complex, these systems become more volatile (or susceptible to cataclysmic events) and must expend more energy to maintain complexity. As more energy is expended, the organization seeks more structure to maintain stability.

STRATEGIC MANAGEMENT

■ **KEY CONCEPT:** Strategic management requires that managers steer the organization through strategic change under conditions of complexity and uncertainty.

The term *strategy* used to mean an analysis of alternatives. In a for-profit business, this might have meant determining what marketing strategy would beat the competition. Today the concept of strategy has taken on a much more cohesive and broader scope and is known as strategic management. **Strategic management** may be defined as an organization-wide task of forming a strategic vision, setting objectives, crafting a strategic plan, implementing and executing the plan, and then over time initiating whatever corrective adjustments in the vision, objectives, strategic plan, and execution are deemed appropriate.

Strategic management

A system of management requiring balancing the demands imposed by external and internal forces with the overall functioning of the organization and using resources in a manner that meets goals and satisfies values

Any system of strategic management involves five steps:

1. Identification of the fundamental values of the organization and the goals and objectives that arise from them
2. Assessment of the organization's external environment—forces outside the organization that may be opportunities or threats
3. Assessment of the organization's resources and capabilities—those things within the control of the organization such as people, facilities, equipment, and money (inputs) that can be allocated to achieve desired goals and objectives (outputs)
4. Identification or formation of the organization's components: (a) subsystems that receive allocated inputs and (b) an organizational structure that includes the subsystems and the relationship of authority, responsibility, and communication (linking processes) that they have with one another
5. Development of the management and decision-making structure

KEY CONCEPT: **Important strategic management concepts are strategic planning, strategic thinking, strategy formulation, total value, strategic success, and systems framework.**

A **strategic plan** guides the organization's decision making. Strategic planning is discussed in greater detail later in this chapter under the heading "Planning."

Strategy formulation requires that management analyze requirements and develop guiding principles for all in the organization. For example, a common strategy is to provide customers with QVST: quality, value, service, and timeliness. McDonald's has used a slight variation on this strategy and has as its guiding principles QVSC—quality, value, service, and cleanliness.

Strategic thinking requires that a manager have a clear business concept based on a thorough understanding of the business and the success factors of the industry.

Fitting strategic management into the systems framework means being equally concerned with the external and internal environments in which the organization operates. A key objective in strategic management is to match the organization's internal capabilities with the external opportunities and threats in order to formulate strategies that will achieve the mission, goals, and objectives of the operation.

The concept of **total value** is critical to organizational success because a business can succeed only when its products and services are perceived as having value. In foodservice, quality, service, and pricing are the keys to survival and success.

Strategic success is a temporary phenomenon that, once achieved, must be pursued continuously. Eight factors that emphasize operating values and attitudes have been identified as important for the achievement of strategic success. They are as follows:

1. **Informed opportunism**—Keeping up to date on the latest information to maintain strategic advantage and flexibility
2. **Direction and empowerment**—Identifying what needs to be done and allowing employees the flexibility to find ways to do it
3. **Friendly facts and congenial controls**—Using financial records as checks and balances but giving managers the freedom to be creative
4. **A different mirror**—Recognizing that ideas can come from many sources, including customers, patients, competitors, and employees.
5. **Teamwork, trust, politics, and power**—Emphasizing teamwork and trust in getting the job done while accepting the inevitability of fighting as a result of power politics
6. **Stability in motion**—Responding to changing conditions while recognizing that some consistency must be maintained and rules may be broken when necessary
7. **Attitudes and attention**—Recognizing the importance of attention in getting work done and that symbolic behavior may make the words come true
8. **Cause and commitment**—Maintaining an awareness of the mission (cause) so that it permeates all actions

Strategic plan

A written document that assesses the current state of the organization and what it should do to achieve its mission, goals, and objectives

Strategy formulation

Various methods that may be employed to help managers develop a strategy for the organization

Strategic thinking

An ongoing process in which significant events are dealt with in a comprehensive manner

Total value

The contribution that management can make to the organization, the customers, the products, and the stakeholders

Strategic success

The achievement of goals and objectives while maintaining operating values

FUNCTIONS OF MANAGEMENT

KEY CONCEPT: **The basic functions performed by managers are planning, organizing, staffing, directing, coordinating, reporting, and budgeting.**

The basic purpose of management has been recognized as the leadership of individuals and groups in order to accomplish the goals of the organization. Henri Fayol, a French mining engineer/manager, recognized that managerial undertakings require planning, organization, command, coordination, and control. Luther Gulick (1937) developed the following seven major functions of management: (1) planning, (2) organizing, (3) staffing, (4) directing, (5) coordinating, (6) reporting, and (7) budgeting. Various combinations of these functions with some modifications, deletions, and additions are found in modern management texts.

POSDCORB, the acronym created from the names of the seven functions described by Gulick, is still widely accepted as describing the basic framework of the manager's job. Some disagreement does exist about whether these functions are common to all levels of management. Others believe that even more functions should be included. Leading, actuating, activating, motivating, and communicating are concepts often fitted into the POSD-CORB framework. That there is a degree of overlapping is evident in the functions themselves and in the efforts to classify them.

Planning

■ **KEY CONCEPT:** The planning function involves a sequence of steps, including writing a vision, philosophy, slogan, mission, strategic plans, intermediate plans, policies, procedures, schedules, and rules, and then implementing, following up, and controlling the plans.

Planning

The function of management that involves developing, in broad outline, the activities required to accomplish organizational objectives and the most effective ways of doing so

The **planning** function, described by Gulick in 1937 and still relevant today, involves developing in broad outline the activities required to accomplish the objectives of the organization and the most effective ways of doing so. Planning is a basic function, and all others are dependent on it. The objective of planning is to think ahead, clearly determine objectives and policies, and select a course of action toward the accomplishment of the goals. Day-to-day planning of operational activities and short- and long-range planning toward department and institution goals are part of this function. Overall planning is the responsibility of top management, but participation at all levels in goal setting and development of new plans and procedures increases their effectiveness.

Vision

The organization's view of the future

The first steps in the planning process are to develop a **vision**, a philosophy or core values statement, a slogan, and a mission statement. Each of these should be simple, easily understood, attainable, measurable, desirable, and energizing. Many commercial foodservices print one or more of these statements on their menus or other printed materials to communicate their business philosophy to their customers.

It is desirable to have each of these developed cooperatively by all members of the organization, not just by top management. The vision is the organization's view of the future; the philosophy contains the organization's set of core values for the attainment of that vision; the slogan is a short, memorable statement of "who we are"; and the mission statement is the summary of the organization's purpose, customers, product, and service. An example of a hospital foodservice's mission statement might be:

> The Department of Hospitality Services at Malibu Hospital is a multifaceted, service-oriented department that provides comprehensive nutrition care, foodservices, and educational programs for the patients, employees, visitors, and members of the community. All programs will be conducted with highest standards of quality and service within budgetary limitations.

Strategic planning

Decision-making based on environmental conditions, competition, forecasts, and resources available

Within multilevel organizations, department mission statements must be written based on the mission statement of the organization. Once these basic planning statements have been written, **strategic planning** can take place. Usually accomplished at the top levels of the management hierarchy, strategic planning involves making some decisions based on environmental conditions, competition, forecasts of the future, and the current and anticipated resources available (Figure 1).

Strategic plans evolve from careful analysis of the company's competitive advantage, threats posed by competitors, environmental forces, customer demands, and ways of measuring how well company goals are being met. The plan should help management make policy and operational decisions, but it should not stifle creativity or prevent managers from dealing effectively with contingencies and changing conditions. It also serves as a means

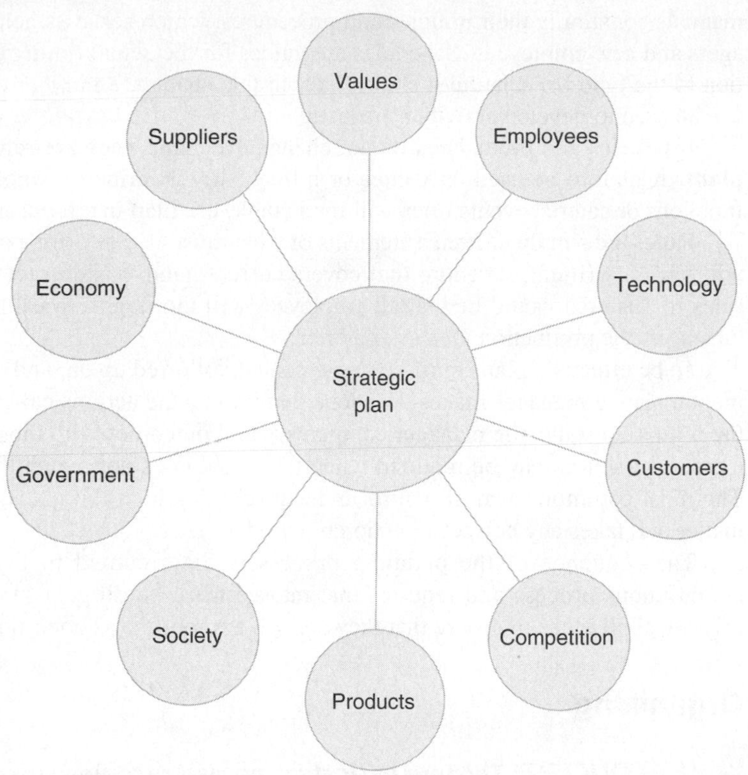

Figure 1 Factors to consider in developing a strategic plan.

of communicating proposed strategy to those in the organization who are responsible for its implementation. A strategic plan may have the following components:

1. A statement of purpose, mission, goals, and objectives of the organization and the measures used to evaluate performance
2. A definition of the desired future of the organization including a statement of identity. What business is the organization in or should it be in, and what kind of company is it or should it be?
3. A description of the competitive advantage of the company
4. A statement of proposed resource allocation to allow for implementation of the plan

Strategic plans are written documents prepared for short- and long-term goals on a periodic basis. Some organizations prepare strategic plans every few years, whereas others write them annually or even quarterly. Regardless of how often they are developed, they are reviewed on a regular basis. The strategic planning document serves as the foundation for intermediate plans, which cover a period of from one to three years. Intermediate planning is based on the strategic plan and begins with the development of policies.

A strategic plan is only as good as the people who contribute to its creation. Involvement of everyone and teamwork are important to both the creation of the plan and its implementation. People support what they create, and department plans must be coordinated with the organization's plan. Planning should be viewed as a continuous process. A strategic plan requires ongoing revision for improvement.

Policies are decision-making guides that are written to ensure that all actions taken by organizational members are consistent with the organization's strategy and objectives. After strategic and intermediate plans have been written, corresponding *operating plans* and budgets may be developed. Operating plans lay out the plans for the current period of time, usually one year or less. They are designed to provide the framework for implementing the strategic and intermediate plans at the departmental level. Operating plans specify the procedures to be used, the schedule to be followed, and the budget to stay within.

Procedures are detailed guidelines for planned activities that occur regularly. These are sometimes called *standard operating procedures (SOPs)*. Many organizations have

Policies

Guides for decision making

Procedures

Detailed guidelines for planned activities that occur regularly manuals containing their policies and procedures, which serve as helpful guides for managers and new employees. Schedules are guides for the actual timing of activities. In addition to the types of schedules shown later in this chapter, a number of formal techniques can be used to develop activity schedules.

If policies and procedures do not change over time, they are referred to as **standing plans**. A plan to be used only once or infrequently is termed a **single-use plan**. Special functions or catered events often call for a single-use plan in a foodservice operation.

Rules are simply written statements of what must be done. For example, a foodservice will have a written procedure that covers correct hand-washing techniques. One of the rules in this area would be that all employees will thoroughly wash their hands when returning to the production area after a break.

To be effective, plans must be implemented, followed up on, and controlled. To implement a plan, a manager makes decisions that initiate the actions called for in the plans. In the follow-up stage, the manager compares actual outcomes with those that were planned. Corrective action may be required when the actual does not match the planned outcome. The most common form of control is feedback, in which the manager monitors performance and takes any corrective action required.

The sequence of the planning process is diagrammed in Figure 2. Planning is a continuous process and requires that management be diligent in conducting periodic reviews of all plans to ensure that they are still appropriate as conditions change.

Organizing

■ **KEY CONCEPT:** The four basic steps necessary to develop the framework of an organization's structure are to (1) determine and define objectives, (2) analyze and classify work to be done, (3) describe in detail work to be done, and (4) determine and specify the relationship between and among workers and management.

Organizing includes the activities necessary to develop the formal structure of authority through which work is subdivided, defined, and coordinated to accomplish the organization's objectives. The organizing function identifies activities and tasks, divides tasks into positions, and puts similar tasks together to take advantage of special abilities and skills of the workers and to use their talents effectively. Perhaps the chief function of the organizing process is the establishment of relationships among all other functions of management.

Standing plans

Policies and procedures that do not change over time

Single-use plan

Plan that is to be used only once or infrequently

Rules

Written statements of what must be done or must not be done

Organizing

The function of management that involves the development of the formal structure through which work is divided, defined, and coordinated

---

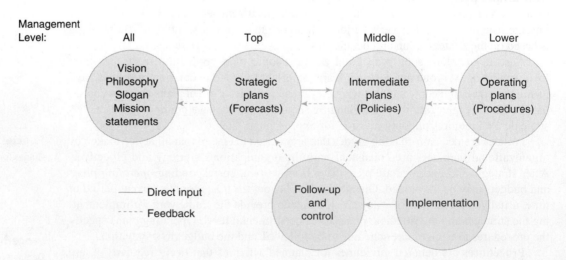

Figure 2 The planning process.

Organizational Structure.   An organization is a system having an established structure and conscious planning, in which people work and deal with one another in a coordinated and cooperative manner for the accomplishment of common goals. The formal organization is the planned structure that establishes a pattern of relationships among the various components of the organization. The informal organization refers to those aspects of the system that arise spontaneously from the activities and interactions of participants.

Whenever several people work together for a common goal, there must be some form of organization; that is, the tasks must be divided among them, and the work of the group must be coordinated. Otherwise, there may be duplication of effort or even work at cross purposes. Dividing the work and arranging for coordination make up the process of organization, and when that is completed, the group may be described as an "organization."

Certain steps are necessary in developing the framework of an organization's structure if goals of an enterprise are to be accomplished and the workers' talents developed to their fullest potential. These steps may be summarized as follows:

1. **Determine and define objectives:** The purpose of every organization dealing with personnel is to accomplish, with the efforts of people, some basic purpose or objective with the greatest efficiency, maximum economy, and minimum effort, and to provide for the personal development of the people working in the organization. Specifically, a foodservice has as its goal the production and service of the best food possible within its financial resources. It is important that these objectives and the plans and policies for their achievement be presented in writing and understood by all responsible.

2. **Analyze and classify work to be done:** This is accomplished by dividing the total work necessary for the accomplishment of overall goals into its major parts and grouping each into like, or similar, activities. Examination of the work to be done will reveal tasks that are similar or are logically related. Such classification may be made by grouping activities that require similar skills, the same equipment, or duties performed in the same areas. There are no arbitrary rules for grouping. In a foodservice, the activities could be grouped as purchasing and storage, preparation and processing, housekeeping and maintenance, and service and dishwashing. Each of these groupings might be broken into smaller classifications, depending on the type and size of the enterprise. With the increasing complexity of foodservice organizations and the trend toward centralization of certain functions, the organizational structure takes on new dimensions and must consider the total management structure as well as the organization of its individual units.

3. **Describe in some detail the work or activity in terms of the employee:** This step is discussed in more detail later in this chapter under "Job Description."

4. **Determine and specify the relationship of the workers to each other and to management:** The work should be grouped into departments or other organizational units, with responsibility and authority defined for each level. It is generally understood that each person assigned to a job will be expected to assume the responsibility for performing the tasks given him or her and that each person will be held accountable for the results. However, persons can be accountable only to the degree that they have been given responsibility and authority. Responsibility without authority is meaningless. An assignment should be specific and in writing. For an organizational structure to become operational, of course, requires the selection of qualified personnel, provision of adequate financing and equipment, and a suitable physical environment. No successful organization structure remains static. It must be a continuing process that moves with changing concepts within the system and with changing conditions in its environment.

Application of the principles of organization and administration to a specific situation should precede any attempt at the operation of a foodservice unit. A detailed plan may be outlined for use as a guide in initiating a new foodservice of any type or for reorganizing an existing one.

KEY CONCEPT: Organizations may be structured on a line, line and staff, or functional basis.

Types of Organizations.   Two types of authority relationships most often found in foodservice operating systems are (1) line and (2) line and staff. Large, complex operations may be organized on a functional basis.

Line Authority.   In the line organization, lines of authority are clearly drawn, and each individual is responsible to the person ranking above him or her on the organizational chart. Thus, authority and responsibility pass from the top-ranking member down to the lowest in rank. In such an organizational structure, each person knows to whom he or she is responsible and, in turn, who is responsible to him or her.

The organizational line structure can grow vertically or horizontally. Vertical growth occurs through the delegation of authority, in which the individual at the top delegates work to his or her immediate subordinates, who redelegate part or all of their work to their subordinates, and so on down the line. For example, the director of a growing cafeteria operation may add an assistant manager, thus creating another level in the chain of command. When the distance from the top to bottom becomes too great for effective coordination, the responsibilities may be redistributed horizontally through departmentalization. In establishing departments, activities are grouped into natural units, with a manager given authority and accepting responsibility for that area of activities. There are several ways of dividing the work, but, in foodservices, the usual way to do it is by function, product, or location. The work may be divided in a restaurant into production, service, and sanitation; in dietetics, by administrative, clinical, and education; in a central commissary, by meat, vegetable, salad, and bakery departments; or by individual schools in a multiunit school foodservice system.

Advantages of the line organization include expediency in decision making, direct placement of responsibility, and clear understanding of authority relationships. A major disadvantage is that the person at the top tends to become overloaded with too much detail, thus limiting the time that he or she can devote to the planning and research necessary for development and growth of the organization. There is no specialist to whom one can turn for help in the various areas of operation.

Staff Authority.   As an enterprise grows, the line organization may no longer be adequate to cope with the many diversified responsibilities demanded of the person at the top. Staff specialists, such as personnel director, research and development specialist, and data processing coordinator, are added to assist the lines in an advisory capacity. The line positions and personnel are involved directly in accomplishing the work for which the organization was created, and the staff advises and supports the line in a **line and staff** organization. A staff position also may be an assistant who serves as an extension of a line officer. The potential for conflict exists between line and staff personnel if the lines of authority are not clearly understood. For example, if a staff specialist recommends a change in procedure, the order for the change would come from the line personnel. Friction may arise if a strong staff person tries to overrule the manager or if the manager does not make full use of the abilities of the staff.

Functional Authority.   Some researchers include functional authority under the staff-type organization, but others consider it to be a distinct type in itself. Functional authority exists when an individual delegates limited authority over a specified segment of activities to another person. In a multiunit foodservice company, for example, the responsibility for purchasing or for menu planning and quality control may be vested in a vice president who then has authority over that function in all units.

Staffing

Staffing is the personnel function of employing and training people and maintaining favorable work conditions. The basic purpose of the staffing function is to obtain the best available people for the organization and to foster development of their skills and abilities.

Line and staff
Support and advisory activities are provided for the main functions of the organization

Staffing
The personnel function of employing and training people and maintaining favorable work conditions

Directing

Directing requires the continuous process of making decisions, conveying them to subordinates, and ensuring appropriate action. Delegation of responsibility is essential to distribute workloads to qualified individuals at various levels. Those delegating responsibility should not do so without detailed instructions on what is expected of the subordinate and the necessary authority to carry out the responsibilities. If a subordinate is not given sufficient authority, the job is merely assigned, not delegated.

A very important part of the directing function is the concern with employees as human beings. Studies have shown that most people work at only 50 percent to 60 percent efficiency, and some investigators place this figure as low as 45 percent. The alert manager is aware that through careful, intelligent guidance and counseling and by effective supervision, the worker's productivity may be increased as much as 20 percent. This may mean the difference between financial success and failure of an enterprise.

Directing
The continuous process of making decisions, conveying them to subordinates, and ensuring appropriate actions

Coordinating

Coordinating is the functional activity of interrelating the various parts of work so they flow smoothly. To function effectively, organizations must be properly designed. Division of work is usually accomplished through departmentalization, or specialization by function, product, client, geographic area, number of persons, or time. Different methods of coordination are required for different types of departmentalization. Management's role in the systems approach is one of coordinating. The manager must recognize the needs of all the parties and make decisions based on the overall effect on the organization as a whole and its objectives.

Coordinating
The functional activity of interrelating the various parts of a process to create a smooth workflow

Reporting

Reporting involves keeping supervisors, managers, and subordinates informed concerning responsibility through records, research, reports, inspection, and other methods. Records and evaluations of the results of work done are kept as the work progresses in order to compare performance with the yardstick of acceptability.

Reporting
Keeping supervisors, managers, and subordinates informed concerning responsibility through records, research, inspection, and other methods

Budgeting

Budgeting includes fiscal planning, accounting, and controlling. Control tends to ensure performance in accordance with plans and is a necessary function of all areas of foodservice. This necessitates measuring quantity of output, quality of the finished product, food and labor costs, and the efficient use of workers' time. Through control, standards of acceptability and accountability are set for performance. A good control system prevents present and future deviation from plans and does much to stimulate an employee to maintain the standards of the foodservice director. The budgeting function should be one of guidance, not command. It is concerned with employees as human beings with interests to be stimulated, aptitudes and abilities to be directed and developed, and comprehension and understanding of their responsibilities to be increased.

Budgeting
Fiscal planning, accounting, and controlling

SKILLS OF MANAGERS

■ **KEY CONCEPT:** **Managers need varying degrees of three skills (technical, human, and conceptual skills), depending on the level in the hierarchy at which the manager is working.**

The most widely accepted method of classifying managerial skills is in terms of the three-skill approach initially proposed by Robert L. Katz (1974). He identified technical, human, and conceptual skills as those that every successful manager must have in varying

Technical skills

Skills that allow a worker to perform specialized activities

Human skills

Understanding and motivating individuals and groups

Conceptual skills

Understanding and integrating all the activities and interests of the organization toward a common objective

Figurehead

Performs the duties of a symbolic, legal, or social nature because of one's position in the organization

Leader

Establishes the work atmosphere within the organization and activates subordinates to achieve organizational goals

Liaison

Establishes and maintains contacts outside the organization to obtain information and cooperation

Monitor

Collects all information relevant to the organization

Disseminator

Transmits information gathered outside the organization to members inside

Spokesperson

Transmits information from inside the organization to outsiders

Entrepreneur

Initiates controlled change in the organization to adapt and keep pace with changing conditions in the environment

Disturbance handler

One who handles unexpected change

Resource allocators

Make decisions concerning priorities for utilization of organizational resources

Negotiators

Deal with individuals and other organizations

degrees, according to the level of the hierarchy at which the manager is operating. Katz contended that managers need all three skills to fulfill their role requirements, but the relative importance and the specific types within each category depend on the leadership situation.

Based on the concept of skill as an ability to translate knowledge into action, the three interrelated skill categories may be briefly summarized as follows: (1) **technical skills**—performing specialized activities, (2) **human skills**—understanding and motivating individuals and groups, and (3) **conceptual skills**—understanding and integrating all of the activities and interests of the organization toward a common objective. Technical skills are usually more important than conceptual ones for lower-level managers. Human skills are needed at all levels of management but are relatively less important for managers at the top level than the low level. Conceptual skills become more important with the need for policy decisions and broad-scale action at upper levels of management.

MANAGERIAL ACTIVITIES AND ROLES

■ **KEY CONCEPT: Managerial roles may be classified as interpersonal (figurehead, leader, and liaison), informational (monitor, disseminator, and spokesperson), and decisional (entrepreneur or initiator, disturbance handler, resource allocator, and negotiator).**

Whereas a number of studies have investigated the personal styles and characteristics of managers, relatively few have researched what managers actually do in fulfilling job requirements. After reviewing and synthesizing the available research on how various managers spend their time, Harold Koontz (1980) reported that Henry Mintzberg designed a study to produce a more supportable and useful description of managerial work. Mintzberg's resulting role theory of management has received attention as a useful way of describing the duties and responsibilities of managers. Mintzberg (1973) defined a role as an organized set of behaviors belonging to an identifiable position. He identified 10 roles common to the work of all managers and divided them into interpersonal (3 roles), informational (3 roles), and decisional (4 roles). Although the roles are described here individually, in reality they constitute an integrated whole. In essence, the manager's formal authority and status create interpersonal relationships leading to information roles and these, in turn, to decisional roles.

The three interpersonal roles of figurehead, leader, and liaison result from the manager's formal authority and status. As a **figurehead**, a manager performs duties of a symbolic, legal, or social nature because of his or her position in the organization. As a **leader**, a manager establishes the work atmosphere within the organization and activates subordinates to achieve organizational goals. As a **liaison**, a manager establishes and maintains contacts outside the organization to obtain information and cooperation.

The three informational roles of monitor, disseminator, and spokesperson characterize the manager as the central focus for receiving and sending of nonroutine information. In the **monitor** role, managers collect all information relevant to the organization. The **disseminator** role involves the manager in transmitting information gathered outside the organization to members inside. In the **spokesperson** role, managers transmit information from inside the organization to outsiders.

The four decisional roles are entrepreneur or initiator, disturbance handler, resource allocator, and negotiator. Managers adopt the role of an **entrepreneur** when they initiate controlled change in the organization to adapt and keep pace with changing conditions in the environment. Unexpected changes require the manager to perform as a **disturbance handler**. As **resource allocators**, managers make decisions concerning priorities for utilization of organizational resources. Finally, managers must be **negotiators** in their dealings with individuals or other organizations. These interlocking and interrelated roles are shown in Figure 3.

Figure 3 Interlocking and interrelated roles of managers.

TOOLS OF MANAGEMENT

█ KEY CONCEPT: **Useful mechanical or visual tools of management are organization charts, job descriptions, job specifications, and work schedules.**

Directors of foodservice commonly use the organization chart as a means of explaining and clarifying the structure of an organization. They also use job descriptions, job specifications, and work schedules to identify personnel and explain their responsibilities to top management and employees. These mechanical or visual means are indispensable in the able direction and supervision of a foodservice. For convenience, these may be called tools of organization and management.

Organization Chart

The **organization chart** may be considered the first tool of management. It graphically presents the basic groupings and relationships of positions and functions. The chart presents a picture of the formal organizational structure and serves many useful purposes, but it does have some limitations. Whereas lines of authority are depicted on the chart, the degree of authority and responsibility at each level is not shown. Informal relationships between equals or between people in different parts of the organization are not evident. For this reason, job descriptions and organization manuals are valuable supplements to the organization chart.

The organization chart is usually constructed on the basis of the line of authority, but it may be based on functional activity or a combination of the two. Functions and positions are graphically presented by the use of blocks or circles. Solid lines connecting the various blocks indicate the channels of authority. Those persons with the greatest authority are shown at the top of the chart and those with the least at the bottom. Advisory responsibility and lines of communication often are shown by use of dotted lines. Organization charts for a hospital is shown in Figure 4 and for a college foodservice in Figure 5.

Figure 5 is an example of a relatively "flat" organizational structure where multiple levels of middle management are eliminated, which results in a broadening of the span of responsibility for all managers. Downsizing and streamlining operations across the country have resulted in previously tall, narrow organization charts becoming much broader and flatter.

Job Description

A **job description** is an organized list of duties that reflects required skills and responsibilities in a specific position. It may be thought of as an extension of the organization chart in that it shows activities and job relationships for the positions identified on the

Organization chart
A graphic representation of the basic groupings and relationships of positions and functions

Job description
An organized list of duties, skills, and responsibilities required in a specific position

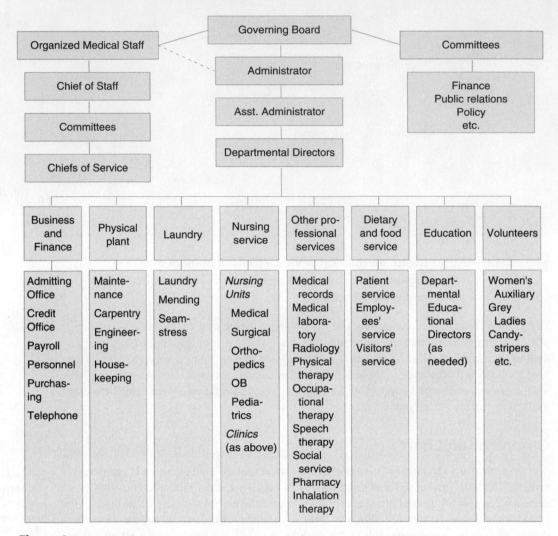

Figure 4 Chart of typical hospital staff organization.

organization chart. Job descriptions are valuable for matching qualified applicants to the job, for orientation and training of employees, for performance appraisal, for establishing rates of pay, and for defining limits of authority and responsibility. They should be written for every position in the foodservice and should be reviewed and updated periodically. In many organizations, the job descriptions are incorporated into a procedure manual or kept in a loose-leaf notebook for easy access.

Job descriptions may be written in either narrative or outline form, or a combination of the two. The format probably will vary according to the job classification; for example, the work of the foodservice employee is described in terms of specific duties and skill requirements, but the job description for the professional position is more likely to be written in terms of broad areas of responsibilities. Most job descriptions include identifying information, a job summary, and specific duties and requirements. The initial job descriptions for a new facility would reflect the responsibilities delegated to each position on a trial basis and subject to early revision. In the case of an established unit, they are developed from information obtained from interviews with employees and supervisors and from observations by the person responsible for writing the job description. A job analysis, in which all aspects of a job are studied and analyzed, may be conducted first to collect information for the job description.

The job description shown in Figure 6 may be useful as a guide. The exact content and format, however, vary according to the position being described and the needs and complexities of the institution.

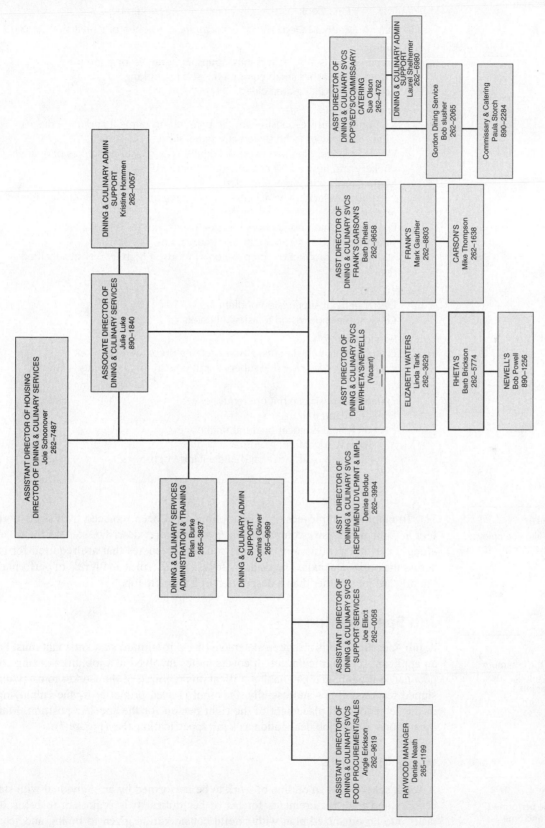

Figure 5 Organization chart for large university dining and culinary services system.
Source: Courtesy of University of Wisconsin–Madison.

Figure 6 Job description; write-up for a cook's position. Job descriptions should be available for all positions in the department.

JOB DESCRIPTION			
Job title:	First Cook	*Date:*	September 2, _____
Job code:	2–26.32 Dept 10	*Location:*	Kitchen of University Cafeteria

Job summary
 Prepares meats and main dishes, soups and gravies for noon meal.
 Cleans and washes small equipment used in cooking.
 Keeps own working area clean.

Performance requirements
 Responsibilities: responsible for the preparation of meat and main dishes, soups and gravies to be served at a stated time.
 Job knowledge: plan own work schedule, know basic principles of quantity food cookery and how to use certain equipment.
 Mental application: mentally alert.
 Dexterity and accuracy: accurate in weighing and measuring of food ingredients and portions.
 Equipment used: food chopper, mixer, ovens, ranges, steam cooker, steam-jacketed kettle, fryer, broiler, meat slicer.
 Standards of production: preparation of foods of high quality in specified quantities.

Supervision
 Under general supervision of dietitian.
 Gives some supervision to assistant cooks.

Relation to other jobs
 Promotion from: Salad maker or vegetable preparation worker.
 Promotion to: Foodservice supervisor (if education and ability warrant).

Qualifications
 Experience desirable but not required.
 Education and training.
  Technical or vocational training: none.
  Formal education: grammar school.
  Ability to read, write, and understand English.

Skills matrix system

An organized plan that allows employees to plan their own professional growth within the organization

To empower employees, job descriptions have been replaced by a **skills matrix system** in some progressive companies. Each skills matrix describes steps in the career ladder along a vertical axis, as well as skills and competencies that are required for each step across the horizontal axis. The skills matrices specify roles and levels of performance for a "family" of jobs, rather than a description of a specific job.

Job Specification

Job specification

A written statement of the minimum standards that must be met by an applicant for a particular job

A **job specification** is a written statement of the minimum standards that must be met by an applicant for a particular job. It covers duties involved in a job, the working conditions peculiar to the job, and personal qualifications required of the worker to carry out the assigned responsibilities successfully. This tool is used primarily by the employing officer in the selection and placement of the right person for the specific position. Many small institutions use the job description as a job specification also (Figure 7).

Work Schedule

Work schedule

An outline of work to be performed, procedures to be used, and time schedule for a particular position

A **work schedule** is an outline of work to be performed by an individual with stated procedures and time requirements for his or her duties. It is important to break down the tasks into an organized plan with careful consideration given to timing and sequence of operations. Work schedules are especially helpful in training new employees and are given to the employee after the person has been hired and training has begun. This is one

JOB SPECIFICATION

Payroll title: First Cook

Department: Preparation Department   *Occupational code:* 2–26.32

Supervised by: Dietitian

Job summary: Prepares meat, main dishes, soups, and gravies for noon meal.

Educational status: Speak, read, write English. Grammar school graduate or higher.

Experience required: Cooking in a cafeteria or restaurant 6 months desirable but not required.

Knowledge and skills: Knowledge of basic principles of quantity food preparation; ability to adjust recipes and follow directions; ability to plan work.

Physical requirements: Standard physical examination.

Personal requirements: Neat, clean; male or female.

References required: Two work and personal references.

Hours: 6:30 A.M. to 3:00 P.M., 5 days a week; days off to be arranged; 30-minute lunch period.

Wage code: Grade 3.

Promotional opportunities: To foodservice supervisor.

Advantages and disadvantages of the job: Location, environment, security.

Tests: None.

Figure 7 Job specification. Example of a typical format used for each job in the department.

means of communication between the employer and employee. Work schedules should be reviewed periodically and adjustments made as needed to adapt to changes in procedures.

An example of a work schedule for a cafeteria worker is given in Figure 8. For food production employees, the individual work schedule would outline in general terms the day's work routine, but it would need to be supplemented by a daily production schedule giving specific assignments for preparation of the day's menu items and pre-preparation for the next day.

Three basic types of work schedules may be used: individual, daily unit, and organization. Because the individual schedule on a daily basis would be too time consuming for most managers, the daily unit schedule is recommended.

The organization work schedule gives the standing assignments by half-hour periods for all employees in chart form. It does not relate specifically to the day's menu. This type of schedule shows graphically the total workload and its division among employees, but it would not be effective unless accompanied by daily assignments or a production schedule.

Scheduling of Employees

Workers may be scheduled successfully only after thorough analysis and study of the jobs to be done, the working conditions, and the probable efficiency of the employees. The menu pattern, the form in which food is purchased, the method of preparation, and the total quantity needed are important factors in determining the amount of preparation time and labor required to produce and serve meals in a given situation. Good menu planning provides for variation in meal items and combinations from day to day, with a fairly uniform production schedule. Workers cannot be expected to maintain high interest and to work efficiently if they have little to do one day and are overworked the next.

Analysis of several sample menus in terms of total labor hours and the time of day required for the amounts and types of preparations is a basic consideration in determining the number of employees necessary in any foodservice. The total estimated work hours required to cover all activities in the organization divided by the number of working hours in the day would give an indication of the number of full-time employees needed. However, careful attention must be given to time schedules so that each employee will be occupied

---

WORK SCHEDULE FOR CAFETERIA COUNTER WORKER

Name: _____

Position—Cafeteria Counter Worker—No. 1
Days off:

5:30 to 7:15 A.M.:
1. Read breakfast menu
2. Ready equipment for breakfast meal
   a. Turn on heat in cafeteria counter units for hot foods, grill, dish warmers, etc.
   b. Prepare counter units for cold food
   c. Obtain required serving utensils and put in position for use
   d. Place dishes where needed, those required for hot food in dish warmer
3. Make coffee (consult supervisor for instructions and amount to be made)
4. Fill milk dispenser
5. Obtain food items to be served cold: fruit, fruit juice, dry cereals, butter, cream, etc. Place in proper location on cafeteria counter
6. Obtain hot food and put in hot section of counter
7. Check with supervisor for correct portion sizes if this has not been decided previously

6:30 to 8:00 A.M.:
1. Open cafeteria doors for breakfast service
2. Check meal tickets, volunteer lists, guest tickets, and collect cash as directed by supervisor
3. Replenish cold food items, dishes, and silver
4. Notify cook before hot items are depleted
5. Make additional coffee as needed
6. Keep counters clean; wipe up spilled food

8:00 to 8:30 A.M.:
Eat breakfast

8:30 to 10:30 A.M.:
1. Break down serving line and return leftover foods to refrigerators and cook's area as directed by supervisor
2. Clean equipment, serving counters, and tables in dining area
3. Prepare serving counters for coffee break period

Hours: 5:30 A.M. to 2:00 P.M.
30 min for breakfast
15 min for coffee break

Supervised by: _____
Relieved by: _____

a. Get a supply of cups, saucers, and tableware
b. Make coffee
c. Fill cream dispensers
d. Keep counter supplied during coffee break period (9:30–10:30)
4. Fill salad dressing, relish, and condiment containers for noon meal

10:30 to 11:30 A.M.:
1. Confer with supervisor regarding menu items and portion sizes for noon meal
2. Clean equipment, counters, and tables in dining area
3. Prepare counters for lunch:
   a. Turn on heat in hot counter and dish warmers
   b. Set out tea bags, cream, ice cups, glasses
   c. Place serving utensils and dishes in position for use
4. Make coffee
5. Fill milk and clean dispensers
6. Set portioned cold foods on cold counter

11:30 A.M. to 1:30 P.M.:
1. Open cafeteria doors for noon meal service
2. Replenish cold food items, dishes, and silver as needed
3. Keep counters clean; wipe up spilled food
4. Make additional coffee as needed

1:30 to 2:00 P.M.:
1. Turn off heating and cooling elements in serving counters
2. Help break down serving line
3. Return leftover foods to proper places
4. Serve late lunches to doctors and nurses
5. Clean equipment and serving counter as directed by supervisor

2:00 P.M.:
Off duty

Figure 8 Work schedule for a counter worker in any type of cafeteria.

during his or her hours on duty. Certain preparations or service duties may require a reduction in the estimated number of full-time workers and the addition of some part-time workers during peak periods in order to maintain the desired standards at an even tempo. A graphic presentation of the estimated work hours needed for each job, as shown in Figure 9, helps to clarify the problems of scheduling and the distribution of the workload.

Working conditions such as the physical factors of temperature, humidity, lighting, and safety influence the scheduling of personnel and affect workers' performance. Of particular importance is the amount and arrangement of equipment. The distance each employee must travel within his or her work area should be kept at a minimum in order to conserve

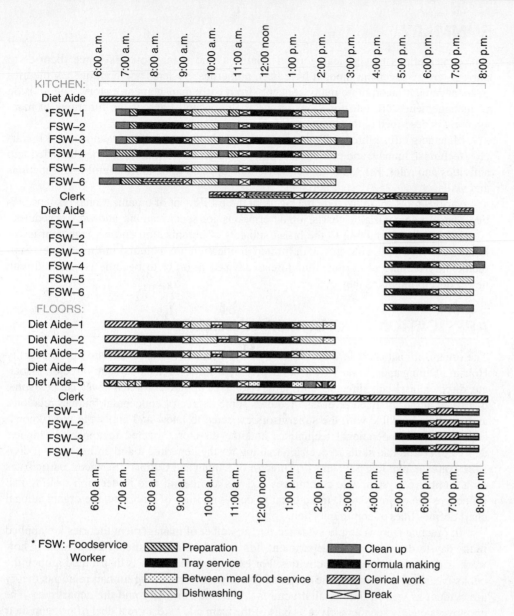

* FSW: Foodservice Worker

- Preparation
- Tray service
- Between meal food service
- Dishwashing
- Clean up
- Formula making
- Clerical work
- Break

the individual's energy and time. Use of mechanical devices in the processing and service of food may decrease the total labor hours needed and increase the degree of skill and responsibility of employees. Arrangement of work areas for efficient operation cannot be overemphasized.

A work distribution analysis chart of the total activities within a department will show where tasks may be eliminated, combined, or modified in the overall picture. The foodservice manager must be sure that the activities are so organized and combined that efficient use is made of the labor hours of each individual worker. Studies may be made to determine a good standard for each procedure, such as the time required for the average worker to combine and shape 25 pounds of ham loaf mixture into loaves in pans for baking. The standards for each procedure should be such that the workers in a particular organization will be able to maintain them. The standard time should be set at a level that the average employee could do 20 percent to 30 percent more work without undue fatigue.

Written schedules clarify the responsibilities of workers and give them a feeling of security. It is wise to include a statement indicating that additional duties may have to be assigned from time to time. However, work schedules must be kept flexible and adjustments made as needed to adapt to the daily menu. Also, the introduction of new food products may decrease the amount of time needed for pre-preparation, as well as the time of cookery; likewise, additional processes may become necessary.

SUMMARY

The contributions of classical, human relations, and management science theories to current-day management thought have been numerous. Systems and contingency theories of management incorporate many concepts from early management history. The division of management work into functions is one such concept. Each of the functions of management is described in this chapter.

Managers utilize three skills in proportion to their place in the organizational hierarchy: technical, human, and conceptual skills. Managerial work may also be classified into activities and roles. For some, this classification appears to be more useful than functions and skills.

Various tools are utilized by managers in the fulfillment of organizational responsibilities. These are organization charts, job descriptions, job specifications, and work schedules.

Information pertaining to the broad subjects of organization and management is voluminous. Only basic concepts with limited application are included in this chapter. Supplementary reading of current literature is advised in order to become acquainted with newer developments as they evolve.

APPLICATION OF CHAPTER CONCEPTS

The organizational chart for the University of Wisconsin–Madison Division of University Housing/Dining and Culinary Services depicts four levels of management: director, associate director, assistant director, and supervisor (see Figure 5). Each level carries some degree of authority. Each level also requires some degree of conceptual, human relations, and technology skills, with the supervisors expected to know and apply the most knowledge relative to operational techniques and the director expected to apply the highest degree of conceptual skills to decision making for the department and entire housing division. For example, Joie Schoonover, Director of Dining and Culinary Services, participates on a number of systemwide committees and has an integral role in decision making that influences the entire system. In addition to depicting lines of authority, the organizational chart defines lines of communication.

In practice there is ample evidence that a number of management theories are applied in the day-to-day work of the department. Tenets of the classical theory are evident in how work is divided into specific activities. For example, production is distributed among the cooks based on units within the scope of services. Aspects of the human relations theory are evident as well in the social structures within the university and the department. The employees clearly see themselves as part of the team and take a great deal of pride in their work and their efforts to please students, faculty, staff, and other customers.

CRITICAL THINKING QUESTIONS

1. In addition to division of labor, what other tenets of the classical theory are evident in the organization design for the UW–Madison Dining and Culinary Services department?
2. Is this a line organization, staff organization, or a line and staff organization? Justify your answer.
3. To whom does the Dining and Culinary Services Director report?
4. If a foodservice worker has a complaint about his or her position, to whom should the employee go first to explain and resolve the issue?
5. Recalling Katz's three skills of managers, describe which positions on the organization chart (Figure 5) will use each skill, predominantly, in performing the functions of the job specified by the position.
6. If advisory responsibility and lines of communication are shown with dotted lines, where on this organization chart would dotted lines be used?
7. What is not shown on this organization chart?

8. To whom do the Assistant Directors of Food Procurement/Sales and Support Services report?

9. Who on the organization chart would be most affected by a change in procurement policy to buy more local products?

10. Describe how this organization chart depicts an interdependent, open system.

CHAPTER REVIEW QUESTIONS

1. Where does organizational design fit on the systems model?

2. Discuss how concepts from the classical, human relations, and management science theories have been incorporated into the modern management theories today.

3. Give several examples of the application of human relations theory used today.

4. Describe the systems approach as it pertains to the management of a foodservice organization. Why is interdependency considered such a key concept in systems theory?

5. Discuss the statement: "A foodservice operation is an interdependent, open system."

6. Explain how contingency theory is really a combination of many other theories.

7. How do strategic management and systems management differ? How are they alike?

8. Explain the difference between a line and a line and staff organization. What are the advantages and disadvantages of each?

9. What are the seven widely accepted functions of management? Compare and contrast the division of managerial work into functions versus roles.

10. List and briefly explain (or diagram) the relationship among Katz's three managerial skills and the manager's level in the organizational hierarchy.

11. List the steps required to establish an organizational structure.

12. Outline the sequence of steps required in an effective planning process. Where do you find some concepts from historical management theory applied to planning?

13. How do job descriptions, job specifications, and work schedules differ? For what purpose is each used?

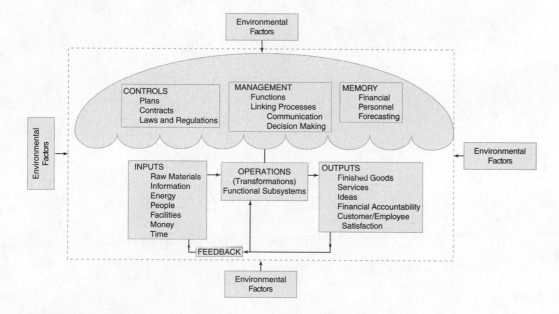

SELECTED WEB SITES

www.business.com   (Business advice, products, and services)
www.ceoexpress.com   (The executive's Internet resource)
mapnp.nonprofitoffice.com   (MAP for nonprofits)
http://www.newgrange.org   (Project management)

Human Resource Management

From Chapter 15 of *Foodservice Management: Principles and Practices*, Twelfth Edition, June Payne-Palacio, Monica Theis.
Copyright © 2012 by Pearson Education, Inc. Published by Pearson Prentice Hall. All rights reserved.

Human Resource Management

StockLife/Shutterstock

STAFFING AND MANAGING HUMAN RESOURCES INVOLVES all of the methods of matching tasks to be performed with the people available to do the work. The acquisition of human resources (job analysis, human resources planning, recruitment, and selection); the development of human resources (placement, orientation, training, performance evaluation, and personnel development); the rewards of human resources (compensation and promotion); and the maintenance of human resources (health and safety, transfer, discipline, dismissal, grievance handling, and labor relations) are all intertwined in this process. Each of these subjects is discussed in this chapter.

An important aspect of the human resources management function is the establishment, acceptance, and enforcement of fair labor policies within an organization. We discuss four areas in which policies are generally established: (1) wages and income maintenance, (2) hours and schedules of work, (3) security in employment, and (4) employee services and benefits. Major federal legislation that has an impact on these organizational policies is included in each section. The chapter concludes with a discussion of labor-management relations, including relevant legislation and the impact of unionization on foodservices.

KEY CONCEPTS

1. Staffing is the managerial function of matching requirements of tasks to be performed with people who have the necessary skills. This is accomplished through effective hiring, placement, promotion, transfer, job design, training, supervision, decision making, performance evaluation, and discipline.

2. Employment needs are outlined in various management tools such as the organization chart, job description, and job specification.

3. Internal recruitment sources include promotions from within and referrals by present employees. The most commonly used external sources are newspaper advertising, employment agencies, schools, and labor unions.

4. An effective hiring process includes a carefully prepared application form and an equally carefully prepared interview.

5. A new employee should be introduced to the job and the company first in a formal orientation program and then in a well-organized training program.

6. Behaviorally anchored rating scales (BARS) are generally considered to be the best and most effective means of performance evaluation.

7. Any disciplinary action taken should be immediate, consistent, impersonal, based on known expectations, and legally defensible.

8. Labor policies have been developed to guide managerial decision making and to commit employees to certain predictable actions.

9. A number of pieces of legislation establish fair labor policies and attempt to balance the power between labor and management.

10. Federal legislation, beginning with the National Labor Relations Act of 1935, has been enacted to allow employees to unionize and engage in collective bargaining.

STAFFING

KEY CONCEPT: Staffing is the managerial function of matching requirements of tasks to be performed with people who have the necessary skills. This is accomplished through effective hiring, placement, promotion, transfer, job design, training, supervision, decision making, performance evaluation, and discipline.

Foodservice has been called the ultimate people business. As the single most important resource in any enterprise, the human factor is the key to success. The ability of foodservice managers to understand people, recognize their potential, and provide for their growth and development on the job is of inestimable worth in helping to create good human relations. Realization by workers that they are useful and important to efficient functioning of the business contributes to their sense of responsibility, ownership, and pride in the organization. An increase in pay alone does not buy goodwill, loyalty, or confidence in self and others. Often just simple changes or considerations such as beautification of the work area, elimination of safety hazards, rearrangement of equipment, modification of work schedules, or even cheerful words of appreciation and encouragement produce incentives that result in increased and improved quality output. Mutually understood and accepted objectives and policies of the foodservice and well-defined channels of communication also contribute significantly to high-level employer-employee relationships.

Beyond good pay and benefits, these characteristics are common to those companies considered the best to work for in the United States: encouraging open communication, flowing up and down; promoting from within; stressing quality to foster a sense of employee pride in output; allowing employees to share in profits; reducing distinctions between ranks; creating as pleasant a workplace environment as possible; encouraging employees to be active in community service; helping employees save by matching funds that they save; and making people feel part of a team. The presence of these characteristics results in a good workplace climate and low absenteeism and turnover of good employees.

Staffing is not simply a synonym for employment. Staffing includes all the methods of matching requirements of tasks to be performed with people having those skills. Hiring, placement, promotion, transfer, job design, and training are all intertwined in this process. People must be hired and promoted who can be trained to perform the necessary tasks, and training must be designed around the needs of the employees and the organization. Staffing may be regarded as an integrated system for moving people into, through, and eventually out of the organization: **integrated staffing**.

Integrated staffing

An orderly plan for moving people into, through, and eventually out of the organization

A detailed plan of organization for a foodservice indicates the number and types of human resources needed, presents their distribution among the various work areas of the service, and shows their work schedules, the provision made for their training, and the responsibilities assigned to each. Far more difficult than the formulation of such a plan on paper is its actual inauguration. Then all the neat little blocks on the chart designating individuals assigned certain responsibilities become persons with diverse energies and loyalties, egocentric ideas, and unclarified codes of values, some skillful, others not, some with acceptable food standards, and others apparently totally lacking in this regard. Left to chance, the introduction of the human element into an orderly plan is likely to plunge it into chaos. With wise selection, intelligent and adequate direction, and careful supervision, the human element vitalizes and enriches the plan.

Foodservices in many large companies have personnel departments responsible for the staffing function. In such organizations, the foodservice director works closely with the personnel department. However, in many small foodservices, personnel management responsibilities are assumed by the director of that department. Thus, the director may be responsible for the organization plans and the procurement, placement, induction, on-the-job training, and supervision of all employees in the department.

Management of human resources presents unique problems that can be solved only by persons with an understanding of human nature, a respect for the personalities of others, and an appreciation of the labor requirements and employment opportunities of the company. Insight into and respect for the rights of all individuals in an organization are the responsibility of the person in charge. These time-honored rights include (1) the right to be treated as an individual and respected as a person; (2) the right to have a voice in one's own affairs, which includes the right to contribute to the best of one's own abilities to the solution of common problems; (3) the right to recognition for one's contribution to the common good; (4) the right to develop and make use of one's highest capabilities; and (5) the right to fairness and justice in all dealings with one's supervision.

As soon as he or she is employed, a worker becomes a member of the group and begins to share in forming that intangible but all-important element termed group morale or group spirit. An understanding, cooperative, and helpful worker contributes to group morale; an irritable, carping, complaining, and obstructive worker destroys it. Many organizations have learned through sad experience how destructive one malcontent member can be to group spirit. Because disciplining workers who are a disturbing force or eliminating them from the work group is neither easy nor pleasant, the selection of those who will build morale rather than destroy it is of great importance.

The skill, craftsmanship, dependability, and regularity of workers and their contribution to group morale in previous positions can determine whether they are chosen as new employees. Certain other qualities indicate probable contributions in the future. For example, capacity for growth, desire for self-improvement in order to render greater service, ambition for promotion, and identification with the firm are all important in the selection of a workforce for tomorrow. However, not every person wants to assume responsibility or to carry out a project to its conclusion. Others may be unwilling to face problem-solving. Some may be overdependent and eager to avoid directing themselves or others. There is a place in the organization for these people as well.

After the foodservice director has considered personnel needs, what the foodservice has to offer in return should be considered. Everybody works smarter when there is something in it for them. Part of the reward is money. Adequate compensation and steady employment are basic to any satisfactory employer-employee relationship.

Another part of the compensation may be intangible; that is, just as employees contribute to the morale or the group spirit of the service, the administration also contributes to their sense of personal satisfaction. The provision of meaningful work and the recognition of achievements are important motivational elements.

A third part of the compensation will be the opportunity to do a good job. Full instructions on accepted procedures and standards and adequate on-the-job supervision are vital to satisfactory performance by workers. Only then will they experience pride in their accomplishments and attain and maintain a high level of performance on the job.

The job should provide opportunity for growth and a reasonable chance for promotion. Workers should have an opportunity to make their service a creative experience. They should be encouraged to regard improvement in techniques as possible and welcome and to feel that suggestions toward this end will be cordially received. They have a right to expect fairness in dealing with management, freedom from misrepresentation and misinformation about the employing organization, a reasonable opportunity for continued education, promotion when earned, and provision for satisfying recreation.

The foodservice director should synthesize the two points of view—the employer's and the employee's—into an adequate, functioning personnel program. Such a program should be characterized by wise selection, careful placement, adequate supervision, and education for the present job and for the future; fair employment policies; services desirable for the comfort and welfare of employees; and record keeping that will facilitate the evaluation and revision, if needed, of the management program.

Skill Standards

The changing nature of today's business environment and labor markets has given impetus to the development of national skill standards by a number of professional organizations. These skill standards define the level of performance necessary to be successful on the job. More specifically, they include the steps involved in completing critical tasks, tools and equipment used, descriptions of possible problems and their responses, and the knowledge, skills, and abilities basic to completing these tasks. Everyone benefits from the use of skill standards:

- Employers can recruit, screen, place, train, and appraise employees more effectively, efficiently, and fairly.
- Workers can know what to expect on the job and be better prepared, thereby increasing their mobility and opportunity for advancement.
- Labor organizations can increase employment security through portable skills and credentials.
- Students can have clear direction to help them set goals and train for future employment.

- Educators can design quality curriculum and instruction consistent with the needs of the industry.
- Consumers can expect high-quality, efficient service from well-trained employees.

THE EMPLOYMENT PROCESS

KEY CONCEPT: **Employment needs are outlined in various management tools such as the organization chart, job description, and job specification.**

Organization charts indicate the number of workers needed in each department of a foodservice. Job descriptions and job specifications outline the specific conditions under which each employee will work, job requirements, training, and other personal qualifications deemed desirable. Such information provides an inventory of employment needs for the foodservice director charged with human resources management.

Recruitment

KEY CONCEPT: **Internal recruitment sources include promotions from within and referrals by present employees. The most commonly used external sources are newspaper advertising, employment agencies, schools, and labor unions.**

The next step is to survey the sources of labor supply and determine which one (or ones) are to be used to bring the open positions to the attention of the best-qualified prospective employees. Minority group members should be actively recruited so that the organization is in compliance with public policy. Labor sources are many and varied, dependent somewhat on which sources are available locally and on the general labor market. Most sources may be classified as either internal or external.

Internal Sources. Promotion of employees to a higher-level position, transfer from a related department or unit, and the rehire of a person formerly on the payroll are examples of internal sources. Promotions or transfers within an organization help to stimulate interest and build morale of employees when they know that on the basis of measured merit they will be given preference over an outsider in the event of a good vacancy. Caution must be taken to ensure that the individual has the necessary personal attributes as well as training and experience for the position open and that equal opportunity employment regulations have not been violated.

An indirect internal source of labor is a current employee who notifies friends or relatives of vacancies and arranges for an interview with the employer. Recruiting labor in this way has advantages and disadvantages. Current employees generally prefer working with those who are congenial, and a pleasant spirit within the group may be built by utilizing this source of labor supply. In contrast, personal ties may be stronger than business loyalties, and inept, unskilled workers may be highly recommended by relatives and friends. Furthermore, a strongly clannish feeling among the workers may lead to an unfortunate generalized reaction against any disciplinary measure, no matter how well justified. The many phases of this situation should be considered before extensive use is made of this source of labor.

External Sources. Some foodservice organizations may plan to fill vacancies by promoting from within; however, replacements will eventually be needed to fill the depleted ranks. The most common external sources are the media, employment agencies, schools, and labor unions.

Advertising. Newspaper advertising and Internet Web sites are a means of reaching a large group of potential applicants. These media sources should cite the qualifications desired; otherwise, many unqualified applicants may respond. Definite statements as to desired training and experience in the foodservice field tend to limit the applicants to those who are truly qualified. Details concerning salary, sick leave, time schedule, and vacations are much better left until the personal interview. The job listings should state whether application is to be made first in person or by letter.

Employment Agencies. Private employment agencies have long served as a means of locating labor. Usually, these agencies are supported by a registration fee charged to persons who are seeking employment. They generally provide a preliminary "weeding out" of would-be applicants, eliminating the unfit. Often these agencies tend to deal with specialized groups in the professional or technical areas and are of most value to those seeking employees on the managerial level.

Federal, state, and local employment agencies are a significant labor source. The value of these agencies lies in the fact that they have studied the employer's needs and have set up the machinery needed to test the aptitudes and skills of the workers. Such procedures benefit foodservice managers who are endeavoring to reduce turnover to a minimum and develop a stable workforce.

Schools. In some localities, vocational and technical schools offer training for the food industry. These graduates are excellent candidates for available foodservice positions. The adequacy of their specific preparation for this work may greatly shorten the period of preliminary training necessary.

Another source, important in the foodservices of colleges and universities, is the student employment office of the college. Utilizing this type of labor offers financial assistance to worthy students and often provides experience to those majoring in food systems management. Perhaps the greatest advantage of student employees to the college foodservice manager is their availability for short work periods during the peak of the service load. However, the labor cost is high because the workers are inexperienced and the labor turnover is great; thus, much energy is expended in introducing new workers to the jobs. The short work periods necessitated by student classroom assignments make the planning of work far more complicated than when full-time employees are used. The immaturity and inexperience of the worker can also result in a waste of food supplies and labor hours unless constant and thorough supervision is provided. The maintenance of high food standards and acceptable service is often much more difficult with student employees than with carefully chosen, well-trained employees of long-time service.

Labor Unions. In organizations where employees are unionized, the labor union may be an important source for workers.

Selection

After the prospective workers have been recruited, the next step is for the employer to select the most capable person available for the particular opening. The cost of hiring, training, and discharging or transferring a worker is too great to allow many mistakes in the employee procurement process. Failure at this point is far more expensive than is commonly recognized.

Recognition of the heavy initial cost of employment means, when the labor market permits, a trend toward careful selection of each appointee.

KEY CONCEPT: An effective hiring process includes a carefully prepared application form and an equally carefully prepared interview.

The application form plays an important role in the employment of any worker. The information requested should be phrased in direct simple statements pertinent to the particular job in which the applicant shows interest, and questions raised should be easily answered. Obviously, quite different information would be required of the person applying for a management position than for a counter worker position. However, both application forms, when completed, must contain biographical data that will provide the employer with all the facts necessary not only to determine the fitness of the applicant for the job, but also to compare the qualifications of all applicants.

The Fair Employment Practice laws adopted by many states make it illegal to ask questions that would be discriminatory because of race, religion, sex, age, marital status, or national origin. After the employee has been hired, such information can be obtained for the individual's personnel records. The manager should check with the personnel department or other authoritative source regarding restrictions in the application form and the interview. References from former employment are usually requested and should be checked.

The Interview. The purposes of the selection interview are (1) to get information—not only all the facts, but also attitudes, feelings, and personality traits that determine "will-do" qualifications; (2) to give information—just as it is essential that the interviewer know all about the applicant, it is also essential that the applicant know all about the establishment and the job; and (3) to make a friend—treat an applicant with the same courtesy that you would give to a customer, because every applicant is a potential customer.

The direct personal interview is advantageous in that the interviewer has the opportunity to become acquainted with the applicant and to observe personal characteristics and reactions that would be impossible to learn from an application form or letter. Also, the great majority of employees of a foodservice are relatively untrained persons, whose qualifications cannot be ascertained in any way other than by a personal interview and by possible communications with previous employers. Documents that could be termed credentials are rarely available; therefore, the personal interview becomes of great importance in making a wise choice. In filling administrative positions, the personal interview serves as a final check of the fitness of a person whose credentials have been considered carefully.

The applicant should be treated as a person whose concern with the decision is as real and vital as that of the employing agency. The job should be discussed in relation to other positions in the foodservice to which the job might lead. Reasonable hopes for promotion should be discussed, and fringe benefits should be presented. Appraisal of the job specifications in terms of the applicant's own fitness should motivate the applicant toward either self-placement or self-elimination.

The development of a successful technique in interviewing requires thought, study, and experience. Some interviewing suggestions include these:

The "Do's" of Interviewing

1. Have a purpose and a plan for the interview—a guided interview pattern.
2. Have on hand during the interview, and study carefully, an analysis of the job, a job description, and a job specification.
3. Provide a private place for the interview, free from interruptions and distractions.
4. Put the applicant at ease; establish confidence and a free and easy talking situation.
5. Use the pronoun *I* very, very sparingly; *we* is much better.
6. Listen with sincere and intensive interest.
7. Do ask questions beginning with *what*, *why*, and *how*. Useful phrases to keep in mind are:
   Would you give me an example?
   For instance . . .
   In what way . . .
   Suppose . . .
8. Do safeguard personal confidences.
9. Do strive to learn not only what the applicant thinks and feels, but also why the applicant thinks and feels that way.
10. Do be pleasant and courteous.
11. Do strive to be a good sounding board or mirror for the applicant's expressions of attitudes, feelings, and ideas.
12. Do ask questions that encourage self-analysis.
13. Do prod, search, and dig courteously for all the facts.
14. Maintain an attitude of friendly interest in the applicant. Make a friend and a customer even if you do not hire the applicant.
15. Do make notes for record purposes, either during or after the interview.
16. Do, immediately after the interview, write a summary on the interview form in the space provided.

Suggestions of things to avoid in interviewing include these:

The "Don'ts" of Interviewing

1. Do not interrupt the applicant.
2. Do not talk too much. Talkative interviews usually are failures.
3. Do not rush the interview. This is not only discourteous, but it also results in failure of the interview.
4. Do not ask leading questions. If the question is worded so that the answer you want is apparent to the applicant, you are actually interviewing yourself.
5. Do not ask questions that demand only a yes or no response.
6. Do not merely talk when the applicant has finished a statement. Use such responses as "I see," "I think I understand," or "What else can you add to that statement?"
7. Do not agree and do not disagree. Be interested but noncommittal.
8. Do not argue, or else the interview is finished.
9. Do not lose control of yourself or the interview.
10. Do not get in a rut. Do not leave any impression with the applicant that the interview is routine and perfunctory.
11. Do not "talk down."
12. Do not express or imply authority. The good employment interview is a free and easy exchange of attitudes and ideas between equals.
13. Do not jump to conclusions. The purpose of the interview is to get information. Appraisal and conclusions will come after the interview.
14. Do not preach or moralize. This is not the purpose of the interview.
15. Do not interview when either you or the applicant is upset.

Depending on the position, there are many good questions that may be asked in the employment interview. For example, asking what were the favorite parts of their previous job is helpful for assessing whether their preferences fit with the job for which they are applying. Asking questions that are unexpected may help in assessing personality, thought processes, energy level, and attitude. Asking an applicant how they might handle a specific job situation is a good way to determine how well he or she would respond in real-life work situations.

Tests. Impressions of the prospective employee gained in the interview and from the follow-up of references are admittedly incomplete. They may be checked or replaced by tests of various types, the most common being intelligence, trade, and aptitude. A number of companies, including foodservices, have improved the results of their selection decisions by the use of psychological tests. These companies have found that the benefits derived from psychological testing far exceed the costs. An applicant's probable tenure, customer relations, work values, and safety record may be predicted with such tests. To be considered legal, all psychological test questions must be job related and legal to ask. In addition, all applicants must be asked the same questions, and scoring methods must be the same for all applicants.

The physical fitness of an applicant for a foodservice appointment is highly important. A health examination should be required of all foodservice workers. Only physically fit persons can do their best work. Quite as important is the need for assurance that the individual presents no health hazard to the foodservice. Managers are well aware of the devastation that might result from the inadvertent employment of a person with a communicable disease.

THE WORKER ON THE JOB

Personnel Records

After an agreement on employment terms has been reached, a record of appointment is made. This becomes the nucleus of the records of the activity and progress of the worker within the organization. Records may be kept on the computer, in card files, or in loose-leaf form. Included among the items listed on the forms are name, address, name of spouse, number of children, other dependents, educational background, former employment (including company and length of time), date of hiring, job assigned, wage rate, whether meals are included, absences with reasons, adjustments in work and wages, promotions, demotions, or transfers with reasons, and information concerning insurance and health benefits. Such complete records are useful in indicating the sense of responsibility and the serious intent of employees, and as a basis for merit ratings, salary adjustments, or other benefits.

Orientation

KEY CONCEPT: A new employee should be introduced to the job and the company first in a formal orientation program and then in a well-organized training program.

The induction of the newly employed worker to the job is a most important phase of staffing. Smith (1984) outlines 10 steps to be included in an orientation program that is designed to challenge the new employee's interest and elicit support for the goals and objectives of the company.

1. **Introduction to the company:** Introductions are simply a matter of identifying the company, where it has been, and where it is going. The key is to make the new employee feel good about the company and begin to instill the pride of belonging, being a part of the company.
2. **Review of important policies and practices:** Policy review will vary from company to company, but certainly must include standards of conduct and performance, an introductory (probation) period of employment, a discipline policy, and a safety policy.
3. **Review of benefits and services:** A review of benefits is crucial. It is not as important to sell a benefits program and all its virtues as it is to communicate what is provided and at what expense. Employees need to appreciate the cost of benefits, and the employer should be able to relate the percentage of payroll spent on their behalf. In addition, discuss services that the employee might not construe as benefits, such as a credit union, parking, food, medical care, discounts, and social-recreational services.
4. **Benefit plan enrollment:** Complete necessary benefit enrollment forms with the assurance that the employee understands his or her options. Provisions should be made to allow the employee to discuss plan options with a spouse before making a commitment.
5. **Completion of employment documents:** Payroll withholding, emergency information, picture releases, employment agreements, equal employment opportunity data, and other relevant and appropriate documents must be completed.
6. **Review of employer expectations:** This deals with employer-employee relationships. Discuss teamwork, working relationships, attitude, and loyalty. A performance evaluation form makes a good topical outline for a discussion of employer expectations.
7. **Setting of employee expectations:** If employees meet company expectations, what can they expect from the company? Training and development, scheduled wage and salary reviews, security, recognition, working conditions, opportunity for advancement, educational assistance programs, counseling, grievance procedures, and other relevant and appropriate expectations should be detailed.
8. **Introduction to fellow workers:** Introduce people a few at a time to let the names be assimilated. Use of name tags is helpful, and so is the buddy system. Assign someone to be a mentor to the new employees, to introduce them, take them to break periods, have lunch with them. A few days is usually enough introduction time.
9. **Introduction to facilities:** Take a standard tour of the facility. This is more effective if you break it into several tours. On the first day, tour the immediate work area and then expand the tour on subsequent days until the facility is covered.
10. **Introduction to the job:** Have your training program in place. Be prepared and ready to get the employee immediately involved in the workflow (Smith, R. E.: Employee orientation. *Personnel Journal,* 1984; 63(12): 43).

Training

After the individual worker has been properly introduced to the job, the employee still needs to be thoroughly trained, especially in the initial period of employment. Familiarity with established operational policies and procedures, presented by management in a well-organized manner, can do much to encourage the new worker and help in gaining self-confidence. Generally, advantages of a good training program include reduction in labor turnover, absenteeism, accidents, and production costs, and an increase in the maintenance of morale, job satisfaction, and efficient production at high levels.

The first step in establishing a training program is to decide when training is needed. Next, determine exactly what needs to be taught and who should receive that training. Goals should be established for the program and an outline developed containing the steps required to help meet those goals.

Adult Training. The unique characteristics of adults as learners must be considered when planning for on-the-job training. Children learn for the future and in order to advance to the next level of learning. Adults, however, learn for immediate application or to solve a present problem. For this reason, they require practical results from the learning experience. Other distinguishing characteristics of the adult learner are a reduced tolerance for disrespectful treatment, the preference for helping to plan and conduct one's own learning experiences, and a broader base of life experiences to bring to the learning activity.

Group Training. Often, training can be given efficiently and economically through group instruction. This type of teaching saves time for the instructor and the worker and also has the advantage of affording the stimulus that comes as the result of group participation. In a foodservice, basic group instruction concerning the policies of management is practical and valuable. Among the areas that might be included are the history and objectives of the organization, relationships of departments and key persons within the particular department, the operational budget as it affects the workers, the preparation and service of food, the sanitation and safety program, and the principles and values of work improvement programs.

Perhaps the most important psychological principle of group training is the use of well-prepared teachers instead of a fellow worker who may have had successful experience in a limited area. Often the stimulation and the inspiration given to the employee by an able instructor are highly motivating and more important in the development of the individual worker than the immediate mastery of routine skills. Tools found to be of value in such an instructional program are audio and visual aids, including films and television; illustrative material such as posters, charts, and cartoons; and demonstrations in which both the instructor and the employees participate. Spending time and money merely showing DVDs in group training classes is wasteful unless the workers have been alerted to the points of emphasis, time is allowed for discussion after the presentation, and follow-up occurs through application on the job. Other psychological principles of group education are not considered here, but they should be understood by those in charge of such programs.

On-the-Job Training. Some large foodservice organizations have inaugurated rather extensive programs to provide on-the-job training of employees, with highly satisfactory results. Important objectives of such programs are (1) to reduce time spent in perfecting skills for the production and service of attractive, wholesome food of high quality at reasonable cost; (2) to avoid accidents and damage to property and equipment; (3) to promote good understanding and close working relationships among employees and supervisors; and (4) to give employees a sense of achievement and prepare them for advancement. In these programs, emphasis is given to certain requirements common to all good job instruction, such as job knowledge, psychological skills, human relations, adaptability, and ability to express oneself. These requirements are necessary for the instructor to be an effective teacher.

Teacher preparation for instruction to be given on the job includes the following tasks:

1. **Break down the job:** List principal steps. Pick out the key points.
2. **Have a timetable:** How much skill do you expect your pupil to have, and how soon?

3. **Have everything ready:** Make sure the right tools, equipment, and materials are at hand.

4. **Have the workplace properly arranged:** Arrange it in the way in which the worker will be expected to keep it.

After the preparation, the teacher sets about with the actual instruction:

1. **Prepare the worker:** Put the worker at ease. A frightened or embarrassed person cannot learn. Find out what is already known about the job. Begin where knowledge ends. Interest the worker in learning the job. Place the worker in the correct position so that the job won't be viewed from the wrong direction.

2. **Present the operation:** Tell, show, illustrate, and question carefully and patiently. Stress key points. Make them clear. Instruct slowly, clearly, and completely, taking up one point at a time, but no more than the trainee can master. Work first for accuracy, then for speed.

3. **Try out the worker's performance:** Test by having the worker perform the job under observation. Have the worker tell and show you, and explain key points. Ask questions and correct errors patiently. Continue until you know the worker knows.

4. **Follow up the worker's performance:** Let the worker perform alone. Check frequently, but do not take over if you can give the help needed. Designate to whom the worker goes for help. Encourage questions. Get the worker to look for key points as progress is made. Taper off extra coaching and close follow-up until the worker is able to work under usual supervision. Give credit where credit is due.

A job breakdown is the analysis of a job to be taught and a listing of the elemental steps of what to do and the key points of how to do them. This serves as a guide in giving instruction so that none of the necessary points will be omitted. Figure 1 is an example of a job breakdown for making change. There should be a job breakdown for every task and job to be performed in the organization.

DVD programs for individual instruction in work methods and procedures have proven to be satisfactory, and although it is time-consuming to prepare such a program, the results appear to justify their use. Slides showing correct techniques are accompanied by oral explanations on tape. For techniques involving motion or rhythm, videotaping may be helpful.

Figure 1 Job breakdown for making change at the cash register. Important steps are "what to do"; key points are "how to do."

Job: Making Change
Equipment and Supplies: Money and Cash Register

Important Steps	Key Points
REGISTER FIRST—WRAP AFTERWARD	
1. Accept money from customer.	1. State amount of sale* "out of" amount received from customer.
2. Place customer's money on plate.	2. Stand in front of cash register. Do not put bill in drawer until after change has been counted.
3. Record the sale on cash register.	3. Check amount of change recorded on viewer.
4. Count change from till.	4. Begin with amount of sale picking up smallest change first, up to amount received from customer.
5. Count change carefully to customer.	5. Start with amount of sale—stop counting when amount is the same as the customer gave.
6. Place customer's money in till.	6. Close the drawer immediately.
7. Deliver change, receipt or sales slip, and merchandise to customer.	7. Say *Thank You*. Let customer know you mean it.
	*Including tax (state and federal).

Encouragement of the worker by the supervisor during the first days on the job and during the training period is important in stabilizing interest and sustaining a sense of adequacy. Informal interviews may serve as a means of determining areas in which help is needed, as well as those in which ability is most marked. Every expression of friendly, courteous interest is appreciated by the worker and aids in a successful adjustment to the new environment.

In addition to the satisfaction attained by establishing pleasant employer-employee relations, the right induction of the new worker has a dollars-and-cents value that cannot be overlooked. An employee who is unhappy, uninterested, and discontented will tend to look for placement elsewhere after a short experience with the company. Then all the money, time, and effort spent in obtaining and introducing the employee to the job will have been lost, and a similar expenditure must be made before another worker can be assigned the task.

Training budgets have been steadily increasing in restaurants, hotels, and fast-food operations because industry experts see employee training not only as a solution to increased turnover, but also as a way to solve other current problems. Among employees and in business, decreased productivity and intense competition have been the stimulants for training programs that are both intensive and progressive.

Performance Evaluation

KEY CONCEPT: Behaviorally anchored rating scales (BARS) are generally considered to be the best and most effective means of performance evaluation.

For maximum effectiveness from the workforce, every employee should know what is expected and how he or she is performing on the job. Workers are entitled to commendation for work well done and to the opportunity to earn greater responsibility, either with or without increased remuneration. One of the responsibilities of management and supervision is the performance evaluation. Management then has an obligation to communicate this information to each worker regarding individual progress. The personal development of, and efficient production by, each worker are of concern to management, but an individual worker cannot be expected to improve if evaluations are not made known or counsel is not made available for assistance. Performance evaluations are used to determine job competence and need for additional training or counseling, and to review the employee's progress within the organization. Ratings made objectively and without prejudice furnish valuable information that can be used in job placement, training, supervision, promotion, replacement, and future recommendations. Careful selection and placement and proper training of employees are prerequisites to a successful evaluation program. The performance evaluation may be accomplished by several methods, including rating scales, checklists, narrative evaluation, personal conferences, and management by objectives.

There are few, if any, objective standards that can be used for measuring subjective personal characteristics such as character, reliability, and initiative. Yet these traits, as they relate to the capabilities, efficiency, and development of each employee, are important to an organization. Such characteristics must be appraised in some way if management is to have an intelligent basis for classifying workers according to rank or grade and, thus, help to provide a standard for salary increases, promotions, transfers, or placement into a job for which the worker is well suited.

Rating procedures have been developed that provide a measurement of the degree to which certain intangible personality traits are present in workers and in their performance on the job. Care should be taken to design the scale to meet the objective desired. Will this estimate of the relative worth of employees be used as a basis for rewards or recognitions or as a tool for explaining to workers why they may or may not be making progress on the job? In the hands of competent administrators, the rating form can be designed to obtain information to accomplish both purposes.

Distinguishable personal traits most likely to affect performance are honesty, initiative, judgment, and ability to get along with other workers. Examples of qualities on a rating chart are quality of work, quantity of work, adaptability, job knowledge, and dependability.

These so-called rating scales, from which the variously known merit, progress, development, or service ratings are derived, are not new in industrial management, although few are directly applicable to foodservices. Some administrators prefer a system of gradation checking where each quality, factor, or characteristic may be marked on a scale ranging from poor to superior, or the reverse, with two or three possible levels within each grade. For example, another format might describe the grade for each factor listed.

Figure 2 is an example of a rating scale with definitions of the various factors attached for use by the rater.

Figure 2 An example of a rating form designed for evaluating a kitchen worker. Comparable forms could be made applicable for each classification of worker.

Associate Rating Form: Kitchen Worker

1. *Job Skill* (Max. points: 25)
   Consider job performance and skill. Does the worker keep up with the work and keep the station clean; make all products uniformly, waste conscious, and economical; work quietly and reasonably fast; refrain from visiting with fellow associates while on duty?

Excellent	25
Good	20
Average	15
Fair	10
Poor	5

2. *Cooperation* (Max. points: 25)
   Consider attitude. Does the worker respond quickly to a call for assistance from a fellow associate? Have a spirit of willingness? Receptive to change and new ideas? Accept new suggestions regarding his/her work?

Excellent	25
Good	20
Average	15
Fair	10
Poor	5

3. *Sanitation* (Max. points: 10)
   Consider health regulations: "No Smoking—Wash Hands When Leaving Rest Rooms." Does worker keep paper, trash, liquids, vegetable leaves, and other foreign materials off floor; keep hot foods hot, and other food under refrigeration?

Excellent	10
Good	8
Average	6
Fair	4
Poor	2

4. *Care of equipment* (Max. points: 10)
   Does worker keep equipment clean and everything returned to proper place, know correct way to operate ovens, steamers, mixers, and other appliances?

Excellent	10
Good	8
Average	6
Fair	4
Poor	2

5. *Safety* (Max. points: 10)
   Does worker work safely and is worker safety conscious? Correct or report all hazards that may cause an accident? Know whereabouts of fire extinguisher and how to use it?

Excellent	10
Good	8
Average	6
Fair	4
Poor	2

6. *Appearance* (Max. points: 10)
   Consider personal cleanliness and neatness. Does worker seem to enjoy the work? Is he/she clean of body? Are clothes clean and appropriate?

Excellent	10
Good	8
Average	6
Fair	4
Poor	2

7. *Attendance* (Max. points: 10)
   Consider regular daily attendance and promptness. Does worker return from 10 minute breaks and meal periods on time?

Excellent	10
Good	8
Average	6
Fair	4
Poor	2

The **critical-incident appraisal method** requires that supervisors identify behaviors that are indicators of excellent or poor performance. Throughout the rating period, records are kept of such critical incidents for each employee. These records are then compared with the previously identified indicators of performance evaluation.

Combining both the rating scale and critical-incident methods led to the **behaviorally anchored rating scale (BARS)** method of performance evaluation. BARS is generally considered the best and most effective means of appraisal. The disadvantage of this method is that the scales are difficult and time-consuming to develop. The steps in developing a BARS are: (1) list all the important dimensions of performance for a job category; (2) collect critical incidents of effective and ineffective behavior; (3) classify effective and ineffective behaviors to appropriate performance dimensions; and (4) assign numerical values to each behavior within each dimension. An example of one specific dimension of a job might be the following:

Customer Service

Skill Description: Greets customers and maintains friendly rapport with them, listens to and handles complaints and issues that arise in a fair and friendly manner with tact and diplomacy.

Rating 1: Demonstrates little ability to get along with customers and usually relies on higher-level managers to resolve issues that arise.

Rating 2: Demonstrates the ability to get along with some customers and is able to resolve complaints and issues that arise about half of the time.

Rating 3: Demonstrates the ability to get along with most customers and is able to resolve most of the issues and complaints that arise.

Rating 4: Demonstrates the ability to get along with customers and listens carefully to them; handles issues and complaints effectively most of the time.

Rating 5: Demonstrates good customer service consistently by greeting customers, developing and maintaining friendly relations, actively listening before commenting; handles complaints and issues effectively at all times.

One of the original purposes of **management by objectives (MBO)** was to simplify and overcome the limitations of the more traditional performance evaluation. This approach emphasizes the setting of measurable performance goals that are mutually agreed on by the employee and the immediate supervisor. At stated intervals, the employee's progress toward the goals is assessed by the employee and by the manager. Participation by employees in the performance evaluation process has resulted in favorable perceptions regarding the performance evaluation interview as well as positive performance outcomes.

Regardless of the rating systems selected, the person making the ratings should be well qualified for the responsibility of evaluating people. Usually the immediate supervisor is in a position to do the best job, because this person can observe activities continuously. However, adequate instructions are needed about the purpose and value of the program so that follow-through with assistance is provided when needed. Also, a thorough explanation and understanding of the factors to be rated is necessary to avoid misinterpretation of the forms or to avoid failure to meet the intended standards. The person who is charged with the responsibility of rating employees must be objective and able to evaluate individuals in terms of the factors to be rated, to be guided by the pattern of performance instead of isolated happenings, to communicate fairly and accurately what is observed, and to be consistent from one time to the next. These are prime requisites of the rater.

An interview is a vitally important part of the performance evaluation process. The purpose of the interview is to provide information and set goals. It should be scheduled in advance, and both employee and supervisor should be prepared. The proper atmosphere for two-way communication must be established. The format should be conversational. In fact, the term *performance evaluation* has been replaced by "Conversation Documents" in some operations. The supervisor should begin with a statement of purpose and then encourage the employee to participate in the dialogue. Total performance, both positive and negative, should be discussed. The evaluation stage of the interview should conclude with

---

Critical-incident appraisal method

Records are kept of both positive and negative occurrences/behaviors for each employee to be used for performance evaluation purposes

---

Behaviorally anchored rating scale (BARS)

Performance evaluation scales that contain specific behaviors identified for each performance level for each job category

---

Management by Objectives (MBO)

An approach to performance evaluation requiring the setting of measurable performance goals that are mutually agreed upon by the employee and the immediate supervisor

a summary and documentation of the interview for the employee's file. In the second stage of the interview, the emphasis should be on setting mutual goals, including personal growth and formulating follow-up procedures. The employee should never be left in doubt about the rating given, or about what must be done to change or improve if there is a need to do so.

A relatively new trend that has been gathering momentum is the implementation of upward feedback performance evaluations, in which employees rate their supervisor's people management skills. Upward feedback performance evaluations have proven to be valuable tools for the improvement of management performance and subordinates' morale. They provide employees with an opportunity to have a say in how they are supervised.

In an effort to encourage the two-way conversation format, it is helpful to give employees some questions to consider prior to the interview. Among questions frequently used are: How could my supervisor help me do my job more effectively? What do I think would help us improve operations within our department?

Promotions and Transfers

On the basis of sound ratings by members of staff, the foodservice manager is fairly able to predict the probable future development of various members of the organization. In the application of a rating scale, one group may rate high. This scale helps to identify the people deserving the stimulus and encouragement toward promotion. The term *promotion* commonly implies an increase in responsibility and salary. Sometimes promotion carries only the opportunity for experience in a desired field. It may mean shorter hours and greater assurance of security. Regardless of the nature of the promotion, it is an expression of appreciation of an individual's worth.

Often a worker found unfit for one job may do well in another. The apparent lack of fitness may arise in the supervisory relationship or in contacts with coworkers. Personal prejudice against a particular type of work or physical inability to do the job may be the cause. In some cases, a minor shift may enable the worker to become a contented and valuable employee. Transfer of an employee who is not finding satisfaction in the current job to another opening within the organization offering a different challenge or opportunity has salvaged many workers. Different jobs may present wide variation in skill requirements, which makes possible the transfer of workers if necessary. Relative levels of difficulty should be considered in placement and in replacement. Continued training of the employee in this new position is critical to the success of a relocated worker.

Discipline

KEY CONCEPT: Any disciplinary action taken should be immediate, consistent, impersonal, based on known expectations, and legally defensible.

Discipline is required when other measures have failed to make certain that workers perform according to accepted standards. Leadership must first ensure that work rules are clear, reasonable, fair, reviewed regularly, and consistent with the collective bargaining agreement. Rules must be disseminated to employees orally and posted in a visible location, and they must be enforced promptly, consistently, and without discrimination. Leadership must set a good example by complying with all rules and requirements.

Any disciplinary action must be undertaken with sensitivity and sound judgment. The supervisor should first thoroughly investigate what happened and why. As a general rule, disciplinary action should be taken in private. Personnel policies usually fit the severity of the penalty to the severity of the infraction, with the steps in progressive discipline ranging anywhere from an informal talk, an oral unrecorded warning or reprimand, a written or official warning, a disciplinary suspension, a demotion or transfer, to a discharge.

As an aid to supervisors, the "hot stove" analogy to disciplinary action is suggested. Experiencing discipline should be like touching a hot stove. The burn gives advance warning and is immediate, consistent, and impersonal:

- **Advance warning:** Everyone knows what will happen if you touch a hot stove. Employees should know what is expected of them.
- **Immediate:** The burn is immediate. Discipline should not be hasty, but should be taken as soon as possible after the infraction.
- **Consistent:** The hot stove burns every time. Disciplinary action should be taken every time an infraction occurs.
- **Impersonal:** Whoever touches the stove is burned. The act, not the person, should be disciplined.

Before taking any disciplinary action, a supervisor should ask these six questions:

1. Was the worker aware of the work rules that were violated?
2. Are the rules reasonable?
3. What rule was violated?
4. Was the investigation fair?
5. Was there substantial evidence of the violation?
6. Are the rules being applied evenly?

After disciplinary action, the employee should be treated as before.

Dismissals

If an employee is terminated without the consent of the employee, the act is termed dismissal. An individual may be discharged because of failure to perform assigned duties, but this should be the final step and should follow counseling, warning, or possibly disciplinary layoff. Each person discharged from a foodservice should be given a terminal or "exit" interview in which strong points are recognized and the reasons for dismissal are dispassionately reviewed. If the situation merits that the employee be recommended for another position, aid should be given in the placement problem. In any event, the discharged employee should not leave the service without having had a chance to speak regarding the dismissal and without being made aware, if possible, of the fair deal given by the supervisor.

Opinions differ regarding the discussion of a dismissal with other employees. If there is a possibility that the incident may foster a sense of insecurity among the group, a presentation of the facts, not necessarily full and complete, may be desirable from the standpoint of group morale. Often, employees understand far more about such situations than the director believes.

Handling Grievances

The wise supervisor gives active supervision; that is, the wise supervisor does not sit at a desk waiting for employees to come with problems. The wise supervisor foresees and is prepared to meet possible difficulties instead of merely waiting for something unpleasant to happen. Grievances are not always expressed in verbal or written form. Supervisors should be alert for symptoms of unexpressed dissatisfaction such as excessive tardiness or absenteeism, decline in quantity or quality of work, change in attitude, or indifference.

Many grievances can be settled by the supervisor and employee on an informal basis. If the employees are unionized, the contract includes formal grievance procedures, which usually include presentation of the grievance in writing and an attempt to settle the dispute at the first-line supervisory level. If this is not possible, the grievance moves through higher levels of authority until settled.

Staff Conferences

Regular staff conferences, department meetings, and the use of rating scales are all valuable in personnel direction. Continued effort to relate workers to their tasks and to the organization as a whole is often expressed in conferences scheduled at regular intervals by the supervisor. At these conferences, points of general interest are presented and suggestions for improvement of the foodservice are exchanged. Knotty problems, such as waste, breakage, and low productivity, that have not been mastered by a direct supervisory approach can be resolved by focusing the interest and awareness of the whole group on them. Never should a staff conference be used for disciplinary action for certain members of the group. As previously stated, the adult worker rarely benefits from public reprimand and unkind ridicule.

In addition to group contact, time should be taken by the supervisor for a talk with each individual worker at least once a week. All employees want to feel that someone is interested in them as an individual and recognizes their present and potential worth to the organization.

Labor Policies and Legislation

KEY CONCEPT: **Labor policies have been developed to guide managerial decision making and to commit employees to certain predictable actions.**

Policies are guides for future action. They should be broad enough to allow some variation in management decisions at all levels, yet offer guidelines for consistency in interpretation, and to commit personnel to certain predictable actions. Policies should not be confused with directives or rules. Policies are adopted to provide meaning or understanding related to a course of action; directives and rules are aimed at compliance.

An important aspect of personnel management is the labor policies accepted and put in force. This is true regardless of the size of the organization. There is an old saying that when two people meet, there is a social problem; when one undertakes a task at the other's behest, there is a labor problem; and when wages are paid for this labor, there is an economic problem. The policies controlling the approach to these problems have slowly developed as civilization has grown and as the number of workers has increased. They have been formed, reformed, and revised, particularly in recent years, because of legislation enacted at federal, state, and local levels.

Policies relating to personnel are known as labor policies. Procurement policies may be related to preferred sources to be used for obtaining applicants, instruments such as tests to be used in selection, or a ratio of employees, such as women to men or minority to majority racial groups to be hired. Policies for development of personnel may concern the type of training programs the company offers, whether or not fees or tuition for continuing education are paid, the amount of time to be allowed from work for personnel to attend classes or meetings, and the bases for promotions and transfers.

Those policies regarding compensation have to do with wage scales to be followed; vacation, sick leave, and holiday pay to be given; bonus or profit-sharing plans to be offered; and group insurance or other benefits that are available to the personnel.

Integration policies refer to whether labor unions are recognized, the way in which grievances and appeals are handled, or the degree of employee participation to be permitted in decision making.

Maintenance policies are about the services to be provided for employees' physical, mental, and emotional health. They may be related to safety measures, compensation for accidents, retirement systems, recreational programs, or other services, all of which are a part of the organizational plan.

Once policies have been developed and accepted, they should be written. The wise employer of today makes available to every worker a copy of the labor-management policies presented in a company handbook. This publication may be an impressive volume of many pages and elaborate illustrations or a few mimeographed sheets; regardless of format, the contents should include information that the worker wants to know about the organization and that the employer wants him or her to know. Employees are not interested in cooperating as members of the team without understanding the policies, especially as these affect them. They want to know what is expected of them and to be kept informed of their accomplishments, the basis for promotion and wage increases, fringe benefits, opportunities for steady work, and the possibilities of any seasonal layoffs.

From the standpoint of the employee, labor policies should be explicit in their provisions for a fair rate of pay, for promotions and transfers, for stabilization of employment, and for ways of keeping jobs interesting so that life does not become mere dull routine. They should offer provisions for fair disciplinary action among employees; recognition of industrial health hazards and provisions for their control; participation in the formulation of future plans and policies of the company, usually expressed by demands for collective bargaining; and certain fringe benefits.

Managers wish to have employees informed of policies about the goals and objectives for which the organization is in business, the goods and services offered, the effect of high productivity as a benefit to both the employee and the company, cost-expenditure ratios and how they affect profits and resulting benefits, and the relationships desired with the public and with other departments of the organization.

There is general agreement on the list of topics that the employer has found must be covered in labor policies conducive to productive management and those desired by employees as vital to satisfactory working conditions. The ones cited by both—wages and income maintenance; hours of work; schedules and overtime provisions; security in employment, including transfers and promotions; a safe and otherwise satisfactory working environment; insurance, retirement, or pension plans; equal employment opportunities; and fair employment practices and civil rights—may be regarded as the major issues in labor policies for most foodservice operations.

These topics can be grouped under four headings: (1) wages and income maintenance, (2) hours and schedules of work, (3) security in employment, and (4) employee services and benefits. Major federal legislation applicable to employment in the private sector is included as appropriate in each of the following discussions.

Wages and Income Maintenance. From the point of view of the worker, the most important characteristic of the wage—the take-home pay received for labor performed—is its purchasing power. This represents the measure of the wants that the worker is able to satisfy and largely determines the adequacy of his or her standard of living, sense of financial security, and identification of self as a worthy and responsible member of the community. In the past, foodservices, like other service organizations, have tended to offer an annual wage rate below that necessary for a fair standard of living. This situation has improved as desirable policies on wages have been adopted and as state and federal laws have been enacted.

The formulation of satisfactory policies regarding wages and other income maintenance is contingent on many factors, such as (1) the desire and intent of the company to pay fair wages to all employees and at the same time to maintain just control over labor costs; (2) recognition of the relationship between the duties and responsibilities of various jobs within the organization and the wages paid; and (3) acknowledgment of individual differences in experience, ability, and willingness to take responsibility. Management has the obligation to reflect such differences in the wage scale established for a particular job and to communicate freely with the workers on these points. Policies based on such considerations will lead to a systematic classification of jobs and wages that could be developed jointly by the employer and the employees. It would then be possible to express the value or worth of each job in terms of wages.

The application of the wage policy to kitchen and dining room personnel would lead to certain groupings, such as:

1. Bus people, pot and pan washers, dishwashers
2. Workers in preliminary or pre-preparation
3. Foodservice groups, including counter workers and waiters or waitresses

4. Cooks' assistants and second cooks, dining room host or hostess, cashiers
5. Cooks, including meat, vegetable, salad, and pastry cooks
6. Supervisors on the nonprofessional level

A wage differential will exist among these groups. Civil service and labor unions, as well as many other organizations, have established steps within each wage level or grade so that employees who merit wage increases may be given such recognition for superior service, although not qualified for advancement to a higher grade or job category.

> **KEY CONCEPT:** **A number of pieces of legislation establish fair labor policies and attempt to balance the power between labor and management.**

The Fair Labor Standards Act of 1938, also known as the Federal Wage and Hour Law, was first enacted to help eliminate poverty, to create purchasing power, and to establish a wage floor that would help prevent another Great Depression. The minimum wage set at that time was $0.40 per hour! The base has gradually increased over the years. The act was amended in 1966, and, under new provisions, most foodservice employees were included for the first time. The minimum wage that year was $1.60, and the law included provisions for gradual increases that would continue as cost of living increased. The act applies equally to all covered workers regardless of sex, number of employees, and whether they are full-time or part-time workers.

The Equal Pay Act, a 1963 amendment to the Fair Labor Standards Act, prohibits employers from discriminating on the basis of sex in the payment of wages for equal work for employees covered by the act. It requires employers to pay equal wages to men and women doing equal work on jobs requiring equal skill, effort, and responsibility that are performed under similar working conditions.

Another provision of the Fair Labor Standards Act of special interest to restaurant foodservice managers relates to wages for tipped employees. In some states, tips received by an employee may be considered by the employer as part of the wages of the employee. The amount of this allowance varies from state to state. A "tipped" employee is a worker engaged in an occupation in which the worker customarily and regularly receives more than $30 a month in tips.

Many foodservice operations employ student workers; this is especially true in colleges and universities, schools, retirement homes, and other homes for congregate living. Minimum-wage laws adopted by various states may make provision for compensation at an adjusted rate below the federal standard. Usually students who work fewer than 20 hours per week are not affected by provisions of such laws.

Unless specifically exempt by this law, all employees must be paid at least 1½ times the employee's regular rate of pay for all hours worked in excess of 40 hours in a work week of seven days. Extra pay is not required for Saturday, Sunday, holiday, or vacation work.

All foodservice managers should become familiar with the state and federal laws regulating minimum wages for their various classifications of employees. Information may be obtained from the nearest office of the Wage and Hour Division of the U.S. Department of Labor.

Unemployment compensation is another piece of federal legislation that, in addition to regular pay for work on the job, partially ensures income maintenance. This nationwide system of insurance to protect wage earners and their families against loss of income because of unemployment was first established under the Social Security Act of 1935. The purpose of this insurance is to provide workers with a weekly income to tide them over during periods of unemployment. Persons covered must have been employed for a specific period of time on a job covered by the law, be able and willing to work, and be unemployed through no fault of their own.

Unemployment insurance is a joint federal-state program, operated by the states with the assistance of the U.S. Department of Labor. Each state has its own specific requirements and benefits. Basically, employers pay a tax based on their payrolls. Benefits to unemployed workers are paid out of the fund built up from these taxes. In most states, firms employing three or four or more workers for 20 weeks throughout the year must participate. Each state law specifies conditions under which workers may receive benefits, the amount they receive, and the number of weeks they may draw benefits. In most states, the employer alone contributes to this fund; in only a few do employees make payment to it. Thus unemployment compensation is an added payroll cost for many foodservice managers and an added benefit to the employees.

Hours and Schedules of Work. The 40-hour work week established under the Minimum Wage and Hour Law is generally in use throughout the United States. Some organizations have adopted a 37½ or a 35-hour week. Time worked beyond 40 hours in a 7-day or 80 hours in a 14-day period (in hospitals or other facilities that care for the sick, elderly, or persons with mental illness) as specified under the law requires extra compensation, as previously noted.

Foodservice managers should carefully consider the schedule of specific hours of the day when each employee is to be on duty. As discussed, many different factors enter into the planning of satisfactory schedules. Employers have a responsibility for scheduling their employees so that their time at work is as needed and is used to their best advantage in order to help control labor costs. Split shifts are almost a thing of the past; straight shifts are usually preferred. An 8-hour day, 5 days a week is common practice also. However, some organizations have experimented with variations, notably a 10-hour day and 4-day week to allow a 3-day off-duty period for the employees and a 12-hour day, 3-day week. Most foodservice organizations have not found this scheduling practical because of the nature of the work to be done.

In addition to the needs of the employer and the organization, consideration is given to the employee and to stipulations in union contracts, if in effect, when planning scheduled time on and off duty for each member of the staff. Most state labor laws require break times for meals and between-meal rest periods for employees, which is a further consideration when planning schedules to cover work that must be done. Familiarity with these regulations is a necessity for the manager.

Security in Employment. One of the major concerns of the working world in recent years is equal opportunity for employment for all persons who desire employment and who are qualified. **Equal employment opportunity (EEO)** is the umbrella term that encompasses all laws and regulations prohibiting discrimination or requiring affirmative action. The **Equal Employment Opportunity Commission (EEOC)** regulations and interpretive guidelines provide guidance to management for compliance with Title VII of the Civil Rights Act of 1964, the Age Discrimination in Employment Act, the Pregnancy Discrimination Act, and the **Americans with Disabilities Act (ADA)** of 1990, all of which are federal EEO statutes.

Most states also have legislation that prohibits discrimination. In some cases, these statutes are broader than the federal laws. Marital status, sexual preference and orientation, race, color, religion, national origin, or ancestry are demographics protected from discrimination in various states. These are designated as fair employment practice laws. A public accommodation law, when in effect, requires that service be given in an equal manner to all persons.

The Civil Rights Act of 1964 stipulates, "No person in the United States shall, on ground of race, color, or national origin be excluded from participating in, be denied the benefits of, or be subjected to any program or activity receiving Federal financial assistance." Title VII under this act extended the provision to include prohibition of discrimination "by employers, employment agencies and labor unions."

Thus, employees who are in covered positions are entitled to be free of unlawful discrimination with regard to recruitment, classified advertising, job classification, hiring, utilization of physical facilities, transfer, promotion, discharge wages and salaries, seniority lines, testing, insurance coverage, pension and retirement benefits, referral to jobs, union membership, and the like. All potential employees have equal opportunity, regardless of background.

Equal employment opportunity (EEO)

The umbrella term that encompasses all laws and regulations prohibiting discrimination and/or requiring affirmative action

Equal Employment Opportunity Commission (EEOC)

Provides guidance to management for compliance with EEO statutes

Americans with Disabilities Act (ADA)

Prohibits discrimination against qualified persons with disabilities in all aspects of employment

In 1974, Title VII of the Civil Rights Act was amended to include prohibition against discrimination based on religion and sex. Then, in 1978, sexual discrimination was further broadened with the passage of the Pregnancy Discrimination Act, which prohibited discrimination due to pregnancy, childbirth, or related medical conditions.

The Civil Rights Act of 1991 increases the likelihood that employees will sue because discrimination cases will be easier to win and the damages that are awarded would be more substantial. This act does not make anything illegal that was not already illegal, but it does relax the burden of proof and make possible recovery for pain, suffering, and punitive damages.

The Age Discrimination in Employment Act of 1967 promotes the employment of the older worker, based on ability instead of age. It prohibits arbitrary age discrimination in employment and helps employers and employees find ways to meet problems arising from the impact of age on employment. The act protects most individuals who are at least 40 but less than 70 years of age from "discrimination in employment based on age in matters of hiring, discharge compensation or other terms, conditions, or privileges of employment."

Title VII of the 1964 Civil Rights Act as amended makes sexual harassment illegal. This law holds only the employer liable; a sexually harassing employee is not liable. **Sexual harassment** takes two forms and is a form of sexual discrimination that violates federal, state, and most local laws. The first form is "quid pro quo" and occurs when a supervisor either rewards or punishes a subordinate for providing or not providing sexual favors. The second form is the "hostile environment," which occurs when an employee's ability to work, take pride in their work, or desire to stay in the position is undermined by an atmosphere infused with unwelcome sexually oriented or otherwise hostile conduct created by supervisors or coworkers.

Sexual harassment

Unwanted sexual advances, or casual, verbal, or physical conduct of a sexual nature

Factors that courts consider as creating a hostile environment include the following:

- Sexually oriented comments, photos, or graphics at the workplace
- Unwanted verbal or physical contact or gender-specific abusive comments
- The frequency or pervasiveness of the misconduct
- The employer's failure to investigate complaints and take quick corrective action

To prevent sexual harassment and liability, foodservices should have written anti-harassment policies and procedures on file; send out regular notifications through memos and meetings that sexual harassment will not be tolerated and that supervisors must treat all subordinates fairly and with respect; hold regular anti-harassment seminars that are mandatory for all supervisors; train all employees on the policies and procedures; take quick action on all complaints; and protect victims and witnesses from retaliation.

The Americans with Disabilities Act of 1990 prohibits discrimination against qualified persons with disabilities in all aspects of employment from application to termination. No job may be denied an individual with a disability if the individual is qualified and able to perform the essential functions of the job, with or without reasonable accommodation. If needed, an employer must make the reasonable accommodation unless it would result in undue hardship for the employer. Existing performance standards do not have to be lowered, but such standards must be job related and uniformly applied to all employees and applicants for that particular job. Equal opportunity must be provided to individuals with disabilities to apply and be considered for a job. The applicant cannot be asked preemployment questions regarding his or her disability, but the applicant can be asked about his or her ability to perform specific job functions. He or she may also be asked to describe or demonstrate how these job functions could be accomplished. Medical histories and preemployment physical exams are not allowed under the ADA legislation; however, the job offer may be conditional depending on the results of a postoffer physical exam. This exam must be required of all applicants in the same job category. Tests for the use of illegal drugs are not considered to be physical exams under the ADA and are, therefore, still legal.

Quotas

An almost always illegal fixed, inflexible percentage or number of positions that an employer decides can be filled only by members of a certain minority group

Quotas are fixed, inflexible percentages or numbers of positions that an employer decides can be filled only by members of a certain minority group. This is a form of reverse discrimination and is almost always illegal.

Affirmative action does not involve the setting of specific quotas but rather the desire to reach general goals to increase the numbers of women and minorities in specific positions. Required for certain federal contractors, affirmative action is legal if ordered by a court to remedy past discrimination or if limited in time and scope. Currently, the continued existence of affirmative action policies is being hotly debated based on the assertion by some that it results in reverse discrimination.

In an effort to stem the tide of illegal immigrants coming into the country, Congress passed the Immigration Reform and Control Act in 1986. This act makes it illegal to recruit or hire persons not legally eligible for employment in the United States. Employers must complete an I-9 form for each employee to verify eligibility to work in the United States. Further, any employer who has four or more employees is prohibited from discriminating against employees or job applicants on the basis of national origin or citizenship status.

As can be seen, our economic society is characterized by many areas of friction in industry. Students of labor quite generally agree that in no area is there an economic problem more important to human beings than security of job tenure, which means assurance of the satisfaction of physical needs, a place in the esteem and affection of others, an opportunity for self-expression, and a chance to enjoy leisure. The three risks that more than any others tend to make the position of most wage earners in industry insecure are unemployment, physical impairment, and old age. The definition for unemployment used by the Bureau of Census in making its enumeration is: "Unemployment may be described as involuntary idleness on the part of those who have lost their latest jobs, are able to work, and are looking for work." This definition is obviously narrow, because it excludes all those persons who are unwilling to work, are unemployable because of physical or mental disabilities, or are temporarily idle for seasonal reasons. However, the definition covers the group whose unemployment usually arises from conditions inherent in the organization and management of industry.

Problems of tenure must concern all persons charged with the direction of the foodservice industry. Fortunately, foodservices on the whole lend themselves to steady employment, and many managers take pride in the long tenure of large numbers of their workers. Sometimes, however, the workers' acceptance of tenure as a matter of course brings definite problems such as laxity and inefficiency in the performance of assigned tasks and lack of interest in improved practices. Standards of performance in some instances have been lowered as security of employment has been ensured. Personnel policies should cover such contingencies.

Employee Services and Benefits.   Benefits that employees receive often represent as much as 39 percent of wages earned. Some of these are so taken for granted that they are scarcely realized or appreciated by those who receive them. Yet if such services were not provided, the lack would be acutely noticed. Managers recognize the humanistic desirability of making available certain programs and services in addition to a fair wage for their employees' comfort and well-being. A less altruistic point of view may cause managers to offer those same benefits in order to compete in the job market and attract desirable applicants.

Extra benefits, sometimes called fringe benefits, fall into three general groups: (1) health and safety, (2) economic services and benefits, and (3) convenience and comfort. The first, *health and safety*, is an important basic factor in all personnel matters. This factor affects social and economic life, being of interest not only to the employee but to the employer and the public as well. Time lost because of illness and accidents is expensive for both management and labor, results in lowered productivity and increased losses for the employer, and directly affects the income of the employee. Maintaining the good physical condition of employees is economically desirable as well as necessary for achievement of the many goals of the department. Also, managers of any foodservice recognize that the health of the worker may affect the health of the public through both direct and indirect contact.

Safe working conditions are of first importance to employer and employee alike. A foodservice does not present the identical hazards found in any other industry, but it does duplicate some of those found in several industries. Falls, burns, shocks, and cuts are possible, as they are in any other place where mechanical equipment is used. It is the responsibility of the manager to see that safeguards are maintained, that the equipment is kept in safe condition, and that all working conditions are safe and clean.

The **Occupational Safety and Health Act of 1970 (OSHA)** has forced managers to look critically at working conditions and to bring any that are undesirable up to a standard demanded by law. Every employer covered by the law is required to furnish employment and places of employment that are free from recognized hazards that are causing or are likely to cause death or serious physical harm and must comply with all safety regulations promulgated by the Secretary of Labor in accordance with the provisions of the Act.

Another benefit for employees is provided for in the **workers' compensation insurance** program. This legislation is administered by the states, and the liability insurance premiums are paid by employers. Workers' compensation laws are based on the theory that the cost of accidents should be a part of production costs, the same as wages, taxes, insurance, and raw materials.

This insurance covers employers' liability for the costs of any accident incurred by an employee on or in connection with the job. The workers must show that they were injured on the job and the extent of their injuries. Compensation laws state the specific amount of payment allowed for each type of injury in addition to hospital, surgical, and, in case of death, funeral expenses. All foodservice directors will need to determine, through their state department of labor, who can be covered by workers' compensation, the methods of payments, and the amount of benefits to which the worker is entitled.

The Family and Medical Leave Act of 1993 gives employees a maximum of 12 weeks of unpaid and job-protected leave per year for themselves, or a spouse, parent, or child with a serious health condition.

Health and accident insurance plans provide some assistance to employees who may become ill or who are injured off the job. Fear of injury or illness is the cause of much worry, even when an insurance plan is available to employees. Without it, many workers would be in financial straits if they were compelled to pay medical and hospital bills on their own.

Many forms of health and accident insurance are available for groups. In some cases, the company alone pays for the employees; in others, it is jointly borne by the company and those who participate in it. Through labor union efforts and the efforts of concerned managers, an increasing number of health services are being made available to employees, many at employer expense. Flexible benefit plans, which allow the employee to choose from a wide array of benefit options, are gaining in popularity. Whereas early benefit plans included only health and retirement, employees can now often choose profit sharing; stock ownership benefits; legal, educational, and child care assistance; dental and vision insurance; and life insurance, depending on their own particular needs and wants.

The extent to which foodservices provide these benefits to employees usually depends on the size of the organization and the facilities it has available, for example, the emergency room of a hospital and the concern of those at the decision-making level.

The second group of employee services and benefits are those labeled *economic*. Most of the programs discussed so far provide some economic benefit to workers, even if indirectly. All insurance plans undoubtedly could be put under this classification instead of putting some under the classification of health and safety. However, benefits to be discussed in this economic group have a direct monetary value in returns to the employee; the employer carries the cost of some, and others are shared by the employee.

Social Security benefits are provided by the Social Security Act, a nationwide program of insurance designed to protect wage earners and their families against loss of income due to age, disability, and death. A designated percentage of the salary of each employed person must be withheld from his or her wages and the same amount from the business added to the Social Security Fund, or to a comparable retirement-system fund if a nonprofit type of organization is involved. Provisions and benefits of Social Security change from time to time, so details soon become outdated. Managers must keep in touch with their local Social Security office to stay informed of current changes.

Occupational Safety and Health Act of 1970 (OSHA)

Requires employers to furnish employment free from safety hazards

Workers' compensation insurance

A program administered by the state in which premiums are paid by the employer to cover employee accidents

Social Security

A federal program of insurance to protect wage earners and their families against loss of income due to age, disability, and death

Other economic benefits offered by some organizations to their employees may include group life insurance programs, profit-sharing plans, and pensions or retirement plans. All of these add to the economic security of those who continue in the service of a particular organization long enough to build a fund that is significant for them after regular employment ceases, because of either retirement or death. Vacations, holidays, and sick leave, all with pay, are other forms of fringe benefits for personnel. Properly administered, they are of advantage to the organization as well.

Employee convenience and comfort benefits make up the third group of fringe benefits. Services provided for the comfort or convenience of employees can be a long list and include, among others, adequate rest and locker rooms, meal service available to employees often at reduced or at-cost levels, free medical service on an emergency basis, credit unions, and recreational facilities. Educational tuition or fees for personnel to attend workshops or classes for self-development and skill development is also included among these benefits. These types of benefits help to build a loyal, contented working group with high morale.

Although many of the labor laws enacted are directed toward the protection of specific groups, the regulations applicable to all workers are well established. Familiarity with federal, state, and local laws applying to foodservice employees is obligatory for every foodservice administrator and manager. Only then can labor policies be of benefit to both the worker and his or her organization and be put into action for implementation.

LABOR-MANAGEMENT RELATIONS

■ **KEY CONCEPT:** **Federal legislation, beginning with the National Labor Relations Act of 1935, has been enacted to allow employees to unionize and engage in collective bargaining.**

Foodservice managers are concerned with problems arising from directing employees' activities, that is, in handling the people who must translate the policies, procedures, and plans into action. When groups of people work together, the potential for conflict always exists. Some people must manage, and some must carry out the technical operations. Everyone wants more of whatever improves his or her position. The closer the relationship between the employee and manager, with open and free discussion on both sides, the less danger there is that grievances will arise.

Many foodservices are so small that the relationship between employer and employee is immediate and direct. Under such circumstances, discussion of mutual concerns is possible right in the workplace. Face-to-face contact tends to develop a sense of real association and mutual interest. Employees with a somewhat complete picture of a relatively small business may see their job in relation to the whole. Many services, however, are so large that there is limited personal contact between employer and employee. Workers may feel there is little chance for the individual to be recognized as an important person in the organization. Also, they may not have an overall view of the business that would make possible self-evaluation of their own jobs in terms of the whole. Workers engaged in a limited phase of total large-scale production may find that they lack the direct contact that tends to humanize employer-employee relationships in a small foodservice.

Legislation

Managers who are not attuned to the concerns of employees, who do not recognize that a small complaint or conflict that arises is probably a symptom of a deeper problem, and who fail to investigate and correct the situation are opening the door for labor unions to come in to represent the employees better.

During the years, much legislation has been enacted to attempt to balance the power between labor and management. In 1935, the passage of the Wagner Act (or **National Labor Relations Act [NLRA]**) was the beginning of positive support of unionization and

National Labor Relations Act (NLRA)

Established the National Labor Relations Board (NLRB); regulates the right of employees to join a union, and provides for collective bargaining. Also known as the Wagner Act

collective bargaining by the federal government. Prior to this legislation, workers had been exploited by management. This exploitation is documented in court cases as early as 1806. The terms of the Wagner Act regulate employees' rights to join a union, prohibit unfair management practices, prohibit management from interfering with their employees who wish to join a union and from discriminating against those who do join, and require employers and union members to bargain collectively (an obligation to meet and discuss terms with an open mind, but without being required to come to an agreement). The majority of today's collective bargaining agreements provide for an impartial arbitrator to hear and decide grievances under the bargaining agreement. The NLRA also established the National Labor Relations Board (NLRB) to administer and interpret the provisions of the act.

These procedures are followed in unfair labor practice cases: (1) A private party files a charge that an unfair labor practice has been committed; (2) the regional office at which the charge is filed investigates the case and decides whether to proceed with the complaint; (3) if the regional director issues a complaint, an attorney from the regional office will prosecute the case; (4) if the case is not settled at this level, a hearing is necessary with a staff attorney representing the NLRB controlling the case; and (5) finally, an administrative law judge hands down a recommended decision and order.

One of the major responsibilities of the NLRB is to determine whether employees should be represented by a union. Employees usually initiate a union campaign if they desire union representation. At least 30 percent of the employees in the bargaining unit must support their petition to the NLRB; this support is shown by employees' signatures on authorization cards. These cards are investigated and authenticated by the NLRB before the board orders that an election be held. The secret ballot election is conducted, and the results are tabulated by an NLRB representative. If the union wins the election, a contract is then drawn up, and the union designates a bargaining unit employee as its union "steward." This person handles the union business in the workplace.

Employees of hospitals operated entirely on a nonprofit basis were exempt from the original NLRA. However, an amendment to the NLRA brought nonprofit hospitals under the provisions of the act. In such situations, dietitians may be called on to defend their positions as "management" instead of as "labor."

The Taft-Hartley Act (or **Labor-Management Relations Act**), passed in 1947, was enacted to offset some of the power leading to unfair practices that labor unions seemed to acquire after 1935. Among other provisions, it prevents unions from coercing employees to join, outlaws the **union shop** (which requires an employee to become a member of the union in order to retain a job) and the **closed shop** (which obligates an employer to hire only union members and to discharge any employee who drops union membership), and makes it illegal for unions to refuse to join in **collective bargaining**. This statute marked a shift away from encouragement of unionization to a more neutral position on the part of the federal government.

Further legislation, passed in 1959, was the Landrum-Griffin Act (or **Labor-Management Reporting and Disclosure Act**), which is in the interests of both labor and management but especially favors the individual labor union member. It contains a bill of rights for union members, requires certain financial disclosures by unions through a specified reporting system, prescribes procedures for the election of union officers, and provides civil and criminal remedies for financial abuses by union officers.

The labor legislation discussed and the areas of human resources management on which it makes an impact are summarized in Table 1.

There are numerous reasons for employers to become targets of union organizing attempts or for employees to turn to a union. Chief among these reasons are poorly developed or administered personnel policies and practices, or a breakdown in some facet of employer-employee relations. A number of steps should be taken by managers long before organizational attempts begin. Most important among them is a review of personnel policies and employee relations, making every effort to maintain good personnel practices, put policies into writing, and communicate them to employees with frequent reviews and discussions.

The impact of unionization on foodservices may be great for those who are naive in the ways of collective bargaining. Legal counsel to assist in negotiating a fair, workable

Labor-Management Relations Act

Prevents unions from coercing employees to join, outlaws union and closed shops, and provides for collective bargaining. Also known as the Taft-Hartley Act

Union shop

Illegal practice that requires an employee to become a member of a union in order to keep a job

Closed shop

Illegal practice that obligates an employer to hire only union members

Collective bargaining

An obligation to meet and discuss terms with an open mind

Labor-Management Reporting and Disclosure Act

Contains a bill of rights for union members that requires financial disclosures, prescribes union officer election procedures, and provides civil and criminal remedies for financial abuses. Also known as the Landrum-Griffin Act

Table 1   Selected labor legislation classified by the relevant area of human resources management.

ACQUISITION OF HUMAN RESOURCES	DEVELOPMENT OF HUMAN RESOURCES	REWARDING OF HUMAN RESOURCES	MAINTENANCE OF HUMAN RESOURCES
Equal Pay Act, 1963	Equal Pay Act, 1963	Fair Labor Standards Act, 1938	State Fair Labor Practices Act, 1913
Civil Rights Act, 1964	Civil Rights Act, 1964	Equal Pay Act, 1963	Wagner Act, 1935
Age Discrimination in Employment Act, 1967	Age Discrimination in Employment Act, 1967	Civil Rights Act, 1964	Social Security Act, 1935
Civil Rights Act, 1974	Civil Rights Act, 1974	Age Discrimination in Employment Act, 1967	Taft-Hartley Act, 1947
Pregnancy Discrimination Act, 1978	Pregnancy Discrimination Act, 1978	Civil Rights Act, 1974	Landrum-Griffin Act, 1959
Immigration Reform and Control Act, 1986	Immigration Reform and Control Act, 1986	Pregnancy Discrimination Act, 1978	Civil Rights Act, 1964
Americans with Disabilities Act, 1990	Americans with Disabilities Act, 1990	Immigration Reform and Control Act, 1986	Age Discrimination in Employment Act, 1967
Civil Rights Act, 1991	Civil Rights Act, 1991	Americans with Disabilities Act, 1990	Occupational Safety & Health Act, 1970
		Civil Rights Act, 1991	Civil Rights Act, 1974
			Pregnancy Discrimination Act, 1978
			Immigration Reform and Control Act, 1986
			Americans with Disabilities Act, 1990
			Civil Rights Act, 1991
			Family and Medical Leave Act, 1993

contract for both labor and management is to be encouraged. If unionization is to become a reality, it is important to create a favorable climate for cooperation and to make certain that the negotiator understands the economic as well as the administrative problems of a foodservice operation, such as scheduling required to cover meal hours; the services necessary, especially to patients in health care facilities; the equipment to be used; and the prices charged in relation to the labor costs.

Certain rights of management may be lost when unionization takes place, because some of the authority but little of the responsibility will be shared with the union. Some of the freedoms lost are the right to hire, discharge, change work assignments and time schedules, set wages and fringe benefits, change policies without appeal, discipline workers without being subject to appeal to the union, and receive and act on grievances directly The right to use volunteer workers in the department may also be lost.

It is imperative, therefore, that the collective bargaining agreement contain a management rights clause. There are two major categories of management rights clauses. One is a brief, general clause not dealing with specific rights, but with the principle of management rights in general. The other is a detailed clause, which clearly lists areas of authority that are specific to management.

Certain cost increases should also be noted, such as the time lost from the job by the person selected to be the union steward and the cost of management support to the union based on a given sum per member per month in contributions.

The nature of labor organizations and the methods they use differ according to the understanding and goals of the leaders and members; their convictions as to remedies needed;

and by legal and other forms of social control. Ordinarily, management and organized labor have different approaches to solving their problems. This often leads to long hours of negotiations before a satisfactory mutual agreement can be reached. It is important that each group try to see the other's viewpoint with fairness and with an honest belief in the good faith of the other.

SUMMARY

The management of human resources has long been a very important part of a manager's job. Like other managerial functions, it has grown throughout the years. In the past, human resources management consisted of hiring people for vacant positions. Today, because of increasing environmental complexities and organizational sophistication, staffing is just one step in a multistage human resources process. At the heart of this process are the very valuable (and perhaps most valuable) resources of any organization—the people. And, people require careful nurturing and constant attention to the moral and legal issues involved in their employment.

This chapter has explored the entire employment process including methods of recruitment and selection, orientation and training, various ways of conducting performance evaluation, discipline, dismissal, and handling grievances.

The existence of written labor policies to cover each of these steps in the process is advocated. In addition, policies should be in place for wages and income maintenance, hours and schedules of work, security in employment, and employee services and benefits. The foundation for writing these policies should be the major federal legislation that exists in each of these areas. These laws are described with the title, date of passage, and the intent of each given.

The passage of the Wagner Act in 1935 established the right of employees to join a union and engage in collective bargaining. The impetus for this legislation was the exploitation of workers by management. Since that time, several more pieces of federal legislation have been enacted to attempt to balance the power of labor union leadership, labor union members, and company management. The chapter concludes with a discussion of the impact of unionization on foodservice management.

APPLICATION OF CHAPTER CONCEPTS

Training of foodservice personnel is an ongoing and oftentimes challenging process. Of utmost importance is training in the area of food safety. The University of Wisconsin–Madison foodservice department has a policy that all employees are ServSafe trained and that all managers and all chefs are ServSafe Certified.

The training is offered once a year during the break between semesters in January. The training program takes 12 hours to complete, which includes the certification exam. The first day is scheduled from 7 A.M. to 3:30 P.M. with two 15-minute breaks and half an hour for lunch. The second day is from 7 A.M. to 11 A.M. with one 15-minute break. The exam is given during the last hour of the class. Employees are paid at their regular hourly rate for the time spent in the class.

The National Restaurant Association ServSafe course materials include a participant's workbook that costs approximately $40 per participant, a PowerPoint slide program with lecture notes for the trainer's use, videos (from 11 to 37 minutes long), the certification exam, and certificates for those who pass the exam. The materials for the presentation of the course content may be used at the trainer's discretion.

A typical class profile would be:

1. Class size: 20 to 40 participants
2. Age: 18 to 70+ years
3. Gender: equal number of males and females
4. Level of work responsibility: from culinary workers to top administrators

5. Education: GED to MBA or master's degree
6. English proficiency: some English as a second language to very proficient
7. Food safety training experience: from none to some previously certified

CRITICAL-THINKING QUESTIONS

1. What are the benefits of this type of in-service training program from the perspective of the foodservice department, management, employees, and the customers?
2. What are the disadvantages of this type of training program?
3. What issues might arise because of the time required to complete the course?
4. If you were the trainer, how would you make use of the supplied course materials to ensure that participants best learn the content?
5. What factors need to be taken into consideration when presenting the material?
6. Considering the size and profile of the class, what issues would the trainer need to be prepared to address?
7. Suggest some innovative ways in which the trainer could make sure that everyone was engaged in the course material.
8. Considering the cost of the ServSafe program in terms of materials and labor hours, suggest some alternative ways to ensure that the foodservice staff knows food safety.
9. Which of the class demographics is likely to be the most difficult to manage?
10. Because the class is only given once a year, how might the safe food handling practices be reinforced in employees' minds throughout the year?

CHAPTER REVIEW QUESTIONS

1. Name the characteristics beyond good pay and benefits that are common to the companies considered the best to work for in the United States today.
2. What are the rights of individuals in an organization?
3. Identify the tasks that are included in the staffing function of management.
4. Graph an integrated staffing system.
5. List and briefly describe the sources of potential employees.
6. Discuss the purposes of the employment interview.
7. Describe what should be included in an employee orientation program.
8. List the five teaching steps that should be included in an on-the-job training program.

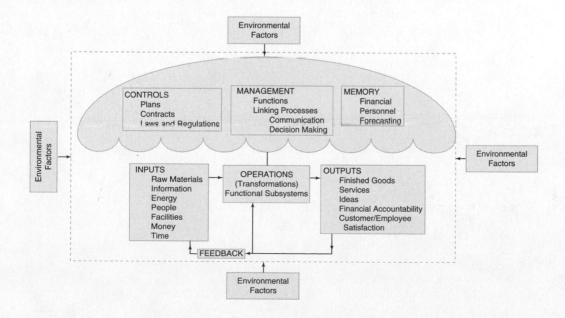

407

9. What are the purposes of the performance evaluation interview?
10. Discuss when and how disciplinary action should be taken.
11. What are the five steps recommended for good decision making?
12. Identify legislation that has had an impact on foodservice management operations.
13. Discuss the impact of unionization on a foodservice management operation.
14. Define the term *policy*.

SELECTED WEB SITES

www.ceoexpress.com   (The executive's Internet resource)
www.intel.com   (Intel computer processors)
www.monster.com   (Career advice, job search tools)

Leadership

Leadership

Monkey Business Images/Shutterstock

UNTIL RECENTLY, THE BUSINESS WORLD HAS PAID SCANT attention to motivating people and managing change. This chapter begins with the subject of motivation and ends with managing change, two concepts that now are seen as critical to leadership effectiveness.

"Managers are people who do things right, while leaders are people who do the right things" (Bennis, W., and Nanus, B.: *Leaders: The Strategies for Taking*

Charge. New York: Harper & Row, 1985). This is just one of many definitions of leadership that may be useful in understanding this very important concept. Another way of looking at leadership is that leading is establishing direction and influencing others to follow that direction willingly.

Organizational effectiveness depends not only on the financial and physical resources of a company but also on the skills, abilities, and motivation of its employees. Regardless of how carefully those employees have been selected and trained, it is difficult to ensure that they will be motivated to apply their full energies to the job. One of the greatest challenges facing a manager is understanding the differing needs of an individual and thus the forces that will motivate him or her to be a productive employee. Balancing the roles of manager and leader is yet another challenge. It is possible to be one and not the other. In today's business environment, however, the ability to be both is essential.

As leaders, those individuals who assume the management of foodservice organizations will be successful to the degree that they are willing to assume responsibility and are able to maintain good human relations. The goals and objectives of the department cannot be attained by the manager alone; working satisfactorily with and through other people constitutes the major part of the job.

Most people may assume that no organization can achieve its goals and plans without leadership. This assumption is generally valid, but what is meant by leadership? In this chapter, the difference between leadership and management is discussed, and the characteristics displayed by managers and leaders in managerial positions are compared. The question raised is, are they, indeed, different?

The topic of leadership effectiveness is of special interest. A historical view of leadership is presented that traces the evolution of effective leadership theories from the era of scientific management to the present-day systems concept and contingency approach. The major contributions of each period are summarized. The judicious use of power is an important factor in leadership success. Therefore, an understanding of how a leader acquires and uses power is essential.

Communication is another factor key to effective leadership. Some of the barriers to successful communication are described, as well as some techniques to improve in this area.

Although profit and productivity are still major goals of leadership, managerial ethics and social responsibility have assumed equal importance. This chapter concludes with a discussion of the ethical and social responsibilities required by leaders in today's foodservice industry.

KEY CONCEPTS

1. An individual's motivations stem from energizing forces within the individual (needs, attitudes, interests, and perceptions) and within the organization (rewards, tasks, coworkers, supervisors, communication, and feedback).

2. Leadership is the activity of influencing other people's behavior toward the achievement of desired objectives. Management is the function of running an organization by effectively and efficiently integrating and coordinating resources in order to achieve desired objectives.

3. As a leader, the foodservice manager must empower employees by clearly communicating the organization's mission, accepting the responsibility for leading the group, and earning employees' trust.

4. Early theories of leadership include scientific management, in which a leader's role was to motivate employees with rewards of money, and human relations theory, in which a leader improved productivity by showing an interest in the employee as an individual.

5. McGregor's Theory X and Theory Y are based on the idea that a leader's attitude toward employees has an impact on job performance and may lead to different management strategies.

6. Situational management theory holds that effectiveness as a leader depends on the characteristics of the leader and the subordinates as well as the situational variables involved.

7. The **contingency theory** of leadership holds that there is no one "best" style of leadership but that style must be adjusted to fit the situation.

8. Leaders acquire power from their ability to reward and punish, position in the organization, expertise, and personal characteristics.

9. Communication, or the constant development of understanding among people, is central to leadership effectiveness.

10. Effective communication means that there is successful transfer of information, meaning, and understanding from a sender to a receiver.

11. Types of communication include oral, written, visual aids, body language, facial expressions, gestures, and actions. The effectiveness of communication can be improved by using multiple forms of communication.

12. Barriers to effective communication can be overcome by being aware of their existence and employing some of the suggested techniques and improving communication.

13. In this era of constant change, an understanding of change management is critical to leadership effectiveness. A good leader systematically faces the challenges presented by the ever-changing conditions in the foodservice industry.

Contingency theory

Holds that managerial activities should be adjusted to fit the situation

MOTIVATION

> **KEY CONCEPT:** An individual's motivations stem from energizing forces within the individual (needs, attitudes, interests, and perceptions) and within the organization (rewards, tasks, coworkers, supervisors, communication, and feedback).

Motivation is the sum of energizing forces internal (individual) and external (organizational) to an individual that results in behavior. It is not possible to motivate another person to do anything he or she does not want to do. Motivation must come from within the person. It is only possible to create an environment in which a person becomes self-motivated. To do this, a leader must understand the concept of human motivation.

History of Motivational Theories

Abraham Maslow's (Figure 1) 1954 classic research on motivational theory has provided the foundation of most current thinking in this area (Maslow, A. H.: *Motivation and Personality.* New York: Harper & Row, 1954). According to Maslow's need hierarchy theory, a person is motivated by his or her desire to satisfy specific needs. These needs are arranged in a hierarchical order (Figure 2). Maslow theorized that only an unsatisfied need motivates behavior; when a need is satisfied, it is no longer a primary motivator; higher order needs cannot become motivating forces until preceding lower order needs have been satisfied; and, finally, people want to move up the hierarchy.

A second theory of motivation based on needs was proposed by McClelland in 1961 (McClelland, D. C.: *The Achieving Society.* Princeton, NJ: Van Nostrand, 1961). Achievement motivation theory holds that an organization offers an individual the opportunity

Figure 1 Abraham Maslow (1908–1970), psychologist and founder of humanistic psychology.

to satisfy three needs: the need for power, the need for achievement, and the need for affiliation. Depending on the individuals' particular needs, they will be motivated by tasks that provide an opportunity to attain that need.

Both Maslow and McClelland based their theories on differences among people. In contrast, organization theories of motivation emphasize task elements with less consideration of individual differences. Herzberg's (1959) dual-factor theory or motivation-hygiene theory purports that factors such as achievement, recognition, responsibility, opportunity for advancement, and the work itself are all motivators, whereas factors such as the company policies, supervision, salary, working conditions, and interpersonal relations are hygiene factors (Hertzberg, F., Mausner, V., and Snyderman, B.: *The Motivation to Work.* New York: Wiley, 1959). Hygiene factors do not motivate but simply prevent dissatisfaction and act as a precondition for motivation by motivators.

Operant conditioning is a second theory of motivation based on organizational factors, developed from the work of E. L. Thorndike and B. F. Skinner (Skinner, B. F.: *Contingencies of Reinforcement.* New York: Appleton-Century-Crofts, 1969). The basic idea behind operant conditioning is that people will perform in order to receive rewards and avoid punishment.

Expectancy theory combines individual factors and organizational factors into a theory of motivation based on the interaction of the two. Expectancy theory states that people make decisions about their behavior on the expectation that the choice they make is more likely to lead to a needed or desired outcome. The relationship between behavior and outcome is affected in complex ways by individual and organizational factors. Victor Vroom is renowned for his work on expectancy theory (Vroom, V.: *Work and Motivation.* New York: Wiley, 1964).

Expectancy theory

Theory that states motivation is a function of the person's ability to accomplish the task and his or her desire to do so

Figure 2 Hierarchy of needs.

Self-actualization needs
(Reaching one's potential)

Self-esteem needs
(Recognition, status, achievement)

Social needs
(Love, belonging, acceptance, friendship)

Safety needs
(Security, freedom from fear, protection from harm)

Physiological needs
(Food, water, air, shelter, clothing, sex)

Current Thinking on Motivation

As with leadership, much has been written about the concept of motivation. Motivation is still not clearly understood and, more often than not, is poorly practiced. One problem is the common myths that exist. Some examples of these myths are as follows:

1. It is possible for a manager to motivate an employee.
   > Not really—Motivation must come from within. A manager can only create an environment in which employees motivate themselves.
2. Money is a good motivator.
   > Not really—The satisfaction of lower-level needs such as money, job security, and nice facilities can help employees from becoming less motivated, but it does not help them to become more motivated.
3. Fear is a good motivator.
   > Fear is a very good short-term motivator but very often is a demotivator for the long term.
4. What motivates me, the manager, will motivate my staff.
   > Different people are motivated by different things, and those things may change with time. Managers need to know what motivates each of their employees.

Some basic principles to remember when attempting to create an environment conducive to self-motivation are as follows:

1. Work to align the goals of the organization with the goals of employees. Allow employees to identify their own goals.
2. Work to understand what really motivates each employee. This can be done by asking them, listening to them, and observing them.
3. Recognize that supporting employee motivation is an ongoing process to sustain a motivational environment in ever-changing organizations.
4. Support employee motivation with organizational systems such as policies and procedures to help ensure clear understanding and equitable treatment.

LEADERSHIP

KEY CONCEPT: Leadership is the activity of influencing other people's behavior toward the achievement of desired objectives. Management is the function of running an organization by effectively and efficiently integrating and coordinating resources in order to achieve desired objectives.

Leadership is one of the most observed and least understood phenomena throughout the world; in fact, there are more than 130 definitions of the term. After many studies, researchers have concluded that there is no common set of factors, traits, or processes that identifies the qualities of effective leadership.

Leadership, like the concept of management, means different things to different people—ranging from being the first to initiate a change to inspiring bravery on the battlefield. This fact has caused many to use other, more definitive terms, such as *activating* or *influencing*. At times, the terms *leadership* and *management* have been used synonymously. However, leadership is essentially the business or activity of trying to influence people to strive willingly to attain the goals and plans of the organization. Management is the function of running an organization from a conceptual or policy standpoint. Leadership may then be defined as working with people to get them to produce willingly the results the leader wants or needs to accomplish.

Although managers and leaders both have minds and souls, they tend to emphasize the use of one over the other as they function in the organization. That is, the mind represents the analytical, calculating, structuring, and ordering side of tasks, whereas the soul represents the visionary, passionate, creative, and flexible side. Some believe that managers and leaders are very different kinds of people who differ in motivation, personal history, and how they think and act. Others believe that the same people can act as managers in one situation and as leaders in another depending on the needs of the situation. Management and leadership require different responses to different demands, and there are situations when each is required. The key is to be able to employ different roles at different times.

Past research has found that subordinates respond to authority alone to do the bare minimum to maintain their jobs, but to raise effort toward total capability, the manager must induce devoted response on the part of subordinates by exercising leadership. Leadership has been viewed as a special form of power involving relationships with people. These relationships are developed when leaders successfully fuse organizational and personal needs in a way that allows people and organizations to reach levels of mutual achievement and satisfaction. This can be an exceedingly difficult task. Each employee is different with different motivations, ambitions, interests, and personalities. As a result, each must be treated differently. Work situations differ. How managers can handle these divergent factors effectively has been the subject of study for many years. Such research, both past and present, can be used to improve managerial leadership effectiveness.

KEY CONCEPT: As a leader, the foodservice manager must empower employees by clearly communicating the organization's mission, accepting the responsibility for leading the group, and earning employees' trust.

Management guru Peter Drucker (1992) contends that the essence of leadership is performance—not charisma or a set of personality traits (Drucker, P. F.: *Managing in the Future.* New York: Truman Talley/E. P. Dutton, 1992). He states that there are three basic requirements for effective leadership:

1. The leader must think through the organization's mission, defining it and establishing it, clearly and visibly. Any necessary compromises made are compatible with the leader's mission and goals, and standards are maintained.
2. The leader sees leadership as a responsibility, not a rank or privilege. The effective leader accepts responsibility for subordinates' mistakes but sees their triumphs as triumphs. For this reason, effective leaders do everything possible to surround themselves with able, independent, and self-assured people.
3. Last, the leader must earn trust. This means that a leader's actions and professed beliefs must be congruent. Drucker states that being a good leader is not based on being clever but on being consistent, and that these are the same characteristics required of a good manager.

Others agree with Drucker's ideas and, based on further research, have found that managers must grow to become leader-managers. They put forth four essential traits of effective leadership: (1) the capacity to engage people and draw them to a compelling vision of what is possible; (2) the ability to communicate their vision in a way that allows people to make it their own and give it personal meaning; (3) trust, total reliability, and integrity, as well as the performance of actions that are congruent with their vision; and (4) the possession of high regard for self and others. The combined effect of these personal characteristics empowers people by (1) making them feel significant, (2) focusing on their developing competence rather than their failures, (3) creating a shared sense of community, and (4) making work exciting and worthy of dedicated commitment.

As a leader, then, the foodservice manager has the task of empowering employees by clearly establishing and communicating the organization's mission, accepting the responsibility of leading the group, and earning employees' trust by showing a high regard for self and others. An empowered team is necessary to create an effective, smoothly operating work unit.

The Traditional Leadership Role

■ **KEY CONCEPT:** Early theories of leadership include scientific management, in which a leader's role was to motivate employees with rewards of money, and human relations theory, in which a leader improved productivity by showing an interest in the employee as an individual.

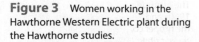

Scientific management

Popular theory in the early 1900s, concerned primarily with the "best" method and "right" wage for a job

Scientific management was founded on the belief that the main common interest of both the organization and the employee was money, and only money. The leader-manager's role consisted of issuing orders and handing out rewards and punishments. The founders of the scientific management theory, such as Frederick W. Taylor (Taylor, F.: *The Principles of Scientific Management.* New York: W. W. Norton, 1911) and Frank and Lillian Gilbreth (www.lib.purdue.edu/spcol/manuscripts/fblg), were primarily concerned with the best method and "right wage" for doing the job. The employee was viewed as a machine or tool. This type of thinking met the needs of the day. But times change. The practices of the scientific management movement began to be questioned in the late 1920s.

Human Relations Approach. The turning point came as a result of the Hawthorne studies. Western Electric Company conducted some experiments at their Hawthorne plant outside Chicago to determine the relationship between the physical working environment and productivity (Figure 3). Lighting was one variable that was tested. Researchers were surprised to find that no matter how they varied the intensity of the lighting, productivity increased. They concluded that the level of performance had nothing to do with the lighting intensity but rather was a result of the interest shown in the worker as a person rather than as a machine. Thus, the human relations theory era was born. Human relationists such as Mayo, Maslow, Roethlisberger, and Dickson brought a more tolerant approach to the leadership of people—consideration of the individual and an understanding of why people work. The theory was good. The implementation, in many cases, was poor.

Newer Approaches to Leadership

■ **KEY CONCEPT:** McGregor's Theory X and Theory Y are based on the idea that a leader's attitude toward employees has an impact on job performance and may lead to different management strategies.

Theory X and Theory Y. The human relations movement began to lose favor in the early 1950s. McGregor (1985) introduced his Theory X and Theory Y analysis of leadership

Figure 3 Women working in the Hawthorne Western Electric plant during the Hawthorne studies.

Figure 4 A comparison of Theory X and Theory Y.

Theory X Beliefs	Theory Y Beliefs
Most people dislike work and will avoid it if possible.	Exerting physical and mental effort at work is as natural as play or rest.
Most people must be coerced, controlled, directed, or threatened with punishment to get them to exert effort to achieve organizational objectives.	Most people will exercise self-direction and self control to achieve organizational objectives to which they are committed.
Most people prefer to be directed, want to avoid responsibility, have little ambition, and want security above all other needs.	The degree of commitment to objectives is dependent on whether achievement will satisfy higher order needs.
	Most people not only accept but seek responsibility.
	Employees have as much imagination, creativity, and ingenuity to solve organizational problems as do supervisors.
results in	results in
Leadership Style	**Leadership Style**
The leader makes all decisions. Employees are carefully supervised in carrying out assigned tasks. Leaders are autocratic and must push employees in order to have an effective work group.	Employees are involved in decision making and left to their own devices to carry out assigned tasks. Leaders are supportive and encouraging in order to have an effective work group.

strategies, suggesting that the basic attitude of a manager toward employees has an impact on job performance (McGregor, D.: *The Human Side of Enterprise.* New York: McGraw-Hill, 2001). He divided these supervisory attitudes into two categories—Theory X and Theory Y. The **Theory X** attitude was held by the traditional and "old-line" managers and is pessimistic about employees' abilities and skills. **Theory Y** was the attitude held by the emerging manager of the 1960s and 1970s and is optimistic. However, again implementation was the problem. Managers trained in Theory Y management found that, in many cases, the resulting job performance did not yield the desired level of quality (Figure 4).

■ **KEY CONCEPT:** **Situational management theory holds that effectiveness as a leader depends on the characteristics of the leader and the subordinates as well as the situational variables involved.**

Situational Management. The work done at Ohio State University and by Blake and Mouton (Blake, R. R., and Mouton, J. S.: *Executive Achievement: Making It at the Top.* New York: McGraw-Hill, 1986), as well as others, culminated in the theory that effectiveness as a leader depends on a multiplicity of factors, not only human behavior and motivation. The **situational management** approach concentrates on the theory that leadership effectiveness is a function of the individual leader (including traits and personalities), of that leader's subordinate (including attitude toward working, socioeconomic interests, and personality), and of the situational variables involved.

Because followers are the ones who determine whether a person possesses leadership qualities, the expectations of followers have been studied. The characteristics that followers most admire in superiors have been found to be honesty, competence, a forward-looking attitude, and inspiration.

Theory X

The traditional set of managerial assumptions that employees have an inherent dislike of work and will avoid it if possible

Theory Y

The attitude held by the managers of the 1960s and 1970s that employees, under the proper conditions, will seek and accept responsibility, be motivated to achieve organizational objectives, and will exercise creativity and imagination in solving organization problems

Situational management

Effectiveness of a leader is a function of the individual leader, the subordinate, socioeconomic interests, and situational variables

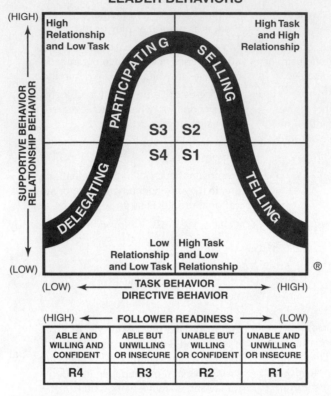

Figure 5 Style of leader with matching performance readiness of follower(s).
Source: P. Hersey, K. Blanchard, and D. E. Johnson, *Management of Organizational Behavior: Leading Human Resources*, 9th ed. (Upper Saddle River, NJ: Pearson Education, Inc. 2008, 2001). ISBN 13: 978-0-13-144139-2. © Copyright 2006 Reprinted with permission of the Center for Leadership Studies, Inc. Escondido, CA 92025. All rights reserved.

Early studies at Ohio State University attempted to define more global leader type behaviors. Two separate and distinct dimensions of leader behavior were identified—initiating structure and consideration. **Initiating structure** refers to the relationship between the leader and the members of the work group in seeking to establish well-defined patterns of organization, channels of communication, and procedures. **Consideration** refers to behavior that indicates friendship, mutual trust, respect, and warmth in the relationship between the leader and the work group. This was the first study to plot leader behavior on two axes. Leadership quadrants drawn from the Ohio State studies are illustrated in Figures 5 and 6. The effects of initiating structure on employee satisfaction and performance have been found to depend entirely on the situation. Research has shown that consideration behavior is positively related to employee satisfaction, but its effect on performance is unclear.

Initiating structure

The relationship between the leader and the members of a work group

Consideration

Behavior that indicates friendship, mutual trust, respect, and warmth between the leader and the work group

Figure 6 Interpretation of the situational leadership model.
Source: Bolman, Lee G., and Deal, Terrence E. *Reframing Organizations: Artistry, Choice, and Leadership*, p. 418. Copyright © 1991 by Jossey-Bass, Inc., Publishers. Used with permission.

High Relationship — Low Task: Leadership through Participation. Use when followers are "able" but "unwilling" or "insecure."	High Relationship — High Task: Leadership through Selling. Use when followers are "unable" but "willing" or "motivated."
Low Relationship — Low Task: Leadership through Delegation. Use when followers are "able" and "willing" or "motivated."	Low Relationship — High Task: Leadership through Telling. Use when followers are "unable" and "unwilling" or "insecure."

In 1971, a theory was proposed that helps to explain the situational nature of the initiating structure dimension of leader behaviors. Called the **path-goal theory** of leadership, it states that the functions of a leader should consist of increasing personal rewards for subordinates for goal attainment and making the path to these rewards easier to follow by clarifying it, removing and reducing roadblocks, and increasing opportunities for satisfaction along the way. This theory is based on the expectancy theory of motivation, which states that motivation is a function of both the person's ability to accomplish the task and his or her desire to do so. In the late 1960s, the theory that leadership effectiveness is contingent not only on leadership style but also on the attitude and outlook of the follower and the situational constraints came to be accepted.

Path-goal theory
Functions of a leader should consist of increasing personal rewards and clarifying pathways for goal attainment for subordinates

KEY CONCEPT: The contingency theory of leadership holds that there is no one "best" style of leadership but that style must be adjusted to fit the situation.

Effective leadership in any given situation is dependent on a number of circumstances—for example, how structured the task involved is, whether the leader has any power as perceived by subordinates, and how well the leader gets along with subordinates. In very "favorable" or in very "unfavorable" situations for getting a task accomplished by group effort, the task-oriented management style works best. In intermediate situations, the human relations style is more successful.

In 1958, Tannenbaum and Schmidt wrote a now-classic article, "How to Choose a Leadership Pattern" (*Harvard Business Review* 1958; 36(2): 95–101), in which they described how a manager should successfully lead his organization. Fifteen years later, they reconsidered and updated their original statements to reflect new management concepts and societal changes. The revised continuum of manager–nonmanager behavior is shown in Figure 7.

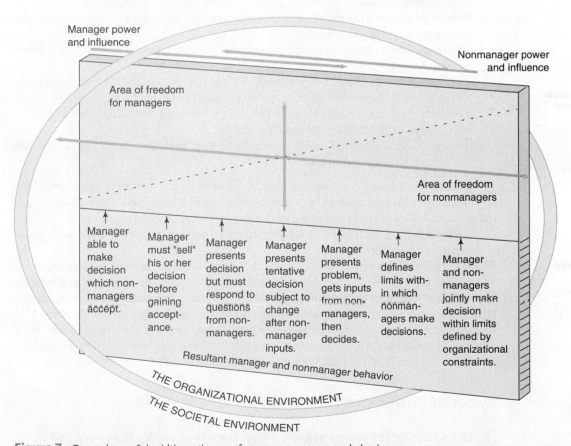

Figure 7 Tannenbaum-Schmidt's continuum of manager–nonmanager behavior.
Reprinted by permission of *Harvard Business Review*. An exhibit from "How to choose a leadership pattern" by Robert Tannenbaum and Warren H. Schmidt (May/June 1973). Copyright © 1973 by the President and Fellows of Harvard College; all rights reserved.

419

The total area of freedom shared by managers and nonmanagers is constantly redefined by interactions between them and the forces in the environment. The points on the continuum designate types of manager and nonmanager behavior that are possible with the amount of freedom available to each. This continuum allows managers to review and analyze their own behavior within the context of alternatives available. It is important to recognize that there is no implication that either end of the continuum is inherently more effective than the other. The appropriate balance is determined by forces in the manager, in the nonmanager, and in the particular situation. The model also suggests that neither manager nor nonmanager has complete control. The nonmanager always has the option of noncompliance, and managers can never relieve themselves of all responsibility for the actions and decisions of the organization.

Also based on the premise that there is no one best way to influence people, the situational leadership model (see Figure 5) bases the recommended style of leadership on (1) the amount of guidance and direction (task behavior) a leader gives; (2) the amount of socioemotional support (relationship behavior) a leader provides; and (3) the readiness (maturity) level that followers exhibit in performing a specific task, function, or objective. Each of the leadership styles shown (delegating, participating, selling, and telling) is a combination of task and relationship behavior (the two dimensions identified in the Ohio State studies).

Servant leadership is currently receiving much attention in all of society even though it was first proposed in a 1970 essay by Robert K. Greenleaf, a management researcher at AT&T and a lifelong philosopher (Greenleaf, R.: *Servant as Leader.* Indianapolis, IN: Greenleaf Center for Servant Leadership, 1970). This powerful, but slow-growing, movement has much to offer the business community. According to Greenleaf, **servant leaders** embody these principles:

- *They are servants first.* They have to make a conscious choice to aspire to lead.
- *They articulate goals.* Today these goals are often called a vision.
- *They inspire trust.* This trust is built on confidence in the leader's values, competence, judgment, and goal-oriented spirit.
- *They know how to listen.* In facing any problem, they seek first to understand and then to be understood.
- *They are masters of positive feedback.* People are shown unqualified acceptance while, at times, their behavior or performance may not be accepted.
- *They rely on foresight.* Servant leaders have a sixth sense that allows them to fill in information gaps necessary for decision making.
- *They emphasize personal development.* To remedy problem situations, the servant leader makes changes within herself first.

An example of a servant leader is Frances Hesselbein, the woman responsible for the revitalization of the Girl Scouts organization in the United States. Hesselbein defined leaders as "not a basket of tricks or skills. (Leadership) is the quality and character and courage of the person who is the leader. It's a matter of ethics and moral compass, the willingness to remain highly vulnerable."

It is probable that most people are able to operate within a narrow band of preferred ways of leading and tend to use these styles over and over. Self-development and training should be directed to a wider range of styles for use in the appropriate situations. Ideally, persons in foodservice management positions should accept as a personal philosophy that their human resources are their greatest assets and that to improve their value is not only a material advantage but a moral obligation as well. The historical view of leadership and the contributions of each of the periods is summarized in Figure 8.

Types of Power and Their Use

> **KEY CONCEPT:** Leaders acquire power from their ability to reward and punish, position in the organization, expertise, and personal characteristics.

Servant leaders

The servant leader is motivated by a natural desire to serve, not to lead, and puts others before himself

Scientific Management—1910 to 1926	
Taylor and Gantt	The one best way
F. and L. Gilbreth	"Efficiency" and work simplification
Human Relations—1926 to 1947	
Mayo	Employees must be treated like people, not machines
Roethlisberger and Dickson	Satisfaction in work
Maslow	
The Behavioral Scientists—1947 to 1967	
McGregor	Under the right conditions, people will manage themselves
Argyris	People work best when their social and psychological
Likert	needs are met
Drucker	
Herzberg	
The New Thinkers—1967 to 2000	
Reddin	The situation, the type of work, and the type of manager
Tannenbaum and Schmidt	all determine the most appropriate leadership style
Hersey and Blanchard	There is no "one best way"
Blake and Mouton	
House	

Figure 8 A summary of the historical view of leadership.

The term *power* often evokes negative feelings. To some, the use of power means that people are being manipulated, coerced, controlled, or dominated. However, power always exists in an organization, and understanding how to manage it and the positive aspects of the proper use of power is an important part of the leadership role.

Because of his or her position in the organization, a leader possesses *position power*; because of personal characteristics or expertise, she or he may also possess *personal power*. Power is used to influence the behavior of others, an important part of a leader's job. Some of the specific ways that leaders acquire power were identified by French and Raven (1959) in a now-classic study (French, J. R. P., and Raven, B. H.: The bases of social power. In D. Cartwright (ed.), *Studies in Social Power*. Ann Arbor: University of Michigan Press, 1959). They are:

Coercive power: Followers believe that the leader has the authority to punish them and the punishment will be unpleasant, such as a salary reduction, a demotion or termination, or assignment to unpleasant tasks.

Reward power: Followers believe that the leader has the authority to reward them, and the rewards will be pleasant such as an increase in salary, a promotion, or assignment to preferred tasks.

Legitimate power: Followers believe that the leader has the right to give directions because of his or her position in the organization.

Expert power: Followers believe that the leader has expertise or knowledge that will be of help to them (Figure 9).

Referent or charismatic power: Followers believe that the leader has charisma or personal characteristics that result in admiration and respect and therefore want to follow that leader (Figure 10).

Expert and referent power evolve from the traits, skills, and beliefs of the leader and can be thought of as personal power, whereas coercive, reward, and legitimate power are all based on the organization's support of the leader and are considered position power. Any type of power, when properly used, is of value to a leader. However, personal power always outlasts position power. Position power without personal power is minimally effective. The combination of the two, however, can be a powerful force and accomplish great

Figure 9 Team members listen intently to the coach who possesses more than one type of power.
Source: Monkey Business Images/Shutterstock.

things. To be most effective, leaders should develop as many sources of power and influence as possible.

In the end, what separates the effective leader from the ineffective one is how the power that one possesses is used. Power should be used judiciously and shared whenever possible. Sharing power means that leaders should seek the advice and counsel of others, include them in briefings and meetings, expand their authority, let them know their efforts have a positive impact on the organization, delegate significant assignments to them, and bring them into the decision-making circle. When power is used in this way, it promotes organization-focused loyalty, high morale, initiative, and individual growth.

Effective Communication

KEY CONCEPT: Communication, or the constant development of understanding among people, is central to leadership effectiveness.

One leadership model shows the central role of communication for leadership effectiveness. In this model, communication is the glue that binds the behavior between leader and

Figure 10 Shuttle Commander Eileen Collins, the first woman to command a space shuttle, July 1999.

follower. The messages transmitted between them present the styles, attitudes, values, motives, skills, and personality variables that are possessed by the leader. The amount of control exerted will vary depending on the situation, task, personnel, and the interrelationships of these components. Good communication is a critical component of effective leadership. It is the process that links all of the management functions. In fact, estimates indicate that between 70 percent and 90 percent of a manager's time is spent communicating.

> ■ **KEY CONCEPT:** **Effective communication means that there is successful transfer of information, meaning, and understanding from a sender to a receiver.**

Communication can be defined as the constant development of understanding among people. It is not necessary to have agreement, but there must be mutual understanding for the exchange to be considered successful. For a leader to lead, directions must be followed. For directions to be followed, they must be understood. The best plans will fail if communication is not comprehended. It is almost certain that no message will be transmitted or received with 100 percent accuracy. The average employee remembers:

10 percent to 15 percent of what is heard
15 percent to 30 percent of what is heard and seen
30 percent to 50 percent of what is said
50 percent to 75 percent of what is done

but remembers

75 percent of what is done with proper instruction

Proper instruction includes hearing, seeing, saying, and doing, and then repeating it all again.

Channels of Communication. An organization's channels of communication can be divided into the formal channel (that established by the organizational structure) and the informal channel. In the formal channel, communication can be downward, upward, or horizontal. Communication from the top down is the most frequently used channel. Equally important is the upward flow of information. Management should encourage the free flow of suggestions, complaints, and facts.

The informal channel of communication includes the grapevine. News acquired through the grapevine contains some factual information but, most of the time, it carries inaccurate information, half-truths, rumors, private interpretations, suspicions, and other kinds of distorted information. The grapevine is constantly active and spreads information with amazing speed, often faster than formal channels.

An alert manager acknowledges the grapevine's presence and tries to take advantage of it, if possible. The grapevine can carry a certain amount of useful information. It can help to clarify and disseminate formal channel information. Rumors and inaccuracies should be dispelled by stating the facts to as many people as possible.

> ■ **KEY CONCEPT:** **Types of communication include oral, written, visual aids, body language, facial expressions, gestures, and actions. The effectiveness of communication can be improved by using multiple forms of communication.**

Oral, or spoken, communication is the most common form of communication and is generally superior. Oral communication takes less time and is more effective in achieving understanding. Face-to-face communication has the advantage of also providing information through body language, personal mannerisms, and facial expressions. Oral communication should be used when (1) instruction is simple, (2) quick action is required, (3) a method to be followed needs to be demonstrated, (4) privacy is required, and (5) employees have proven they are capable and meet their commitments.

Written communication should be used in some circumstances, particularly when (1) a policy or some other authority is being quoted, (2) employees are to be held strictly accountable, (3) a record is needed, (4) employees are inexperienced, and (5) distance makes oral communication impossible. A well-balanced use of both oral and written communication is often very effective.

Other types of communication include visual aids, gestures, and actions. Visual aids, such as pictures, charts, cartoons, symbols, and videos, can be effective, particularly when used with good oral communication. "Actions speak louder than words" is sage advice to any manager. Gestures, handshakes, a shrug of the shoulders, a smile, and silence all have meaning and are powerful forms of communication to subordinates.

KEY CONCEPT: **Barriers to effective communication can be overcome by being aware of their existence and employing some of the suggested techniques and improving communication.**

Some of the barriers to communication have to do with the language used, the differing backgrounds of the sender and receiver, and the circumstances in which communication takes place. The receiver hears what he or she expects to hear and may shut out or ignore what is not expected. There is a tendency to infer what is expected even when it has not been communicated. Senders and receivers have different perceptions based on their different backgrounds. It is important to consider where the other person "is coming from." Receivers evaluate the source and interpret or accept communication in light of that evaluation. A trusted and respected leader will have more open channels of communication than a leader who does not command trust and respect. Conflicting information is often ignored. Different people most often attach various meanings to certain words. The sender or communicator not only must choose words that convey the meaning to the receiver but also must give attention to the message transmitted by nonverbal cues. Body language and facial expression often say more than the words they accompany. A receiver who is emotionally upset often stops listening in order to think about what he or she will say next. Noise and the environment often form a physical barrier to communication. There is a right place and a wrong place to conduct good communication, just as there is a right time and a wrong time.

A network breakdown occurs when there is a disruption or closure of a communication channel. This can be caused by a number of factors, both intentional and unintentional. Some reasons for the network to break down are forgetfulness, jealousy, fear of negative feedback, and to gain an edge over the competition. Information overload occurs when people receive more information than they are able to process. Time pressures on the sender form a barrier to effective communication because of hastily developed messages, use of the most expedient (often, not most effective) channel, and allowing insufficient time for feedback. These barriers to successful communication are summarized in Figure 11.

Improving Communication. Communication is not a one-way process. One of the most important parts of effective communication is to listen to the reply, which may be words, facial expression, body language, or even silence. The evaluation of feedback can tell much about how the message has been received. Empathy or the ability to put yourself in the receiver's shoes in a conversation can also be crucial to mutual understanding.

Face-to-face communication is advantageous to use, when possible, because of the ability to gain immediate feedback from multiple channels, such as oral, facial expression, and body language. Long, technical, and complicated words should be avoided as much as possible. To secure understanding, repeating information using slightly different words, phrases, or approaches is often effective. Being sensitive to the receiver or being able to put yourself in the receiver's place can improve communication. One should be aware that some words or phrases can have symbolic meaning to others and avoid using them. Proper timing is also important. The old maxim "criticize in private, praise in public" is an example of timing. Reinforcing words with congruent actions has already been discussed as essential

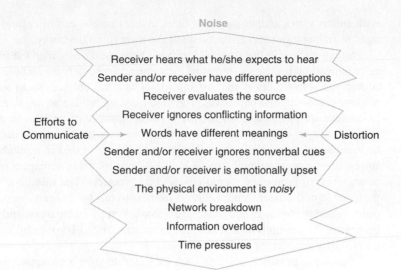

Figure 11 Barriers to successful communication.

to effective communication. Finally, an atmosphere of openness and trust, fostered by self-disclosure, builds healthy relationships that contribute to effective communication. These methods to improve communication are summarized in Figure 12.

Ethics and Social Responsibility

The major goals of administrative leadership in the scientific management era were profit and productivity. Today, leadership in organizations involves managerial ethics and social responsibility as well. A leader has high ethical standards that inspire trust, loyalty, and effective leader-follower relationships. Among the ethical challenges facing foodservice managers today are identifying and understanding different cultural values, dealing with unethical behavior in the organization, balancing the organization's need to know with the employees' rights to privacy, balancing management and employees' rights, and identifying and implementing programs to ensure that the organization is operating in a socially responsible manner. Some areas of each of these are controlled by government regulatory agencies and legal mandates, but many other areas are not.

Ethics can be defined as the rightness or wrongness of actions and as the goodness or badness of these actions' objectives. Many professional organizations have a code of ethics that provides guidelines for their members to use in their work with others. A bill of rights for employees also provides a valuable set of guidelines for managers to use in dealing

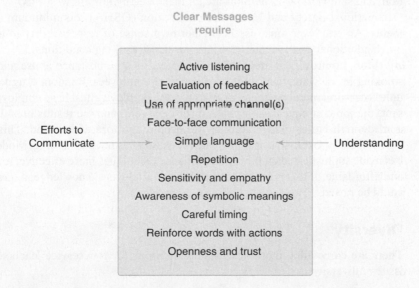

Figure 12 Ways to improve communication to achieve mutual understanding.

425

with subordinates and, at the same time, assures employees of certain rights, such as the right to follow a grievance procedure or the right to a safe workplace.

Social responsibility is an ethical issue because it deals with the goodness or badness of organizational actions in terms of their impact on society as a whole. The classical view of social responsibility is that organizations have no obligations to society other than to achieve organizational objectives. The modern view holds that organizations must operate to achieve the greatest good for the greatest number of people. In other words, social responsibility is demonstrated when a company goes beyond profit maximization in order to benefit society in other ways. This may be demonstrated in a number of ways. On the lowest level, organizational "image building" occurs when managers support good causes in an effort to promote the company and its products. The middle-of-the-road approach includes "good citizenship," which is demonstrated by company support of charities or public interest issues, employee time off to work in problem areas, and employee wellness programs. At the highest level is "full corporate social responsibility," demonstrated by enthusiastic support for social problems.

The areas in which managers are expected to take a proactive, socially responsible stance include the environment, minority group relations, consumer responsibility, and employee rights. Foodservice has a major impact on the environment. Conservation, including the wise use of water and energy, and pollution prevention are real concerns for the industry, as well as being economically and socially mandated practices. The major pollution concern for foodservice is solid waste management. The National Restaurant Association (the representative of 636,000 foodservice units) lends its full support to socially responsible, multitiered solutions to the solid waste crisis. To be successful, such a solution would require the integration of recycling, source reduction, incineration, and landfilling, and the support of local and state government. Policies for solid waste management depend on (1) cooperation of customers to sort and separate solid waste, (2) interest and support of employees and management, (3) the ability to store waste, (4) the cost of transporting waste to recycling centers, (5) the availability of buyback centers or reclaimers, and (6) a market demand for recycled products.

Social responsibility in minority group relations means going beyond the minimum Equal Employment Opportunity Commission (EEOC) requirements and actively recruiting and promoting members of minority groups, as well as training them if they lack necessary entry-level skills.

Responsibility to consumers in the foodservice field means ethical pricing and advertising practices. It also means serving good-quality food that has been prepared under the most sanitary conditions humanly possible.

In the area of management and employee rights, several areas of social responsibility are important. Freedom of speech, assembly, due process of law, privacy, fair compensation, and safe working conditions are all mandated by law. As with EEOC regulations, the Occupational Safety and Health Administration (OSHA) sets minimum safety requirements. An employer must use his or her own sense of responsibility to determine how much additional cost to incur to ensure the safest working conditions.

More controversial areas of employee rights are substance abuse and drug testing, smoking in the workplace, and surveillance of employees. Random drug testing is illegal unless certain criteria are met. For example, the employer must have employee written consent, the job consequences of abuse must be severe, and the results must be held strictly confidential. No-smoking facilities are becoming more widespread. This threatens the rights of the smoker; however, thus far, opposition has not been strong. Modern technology has made sophisticated employee surveillance techniques more effective, readily available, and affordable. If this practice occurs without employees' knowledge, a question of ethics could be raised.

Diversity

There are compelling moral and business reasons for foodservice leaders to address the issue of diversity.

Diversity often requires changing an organization's culture so that everyone feels welcome and able to participate at a very high level. This organizational change should be part of a strategic long-term effort and requires good leadership and the active support of the organization's top-level management. In order to avoid the past failures of diversity initiatives, management should remember the following:

- Diversity is an outcome; it is not something you do. Therefore, diversity should not be implemented as a program but as a process.
- Diversity should be the focus of every department and not simply delegated to the human resources department, where it will get spasmodic attention.
- Much can be learned from others in the community who have made diversity a priority.
- The business results of diversity should be measured. These may include employee retention, recruiting numbers, and operating measures.
- Use trained facilitators when holding diversity-training programs.
- Separate diversity from affirmative action. Affirmative action is a government-mandated program that focuses on race and gender and is aimed at changing historic patterns of discrimination. It is seen as an unwelcome imposition by most organizations.
- Diversity efforts require the use of change management processes.
- Diversity should be voluntary, internally driven, and focused on increasing innovation.

Diversity requires a long-term commitment in which results are measured in years, not months or weeks.

Functional Responsibilities and Skills Required

Certain basic responsibilities are common to all foodservice managers in whatever type of organization they are employed. Most of the responsibilities that are specific to foodservice include the following:

- Establishment of goals, objectives, and standards
- Personnel selection, education, and maintenance of an effective staff
- Overall planning and delegation of work to be done; scheduling of workers
- Purchase of food, equipment, and supplies according to specification
- Planning for physical facilities and equipment needs
- Supervision of all technical operations: production, delivery and service of food, sanitation, safety, security
- Financial planning and control

These responsibilities may be classified under the functions of management.

Effective administrative leadership is a professional responsibility. Some of the key characteristics of successful—and, thus, professionally responsible—leaders are:

1. **Sense of responsibility**—This may mean sometimes subordinating personal desires to the needs of the organization or the profession.
2. **Technical and professional competence**—The input of others to make decisions may provide guidance, but the final decision will require personal technical and professional knowledge and skills.
3. **Enthusiasm**—Honest, genuine enthusiasm for the goals and plans of the leader are vital to the generation of commitment and enthusiasm on the part of employees. New directions and unfamiliar areas should be sought without reluctance.
4. **Communication skills**—Communication is one of the vital linking processes that holds the organization together. It is a key variable in leadership effectiveness. Verbal, written, and nonverbal communications should be understood and utilized effectively. Active listening, avoiding distortion, is a key to good communication.
5. **High ethical standards**—Ethical standards are the basis of all group interaction and decision-making processes. Therefore, they play a key role in the leadership function.

Professional ethics requires leaders to maintain high standards of personal conduct in all situations so that employees may rely on their actions. Integrity is demonstrated when concern for company interests is greater than personal pride.

6. Flexibility—Leaders must have the ability to take whatever comes along and thrive on it. This requires an understanding and acceptance of the fact that no two people or two situations are ever exactly alike. Approaches must be adapted. Change and stress must be understood and managed.

7. Vision—An ability to see the organization as a whole made up of interdependent and interrelated parts—to see where it is going and how it can get there—is necessary for effective leadership. Leaders with ideas and images that can excite people and develop timely and appropriate choices will inspire those they lead (Lester, 1981).

Supervision

Supervision encompasses coordinating, directing, and leading the work of employees to accomplish the organization's goals. In small foodservice systems, the total supervisory function may be the responsibility of the manager. In larger systems, the supervision of the day-to-day technical operations may be delegated to foodservice supervisors, dietetic technicians, or cook-managers. The manager is thus able to concentrate on planning, policy and goal setting, and interdepartmental relationships, and on solving overall problems of the department. In a large department, the director, chief dietitian, or other administrator may delegate these management functions in part to other professionally trained staff.

When responsibility and authority are delegated, management must provide guidance so that the supervisor understands the limits of authority, that is, what decisions can be made without consultation and what actions can be taken on one's own. Management has a responsibility for training supervisors so that they can solve problems and meet emergencies.

The supervisor represents both management and employees. In a foodservice unit, as with industry in general, the supervisor is one of the key persons in the organization. The supervisor is the one to whom the employees look as a representative of management, whereas to management the supervisor represents the working force. Both groups, therefore, are interested in the quality of the supervision as represented by this staff member. The supervisor must be able to interpret the objectives and policies of the company to the employees in such a way as to encourage their cooperation and elicit their confidence and to inspire and lead employees as evidenced through fair and intelligent dealings with them and through the personnel program.

Throughout an employee's term of service, supervision should play a large part in relating the employee to the task and to coworkers. When the probation period is over and the employee is regarded as a member of the permanent staff, familiar with the task and able to perform it, supervision is still necessary to maintain interest and provide for personal growth. To a large extent, recognition and approbation by superiors remain potent incentives to the average worker. The supervisor must accept the responsibility of finding and using incentives that lead to sound development. Adjustments in work assignments to meet changes in the individual's abilities and interests are wisely made only when supervision is adequate, in both kind and amount.

Routine Supervision.   Routine supervision varies with the situation, but it is, for the most part, a matter of personal contact reinforced through checking by observations, records, and charts. Routine supervision may consist of greeting employees each day by name; checking for cleanliness, appearance, and state of health; checking menus and work schedules; making work assignments; explaining to employees any instruction they seem not to understand; checking continuously for quality and quantity of production and service; inspecting for sanitation of work areas and equipment; and, in general, maintaining good working conditions. The supervision of personnel is too often left to chance or to the "free time" that never seems a part of the foodservice manager's busy day. To avoid hit-and-miss contact with employees, the wise supervisor sets aside a certain time each day for checking on the work in progress and for stimulating interest and cooperation in the individual and in the group. Schedules are needed for checking daily, weekly, and periodic jobs. Checking at the end of the day to see that the work as scheduled has been carried out completes the "routine" supervision.

Decision Making

Much of the supervisor's time is spent making decisions and solving problems. Decision making can be thought of as the generic process, whereas problem solving is one type of decision making that applies to a specific situation.

The ability to make decisions in a timely and logical manner is an important skill for supervisors to possess. Better decisions are likely to be made when a number of steps are followed in the proper sequence. These steps are to (1) define the situation—nothing is as useless as the right answer to the wrong question—and then analyze the situation, (2) identify the objectives desired, (3) develop many alternatives—**brainstorm**—and then think them through considering the consequences of each, (4) conduct an evaluation of the alternatives, (5) choose the alternative with the most positive consequences and the least negative consequences, (6) select strategies to implement the chosen alternative, and (7) follow up by monitoring and evaluating the decision (Figure 13).

Brainstorm

A technique for generating ideas about problems and opportunities for improvement

The following questions also need to be asked and answered:

1. Who should make the decision? Should input from others be solicited? Should the decision be delegated, or should you make it alone?
2. What time factors are involved? Are deadlines involved? How much time is available to gather data?
3. Is enough information available, or is more needed? In gathering more information, is a specialist needed?
4. What forces will act against the decision, and what forces will act for it?
5. What risks are involved in the decision? There may be positive and negative consequences in terms of finances, time, effort, human relations, and commitment.

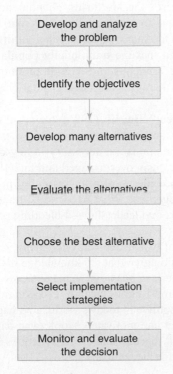

Figure 13 The seven-step decision-making process.

Change Management

▎ **KEY CONCEPT:** **In this era of constant change, an understanding of change management is critical to leadership effectiveness. A good leader systematically faces the challenges presented by the ever-changing conditions in the foodservice industry.**

Change management

The process, tools, and techniques to manage people effectively and the associated human resource issues that surface when implementing changes

---

Accelerated change has become an important part of organizational life. Understanding that people in an organization respond to change in distinct and predictable ways is the foundation of **change management**. Change management has its roots in the two areas of business process improvement and psychology. Business process improvement encompasses total quality management (TQM) and business process reengineering (BPR) and focuses on organization change such as new processes or restructuring. Psychology contributes an understanding of the importance of the "human side" of change in the workplace.

The process has three phases: (1) preparing for change; (2) managing change; and (3) reinforcing change. In phase 1, the leader defines the management strategy and forms and prepares the change management team. Phase 2 involves the development of change management plans and taking action and implementing the plans. Change is reinforced in phase 3 by collecting and analyzing feedback, diagnosing gaps and managing resistance, and implementing corrective actions and celebrating successes.

SUMMARY

Leadership is widely touted as a cure-all for organizational problems. It is also widely misunderstood—a fact that can result in oversimplified advice to managers. Leadership in foodservice organizations can be defined as the privilege of having the responsibility to direct the actions of others in carrying out the purposes of their organization. This can be accomplished at various levels of authority, but at all levels the leader is accountable for both successes and failures. Many researchers believe that they can systematize or develop models to capture the elusive nature of the leadership phenomenon; however, there are just as many researchers who believe that it cannot be systematized or modeled. This latter group contends that there are too many variables inherent in the environments in which the leader must function and that the traditionally popular models of leadership, such as the **managerial grid**, the Tannenbaum-Schmidt continuum, and the Hersey-Blanchard situational model, neglect many of the most critical challenges that leaders must face.

Managerial grid

A graphical representation of management styles based on the relationship between concern for people and concern for production

---

Managers and leaders—are they different? Bennis (1985) makes this insightful distinction between managers and leaders: "Managers do things right," whereas "leaders do the right things." He contends that both functions are necessary in any organization, but that American businesses today are dangerously overmanaged and underled. Drucker (1992) agrees and suggests that leadership is made up of a few essential principles, the very same ones that constitute effective management. What needs to be done now is the integration of all the principles of management and leadership—a blending of innovation, stability, order, and flexibility.

Clearly, leadership has been the subject of exhaustive study for many years and will continue to be studied. Many researchers would agree that the knowledge that we already have is enough to improve the situation in American business. Managers now need to do a better job of applying what is known about motivation, change, and communication in order to become leader-managers. To be competitive in today's world, a manager must not only make a profit but also develop competent and motivated people who can adapt rapidly to changing technology and markets, work together and create synergies, and interact with customers as though they were speaking for the company.

Table 1 Differences between the old and new styles of leadership.	
OLD LEADERSHIP STYLE	**NEW LEADERSHIP STYLE**
Power is concentrated with the leader.	Power is distributed throughout the team.
The leader is accountable and controls the organization.	The leader is accountable but surrenders control of the organization to teams.
The leader defines the vision, mission, and goals of the organization.	The leader defines the vision and mission of the organization. The team defines the goals of the organization.
The leader makes decisions. Employees implement decisions.	Each team member has input into the decision-making process. Decisions are agreed to by the whole team.
Individuals are recognized for achievement.	The team is recognized for achievement.
The leader takes credit for the end product of employees' work.	The team takes credit for the end product of the team's work.

Many see the need for a new team-based style of leadership in which the power of ideas is recognized over the power of position. The differences inherent in this new style are highlighted in Table 1. This style requires that the leader do the following:

1. Build trusting relationships within the team by being empathetic, providing an honest and sincere appreciation for work, keeping confidences, being a good listener, and maintaining high ethics.
2. Build a unified team by creating a shared sense of purpose, creating an environment where goals are considered team goals, recognizing and appreciating people for their individual differences, making each person responsible for the team product, building the confidence of each team member, becoming involved and staying involved, and becoming a mentor.
3. Establish a clear communication style by fostering trust, accepting others' viewpoints, and being consistent in interactions with others.
4. Solve problems creatively by including all members of the team in the problem-solving process.
5. Develop an enthusiastic motivating style by including all members of the team in the decision-making process, giving all members of the team ownership in the end products, providing some form of recognition at the end of a project, and keeping the team focused on its goals and objectives.
6. Become a flexible and courageous risk taker and decision maker.
7. Use power wisely.

A comprehensive study recently published found that today's most effective leaders are humble and strong-willed and that, even though they hold positions of great power, they shun the attention of celebrity. They channel their ambition toward the goal of building a great company. Compellingly modest with unwavering resolve, they set up successors for success. In the end, leadership is not about being "in charge," but rather it is about "leading the charge."

APPLICATION OF CHAPTER CONCEPTS

The Priorities and Strategies for the next four years at the University of Wisconsin–Madison Division of Housing are clearly communicated to all employees. They are based on the following guiding principles:

Mission: Be the place where everyone wants to live
Ethical Responsibilities: Keep our promises, speak the truth, avoid harm, repair harm when it is done, practice justice.

Diversity Statement: Each individual brings uniqueness to our community. All are valued for who they are and their skills and contributions. We actively seek this diversity and work hard to help all staff and all residents feel that they are affirmed members of the community. By working together, we can create and maintain work and living environment in which no individual is advantaged or disadvantaged for being different and where everyone has the opportunity to develop their potential and contribute fully to our community. We know that our residents and staff will thrive as a result.

The Priorities and Strategies are:

1. Sustain our business
2. Sustain our environment
3. Enhance supervisors' effectiveness
4. Take full advantage of technology

Focusing on #3, the goal is to create an environment, structures, processes and systems that will make it possible for all supervisors to be successful. One of the strategies to achieve this goal is to develop and implement a training program to enhance supervisors' effectiveness. Listed to be included in this training program are: leadership standards and operating principles of the division; critical thinking; how to create a positive workplace climate; how to become a skilled trainer; how to do interviewing, selection, and performance reviews; and communication.

CRITICAL-THINKING QUESTIONS

1. What style of leadership is being employed at the UW–Madison Division of Housing?
2. What types of leadership activities would you attempt to avoid in this particular setting?
3. Describe how communication would be different based on this style of leadership. What specific words would be used frequently?
4. Why would this supervisory training program be potentially motivating for supervisors? Why might it be demotivating?
5. Who should do the training?
6. What kind of "noise" might be a barrier to communication during training sessions of the type listed?
7. What principles of good communication should the trainer employ during the training sessions?
8. Prioritize, from most to least important, the six topics listed for the supervisors' training based on your knowledge of supervision from places you have worked.
9. How might expectations for leadership in the Director's position vary from that of the Dining and Culinary Services Assistant Directors?
10. Where does leadership fit in the systems model?

CHAPTER REVIEW QUESTIONS

1. Explain the need hierarchy, achievement motivation, motivation-hygiene, operant conditioning, and expectancy theories of motivation. Describe one management strategy using each of these theories.
2. Compare and contrast the concepts of management and leadership.
3. Describe the difference between McGregor's Theory X and Theory Y approaches to leadership.
4. Trace the history of leadership theories, and describe the contributions that each theory has made to the current approaches.
5. What is situational leadership?

6. Describe how the Tannenbaum-Schmidt continuum of manager behavior fits into a contingency theory of leadership.
7. Define the five types of leader power and give an example of the judicious use of each.
8. Define communication.
9. List the various modes of communication that are used in an organization and give an example of each.
10. List and briefly describe some of the barriers to good communication.
11. Describe some ways in which communication can be made a two-way process.
12. Identify some other techniques that may be used to improve communication.
13. Describe how social responsibility has been legally mandated.
14. Discuss a foodservice manager's professional responsibilities.

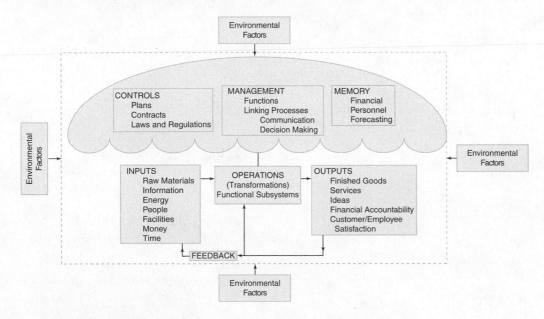

SELECTED WEB SITES

www.adrr.com (Mediation and dispute resolution resources site)

http://alumnus.caltech.edu/~rouda/background.html (Background and theory for large scale organizational change methods)

www.bartleby.com (Literature online)

www.bsr.org (Consulting, research, and collaboration for business strategies and solutions)

http://business-ethics.com (*Business Ethics*, the magazine of corporate responsibility)

www.ceoexpress.com (The executive's Internet resource)

www.corpwatch.org (Holding corporations accountable)

www.fastcompany.com (Articles on technology, design, ethonomics, leadership, and more)

http://first.emeraldinsight.com (Strategic management research)

http://humanresources.about.com (Human resources articles)

www.influenceatwork.com (Principle of influence)

www.managementhelp.org (Free management library)

http://mapnp.nonprofitoffice.com (MAP for nonprofits)

http://money.cnn.com/magazines/fortune/ (*Fortune* magazine)

www.prosci.com (Prosci, an independent research company in the field of change management)

www.publicpolicy.umd.edu/leadership (University of Maryland School of Public Policy leadership association)

www.queendom.com (Test Web site)

www.tqmpapers.com (Research papers on total quality management)

www.women-unlimited.com (Women Unlimited, a resource for cultivating leadership in women)

Performance Improvement

Rod Ferris/Shutterstock

PERFORMANCE IMPROVEMENT, IN TODAY'S ECONOMIC environment, may very well be the most important management activity. Predictions are that it will continue to be the biggest and toughest challenge facing managers during the next few decades. But, exactly what is performance improvement, and how can it be achieved and measured? **Performance improvement** may be defined as the continuous study and adaptation of a foodservice organization's functions and processes to increase the probability of achieving the desired outcomes and to better meet the needs of customers, patients, and other users of the services.

One of the key tenets of total quality management is continuous performance improvement. For the past six decades numerous models have been used by organizations to implement programs that will result in ongoing improvement in their operations. No matter which method is chosen, they are all designed to answer the following fundamental questions:

- What are we trying to accomplish?
- How will we know that a change is an improvement?
- What change can we make that will result in improvement?

From Chapter 16 of *Foodservice Management: Principles and Practices*, Twelfth Edition, June Payne-Palacio, Monica Theis.

Performance Improvement
The continuous study and adaptation of a foodservice organization's functions and processes to increase the probability of achieving the desired outcomes and to better meet the needs of customers, patients, and other users of the services

Productivity
A measure or level of output of goods produced or services rendered in relation to the input in terms of resources used

One such program in widespread use today is the PDCA (Plan, Do, Check, Act) cycle. This cyclical method includes: devising a plan for improvement, implementing the plan, collecting and analyzing data to determine whether the plan worked, and taking action to standardize or improve the process.

Six Sigma is a highly disciplined approach to performance improvement that helps organizations focus on developing and delivering near-perfect products and services. Combined with the principles of lean manufacturing, Lean Six Sigma focuses on the elimination of waste in the food production system.

A number of statistical tools and other processes are helpful in the TQM approach. Examples of KRAs (key result areas)/KPIs (key performance indicators), baseline and benchmarking measurements, brainstorming, flow charts, check sheets, cause-and-effect diagrams, Pareto charts, scatter diagrams, histograms, sociotechnical systems, statistical process control, just-in-time (JIT), and the use of ISO 9000 standards are included in this chapter.

Productivity, the ratio of output to input, can be used as a measure of quantitative performance improvement. However, using the output/input ratio as a definition of productivity in the practical world of foodservice today is inadequate and somewhat irrelevant. A wider conception of productivity, which encompasses factors such as product quality and customer satisfaction, is necessary. In addition, any attempt at performance improvement must take into consideration the people involved. The human factor in any performance improvement program cannot be overlooked. An understanding of human nature on the part of management and improvement in the overall quality of work life are critical components of any productivity improvement program.

People "working smarter" is also believed to be a critical component for improvement in performance in foodservice operations. Increased production with less human effort has been an objective in the foodservice industry for years. Some methods for designing effective and efficient ways of accomplishing work are included in this chapter. This work design must consider improved job content, a safe and healthy work environment, and work simplification.

A step-by-step procedure for implementing a productivity improvement program is outlined in this chapter. One very important step requires that the job be broken down into its component parts in detail. This may be accomplished by work sampling, a pathway or flow diagram, operation and process charting, or micromotion studies, each of which is discussed briefly.

KEY CONCEPTS

1. Performance is a measure of the results (outputs) achieved. Therefore, performance improvement is systematically making changes to enhance the organization's desired results.

2. Total quality management (TQM) is a management process and set of disciplines that are coordinated to ensure that the company consistently meets or exceeds quality standards as set by customers and other stakeholders.

3. The PDCA (Plan, Do, Check, Act) cycle is a continuous quality improvement model consisting of a logical sequence of four repetitive steps.

4. Six Sigma is a highly disciplined approach to performance improvement that helps organizations focus on developing and delivering near-perfect products and services.

5. TQM tools include KRAs (Key Result Areas) and KPIs (key performance indicators), baseline and benchmarking measurements, brainstorming, flow charts, check sheets, cause-and-effect diagrams, Pareto charts, scatter diagrams, histograms, sociotechnical systems, statistical process control, just-in-time (JIT), and the use of ISO 9000 standards.

6. Productivity is a measure or level of output of goods produced or services rendered in relation to input in terms of time (labor hours, minutes, or days), money spent, or other resources used.

7. **Quality of work life (QWL)** is a term that has been used to describe values that relate to the quality of human experience in the workplace. QWL is affected by a composite of factors on the job, including factors that relate to work itself, to the work environment, and to the employee personally.

8. The goals of work design are to improve the content of the job, to provide a safe and healthy work environment, and to design a staff of fit people, an optimum work environment, and work simplification.

9. The fundamental principles of motion economy may be applied to foodservice operations in order to improve productivity.

10. Methods that can be used when conducting a productivity improvement study include work sampling, pathway or flow diagrams, operation and process charting, and micromotion studies.

Quality of work life (QWL)

An approach to management that takes into consideration the quality of human experiences in the workplace

> **KEY CONCEPT: Performance is a measure of the results (outputs) achieved. Therefore, performance improvement is systematically making changes to enhance the organization's desired results.**

It has been said that if you do not change faster and more effectively than your competitors, you will be gone! Today no foodservice can afford to remain static for long. Instead, it must keep pace with the socioeconomic changes and technological developments in food and equipment and their effects on the overall pattern of operation. Changes in consumer attitudes and behavior, labor and energy costs, regulatory considerations, and the general economic environment have created new and challenging problems. The present-day foodservice consumer shows a much greater awareness of value and food safety requirements and demands quality food and efficient service at a reasonable price.

Performance improvement may be defined as the continuous study and adaptation of a foodservice organization's functions and processes to increase the probability of achieving the desired outcomes and to better meet the needs of customers, patients, and other users of the services. Performance is a measure of the results (outputs) achieved. Using Systems Model terminology, *performance improvement*, therefore, refers to measuring the outputs, then modifying the inputs or transformational processes to increase the quality of the outputs; the quantity of the outputs, efficiency; and/or the effectiveness of the transformational processes.

In a foodservice, the performance improvement mindset means doing whatever it takes to ensure the best service, the best food, highest levels of customer/patient/employee satisfaction, and financial success. The key to achieving these outcomes is to continuously examine all parts of the system seeking opportunities for improvement in order to benefit customers, improve results, and maximize quality and efficiency.

TOTAL QUALITY MANAGEMENT

> **KEY CONCEPT: Total quality management (TQM) is a management process and set of disciplines that are coordinated to ensure that the company consistently meets or exceeds quality standards as set by customers and other stakeholders.**

Total Quality Management. An understanding of what is referred to as **Japanese-style management or Theory Z** has led to the adoption of some form of TQM methods in the majority of organizations in the United States.

Total quality management (TQM)

A management process and set of disciplines that are coordinated to ensure that the company consistently meets or exceeds quality standards as set by customers and other stakeholders

Japanese-style management or Theory Z

Theory of management in which workers are seen as the key to increased productivity

Principles of TQM

The Fourteen Points of Management of Dr. W. Edward Deming (1982), one of the most prominent pioneers in the quality movement, represent for many the essence of TQM:

1. Create constancy of purpose for improvement of product and service.
2. Adopt the new philosophy. (Obstacles must be removed and transformation of organizations is needed.)
3. Cease dependence on mass inspections. (Quality must be designed and built into the processes, preventing mistakes and/or poor quality rather than having to fix them after they have occurred.)
4. End the practice of awarding business on the basis of price tags alone. (Organizations should establish long-term relationships with (single) suppliers.)
5. Improve constantly and forever the system of production and service. (Management and employees must search continuously for ways to improve quality and productivity.)
6. Institute training. (Training at all levels is a necessity, not an option.)
7. Adopt and institute leadership. (Managers should lead not supervise.)
8. Drive out fear. (Employees should feel secure enough to express ideas and ask questions.)
9. Break down barriers between staff areas. (Working in teams will solve many problems and improve quality and productivity.)
10. Eliminate slogans, exhortations, and targets for the workforce. (Problems with quality and productivity are caused by the system, not by individuals. Posters and such cause frustration and resentment.)
11. Eliminate numerical quotas for the workforce and numerical goals for people in management. (In order to meet quotas, people will produce poor products and reports.)
12. Remove barriers that rob people of pride of workmanship.
13. Encourage education and self-improvement for everyone.
14. Take action to accomplish the transformation. (Commitment on the part of both management and employees, at all levels, is required.) (Deming, W. E.: *Quality, Productivity, and Competitive Position.* Cambridge, MA: MIT Press, 1982)

TQM is based on the systems approach to management, namely, that the organization is viewed as a system of interrelated, interdependent parts. Fundamental to TQM is the fact that the organization is the focus of management, not the individual. The objective in TQM is to identify barriers to quality, satisfy internal and external customers, and create an atmosphere of continuous improvement.

TQM consists of five major subsystems:

1. A customer focus
2. A strategic approach to operations
3. A commitment to human resource development
4. A long-term focus
5. Total employee involvement

All operations should center attention on satisfying customer needs by striving for continuous improvement in all areas. Personnel need to be trained in the TQM philosophies, with strong encouragement to participate in operating decisions. A teamwork mentality is essential to TQM. Finally, current decisions need to be evaluated based on their long-term rather than short-term consequences. As in the systems model, these five subsystems are interrelated and interdependent. Not one of them can be left out and still have the system operate effectively.

At the heart of the TQM approach is the acceptance that variability is a natural and omnipresent condition. In the systems model, inputs are "transformed" into outputs, outputs are evaluated, and adjustments made according to the feedback received. This is exactly where **quality assurance** (QA) is used. QA involves checking for adherence to quality standards or specifications after the product has been produced. QA measurements include food temperatures, portion sizes, nutrient content, and so on. However, even though QA measures are important, they have been found to foster an inspection mentality

---

Quality assurance

The process of checking for adherence to quality standards or specifications after the product has been produced

that does not encourage empowerment or a sense of teamwork to improve quality when used alone.

In the TQM concept of variation, the focus shifts from the outputs to the transformation process. Reducing variation in transformational activities within the organization is seen as the key to improving productivity and quality. Management moves from a policing role to that of coach, mentor, facilitator, and sponsor. This allows the management team to empower employees to work on quality improvement. Quality must first be assured within the system before it can be provided in the products or outputs.

Deming maintained that 90 percent of variation is due to systematic factors such as procedures, supplies, and equipment not under the employees' control. It is, therefore, management's responsibility to reduce variation and to involve employees in the continuous improvement of system processes.

TQM requires that management operate on the assumption that employees want to do their jobs well, are motivated, and have self-esteem, dignity, and an eagerness to learn. What has been called "a blinding flash of the obvious" because of its simplicity is that a well-managed organization takes advantage of all of its brain power. TQM requires a paradigm shift in the meaning of work and the system that supports it. One small part of the new paradigm is the requisite change in the way managers make decisions, allocate resources, and appraise employees.

To be an effective TQM manager, five key competencies have been identified. They include the ability to:

1. Develop relationships of openness and trust
2. Build collaboration and teamwork
3. Manage with statistical tools and quality processes based on collected facts
4. Support results through recognition and rewards
5. Create a learning and continuously improving organization

One of the key tenets of TQM is continuous performance improvement. For the past six decades, organizations have used numerous models to implement programs that will result in ongoing improvement in operations. No matter which method is chosen, they each are designed to answer the fundamental questions:

- What are we trying to accomplish?
- How will we know that a change is an improvement?
- What change can we make that will result in improvement?

The PDCA Cycle

KEY CONCEPT: The PDCA (Plan, Do, Check, Act) cycle is a continuous quality improvement model consisting of a logical sequence of four repetitive steps.

The **PDCA Cycle** (Figure 1) enjoys widespread use today. This cyclical method includes devising a plan for improvement, implementing the plan, collecting and analyzing data to determine whether the plan worked, and taking action to standardize or improve the process.

1. PLAN (prepare for implementation):
   a. Analyze the processes.
   b. Be open-minded and flexible.
   c. Brainstorm.
   d. Be selective.
   e. Be persistent.
   f. Listen to employees' problems regarding their jobs.
   g. Learn from others, particularly from the best.
   h. Establish the objectives and processes necessary to deliver results in accordance with expected output.

PDCA Cycle

A continuous quality improvement model consisting of a logical sequence of four repetitive steps—Plan, Do, Check, Act

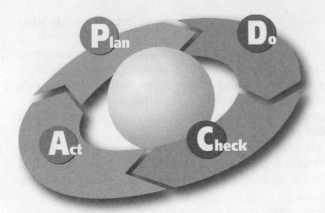

2. DO (execute the plan, taking small steps in controlled circumstances): Train and develop employees and management on how to use these tools:
   a. The TQM approach to work, including the new roles for managers and for employees and the fundamentals of teamwork.
   b. TQM tools for problem solving and measurement.
   c. TQM programs for improvement of work processes.
3. CHECK (check and study the results, develop and implement tools, programs, and performance improvement strategies):
   a. Establish goals, timebound steps, and methods to implement an improvement.
4. ACT (take action to standardize or improve the process. Review, measure, and evaluate the results, then replan as needed).

Six Sigma

Six Sigma

A highly disciplined approach to performance improvement that helps organizations focus on developing and delivering near-perfect products and services

Figure 2 The often-used symbol for Six Sigma is shown in the center of this diagram.

■ **KEY CONCEPT:** **Six Sigma is a highly disciplined approach to performance improvement that helps organizations focus on developing and delivering near-perfect products and services.**

Among the newest of the performance improvement models is Six Sigma® (Figure 2), a trademark of Motorola that was first introduced in 1986. The word "sigma" is from the

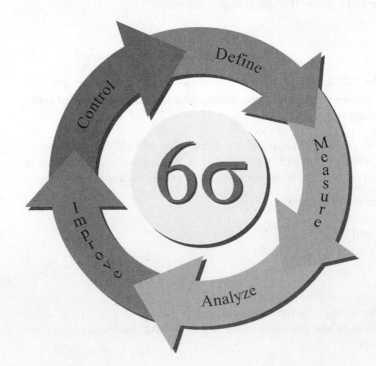

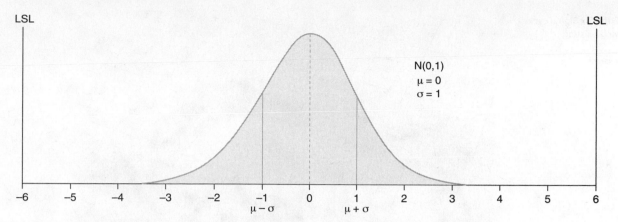

Figure 3 The graph of the normal distribution, which is the foundation of the Six Sigma model.

Greek and is a statistical term that measures by how many standard deviations a process deviates from perfection (Figure 3). The higher the sigma number, the closer to perfection. One sigma is not very good, whereas six sigma is 3.4 errors per million. The idea behind this approach is that if you can measure how many errors occur in a process, you can systematically determine how to eliminate them and get as close to zero as possible.

The differences between Six Sigma and earlier performance improvement programs include:

- A clear focus on achieving measurable and quantifiable financial returns
- An increased emphasis on strong and passionate management leadership and support
- The identification of key roles to lead and implement, Executive Leadership, Champions, Master Black Belts, Black Belts, and Green Belts
- A clear commitment to making decisions based on verifiable data, rather than assumptions and guesswork

In Six Sigma programs the PDCA cycle has been reformulated as *"Define, Measure, Analyze, Improve, Control" (DMAIC)* designed for improving existing processes (Figure 4) and *Define, Measure, Analyze, Design, Verify & Validate (DMADV)* for creating new products or processes (Figure 5). The steps in DMAIC are:

- *Define*—goals that are consistent with customer desires and organizational strategy
- *Measure*—key aspects of the current process and collect relevant data
- *Analyze*—the data to determine cause-and-effect relationships making sure that all factors are considered
- *Improve*—the process based on the data analysis
- *Control*—by pilot testing changes, set up control methods, and continuously monitor the process in order to standardize it and maintain gains.

DMADV steps are:

- *Define*—establish the project purpose and scope
- *Measure*—customer desires are turned into Critical to Quality (CTQ) characteristics
- *Analyze*—Innovative concepts are generated and the best are selected
- *Design*—selected designs are developed and tested
- *Verify & Validate*—design requirements are verified and validated against intended use prior to implementation and control.

Lean Six Sigma

Six Sigma has been combined with principles from **lean manufacturing** to yield a program called **Lean Six Sigma** in which the focus on reducing waste is added to the original Six Sigma concept. In lean manufacturing the goal is to use the correct concept/tool/technique to improve quality, cost, and delivery in a waste-free environment. Waste is defined

Lean manufacturing

A compilation of world-class practices with the goal of using the correct concept/tool/technique to improve quality, cost, and delivery in a waste-free environment

Lean Six Sigma

A performance improvement program in which the focus on reducing waste has been added to the original Six Sigma concept

Figure 4 DMAIC, the Six Sigma cycle designed for improving existing processes.
Source: Yabresse/Shutterstock.

Figure 5 DMADV, the Six Sigma cycle designed for new products and processes.
Source: Yabresse/Shutterstock.

as anything that does not add value in the customers' eyes and for which they are unwilling to pay. Included in a list of possible sources of waste are overproduction, waiting or idle time, transport time, overprocessing, excess inventory, motion, correction of defects, and people skills. The goal of Lean Six Sigma is the total elimination of waste.

TQM Tools

KEY CONCEPT: **TQM tools include KRAs (key result areas) and KPIs (key performance indicators), baseline and benchmarking measurements, brainstorming, flow charts, check sheets, cause-and-effect diagrams, Pareto charts, scatter diagrams, histograms, sociotechnical systems, statistical process control, just-in-time (JIT), and the use of ISO 9000 standards.**

Quality standards can be made more quantifiable by establishing **key result areas** (KRAs) also known as KPIs **(key performance indicators)** such as food and service quality, financial management, human resource management, productivity, planning and marketing, and facilities management. Within each KRA, measurable and quantifiable critical factors are listed. An example of the use of KPIs is shown in Figure 6. Here the secondary lunch participation rate in a district's schools is one of the KPIs used to measure food and service quality.

Brainstorming is a useful technique for generating ideas about problems and opportunities for improvement. Check sheets are used to show exactly what is happening and how often. It is a method of collecting data based on observations and may show a pattern of opportunities for improvement. A sample check sheet is shown in Figure 7. A **cause-and-effect diagram**, often referred to as Ishikawa's **fish diagram**, is used to focus on the different causes of a problem. This focus consequently allows for the grouping and organizing of efforts to improve a process. A fish diagram is shown in Figure 8. **Pareto charts** illustrate the relative importance of problems. They are essentially bar charts where the strategy is to work on the tallest bar or problem that occurs most frequently. A Pareto chart is shown in Figure 9. A scatter diagram is a tool used to determine the strength of a relationship between two variables and to determine the impact on one variable when the other is changed. A scatter diagram is shown in Figure 10. Control charts are trend graphs that show variations in quality measurements over time. A run chart is a trend graph that shows the frequency or amount of a given variable over time. Examples of control and run charts are shown in Figure 11. A histogram is a graphic means of depicting any frequency data that have been collected (Figures 12 and 13).

Baseline measurements provide the starting point in a TQM program against which progress and overall performance toward targets or goals may be assessed. Benchmarking is the TQM measurement tool that provides an opportunity for a company to set attainable goals based on what other companies are achieving. Included in the benchmarking process is a profiling of the company and how it attained its results.

Companies have used a number of other programs to improve work processes. The primary ones include **sociotechnical systems (STS)**, **statistical process control (SPC)**, **just-in-time (JIT)** production and inventory control, the **ISO 9000** program of the International Organization for Standardization. Briefly, STS begins with an analysis of the existing flow diagram, focusing on improvements in technical systems such as transportation, data capturing, and workstations. SPC uses such statistics as mean/average, range, and variation/standard deviation to establish control limits for a process. JIT is a production/inventory management system that establishes a system of producing and supplying products at the right time, in the right amount, with neither defects or waste and links suppliers and customers to minimize total inventory-related costs. ISO 9000 is a series of standards that represent international consensus on good management practices. These standards are designed to be used as guidelines for effective quality management systems that establish a framework for continuous improvement.

Key result areas/key performance indicators

Quantifiable and measurable quality standards

Cause-and-effect diagram/ fish diagram

Used to focus on the different causes of a problem that allows for grouping and organizing efforts to improve a process

Pareto chart

Bar charts in which the strategy is to work on the tallest bar or problem that occurs most frequently

Baseline measurements

In total quality management, data against which progress toward goals may be assessed

Sociotechnical systems (STS)

A program to improve work processes that begins with an analysis of the existing flow diagram focusing on improvements in technical systems

Statistical process control (SPC)

A program to improve work processes that uses statistics to establish control limits for a process

Just-in-time (JIT)

A production/inventory management system that establishes a system of producing and supplying products at the right time, in the right amount, with neither defects or waste and links suppliers and customers to minimize total inventory-related costs

ISO 9000

A series of five international standards that describes elements of an effective quality system

Council of the Great City Schools

Lunch Participation Rate

Total number of lunches served daily *divided by* average daily attendance

Why This Measure Is Important

High participation rates can indicate a high level of customer satisfaction with the school lunch program. Student customers are attracted to quality food selections that are appealing, quick to eat, and economical. High rates can also show that students get their food fast and have plenty of time to eat and socialize. Program revenue can significantly increase when a large percentage of students participate in the lunch program. Furthermore, the federal reimbursement rates for free and reduced-price students who participate in the lunch program can also contribute significantly to revenue.

Factors That Influence This Measure

- Dining areas that are clean, attractive, and "kid-friendly"
- Adequate number of Point of Sale (POS) stations to help move lines quickly and efficiently
- A variety of menu selections
- Number and length of meal times determined by school administration
- Adequate time to eat
- Seating capacity
- The quality of customer service shown to students

Analysis of Data

- FY 07 = 28 districts provided reasonable responses; FY 06 = 27 districts; FY 05 = 24 districts
- FY 07: High = 85.3%; Low = 11.5%; Median = 61.1%
- The upper quartile of districts have participation rates of 73% to over 85%, while the lowest quartile reports 54% down to only 11.5%
- Numerous districts reported their annual number of lunches served, rather than the average daily. If that was the case, we divided the annual number of lunches served by the total number of school days to determine an average number of lunches served. We then divided this number by the average daily attendance.

Figure 6 An example of a KPI for a school foodservice.
Source: Council of the Great City Schools.

Performance Measurement
& Benchmarking for K12 Operations

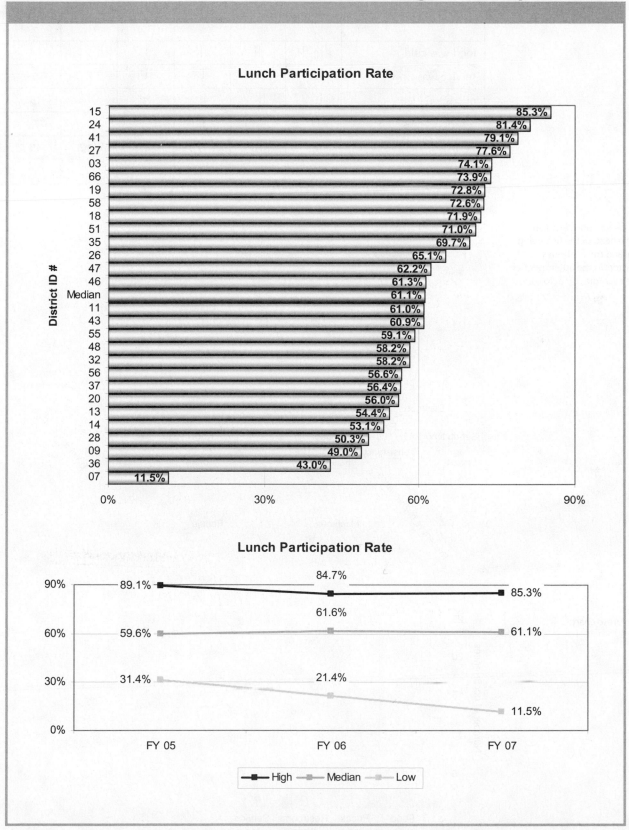

Lunch Participation Rate

Lunch Participation Rate

Figure 6 *(Continued)*

Figure 7 A check sheet for collating data.

Problems: Customer Complaints	Week one					
	Mon	Tue	Wed	Thu	Fri	Total
food was cold	⊬⊬⊬ I	II	IIII	I	⊬⊬⊬ I ⊬⊬⊬	24
service was slow	II	I	I	I		5
prices too high	III	II	II	⊬⊬⊬	I	13
restrooms messy	I	⊬⊬⊬	I			7
TOTAL	**12**	**10**	**8**	**7**	**12**	**49**

Figure 8 A cause-and-effect fish diagram with the head of the fish being the quality goal and the fishbones representing factors in the attainment of that goal. Some examples of factors are shown.

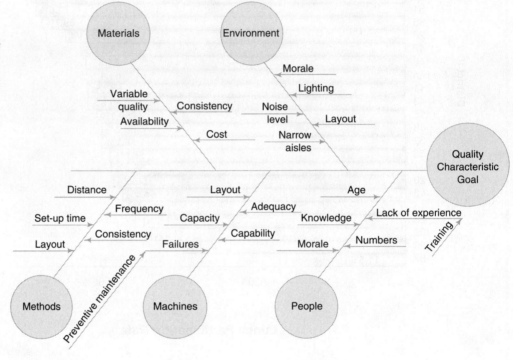

Figure 9 A Pareto chart.

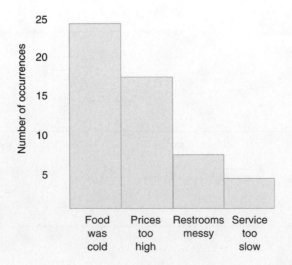

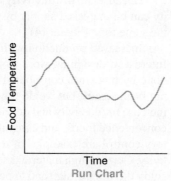

Figure 10 A sample scatter diagram.

P – Poor   G – Good
N – Needs improvement V – Very good
F – Fair   O – Outstanding

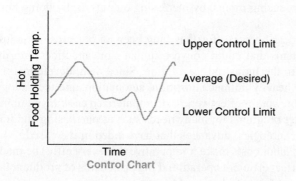

Figure 11 Samples of control and run charts.

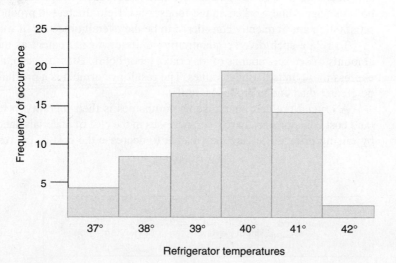

Figure 12 A sample histogram.

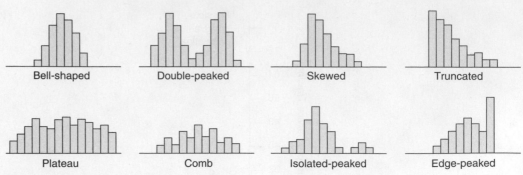

Figure 13 Some common histogram patterns.

INCREASING PRODUCTIVITY

KEY CONCEPT: **Productivity is a measure or level of output of goods produced or services rendered in relation to input in terms of time (labor hours, minutes, or days), money spent, or other resources used.**

The discussions thus far on improving performance have concentrated more on the qualitative aspects of work performance than on the quantitative aspects. However, any attempt at performance improvement must include a consideration of such quantitative aspects.

Productivity ratio
Outputs divided by inputs

Because the **productivity ratio** is calculated by dividing outputs by inputs, productivity can be increased simply by reducing inputs, by increasing outputs, or by doing both at the same time (Figure 14).

Increased production with less human effort has long been an objective in industry. Interest in designing work systems that could convert human work practices into those done by machines contributed to the Industrial Revolution. Since then, development has not been steady, but we do rely heavily on mechanization, automation, and technology to increase productivity and develop worker effectiveness. Computerized cooking equipment, convenience foods, and computer programs for many needs such as purchasing and inventory control are examples of technological advances that have aided in increased productivity. Current high material and labor costs make it imperative that every effort be made to study the work design and to perfect efficient operation if high standards of production and quality of products are to be maintained at a reasonable cost.

Simplification of tasks and techniques that is designed to decrease worker fatigue is an effective aid to good management and is accorded wide recognition and attention by both managers and workers in the foodservice field. Increased productivity and employee satisfaction are frequently considered to be the overall objective of work design.

To relate such diverse quantitative units of measurement as number of meals and amounts of service, pounds of materials, labor hours, Btus, and capital equipment, we can express these units in dollar values. The resulting formula is a profitability ratio that must be greater than one to produce a profit.

A crucial problem facing some companies is their inability, because of competition (and cost containment), to recover increases in the cost of materials, labor, or other resources by raising prices. They are also unable to decrease the cost of the resources or substitute

Figure 14 The productivity ratio.

Productivity Ratio: $\dfrac{\text{Output (i.e. Products, Services, Financial Data)}}{\text{Input (i.e. Raw Materials, Money, Time, People)}}$

others. Therefore, if the profit margin is to be maintained or increased, productivity must be improved.

In foodservice organizations, productivity is measured using indicators such as meals per worked hour, meals per paid hour, meal equivalents per worked hour, meal equivalents per paid hour, transactions per worked hour, and transactions per paid hour. When measured for successive periods, these productivity indicators show a trend. Comparisons can also be made between similar institutions using benchmarks.

Quality Management Approaches to Productivity Improvement

> ▋ **KEY CONCEPT:** Quality of work life (QWL) is a term that has been used to describe values that relate to the quality of human experience in the workplace. QWL is affected by a composite of factors on the job, including factors that relate to work itself, to the work environment, and to the employee personally.

People are the key factor in improving productivity. If productivity is to be improved, both the nature of people and the organizations in which they work must be understood. People are the highest order of resources and, as such, are responsible for controlling and utilizing all other resources.

If improving the productivity position of an organization is directly traceable to people, then it follows that achieving a better bottom line of productivity must be everybody's business. Managers must be capable of utilizing the human resources of the organization and use a systems approach to productivity improvement in which all members of the organization are involved.

Increased productivity means motivation, dignity, and greater personal participation in the design and performance of work in the foodservice organization. It means developing individuals whose lives can be productive in the fullest sense.

A study of 195 U.S. companies found that management ineffectiveness was by far the single greatest cause of declining productivity and that the only successful effort to raise productivity was an integrated QWL approach.

QWL is a multifaceted concept. Incentive plans such as a contingent time-off plan under which the company agrees to award specific time off if the workers perform at an agreed-on level have been successful in improving productivity. Such factors as reducing worker fears, providing opportunity for advancement, implementing job enrichment by adding responsibility, budget, or staff to the job, allowing the exercise of professional skills, and improving communication skills also aid in increasing productivity.

A classic study conducted a number of years ago by Kahn and Katz (Kahn, R. L., and D. Katz: Leadership practices in relation to productivity and morale. In D. Cartwright and A. Zander, eds., *Group Dynamics Research and Theory*. 2nd ed. New York: Harper & Row, 1960), two behavioral science researchers found that a particular leadership style was more effective in increasing productivity and employee satisfaction. The characteristics of this style of leadership are (1) general supervision rather than close, detailed supervision of employees; (2) more time devoted to supervisory activities than to doing production work; (3) much attention to planning of work and special tasks; (4) a willingness to permit employees to participate in the decision-making process; and (5) an approach to the job situation that is described as being employee-centered, that is, showing a sincere interest in the needs and problems of employees as individuals, as well as being interested in high production.

Increased involvement of workers in their organizations has received much attention in the past few years. Today's workers no longer want to be separated from responsibility. Productivity appears to be maximized when a unity of purpose and a feeling of ownership exist among employees. This unity is created when the greatest possible responsibility is given to the lowest possible levels of the organization; compensation systems are designed so that employees are salaried with incentive earnings tied to competence and performance;

the greatest degree of involvement and consensus is sought from all levels; and management exhibits unity with the employee.

In addition to these characteristics, improvements in resources (supervision, methods, and technology) to facilitate greater effectiveness and reduce frustrations seem effective in improving productivity and employee satisfaction.

The QWL approach, in essence, attempts to replace the typical adversarial relationship between management and employees with a cooperative one. The key words of QWL are cooperation, trust, involvement, respect, rapport, and openness.

Work Design

█ **KEY CONCEPT:** **The goals of work design are to improve the content of the job, to provide a safe and healthy work environment, and to design a staff of fit people, an optimum work environment, and work simplification.**

The overall objectives of work design are to increase productivity and employee satisfaction. The specific objectives are to improve the content of the job, to provide a safe and healthy work environment, and to design a staff of fit people, an optimum work environment, and effective and efficient work methods.

Job content in foodservice systems is being improved through automation of the production and distribution systems. Food factories and commissary-type operations employ large-volume equipment in long, integrated production runs to prepare one specific product at a time. This system makes possible a more orderly pace and, usually, more desirable work hours.

Another approach to changing job content is to redelegate some parts of the job. A growing number of jobs are becoming encumbered with routine "busy work" that has little or no value and that could be delegated to less-skilled employees. High levels of productivity, profitability, motivation, and morale are dependent on allowing employees to do what they have been trained and paid to do. The ingredient room where foodservice employees weigh, measure, and assemble all the ingredients for each production formula is an example of this downward shift of responsibility. Such work would normally be performed by a cook, chef, or cold prep person. The use of support personnel such as dietetic technicians and assistants is another example. Delegation of this type must be done carefully. It is a complex process requiring skill in planning, organizing, and controlling. The different needs and abilities of employees must be effectively managed.

Providing a safe and healthy work environment is both economically and sociologically important. From an economic standpoint, accidents and job-related illnesses are extremely costly in terms of productivity. The Occupational Safety and Health Administration (OSHA) found that musculoskeletal disorders (MSDs) are a serious national problem that are caused by work and nonwork activities and there are workplace interventions that can reduce the problems. In 2001, OSHA developed an ergonomics program rule requiring employers to put in place an ergonomics program for any task that has caused even one certified MSD. In addition to this legislation, the safety and health of the workforce is the responsibility of its management and is discussed further in the sections that follow.

In order to improve productivity, large foodservice operations are using more sophisticated, mechanized, and computerized equipment to perform repetitive operations. Robots are delivering food to hospital patients, as well as carrying medical records and pharmaceutical supplies. The robot shown in Figure 15 moves around independently. Once its departure point and destination have been programmed in on the simple keyboard, the robot uses the building map in its memory to determine its route. Obstacles in its path are detected by sensors and a video camera. Doors and elevators can be opened and operated by radio signals from the robot.

Probably the greatest change that will be evident in the future planning of foodservice facilities is the physical arrangement of spaces and equipment to increase the productivity

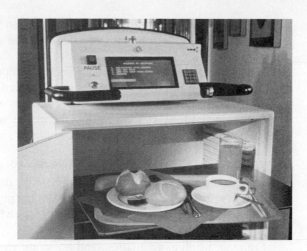

Figure 15 A robot used to deliver hospital trays.

of workers. To enable equipment and workers to combine productively requires the use of the science variously known as ergonomics, human factors, or human engineering. By using methods developed from these disciplines, tasks, equipment, and working environment can be adapted to the sensory, perceptual, mental, and physical attributes of the human worker. The employee works best when the equipment is designed for the job to be done, is geared to the employee's capabilities, and is well placed in pleasing surroundings.

To maximize productivity in foodservice, adherence to these principles of human engineering is important:

1. Design and arrangement of equipment should be such that the equipment's use requires a minimum application of human physical effort.

2. Only essential information should be provided for the equipment, and this should be presented when and where it is required with maximum clarity. It should be arranged in a step-by-step order.

3. Control devices on equipment should be easily identified, minimum in number, logical in placement, and in consonance with displays in operation. They should relate precisely to the functions they control.

4. Equipment should be designed to provide maximum productivity while utilizing the worker's physical and mental attributes most effectively. It should take into account the dimensions of the worker and his or her strengths.

5. Equipment should be selected on the basis of need in utilizing specific ingredients to prepare a selected menu, grouped in most used combinations, and arranged in order of most frequent interuse, proceeding from left to right. Those tasks demanding the greatest skill should be grouped around the worker having these skills, and worker movements to provide for his or her needs should be minimal.

6. The environment in which the foodservice worker operates should be designed and controlled to allow the worker to be most productive, comfortable, and happy on the job. This control involves consideration of lighting, facility and equipment coloration, temperature, humidity, noise, odors, facility design, floor conditions, and safety, among others.

One of the goals of human engineering is the prevention of fatigue. The manager of a foodservice may find that the fatigue of some workers, with a resultant drop in their energy, enthusiasm, and production output, is due to external factors beyond his or her control, such as irregularities in the home situation, extraordinary physical exertion away from the job, or a nutritionally inadequate food intake. However, in the organization, while the workers are on the job, there are unlimited opportunities to study causes of fatigue and possibly to correct them.

Certain psychological factors such as attitude of disinterest in and boredom with the job, dislike of the supervisor, or a low rate of pay may contribute to the fatigue and low output of some workers, but such situations often can be improved through changes in personnel policies and administration. Emphasis in this section is relative to the environmental and physical factors on the job that can affect fatigue and on performance improvement methods.

With a given set of working conditions and equipment, the amount of work done in a day depends on the ability of the worker and the speed at which that person works. The fatigue resulting from a given level of activity depends on such factors as (1) hours of work, that is, the length of the working day and the weekly working hours; (2) number, location, and length of rest periods; (3) working conditions such as lighting, heating, ventilation, and noise; and (4) the work itself.

The amount of reserve energy brought to the job varies with individuals. Some workers can maintain a fairly even tempo throughout the day, whereas others tire rather quickly and need to rest periodically to recoup nervous and physical energy. Short rest periods appropriately scheduled tend to reduce fatigue and lessen time taken by employees for personal needs.

Lighting, heating, ventilation, and noise are environmental factors that often contribute to worker fatigue. Satisfactory standards for the lighting of kitchen areas is 35 to 50 foot-candles on work surfaces with reflectance ratios of 80 for ceiling, 30 to 35 on equipment, to a minimum of 15 for floors. Temperature and humidity also influence worker productivity. A desirable climate for food preparation and service areas is around 68°F to 72°F in the winter and 74°F to 78°F in summer, with relative humidity of 40 percent to 45 percent. Higher temperatures tend to increase the heart rate and fatigue of most workers. Air conditioning in hot and humid locales is considered a necessity, whereas in some parts of the country a good fan and duct system is satisfactory to change the air every two to five minutes. Hoods over cooking equipment provide for the disposal of much heat and odor originating from these units. Noise has a disturbing and tiring effect on most people. Effective control of the intensity of noise in a foodservice area is possible through precautionary measures such as installing sound-absorbing ceiling materials, using rubber-tired mobile equipment and smooth-running motors, and training employees to work quietly.

Much has been written about the value of the study of physical facilities and the procedures followed in specific jobs. These studies are aimed at increasing efficiency in the operation of a foodservice. A thorough analysis of a floor plan, on paper or in actuality, provides a basis for decisions regarding changes needed in order to make the most compact arrangement possible, yet provide adequate equipment in an efficient arrangement. Detailed studies of activities within an organization often reveal that cost and time requirements are high because of unnecessary operations and excess motions used by the workers in the performance of their jobs. When proper adjustments are made in both the physical setup and the work procedures, the conservation of energy of the workers, increased production, and a reduction in total person-hours should result. Such studies have proved highly effective in the simplification of effort in both repetitive and nonrepetitive activities and apply either in a new situation or where long-established procedures have become accepted practices.

What has become known as work simplification began in the late 1920s. An industrial engineer, Allan H. Mogensen, developed the philosophy as a result of his work at Eastman Kodak. He found that workers were creative in thwarting his attempts to prescribe more efficient methods and, when not under surveillance, would develop more productive methods that would enhance their rewards. He reasoned that this creativity could be harnessed in a way that would enable every employee to be his or her own industrial engineer. Thus, the slogan "Work smarter, not harder" emerged.

Work simplification is more than a technique or set of how-to-do-its. It is a way of thinking or a philosophy that there is always a better way. The emphasis is on the elimination of any uneconomical use of time, equipment, materials, space, or human effort. Conservative estimates show that through an effective work simplification program, foodservice worker productivity can be increased by 20 percent to 50 percent.

Employee interest, understanding, and cooperation are essential to the successful operation of a work simplification program. Thinking through and planning before starting any task are necessary if it is to be accomplished efficiently and in the simplest manner possible. The elimination of wasted effort is easy once the worker becomes "motion conscious," learns to apply the principles that may be involved, and sees objectively the benefits of changed procedures. Such benefits can be evidenced by lessened worker fatigue, safer and better working conditions, better and more uniform quality production, and possibly higher wages through increased production. Agreeing to and understanding the objectives and realizing that benefits will be shared mutually by workers and management are factors for success. Soliciting and incorporating suggestions for job improvement methods from the workers is conducive to enthusiastic interest and participation. Usually, any employee resistance to change in established work routines can be overcome by a proper approach by management before and after the inauguration of a work simplification program. Selecting personnel with the personality to be leaders and training them for leadership in this work are of prime importance to its implementation.

Principles of Motion Economy

KEY CONCEPT: The fundamental principles of motion economy may be applied to foodservice operations in order to improve productivity.

The same principles of motion economy outlined by Ralph M. Barnes in the 1930s are valid for foodservice operations today. Analysts, supervisors, and designers need to have an understanding of these principles and the ability to interpret them to workers effectively before job breakdown studies and revisions in procedures, arrangement of work area, and equipment are inaugurated. A summary of some fundamental principles of motion economy most relevant to foodservice follows:

- Your two hands should begin and end their motions at the same time and should not be idle at the same time, except during rest periods.
- Motions of your arms should be made in opposite and symmetrical directions simultaneously.
- Hand motions should be smooth and continuous.
- Good lighting is essential for visual perception.
- The height of the worktop and chair should allow for sitting and standing wherever possible.
- A work chair should permit good posture.
- Combine tools whenever possible.
- Pre-position tools and materials, having a definite, fixed place for everything used.
- Handles and cranks should allow for maximum contact with the surface of the hand.
- Arrange work to allow for an easy, natural rhythm.
- Use drop delivery whenever possible.
- Tools, materials, and controls should be located directly in front of the worker and arranged to allow for the best sequence of motions.

Practical application of most of these principles can be made easily in the foodservice field and results in eliminating wasted motion, thereby improving productivity; increases ease of workers' tasks; reduces fatigue; and minimizes cumulative trauma such as tendonitis and carpal tunnel syndrome. A few specific examples of application follow:

- To serve food onto a plate at the counter, pick up plate with left hand and bring it to a center position while the right hand grasps the serving utensil, dips the food, and carries it to the plate, both operations ending simultaneously; when panning rolls, pick up a roll in each hand and place on the pan.
- Stir a mass of food easily and with minimum fatigue by grasping the handle of a wire whip (thumb up) and stirring in a circular motion instead of pushing the whip directly back and forth across the kettle. The principles of momentum and smooth, continuous motion of the hands are also applied in this same example, because greater force may be gained easily at the beginning of the downward and upward parts of the cycle.

- Gain and maintain speed in dipping muffin or cupcake batter through the use of rhythmic motions; use regular and rhythmic motions in slicing or chopping certain vegetables and fruits with a French knife on a board.
- When chopping vegetables into a bowl, position the cutting board on the worktop adjacent to a sink and place the bowl in the sink. Use the back of the knife blade to drop deliver the chopped vegetables into the bowl.
- Store mixer attachments and cooking utensils as close as possible to their place of use; remove clean dishes from the dishwasher directly to carts or dispensing units that fit into the serving counter; store glasses and cups in the racks in which they were washed; cook certain foods in the containers from which they will be served.
- Install water outlets above the range, tilting skillets, and steam-jacketed kettles so utensils can be filled at point of use.
- For breading foods, arrange the container of food to be breaded, flour, egg mixture, crumbs, and cooking pan in the correct sequence so that no wasted motions are made.
- Provide some means of adjusting height of work surface to the tall and short worker; include one or two adjustable-height stools in the list of kitchen equipment.
- Provide knee lever–controlled drain outlets on kitchen sinks; install electronic-eye controls on doors between the dining room and kitchen.

Tools for Assessing Productivity

KEY CONCEPT: Methods that can be used when conducting a productivity improvement study include work sampling, pathway or flow diagrams, operation and process charting, and micromotion studies.

The objective of whichever method is chosen is to gain a complete and detailed picture of the process, regardless of the method of recording.

Work sampling is a tool for fact-finding and is often less costly in time and money than a continuous study. It is based on the laws of probability that random samples reflect the same pattern of distribution as a large group. The primary use of work sampling, rather than observing the detailed activities of a repetitive task, is to measure the activities and delays of people or equipment and determine the percentage of the time they are working or idle. The shorter and intermittent observations are less tiring to both the worker and the observer than continuous time studies; several workers can be observed simultaneously; interruptions do not affect the results; and tabulations can be made quickly on data-processing equipment, although neither management nor workers may have the necessary knowledge of statistics. This process is sometimes known as random ratio-delay sampling.

A **pathway chart** or **flow diagram** is a scale drawing of an area on which the path of the worker or movement of material during a given process can be indicated and measured, but with no breakdown of time or details of the operation. The distance traveled as the worker moves about in the performance of a task is measured by computing the total length of lines drawn from one key point to another simultaneously with the worker's movements and multiplying by the scale of the drawing. A more convenient method is to set up pins or string supports at key points on a scale drawing of the worker's area and wind a measured length of string around the supports as the worker progresses from one position to another.

Operation charts can be used as simple devices to record, in sequence, the elemental movements of the hands of a worker at a given station, without consideration for time. A diagram of the work area might head the chart, with the observed activities of both hands listed in two columns—left side for left hand, and right side for right hand. In such a chart, small circles are usually used to indicate transportation and large circles to denote action. Analysis of the chart gives a basis for reducing transportation to the lowest degree possible

Work sampling

Random sampling of work to measure the activities and delays of people or equipment to determine percentage of productive time

Pathway chart/Flow diagram

A scale drawing of an area on which the path of the worker or movement of material during a given process may be indicated and measured. Also called a flow diagram

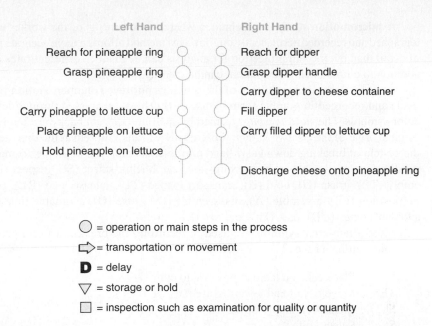

Left Hand   Right Hand

Reach for pineapple ring   ○   ○   Reach for dipper

Grasp pineapple ring   ○   ○   Grasp dipper handle

         Carry dipper to cheese container

Carry pineapple to lettuce cup   ○   ○   Fill dipper

Place pineapple on lettuce   ○   ○   Carry filled dipper to lettuce cup

Hold pineapple on lettuce   ○

         ○   Discharge cheese onto pineapple ring

Figure 16 Operation chart showing movement of the two hands in making a pineapple and cottage cheese salad.

○ = operation or main steps in the process

⇨ = transportation or movement

D = delay

▽ = storage or hold

☐ = inspection such as examination for quality or quantity

and for replanning the work area and procedures. It is important that both hands be used simultaneously and effectively. A chart showing the procedures used in making a pineapple and cottage cheese salad is given in Figure 16. The lettuce cup had been prearranged on the plate.

A simple listing of the procedures and times used in the preparation of a menu item can be made and used to improve either the physical setup or the method—for example, observing the cook mixing and portioning meat balls, beginning at the worktable. A sample procedure chart is shown in Table 1.

Table 1 A sample procedure chart.

APPROXIMATE DISTANCE (ft)	TIME (min)	DESCRIPTION OF OPERATION
6	9:00	Fasten bowl and beater in position on mixer
15	9:01	Go to refrigerator for milk, ground meat, and other weighed recipe ingredients (use cart)
15	9:035	Return to mixer
3	9:04	Place seasonings, eggs, milk, and cut-up bread in mixer bowl
	9:05	Mix slightly (observe)
	9:06	Add meat and mix to blend (observe)
3	9:075	Remove beater and take to wash sink
5	9:085	Lift bowl of meat mixture to low bench near worktable
50	9:09	Assemble portion tools and pans
	9:10	Portion onto pans with number 12 dipper
	9:25	Complete portioning

A **micromotion study** is a technique whereby movements of the worker may be photographed and recorded permanently on film. This method affords a more accurate presentation of detail than others, and projection for analysis can be made at different rates of speed. In addition, the time of each movement can be recorded.

A detailed motion breakdown of the activities portrayed on micromotion film is easily made and recorded in graphic form by use of **therbligs**, expressed through letter, line, or color symbols. The word *therblig*, formed by spelling *Gilbreth* backward but retaining the original order of the last two letters, was coined by Frank Gilbreth at the time he introduced the system of breaking down basic hand movements employed in job performance into 17 subdivisions or elements. The therbligs are search (Sh), select (St), inspect (I), transport empty (TE), grasp (G), hold (H), transport loaded (TL), release load (RL), position (P), preposition (PP), assemble (A), disassemble (DA), use (U), avoidable delay (AD), unavoidable delay (UD), plan (Pn), and rest (R).

Most often letter symbols are used in recording the breakdown of a procedure, for example, cutting a cake:

P	Place cake on table in position to cut
TE	Move right hand toward knife rack
Sh	Look over supply of knives
St	Select knife
G	Take knife in right hand
TL	Move knife to cutting position above cake
U	Cut cake

Any human activities can be analyzed by this system as a basis for eliminating unnecessary and excess motions in formulating an improved procedure.

The **chronocyclegraph** is a photographic technique designed to show motion patterns of hands performing rapid repetitive operations. It is made by attaching lights to the hands, which show as dotted lines on the finished photograph. The entire workplace must be included in order to study the relationship of the worker and direction of his or her hand movements to the work setup. Complete calculation of velocity and acceleration of hand motions is limited by the two-dimensional nature of this technique.

Applications of Productivity Improvement

Analysis of the data accumulated in the study of the work situation and the methods used in a foodservice may show that certain changes could be made immediately, whereas others involve time, money, and an educational program for the workers. No one set of rules can be used to bring about the desired improvements, but through the cooperative effort of management and worker groups, many things can be made possible. A few suggestions for improvements follow.

One of the first steps in a job improvement plan is to try to *eliminate unnecessary operations, delays, and moves* without producing deleterious effects on the product or worker. Habit plays an important part in people's work routines, and it is easy for them to continue in the old pattern; for example, even though most employees know that working with two hands is more efficient, they will continue to use one hand to hold something while the other hand does all the work. A common example of good practice is to have one person fill and deliver storeroom requisitions once a day instead of each employee going to the storeroom for single items as needed.

Operations can be combined as in the making of certain types of sandwiches when the butter could be combined with the spread mixture and applied in one operation instead of two. Other examples of simplified practice are the one-bowl method for combining ingredients for cakes, and cutting a handful of celery stalks at one time instead of one at a time.

A change in sequence of operations to make the most efficient use of time and equipment and to reduce distance is important. Instead of trying to pare and cut dry, hard squash, put it into the steamer for a short time until the hard cover softens; then it can be pared and cut quickly and easily.

The selection of multiple-use equipment reduces to a minimum the items needed. A mixer with all of the chopper, slicer, and grinder attachments might be more desirable for a given situation than the purchase of a chopper in addition to the mixer without attachments. Where and when the item will be used determines its best location. A mixer to be used in only one department should be located convenient to that center of activity, whereas a piece of equipment shared by two departments would be located between the two, but nearest and most accessible to the department requiring the heaviest and most frequent usage. Duplication of some equipment can be compensated in reduced labor hours required for certain jobs.

Equipment can be relocated or removed entirely to facilitate a more direct flow of work in any area. To reduce time-wasting "searches," a definite place should be provided for every item; in a well-regulated foodservice, everything is kept in the designated location except when in use. This storage location or prepositioning of the items should be convenient to the center of their first use; for example, the bowls, beaters, and attachments for the mixer should be stored next to or underneath the machine, and the cook's knives stored in a drawer or on a rack at the cook's table. Some kitchens may have retained a meat block, even though pan-ready meats are now used. Others may have more range space than is needed for modern cooking. In either case, the removal of certain equipment would provide space for more efficient utilization. Some kitchens may need additional equipment to provide adequate physical facilities for satisfactory operation. Most pieces of kitchen equipment are designed as labor-saving devices and can do many times the amount of work that could be accomplished by hand in a comparable time; they should be used whenever feasible.

Improvements in design and operation of kitchen equipment influence the method of operation. Automatic timing, temperature-control devices, and computer programming release the worker for other duties more than was possible when frequent checking and manual control were necessary.

The *reduction of transportation or movement of materials and equipment* often can be made through rearrangement of equipment, mobile equipment, and the use of carts to transport many items at one time. The relation of the receiving, storage, and preparation areas requires careful planning to be sure that the flow of the raw product through preparation and service is kept direct and in as condensed an area as practicable. Some delays in operation can be avoided by the installation of additional equipment; by a change in the sequence of operation, such as the assembly-line technique in pie making; by training the workers to use both hands at one time and to practice certain shortcuts in preparation; or by a better understanding of the timing standard for various processes.

The use of a different product could become a deciding factor in changing the method of procedure. The present tendency is toward the increased use of prepared foods. Peeled carrots and potatoes; hard-cooked and peeled eggs; peeled and sectioned citrus fruit, salad mixes, and frozen vegetables; basic mixes for baked products; and frozen-portioned cookie dough are only a few of the items that definitely change the preliminary procedures necessary in many food production jobs.

Considering these suggestions and other factors peculiar to the situation provides a basis for outlining an improved method that can be tried and reevaluated for further streamlining. The advantages to be gained from such a revision are indicated by comparing the summaries at the top of Figures 17 and 18.

■ **KEY CONCEPT:** **All improvement requires change, but not all change will result in improvement.**

To increase the chance that a change will result in a sustained improvement, the principles of change management, should be considered. Research has shown

PROCESS CHART

Present ☒   Proposed ☐

FILE NUMBER   Page

SUMMARY		No.	TIME ( )		
OPERATIONS	O	1,546		TASK or JOB	Dishwashing Procedure, Operations I Scraping Trays
INSPECTIONS	□	0		DEPT.	10th Floor Pantry
MOVES	⇨	99		EQUIPMENT TOOLS etc.	Scraping counter, prerinse counter with disposal unit, trash can, carts, cloth
DELAYS	D	70			
UNITS PRODUCED: 70 trays			1½ hr.	OPERATOR	Pantry Worker A
TOTAL DISTANCE MOVED				ANALYST	DATE March 20

Descriptive Notes	Activity	Dist.	Time	Analysis notes
Rinses cloth at sink.	⊗ □ ⇨ D			Damp cloth is used to wipe trays.
Carries cloth to scraping table.	O □ ⊗ D	8' 6"		
Brings loaded cart into pantry from hall.	O □ ⊗ D	5' 6"		Positions cart at left of operator. Each cart holds 6-9 trays.
Moves to side of table.	O □ ⊗ D			
Takes tray from cart and places on scraping table.	⊗ □ ⇨ D			
Moves around in front of table.	O □ ⊗ D	1' 0"		
Changes position of tray.	O □ ⇨ ⊗			Convenient position for working.
Places tray on stack of empty trays.	⊗ □ ⇨ D			
Pulls menu from tray.	⊗ □ ⇨ D			
Places name card on tray at extreme right of scraping table.	⊗ □ ⇨ D			Name cards in stacks by sections.
Picks up salt and pepper with left hand.	⊗ □ ⇨ D			
Places salt and pepper on tray with name cards.	⊗ □ ⇨ D			
Empties coffee pots into disposal.	⊗ □ ⇨ D			
Places empty coffee pots on prerinse counter.	⊗ □ ⇨ D			
Picks up plate and scrapes waste into disposal.	⊗ □ ⇨ D			
Adds plate to stack on prerinse counter.	⊗ □ ⇨ D			
Picks up creamer and empties contents into disposal.	⊗ □ ⇨ D			
Places creamer on prerinse counter.	⊗ □ ⇨ D			
Places cup and saucer on prerinse counter.	⊗ □ ⇨ D			Saucers stacked.
Removes glasses from tray and empties contents into disposal.	⊗ □ ⇨ D			
Places empty glasses upside down in wash rack on prerinse counter.	⊗ □ ⇨ D			
Picks up bowl with right hand.	⊗ □ ⇨ D			
Transfers bowl to left hand.	O □ ⊗ D			Unnecessary handling. Rubber scraper better tool.
Scrapes waste food from bowl with spoon into disposal.	⊗ □ ⇨ D			
Stacks bowls on prerinse counter.	O □ ⊗ D			

Figure 17   Process chart of tray scraping as observed in a hospital floor-service pantry.

that the most successful improvements have resulted from changes that:

1. Were innovative
2. Were tested first for a short period of time on a small-scale basis
3. Did not require additional resources
4. Resulted in simpler systems
5. Motivated participants in the change
6. Satisfied diverse and changing viewpoints

PROCESS CHART

Present ☐   Proposed ☒

SUMMARY		No.	TIME ( )	TASK or JOB	Dishwashing Procedure, Operations I Scraping Trays
OPERATIONS	○	1,024		DEPT.	10th Floor Pantry
INSPECTIONS	☐	2		EQUIPMENT TOOLS etc.	Scraping counter, prerinse counter with disposal unit, trash can, carts, pan, rubber scraper
MOVES	⇨	13			
DELAYS	D	0			
UNITS PRODUCED: 70 trays			1 hr. total	OPERATOR	Pantry Worker A
TOTAL DISTANCE MOVED			117 feet	ANALYST	DATE March 20

Descriptive Notes	Activity	Dist.	Time	Analysis notes
Rinses cloth at sink and fills pan with water.	⊗☐⇨D			Cloth is rinsed several times during operation.
Carries cloth and pan to scraping table.	○☐⊗D	7' 0"		Pan of water at counter reduces trips to sink.
Goes to silver storage unit.	○☐⊗D	4' 9"		
Gets rubber spatula from drawer.	⊗☐⇨D			
Returns and places spatula on scraping table.	○☐⊗D	5' 0"		
Brings loaded cart into pantry from hall.	○☐⊗D	5' 6"		Pre-positioned tray on scraping counter facilitates placement of name cards, and salts and peppers.
Takes tray from cart and places on scraping table.	⊗☐⇨D			
Picks up salt and pepper and places on tray at extreme right of worker.	⊗☐⇨D			
Places name-card holder with menu on same tray.	⊗☐⇨D			Menu pulled after name-card holder is on tray while hand is in position. Drops menu on table; all menus later put into trash can at one time.
Scrapes waste food from bowl with rubber scraper.	⊗☐⇨D			
Stacks bowls on prerinse counter.	⊗☐⇨D			All refuse from one tray scraped into one dish; then, into disposal.
Places silver in rack on prerinse counter.	⊗☐⇨D			
Removes glasses from tray, empties contents into disposal.	⊗☐⇨D			
Places glasses upside down in wash rack on prerinse counter.	⊗☐⇨D			
Empties coffee pot and creamer into disposal, transfers directly to dish rack.	⊗☐⇨D			Both hands used simultaneously. Movements combined or continuous wherever possible.
Removes paper tray-cover, folds once and places in trash can.	⊗☐⇨D			
Wipes off bottom of tray, places on stack then wipes off top of tray.	⊗☐⇨D			Handling of each tray reduced to a minimum.
Reaches to cart for next tray.	○☐⊗D			
Operations repeated until all trays are scraped.	○☐⊗D			

Figure 18 Process chart of same operation as shown in Figure 17 after a study and revision of the original procedures had been made. By changing the sequence of operations and moving the tray cart near the working area, the operations, moves, and delays were reduced materially.

SUMMARY

Continuous improvement of quality and quantity of products and services is essential for an organization to be successful today. It is not enough to make a one-time attack. Continuous improvement efforts are required. Performance improvement is systematically and continuously making changes to enhance the organization's desired results.

TQM is a management process and set of disciplines that are coordinated to ensure that the company consistently meets or exceeds quality standards as set by customers.

The PDCA Cycle is one continuous quality improvement model consisting of a logical sequence of four repetitive steps—Plan, Do, Check, Act.

Six Sigma is another approach to performance improvement that helps organizations focus on developing and delivering near-perfect products and services. And, Lean Six Sigma combines a focus on waste with the original Six Sigma concept.

Some TQM tools include KRAs (Key Result Areas), baseline and benchmarking measurements, brainstorming, flow charts, check sheets, cause-and-effect diagrams, Pareto charts, scatter diagrams, histograms, sociotechnical systems, statistical process control, just-in-time (JIT) inventory control, and ISO 9000.

Productivity is a measure or level of output of goods produced or services rendered in relation to input in terms of time (labor hours, minutes, or days), money spent, or other resources used.

Quality of work life (QWL) is a term that has been used to describe values that relate to the quality of human experience in the workplace. QWL is affected by a composite of factors on the job, including factors that relate to work itself, to the work environment, and to the employee personally.

The goals of work design are to improve the content of the job, to provide a safe and healthy work environment, and to design a staff of fit people, an optimum work environment, and work simplification.

The fundamental principles of motion economy may be applied to foodservice operations in order to improve productivity.

Some methods that can be used when conducting a productivity improvement study include work sampling, pathway or flow diagrams, operation and process charting, and micromotion studies.

APPLICATION OF CHAPTER CONCEPTS

The University of Wisconsin–Madison foodservice department is involved in an ongoing campus-wide performance improvement project. This project entitled, Administrative Process Redesign (APR), was initiated in response to tighter budgets, pending staff retirements, and ongoing technological changes. The overall goal is to utilize expertise from within the university to address these problems in new ways and to develop lasting solutions that satisfy their customers.

The Mission Statement for the APR project states: "The . . . project provides UN–Madison with a framework for administrative efficiency, improving how we deliver effective services to the campus community and changing how we interact with one another." Specific goals include:

- Identify key administrative processes and business practices that can be streamlined, standardized, simplified, and automated to make work more efficient and improve service delivery. Design and implement new processes and applications to ensure work standardizations.
- Develop models for staff reorganization to support the recommendations for processes and system changes based on best practices, campus needs, and data analysis.
- Engage the campus in an inclusive and transparent project so all stakeholders are involved in the recommendations for change and prepared to successfully implement the agreed-on best business practices and recommended models for improved service delivery.

Lean Six Sigma was chosen as the redesign methodology because it offered the strength and scale needed for this complicated, cross-campus process redesign. Now that the project has begun its third year, three significant challenges have presented themselves: (1) moving redesign teams from solutions to implementation, (2) choosing impactful projects while balancing limited resources, and (3) trying to move fast enough to meet the urgency. Focusing on just the first challenge, the annual report from APR stated:

> Implementing solutions takes longer than expected. Impediments to implementation among some of the . . . training teams . . . included difficulty identifying process owners in a decentralized campus environment, timidity in initiating contact with the sponsors who approved their solutions, a lack of awareness that "approval" meant permission to pursue implementation of their solutions, and an inability to get in the queue for technical resources. As a result, teams sometimes lost their momentum, adding to the delay.

To resolve these issues, teams were provided with greater support by assigning a Black Belt Six Sigma expert to each team, selected for their subject matter expertise, encouraging teams to update their sponsors at each step of the Six Sigma process improvement method (DMAIC), and receiving assurance of priority consideration for technical resources.

CRITICAL-THINKING QUESTIONS

1. What advantages does the goal of using of university expertise versus hiring outside consultants offer when making strategic decisions?
2. How does the Mission Statement relate to the initial reasons for this performance improvement project?
3. How would the use of Lean Six Sigma differ from any previous performance improvement programs?
4. If the goal of Lean Six Sigma is the total elimination of any kind of waste, what are possible areas of focus for the foodservice department?
5. From reading the case study, where on the DMAIC cycle does the last paragraph fit?
6. Go to www.valuebasedmanagement.net and click on Kaizen philosophy. What does *Kaizen* mean? What are the five founding elements of this philosophy? Does the UW–Madison APR incorporate these elements in its program?
7. Research how Kaizen differs from Six Sigma.
8. Brainstorm some possible solutions to the other two challenges facing the process teams.
9. Looking at the first goal listed, suggest some ways that the foodservice might be able to streamline, standardize, simplify, or automate their work.
10. How does the third goal comply with the principles of change management?

CHAPTER REVIEW QUESTIONS

1. Why are issues such as performance improvement, productivity, and TQM so important in today's work environment?
2. What are the goals of any performance improvement program?
3. How is performance improvement related to TQM?
4. Give some foodservice management examples of Quality Assurance measures, other than those given in the chapter.
5. What is one way of reducing variation in transformational activities within a foodservice operation that might result in performance improvement?
6. How does Six Sigma differ from the PDCA Cycle model of performance improvement?
7. What are primary goals of lean manufacturing?
8. Define productivity as it relates specifically to foodservice management.
9. Describe the quality of work life (QWL) concept. What are some key words that embody the QWL approach?
10. What are the overall objectives of work design?

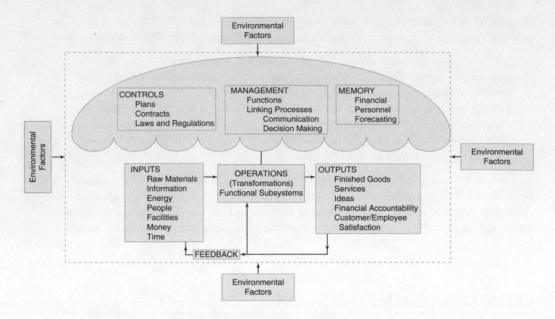

11. List and briefly discuss some environmental factors that can minimize worker fatigue.
12. List and briefly explain the principles of motion economy.

SELECTED WEB SITES

www.asfsa.org   (School Nutrition Association)

www.ceoexpress.com   (CEOExpress, the executive's Internet)

www.ers.usda.gov   (USDA Economic Research Service)

www.foodservice.com   (The first online community for the foodservice industry)

www.fsdmag.com   (*FoodService Director* magazine)

www.icongrouponline.com   (Reference publications for the twenty-first century)

www.nfsmi.org   (National Food Service Management Institute, child nutrition program)

www.osha.gov   (U.S. Department of Labor Occupational Safety and Health Administration)

www.valuebasedmanagement.net   (Value Based Management.net)

Financial Management

Serhiy Kobyakov/Shutterstock

FINANCIAL PLANNING AND ACCOUNTABILITY FOR THE

foodservice organization are major responsibilities of the manager. Cost effectiveness is essential if operations are to be successful, especially with today's economy and competitive market. Every person responsible for the financial management must know, day to day, what transactions have taken place and how they compare with established goals. Otherwise, downward trends may not be detected in time to take corrective action before financial disaster occurs.

From Chapter 17 of *Foodservice Management: Principles and Practices*, Twelfth Edition, June Payne-Palacio, Monica Theis.

In addition, other stakeholders need financial data in order to make wise decisions. For example, owners, investors, lenders, and creditors will require accurate and timely financial information in order to decide whether to build or renovate facilities, monitor current business condition, or invest money in a business.

Accounting is the tool used by managers to record financial transactions, summarize them, and then accurately report them. The branches of accounting include financial accounting, cost accounting, tax accounting, auditing, and managerial accounting. Each of these branches focuses on providing financial information for different purposes. Each is briefly summarized in this chapter. Generally Accepted Accounting Principles have been established to ensure that financial reports are more standardized, accurate, reliable, and understandable for all users. The principles of most interest to the foodservice industry are described in this chapter.

The primary purpose of this chapter is to provide basic information necessary for managers to be able to (1) maintain records of day-to-day operations, (2) prepare and use financial statements, (3) manage revenues and expenses, (4) develop accurate forecasts using financial records, (5) plan budgets, and (6) determine what kinds of corrective action can and should be taken to keep financial operations in line with preestablished goals. A thorough understanding of this basic information will help the foodservice manager make operational decisions that are in the best interests of the organization.

KEY CONCEPTS

1. Financial management is an important management function and requires knowledge of fundamental accounting techniques.

2. Careful record keeping is essential for monitoring day-to-day financial data and to serve as the foundation of financial statements.

3. The Income Statement is a summary of financial information for a defined accounting period.

4. The Balance Sheet provides information about the value of a business and how well its assets have been used to meet the financial goals of the operation.

5. Ratio analysis is widely used in the foodservice industry. Various ratios are useful for comparing present performance to a previous time period; to another company's performance; to industry averages; and/or to budgeted figures.

6. Many factors affect menu pricing, and all must be considered in order to assign financially viable menu prices.

7. An important aspect of managerial accounting is the management of costs.

8. A budget is a financial plan developed to help achieve future goals.

9. Several different types of budgets are used in organizations, including the operating, cash, and capital budgets.

ACCOUNTING FUNDAMENTALS

■ **KEY CONCEPT: Financial management is an important management function and requires knowledge of fundamental accounting techniques.**

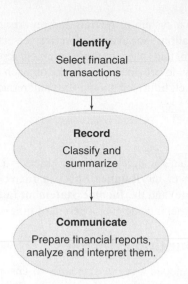

Figure 1 The accounting information system.

Identify
Select financial transactions

Record
Classify and summarize

Communicate
Prepare financial reports, analyze and interpret them.

Purpose of Accounting

Accounting may be defined as an information system that identifies, records, and communicates the economic events of an organization to interested users. Simply stated, the accountant selects financial transactions (identification); records, classifies, and summarizes these transactions (recordation); and prepares financial reports and analyzes and interprets them for users (communication) (Figure 1).

Branches of Accounting

Financial accounting is the branch of accounting that focuses on recording, summarizing, and reporting financial transactions that include **revenue** (money taken in), **expense** (the cost of everything required to operate the business), **profit** (what remains after all expenses have been paid), **assets** (items owned by the business), **liabilities** (amounts the business owes), and **owners' equity** (the difference between assets and liabilities is equal to the claim that owners have on the assets).

Cost accounting focuses on classifying, recording, and reporting business expenses.

Tax accounting deals with the accurate and timely filing of tax forms, payments, and documents required by the government. For foodservice operations this may include such government levies as income taxes, sales taxes, and payroll taxes.

Auditing is the branch of accounting that is concerned with the truthfulness and accuracy of financial reports. **Auditors** are individuals who conduct independent verification of a business's financial records. This verification is called an audit. The purpose of an audit is to point out weaknesses and/or irregularities and to prevent accounting fraud.

Managerial accounting is the branch of accounting where transactions are recorded and analyzed for the purpose of making management decisions. In order to practice managerial accounting, a person needs to be very knowledgeable about basic accounting principles and about the segment of the foodservice industry in which he or she is working.

Uniform System of Accounts

To assist managers in their financial responsibility, many specific areas of the industry have developed a **Uniform System of Accounts**. This is an agreed-upon system of accounting for that particular segment of the industry. The National Restaurant Association, for example, has developed the Uniform System of Accounts for Restaurants (USAR).

Large organizations where foodservice is but one of several departments, such as hospitals, colleges and universities, and hotels or motels, have their own accounting or finance departments. In these situations, the foodservice manager works closely with the CFO

Accounting
An information system that identifies, records, and communicates the economic events of an organization to interested users.

Financial accounting
The branch of accounting that focuses on recording, summarizing, and reporting financial transactions that include *revenue* (money taken in), *expense* (the cost of everything required to operate the business), *profit* (what remains after all expenses have been paid), *assets* (items owned by the business), *liabilities* (amounts the business owes), and *owners' equity* (the difference between assets and liabilities is equal to the claim that owners have on the assets).

Revenue
Money taken in

Expense
The cost of everything required to operate the business

Profit
What remains after all expenses have been paid

Assets
Items owned by the business

Liabilities
Amounts the business owes

Owners' equity
The difference between assets and liabilities, equal to the claim that owners have on the assets

Cost accounting
Focuses on classifying, recording, and reporting business expenses

Tax accounting
Deals with the accurate and timely filing of tax forms, payments, and documents required by the government

Auditing
The branch of accounting that is concerned with the truthfulness and accuracy of financial reports

Auditors
Individuals who conduct independent verification of a business' financial records

Managerial accounting

The branch of accounting where transactions are recorded and analyzed for the purpose of making management decisions

---

Uniform System of Accounts

An agreed-upon system of accounting for a particular segment of the industry

---

The Accounting Formula

Assets = Liabilities + Equity

Balance Sheet

A financial summary of the health of the business on a given date

---

Income Statement

A financial report that includes the revenue, expenses, and net income over a period of time

---

Generally Accepted Accounting Principles (GAAP)

A set of standards to be used when recording financial transactions

(chief financial officer) to develop a system of records and reports most suitable to the needs of the operation. In many situations, however, the foodservice manager generates his or her operating data for close control and speedier, more complete reports than may come from a central business office. They do provide good checks on each other, however, and managers of both departments are well informed about needs and requests presented in the budgeting process.

The Accounting Formula

The Accounting Formula states that for every business Assets = Liabilities + Equity. This formula forms the foundation of the **Balance Sheet** (a financial summary of the health of the business on a given date) and the **Income Statement** (a financial report that includes the revenue, expenses, and net income over a period of time).

Generally Accepted Accounting Principles

The accounting profession has developed a set of standards to ensure the accuracy and readability of financial records. **Generally Accepted Accounting Principles (GAAP)** are a set of standards to be used when recording financial transactions. Among the most critical of the standards are the following principles:

- **Distinct business entity**—a business's financial transactions must be kept completely separate from those of the owners
- **Going concern**—the assumption that the business will be ongoing indefinitely and thus, assets are recorded at the price paid for them and not at replacement value
- **Monetary unit**—financial statements must be prepared in a specific currency denomination, such as dollars in the United States
- **Time period**—the time period of the financial statements must be reported
- **Cost**—all business transactions must be recorded at their cash cost
- **Consistency**—a business must consistently use one system to record transactions. For example, in accrual accounting, revenue is recorded when it is earned. In cash accounting, revenue is recorded when it is received
- **Matching**—expenses incurred should closely match the actual revenue those expenses generated
- **Materiality**—if the value of an item is not significant, then other accounting principles may be ignored if is not practical to use them
- **Objectivity**—there must be evidence (such as sales slips, invoices, guest checks) to back up the financial transactions reported
- **Conservatism**—accountants must be conservative when reporting revenue and realistic when reporting expense and other liabilities
- **Full disclosure**—requires that footnotes on the financial statements disclose any past or future events that could affect the financial health of the business

FINANCIAL RECORDS

■ **KEY CONCEPT:** Careful record keeping is essential for monitoring day-to-day financial data and to serve as the foundation of financial statements.

Knowledge of the day-to-day financial transactions and an awareness of "where the money is going before it is gone" are ongoing responsibilities of the foodservice manager. The use of records is essential for providing readily available operating data.

Numbers, types of records, and frequency of documentation will vary depending on the type of organization. For example, a school may offer only one meal per day: a USDA lunch program, Monday through Friday, for the academic year. At the other extreme, an employee cafeteria in a high-volume industrial plant may offer service 24 hours a day, 7 days per week.

Most financial record keeping and reporting in foodservice operations are computerized. This is often a part of a comprehensive management information system that links up with other functions that influence the financial well-being of the foodservice operation. These functions include purchasing, receiving, inventory, and production. Data required for computer input are essentially the same as those for manual record keeping; forms and procedures vary. Good manual control and decisions on what information should be provided by computer are prerequisites to a good computerized control system. Designing appropriate forms for data organization is the first step in setting up either a manual or computerized system.

Records for Control

Records deemed essential for a foodservice operation include those used to collect data on the major phases of the operations. These records may be classified by function: purchasing and receiving, storage and storeroom control, production and service of food, cash transactions, operating and maintenance, and personnel. The following are some examples of records by functional category.

Purchasing and Receiving Records

> Purchase orders
> Invoices
> Receiving records
> Requisitions
> Discrepancy reports

Storage and Storeroom Records

> Requisition or storeroom issue records
> Perpetual inventory
> Physical inventory

Food Production

> Menu
> Standardized recipes
> Portion control standards
> Production schedule and leftovers report
> Forecasts and tallies

Service Records. Service records are those documents used to collect and track actual demand for eating occasions and individual menu items. The data derived from these records are referred to as volume indicators. In other words, they are used to predict the volume of business per service unit for the upcoming fiscal year. Examples of individual service unit records follow in Figures 2 to 4.

A set of records needs to be established for each service unit within an organization in order to control and monitor costs and to provide the database necessary to forecast future budgets.

Income and Expense Records. A record of daily transactions is essential for preparation of monthly financial statements. Managers must know the sources and amounts of income and where that income goes. Several records are needed to provide this information in a simplified way.

Sales and Cash Receipts. Business procedures are needed for accounting of cash received in foodservice operations. Cash registers provide a relatively safe place for money during serving hours and also provide accurate data on number of sales made and total cash

Monthly Census Report

Name of Organization _____

Date _____ Month _____ 20____ Year

Day/ Date	Regular Guest Count					Employee Meals					Special (Catering) Functions					Grand Totals	
	Break- fast	Lunch	Dinner	Totals		Break- fast	Lunch	Dinner	Totals		Break- fast	Lunch	Dinner	Totals			
				Today	To Date				Today	To Date				Today	To Date	Today	To Date
Su 1																	
Mo 2																	
Tu 3																	
——																	
Tu 31																	

Figure 2 Census record-keeping form, which is adaptable to commercial foodservice. The "To Date" figures are cumulative for the month.

MONTHLY MEAL COUNT

Hospital

Date _____ 20 ____
mo.

	Patient Meals					Personnel Meals					Patient and Personnel	
				Total Meals					Total Meals		Total Meals	
Date	Break-fast	Lunch	Dinner	Today	To Date	Break-fast	Lunch	Dinner	Today	To Date	Today	To Date
1												
2												
3												
—												
30												
31												

Figure 3 Meal count summary sheet suitable for health care facilities.

Name of Foodservice

Organization _____   Function _____
Date _____ Time _____   Arranged by _____
Room _____   Address _____
Number Guaranteed _____ Served _____   Phone No. _____
Price _____   Booked by _____ Date _____
Total Charge _____   Approved by _____

Menu	Details
	Setup
	Speaker's Table
	Flowers
	Music
	Public Address
	Tickets
	Misc.

Guarantees are not subject to change less than 24 hours in advance of party. We are prepared to serve 10% in excess of the number guaranteed.

Copies: Manager
Food Director
Catering
Maintenance
Kitchen
Accounting

Accepted _____

Union Office _____

Figure 4 Catering agreement form also serves as a record of numbers served.

```
                        Univ of Wisc Madison
                          Point-of-Sale
                    Time Period Sales/Patron Analysis
                      Report For:  Mon 05/03/99
                         CARSON'S CARRYOUT

Readers: CARSN1 CARSN# SP EVT
```

Time Period: 1 All Day	PERIOD					CUMULATIVE				
Time	Patron Count	Percent of Total	Sales	Percent of Total	Average Check	Patron Count	Percent of Total	Sales	Percent of Total	Average Check
03:30PM - 04:00PM	17	1.87	58.94	1.91	3.47	402	44.22	1283.35	41.60	3.19
04:00PM - 04:30PM	30	3.30	84.78	2.75	2.83	432	47.52	1368.13	44.35	3.17
04:30PM - 05:00PM	22	2.42	87.04	2.82	3.96	454	49.94	1455.17	47.17	3.21
05:00PM - 05:30PM	60	6.60	201.38	6.53	3.36	514	56.55	1656.55	53.70	3.22
05:30PM - 06:00PM	94	10.34	334.89	10.86	3.56	608	66.89	1991.44	64.55	3.28
06:00PM - 06:30PM	79	8.69	306.19	9.93	3.88	687	75.58	2297.63	74.48	3.34
06:30PM - 07:00PM	86	9.46	300.66	9.75	3.50	773	85.04	2598.29	84.23	3.36
07:00PM - 07:30PM	77	8.47	284.84	9.23	3.70	850	93.51	2883.13	93.46	3.39
07:30PM - 08:00PM	59	6.49	201.76	6.54	3.42	909	100.00	3084.89	100.00	3.39

Figure 5   Cash report form to be filled in by cashiers using cash registers.
Courtesy of the University of Wisconsin–Madison Division of Housing.

received. Larger organizations use cash registers of varying degrees of sophistication including electronic point-of-sale (POS) computer terminals. These produce summary printouts and proofs of cash collected, which can replace the use of the cash register record shown in Figure 5. The POS terminal can be programmed to provide as much information and detail as management desires, which can include the following:

- Number of sales
- Total sales dollars by cash, check, credit or debit card
- Tax collected
- A total customer count of those who paid by cash and a count by number of those customers who received meals other than by the cash system
- The total number of servings for each type of food, such as entrées, vegetables, desserts, salads, and beverages (menu tally)
- The dollar volume for each type of food sold
- Sales transactions by incremental day-part

The computer can also perform the following tasks:

- Print an itemized receipt for each customer
- Calculate automatically the change to be returned to the customer and print the transaction on the receipt
- Report totals and productivity by hour or shift

A record of income from sales other than cash sales and of payments made for all expense items is also essential. A *cash receipts and disbursements book* is used by bookkeepers to record these transactions. Also, they can be kept by computer. Sample forms of

Cash Receipts Record (a)

Name of Organization _____ Month _____ 20 ____

Date	Total Amount Received	Source of Income					
		Food Sales	Beverage Sales	Accounts Paid	Misc. Sales	Other	
						Source	Amount
1							
2							
3							
4							
—							
31							
Totals							

Cash Disbursements Record (b)

Name of Organization _____ Month_____ 20 ____

Date	Name of Account	Check No.	Amount Paid	Classification of Expense Accounts					
				Food	Beverages	Supplies	Utilities	Payroll	Rent
1									
2									
3									
4									
—									
31									
Totals									

Figure 6 Sample cash receipts and cash disbursements forms for financial control. Income sources and expense accounts vary with type of operation. Totals on each form are posted to the appropriate classification column.

the two parts of the cash record are shown in Figure 6. These should be filled in daily, posting the disbursement amounts from bills received and paid by check, the cash received from the cash register reports, and reports of any other cash payment received. The data and information presented here are basic for either manual or computerized record keeping.

No records, however carefully designed, are of value unless they are kept *daily*, are *accurate*, and are *used by management*.

The Income Statement

■ **KEY CONCEPT: The Income Statement is a summary of financial information for a defined accounting period.**

Financial data collected in the reports in the previous section must then be summarized in a standardized format for use by all stakeholders in the business. The Income Statement is one such summary. The Income Statement (also called a Profit and Loss Statement [P & L] or a Statement of Operations) shows whether the business made or lost money during the period being reported. For this reason it presents important information to all stakeholders

Figure 7 Sample income statement.

My Place Cafe INCOME STATEMENT for March 31, XXXX			
Food Sales		$ 60,000	
Cost of Goods Sold			
Inventory, March 1, 2010	$ 21,000		
Add: Purchases for March	25,200		
	$ 46,200		
Less: Inventory March 31, 2010	22,200		
Total Cost of Food Sold		$ 24,000	40%
Gross Profit		$ 36,000	
Labor Cost			
Salaries & Wages	$ 18,000		
Fringe benefits	2,400		
Social security taxes	900		
Total labor cost		$ 21,300	35.5%
Operating Expenses			
Office expenses	$ 1,050		
Laundry & uniforms	750		
Utilities	2,100		
Repairs & maintenance	900		
Printing & advertising	600		
General expense	1,500		
Depreciation	1,650		
Taxes	375		
Insurance	675		
Interest on notes & mortgage	900		
Total operating expense		$ 10,500	
Total labor & operating expense			$ 31,800
Net Income			$ 4,200 7.0%

of the operation. Owners can see the effectiveness of the manager they have hired. Investors and creditors are provided with an indication of whether their investment is a good one. Creditors read an income statement to determine whether to extend credit to the operation. Managers use the income statement to determine their effectiveness and ability to run a profitable operation.

An important difference between the Income Statement and the Balance Sheet is that the Income Statement represents a period of time and the Balance Sheet represents a given point in time. An Income Statement is said to be *dynamic*, whereas the Balance Sheet is *static*.

An example of an Income Statement is shown in Figure 7. The format may vary slightly depending on the specific type of operation. The USAR is a good guide for establishing the format.

Sales or revenues include the cash receipts or the funds allocated to the operation for the period of time covered by the report. The cost of food sold in a foodservice establishment is calculated using the following procedure:

Inventory at the beginning of the period	$XXX
Plus purchases made during the period	+ XXX
Equals total value of available food	= XXX
Less inventory at the end of the period	– XXX
Equals cost of goods sold during the period	$XXX

MY PLACE BISTRO
Profit and Loss Statement

SALES				
Food	$ 62,145	81.1%	$ 585,808	78.2%
Liquor	8,274	10.8%	94,388	12.6%
Beer	3,264	4.2%	37,456	5.0%
Wine	2,973	3.9%	31,463	4.2%
TOTAL SALES	76,656	100.0%	749,115	100.0%
COST OF SALES				
Food	21,440	34.5%	200,346	34.2%
Liquor	2,358	28.5%	21,520	22.8%
Beer	969	29.7%	8,989	24.0%
Wine	1,178	39.6%	11,798	37.5%
TOTAL COST OF SALES	25,945	33.8%	242,653	32.4%
GROSS PROFIT	50,711	66.2%	506,462	67.6%
CONTROLLABE EXPENSES				
Salaries & Wages	22,929	29.9%	215,745	28.8%
Employee Benefits	3,290	4.3%	32,212	4.3%
Direct Operating Expenses	6,274	8.2%	44,198	5.9%
Music & Entertainment	150	0.2%	1,498	0.2%
Marketing	1,624	2.1%	17,229	2.3%
Utilities	2,341	3.1%	22,474	3.0%
General & Administrative Expenses	2,708	3.5%	27,718	3.7%
Repairs & Maintenance	1,507	2.0%	13,484	1.8%
TOTAL CONTROLLABLE EXPENSES	40,823	53.3%	374,558	50.0%
CONTROLLABLE PROFIT	9,888	12.9%	131,904	17.6%
OCCUPANCY COSTS				
Rent	4,590	6.0%	44,947	6.0%
Property Taxes	824	1.1%	8,240	1.1%
Other Taxes	103	0.1%	1,498	0.2%
Property Insurance	600	0.8%	5,993	0.8%
TOTAL OCCUPANCY COSTS	6,117	8.5%	60,678	8.1%
INCOME BEFORE INTEREST & DEPRECIATION	3,771	4.9%	71,226	9.5%
Interest	220	0.3%	2,248	0.3%
Depreciation	1,124	1.5%	11,236	1.5%
INCOME BEFORE TAXES	$ 2,427	3.2%	57,742	7.7%

Figure 8 Income statement showing liquor, beer, and wine.

A foodservice operation that sells alcoholic beverages, as well as food, would include separate listings for sales and cost of sales for alcohol, beer, and wine on the income statement. An example of this part of an income statement for a restaurant is shown in Figure 8.

Gross profit or income is calculated by subtracting cost of goods sold from sales or revenue. The remaining expenses may be categorized as controllable or noncontrollable or, as in the example, labor costs and operating expenses. The net profit or loss is calculated by subtracting labor and other operating expenses from gross profit.

The figures for preparing this statement are taken from the cash ledger, income and disbursements, and from the beginning and ending physical inventory figures. A simple summary of the profit and loss statement is shown here:

	Income (sales)
Less:	Cost of food sold
Equals:	Gross profit
Less:	Labor, overhead, and operating costs
Equals:	Net profit or loss

Percentage ratios of the major items of expense and of the profit to the sales are included on the income statement for better interpretation of operations, because dollars and cents figures, in themselves, have little meaning here. The percentage figures are determined by dividing each expense item *by* total income, that is, the percentage of income that is spent for food, labor, other expenses, and a profit or, if expenses exceed income, a loss.

As with the daily food-cost report, a cumulative statement of profit and loss, recorded month by month, together with the budgeted figures gives comparative data for the manager's use.

If this report is to be effective, it must be completed and available as early in the month as possible. Reports coming to the foodservice manager's desk a month or six weeks after the end of the operating period have little or no control value at that late date. The amount of profit or loss should be no surprise, however, to the manager who has used the daily reports to "keep a finger on the pulse of operations."

The Balance Sheet

■ **KEY CONCEPT:** **The Balance Sheet provides information about the value of a business and how well its assets have been used to meet the financial goals of the operation.**

The Balance Sheet (Figure 9) is a listing of assets, liabilities, and capital of an operation as of a specific date. The assets are categorized as current or fixed. Current assets in-

Figure 9   Sample balance sheet.

My Place Yacht Club
BALANCE SHEET
December 31, XXXX

Assets		Liabilities & Members' Equity	
Current Assets		**Current Liabilities**	
Cash on hand & in checking	$ 7,360	Accounts payable	$ 14,290
Cash in savings	2,760	Accrued expenses	4,445
Accounts receivable	33,639	Mortgage payable, current	12,000
Inventory	2,665		$ 30,735
	$ 46,424		
Fixed Assets (Estimated value)		**Long-Term Liabilities**	
Capital improvements	$ 14,428	Mortgage payable	$ 185,025
Furniture, fixtures, and		Less current portion	12,000
equipment	25,000		$ 173,025
Clubhouse & docks	200,000		
Land	180,000		
	$ 419,428		
Other Assets		**Members' Equity**	
Prepaid expenses	$ 2,844	Capital stock	$ 23,500
Escrow account	3,000	Surplus	224,000
Membership fees	9,940	Reserves	8,975
	$ 15,784	Net income	30,401
			$ 286,876
Funded Reserves			
Building and depreciation	$ 5,000		
Dock replacement	4,000		
	$ 9,000		
		TOTAL LIABILITIES AND	
TOTAL ASSETS	$ 490,636	MEMBERS' EQUITY	$ 490,636

clude cash and other assets that will be converted to cash in a short period of time, usually a year or less. Cash includes cash on hand, cash in savings and checking accounts, electronic fund transfers from credit card companies, and CDs (certificates of deposit). Assets that will be converted to cash in a short period of time include accounts receivable, inventories, prepaid expenses, and marketable securities.

Fixed assets are permanent, such as long-term investments, buildings, furniture, fixtures, land, large and small equipment, linen, china, and glassware. Because these fixed assets lose value over time, their value is adjusted by deducting an accumulated depreciation.

Some operations may have other assets and funded reserves to be used for future improvements.

Liabilities are classified as current or long-term. Current liabilities are those that must be paid within the period of a year, such as food and supplies, taxes, salaries, wages, interest, and part of the mortgage. Long-term liabilities are those that will not be paid within the coming year. These include long-term debt, mortgages, lease obligations, and deferred income taxes.

The Capitol or Equity section of the Balance Sheet includes the portion of the business that represents the owners' interest. The ownership in for-profit businesses may be a proprietorship (owned by a single individual), a partnership (owned by two or more people), or a corporation (owned by stockholders). Retained earnings is the final entry in the equity section of the balance sheet. Retained earnings represents the profit that has not been distributed as dividends. If net losses have occurred, this number may be negative.

As shown on the sample Balance Sheet, the fundamental Accounting Formula

$$\text{ASSETS} = \text{LIABILITIES} + \text{EQUITY}$$

is always followed on the bottom line of the Balance Sheet.

Ratio Analysis

KEY CONCEPT: **Ratio analysis is widely used in the foodservice industry. Various ratios are useful for comparing present performance to a previous time period; to another company's performance; to industry averages; and/or to budgeted figures.**

Figures presented on an income statement have little meaning unless they are compared in some way. A ratio is a mathematical expression of the relationship between two numbers and may be presented as follows:

- **Common ratio:** that is, 2 to 1 or 2:1, ratio of food sales to liquor sales
- **Percentage:** that is, %, food cost as a percent of sales
- **Turnover:** that is, number of times inventory turns over in a month
- **Per Unit Basis:** for example, a per-dollar basis, that is, dollars generated per seat in a restaurant

Ratios are classified into categories depending on the question they are designed to answer:

- Liquidity—is the organization able to pay its bills when they are due?

Current Ratio = Current Assets to Current Liabilities

Quick (Acid-Test) Ratio = Cash + Accounts Receivable + Marketable
Securities to Current Liabilities

- Solvency—is the organization able to meet its long-term financial obligations?

$$\text{Solvency Ratio} = \text{Total Assets to Total Liabilities}$$

$$\text{Debt to Equity Ratio} = \text{Total Liabilities to Total Owner's Equity}$$

- Activity—how effectively is the organization using its assets?

$$\text{Food Inventory Turnover} = \frac{\text{Cost of Food Sold}}{\text{Average Food Inventory}}$$

Note: Average Inventory is $\dfrac{\text{Beginning Food Inventory} + \text{Ending Food Inventory}}{2}$

The same formula may be used to calculate the Beverage Inventory Turnover.

- Profitability—how effective is management in generating sales, controlling expenses, and providing a profit?

$$\text{Profit Margin} = \frac{\text{Net Profit}}{\text{Sales}}$$

$$\text{Return on Equity} = \frac{\text{Net Profit}}{\text{Equity}}$$

$$\text{Return on Assets} = \frac{\text{Net Profit}}{\text{Total Assets}}$$

- Operating—how successful is the organization in generating revenues and in controlling expenses?

$$\text{Sales Mix} = \text{Food Sales to Beverage Sales}$$

Catering to Vending to Cafeteria Sales

$$\text{Average Customer Check} = \frac{\text{Total Sales}}{\text{Number of Guests Served}}$$

$$\text{Seat Turnover} = \frac{\text{Covers Served}}{\text{Number of Seats}}$$

$$\text{Food cost percent} = \frac{\text{Cost of Food Sold}}{\text{Food Sales}}$$

$$\text{Labor cost percent} = \frac{\text{Cost of Labor (Salaries, Wages, Benefits)}}{\text{Total Sales}}$$

$$\text{Beverage cost percent} = \frac{\text{Cost of Beverages Sold}}{\text{Beverage Sales}}$$

$$\text{Food cost per patient or per student} = \frac{\text{Food Cost}}{\text{Number of Patients/Students Served}}$$

$$\text{Meals per labor hour} = \frac{\text{Number of Meals Served}}{\text{Number of Labor Hours Needed to Produce the Meals}}$$

$$\text{Labor minutes per meal} = \frac{\text{Minutes of Labor Time to Produce Meals}}{\text{Number of Meals Served}}$$

$$\text{Meals per full-time equivalent} = \frac{\text{Number of Meals Served}}{\text{Number of FTEs to Produce the Meals}}$$

Figure 10 shows how a ratio may be used as a benchmark. An operating ratio, labor costs per revenue, is graphed using a bar chart for the various school districts and a line graph to show the low, median, and high average percentages for three successive years.

Council of the Great City Schools

Labor Costs per Revenue

Total department labor expenses, plus benefits and taxes, plus workers' compensation costs *divided by* total revenue

Why This Measure Is Important

This measure is important because labor contributes the largest expense that foodservice revenue must cover. The expense is largely controlled by school boards because they establish salary schedules and benefit plans, and give raises. However, directors can control labor cost by implementing productivity standards and staffing formulas.

Factors That Influence This Measure

- District policies for health benefits for employees and dependents
- District policies for Retirement benefits
- Number of annual work days
- Number of annual paid holidays
- Staffing formulas
- Productivity Standards
- Salary Schedule
- Union contracts
- Type of menu items

Analysis of Data

- FY 07 = 48 districts provided reasonable responses; FY 06 = 48 districts; FY 05 = 45 districts
- FY 07: Low = 34.7%; High = 80.9%; Median = 49.0%

Figure 10 Sample of the use of ratio analysis for benchmarking purposes.
Source: Council of the Great City Schools.

Figure 10   (*Continued*)

**Performance Measurement
& Benchmarking for K12 Operations**

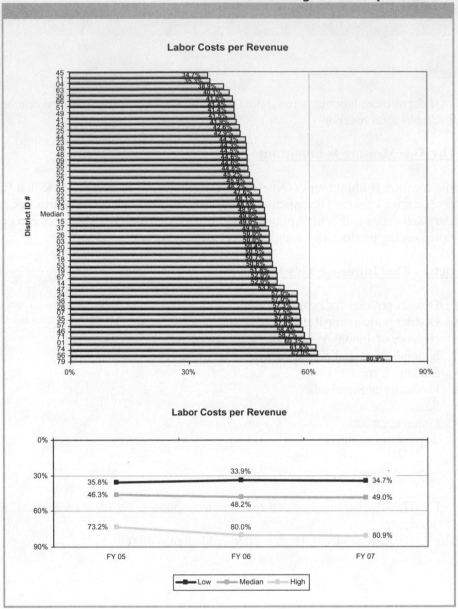

MANAGEMENT OF REVENUE AND EXPENSE

Pricing

▎ **KEY CONCEPT:** Many factors affect menu pricing, and all must be considered in order to assign financially viable menu prices.

One important responsibility of foodservice managers is to determine a sound basis for establishing the selling price for food. Haphazard methods may lead to financial disaster or the dissatisfaction of the customers. When making a purchase, customers seek good value for the price they are paying. So the manager's goal should be to establish menu prices that reflect a good price/value relationship in the minds of customers while also achieving a profit for the operation.

Some of the most common factors that influence menu pricing are:

- Local competition (an important consideration when setting menu prices)
- Level of service (as service increases, costs increase, therefore price must increase)
- Type of customer (who are the customers and what do they value?)
- Product quality (level of quality is determined by customers' desires and operational goals)
- Portion sizes (the size of portions served has a significant effect on menu price)
- Ambiance (prices may be higher if supported by product quality and ambiance)
- Meal period (diners expect to pay higher prices at dinner than at lunch)
- Location (a good location will support higher prices than a poor one)
- **Sales mix** (sales mix is the frequency with which menu items are selected by customers and may have the most influence on setting realistic menu prices)
- Food and labor costs (food and labor costs vary from area to area)
- Desired profit margin (a nonprofit operation will set prices to break even, whereas a for-profit business will determine its desired profit margin)

Sales mix
The frequency with which menu items are selected by customers

There are two basic approaches to menu pricing in wide use today: the marketing approach and the cost approach. The marketing approach seeks to align pricing with customer expectations. For example, a fine-dining restaurant, when setting entrée prices, knows that customers will pay for top quality, whereas a fast-food operation sets prices based on customers' perceived value for each dollar spent. The goal for both operations is to maximize volume and maintain a competitive position in relation to other operations in the same market.

Cost approaches to pricing take into consideration the operation's costs and profit goals. The two most commonly employed cost approaches are the food cost percentage method and the item contribution margin.

The food cost percentage method is based on the raw-food cost of menu items plus a pricing factor to give a selling price appropriate for the type of organization and the desired food cost percentage level that the foodservice wishes to maintain. The formula for determining selling price based on food cost percent is:

$$\text{Selling Price} = \text{Item Food Cost} \times \text{Pricing Factor}$$

The *raw-food cost* is found by costing the standardized recipe for each menu item. An example of a costed recipe is shown in Figure 11. Storeroom purchase records provide the price of ingredients to use in costing the recipes. Many foodservices have the costed recipes and storeroom records on computer, and they use programs to update recipe costs as ingredient prices fluctuate.

The **pricing factor** is determined by dividing the desired food cost percentage that the foodservice wishes to maintain into 100 (representing total sales or 100 percent). The resulting figure is called the *pricing* or *markup factor*. This is the figure by which the raw-food cost is multiplied to obtain a selling price. To illustrate, assume the foodservice wishes to maintain a 40 percent (of income) food cost:

Pricing Factor
Determined by dividing the desired food cost percentage that the foodservice wishes to maintain into 100 (representing total sales or 100 percent); it is then used to multiply the food cost to arrive at the menu price

$$\frac{100 \text{ (represents total sales)}}{40 \text{ (percent of income for food)}} = 2.5$$

2.5 is the pricing factor.

Cost of a portion in Figure 11 is .3498 × 2.5 = $.874, or .87, the suggested selling price.

The pricing factor cannot be used alone, however, to calculate selling price. There are many "free" items given with a meal that must be factored in—salt and pepper, condiments, sugar and cream, and jams, jellies, and sauces. These do not show up in recipe costing, but they must be accounted for.

Also, it is imperative that the foodservice manager know not only the raw-food cost of menu items but also the cost of the many hidden losses in preparation, cooking, and serving, which if not controlled add appreciably to the total food cost. Overproduction and unavoidable waste likewise add to the costs, and the wise manager analyzes these, controls

Figure 11 A costed recipe is the basis for establishing selling price.

Name of product	Quiche Lorraine	Size of Pan	12 x 20 x 2
Yield (total quantity)	2 pans	How Portioned	4 x 6: 24/pan
Size Portion	7 oz	Date Prepared	8/31/97
No. of Portions	48	Prepared by	L.L.

NUMBER OF SERVINGS: 48

INGREDIENTS	EP Weight	Measure	AP Weight	Measure	Unit Price	Cost
Flour, pastry			3 lbs 2 oz		.523/lb	$1 .6343
Salt, cooking			2 oz		.058/lb	.0072
Shortening			1 lb 12 oz		.73/lb	$1 .277
Water		2½ c				—
Onion, chopped	4.2 qt		4.5 oz		.238/lb	.0069
Milk		1 gal			2.44/gal	$2 .44
Swiss cheese, grated			2 lb		2.95/lb	$5 .90
Eggs, fresh, whole		3 doz			.68/doz	$2 .04
Mustard, dry			1/2 oz		.92/lb	.0287
Ham, ground (optional)	1 lb 4 oz				2.72/lb	$3 .40

Procedure:	Total Cost $16.7941
	Portion Cost .3498

what is possible, and considers the other when establishing selling prices. To compensate for these "unproductive and hidden costs," many foodservice managers add 10 percent (or some such standardized amount) to the recipe cost before markup. Thus, in the illustration given, the suggested selling price of 87 cents would be changed:

$$\text{Raw-food cost of } \$.3498 \times .10 = .03498$$
$$+ .3498 = \$.3848$$
$$\times 2.5 = .961, \text{ or } \$.96, \text{ a more realistic selling price.}$$

Pricing of table d'hôte and other combination menus usually found on printed menus in commercial foodservices follows the same procedure as illustrated. However, all items that are served together at one price (such as meat, potato, vegetable, salad, and beverage) are costed out, and the total raw-food cost is obtained before the pricing factor is used to calculate the selling price.

Obviously, the exact calculated price cannot be used when a fraction or an "awkward" number results. Such numbers are *rounded up* to the nearest reasonable figure; $1.87 might become $1.90 or even $2, for example.

The **item contribution margin (sometimes called item gross profit margin)** is the amount that remains after the food cost of a menu item is subtracted from the selling price of that item. This margin is, therefore, the amount that contributes to paying for labor cost and other expenses and to a profit. To calculate a menu price using the item contribution margin, the following formula is used:

Item Contribution Margin (sometimes called Item Gross Profit Margin)

The amount that remains after the food cost of a menu item is subtracted from the selling price of that item

Selling Price = Item Food Cost + Desired Item Contribution Margin

Managerial Accounting for Costs

KEY CONCEPT: An important aspect of managerial accounting is the management of costs.

Costs may be classified into several categories: fixed and variable, controllable and non-controllable, direct and indirect are just some of the major classifications. **Fixed costs** remain constant despite increases or decreases in sales volume, such as rent. **Variable costs** increase when sales volume increases and decrease when sales volume decreases; an example is food cost. **Controllable costs** are those costs over which a manager has control, whereas **noncontrollable costs** are those that a manager cannot control. **Direct costs** are those that are easily attributed to a specific area of an operation. **Indirect costs (also called overhead)** are not easily attributable to a specific area. The remainder of this section focuses on variable and controllable costs.

A critical step in achieving a good financial position involves the manager making follow-up decisions and taking actions after review of the records and reports. If operations are in line with the budget plan, no action is indicated. If, however, costs are excessively high and profits not as predicted, or volume indicators are lower than anticipated, a review of the many factors involved in cost control is necessary. There are, however, many alternatives to consider before risking customer satisfaction by raising prices or discontinuing valued services. These actions may be required eventually, but not as a first approach.

Managers search for causes of deviations from the expected by reviewing the many factors that have a bearing on costs. These include every activity in the department. A brief review of some of these factors is provided here. Table 1 summarizes some of the key questions that the manager should consider when analyzing budget deviations.

Fixed costs
Costs that remain constant despite increases or decreases in sales volume

Variable costs
Costs that increase when sales volume increases and decrease when sales volume decreases, such as food cost.

Controllable costs
Those costs over which a manager has control

Noncontrollable costs
Costs that a manager cannot control

Direct costs
Costs that are easily attributed to a specific area of an operation

Indirect costs (also called overhead)
Costs that are not easily attributable to a specific area

Table 1   Some factors to consider when analyzing budget deviations.

FACTOR	KEY ANALYTICAL QUESTIONS
Food costs	
Menus, menu costing, selling price	1. How many choices are offered? 2. What are the food and labor costs of each menu item? 3. Which items are most profitable? 4. How many of each item are sold? 5. Could menu items be better merchandised?
Purchasing	1. Are appropriate specifications used? 2. Has prime vending or group purchasing been considered? 3. Has buyer kept current with market trends and conditions?
Receiving	1. Are deliveries checked against the purchase order? 2. Are qualities and quantities verified with specifications?
Storage	1. How does current turnover rate compare with previous calculations? 2. Is there opportunity for theft? 3. Are storeroom requisitions controlled? 4. Are store areas properly arranged to minimize spoilage? 5. Are proper temperatures maintained in all storage units?
Food production	1. Are standardized recipes available and used? 2. Has establishing a central ingredient assembly been considered? 3. Is production equipment adequate and well maintained? 4. Are forecasts accurate and followed by production staff?

(continued)

Table 1 (*Continued*)

FACTOR	KEY ANALYTICAL QUESTIONS
Portion size	1. Have portion sizes been established for each menu item? 2. Are employees aware of the portion sizes, and have they been trained in portion control? 3. Are appropriate and adequate portioning utensils available for employee use?
Employee meals	1. Have the costs of employee meals been calculated? 2. Are proper accounting methods used to justify these costs?
Labor costs	
Type and extent of service offered	1. Can more self-service opportunities be offered without sacrificing customer satisfaction?
Hours of service	1. Is there enough customer volume to justify current hours of service? 2. What merchandising techniques can be implemented to stimulate sales during slack times? 3. Are there tasks done at peak times that could be transferred to slack times?
Physical plant	1. Is equipment arranged logically to minimize human energy expenditure? 2. Are carts available and are size and number adequate to minimize trips to storage areas? 3. Does sharing equipment delay production?
Personnel policies and productivity	1. Have production standards been determined and communicated to the employee? 2. Are employees properly trained and supervised to ensure that productivity standards are met? 3. Can overtime expenditures be justified?
Supervision	1. Are supervisors monitoring departmental activities? 2. Do supervisors recognize key productivity times and take action to ensure that standards are met? 3. Does supervisor know how to allocate resources on a day-by-day basis to keep within budgetary guidelines?
Operating and other expenses	
Maintenance and repair	1. Is a preventative maintenance system defined and used? 2. Can repair costs be justified compared to equipment replacement? 3. Are employees trained to report broken equipment?
Breakage	1. Are records of china and glass breakage kept and summarized periodically to monitor changes in amounts broken? 2. Are employees aware of costs? 3. Are proper handling techniques used to minimize breakage?
Supplies	1. Do employees have access to supplies? 2. Are procedures for use of chemicals established to minimize waste?
Energy and utility costs	1. Does preventative maintenance include energy efficiency check? 2. Is equipment used properly to minimize energy utilization?

Purchasing.   Purchasing methods and procedures should be reviewed as part of the cost control process.

The market is ever changing, and the buyer must keep abreast of new developments and learn what best suits the needs of the foodservice and at the most advantageous price. Specifications may need to be changed from time to time according to market trends. Certain costs are controlled through wise purchasing by an informed, capable buyer who is alert to ever-changing market conditions and has knowledge of new products as they become available.

Receiving.   Losses may easily occur at the point of receiving goods if management is negligent about checking in orders as they are received. This task may be entrusted to an assistant, but should be done by someone with managerial authority.

Storage and Storeroom Control.   Protection of the company's large investment of money in the food after it is purchased and received contributes greatly to overall cost control. It has been said that one should buy only the amount that can be used at once or stored adequately. Furthermore, one should store only what is essential for limited periods of time because unnecessarily large inventories tend to increase the possibility of loss through spoilage, waste, or theft, in addition to tying up money unnecessarily.

The value of the inventory can be monitored by calculating the turnover rate, which is a measure of how many times storeroom goods are used and replenished during a specified time period. (See the Inventory Turnover formula in the ratio section of this chapter.) A turnover of three to five times a month is fairly average for many foodservices, although this varies considerably. A small fast-food restaurant in a large city may have a higher turnover of inventory, because foods are used quickly and deliveries can be made frequently. In contrast, a large university that is located in a somewhat geographically isolated area may keep a large inventory of staple items to carry it through a school year, and so the inventory turnover would be lower.

If the turnover rate is excessively high, it may indicate a shortage of funds to purchase in sufficient quantities, and purchases are made in small amounts that are used almost at once. This is an expensive method. It may also limit the foodservice's credit rating and ability to buy competitively.

If the turnover rate is low, too much stock may be remaining on the storeroom shelves too long, or many items may be left unused. Managers should check the inventory from time to time and include on the menu those items that need to be "moved" before they deteriorate and result in waste.

Food Production: Preparation, Cooking, and Leftovers Control.   Foodservice managers are well aware of the many costs and potential losses that can occur in the production of food for service. Foodservice workers, although well trained, need continuous supervision to ensure that standardized recipes are used properly, and equipment is operated appropriately to minimize preparation losses.

Reducing the amount of leftover prepared foods is another step that can be taken toward cost containment. The manager's ability to forecast accurately the number of portions that are used or sold is critical and should not be based on guesswork or left to the cooks to decide how much to prepare. Rather, the use of records to show *amounts prepared, amounts sold or used*, and *amounts left* gives a realistic basis for forecasting quantities required the next time an item is served.

Portion Size and Serving Wastes.   An established portion size is part of the standardized recipe and is one basis for costing and setting the selling price. The size of a portion or serving to be offered to the consumer is a management decision and must be communicated in writing to the employees.

One means of ensuring standardized portions is to know size and yield of all pans, measures, ladles, and other small equipment used in the serving. For example, if one gallon of soup is to yield 16 one-cup servings, accurate measurements must be made of both the original quantity and the amount taken up in the ladle. A one-cup ladle should be provided for the server's use, not a three-quarter cup or some other size, to obtain the standard portion. Other appropriate-size serving equipment should be used for other food items.

Employees' Meals. Sometimes employees are given a discount on their meals or are charged at-cost prices rather than the usual marked-up selling price. The value of food consumed by employees should be of real concern to management in attempting to better control both food and labor costs. The philosophy of management regarding employees' meals—to charge for them or not—varies with the individual institution. Managers should question the present policy in view of overall cost control. If meals are provided, their value must be determined for use in the financial statement.

Meals provided as part of employees' compensation should be handled as a labor cost, not food cost, in the profit and loss statement. A cost determination of the value of the meals is made by management, and the total of all employees' meals is deducted from the "cost of food sold" and added to "labor" as an employee benefit to reflect their true place in financial accounting.

Labor Cost Control. Labor costs represent a major component of the total foodservice expense in most organizations today. Until recent years, food was first in importance, and labor was second. Together, food and labor made up around 75 percent of the total expense. With ever-increasing wage rates and employee benefits, it now is estimated that labor constitutes 50 percent to 70 percent of the total, as an overall average.

However, there are so many variables in each situation that even "averages" have little meaning. Restaurants with full table service in luxurious surroundings and French-style service have quite a different labor cost than a serve-yourself buffet operation. In the first case, the income per meal may be $30; in the second, $3.95. The labor cost may be 50 percent in each case—$15 for labor in the luxury restaurant and $1.98 in the self-service establishment—but each shows the same *percentage* of income spent for labor. Dollar figures need to be closely monitored in any evaluation, and managers should not rely on percentages only.

Production employees can prepare more servings of most menu items with little extra time expenditure; supervisors can handle a somewhat larger volume of trade during their time on duty; and probably no additional office help would be required as the volume of business increases. Good managers should be able to determine when additional labor is required to handle increased volume. Generally speaking, the greater the volume of business, the greater the returns on labor dollars spent. Labor costs are less controllable than food costs, and their percentage of payroll costs to sales fluctuates with sales. It is impractical, if not impossible, to change the number of employees day by day in proportion to the number of customers, patients, or students, as one might change the menu to meet fluctuating needs. Therefore, it is necessary to consider ways to get full returns from the payroll dollar. Several ratios shown in the ratio analysis section of this chapter may be used to evaluate labor costs: meals/labor hour, meals/FTE, labor minutes/meal.

Type of Foodservice System. Foodservice organizations faced with excessively high labor costs might investigate the feasibility of converting to another system that requires less labor. Or, if a complete conversion is not possible, consideration could be given to the use of more prepared frozen food items, thus reducing labor time and cost for food production.

Type and Extent of Services Offered. The extent of service offered within the organization affects total labor costs. In cafeterias, for example, the patrons may carry their own trays and bus their own soiled dishes, or if table service is used, the ratio of servers to guests varies as does the cost of labor. If the menu and service are simple, one server is able to serve many guests. When the formality of dining calls for personalized service and several echelons of dining room employees from the maître d' to the head waitperson, server, wine steward, coffee server, and bus person, we can easily understand the high cost of labor in such establishments.

Hours of Service. The hours of service determine the number of "shifts" of personnel as well as the total number of labor hours required to accomplish the work. The hospital cafeteria that is open 7 days a week and serves four or five meals daily—breakfast, lunch, dinner, night supper, and 3 A.M. lunch for the night workers—demands a larger complement

Name of Foodservice					
Date ____ AM	Number of Customers	Amount of Sales	Average Sales	Labor Hours	Labor Cost
7:00–7:15					
7:16–7:30					
7:31–7:45					
(etc.)					

Figure 12 Records of census and sales by time segments give managers data helpful for evaluating and scheduling personnel.

of employees than does the school lunchroom that serves only one meal per day for 5 days. The restaurant that is open 24 hours a day, 7 days a week, uses a different labor schedule than the one that is open for business 10 to 12 hours a day, 6 days a week. Each situation has a different labor-cost expense.

Records of patronage and sales by 15-minute time segments throughout the serving period provide valuable data for management when evaluating labor needs and scheduling. Electronic or computer POS cash registers provide such data; small foodservices use a simple form such as that shown in Figure 12 for posting such data.

Physical Plant: Size and Equipment Arrangement. An efficient kitchen arrangement and a convenient location are positive factors in labor-cost control. The foodservice manager may not be the one responsible for the kitchen plan, but if he or she "inherited" one that is poorly arranged, some changes may be necessary. Work flow and productivity analysis provide information to determine whether changes are needed.

Menu and Form of Food Purchased. Many questions can be asked about the menu and form of food purchased as they affect overall labor costs. The number of menu choices offered, the complexity of preparation involved, the labor time and cost required, and the number of dishes to be washed, resulting from the menu items served, are only a few costs. Studies to determine the exact labor time and cost involved in preparing foods from the raw state versus the food and labor costs of using convenience foods give a preliminary basis for decisions on which form of food to buy.

Personnel Policies and Productivity. Labor is a commodity that cannot be purchased on short notice. The careful selection and placement of workers are basic to reducing turnover and its inherent costs. A study of overall personnel policies, including wage scales and employee benefits, can give managers possible clues to remedy excessive labor costs. However, the most important aspect of labor cost is probably employee productivity. Ineffective management is the single greatest cause of declining, or poor, productivity. Good supervision is vital to holding labor costs in line.

Supervision. Supervision is a major factor in the labor-cost picture. The effects of good or bad supervision cannot be underestimated when evaluating total labor cost. Good supervision ensures adherence to established policies and rigid control of work schedules and standards, and it influences employee morale; productivity is high, and management receives fair returns on the labor dollar invested.

Too often, however, administration views supervision costs as excessive and attempts to cut labor costs by replacing competent, well-trained supervisors with inexperienced, immature ones. Sometimes an experienced but unqualified person is promoted from the ranks to assume supervisory duties at a relatively low cost. Rarely does such replacement prove satisfactory. Neither the inexperienced nor the experienced untrained worker is able to see the full view of the foodservice operation. Usually the costs begin to rise until any slight saving entailed in the employment of an untrained director is absorbed many times over. Money spent for efficient supervision brings high returns in economic value to the organization. There is no substitute for good supervision.

Operating and Other Expenses. Control should not end with consideration of food and labor costs only; 12 percent to 18 percent of the departmental budget will probably be used for other items classified as overhead and operating expenses. These include utilities, laundry and linen supplies, repairs, replacement and maintenance, telephone, printing, paper goods, office supplies and cleaning materials, depreciation, rent or amortization, and insurance and taxes.

In addition, there is a real concern for conservation of energy resources within all foodservice establishments. Not only does conservation meet a national need, but it also helps to reduce departmental operating costs.

Maintenance and Repair. A planned maintenance program with the services of a maintenance engineer helps prevent breakdowns, extends the life of the equipment, and is usually a cost-effective procedure.

Breakage. Excessive breakage quickly adds to operating costs. Procedures should be in place to document breakage, and employees should be well trained on materials handling to prevent excess breakage.

Supplies. Supplies include linens, paper goods, cleaning compounds, dishwasher detergents, office supplies, and similar items. Although these items may be considered small in relation to other costs, any waste is costly. Accurate accounting of these items helps control costs.

Energy and Utility Costs. The energy "squeeze" of the 1970s made most foodservice managers and equipment manufacturers well aware of the need for conservation. New equipment designs are energy efficient, and managers continue to seek ways to conserve and to reduce utility bills.

Food Costs. Food is the most readily controlled item of expenditure and the one subject to greatest fluctuation in the foodservice budget. If control of food costs is to be effective, efficient methods must be employed in planning the menu, purchasing, storing, preparing, and serving. The expenditures for food vary greatly from one type of institution to another and often for institutions of the same type because of the form of food purchased, the amount of on-premise preparation, geographic location, and delivery costs.

In spite of the variation in the amounts spent for food, the underlying bases of food-cost control are the same for all types of foodservices. The effectiveness of control is determined by the menu; menu costing and establishment of the selling price; the purchasing, receiving, storage, and storeroom control procedures; methods used in the production of food, including pre-preparation, cooking, and use of leftovers; and portion size.

Menus. Menu planning is the first and, perhaps, the most important step in the control of food costs. The menu determines what and how many foods must be purchased and prepared. Knowledge of these food costs, as well as labor cost and intensity, and the *precosting* of the menu to determine whether or not it is within budgetary limitations are essential for control procedures.

Menus that provide extensive choices require preparation of many kinds of foods, several of which may not be sold in quantities sufficient to pay for their preparation. If a widely diversified selection is offered, the investment of too large a sum in food or labor for its preparation can result. Also, it may result in carrying an extensive inventory of small quantities of food items, or of foods infrequently used.

Foodservice managers should remember also that although menus are made some days or even weeks in advance, they can be adjusted daily to the inventory of food on hand and to local market conditions. Waste can be prevented only by wise utilization of available supplies, which helps to keep food costs under control.

ACCOUNTING INFORMATION FOR PLANNING

> ■ KEY CONCEPT: A budget is a financial plan developed to help achieve future goals.

Just as the Income Statement informs a manager about *past* performance, the Budget is developed to help achieve *future* performance. The Budget tells the manager what must be done to attain desired profit and cost objectives.

The financial goals of various foodservices differ. Some operations are in business to make as large a profit as possible; others are nonprofit but seek to provide the best possible food and service that their available resources allow. In all situations, having some type of financial plan (budget) in place is the key to achieving desired departmental goals. Without such a guide, problems may arise before management is aware of them and could lead to financial downfall.

Budgeting

A **budget** is based on factual data from past records of income, resource expenditures, and business volume. Consideration for any anticipated changes that may affect future operations is also essential for budget development.

Budget
A financial plan developed to help achieve future goals

The Systems Model

For any foodservice that is just beginning operation, a detailed budget based on historical data will not be possible. Because the service has not operated previously, no records of past operations are available on which to base a plan. In these situations, management cannot use past trends as the basis for the budget but must rely instead on a combination of known facts. For example, the manager of a restaurant may rely on industry-wide data for similar operations. There are also standard financial formulas for the food and hospitality industry that may be used to determine anticipated revenue and costs. These are available through trade associations such as the National Restaurant Association.

With the current emphasis on cost containment and better management of all resources, it is important that foodservice managers understand the budget planning process and the techniques used to prepare a realistic budget. Too many managers operate without a budget as a guide because it is time-consuming to prepare, predictions are difficult, and incomplete records fail to provide the necessary data. The value of a budget and the budgeting process must be clearly understood and accepted by management; otherwise, if one is planned, it may be an empty gesture, not used for its intended purpose.

Value of a Budget. To some, the word *budget* has the connotation of curtailed spending and inflexibility and, therefore, is undesirable. In reality, a budget is a valuable management tool that can and should serve as a guide for allocation of resources and for comparison with actual operations—the basis for financial control.

The advantages of budget planning and development are many, far outweighing any potential disadvantages. Consider these advantages:

1. Budget planning forces management to seriously consider the future directions and development of their department and to reaffirm old or establish new financial goals.

All those with decision-making authority in the department should be involved in the budget planning process.

2. The budget planning committee's review of previous expenditures provides an evaluation process and a base for justifying future requests for funds.

3. A budget is an important control device because it documents goals and objectives in a quantified manner. It gives a standard for comparison against actual transactions. Deviations from the anticipated (budgeted) income and expenditures are evident and can be corrected or justified as they occur.

4. Because persons involved in planning establish the priorities of need, they are more likely to be committed to staying within the limits they were responsible for setting.

5. A budget establishes goals for profit and revenue.

6. A budget provides for continuity in the event of management turnover.

7. A budget documents plans for anticipated changes due to inflation, increases in the cost of living, and other economic indicators.

8. The budget serves as a communication tool for management.

Disadvantages of the budget process are minor compared with the positive results of having a budget for a guide. Such disadvantages include the following:

1. A budget that is rigid is often ignored as unworkable. Budgets should be flexible and adjustable according to changing situations.

2. Budget preparation is tedious, requires time, and takes personnel away from other management activities.

3. Unless the entire managerial staff is in support of budgeting and cooperates in the preparation and use of the budget, the process may become merely a gesture and have limited value.

4. Departments within the organization may vie with each other for funds, which could cause undesirable competition and interdepartmental friction.

5. For implementation purposes, budgets must be planned far in advance of actual activities. Unanticipated changes in the economy or the organization itself may alter all budget predictions.

KEY CONCEPT: Several different types of budgets are used in organizations, including the operating, cash, and capital budgets.

Although there are many types of budgets, all have the same intent: to determine how much money (or other resources) is available and at what rate it is to be spent. It is then the manager's responsibility to allocate that amount to cover various expenses plus allow for a margin of profit when appropriate.

The following are descriptions of some types of budgets commonly used by foodservice managers.

Master Budgets. The *master budget* coordinates every aspect of the operation. The master budget in practice is actually a compilation of several small budgets. Composition will vary among organizations, but the master budget will minimally include the operating and capital budgets. Other potential items are cash, sales, and labor, which may be separated out from the operating budget.

Operating Budget. The *operating budget* is a plan that minimally includes revenues and expenses. It is a forecast of revenue (sales), expenses, and profit for a specified period of time or *fiscal year*. The operating budget serves as the guide for day-to-day operations of the department and is an important component of the control process as it is used for financial decision-making. The operating budget includes the *statistics budget*, which is an estimate of the volume of sales in commercial operations or services in noncommercial operations.

Budget figures are based on historical data from records of past performance. Categories of performance differ between commercial and noncommercial operations. For example, commercial operations use number of sales and covers as the primary indicators of performance, whereas noncommercial operations use a number of other indicators such

Revenues	
Cafeteria sales	$126,000
Vending	42,000
Catering	63,000
Total revenue	$231,000
Expenses	
Food	$215,000
Labor	221,000
Cleaning supplies	3,300
Silverware and china	3,500
Paper supplies	9,600
Kitchen utensils and non-capital equipment	1,000
Maintenance contracts	100
Equipment rental	1,000
Uniforms	800
Office supplies	1,100
Photocopying	125
Postage	90
Print shop	1,000
Instructional materials	100
Travel and registrations	1,500
Total expenses	$459,215

Figure 13 Sample operating budget with fixed dollar values: Department of Food and Nutrition Services operating budget.

as resident census in long-term care facilities, meal participation in schools, and meal equivalents per patient day in hospitals. These groups of performance data are sometimes referred to as *volume indicators* and provide the basis for future projections of activity and costs. All operations monitor historical data on expenses including food, supplies, labor, energy, and overhead expenses. These expense budgets are included in the operating budget along with the *revenue budget*, which is a projection of the expected or anticipated income for the financial time period (Figure 13).

Cash Budgets. A *cash budget* is developed to project the receipt of revenue and the expenditure of funds. The purpose of this budget is to determine if funds will be available when needed in order to meet the financial obligations or demands of the operation. The cash budget is an illustration of the inflow and outflow of cash, thereby identifying the amount of cash on hand at any given time.

Capital Budgets. A *capital budget* is a long-term plan prepared to estimate or predict the costs of capital outlays or expenditures and their financing. Examples of capital expenditures include equipment replacement, renovation projects, and facility expansion. Items addressed in the capital budget are often defined by a dollar value. For example, an organization may define capital as any items valued at or more than $1,500.

Various methods of establishing line item amounts within individual budgets are used by organizations. The following is a summary of three common methods: fixed, flexible, and zero-based.

1. **Fixed:** A fixed budget is a set dollar amount based on a set, predetermined level of activity or transactions. It is generally based on past activity indicators such as sales and costs with some consideration for future change. Fixed budgets can be quite rigid but are common, especially in publicly held institutions where funding is tight and there are limited or no opportunities to generate revenue. The operating budget in Figure 12 is an example of the fixed dollar concept.
2. **Flexible:** A flexible budget, as opposed to a fixed budget, gives a dollar range for low to high levels of predicted activity. This type of operating budget is developed to reflect the variability in performance activities as expressed in volume indicators. For example, if volume of business goes up in a cafeteria, then the manager has the flexibility to spend more

on resources needed to accommodate the higher demand. It is more flexible compared with the fixed budget but more difficult to use as a control tool.

3. **Zero-based:** The *zero-based budget* (ZBB) is newly developed each fiscal year starting with a "blank piece of paper." This approach requires that the manager prepare a budget for each activity of the department, thereby forcing the manager to evaluate all activities each year and justify every request for funds. Zero-based budgets are commonly used for capital requests such as equipment and renovation projects.

Steps in Budget Planning

As mentioned, budgets are time-consuming to prepare and require thought-provoking effort on the part of all who are involved. A timetable is generally set up for the various phases of planning, implementation, control, and evaluation. The schedule must allow ample time for careful completion of the budget process so it can be evaluated and approved well in advance of the beginning of the next fiscal period. Budget planning as a joint endeavor represents many points of view. Final agreement by participants should ensure a fair allocation of funds relative to the mission of the organization.

The budget planning process includes several distinct phases; each one derives information from the one before:

- The *evaluation phase* dissects an operation's past performance and identifies those factors that are likely to influence future activities.
- The *preparation* or *planning phase* uses information from the evaluation phase to forecast and prepare the first draft of the budget.
- The *justification phase* is a time of review, revision, and final approval. This process involves persons in organizational administration, such as the CFO, who have the authority to allocate funds.
- The *implementation* or *execution phase* translates the budget expenditures into the operation functions.
- The *control phase* is an ongoing monitoring process to ensure that operations stay in line with budgeted predictions.

More specifically, the following steps are usually included in planning the foodservice budget:

1. Collect operating data from records and reports. (See previous section in this chapter.)
2. Study these data and evaluate them against departmental goals. Information reviewed should cover actual operating and budget variance figures from the previous three or four years with justification or explanation of variances; income and expense trends; sales reports and statistics; menus, prices, customer selection, portion sizes, and food cost per portion; and labor statistics such as the number of employees, their duties, schedules, and wage rates.
3. Analyze and discuss any factors that can affect future operations. These include both external (outside the organization) and internal (within the organization) influences that can be identified as having a possible effect on foodservice costs or activities in the future. Examples of *external* factors are the local economy, actions by government (change in taxes or laws), changes in utility costs, new construction that might bring in new business or divert traffic and so reduce patronage, or increases in competition. Examples of *internal* factors are a planned addition to the facility that will change the number of persons to be served; a change in type of foodservice system such as going from conventional to assembly/serve; converting to computerized record keeping; or change in hours of service to better accommodate patrons.
4. Discuss and plan for new goals or activities desired, such as a remodeling project, purchasing new equipment, or a new service (such as catering) to be offered.
5. Set priorities and make decisions on what can be included in the budget for next year. In establishing budgetary priorities, the manager must weigh the relative value of a funding request against the contribution that the request makes toward the mission of the organization. For example, a manager in a school may need to justify how a new refrigerator at $30,000 will make a contribution to the educational goals for the district's children.

6. Write the budget for presentation. Although there is no established format for the formal write-up of the budget, it contains an organized listing of expected income, classified according to sources, and the categorized list of all expense items. Usually a form similar to the one shown in Figure 14 is used as a work sheet to organize data in the budget. Writing the budget follows these steps:

   a. List all sources of expected income. Figure 15 illustrates those for a college residence hall where income comes from student board fees. Commercial operations derive income from cash sales. Record this year's dollar figures for each of the sources of income and then the anticipated changes for the next budget period. Calculate and record the total expected income.

   b. Classify and list the items of expense with the cost calculated for each. Basically, these are food, labor, overhead (for example, fixed costs such as amortization or rent, taxes, and insurance), and operating costs (for example, utilities, telephone, and supplies).

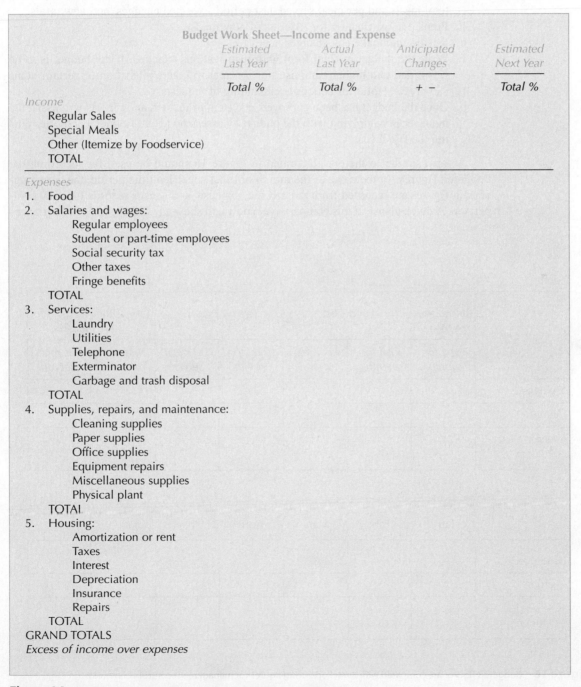

Budget Work Sheet—Income and Expense

	Estimated Last Year	Actual Last Year	Anticipated Changes	Estimated Next Year
	Total %	Total %	+ −	Total %
Income				
Regular Sales				
Special Meals				
Other (Itemize by Foodservice)				
TOTAL				
Expenses				
1. Food				
2. Salaries and wages:				
Regular employees				
Student or part-time employees				
Social security tax				
Other taxes				
Fringe benefits				
TOTAL				
3. Services:				
Laundry				
Utilities				
Telephone				
Exterminator				
Garbage and trash disposal				
TOTAL				
4. Supplies, repairs, and maintenance:				
Cleaning supplies				
Paper supplies				
Office supplies				
Equipment repairs				
Miscellaneous supplies				
Physical plant				
TOTAL				
5. Housing:				
Amortization or rent				
Taxes				
Interest				
Depreciation				
Insurance				
Repairs				
TOTAL				
GRAND TOTALS				
Excess of income over expenses				

Figure 14 Budget planning work sheet, adaptable for use in any foodservice.

Figure 15 Income sources planning form.

Sources of Income	Income Past Period	Anticipated Increase	Anticipated Decrease	Anticipated Income
Board fees				
Cafeteria receipts				
Guest meals				
Special meals				
Catering				
Special food orders				
Miscellaneous				
Total				

c. Add other pertinent data, such as number of meals served, labor hours for both total meals and per meal served, last period, expected changes, and new totals.

d. Prepare a justification for requests of new funds.

e. Review and make any changes necessary.

f. Write the budget in final form with justifications attached. If the budget is to be forwarded to a higher administrator for approval, an explanation of certain items can prove helpful for better understanding of requests.

g. Once the budget has been approved, a system of records and reports will assist the manager in complying with the budget by assessing actual financial activities during the fiscal year.

A form similar to the one illustrated in Figure 16 should be used for recording the budgeted figures. At the close of the month or other specified time period, the actual operating figures are recorded from the income, expense, and census records for easy comparison. A quick glance at this comparative report will show any discrepancies or variances

Name of Food Service

Month _____, 20 _____

	Number of Meals	Food Cost		Payroll Expense		Other Costs and Expenses	
	Total for month	Total for month	Per meal served	Total for month	Per meal served	Total for month	Per meal served
Budgeted							
Actual							
Over + – Under							

Cumulative for Year to Date

	Jan.	Feb.	Mar.	April	May	June	etc.
Budgeted							
Actual							
Over + – Under							

Figure 16 Budgeted figures are compared with actual operating figures for management control of finances.

between anticipated and actual business. Any deviation—positive or negative—should be analyzed to determine the reasons for the deviation and to plan corrective action. The data on the comparative form should be used in connection with information from the daily food cost report and income statements to evaluate activities and decide what actions to take.

SUMMARY

Good financial management is essential for the success of every foodservice operation. Financial planning and accountability are the responsibility of the foodservice manager. A basic understanding of accounting and financial management concepts is necessary to analyze the financial performance of the foodservice department and to make appropriate decisions for allocation of available resources. Managers must have knowledge of the techniques used to control costs and to provide data for sound financial decision making. The following four actions are basic to achieving financial credibility on the part of the manager and, when followed, should provide a guide to achieving the desired success:

1. Knowing what is being accomplished through a system of records that provides pertinent data on current operations
2. Using the data from the records to evaluate progress that has been made toward reaching set goals
3. Taking corrective actions as necessary to bring operations in line with financial objectives
4. Setting financial goals and objectives to be attained, usually through a planned budget

The foodservice manager must recognize that the budget is the key management tool for financial planning and that he or she must take an active role in budget development and implementation. Understanding and getting involved in the budget planning process ensure a managerial commitment to the financial goals of the department.

APPLICATION OF CHAPTER CONCEPTS

Frank's Place is the main University Housing dining unit located within a housing commons. Frank's Place has cafeteria-style service with cereal, salad, and sandwich bars. A wide variety of prepared entrées, à la carte items, and beverages are offered. Those who live in the residence halls may easily take food back to their rooms and place the soiled dishes in the trash rooms located on each floor for pickup by the foodservice employees. Frank's offers breakfast, lunch, dinner, and late night snacks with a menu that changes daily. The Housing Division states, "We have a responsibility to provide the highest quality food at reasonable prices for our residents. Residents pay for overhead costs as part of their room rates, so their purchase price reflects only the cost of food. Students pay the posted prices and cash customers pay an additional 60% of the posted price. A selection of some menu items and posted prices are listed below:

Creamy Beef Stroganoff with Wide Egg Noodles	$2.99
Chocolate Layer Cake	$1.39
Teriyaki Garlic Beef & Cheese Salad	$3.35
Chicken Breast Satay with Peanut Sauce	$1.33
Breaded Chicken Tenders	$2.79
Supreme Burger	$2.74
Chicken Breast Supreme on a Bun	$2.69
Vegan Boca Burger	$1.95
Breaded Onion Rings	$1.25
Roasted Turkey & Bacon Ciabatta	$2.69
Tuna Salad Fruit Plate	$2.99
Vegetable Egg Roll with Fried Rice	$1.95
Cookie	$.49

Figure 17 The coauthor of this text harvests an assortment of vegetables (including carrots, beets, and lettuce) from the campus vegetable garden to supply Frank's Place as a part of a new food initiative.

Several foodservice operations, not affiliated with the university, are located within walking distance of campus. A fast-food operation offers a comparable burger to the Supreme Burger, chicken tenders, a veggie burger, and breaded onion rings. A chain restaurant offers beef stroganoff, chocolate cake, and a tuna salad with fruit. An Asian-themed restaurant offers vegetable egg roll with fried rice, chicken breast satay with peanut sauce, and a teriyaki beef salad on its menu. And, a sandwich shop serves a chicken breast sandwich on a bun, a turkey and bacon ciabatta, and fresh-baked cookies on its menu.

Fresh produce from a vegetable garden located just across the parking lot from the foodservice is used daily in the menu at Frank's Place. This locally grown food initiative is in the early stages of implementation. At this point the garden is far from being able to produce all of the produce required by Frank's Place. But, it is a beginning (Figure 17).

CRITICAL-THINKING QUESTIONS

1. Using the marketing approach to menu pricing, what would management need to do before establishing the selling prices?
2. Some selling prices at the local fast food establishment are: Deluxe Burger $2.43, Onion Rings $.99, Chicken Tenders $1.99, and Veggie Burger $1.99. Given these prices, should any of the prices charged by Frank's Place be reconsidered? If so, why?
3. Using the food cost percentage method of establishing menu prices, what would management need to do first?
4. "Students pay the posted prices and cash customers pay an additional 60% of the posted price." What is the desired food cost percent for this operation?
5. Frank's Place wants to offer lasagna as a new dinner special. The raw food cost is $1.75, and 10% is to be added for hidden costs and unproductive costs. The desired food cost percentage is 40%. What should be the selling price? For cash customers? For residential students?
6. If the total sales for the month of April at Frank's Place was $240,000 and the total cost of food used was $92,500, what was the food cost percentage for this month? Given this answer, what should management do?

7. If the budgeted amount for food purchases each month for Frank's Place is $80,000, how can the April discrepancy be explained?
8. What impact would the incorporation of locally grown produce have on the overall food cost at Frank's Place?
9. In what ways could the desired food cost percentage of an item be achieved without raising its selling price?
10. The roasted turkey and bacon ciabatta is a very popular item. If the raw food cost of this item is $2.15, is the selling price for cash customers within the desired food cost percentage range?

CHAPTER REVIEW QUESTIONS

1. Why is knowledge of accounting standards and uniform systems of accounts important for a foodservice manager?
2. How do an income statement and balance sheet differ, and who is likely to use each?
3. What are the major requirements for any record-keeping system?
4. What is the formula for determining food-cost percentage?
5. How are standards for food-cost percentages set?
6. Define markup. How is it calculated?
7. What three ratios are commonly used to analyze labor productivity and costs?
8. How are benchmarking and ratio analysis related?
9. What is the purpose of the budget?
10. Describe the three phases of budget planning.

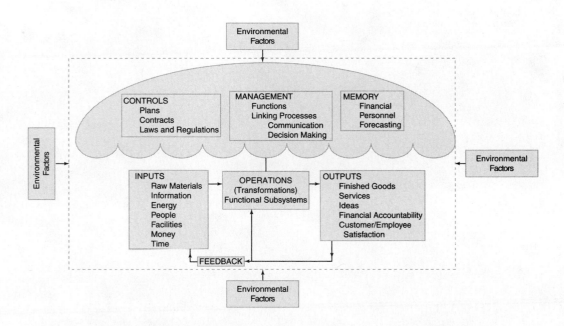

SELECTED WEB SITES

http://www.healthcarefoodservice.org (The Association for Healthcare Foodservice, a society for professionals and suppliers in the self-operated healthcare foodservice industry)

www.hotelschool.cornell.edu/research/library/tools/industry/food.html (Cornell University School of Hotel Administration)

http://monkeydish.com (Web site powered by *Restaurant Business* magazine)

http://researchandmarkets.com (World's largest market research resource)

http://www.restaurant.org (The National Restaurant Association)

Marketing

From Chapter 18 of *Foodservice Management: Principles and Practices*, Twelfth Edition, June Payne-Palacio, Monica Theis.

Marketing

Alexey Averiyanov/Shutterstock

MARKETING HAS BEEN AN ESSENTIAL MANAGERIAL

function of commercial foodservice operations since their inception. More recently, managers of noncommercial operations (such as hospitals, long-term care facilities, schools, and universities) have recognized the value of marketing principles as a means to survive in a highly competitive industry where resources are increasingly scarce and costly. Serving good food is not enough. Today's customer is more sophisticated and has higher expectations for food and service than ever before. Good food must at minimum be accompanied by excellent service and good value per price. Other, yet variable, aspects of value include presentation, convenience, and nutrition. Increasingly consumers are interested in aspects of food and service that historically were not valued as part of a business transactions. Factors such as sustainability, animal rights, and treatment of workers are now considered by some consumers before a purchase is made. Acknowledging and accommodating these attributes can create a competitive edge or *point of difference*—the point at which a customer chooses one foodservice over another.

A food manager does not need a business degree in marketing to develop a successful marketing program for a foodservice operation. This chapter introduces the reader to the basic principles of marketing and offers suggestions on how to develop and implement a successful program. It begins by defining some key marketing terms and concepts. Subsequent sections describe the unique aspects of the marketing process in foodservice. The final section describes promotions planning appropriate for foodservice operations. Guidelines are offered on how to plan and implement a specific promotion. The branded concept, as a means of increasing sales, is addressed as well.

KEY CONCEPTS

1. Marketing is a business strategy designed to attract customers and influence their purchasing behaviors.

2. Marketing is a cyclical process driven by the results of market research and strategic planning.

3. Market segmentation divides a total market into groups of people with unique wants and needs.

4. The marking mix represents the package of approaches that organizations use to attract the attention of a target market.

5. Foodservice operations have unique characteristics that influence the application of marketing principles.

6. Successful marketing is based on careful planning, implementation, and evaluation of strategies.

7. Promotions are specific and well-planned events to attract customers and influence perception or buying behaviors.

8. Success of a promotion is based on the type of promotion and its objective.

9. Successful promotions require careful planning to ensure desired outcomes.

10. Branding and branded concepts can expand customer base and generate new revenue.

MARKETING DEFINED

KEY CONCEPT: Marketing is a business strategy designed to attract customers and influence their purchasing behaviors.

Today, the word **marketing** is used in many contexts. In this chapter, marketing is examined as a specific organizational function that influences promotional activities in a foodservice. One definition of marketing is provided by the American Marketing Association (AMA) and defines marketing as an organizational function and a set of processes

Marketing
Activities directed at satisfying the needs and wants of customers

Marketing concept

The management philosophy that determining and satisfying the wants and needs of customers is the primary objective of an organization

for creating, communicating, and delivering value to customers and for managing customer relationships in ways that benefit the organization and its stakeholders. The **marketing concept** is a business philosophy whereby resources and activities are diligently directed toward satisfying the needs and wants of customers through an exchange process, with the obvious understanding that outcomes contribute to the bottom line.

In today's business environment of shrinking resources and increased competition, it is more important than ever for organizations, including foodservices, to take a strategic approach to marketing. However, it is important for the manager to adopt this philosophy and empower the employees to put customer needs first; without the customer, after all, there would be no foodservice organization. The marketing concept implies having the vision and flexibility to change with customers' evolving needs, wants, and demands.

Marketing activities identify and attract customers to an organization and its products and services. Until recently, marketing was not recognized as a valuable function in non-commercial settings. However, the health care and education industries have faced numerous challenges, including increased costs, increased government regulation, decreased government reimbursements, and competition for customers. As a result, many hospitals and long-term care facilities are struggling to maintain or increase their patient numbers. Schools, colleges, and universities are challenged by competition from nearby restaurants and "brown baggers." There is no such thing as a captive audience.

The foodservices of these organizations can play an important role in attracting and keeping customers by producing good-quality food, offering excellent service, and increasing customer awareness of their availability. For example, good food and service can be a key factor in whether a family is willing to admit a family member to a long-term care facility. Variety and excitement in the school cafeteria can prompt a student to choose the cafeteria over a nearby fast-food restaurant for lunch. Furthermore, patients satisfied with their food are more likely to comment favorably on their entire hospital stay.

Marketing is indeed a customer-centered, customer-driven process that includes specific and strategic activities. Figure 1 illustrates the marketing cycle. Steps include (1) identification of customers; (2) development of products, pricing, and distribution; (3) customer purchases; (4) generation of profits; and (5) appropriate action based on profits and customer feedback.

Figure 1 The marketing cycle.

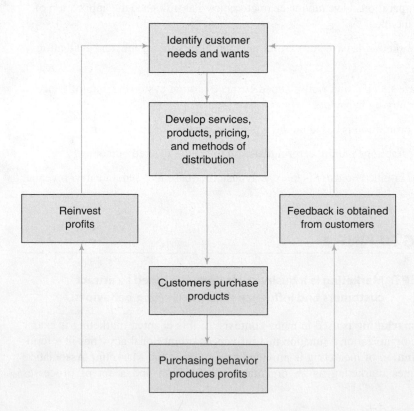

Marketing operates in a dynamic environment influenced by external and internal forces. Outside forces include politics, the economy, government regulation, laws, social pressures, technology, local competition, industry trends, and, of course, customer attitudes and behavior. Inside influences can include organizational goals, budgetary constraints, and departmental policy.

THE MARKETING CYCLE

■ **KEY CONCEPT: Marketing is a cyclical process driven by the results of market research and strategic planning.**

The **marketing cycle** begins by identifying the customers who make up the potential market.

The market, or **target market**, is defined as a segment of a population that, as individuals or organizations, have needs for products and possess the ability, willingness, and authority to make a purchase. To begin identifying the target market, the manager should consider the following questions:

* Who are our current customers? Are we meeting their wants and needs?
* Who and where are our potential customers?
* What do we have or what can we create to attract new customers?

For example, the director of a school lunch program may find that potential customers include students who currently bring their lunch or go home, as well as teachers, staff, and visitors who have not previously participated in the lunch program. Numbers can be estimated by calculating total student enrollment, total teaching and support staff, and the estimated number of visitors to the school each day. Additional customers might include an older adult population of the community, who may participate in a congregate meal program at the school. Finally, the unique needs of each group must be identified. These unique needs may include the desire for grab-and-go options or bagged lunches for the student, familiar or traditional foods for the older adults, and fresh, local, and organic for the teachers and staff. Specifically, the manager or marketing team needs to identify what aspects of food and service have real or perceived value to potential and existing customers. Further judgment needs to be made on whether these customers will be willing to pay money for these aspects or values.

■ **KEY CONCEPT: Market segmentation divides a total market into groups of people with unique wants and needs.**

Answering these questions helps the manager begin to define the market segments. **Market segmentation** divides the total market into smaller groups of people with similar product needs. Categories of customers emerge based on demographics, geographic location, psychographics, and product preference.

Demographic segmentation refers to the statistical data on customer profile characteristics such as age, sex, income, and educational background. **Geographic segmentation** categorizes customers according to where they live. **Psychographic segmentation** refers to customers of similar lifestyles, attitudes, and personalities. Finally, *product preference* is segmentation by customer behavior exhibited in a foodservice operation.

Once the needs and wants of potential customers have been identified, the manager can proceed with the marketing process by developing the products and services necessary to satisfy, if not exceed, these needs and wants. A product may be an object, service, or idea. It must also be available at the right place at the right time and be priced appropriately so that the customer identifies it as meeting a need, is willing to pay for the product, and prefers the product over that offered by the competition. To this end, the marketing process must be customer oriented and customer driven.

Marketing cycle

A recurrent series of activities designed to meet the wants and needs of customers; the cycle is driven by customer feedback

Target market

A market segment identified by the seller as having specific wants or needs

Market segmentation

The process of placing customers into groups of like characteristics such as by demographics or geographic location

Demographic segmentation

Dividing or segmenting a market into groups of people based on variables such as age, sex, income, education, religion, and race

Geographic segmentation

Dividing a market into different units based on variables such as nation, state, region, city, or neighborhood

Psychographic segmentation

Dividing a market into groups based on variables such as social class, lifestyle, or personality traits

THE MARKETING MIX

▌**KEY CONCEPT:** **The marketing mix represents the package of approaches that organizations use to attract a target market.**

A well-defined marketing program includes four elements: product, place, price, and promotion. These elements, often called the four P's of marketing, and their unique combinations in any marketing program are called the marketing mix.

Product is the unique combination of goods and services that satisfies a want or need. The product can be objects, services, ideas, places, or an organization. It is what is produced based on knowledge of the market and what is ultimately sold. Foodservice products include all items on the menu, as well as the many types of service options, such as cafeterias, vending machines, and catering, and other desirable attributes, such as pleasant atmosphere and convenient hours of service.

Place includes distribution and how products are sold. Products must be available at the right time and place, convenient for customers. Many foodservices today are accommodating customer desires for speed and convenience. For example, large-scale hospitals often set up mobile cafeterias or kiosks on nursing units during busy lunch periods as a convenience for medical staff with limited break time. Many organizations are opening food courts similar to those seen in shopping malls.

Price is the amount of money charged for a product or the sum of the values customers exchange for the benefit of the product. Strategic pricing encourages the customer to make a purchase, contributes to product image, and allows products to compete in the market. For example, a cafeteria manager may offer coffee at a reduced price during slow periods knowing that a customer is likely to make additional purchases such as sweet rolls, pie, or popcorn (see Figure 2).

Promotion involves all communication with the customer. It introduces the customer to, or increases customer awareness of, the available product. (Promotion is discussed in more detail later in the chapter.)

MARKETING FOR FOODSERVICE OPERATIONS

▌**KEY CONCEPT:** **Foodservice operations have unique characteristics that influence the application of marketing principles.**

Unique Aspects of Foodservice Marketing

Marketing in foodservice requires a unique approach, because unlike some industries, foodservice includes a service component. Service is the application of human or mechanical efforts to people or objects. Service industries such as foodservices differ from most manufacturing industries in product, customer contact, perishability of inventory, and distribution.

Product

Food provided by a foodservice operation is consumed but not possessed, which distinguishes it from other consumer goods such as appliances. Food as a product is unique in that it has both a tangible and an intangible component. The food itself is the *tangible* component, meaning that it is capable of being perceived by the buyer through smell, touch, taste. Service is *intangible* in that it cannot be seen, touched, tasted, or possessed, yet the consumer is very much aware of its presence and certainly aware of its absence. For example, customers are quick to notice lack of friendliness or indifference on the part of wait staff.

Customer Contact

The customer takes a more active role in the marketing function in a service industry. For example, in many cafeterias, patrons help themselves to displayed foods or, in the case of

Figure 2 An example of a preferred customer coupon.
Source: Courtesy of the University of Wisconsin–Madison Division of Housing Dining and Culinary Services. Used with permission.

table service, there is direct and frequent customer-employee contact. Each contact represents an opportunity for the foodservice to market not only the food product but the organizational image as well.

In the cafeteria self-serve situation, the foodservice operation has the opportunity to entice the customer with attractive, well-designed displays. Table service offers more direct and personal contact. For example, wait staff can be trained to anticipate customer wants and needs such as a beverage refill or readiness with the check. One negative customer-employee interaction can generate lasting dissatisfaction that may result in the loss of business not only from the unhappy customer, but also from all potential customers that the dissatisfied customer influences through word of mouth.

Perishability

Food is unique in that it is highly perishable and difficult to store in inventory. Unlike a tangible product, such as a television set, which can be stored in a warehouse during low-demand periods, food is highly perishable. If it is unsold or simply not used, it is lost income, or waste. For example, if the customer count is lower than expected in a cafeteria or school, these potential sales are lost forever, and food prepared ahead of time is wasted.

Distribution

In many types of foodservice operations, food must be prepared in advance, held either hot or cold, and transported for distribution. For example, many elementary and high schools receive their food from commissary foodservice operations. Without careful consideration of the conditions during holding and transport, food quality can deteriorate significantly and, thus, it can be rejected by the paying customer.

> █ **KEY CONCEPT:** **Successful marketing is based on careful planning, implementation, and evaluation of strategies.**

MARKETING AS A MANAGERIAL FUNCTION

Management must recognize marketing as an essential function, similar to traditional management functions of organizing, leading, and controlling.

Common marketing mistakes include the following:

- Lack of planning
- Improper budgeting
- Poorly defined goals and objectives
- Lack of product development
- Inadequate program evaluation

With a clear vision of, and a commitment to, the organization's mission, the wise manager will develop a marketing program that includes planning, implementation, and evaluation.

Planning

Planning begins with a clear understanding of, and a commitment to, the goals and objectives of the marketing plan. In other words, the manager should ask: "What are we as an organization or a department trying to do?" "What do we hope to accomplish?" For example, is the purpose of the marketing program to attract new customers, retain current customers, or influence specific purchasing behaviors?

This self-analysis sometimes comes about through a formal process referred to as a SWOT analysis. SWOT stands for strengths, weaknesses, opportunities, and threats. By carefully considering each of these relative to its operation, the management team can determine what it can uniquely offer that can satisfy a recognized need for a particular target market. For example, a dining division for a college might identify food quality at a reasonable price as a strength, or it might identify a lack of contemporary dining rooms that appeal to a young market as a weakness. Opportunities could include providing catering services to the employees of a nearby building. A threat might be the close proximity of restaurants that compete for student food dollars. Such an analysis can create an awareness of what a foodservice has and what it can develop to be more appealing to targeted customers.

General goals need to be defined as part of the organization's long-term or strategic planning. For a goal to become reality, specific objectives must be established. Objectives must be clear and, for purposes of program evaluation, they must be measurable. Responsibility for achieving the objective through specific activities should be assigned and a timetable established for meeting the objective. For example, the goal for a hospital cafeteria may be to increase patronage by employees and visitors. A specific objective would be to increase by 10 percent the number of customers using the cafeteria between 11 A.M. and 1 P.M.

Personal interviews or focus groups with potential customers and surveys such as the one shown in Figure 3 are appropriate methods to determine the food and service preferences of the target market. Using the results of the interviews and surveys, the manager can create specific plans to achieve the objectives. Without specific action plans, well-defined objectives may be abandoned, and desired goals will not be met.

Implementation

Implementation is critical to keep objectives from becoming good intentions that never materialize. This involves empowering staff to embrace the marketing plan, training

THE BAYSIDE CAFETERIA

We invite you to rate our food and service to help us improve the quality of our cafeteria. Please circle one choice in each category; (5 = very satisfied, 3 = meets expectations, 1 = dissatisfied). Please comment on ratings of 3 or less.

1. Food: 5   4   3   2   1
   Comments:

2. Price/Value: 5   4   3   2   1
   Comments:

3. Prompt Service: 5   4   3   2   1
   Comments:

4. Courtesy: 5   4   3   2   1
   Comments:

5. Atmosphere: 5   4   3   2   1
   Comments:

When and how often do you use the cafeteria? (Check all that apply and indicate the number of times per week).

                              No. of times/week
Breakfast   ____   ____
Morning break   ____   ____
Lunch   ____   ____
Afternoon break   ____   ____
Dinner   ____   ____

What food items would you like to see added to the cafeteria selections?
1._____
2._____
3._____
4._____
5._____

Please use the space below for additional comments and suggestions. Thank you.

Figure 3 Survey designed to determine preferences of current and potential cafeteria customers.

employees to execute the plan successfully, defining and developing the promotion plans, effectively communicating marketing messages, and providing support to enable the plan to succeed. Part of this support includes implementing procedures to evaluate the success of the marketing plan.

Evaluation

Evaluation is the process of determining the success of a plan as implemented. The manager must measure the degree to which the previously established objectives were achieved. For example, if the foodservice manager sets an objective of increasing school lunch participation by 5%, then the manager must review daily meal counts to determine if that objective was actually achieved through marketing plans that were executed. The knowledge gained from this evaluation can be used to refine objectives and action plans.

Marketing programs, in particular, are costly in terms of time and resources; therefore, management must take steps to ensure that there is an actual, measurable return on this investment. Logically, the evaluation strategies come after implementation of the program and after a specific amount of time has passed.

PROMOTIONS IN FOODSERVICE OPERATIONS

■ **KEY CONCEPT: Promotions are specific and well-planned events to attract customers and influence perception or buying behaviors.**

As described, marketing is a process of identifying customers and their needs and developing products to satisfy those needs. Promotions, on the other hand, are distinct activities used continually to pique the interest of customers in an effort to stimulate repeat business, as well as generate new business. The most common activity in foodservice is that of the sales promotion.

Sales Promotion

As discussed earlier in this chapter, promotion is one of the four P's of a marketing program. Promotion is a distinct function, different from merchandising and advertising. It is the function of influencing the customer's purchase and repurchase behavior, with a primary goal of increasing patronage and, in turn, improving sales and profit. Promotion can also be used for a number of nonprofit goals, such as increasing public awareness of a facility's services.

By planning, implementing, and evaluating promotional strategies, the manager can accomplish several goals. These goals are to (1) present information to the customers, (2) reinforce desired purchasing behavior to stimulate repeat business, (3) stimulate first-time business by arousing curiosity, and (4) enhance the image of an organization. Such strategies are appropriate for all types of foodservices. Obviously promotions are necessary for cafeterias, vending, and catering, which rely on a profit. There are, however, many other reasons for understanding the basics of promotional marketing.

■ **KEY CONCEPT: Success of a promotion is based on the type of promotion and its objective.**

There are two categories of promotions. First, there are the *share-of-market* promotions. These are financial, volume-based activities designed to increase patronage, sales, or a combination of the two. Second, there are *share-of-mind* promotions, which seek to influence the customer's preference or feelings about a particular facility or product. Both of these can be used in noncommercial and retail foodservices.

■ **KEY CONCEPT: Successful promotions require careful planning to ensure desired outcomes.**

Promotion Planning

Promotion planning begins just like any other managerial function—by establishing clear, measurable objectives. The primary objectives of promotions are to increase the frequency of customer visits and the level of customer satisfaction. Figure 4 suggests specific topic objectives for various types of foodservice operations. It is important to note that measures would need to be added to each of these in order to use them as an evaluation strategy. For example, a measurable objective for increasing participation in a school lunch program would be to extend the objective statement as follows: Increase participation in the school lunch program by 5% within one school year.

The manager can generate ideas for specific objective(s) by asking the following questions:

1. What is it that we are trying to accomplish with this promotion?
2. Is it consistent with our mission statement?
3. Is it designed to meet customer needs?
4. How can we evaluate or measure the success of this promotion?

Figure 4 Examples of topics for promotions objectives.

Schools
  Increase participation in the school lunch program.
  Increase total à la carte sales.
  Create an awareness of a new product.
Hospital Cafeteria, Vending
  Increase average total profit.
  Increase beverage to food ratio.
  Increase salad and dessert sales.
Long-Term Care Facilities
  Increase awareness of nutritional value of food.
  Increase awareness of special services.
  Increase family participation in holiday meals.

In contrast to marketing and merchandising, promotions are generally designed to run for a short period of time but may be extended or repeated if the objectives remain desirable. For example, a school may try a special promotion during National School Lunch Week to increase participation by offering a free dessert with each meal. If highly successful, the foodservice manager may wish to repeat the promotion at another time during the school year.

Some guidelines for the development, implementation, and evaluation of a successful promotion are as follows:

1. Plan well in advance—at least one to three months before the event is to take place.
2. Establish goals and objectives.
3. Know the current and potential customers.
4. Select a promotional idea consistent with customer need and the organization's mission.
5. Seek advice and ideas from internal and external sources.
6. Verify availability of financial resources and compare costs of promotion to expected benefits.
7. Design a written plan for implementation and review the plan with employees.
8. Execute the plan, paying careful attention to all details.
9. Evaluate the results against the planned objectives and make changes as necessary for future promotions.

There are numerous means by which promotion objectives can be met, including coupons, contests, discounts, combination pricing, signs, special events, menu boards, and theme days. The illustrations shown in Figures 5 to 8 are examples of promotions used in various types of foodservice organizations.

■ **KEY CONCEPT:** **Branding and branded concepts can expand customer base and generate new revenue.**

BRANDING

Since the beginning of the 1990s, there has been an explosion in the use of *branding* and the **branded concept** as a marketing strategy in all segments of the foodservice industry. The catalyst behind this phenomenon is one of economics. All foodservice operations, and particularly those traditionally recognized as noncommercial, are under increasing pressure to operate "in the black." This pressure has resulted in a paradigm shift referred to as the commercialization of noncommercial operations. For example, many hospital cafeterias are no longer subsidized by their parent organization. Instead, these foodservice operations are expected to at least break even (that is, generate enough revenue to cover expenses) or actually generate a profit, thereby contributing to the financial well-being of the organization. Traditionally, noncommercial foodservices such as those in hospitals and schools

Branded concept

A marketing strategy that communicates a recognized brand to customers

Figure 5 Example of a gift certificate redeemable in a cafeteria.
Source: Courtesy the University of Wisconsin–Madison, Division of Housing; Dining and Culinary Services. Used with permission.

have relied on familiar revenue-generating options such as catering, vending, and take-out foods to boost income. Branding and the branded concept began to emerge in the early 1990s and have continued to gain in popularity ever since. It is important for today's foodservice manager to understand what branding is, why it has the potential to work as a marketing strategy, the types and variations of branding, and management issues such as deciding which branded items to use and how to avoid potential pitfalls of branding.

As a marketing strategy, *branding* refers to the use of nationally or locally labeled products for sale in an existing foodservice operation. In foodservice operations, branding is used specifically to increase sales through brand promotions that are designed to woo new customers and increase the average amount of individual transactions. In practice, branding takes many forms. The most popular are retail-item, restaurant, and in-house branding.

Retail-item branding, also referred to as manufacturer's branding, has been used for years and simply refers to the sale of nationally recognized items in existing foodservice operations. Examples include Skippy peanut butter in school lunch programs and Kraft salad dressings in hospital cafeterias. *Restaurant branding*, on the other hand, is a far more recent approach to branding and refers to the inclusion of a national restaurant chain in an existing operation. This approach may vary from the purchase of a franchise (such as a McDonald's in the lobby of a hospital) to contracting with a chain restaurant for periodic sales (such as offering Pizza Hut pizza in a school cafeteria once a month). Figure 9 is one example of how branding is used in onsite foodservices. There is at least one variation to branding with nationally recognized chains and that is to contract with a popular local or regional brand. For example, schools in some Midwest states can contract with Rocky Rococo Pizza in an effort to increase the variety of branded products and maintain interest in the school lunch program.

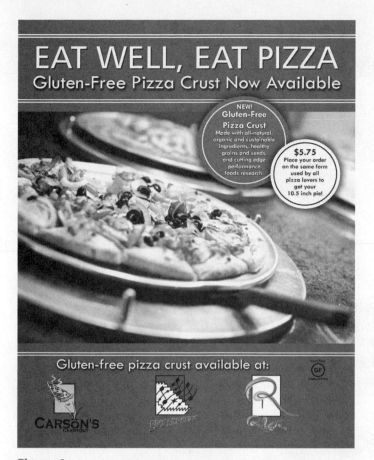

Figure 6   Examples of promotions for a university foodservice.

Source: Courtesy of the University of Wisconsin–Madison, Division of Housing, Dining and Culinary Services. Used with permission.

Another major type of branding is *in-house* or *signature branding*. Signature brands are items prepared within a specific foodservice operation and identified as unique to that operation. For example, a hospital cafeteria may sell a line of sandwiches that customers identify with that cafeteria and recognize for their consistent high quality. The foodservice, in turn, can take that line, develop it as an in-house brand, and promote it using a specially designed logo and other item-specific promotional materials. This approach is sometimes used to offset the potential for "cannibalization" of in-house items when national or local branding is introduced. The in-house brands are designed to compete side by side with the other brands for sales.

A more contemporary term related to branding is that of the *branded concept*. This term refers to a complete marketing package that communicates a recognized and consistent brand identity to the customer. This package is developed and made available by the commercial company and generally consists of two components. The first is the entire point-of-sale environment, which includes all of the materials with logos that are used to promote a specific product or line of products. Examples include product packaging, signage (including menu boards), staff uniforms, table tents, and flyers. The second component of the branded concept refers to the management resources made available through the commercial company. Resources include purchasing assistance, production tools, such as recipes, and service suggestions. Commercial companies currently participating in this practice include Starbucks, Chick-fil-A, and Subway.

The success of branding and the branded concept is based on the premise that customers are willing to pay more for a branded product. Part of this success can be attributed to the fact that brands are recognized and trusted. More important, however, relative to the growth of branding in today's operations, is the psychological phenomenon that customers are willing to pay for *perceived* quality and value. So even though a product prepared by a

Scandinavian Dinner

April 26 in All Full-Service Dining Rooms

Menu Includes:

Mock Glogg
Traditionally a spiced wine served hot, we are offering a tasty non-alcoholic version.

Lefse
Sometimes called a Scandinavian tortilla, lefse is a very tasty, soft flatbread made from potato.

Fruktsoppa
A traditional fruit soup from Sweden made with apples, apricots, raisins and delicious produce.

Rommegrot
A Norwegian cream pudding.

Traditional Swedish Meatballs and a wonderful meatless version made with walnuts.

Poached Salmon

Potato Pancakes

Boiled Potato Wedges

Swedish Cucumber salad

Lingonberries and Cream

Earth Day Dinner Celebration
April 22
4:30 - 8:30 p.m.
Frank's Place

UNIVERSITY HOUSING
DINING AND CULINARY SERVICES

Figure 7 Examples of cafeteria menu flyers to increase customer awareness of special events.
Source: Courtesy of the University of Wisconsin–Madison, Division of Housing, Dining and Culinary Services. Used with permission.

Figure 8 Promotional table tent for a theme day.
Source: Courtesy of the University of Wisconsin–Madison, Division of Housing, Dining and Culinary Services. Used with permission.

Figure 9 Java Coast coffee kiosk.
Source: Courtesy of the University of Wisconsin
Hospital and Clinics, Foodservice Department.
Used with permission.

foodservice may be bigger, better, and less expensive, consumers will still prefer and pay more for a brand they recognize and trust.

It follows, then, that with careful planning and implementation, a foodservice manager can anticipate the following advantages and outcomes from branding:

- Increased volume of business
- Increased per-capita spending resulting in higher average receipts
- Increased revenue
- Increased crossover traffic to in-house brands (that is, customers are attracted to the branded items but will also purchase in-house items).

Each of these advantages contributes to the ultimate goal of improved customer satisfaction.

Branding, with all of its attractive advantages, does not, however, come without its potential pitfalls. Contracts and agreements must be carefully negotiated to ensure that responsibilities and obligations are clearly understood by all parties involved. Pricing of branded items must be carefully considered because customers are well aware of the street prices for popular, national brands. Managers may also have to respond to employee fear of contracting with commercial companies. Depending on the degree to which branding is incorporated into an existing foodservice, it may mean a reduction of in-house staff.

To offset these risks, foodservice managers should carefully study branding and the branded concept before signing a contract or agreement with a commercial company. The decision-making process for brand selection should begin with careful evaluation of the target market of existing and potential customers. Actual and perceived value as defined by the customer must be clearly understood. From there, the selection process should focus on products with the potential for the greatest gross profit. The overall financial investment must be carefully considered. For example, implementing branding and the branded concept in an existing cafeteria may require additional operations or facility renovation. These and other potential investments must be carefully weighed against the potential for increased revenue and other less tangible advantages such as improved customer satisfaction.

SUMMARY

Marketing has been an essential function of commercial foodservice operations for a long time. In recent years, managers of noncommercial operations (such as hospitals, long-term care facilities, schools, and universities) have recognized the value of marketing principles as a means to survive in a highly competitive industry with limited resources and ever-increasing costs.

Foodservice managers today must have a sound knowledge base of marketing terminology, the marketing cycle, the marketing concept, and the unique aspects of marketing in a foodservice in order to implement a program successfully. Implementation includes carefully planned training for foodservice employees and an evaluation strategy to assess the degree to which the program objectives were achieved.

Merchandising and promotions are very important activities related to a marketing program. The foodservice manager must become familiar with promotion design, planning procedures, implementation, and evaluation strategies as a means to gain the competitive edge and retain or attract new customers to the foodservice operation.

APPLICATION OF CHAPTER CONCEPTS

The Housing Division at the University of Wisconsin–Madison includes a marketing department. In the context of Housing's mission, "where everyone wants to live," the marketing department builds strategic marketing plans with the goal of enticing students to live in campus housing. Although the Division of Dining and Culinary Services (DCS) does not have a marketing plan of its own, it works closely with the marketing department to promote dining services as a highly valued service within the Housing Division. In fact, the DCS division tweaks the mission a bit with the statement "where everyone wants to eat."

In that spirit, the DCS launches a number of promotions each year with the primary goal of creating and maintaining interest in its dining program for residents and cash customers alike. Other intents of promotions are to:

- Introduce new products such as organic pasta sauce
- Roll out new services such as extended hours at one of the coffee houses
- Fulfill an educational mission: a dinner of local products with area farmers in attendance to discuss their products and farming practices

Each year, despite extensive choice in food and hours of service, the DCS finds that residents start to get a bit bored with the fare. In recognition of this, the DCS launches a number of promotions each academic year that they term "monotony breakers," and the purpose is strictly fun. A number of concepts have been wildly successful: a pirate dinner featuring employees in costume, and breakfast at midnight where residents are invited to wear their pajamas. As fun as the concepts are, they take a great deal of planning to ensure that they work from an operations perspective, are "budget friendly," and trigger results based on promotion-specific objectives.

CRITICAL-THINKING QUESTIONS

1. What is the primary focus of the marketing department for the Division of Housing at UW–Madison?
2. How do the products and services offered through the Dining and Culinary Services unit link with the marketing department?
3. How does the concept of a marketing cycle relate to products and services offered through the Dining and Culinary Services unit?
4. What is the marketing mix for the Dining and Culinary Services unit of UW Housing?
5. What are some unique challenges that the Dining and Culinary Services unit needs to consider that perhaps are not so pronounced in a local restaurant?

6. What are some advantages that the Dining and Culinary Services unit has that a local restaurant may not have?
7. What ideas do you have for maintaining, if not increasing, interest in dining services through promotions?
8. The Dining and Culinary Services unit works to identify "wacky" ideas to generate interest through promotions but also is careful to never offend. How might this sensitivity influence the types of promotions offered?
9. What branded concepts might be most valuable in a setting such as the Dining and Culinary Services at UW Housing?
10. Do you think branding will grow or fade in the next few years on college campuses? Why or why not?

CHAPTER REVIEW QUESTIONS

1. What is marketing, and why is it referred to as a cyclical management function?
2. What is a target market? How can it be identified and segmented?
3. What are the elements of a marketing mix? What factors influence this mix in a given foodservice operation?
4. Differentiate between tangible and intangible components of a foodservice product.
5. What is a promotion, and how does it link to marketing?
6. Why is it important to establish clear goals and objectives for promotions?
7. What is the difference between a share-of-mind and a share-of-market promotion?
8. Define *branding* and the *branded concept*.
9. Why is branding so popular today, particularly in noncommercial foodservices?
10. Define and give examples of the major types of branding.

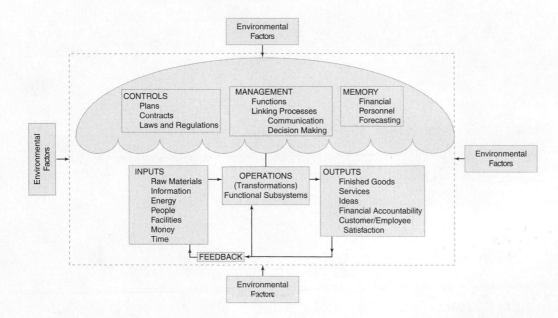

SELECTED WEB SITES

www.marketingpower.com   (The American Marketing Association)
www.census.gov   (U.S. Census Bureau)

OBJECTIVES OF COOKING

The basic objectives of cooking are to enhance the flavor of food and the attractiveness of the original color, form, and texture; to destroy harmful organisms and substances to ensure that food is safe for human consumption; and to improve digestibility.

BASIC COOKING METHODS

Cooking methods are classified as dry heat or moist heat. *Dry heat* methods are those in which the heat is conducted to the food by dry air, hot metal, radiation, or in a minimum amount of fat. Roasting, baking, broiling, grilling, griddling, and frying are examples of dry heat methods. *Moist heat* methods are those in which the heat is conducted to the food product by water or steam. Examples are boiling or simmering, stewing, blanching, poaching, braising, and steaming.

The method used depends on the type and quality of the food and availability of equipment. Different cooking methods are suitable for different kinds of food. For example, tender cuts of meat usually are prepared using a dry heat method, whereas a less tender cut should be cooked using moist heat. The following is a summary of common cooking methods.

Baking. Cooking by dry heat, usually in an oven.

Time and temperature: Baking temperature is determined by type of food and equipment. Oven load and size of containers must be considered when figuring required cooking time.

Equipment: Oven (deck, revolving, conveyor, range, or convection). A convection oven reduces cooking time by 10 to 15 percent and cooks at a temperature 25°F to 50°F lower than a traditional or conventional oven.

Barbecuing. Cooking on a grill or spit over hot coals, or in an oven, basting intermittently with a highly seasoned sauce.

Typical products: Meat, poultry.

Blanching. Cooking a food item partially and briefly. Food usually is blanched in water, although some foods, such as French fries, are blanched in hot fat. To blanch in water, the food is placed in rapidly boiling water and held until the water returns to a boil, then quickly cooled in cold water.

Equipment: Steam-jacketed or other type of kettle.

Typical products: Vegetables or fruits; to set the color and destroy enzymes, or to loosen skins for easier peeling.

Boiling. Cooking food in a liquid that is bubbling rapidly.

Time and temperature: The temperature of boiling water is 212°F at sea level. This point is raised by the presence of solids in the water and lowered by higher altitudes. At 5,000 feet, water boils at about 203°F; therefore, it takes *longer* to boil foods at high altitudes because of the lower boiling temperature.

Equipment: Steam-jacketed kettle, stock pot, or other kettle on top of the range.

Typical products: Vegetables, pasta, cereals, rice. Not generally used for high-protein foods (meat, fish, or eggs) because heat toughens the protein, and the rapid movement of boiling breaks delicate foods. This type of food is usually brought to a boil, then the heat is reduced to simmering temperature for the rest of the cooking period.

Braising. A method of cooking that combines cooking in fat with the addition of moisture. Food is browned in a small quantity of fat, then cooked slowly in liquid in a covered utensil.

Equipment: Tilting frypan or steam-jacketed kettle. For smaller amounts, a skillet or wok may be used. After the moisture is added to the browned food, the product may also be finished in the oven at a low temperature.

Typical products: Meats, poultry.

Broiling. Cooking by radiant heat. Food is placed on a rack either below or between the gas or electric heat source. The rack is positioned 3 to 6 inches from the heat source, depending on the type and intensity of the heat. The temperature required depends on the thickness of the food. Traditional broilers lack precise temperature controls, and food must be closely monitored during cooking. In *panbroiling*, food is cooked without fat in a frypan. If fat is not poured off as it accumulates, the process becomes panfrying.

Equipment: Specially designed broilers for institutional use.

Typical products: Tender cuts of meat (steaks, chops), fish, poultry.

Deep-Fat Frying. Cooking by submerging food in hot fat. In this type of cooking, some of the medium becomes part of the food during the cooking process, and it is not unusual for foods to absorb 10 to 20 percent of fat during frying. Foods may be dipped in a breading or batter before frying to form a protective coating between food and fat and to give the product crispness, color, and flavor. A well-prepared deep-fat fried food should have minimum fat absorption, an attractive golden color, a crisp surface or coating, and no off-flavors imparted by the frying fat. For the production of a high-quality product, use a good-quality fat with a high smoke point, avoid overloading the baskets, fry at proper temperatures, and avoid frying strongly and mildly flavored foods in the same fat. About 10 to 30 percent of the fat should be replaced with fresh fat before each daily use. Modern fryers are equipped with automatic basket lifts, fat temperature sensors, and computerized timers to aid in the consistent production of good fried foods. Thermostatic control and fast recovery of fat temperature permits the rapid production of consistent quality fried foods.

From Appendix A of *Foodservice Management: Principles and Practices*, Twelfth Edition, June Payne-Palacio, Monica Theis.

Equipment: Deep-fat fryer. Pressure fryers and convection fryers are recent developments that reduce the frying time, thus enabling large-volume foodservices to produce fried foods more rapidly. Pressurized fryers are used most frequently in foodservice operations specializing in fried chicken.

Typical products: Fish, shellfish, chicken, vegetables, meat.

Fricasseeing. Browning in fat, then simmering in gravy. Similar to braising, but moisture is in the form of gravy rather than water or other liquid.

Equipment: Tilting frypan, steam-jacketed kettle.

Typical products: Chicken, some meat cuts.

Frying. Cooking in fat or oil. See Deep-Fat Frying, Ovenfrying, Panfrying, and Sautéing for frying methods.

Griddling. Cooking on a solid cooking surface. Food is placed on a flat surface and cooked with or without a small amount of fat.

Equipment: Griddle.

Temperature: The temperature on a griddle is adjustable and is lower than on a grill (usually around 350°F).

Typical products: Meat, eggs, pancakes, sandwiches.

Grilling. Cooking on an open grid over a heat source.

Equipment: Grill, with heat source of charcoal, an electric element, or gas-heated element.

Typical products: Meat, fish.

Ovenfrying. High-temperature cooking in an oven. Food is placed on greased baking sheets, with melted fat brushed or drizzled over it, and baked in a hot oven (usually 400°F to 450°F). The resulting product resembles fried or sautéed food. This method is used when deep-fat fryers are not available or are inadequate to handle the production demand, usually in large health care facilities or other noncommercial foodservice operations.

Typical products: Chicken pieces, fish fillets.

Panfrying. Cooking in a moderate amount of fat in a pan over moderate heat. The amount of fat depends on the food being cooked. Only a small amount is used for eggs, whereas more may be needed for panfried chicken. Most foods must be turned at least once for even cooking. Some larger foods may be removed from the pan and finished in the oven, to prevent excessive surface browning.

Equipment: Skillet, tilting frypan.

Typical products: Meat, chicken, eggs, potatoes, onions.

Poaching. Cooking by immersing food in hot liquid maintained at simmering temperature. Food is added to hot liquid and simmered, keeping the temperature below boiling.

Equipment: Tilting frypan, steamer, oven, or a shallow pan on the range top.

Typical products: Fish, eggs out of the shell, fruit.

Roasting. Baking of meat or poultry (uncovered) in an oven. Cooking uncovered is essential to roasting, because if the meat or poultry is covered with a lid or aluminum foil, the steam is held in, changing the process from dry-heat to moist-heat cooking.

Equipment: Oven (range, deck, revolving, range, or convection).

Typical products: Poultry, tender cuts of beef, pork, lamb, or veal.

Sautéing. Cooking quickly in a small amount of fat. Food is placed in a preheated skillet with a small amount of fat and cooked quickly. Food should be cut or pounded to an even thickness and not overcrowded in the pan. After a food is sautéed, wine or stock is frequently added to dissolve brown bits of food sticking to the sides or bottom of the pan, a process called deglazing. Generally, this liquid is served with the sautéed item.

Equipment: Skillet, tilting frypan.

Typical products: Poultry, fish fillets, tender cuts of meat.

Searing. Browning of food in fat over high heat before finishing by another method.

Equipment: Skillet, tilting frypan.

Typical product: Meat.

Simmering. Cooking of food in liquid below the boiling point. Liquid should be kept at a temperature ranging from 185°F to just below the boiling point. Most foods cooked in a liquid are simmered because the higher temperatures and intense bubbling of boiling may be detrimental to the texture and appearance of the food. Food may be brought to the boiling point first, then the heat reduced for the rest of the cooking period.

Equipment: Steam-jacketed kettle, stock pot, or other kettle on top of the range.

Typical products: Soups, sauces, meat, poultry.

Steaming. Cooking by exposing foods directly to steam. Steam cookers provide for controlled cooking in constant temperatures. Food properly cooked in a pressure steamer is evenly cooked, retains a high vitamin content as well as its natural color and flavor, and suffers less of the usual cooking losses, such as shrinkage caused by prolonged cooking, boiling over, or burning. Pressure steaming is an extremely rapid method of cooking and must be carefully controlled and timed.

Equipment: Steamers may be low pressure, high pressure, or zero pressure. High-pressure steam cookers are used primarily for fast cooking and small-batch cookery of vegetables. In a zero convection, a fan circulates the steam throughout the steamer cavity. Most steamers are designed to accommodate standard-size pans that can be used directly on the serving counter. Steam is the source of heat in jacketed kettles, but is not the cooking medium. The heat is transferred through the walls of the inner lining of the kettle by conduction, but no contact between food and steam is possible. The temperature is higher than in a double boiler because the steam is under pressure. The temperature increases with increase in pressure.

Typical products: Vegetables, fruits, poultry, dumplings, pasta, rice, cereals.

Stewing. Cooking in a small amount of water, which may be either boiling or simmering. Whether a food is to be simmered, stewed, or boiled, the liquid usually is brought to a full boil first. This compensates for the lowering of the temperature when the food is added. The heat is then adjusted to maintain a steady temperature.

Equipment: Steam-jacketed kettle, tilting frypan, kettle on top of the range.

Typical products: Meat, poultry, fruit.

Stir-Frying. Cooking quickly in a small amount of oil over high heat. Food is cut into uniform strips or small pieces and cooked quickly in a small amount of oil. A light tossing and stirring motion is used to preserve the shape of the food.

Equipment: Tilting frypan, skillet, wok.

Typical products: Vegetables, chicken, pork, tender beef, or shrimp.

COOKING METHODS FOR SPECIFIC FOODS

Most foods are cooked by one of the basic methods described in the previous section. Broiling, frying, baking, and simmering are standard processes in food preparation, but there may be variations in exact procedures because of the type of product, available equipment and personnel, and the size and character of the operation. The following information is given to augment the basic definitions previously provided.

Meat

Cooking Methods. Depends on the quality and cut of meat and the quantity that must be prepared at one time. For *beef,* dry heat (broiling, roasting) is generally used for tender cuts, and moist heat cookery (braising, stewing, simmering) for the less tender cuts. Lower grades of meat and the less tender cuts of higher-quality beef may be tenderized by scoring, cubing, or grinding or by the addition of enzymes. Adding tomatoes or vinegar to a meat mixture also has a tenderizing effect. For *veal, pork,* and *lamb,* practically any cut but the shank may be cooked by dry heat, although broiling is not as desirable for pork or veal as it is for lamb or beef. Veal, because of its delicate flavor and lack of fat in the tissues, combines well with sauces and other foods.

Roasting. The time-weight relationship expressed in minutes per pound can be used as a guide, but the most accurate way to determine the doneness of a roast is with a meat thermometer that registers the internal temperature. For ease in roasting and handling, roasts to be cooked together should be uniform in size. Frozen meat generally is thawed in the refrigerator before cooking to reduce both time and heavy drip losses during preparation. Roasts will continue cooking for a period of time after removal from the oven, and the internal temperature of the roast may rise as much as 5°. The roast should be allowed to sit or rest in a warm place for 15 to 20 minutes before it is carved. The roast becomes more firm, retains more of its juices, and is easier to carve. When cooking a number of roasts, it is possible to offer meat at different stages of doneness by staggering the times that roasts are placed in the oven. The well-done roasts are started first and, when done, are removed from the oven, allowed to stand 20 minutes, sliced, and placed in pans in the warmer or in the oven at low heat. The rare meat is put in the oven last and, when the thermometer reaches 125°F, is removed from the oven, sliced, and sent directly to the serving area. For optimum quality, roasts are cooked and sliced just before serving. However, this may not be possible in some foodservice operations. If the meat must be cooked the day before or several hours prior to serving, the quality is better if the cooked roasts are stored in the refrigerator, then sliced and reheated before serving rather than refrigerating and reheating the sliced meat.

Time/Temperature. Yield is an important factor in the cooking of meat. Reduction in the yield of cooked meat may occur as cooking losses or as carving or serving losses. Shrinkage during cooking usually is the major loss involved, and it may range from 15 to 30 percent. Some shrinkage occurs regardless of the cooking method, but the cooking temperature and the cooking time have a direct bearing on the amount of shrinkage. Low temperatures generally result in fewer cooking losses and the most palatable product. If cooked too long, meat dries out and tends to be less tender. Even meat that requires moist heat and a comparatively long cooking time to become tender will be less tender when overcooked.

Poultry

Cooking Methods. Broiling (if not too large), panfrying, deep-fat frying, ovenfrying, roasting, barbecuing, fricasseeing, stewing, broasting.

Time/Temperature. Moderate heat for tender, juicy, and evenly done meat. High temperatures result in stringy, tough, and unappetizing meat. When roasting, use a thermometer placed in the thickest part of the breast or inner part of the thigh muscle. Make sure the bulb does not rest against a bone. Temperature should reach 170°F to 180°F. Poultry usually is cooked well done, but overcooking results in loss of juiciness. Many foodservices prefer to purchase boneless turkey roasts or rolls for convenience in roasting, slicing, and portion control. Cooking time for ready-to-cook rolls is longer in minutes per pound than for whole turkeys, but the total cooking time is less. Stuffing or dressing should be baked separately and served with the roasted sliced meat.

Fish

Thawing. Frozen fish steaks or fillets need not be thawed before cooking unless they are to be breaded, but any defrosting should be at refrigerator temperature and only long enough to permit ease in preparation. Thawing at room temperature is not recommended. Once thawed, fish should be cooked immediately and never refrozen. Frozen breaded fish portions should not be thawed before cooking.

Cooking Methods. Deep-fat frying, panfrying, ovenfrying, broiling, baking, poaching. The best cooking method is determined by size, fat content, and flavor. Baking and broiling are suitable for fat fish, such as salmon, trout, and whitefish. If lean fish is baked or broiled, fat is added to prevent dryness, and it often is baked in a sauce. Lean fish, such as haddock, halibut, and sea bass, are often poached, simmered, or steamed, although they may be broiled or baked if basted frequently. Fish cooked in moist heat (poaching) requires very little cooking time and usually is served with a sauce. Frying is suitable for all types, but those with firm flesh that will not break apart easily are best for deep-fat frying. Whatever the method, fish should be served as quickly as possible after cooking for optimum quality.

Equipment. Deep-fat fryer, skillet, tilting frypan, oven, steamer.

Time/Temperature. Low to moderate heat. Allow extra time for frozen fish that is not defrosted. Fish should be cooked only until the flesh is easily separated from the bones.

Eggs

Cooking Methods. Poaching, frying, scrambling, and cooking in the shell.

Poaching. Cooked to order in a shallow pan of hot water on top of the range, or in quantity, a counter pan deep enough to permit 2 to 2½ inches of water to cover the eggs is used. Eggs should be broken onto saucers and slid into the water toward the side of the pan. The water should be simmering when the eggs are added. The addition of 2 tablespoons of vinegar and 1 tablespoon of salt to 1 gallon of water prevents whites from spreading. Poaching may be done in a shallow pan on the range top or in the oven, tilting frypan, or steamer.

Frying. Usually cooked to order in a frypan or on a griddle. Eggs cooked on a griddle are more apt to spread than those cooked in a small frypan, and so are less attractive. To prevent toughening, eggs should not be fried at a high temperature.

Scrambling. Cooked to order in a frypan or griddle, or in quantity in the steamer or oven. The addition of milk to the eggs keeps them from drying, and medium white sauce added in place of milk prevents the eggs from separating and becoming watery when held on the serving counter.

Cooked in the Shell. In a pan on top of the range, an automatic egg cooker, a wire basket in the steam-jacketed kettle, or in a steamer. If eggs are brought to room temperature before cooking, the shells will not crack when heat is applied.

Time/Temperature. Avoid high temperatures and long cooking times. Eggs should be cooked as close to service as possible or cooked to order.

Pasta and Cereals

Pasta. Pasta is cooked uncovered in a large amount of boiling water in a stock pot or steam-jacketed kettle until tender but firm (*al dente*), then rinsed with cold or hot water and drained. If pasta is to be combined with other ingredients in a casserole, it should be undercooked slightly. If the pasta is not to be served immediately, it may be drained and covered with cold water. When pasta is cold, drain off water and toss lightly with a little salad oil. This will keep pasta from sticking or drying out. Cover tightly and store in the refrigerator. To reheat, place pasta in a colander and immerse in rapidly boiling water just long enough to heat through; or reheat in a microwave oven.

Rice. Rice is cooked in a steamer, the oven, or by boiling. It is cooked until all of the water is absorbed, so the right proportion of rice to water and the correct cooking time are important. Converted or parboiled long-grain white rice requires slightly more water and a longer cooking time than does regular long-grain or medium-grain rice. The cooking time for brown rice is almost double that of white rice.

Cereals. Cereals in quantity are generally cooked in a steam-jacketed kettle or steamer, but they may be prepared in a heavy kettle on top of the range. Add cereal and salt to boiling water, using a wire whip. Stir until some thickening is apparent, then reduce the heat and cook until the cereal reaches the desired consistency and the raw starch taste has disappeared. Cereal should be thick and creamy but not sticky. Overstirring or overcooking produces a sticky, gummy product.

Fruits and Vegetables

Pre-preparation. Fresh fruits should be washed to remove surface soil, sprays, and preservatives before they are served raw or cooked. Apples, bananas, and peaches discolor rapidly after peeling, so they should be immersed in pineapple, orange, or diluted lemon juice. Fruits also may be treated with ascorbic acid or other preparations that prevent oxidation. Berries deteriorate rapidly, so washing should be scheduled as near service as possible. A small amount of sugar sprinkled over the berries after cleaning keeps them fresh-looking.

Fresh vegetables should be washed, trimmed, peeled if necessary, and cut into even-sized pieces for cooking. Preparing fresh vegetables too far in advance causes them to discolor. Covering prepared vegetables with cold water helps retain color but reduces their nutritive value if they are held too long. Many foodservice operations have taken the preliminary preparation of fruits and vegetables out of the individual kitchens; they either centralize this function or buy convenience products that have some or all of the pre-preparation completed. Peeled potatoes and carrots, washed spinach and other leafy vegetables, cut vegetables ready for cooking, and peeled and sectioned citrus fruits and fresh pineapple are examples.

Cooking Methods. Steaming, boiling, baking, frying.

Equipment. Steamer, steam-jacketed kettle, tilting frypan, kettle on top of the range.

Whatever method is used, vegetables should be cooked in as small a quantity at one time as is feasible for the type of service. The needs of most foodservices can be met by the continuous cooking of vegetables in small quantities. Vegetables should be served as soon as possible after cooking for optimum quality and should be handled carefully to prevent breaking or mashing. Appearance is important to customer acceptance of vegetables, as is the seasoning. Frozen vegetables are cooked by the same methods used for fresh vegetables, but because frozen vegetables have been partially cooked, the final cooking time is shorter than for fresh products. Most frozen vegetables do not need to be thawed; they can be cooked from the frozen state and placed directly into steamer pans or boiling salted water. Exceptions are vegetables that are frozen into a solid block, such as spinach and winter squash. Results are more satisfactory if they are thawed in the refrigerator first for more even cooking.

To *steam*, place prepared vegetables not more than 3 to 4 inches deep in stainless steel inset pans. Perforated pans provide the best circulation, but if cooking liquid needs to be retained, use solid pans. To *boil*, add vegetables to boiling salted water in a steam-jacketed kettle or stockpot, in lots no larger than 10 pounds. The amount of water used in cooking all vegetables is important for retention of nutrients: the less water used, the more nutrients retained. Addition of baking soda to the water also causes loss of vitamins. Mature root vegetables that need longer cooking require more water than young, tender vegetables. Spinach and other greens need only the water clinging to their leaves from washing. Cover and bring water quickly back to the boiling point. Green vegetables retain their color better if the lid is removed just before boiling begins; strong-flavored vegetables, such as cabbage, cauliflower, and Brussels sprouts, should be cooked uncovered to prevent development of unpleasant flavors. To *stir-fry*, cut vegetables diagonally or into small uniform pieces. Heat a small amount of oil in a wok, tilting frypan, or steam-jacketed kettle. Cook and stir until vegetables are coated with oil. A small amount of liquid is usually added and the vegetables cooked, covered, until tender but crisp.

One of the main purposes of cooking vegetables is to change the texture. During the cooking process, however, the color and flavor may be altered and some loss of nutrients may occur. The degree to which these characteristics change determines the quality of the cooked vegetables. Many factors affect cooking time, including the type and maturity of the vegetable,

the presence of acids, the size of the pieces, and the degree of doneness. Vegetables are considered done when they have reached the desired degree of tenderness. The starch in vegetables also affects texture. Dry starchy foods, such as beans or lentils, must be cooked in enough water so that the starch granules can absorb moisture and soften. Most starchy vegetables, such as potatoes and yams, have enough moisture of their own, but they must still be cooked until the starch granules soften. Color is a major factor in consumer acceptance of vegetables, so methods of cookery that retain color, as well as nutritive value, should be selected. The green pigment chlorophyll is the least stable of food pigments, and considerable attention is given to preserving this color in vegetables. Chlorophyll is affected by acid to produce an unattractive olive-gray color. Vegetables are slightly acidic in reaction, and when cooked, the acid is liberated from the cells into the cooking water. Fortunately, much of the acid is volatile and given off in the first few minutes of cooking. If an open kettle is used for cooking green vegetables, the volatile acids may escape easily, aiding in the retention of the green pigment.

Canned vegetables are heated in a steam-jacketed kettle, stockpot, steamer, or oven. Overheating, as with overcooking of fresh and frozen vegetables, results in further loss of nutrients and a soft-textured, unattractive, and poor-flavored product.

Dried vegetables are soaked before cooking to restore the water content and to shorten the cooking time. Legumes will absorb enough water to approximately double their dry weight, with an attendant increase in volume. The length of the soaking period depends on the temperature of the water, with warm water cutting the soaking time to about half. The vegetable may be covered with boiling water, let stand for 1 hour, then cooked until tender; or they may be covered with cold water and soaked overnight, drained, then cooked.

Small batch or continuous cooking of vegetables throughout the meal service is the most satisfactory way to obtain high-quality products. Quantities of not more than 10-pound lots, and preferably 5-pound batches, should be cooked at intervals as needed. High-speed steamers and small tilting steam-jacketed kettles behind the service line are the most useful kinds of equipment for batch cooking of vegetables.

Salads

Preparation of Ingredients. Salad greens should be clean, crisp, chilled, and well drained. Wash in a spray of water or in a large container of water, shake off excess moisture, drain thoroughly, and refrigerate. All ingredients for salads should be chilled thoroughly and drained when necessary.

Arrangement. To make salads efficiently, prepare all ingredients and chill. Arrange salad plates or bowls on trays that have been lined up on a worktable. Place a leafy underliner on each plate, then add the body of the salad to the plates. This may be a mixed salad, measured with a dipper or scoop, or it may be a placed salad in which individual ingredients are arranged on the underliner. Chopped lettuce placed in the lettuce cup gives height to the salad. Top garnishes add the final touch of color and flavor contrast. The trays of salads are then refrigerated until service but should not be held more than a few hours or the salads will wilt. Dressings generally are served separately or added just before serving, except in potato salad and some entrée salads where flavor is improved by standing 2 to 4 hours after mixing.

Salad Bar. The basic salad bar consists of salad greens with a variety of accompaniments and dressings. Lettuce usually is the main ingredient, but other greens and accompaniments are usually added. In addition to vegetables and fruits, chopped hard-cooked eggs, crumbled crisp bacon, croutons, shredded cheese, cottage cheese, cabbage slaw, pasta salads, molded fruit gelatin, and other prepared salads often appear on salad bars. A variety of dressings is offered. The salad bar should be attractively presented and the salad ingredients kept cold. A logical arrangement places chilled plates or bowls on ice first, near the greens, followed by the accompaniments, the prepared salads, and, finally, the dressings. The salad bar offers an opportunity for creativity and can be an effective merchandising tool.

Sandwiches

Sandwiches may be prepared to order in commercial foodservice operations by pantry workers and/or short-order cooks. Fillings are made and refrigerated, margarine or butter is softened, lettuce is cleaned and crisped, and other ingredients prepared ready for assembling. Ingredients should be arranged for maximum efficiency, with everything needed within easy reach of both hands.

In large quantity, all sandwiches needed may be made and refrigerated until service or, in cafeteria service, may be assembled a few at a time. Hot sandwiches may be made up and grilled or baked as needed, or for cafeteria service, the fillings may be cooked and the sandwiches assembled on the cafeteria counter. An efficient workstation should be set up for making sandwiches and an assembly-line procedure used. Place bread slices on a baking sheet or tray and brush with margarine, butter, or mayonnaise, then spread or place the filling, according to the type of sandwich being made, on all slices on the tray. Add the top bread slices to all the sandwiches. For grilled sandwiches, brush the top and bottom slices with melted margarine or butter. Measure fillings with a dipper or scoop and portion sliced meat or cheese according to count or weight. The recipes or instruction sheets should include the directions for portioning.

Sanitation is important in the making of cold sandwiches because of the amount of handling involved and because they are not cooked. Mixed fillings containing meat, poultry, fish, eggs, or mayonnaise should be prepared the day they are to be served, and only in such quantities as will be used during one serving period. Fillings should be refrigerated until needed, and if sandwiches are made ahead they, too, should be refrigerated. Lettuce should be omitted from sandwiches to be stored for some time in the refrigerator because the lettuce will wilt and become unappetizing.

Soups

Most soups can be classified as clear or unthickened, and cream or thick. *Clear* or *unthickened* soups are based on a clear, unthickened broth or stock. Vegetables, pasta, rice, meat, or poultry products may be added. *Bouillon* is a clear soup without solid ingredients. *Consommé* is a concentrated flavorful broth or stock that has been clarified to make it clear and transparent. *Broth* or *stock*, the basic ingredient for all clear soups, is made by simmering meat, poultry, seafood, and/or vegetables in water to extract their flavor. Brown stock, made from beef that has been browned before simmering, and white or light stock, made from veal and/or chicken, are the stocks used most often. Because the making of stock is so time consuming, many foodservice operations use concentrated bases, which are mixed with water to make flavored liquids similar to stocks. Bases vary in quality, with the best products being composed mainly of meat or poultry extracts. These are perishable and must be refrigerated. Many bases have salt as their principal ingredient, so it is important to read the list of ingredients on the label. When using these bases, the amount of salt and other seasonings in the soup recipe may need to be adjusted.

Cream or *thick* soups are made with a thin white sauce combined with mashed, strained, or finely chopped vegetables, chicken, fish, or meat. Chicken stock may be used to replace part of the milk in the sauce to enhance the flavor. *Chowders* are unstrained, thick soups prepared from seafood, poultry, meat, and/or vegetables. *Bisques* are mixtures of chopped shellfish, stock, milk, and seasonings, usually thickened. *Purees* are soups that are naturally thickened by pureeing one or more of their ingredients.

Sauces

Basic to many sauces is a *roux*, which is a cooked mixture of equal parts by weight of fat and flour. A roux may range from white, in which the fat and flour are cooked only for a short time, to brown, cooked until it is light brown in color and has a nutty taste and aroma.

Many meat and vegetable sauces are modifications of basic recipes, such as white sauce, bechamel sauce, and brown sauce. *White sauce* is made with a roux of fat, usually margarine or butter, and flour, with milk as the liquid. White sauce is used as a basis for cream soups, as a sauce for vegetables, and as an ingredient in many casseroles. *Bechamel sauce* and its variations use milk and chicken stock as the liquid and are generally served with seafood, eggs, poultry, or vegetables. *Brown sauce* is made with a well-browned roux and beef stock and is used mainly with meats.

Bakeshop Production

Breads, cakes, cookies, pies, and other desserts may be produced in a separate bakeshop or made in an area of the main kitchen in which ovens, mixers, and other equipment are available. Although some foodservice operations purchase all or some of these items already prepared, others prefer to make these on the premises either from mixes or "from scratch."

The choice of baking mixes influences the finished product and should be made only after testing and comparing more than one brand. Some large foodservices contract with manufacturers to make mixes to their specifications. If mixes are used, the baked product may be individualized by variations in finishing and presentation. For example, a basic white cake may be baked as a sheet cake or made into a layer cake by cutting the sheet cake into two pieces and placing one on top of the other. A variety of icings may be used with a basic plain cake. Many possibilities exist also when making up plain or sweet roll dough.

If mixes are not used for breads and cakes, balanced formulas should be developed and standardized for the pan sizes used in the foodservice. Many variations are possible if good basic recipes are developed for butter, white, and chocolate cakes, and for biscuits, muffins, and rolls. An important factor in successful bakeshop production is the weighing and portioning of batters and doughs. Each recipe should include information on what size of pan to use and the weight of batter for each pan for products such as cakes, coffee cakes, and loaf breads; the weight of each roll or bun; and the size of dipper for muffins and drop cookies.

A baking sheet 18 × 26 inches and 1½ inches deep with straight sides is used for cakes, cookies, and some quick breads. A half-size baking sheet 12 × 18 inches is often used and is especially good for layer cakes. If a baking pan 12 × 18 inches, or 12 × 20 inches, with 2½- to 3-inch sides is used, special attention must be given to the amount of batter in the pans. Loaf pans for pound cakes and quick breads, and tube pans for foam cakes, vary in size and should be selected according to the size of serving desired. Pans should be prepared before mixing of the products begins. Pans for angel-food and sponge cakes are not greased; baking powder biscuits and cookies with high fat content are usually placed on ungreased baking sheets. Most other pans are either lightly greased, greased and floured, or covered with a parchment paper liner.

The contents of this appendix provide a basic overview of equipment that was available at the time it was written. Because this is an area that is constantly changing, careful research should be done before making any equipment decisions. Visiting factories, talking to manufacturers and sales representatives, testing equipment, consulting kitchen designers, and attending trade shows are ways for a foodservice manager to update his/her knowledge in the area.

The current goals of all types of equipment design are improved performance, reduced energy usage, efficient use of space, reduced labor, durability, ease of cleaning/operating/servicing, and multitasking capability. Long before "sustainable design" became an international movement, foodservice equipment designers were developing equipment that was more energy efficient and consumed less water and less electricity while in use.

The individual characteristics of the foodservice operation and its needs will determine which choices should be made for each piece of equipment purchased.

COOKING EQUIPMENT

Ranges

In commercial foodservice terminology, *range* refers to the cooktop unit. A variety of cooktops and combinations of these are available (Figure 1). *Open burners* for gas flames or electric coils are the most popular and are usually associated with short-order preparation (Figure 2). Heat is concentrated under kettles; burners come in different sizes to fit the various size pans from small saucepans to large stock pots; heating elements and grates are simple in design, easily removable for cleaning; gas cones are elevated so combustion and ventilation

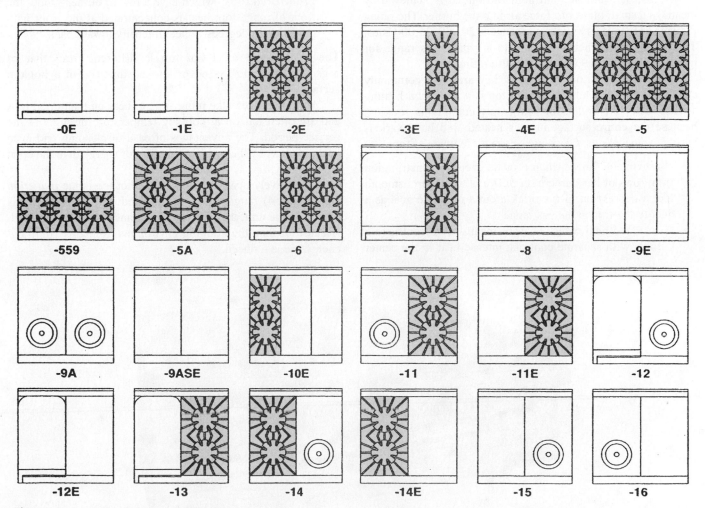

Figure 1 Chart of heavy-duty gas range tops.
Source: Courtesy of the Montague Company, Hayward, CA.

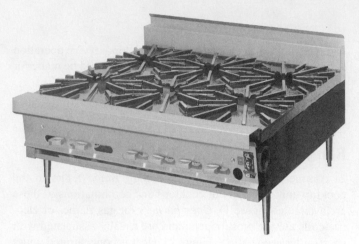

Figure 2 Open-top range.
Source: Courtesy of the Montague Company, Hayward, CA.

Figure 3 Combination closed-top (uniform hot top) and graduated hot top range.
Source: Courtesy of the Montague Company, Hayward, CA.

can be complete; burners can be turned on and off as needed; instant heat is available; and high Btu output is achieved by means of a small blower to force air into the burner. The rating for each burner of a typical sauté range is 20,000–35,000 Btus. This is powerful when compared to a typical gas range for home use that has a 9,000–15,000 Btu rating.

Closed burners, or *hot tops* as they are most commonly called, are ranges where the entire top is a flat metal heating surface. They are styled for heavy-duty continuous cooking, because the entire surface area is heated, and have various burner arrangements. Gas ranges have these types of tops:

- **Uniform hot tops**, which provide even heat distribution from rows of bar burners set in fire brick under a smooth top; a depression in the brick around the edge acts as a duct to the flue in the gas range
- **Graduated heat**, which heats by means of concentric ring burners with separate controls; intense heat in the center

(approximately 1,100°F) to low heat at the edge (450°F) (Figure 3 shows a combination uniform hot top and graduated hot top range); projections on the underside of the top help direct heat to edges
- **Front-fired tops**, which have a row of burners under the front of range top; heat is concentrated at the front with gradation in degrees of heat intensity toward back

The top surface of a hot top is different from that of a griddle, and food is never cooked directly on a hot top surface.

Hot top ranges take more time to heat up than open tops and are often left on at cooking temperature throughout the service period. The advantages of ease of cleaning and even heat are offset by the much greater use of energy than the open burner ranges.

A relatively new variation on the hot top is the *induction top* (Figure 4) range. Heat is generated only when a pan is placed on the unit, and only utensils transfer heat to the food. Because of this, the cooking environment remains cool, and energy use is reduced.

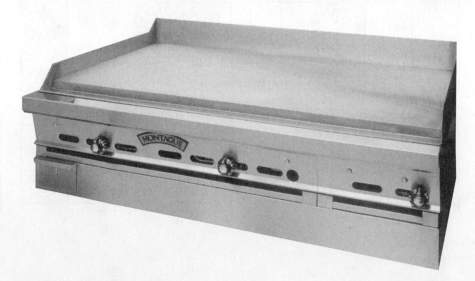

Figure 4 Induction hot top range.
Source: Courtesy of the Montague Company, Hayward, CA.

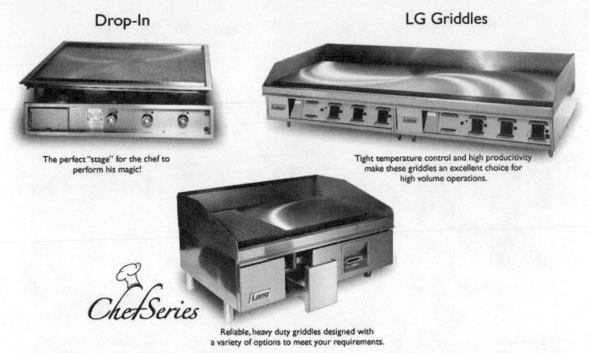

Drop-In

The perfect "stage" for the chef to perform his magic!

LG Griddles

Tight temperature control and high producitivity make these griddles an excellent choice for high volume operations.

ChefSeries

Reliable, heavy duty griddles designed with a variety of options to meet your requirements.

Figure 5 Three styles of griddle top ranges.
Source: Courtesy of Star Manufacturing International, Inc., St. Louis, MO.

Griddle tops are designed for food to be cooked directly on the range top surface (Figure 5). Griddles are usually 3/4- or 1-inch thick and have separate temperature controls for every two feet of surface length. Because fat is involved with griddle cooking, splatter guards around the perimeter and grease troughs are important parts of a griddle top. Griddles are available with a grooved surface to provide food with a broiled appearance.

The popularity of Asian food has led to the introduction of *wok top ranges*, which are variously called Chinese ranges, chop suey–style ranges, and guangdong-style ranges (Figure 6). Some operations also find a *stock pot range* useful (Figure 7).

Figure 6 A wok range.
Source: Courtesy of the Montague Company, Hayward, CA.

Figure 7 A stock pot range.
Source: Courtesy of the Montague Company, Hayward, CA.

Maximizers

Electric, 30", 36" & 60"

Maximize your cooking space with Lang's 30"
electric convection oven and range combination

Lang offers traditional electric ranges which are available
with either conventional or convection ovens, plus your choice
of griddle, hot top and French plate top sections.

Figure 8 Two range ovens.

Source: Courtesy of Star Manufacturing International, Inc., St. Louis, MO.

As shown in Figure 1, manufacturers will build any combination of burners and hot tops in approximately 12-inch widths. Cooktops can then be combined with a variety of choices to put above and below them. Below-range options include an oven (Figure 8), storage cabinet (Figure 9), refrigeration (Figure 10), or no base (the range is mounted on a tabletop) (Figure 11). A flue-riser is usually mounted above the range to prevent splatters on the back wall and to direct flue gases to the exhaust hood. At the top of the flue-riser, choices include one or two shelves (Figure 12), a *salamander broiler* (Figure 13), or a *cheesemelter* (Figure 14).

Ranges are available in two weights:

1. Heavy-duty ranges: Durable and well suited for large-volume foodservice operations with constant usage, as in hotels, large restaurants, colleges, hospitals. Approximate sizes of sections: electric—36 inches wide, 36 inches deep, 32 inches high; gas—31 to 34 inches wide, 34 to 42 inches deep, 33 to 34 inches high.

2. Medium weight or restaurant type: Lighter in construction than heavy-duty ranges and used where demands are less constant, such as in short-order cooking, or where use is intermittent, such as in churches and clubs. Complete units, 6, 8, or 10 burners, or combination with fry-top and/or even-heat top; 1 or 2 ovens. Approximate size 35 to 64 inches wide, 27

Figure 9 A range with cabinet below.

Source: Courtesy of the Montague Company, Hayward, CA.

Figure 10 A range with refrigeration below.
Source: Courtesy of the Montague Company, Hayward, CA.

to 32 inches deep, 34 inches high; ovens, 26 inches wide, 22 inches deep, 15 inches high.

Range sections are often joined to other modular units, such as broilers and fryers, to make a complete cooking unit (Figure 15). The *Euro-style range,* sometimes called Waldorf or Island-style range, is gaining in popularity, especially in upscale operations and display kitchens. The modular equipment in the Euro-style range is back-to-back (Figure 16).

Two-Sided Cookers

Often called a *clamshell*, this type of cooker offers the benefits of both a griddle and a grill (Figure 17). Some models sandwich

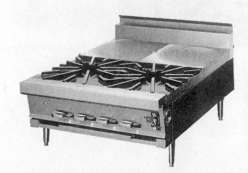

Figure 11 A tabletop range with optional legs.
Source: Courtesy of the Montague Company, Hayward, CA.

Figure 12 A range with shelves above.
Source: Courtesy of the Montague Company, Hayward, CA.

Figure 13   A range with a salamander above.

Source: Courtesy of the Montague Company, Hayward, CA.

electric cookers are available and are constructed of stainless steel, varying in widths from two to six feet. The platens are made of cast iron, highly polished steel, cold-rolled steel, or a chrome finish.

A relative newcomer in two-sided cooking technology is the *steam shell cooker*. As shown in Figure 18, the steam shell works by circulating steam below the cooking surface. This allows for near-instant temperature recovery and even surface heat when cold food is placed on the griddle. Steam is disbursed to the food when the lid is closed, which reduces cooking time and allows food to retain moisture and natural flavors. The growing popularity of panini-style toasted sandwiches on crusty breads makes a sandwich toaster such as the one shown in Figure 19 a good addition. The toaster adds grill marks to the bread.

Broilers

Salamanders and *cheesemelters* are types of broilers (see Figures 13 and 14). Salamanders are designed to broil, brown, finish, and reheat food products. Cheesemelters provide a finishing touch on a variety of foods and are used heavily for Mexican and Italian dishes.

Hearth-type or open-top broilers utilize a heavy cast iron grate horizontally above the heat source. Charcoal or chunks of irregular size ceramic or other refractory material

food between a heated top and bottom plate, or platen. This eliminates the need for turning. Other models utilize a bottom plate and an infrared, noncontact broiler on top. Both gas and

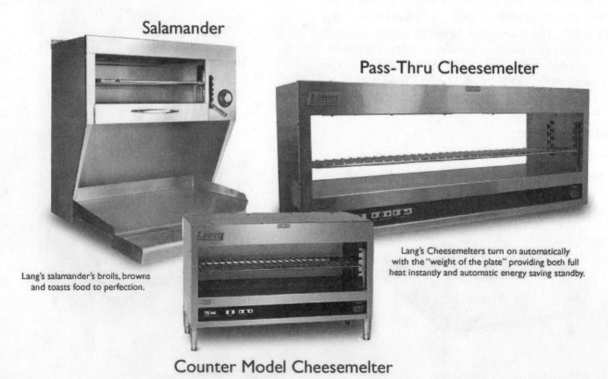

Salamander

Pass-Thru Cheesemelter

Counter Model Cheesemelter

Lang's salamander's broils, browns and toasts food to perfection.

Lang's Cheesemelters turn on automatically with the "weight of the plate" providing both full heat instantly and automatic energy saving standby.

Figure 14   Three cheesemelters.

Source: Courtesy of Star Manufacturing International, Inc., St. Louis, MO.

Figure 15 A bank of modular cooking equipment.
Source: Courtesy of the Montague Company, Hayward, CA.

above gas or electric burners form the radiant bed of heat. Juice and fat drippings cause smoking and flaming that necessitate an efficient exhaust fan over the broiler. These are available in multiple sections of any desired length (Figure 20).

Deep Fat Fryers

Deep fat fryers are made of chromium-plated steel or stainless steel and have an automatic temperature control with signal light and timer; quick heat recovery; cool sediment zone; self-draining device; and easy removal of sediment and filtering of

Figure 16 Euro-style range unit.
Source: Courtesy of the Montague Company, Hayward, CA.

fat. Capacity is expressed in pounds of fat or pounds cooked per hour, and fuel input is used to determine production capacity. These should fry from 1½ to 2 times the weight of fat per hour.

Types: Fryers are available in these types:

1. **Deep fat fryers:** Sizes from 11×11 to 24×24 inches with fat capacities of 13 to 130 pounds. Models are available as freestanding, counter, or built-in, single, or multiple units (Figure 21). The bank of deep fat fryers shown in Figure 22 is computer-controlled to automatically control temperature and cooking time. There are three types of fryers in this category: open-pot, tube-style, and flat-bottom. They are available in varying sizes, from 11×11 to 24×24 inches with oil (shortening) capacities of 13 to 130 pounds; the menu will help determine the right type and size of fryer.

2. **Pressure deep fat fryers:** Equipped with a tightly sealed cover, allowing moisture given off during cooking to build up steam pressure within the kettle; cooking is accomplished in approximately one third of the normal time.

3. **Semiautomatic speed production model:** Equipped with conveyer to permit continuous batch cooking and automatic discharge of product as completed.

4. **Convection deep fat fryers:** Combine convection cooking, continuous fat filtration, and a heat exchanger to produce an energy-efficient, highly productive piece of equipment (Figure 23).

Installation: Adequate ventilation is necessary, venting into hood recommended; flue venting from fryer to general

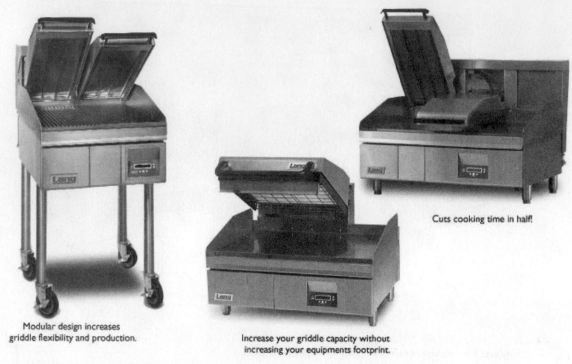

Modular design increases
griddle flexibility and production.

Cuts cooking time in half!

Increase your griddle capacity without
increasing your equipments footprint.

Figure 17 Two-sided clamshell cookers with a griddle on the bottom and a broiler on the top.
Source: Courtesy of Star Manufacturing International, Inc., St. Louis, MO.

vent flue is not desirable; table or work space adjacent to fryer is necessary.

Tilting Frypan

A versatile piece of equipment, a tilting frypan can be used as a frypan, braising pan, griddle, kettle, steamer, thawer, proofer,

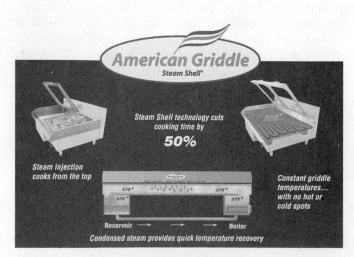

Figure 18 How the steam shell griddle works.
Source: Courtesy of American Griddle, Fort Wayne, IN.

bagel maker, oven, or food warmer-server. It eliminates most top-of-range cooking, provides for one-step preparation of many menu items, and can double as a sink to assist with cleanup chores if necessary. All interior and exterior surfaces are of heavy-duty stainless steel. Features include a contoured pouring spout; one-piece counterbalanced hinged cover; self-locking worm-and-gear tilt mechanism; even-heat smooth flat bottom (either gas or electric); and automatic thermostat heat controls for a wide range of temperatures. This equipment is available in several sizes and capacities as floor models mounted on tubular legs with or without casters, wall-mounted, or small electric table-mounted (Figure 24); conserves fuel and labor; and has quick-connect installation conducive to rapid rearrangement, easy maintenance, and good sanitation. It is easy to clean and reduces use of pots and pans and their washing.

Pasta Cookers

The popularity of Italian food is the impetus for the development of equipment to cook small batches of various kinds of pasta easily. Very similar in appearance to a deep-fat fryer, this equipment allows individual servings of different kinds of pasta to be lowered into boiling water in wire baskets and cooked simultaneously (Figure 25).

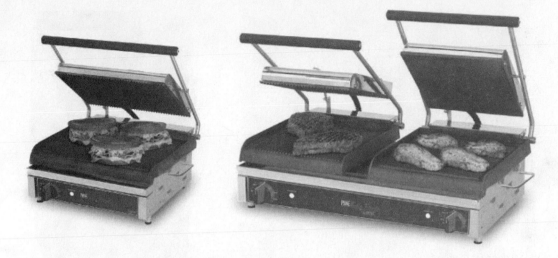

Toasted hot sandwiches on fresh, craft-made breads, flatbreads and crusty rolls are growing in popularity and a delicious way to add a signature item to the menu. A Lang PaneBella® Fresco™ Panini-style sandwich toaster can add variety and boost perceived value for your daily sandwich offerings while adding appetizing grill marks to a variety of foods. The professional Lang PaneBella® Fresco™ Series sandwich toasters are built to last with heavy-duty materials and reliable components unlike import and consumer-grade products not made to stand up to everyday use and abuse.

Figure 19 Panini-style sandwich toasters.

Source: Courtesy of Star Manufacturing International, Inc., St. Louis, MO.

Lang ChefSeries Charbroilers are equipped with a digital electronic timer to ensure products are cooked to the exact time, every time without needing to buy external timers. Fully integrated digital temperature probe eliminates guesswork on when products have reached safe serving temperatures.

Lang charbroilers deliver maximum heat to provide the taste and look of charbroiled menu items.

Figure 20 Charbroilers.

Source: Courtesy of Star Manufacturing International, Inc., St. Louis, MO.

Figure 21   Conventional deep fat fryer.
Source: Courtesy of Frymaster LLC, Shreveport, LA.

Ovens

The two basic oven designs are *still-air radiation*, in which heated air circulates around the outside of the heating chamber and radiates through a lining, and *convection*, where heated air from a heat source is forced over and around food racks by fans located on the rear wall of the oven.

Features include all welded construction of structural steel for durable rigid frames; inner lining of 18-gauge rust-proof sheet metal reinforced to prevent buckling; a minimum of 4 inches of nonsagging insulation on all sides, up to 10 inches in large bakery ovens; thermostatic heat control that is precise between 150°F and 550°F; signal lights and timer; a level oven floor or deck of steel, tile, or transite (concrete and asbestos combination); well-insulated, counterbalanced doors that open level with the bottom of the oven to support a minimum 150-pound weight; nonbreakable hinges; concealed manifolds and wiring; cool handles; a system designed to eject vapors and prevent flowback of condensate; a light that is operated from outside the oven; a steam injector for baking

Figure 23   Convection fryer.
Source: Courtesy of Hobart Corp., Troy, OH.

Figure 24   A tilting frypan.
Source: Courtesy of Groen—A Dover Industries Co.

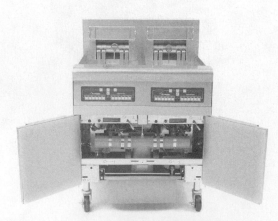

Figure 22   A system of computer-controlled deep fat fryers.
Source: Courtesy of Frymaster LLC, Shreveport, LA.

Figure 25   A pasta cooker.

of hard rolls; thermocouple attachments for internal food-temperature record; and glass windows in doors that are available on request.

Types: Ovens come in these types:

1. Deck: Units stacked to save space; separate heating elements and controls for each unit and good insulation between decks; decks at good working heights; 7 or 8 inches clearance for baking, 12 to 16 inches high for roasting; capacity expressed in number of 18 × 26-inch bun pans per deck; pie, cake, or baking pans should be sized to fit multiples of that dimension; floor space requirements and inside dimensions vary with types. An example of a typical one-section oven of compact design on 23-inch legs is shown in Figure 26):

- **Floor space requirements:** 60½ inches wide, 39½ inches deep without flue deflector
- **Inside dimensions:** 42 inches wide, 32 inches deep, 7 inches high
- **Capacity:** Two 18 × 26-inch bun pans; 24 one-pound loaves of bread; 12 ten-inch pies
- **Btu/hour:** 50,000

2. Convection oven: Forced air circulation cabinet, which uses a high-speed centrifugal fan to force air circulation and guarantee even-heat distribution by an airflow pattern over and around the product in a minimum of time, from one-third to three-quarters of time required in a conventional oven (Figure 27). More cooking is accomplished in smaller space because food is placed on multiple racks instead of on a single deck.

Sizes vary with the manufacturers, but a typical convection oven measures 36 inches wide by 33 inches deep or larger models 45 inches wide by 24½ inches deep. Removable rack glides designed to accommodate 8 or 9 trays or baking sheets,

Figure 26   Deck ovens.
Source: Courtesy of Hobart Corp., Troy, OH.

F Series Ovens

Durability, reliability and economy in one heavy duty package!

G & E Series Ovens

The G & E Series Convection ovens are the workhorses of Lang's Convection oven line. These ovens have stood the test of time in the most demanding foodservice operations.

ChefSeries

Lang's ChefSeries convection ovens are the most advanced ovens in the industry. These ovens can do most of what a combi oven can do at 2/3 less cost.

Figure 27 Three styles of convection ovens.

Source: Courtesy of Star Manufacturing International, Inc., St. Louis, MO.

2 inches apart, thus holding more than other ovens that require greater floor space. Units may be stacked to double the output in the relatively small floor space. Convection ovens must be well insulated; may have interiors of stainless steel or vitreous enameled steel. Shelves and shelf supports lift out for easy cleaning; fitted with inside lights, timer, thermostatic heat control, glass doors or window in doors, removable spillage pan. Quick-connect installation and addition of casters made for flexibility in arrangement. Muffle-type seals on doors for roasting and baking reduce shrinkage because of moisture retention and reduced time for cooking. Figure 28 shows a roll-in plate rack, a roll-in tray rack, and a warmer to be used in conjunction with a convection oven.

3. **Revolving tray or reel ovens:** Flat tray decks suspended between two revolving spiders in a Ferris-wheel type of rotation; compact, space saving; welded steel, heat-tight construction; all parts highly resistant to heat and corrosion; main bearings and entire tray load supported independently of side walls; trays stabilized to keep level and sway proof; each tray equipped with individual emergency release; heavy-duty motor; smooth roller-chain drive, self-adjusting, automatic controls. Example of relative dimensions: four trays, each 96 inches long × 26 inches wide; capacity, twenty 18 × 26-inch

bun pans; outside, 10 feet 2 inches wide, 7 feet 4 inches deep, 6 feet 7 inches high. Small units 3½ feet deep and six-pan units are available for small foodservice operations.

Figure 28 A plate rack with trolley and a pan rack with trolley are designed to roll food directly into a convection oven. The thermal cover fits over both.

Source: Courtesy of Robert Norlander, VP of Marketing, Cleveland Range, Cleveland, OH.

Figure 29 A combination rotary oven.
Source: Courtesy of Hobart Corp., Troy, OH.

4. Rotary ovens: Similar to revolving tray ovens except rotation is on a vertical axis instead of a horizontal one. Both revolving tray and rotary type ovens are most suitable for large-volume baking (Figure 29).

5. Microwave ovens: Electromagnetic energy directed into heating cavity by magnetrons producing microwaves that penetrate food, rapidly and evenly heating water and other polarized molecules within it and causing almost instantaneous cooking of the food; energy produced at given rate is not stored, nor does it heat the air surrounding or the dish containing the food (glass, china, plastic, paper); components include heating cavity of stainless steel, radio-frequency generator, power supply, usually 220 volts, between 30 and 50 amperes; must pass close inspection to ensure safety during use; automatic shut-off before door can be opened. Can be stacked; used extensively for fast reheating of prepared bulk or plated foods, but items can also be cooked quickly and served immediately on the same dish.

6. Combination ovens: (a) an oven that combines a convection oven, pressureless steamer, proof cabinet, and cook-

Figure 30 This combination steamer convection oven is well suited for a small operation.
Source: Courtesy of Groen—A Dover Industries Co.

and-hold oven in a single compact unit (Figure 30); (b) an ultrahigh-speed oven that uses a combination of microwaves and high-velocity convection heat to cook food at speeds that surpass a microwave; and (c) an oven that uses a combination of intense light and infrared energy to cook foods quickly. A "MicroBakery" is shown in Figure 31 that combines a combi oven, proofer, and staging cabinet all within five feet of space.

7. Conveyor ovens: Programmable for temperature/speed/heat zones, typically uses one of three technologies: (a) infrared—a radiant heating process that does not heat the air surrounding the food but transfers heat directly to the surfaces it contacts; (b) jet sweep—sometimes called air impingement; hundreds of air ducts under and over the food sweep away cold air, cooking the food uniformly (Figure 32); (c) convection—fans circulate hot air in the oven cavity.

8. Cook-and-hold ovens: Food temperature rises until nearly done, then burner turns off and a fan continues to circulate stored heat. Once the hold temperature is reached, the burner and fan cycle to maintain heat.

9. Other specialty ovens such as wood-burning ovens and gas-fired brick ovens, often called pizza ovens because of their most common use (Figure 33).

Steam Equipment

Steam may be supplied from a central heating plant, directly connected to the equipment, or generated at point of use, which requires a water connection and a means of heating it to form the steam. Pressures vary according to needs, with an automatic pressure control and safety valve if the supply is above 5 to 8 pounds per square inch (psi). Equipment is made of stainless steel or aluminum for rust resistance and has smooth exterior and interior surfaces for easy cleaning and

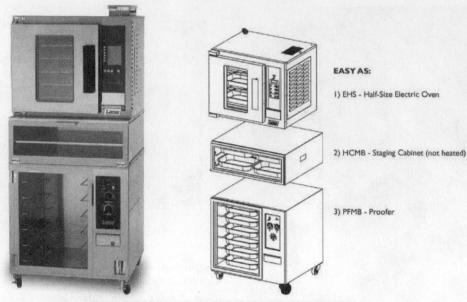

The Lang MicroBakery requires only five square feet of space. It's equipped with a
half-size convection oven, proofer and staging cabinet to provide a compact bakery option
for chain and retail operations with limited space and personnel.

EASY AS:

1) EHS - Half-Size Electric Oven

2) HCMB - Staging Cabinet (not heated)

3) PFMB - Proofer

Figure 31 A convection oven, proofer, and staging cabinet fit into five square feet of space to provide a compact bakery operation.

Source: Courtesy of Star Manufacturing International, Inc., St. Louis, MO.

sanitation; timing and automatic shut-off devices; and concealed control valves. Steam cookers offer fast cooking in two general types: *cabinet cookers* and *steam-jacketed kettles*.

Cabinet Cookers. Steam injected into the cooking chamber comes in direct contact with food. To ensure that steam is clean, the supply may need to be generated on-premise from a tap-water source instead of from the steam system for a group

of buildings. Features include door gaskets to seal; doors of full-floating type, with automatic bar-type slide-out shelves linked to doors; timers and automatic shut-off, and safety throttle valve for each compartment so doors cannot be opened until steam pressure is reduced; perforated or solid baskets for food; and capacity in terms of number of 12 × 20-inch counter pans side by side each shelf or 10 × 23-inch bulk pans. Counter pans are used both for cooking and serving.

Figure 32 This conveyor oven uses air impingement technology.

Source: Courtesy of Lincoln Food Service Products, Inc.

Figure 33 A pizza oven.
Source: Courtesy of the Montague Company, Hayward, CA.

Types: The following types of cabinet cookers are available:

1. Heavy-duty, direct connected steamers: Compartments fabricated to form one-piece body and entire interior of stainless steel; 5 to 8 pounds per square inch with continuous steam inflow and drain-off of condensate; one to four compartments with adjustable shelves; inside dimensions 28 × 21 inches desirable to accommodate two 12 × 20-inch counter pans on each shelf, and 10 to 16 inches high.

2. Pressure cookers: Operate at 15 pounds steam pressure for small-batch speed cooking; reheating frozen meals or thawing and cooking frozen foods; smaller than free-venting cabinets; self-sealing inside door cannot be opened under pressure; 15-pound safety valve and 30-pound gauge; automatic timers and cutoffs. Inside capacities, from 12 to 40 inches wide, 14 to 28 inches high, 18 to 31½ inches deep; one to three cooking compartments.

3. Self-steam-generating (nonpressure): Intended for installations without direct steam supply; requires water (hot preferred) connection and adequate source of heat supply to produce the steam; steam generators fit below cookers; designs and capacities similar to heavy-duty steamers.

4. Pressureless forced convection steamers: High-speed steam cookers with convection generators producing turbulent steam, without pressure, in the cooking compartment. Doors may be safely opened at any time during cooking cycle, and cooking is faster than in the conventional pressure cooker.

Installation: Heavy-duty steamers of cabinet type may have pedestal support or be equipped with feet and have at least 6-inch clearance from floor, or be wall mounted to save space; install in drip pan or floor depression with drain; modular units available in many combinations with other steam equipment (Figure 34).

Steam-Jacketed Kettles. This equipment has two bowl-like sections of drawn, shaped, welded aluminum or stainless steel with air space between for circulation of steam to heat the inner shell (Figure 35). Food does not come in contact with steam. Features include a steam outlet safety valve and pressure gauge; steam pressure inside the jacket that determines the kettle's operating temperature (e.g., 50 psi = 298°F); direct-connected or self-generated steam supply; full or two-thirds jacketed; stationary or tilting; open or fitted with no-drip, hinged and balanced cover; mounted on tubular legs, pedestal, or wall brackets, or set on a table. It has a power twin-shaft agitator mixer attachment for stirring heavy mixtures while cooking (Figure 36), and an electrically operated device to automatically meter water into the kettle is available. It may have a cold water connection to the jacket to cool products quickly after cooking. Its modular design (square jacket) makes it easy to combine with other modular equipment to save space. Basket insets are available for removing and draining vegetables easily.

Types: The following types of steam-jacketed kettles are available:

1. Deep kettles, fully or two-thirds jacketed: Best for soups, puddings, pie fillings.

Figure 34 Compartment pressureless steamers and jacketed kettle powered by a pressure boiler-in-base.
Source: Courtesy of Groen—A Dover Industries Co.

Figure 35   Floor-mounted, stationary steam-jacketed kettle.

Source: Courtesy of Groen—A Dover Industries Co.

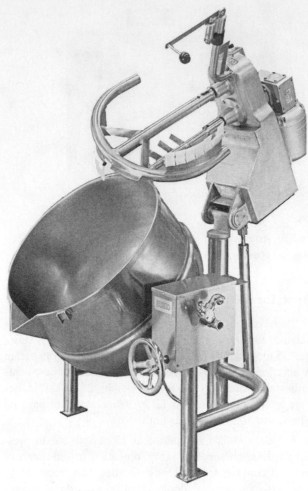

Figure 36   Tilting steam-jacketed kettle with tilt-out twin-shaft agitator.

Source: Courtesy of Groen—A Dover Industries Co.

2. Shallow kettles, always full-jacketed: Suitable for braising and browning meats, stews; prevents crushing of under-layers of food as in deep type.

3. Trunnion or tilting kettles: Mounted on trunnions with tilting device and pouring lip for easy unloading; either power-driven or manual mechanism; self-locking devices to secure kettle in any position; large floor models, or small units mounted to table to form battery; used on deep or shallow-type kettles. Capacities: from 1 quart to 80 gallons; up to 12-gallon size suitable for table mounting and rotation vegetable cookery.

4. Stationary types for liquids or thin mixtures: Tangent outlet for straight-flow drain-off; capacities from 10 to 500 gallons.

Installation: Kettle set for easy draw-off of food; drip into grated drain in floor or table; mixing swivel faucet over kettle to fill or clean; table models at height convenient for workers; adequate voltage or gas supply for self-generating models.

Figures 37 and 38 show equipment designed to be used in the cook/chill or cook/freeze foodservice systems. Food is cooked, packaged in a special airtight and watertight plastic casing at or above pasteurization temperature, chilled rapidly in ice water, and stored up to 45 days in 28°F to 32°F

storage. Pumpable foods are cooked in mixer kettles, pumped into the casings, sealed, and chilled in the tumble chiller. Solid foods, such as roasts, are browned, encased, vacuum-sealed in casings, and then cooked in the cook/chill tank. In this tank, the product is water bath cooked and then rapidly cooled by circulation of ice water in the same tank. Rethermalization may be accomplished in a convection oven, combination oven, a convection steamer, pressure steamer, or steam kettle. Figure 37 shows a cook/chill system designed for a small foodservice operation.

Mixers

Bench models of mixers (Figure 39) are made for use on tables, counters, and back bars; floor models are available. Features include three- or four-speed transmission, ball-bearing action; timed mixing control with automatic shut-off; action designed for thorough blending, mixing, and aerating of all ingredients in bowl; electrically controlled brake; ability to change speeds while in action on some machines; durable

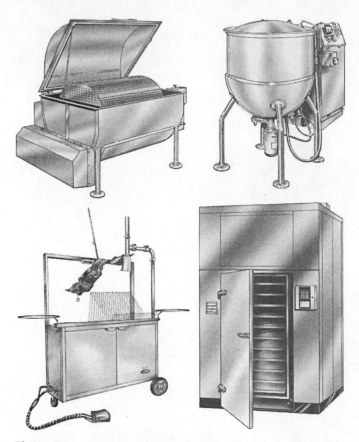

Figure 37 A cook/chill system and its components.
Source: Courtesy of Aladdin Synergetics, Inc.

washable finish as stainless steel or anodized aluminum. Bowls are made of heavily tinned steel or stainless steel. On some models, a safety ring prevents operation of the mixer unless the ring is locked in place (Figure 40).

Standard equipment includes one bowl, one flat beater, one wire whip; other attachments are available such as a dough hook (Figure 41), chopper, slicer, dicer, oil dripper, bowl splash cover, and dolly, purchased separately. Most models have one or two adapters with smaller bowls, beaters, and whips that may be used on the same machine. Capacities are from 5 to 200 quarts.

Choppers, Cutters, Slicers

Some foodservices meet their needs for puréeing, chopping, dicing, shredding, and slicing through the use of mixer attachments; others need specialized pieces of equipment in certain work areas. Various sizes and capacities of such machines are available in pedestal or bench models or mounted on portable stands. A food processor as shown in Figure 42 is useful for puréeing small quantities of food. A typical slicer is shown in Figure 43. All should be made of smooth, noncorrosive metals, have encased motors, safety protectors over blades, and parts removable for cleaning and should slice in horizontal or angle-fed troughs.

Vertical Speed Cutter-Mixer

The high-speed vertical cutter-mixer (VCM) (Figure 44) has a gray enamel cast-iron base, a stainless steel or aluminum bowl, and blades that move at 1,140 rpm. It is designed to mix, cut, blend, whip, cream, grate, knead, chop, emulsify, and homogenize. A counterbalanced see-through bowl cover interlocks with the motor and has an easy tilt design for emptying. It is mounted on a tubular steel frame and has a variety of cutting blades, shafts, and baffles for specific uses. Capacities are 30 and 45 quarts. It can chop 10 heads of lettuce in 3 seconds, make 32 quarts of salad dressing in 60 seconds, grate 20 pounds of cheese in 30 seconds, and make 40 pounds of ham salad in 90 seconds.

Refrigerators

There are three basic categories of refrigerators: reach-ins, walk-ins, and blast chiller/freezers. These can be central or self-contained units. Features include water- or air-cooled compressors; pass-through, cabinet convertible temperatures; efficient nonabsorbent insulation; tight-fitting doors, strong no-sag hinges, strong catches; and all cleanable surfaces and parts. *Reach-ins* are fitted with tray glides to accommodate standard tray sizes or removable wire or slatted stainless steel shelves (Figure 45). *Walk-ins* have portable, sectional, slatted metal shelving. Some reach-in models can be detached from the motor unit to provide portable, temporary refrigerated storage. *Counter units* have individual compressors for salad, frozen dessert, and milk storage areas, and self-leveling dispensers for cold or freezer storage and service. *Ice makers* are central and self-contained units and can make cubes, tubes, or flakes. Capacity is measured in output per hour. Many models and sizes are available. *Water coolers* have a glass filler or bubbler faucet. Capacity depends on cooling volume per hour and size of storage tank. They are designed for convenient storage of clean glasses. *Bottle chillers* have a top opening cabinet, usually found in bar operations. *Wine refrigerators* are reach-in units designed to hold red and white wines at optimal serving temperatures. *Display refrigerators* are reach-ins designed to merchandise products, often with well lit interiors, revolving shelves, and multiple doors for self-service. *Dough retarders* are upright reach-ins or under-counter units designed to hold unbaked dough at a consistent temperature and high humidity. *Undercounter drawers* hold foods at refrigerator or freezer temperatures under a countertop griddle/grill or fryer. *Wall and overcounter* allow wall-mounted refrigeration to provide extra storage over a work or service station.

DISH AND UTENSIL CLEANING EQUIPMENT

Stationary Warewashers

Undercounter or upright, door-type warewashers may be operated by one person and are usually used in small-volume

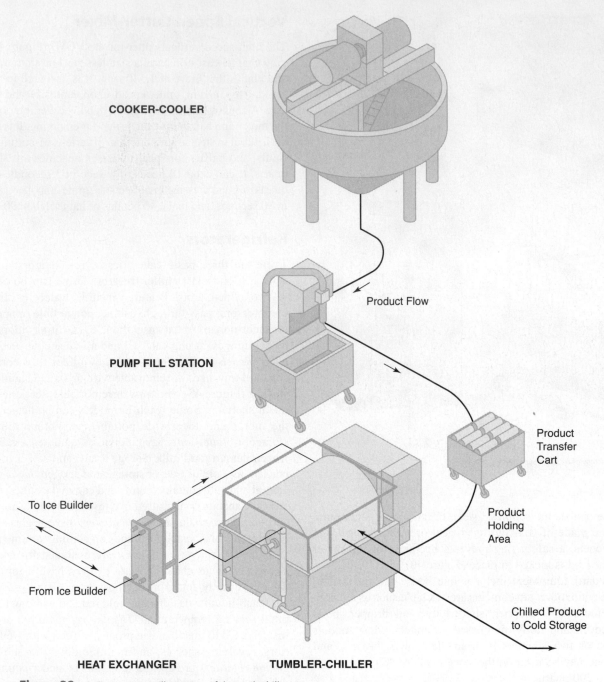

COOKER-COOLER

Product Flow

PUMP FILL STATION

Product Transfer Cart

To Ice Builder

From Ice Builder

Product Holding Area

Chilled Product to Cold Storage

HEAT EXCHANGER   **TUMBLER-CHILLER**

Figure 38   A diagrammatic illustration of the cook-chill process.

operations. Undercounter models are similar to home-style dishwashers in that they may fit under a counter or be free standing. Foodservice models are designed to withstand heavier, more frequent use and to clean faster and with more power, often completing an entire cycle in as little as 90 seconds. Models may include a booster heater, low-detergent alert signal, detergent pump, and pump drains.

Door-type or single-rack warewashers have a 35 to 55 rack per hour capacity and may be designed as a corner or straight-through model.

Moving Warewashers

Rack conveyors are designed to transport racks of ware between wash and rinse arms. They range from single-tank machines capable of washing approximately 125 to 200 racks per hour to multiple tank machines that wash between 250 to more than 300 racks per hour. Optional features may include recirculating prewash and power prewash cycles, corner scraper units, gas-heated and/or low-water models, automatic activators that run the machine only when racks are in it, and automatic loaders and unloaders.

Figure 39 Bench model mixer.
Source: Courtesy of Hobart Corp., Troy, OH.

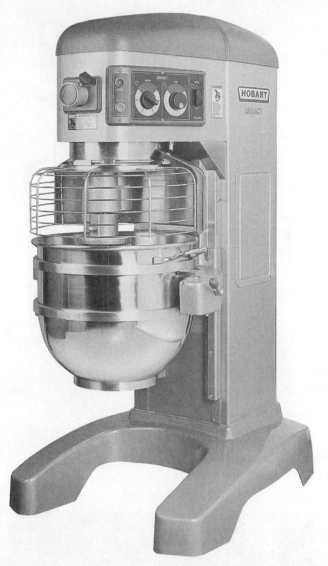

The largest operators require the highest speed warewashers—the flight-type or circular conveyor machines that are capable of handling between 8,000 and 24,000 dishes per hour. Because of the design of the conveyor on a flight-type machine, dishes and trays do not require a rack to move through the prewash, wash, rinse, and final rinse tanks of the machine. Options on this type of warewasher include straight-line or circular configuration, high- or low-temperature operation, customized length (minimum of 13 feet) and width,

Figure 40 Floor model mixer shown with safety guard.
Source: Courtesy of Hobart Corp., Troy, OH.

left-to-right or right-to-left operation, extra water- and energy-saving capability, noise-reducing insulation, custom conveyors, variable speeds, automatic "eyes" to shut off the cycles when no ware is present, dryer attachments, special designs for insulated trays and silverware troughs, and theft-proof/

(a) Flat beater   (b) Wire whip   (c) Dough hook

Figure 41 Mixer attachments.
Source: Courtesy of Hobart Corp., Troy, OH.

Figure 42   Food processor.
Source: Courtesy of Hobart Corp., Troy, OH.

Figure 43   A slicer with an angle-fed trough.
Source: Courtesy of Hobart Corp., Troy, OH.

Figure 44   High-speed cutter-mixer prepares foods in seconds.
Source: Courtesy of Hobart Corp., Troy, OH.

Figure 45   Convenient refrigerator unit may be fitted with pan slides or pull-out shelves; glass doors or same as outside thermal-bonded vinyl finish.
Source: Courtesy of Hobart Corp., Troy, OH.

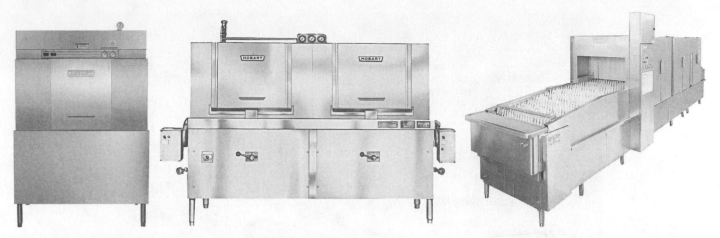

Figure 46 Examples of (a) single-tank, (b) double-tank, and (c) flight-type dishwashers.
Source: Courtesy of Hobart Corp., Troy, OH.

tamper-resistant designs for correctional facilities. Examples of single-tank, double-tank, and flight-type dishwashers are shown in Figure 46.

Specialty Warewashers

Pot and pan/utensil warewashers feature high-pressure water scraping capabilities with a longer wash cycle than standard warewashers. Pot and pan sinks are also available with mechanisms to agitate the wash water such as the Turbowash shown in Figure 47. *Flatware washers* eliminate the problems of nesting spoons and dried-on, difficult-to-clean foods such as eggs that often adhere to flatware. Tray washers are designed to hold all sizes of trays, full sheet pans, and other large, flat-surface items (Figure 48).

Support Systems

Items that may increase efficiency and lower costs in this area are garbage troughs, food waste pulpers, tray accumulators, tray conveyors, blowers and tray dryers, scrape and sort tables, soak sinks, exhaust condensers, automated dispensers, and hot water boosters.

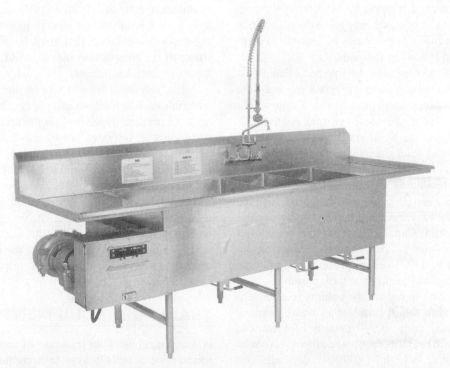

Figure 47 Pot and pan washer.
Source: Courtesy of Hobart Corp., Troy, OH.

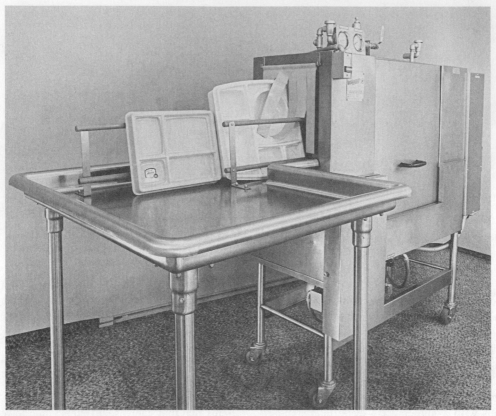

Figure 48   Machine designed especially for washing trays.
Source: Courtesy of Insinger Machine Company.

WASTE DISPOSERS

One system for the disposal of waste may solve the problem in a given situation but, in many cases, it may be feasible to combine two or more of the following methods.

Unit disposers for food waste at vegetable and salad preparation sinks and dish scrapping areas eliminate the need for garbage can collections, storage, and outside pickup unless their installation and use are prohibited by environmental controls. All waste paper, cardboard cartons, wood crates, plastics, tin cans, broken china, and glassware (and garbage) might need to be discharged into trash bins for pickup if incineration of burnable waste is restricted by antipollution regulations in the community.

Can and bottle crushers are capable of reducing this type of disposable bulk up to 90 percent and cut labor costs, refuse space, and cost of pickup. Capacities of models vary from 50 cans and bottles per minute to 7,500 per hour. In the crushing mechanism, rollers set in a "V" design prevent clogging and progressively reduce cans to the smallest bulk possible.

The use of *compactors* to reduce the volume is a convenient and economical aid to the disposal of all waste in many foodservices. One model with 13,000 pounds of force can compact paper, milk cartons, cans, bottles, and food scraps to a minimum 5-to-1 ratio or as high as 200-to-1, depending on the combination of materials. Discharge of the compacted material, up to 50 pounds, into a polybag or carton on a dolly

makes it ready for short-time storage and haul-away. Most machines operate on a 120-volt, 20-ampere outlet, have safety interlocks throughout for operating protection, and a sanitizing-deodorizing spray that may be released at each return stroke of the compaction ram to avoid any objectionable odor from the compacted mass.

The *pulping system* reduces the volume of disposable materials such as food scraps, paper, plastic, and cooked bones up to 85 percent, depending on the mix. Cans, silverware, and some glass are tolerated but are automatically ejected from the pulping tank into a trash box. Durable teeth on a rotating disc and cutters pulp the material in the tank. It is then circulated to a powerful water-press above, reducing the pulp to a semidry form that is forced into a discharge chute to containers for removal as low-volume waste. The water from the press recirculates to the pulping tank. This equipment is available in several sizes. It may be incorporated into the dishwashing system or other area where pulpable waste originates (Figure 49).

TRANSPORT EQUIPMENT

Powered equipment for transport of food and supplies within a foodservice is usually kept to minimum distances by careful planning of area relationships. A thorough study of the advantages, capabilities, and maintenance factors should precede the

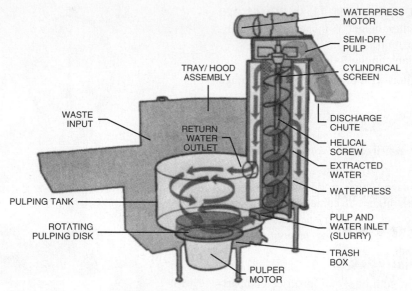

Figure 49 Diagram showing how pulpable waste can be reduced in volume and form.

Source: Courtesy of Hobart Corp., Troy, OH.

selection of a system for a particular situation. Also, automatic and emergency shutoffs, enclosed but easy access to working parts, safety, and cleanability are important features to consider.

Conveyors and Subveyors

Features of this equipment include reverse for two-way service; emergency brakes and safety guards; an automatic stop and start with removal of tray; or continuous flow. *Conveyors* use horizontal transportation and are stationary or mobile units for flexibility of tray or food assembly. *Subveyors* use vertical conveying, intended where space may be limited on a single floor and work or serving units are on different floors.

Monorail and Driverless Vehicles

These types of methods require special equipment and installation. They reduce labor and hand-pushing of carts, are speedy, but are relatively expensive to install. *Monorail* requires an overhead rail and "Amsco" system, a special electronic track under the floor. *Driverless vehicles* are monitored from a control panel, powered by batteries, and are directed over the track to locations on the same floor or to a bank of special elevators that automatically open and close on signal and exit on the assigned floor.

NONMECHANICAL KITCHEN EQUIPMENT

Tables and Sinks

Often fabricated by specification order to fit space and need, tables and sinks are made of stainless steel, No. 12 or 14 gauge, No. 4 grind. Features include welded and polished joinings;

rounded corner construction; seamless stainless steel tubular supports with welded cross rails and braces of the same material; and adjustable inside-threaded stainless steel rounded or pear-shaped feet. Worktables may be fitted with ball-bearing rubber-tired casters, two swivel and two stationary, and brakes on two casters.

Tables. Table tops are made of one sheet without seams; edges integrally finished, rolled edge, raised rolled edge where liquids are used, turned up as flange or splashback with rolled edge. Legs and feet can be tubular, welded, or seamless metal; adjustable; of simple design; and provide a minimum of 6 inches of space between bottom of unit and floor. Drawers operate on ball bearings, equipped with stop, removable. Undershelves: stationary bar, slatted, solid, removable sections; sink or bain-marie (Figure 50).

Figure 50 Kitchen worktable.

Source: Courtesy of Restaurant Equippers. .

Dimensions: Standard, length 48, 60, 72, 84, 96, 108, 120 inches; width 24, 30, 36 inches; height 34 inches; other dimensions by individual specification.

Types: Tables are available in the following types:

1. **Baker's tables:** Fitted with drawers; separate storage bins as specified.

2. **Salad tables:** With or without refrigerated work space and storage, sinks.

3. **Sandwich tables:** Refrigerated storage for fillings; removable cutting boards.

4. **Dish tables:** Well braced sturdy understructure; 3-inch upturned and rolled edges, higher if joined to wall; scrap block, waste drain, sinks for soaking, over-and-under shelves, rack return, tray rest; adequate space for receiving, soiled dishes, clean dishes, preflush.

Sinks. Sinks are available with one, two, or three compartments. Features include all-welded seamless construction, drainboard and splashback integral from one sheet of metal, rolled edges; corners fully rounded with 1-inch radius, coves spherical in shape at intersection of corners; bottom of each compartment scored and pitched to outlet; outlet recessed 5 inches in diameter, 1/2-inch deep, fitted with nonclog waste outlet; partitions: two thicknesses formed of one sheet of metal, folded and welded to bottom and sides of sink; provision for overflow; drainboards pitched to drain into sink; drainboards supported by channel braces to sink legs or wall-bracketed; if longer than 42 inches usually supported by two pipe legs at end away from sink; removable strainer at waste outlet; external level control for outlet valve; stationary or swing faucets.

Dimensions: Standard single compartment, 20, 24, 30, 36, 48, 60, 72 inches long, 20, 24, 30 inches wide, 14, 16 inches deep; two-compartment, 36, 42, 48, 54, 60, 72 inches long, 18, 22, 24, 30 inches wide, 14, 16 inches deep. Others by individual specification; 38-inch height convenient for sinks.

Storage Cabinets, Racks, Carts

Cabinets and racks can be stationary or portable. They can be open or closed and have shelves that are attached, removable, cantilevered, or adjustable. Features include tray slides; sturdy construction of metal or polymer; solid floor; bolted or welded; doors, hinged, or side sliding, side sliding removable, suspension hung. Both stationary or portable types can be heated or refrigerated. Size is determined by needs and space.

Wall-mounted storage and/or workstations can be designed with combinations of grids, shelving, and accessories to store supplies or to transform a traffic aisle by folding down to form temporary workstations.

Scales

A heavy-duty *platform scale* can be built into the floor of the receiving room area for weighing in supplies and food; weight

Figure 51   Receiving area table model scale.
Source: Courtesy of Hobart Corp., Troy, OH.

indicator should be plainly visible from both front and back. *Exact-weight* floor or table models are used in a storeroom, ingredient room, bakeshop, and where recipes are made up (Figure 51). Portion scales are used for weighing individual servings where needed. All types of scales are now available with lighted electronic display (LED) readouts, locking in an accurate weight almost instantly on an easy-to-read screen (Figures 52 and 53).

Cooking Utensils

Cooking utensils should be strong and durable to withstand heavy wear; be made of nontoxic material; be resistant to chipping, dents, cracks, acids, and alkalis; be cleanable; and have even heat spread. Highly polished metal reflects heat, whereas dull metal absorbs and browns food more readily in baking.

Types: A variety of sizes of sauce pans, sauce pots, stock pots, frypans, and roast and bake pans are available:

1. **Aluminum heavy-duty:** double-thick bottoms, extra-thick edge;

2. **Semiheavy:** Lighter weight, uniform thickness, rolled edge;

SERVING EQUIPMENT

Counters

Counters should be designed with an attractive, compact, efficient arrangement for specific foodservice, and be welded and polished in one piece. Hot and cold units should be well insulated and easily cleaned and have separate temperature controls for each unit of heated section and counter guard shields for open food display sections. Portable or built-in self-leveling dish and tray storage may be desired, as well as an adequate tray slide to prevent accidents.

Serving Utensils

Serving utensils come in a variety of sizes of ladles, long-handled spoons, perforated, slotted, and solid; spatulas; and ice cream dippers. They are selected to give predetermined portion size. The capacity or size is marked on ladle handles and on dippers.

Special Counter Equipment

Special counter equipment should have a convenient arrangement and easily operated automatic heat controls.

Types: Special equipment comes in these types:

1. **Coffeemaker:** Urn or battery vacuum makers with cup storage near;

2. **Toasters, egg cookers, grills with hoods; temporary storage cabinets for hot cooked foods, rolls:** Controls for temperature and moisture content; freezer cabinet unit for ice creams; bread dispensers; milk-dispensing machines.

Figure 52 Table model scale with digital readout.
Source: Courtesy of Hobart Corp., Troy, OH.

Self-Leveling Dispensers

Dispensers should have counterweighted springs that bring the platform to a uniform level on removal of items. These are used for foods, dishes, and containers, and for heated, refrigerated, or freezer storage. They can be mobile, stationary, or built-in with open or closed frames of stainless, galvanized, carbon steel or aluminum, and noncorrosive springs.

Types: Dispensers come in the following types:

1. **Tube type:** For plates, saucers, bowls;

2. **Chassis type:** Accommodates square or rectangular trays, or racks, empty or filled; adjustable to vary dispensing height.

3. Stainless steel: Uniform thickness, spot heats over direct fire.

Small equipment includes pudding pans, pie and cake pans, quart and gallon measures, and mixing bowls of lighter-weight metals. Pudding and counter pans should be selected to fit the serving table, refrigerator, and mobile racks for flexibility of use: 12 × 20 inch size is recommended. Clamped-on lids cut spillage losses in transporting prepared foods.

Cutlery

Cutlery is made of high-carbon tooled steel or high-carbon chrome-vanadium steel with full-tang construction and compression-type nickel–silver rivets. Shapes of handles and sizes of items are varied to meet needs. Handle and blade weight should be balanced for easy handling.

Coffeemakers

Coffeemaking equipment falls into two general types: (1) urns for making large quantities of coffee when many people are served in a short period of time and (2) small electronic automatic brewing units for a continuous fresh supply of the beverage. Requirements are fairly simple in either case but are important to the making of an acceptable product. Features

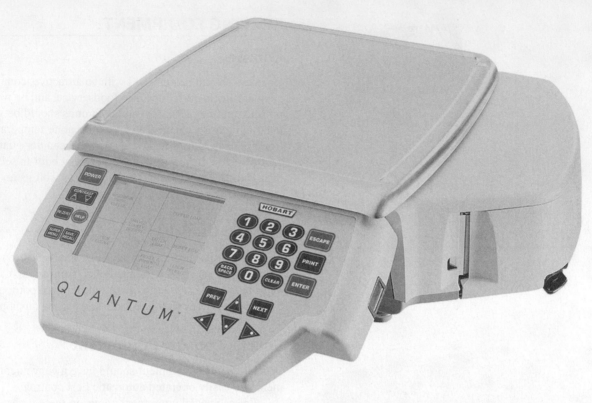

Figure 53 An electronic portion-control food scale gives accurate weight almost immediately on a large LED readout.
Source: Courtesy of Hobart Corp., Troy, OH.

include glass or stainless steel liners for urns and glass or stainless steel decanters for the automatic brewing machines; fluted paper filters; controlled hot water temperature, coffee and water measurement, infusion time, brewing speed, and holding temperatures; equipment is easily cleanable. Installation with quick-disconnect outlets provides for easy relocation of equipment. The use of freeze-dried coffee simplifies the process, reduces time and labor, and eliminates the necessity of discarding coffee grounds.

Mobile Food Serving Carts

Specialized equipment for transporting bulk or served food some distance to the consumer, mobile carts are well insulated, have automatic temperature controls, may require high-voltage outlets; and are engineered for ease in moving and turning. Features include circumference bumper guards; easily cleanable design; combination heated, nonheated, low-temperature, and refrigerated sections; beverage dispensers and other accessories as found on serving counters.

The selection of foodservice equipment by any arbitrary rule would be unwise and ill advised. Each operation must be studied to determine the real needs and purchases made accordingly. The equipment suggested here should serve as only a guide in helping to recall basic considerations regarding various items of equipment.

China

The three types of china are vitrified, semivitrified, and pottery. Of these, only vitrified is considered durable enough for use in most foodservices.

Vitrified china, also known as porcelain, is made of excellent quality clay free from iron, with flint and feldspar added. These materials plus water can be shaped and fired to a high temperature for at least 60 hours, which fuses the mixture into a homogeneous body that is durable and virtually nonabsorbent. At this point, the shaped piece is known as "bisque." The introduction of a metallic ion "alumina" into the body of the materials was a notable improvement in making vitrified china. This enabled the industry to make a thinner, whiter, stronger piece of china with greater edge chip resistance, greater impact strength, and smoother body that has faster surface cleanability than china made without alumina.

The U.S. Bureau of Standards has established three standards for vitrified china for institutional use: (1) *thick:* 5/16 to 3/8 inches thick (which is quite heavy); (2) *hotel:* 5/23 to 1/4 inches thick, with a rolled underedge; and (3) *medium-weight:* sold on the market as "banquet" weight, thinner than hotel weight, with straight edges.

The bureau also tests and sets limits for moisture absorption for each size piece and also tests for durability by use of chipping, impact, and breakage tests under stated conditions. It is essential that the buyer recognize that weight does not mean strength and long life for china. Durability and strength are far more directly related to the quality of materials used and the methods of manufacture employed than they are to weight.

The thick china is commonly used for cafeteria service or other situations where extra-heavy service is demanded of the table appointments. It is clumsy to handle and apt to be unattractive in appearance. All hotel-weight china except cups has a roll under the outer edge that gives the effect of weight and also lessens chipping on the upper side of the plate. This type of china is well adapted for use in operations such as hospitals, residence halls, and restaurants. It is highly resistant to shock, easy to handle, and available in many designs and colors. Banquet-weight china is used extensively in exclusive restaurants, clubs, and the private room service of hospitals. It more closely resembles household dinnerware.

Vitrified heat-resistant ware of good quality is nonabsorbent, stainproof, and withstands high temperatures without crazing or breaking. Items are available in a variety of attractive colors and designs and include coffeepots, teapots, casseroles, ramekins, and individual pudding or pie dishes.

Semivitrified china is a good-quality earthenware that has been fired insufficiently to obtain vitrification. This treatment results in a soft body, which is, therefore, porous and absorbent. Semivitrified china has been given a glaze that seals and finishes the dish, but the glaze may be sensitive to heat shocks and cracks easily. The design may not be permanent, as it is applied after the china is glazed and fired in making semivitrified and semiporcelain china.

Decoration. Three methods are used to put color, designs, and decorations on china: lining, printing, and decalcomania (decals). In *lining*, a line design is applied to the edge or rim of the dish by machine; only one color can be used. In *printing*, any type of design may be applied by stamping or printing on. In *decalcomania*, the design is transferred from a specially prepared paper; any number of colors can be used. After the colored design has been applied on vitrified china by whatever method, the item is dipped into a glaze and fired at a high temperature. The glaze is a molten glass that is applied as a coating to the shaped, fired, and decorated dish and is fused to it. This process seals the surface of the bisque, covers and protects the design, further strengthens the body, makes the surface smooth, and is then highly resistant to chemicals and to cracking, crazing, or marring by physical shock.

Certain colors such as some blue pigments and the application of gold trim are affected by the high temperatures used to fire the glaze, so they may be applied after the glazing process. This design over the glaze is not as satisfactory as an underglaze for institutional foodservice use in most situations. The colors and gold that are put on top of the glaze are less durable and wear away faster than those that are put on under the glaze and protected by it.

Factors in Selection of China. The things to consider when selecting china are its weight and durability, restaurant design, the color and design of the china, budget, the availability of replacements, shapes, sizes, and capacities. In addition, in purchasing china, "firsts"—the most perfect pieces that can be selected from each run of the kiln after the firing process—are the most desirable. They are free from warping, chips, faults in the glaze, thin or uneven glaze, large scars on the underside from the pins on which the china was held during firing, and uneven or poorly applied designs. Other pieces are graded as "seconds" or "thirds," depending on the degree of imperfection. Warped plates are detected by rolling several plates on edge simultaneously. The warped ones show up plainly in the rolling in contrast to the first selection. Close inspection of each piece by experienced workers completes the grading process.

The *color* and *design* of the china selected should be in harmony with the overall motifs and general atmosphere desired in the dining area. Pigments and processes have been so perfected that now there is practically no limit to the color and design possibilities of china. Conservative but attractive designs enhance the beauty of any dining room and ordinarily do not detract from interest in the food. Colors primarily used for the body of china are white, off-white, ivory, buff, or tan. These complement natural food colors and serve as a good background for them. Design colors should harmonize. Gaudy and naturalistic designs in the center of plates seem to leave little room for food. Also, such designs may add 5 percent to 25 percent to the cost of each plate. In contrast, an inexpensive design may be created with a colored edge for the dominant note.

That the choice of china is influenced by the size of the budget is evident. Not infrequently, the budget limits the choice to china with a simple border pattern, which may or may not have artistic appeal. Managers need to weigh values of beauty and durability along with cost in the selection of china. Interest in, and demand for, good design in less expensive china has influenced manufacturers to produce such items.

Another factor that may influence choice is the available designs for which *replacements* can be obtained within a reasonable time period. Stock types of patterns are usually available for immediate shipment. Specially made china, such as that having a monogram or crest, must be ordered weeks in advance. This fact must be considered along with the relatively higher cost of such special china in selecting a pattern for any specific service. Even open-stock types of patterns may be discontinued with limited notice, so the possibility of replacements with identical china or that similar in type should be considered when the initial selection is made.

Another consideration in selecting china is the *shape* of the pieces because there are many different ones on the market. Plates are available with a wide flat 1- to 1½-inch rim; Econo-Rim, which is 1/4- to 3/8-inch rolled under edge, designed to save space on trays and in storage and give extra strength to the edge; and coupe-shape, which is a no-rim design with the body of the plate scooped or slightly concave. Cups are made in a low, wide shape and in a taller, slender shape with a much narrower opening, which holds heat in the beverage longer and stores more easily than the more open shape. In addition, mugs of all sizes and shapes, some footed and some not, have become popular in many foodservices and eliminate the need for saucers.

A wide range of *sizes* and *capacities* of china is available and can vary somewhat from manufacturer to manufacturer. The present trend in purchasing is to limit the number of different-size dishes, supplying one size for several uses. For example, instead of buying both 4-inch bread/butter plates and 6-inch salad/dessert plates, a 5-inch plate to satisfy both uses can be purchased. An alternative to ordering different size bowls for soup, cereals, and similar items is to purchase one size for all. This simplification is advantageous from the standpoint of service, inventory, dishwashing, replacement, and storage.

The size of plates is the measurement from outer rim to outer rim, and that is the size specified when ordering. Cups, bowls, sugar bowls, creamers, and pitchers are specified by capacity in terms of ounces.

Amounts to Purchase. The quantity of dinnerware to be purchased for equipping a foodservice depends on many factors: the seating capacity and total number of people to be served, the length of the serving period, the type of menu and the price of the meal, the kind of service, the dishwashing facilities and whether they are used intermittently or continuously, and the caliber and speed of the employees. Other factors not to be overlooked are the variety of sizes of each item to be stocked and the frequency of use of the piece. For example, if only one size plate is purchased for multiple use as a bread and butter, salad, and underliner plate, fewer total pieces would be required than if three different-size plates had been selected. Also, a larger number of coffee cups used many times a day must be purchased to provide a margin of safety than would be necessary for bouillon cups that may be used only once or twice a week.

Any listing of quantities must be determined by the needs of a particular institution and not by a set formula. Table 1 suggests the number of each item of dinnerware needed per customer in a foodservice using an intermittent dishwashing cycle and might be helpful as a basis for initial planning.

Care. China has a much longer life when handled carefully and cleaned properly. It is believed that most breakage is caused by china hitting against china, and that 75 percent to 80 percent of all breakage occurs in the soiled dish and washing area. Careful training and supervision of the personnel can do much to prevent breakage and keep dishes looking bright and clean. Procedures to reduce the number of times a piece of china is handled will also assist in this. Examples are to separate and stack soiled dishes into like kinds before taking them to the dishroom for washing and to store clean cups and glasses in the racks in which they are washed. Rubber plate scrapers and collars on openings in scrapping tables not only decrease noise but help to reduce breakage of dishes. Also helpful are the use of plastic and other synthetic-coated metal dishracks and plastic or nylon pegs on dishmachine conveyors.

Suitable washing compound and proper temperature of wash and rinse waters, in addition to careful attention throughout the scraping, washing, and stacking and storing of clean dishes, contribute to the life span of china.

The soiled dishes, scraped and ready for the machine, are placed on belts or in racks, so that all surfaces are exposed. Sorting and stacking dishes into piles of dishes in the racks or on the conveyor belt speed washing at both the loading and unloading ends of the machine and ensure better wash action, because there is no overlapping of larger dishes to block the spray. After the washing and rinsing, the china is air dried. Plates of like size are stacked carefully so that the bottom rim of one does not mar the surface of the plate beneath it. Cups and glasses are stored in the wash racks, stacked on dollies, and wheeled to the unit where they will be used next. Plates and bowls likewise may be placed directly from the dishmachine into self-leveling mobile units or onto dish storage trucks where they remain until needed. Thus, breakage is lowered through reduced handling, and fewer labor hours are required for this one-time handling as opposed to storing dishes in a cupboard and then having to remove them when needed.

Generally, breakage is highest on small plates, saucers, and fruit dishes; they are often stacked too high and slide off the trays or carts; handles are broken from cups; and the edges of large, heavy plates may be chipped if plates are stacked carelessly. As a means of reducing breakage through carelessness, it is advisable to make a frequent inventory of stock in circulation. Thus, the workers become aware that a constant check of breakage is being made. Often a price list of china is posted, so the total loss to the foodservice through breakage is made known to the workers. Supervisors, too, should try to determine how and where breakage is occurring. If the breakage seems unreasonably high, they should include corrective procedures in training sessions held for those workers involved in dish handling.

Replacement of china may be made as breakage demands, or provision may be made for a stockroom supply ample for the probable yearly need. In this case, replacements of the storeroom stock can be made following the annual inventory. Managers should be aware of the supply of dishes in circulation

Table 1	Dinnerware needs per customer.
ITEM	**NUMBER PER CUSTOMER**
Cups and Saucers	2–2.5
Mugs	3
Dinner Plates	2–2.5
Salad Plates	2–3
Bowls, Cereal/Soup	1–2
Fruit Dishes	2–3

and make sure an ample quantity is available so service is not slowed because of a lack of clean dishes.

Glass Dinnerware

A popular dinnerware made by the Corning Glass Company is a basic glass in which a percentage of the sand used in its manufacture is replaced with aluminum powder. The resulting dinnerware is strong, thin, well tempered, has a smooth surface, and is highly resistant to stains, heat, scratching, and breakage. It is available in a variety of sizes, shapes, and decorative designs on a white background. The cost is less than that of some high-quality vitrified china dinnerware. The amounts to order and the care of Corning dinnerware are comparable to china.

Plastic Dinnerware

The introduction and availability of synthetic compounds for molded dinnerware have provided competition for china and glass for use in some types of institution foodservices. The history of the development of a suitable and highly acceptable product has been a long one.

Celluloid (1868), an early synthetic thermoplastic compound and a forerunner of modern plastics, was made of cellulose nitrate and camphor. Its nonresistance to heat, high inflammability, and camphor odor and flavor made it unsuitable for dishware. In the next period of development (1908), phenol and formaldehyde were incorporated into a thermosetting compound that was capable of being molded under pressure and heat into forms that would retain their shapes under mechanical strains, at well above the temperature of boiling water. This type of compound has had wide and varied usage, but because of its odor and unattractive brownish color, its use in the foodservice industry was limited mainly to counter and serving trays. The substitution of urea for phenol made it possible to produce a white compound of great strength that would take colors well. The basic cost of this material was high; therefore, it was often made into thin dishes suitable only for picnic or limited use and that could be sold for a reasonably low price.

During World War II, it was found that melamine could be combined with formaldehyde to give a tough resin that could withstand the demands on it in high-altitude flying equipment. This type of melamine plastic compound is now used in the production of dinnerware, often called melamine ware.

The first heavy-duty dinnerware made of melamine-formaldehyde compounds contained a chopped cotton cloth filler. The products had a high tensile and impact strength but were unattractive and limited to a low color range. Compounds made by blending long-fiber, high-grade paper stock with melamine resin and colorfast pigments are used in the production of dinnerware at the present time. This material is known as alpha-cellulose-filled, melamine-formaldehyde, thermosetting

molding compound; the products made from it are available in a wide range of colors and designs.

The melamine compound undergoes chemical change in the molding process under pressure of some 3,000 to 3,500 pounds per square inch at 335°F, which gives the dinnerware pieces a smooth lustrous surface, resistant to scratching, chippage, breakage, detergents, and grease. Also, it is not affected by the hot water used in dishwashing. Because the color pigment is thoroughly blended with the compound before molding, there is no fading of the finished product.

The permanent decoration of melamine dinnerware is made possible by opening the press when the material has just been shaped and adding a melamine-impregnated overlay, with the lithographed side placed down onto the dish. The mold is closed and, during the cure, the overlay becomes an integral part of the base material, and the resulting product has a smooth, wear-resistant, and protective glaze over the design.

Factors in Selecting Plasticware. The U.S. Department of Commerce has established standards for the heavy-duty type of melamine dishes. Foodservices should specify that the ware being purchased complies with Commercial Standards (CS) 173–50 that relate to thickness, resistance to acids, boiling water, dry heat, and the finished product.

Sample pieces of plasticware may be purchased or requested for testing before an order is placed. Special attention should be given to balance and to any marring of the surface by normal cutting and use.

The original cost of plastic dinnerware may be somewhat higher than for medium-weight china, but the replacement costs are estimated to be only about one-tenth of that for china. Differences in shape, density, and balance in design account, in some measure, for the price range in melamine ware. Competition is keen between the molding companies to produce items from this common basic material that are attractive in color and design and that meet the needs of the food industry. A price quotation from several companies should precede purchase.

The choice between melamine or the long-accepted china dinnerware may pose problems for the prospective buyer. The light weight of melamine, which is about one-third that of ordinary dinnerware, its low breakage, minimum handling noise, and attractive colors make it especially acceptable in many types of foodservice operations, especially in hospitals, other health care facilities, and school foodservices. Another advantage is that it can be recycled. Much melamine that is sold today is made from 100% recycled melamine.

One disadvantage of melamine may be staining, scratching, and difficulty in cleaning, although improvements in manufacture have reduced this as a major problem. Although melamine products possess low thermal conductivity, thus eliminating the need to preheat them for service, they may present some dishwashing problems. This ware does not air dry quickly and may remain damp for storage. Bacteriological tests on such dishes, however, indicate no cause for concern

Figure 54 A tray and dinnerware made of polycarbonate.
Source: Courtesy of Cambro Manufacturing Company, Huntington Beach, CA.

over this condition. Melamine cannot resist high heat and as such is not microwave or oven safe.

Today, newer plasticware has been developed from polycarbonates that resists stains, odors, and scratches. These are ideal for schools, cafeterias, day care centers, or health care facilities (Figure 54).

Care. The same care in dishwashing as described for china should be followed for plasticware dishes. However, the staining of cups may require the extra step of soaking them to remove the stain. China cups may also require this step.

Many manufacturers of melamine dinnerware have successfully incorporated stain-resistant compounds into the thermosetting resin, which prevents much of the objectionable staining and adds to the life of this type of dinnerware. The development of new washing compounds and closer attention to washing techniques have eliminated the problem somewhat. Alkaline detergents are recommended for washing. Abrasives cannot be used successfully on plastic surfaces; therefore, chemical rinses must be depended on, preferably those without chlorine. Some users believe that frequent cup replacement is the answer and is justly compensated by the high resistance to breaking, chipping, cracking, and crazing under ordinary conditions, the lightness of weight, the low noise level in handling, the attractive coloring and luster, and the relatively low upkeep and replacement costs.

Amounts to Purchase. The initial stock of plastic dinnerware is comparable to that given for china. Sizes of dishes are also comparable. Another guide for amounts of dinnerware to select for the average foodservice would be an allowance of three times the number of dining room seats for items such as bread and butter plates, salad dishes, dinner plates, saucers, fruit and/or cereal dishes, and four times for cups. The amounts of these and other items would depend much on the menu pattern and other conditions mentioned earlier.

Disposable Dinnerware

One-time use items for table service are available in many different materials, including paper, plasticized paper, clear or colored thin plastics, Styrofoam®, and aluminum foil. They are

available in a wide range of sizes, shapes, colors, and quality by weight. Some are made for use with cold foods only; others withstand considerable heat, making them suitable for oven or microwave use, and for serving hot foods.

The selection of disposable dishware over other types may well be justified, especially for any foodservice using the assembly/serve system and for fast-food, carry-out businesses.

Factors in Selection. Consideration should be given to initial and replacement costs of conventional dinnerware; space and equipment for dishwashing and labor for handling in comparison to the initial and repeat cost of paper or plastic; and its *disposal* and *acceptability* by the persons to be served. In any case, all foodservices should have ready access to some disposable dishware for times of emergency.

Disposal of large quantities of "disposables" poses problems in some situations. The availability on the premises of a large trash compactor is a necessity to handle this waste without undue bulk.

Quantities to purchase are determined by the amount of space to store the large cartons of paper or plastic goods, the relative closeness to a marked supply, and, of course, the number of persons to be served in a given period of time and the menu items offered.

Silver Tableware

Silverware. Quality silverware has been used in discriminating foodservices because of the demands for, and interest of, the residents or clientele in attractive service. It lends dignity and charm to dining tables, perhaps because of the association of the idea that silver, a precious metal, is found where people know and appreciate gracious, comfortable living. Some knowledge of the manufacture of silverware will help the foodservice manager make a wise decision in the selection of this item.

"Blanks" serve as the basic forms for flatware as well as hollow ware. They are made of 18 percent nickel-silver, a metal that gives the utensil the needed strength and resistance to bending or twisting to which institutional silverware is often subjected. The design, shape, and thickness or weight of the blanks should be conducive to heavy wear and beauty.

Nine pounds per gross is the standard weight of blanks of ordinary teaspoons sold for public service. The principal weights of blanks used are heavy, 10½ pounds; regular, 9 pounds; medium, 7½ to 8 pounds. The 9-pound blanks are desirable for hospital tray service, whereas the 10½-pound patterns may be advisable for heavy-duty silverware for certain commercial restaurants and cafeterias. The weight of the blank used influences the price of the silverware.

Flatware blanks are stamped, graded, and rolled until they are the corresponding size of forks or spoons. They are then placed in various presses, and the fork tines or spoon bowls are shaped. In the next step, they are struck with the pattern die, after which the edges are trimmed and smoothed down so that the articles resemble the finished products. Forks should have well-designed tines, durable and heat treated to give maximum strength; both forks and spoons should have heavy reinforced shanks to give the best wearing qualities. After being cleaned and polished, the articles are ready for plating with the silver.

The steps in the manufacture of knives prior to plating differ from those in the making of blanks for forks and spoons. The 18 percent nickel-silver base was found to produce a blade that bent easily and refused to take an edge sharp enough for practical use in cutlery. Stainless steel has become widely used for knife blades, and noncorrosive alloys have been made that prove satisfactory as the base for solid-handle knives that are to be plated. The popular hollow-handle knife, made with the 18 percent nickel-silver as the base of the handle, has been largely replaced by the one-piece stainless steel knife with the plate handle. An improvement in the design of knives was the change in style from the long blade–short handle to the short blade–long handle type that permits the user to press down with the forefinger on the back of the handle instead of on the narrow edge of the steel blade.

Manufacturers of better qualities of flatware use an intervening step between the making of the blank and its plating. Reinforcements of an extra disc of silver are made on blanks at the point of greatest wear: the heel of the bowls of spoons and the base of fork tines Such treatment is referred to as overlay, sectional plate, or reinforced plate, and it increases the length of wear by many times.

The plating of silverware is accomplished by electrolysis. Pure silver bars or ingots are placed around the side of a plating tank, and the articles to be plated are hung in the solution in the tank. By means of an electric current, the silver passes from the bars and is deposited on the blanks; the length of time and the strength of the current determines the amount of silver deposited.

After the articles are removed from the plating tank, they are sent to the finishing rooms. Better grades are burnished, or rubbed under pressure with a round pointed steel tool, to harden and smooth out the plate. It is then polished and colored. The better qualities of silverware are given extra burnishing. The various finishes are *butler* or dull finish, *hotel finish* or medium bright, and *bright*. The finishes are obtained by using different types of buffs and polishing compounds and by carrying the polishing process to different degrees.

The plating of institutional silverware is heavier than for the silverware generally used in the home, the most common institution ware being known as *triple plate*, or three times full standard. In triple plate, 6 ounces of pure silver has been applied to one gross of teaspoons, with other items in proportion—for example, tablespoons with 12 ounces of silver to the gross. A much lighter plating known as *full standard* carries a deposit of 5 ounces of pure silver to the gross of tablespoons and only 2½ ounces to the gross of teaspoons. *Half standard*, as its name implies, carries half the amount of silver deposit of full standard. Full standard plate quality is the lightest grade recommended for use in institutions.

The leading manufacturers of silverplate generally make, under their own trade name, a better quality of silverplate than those noted earlier. An example of such silverware is heavy hotel teaspoons, which weigh 11½ to 12 pounds per gross. An extra-heavy plate deposit is used on 10½-pound blanks in their production. The silver overlay on the tips and backs of bowls and tines is usually invisible on any 10½- and 11-pound qualities. The heavy, finely finished metal blanks, the heavy plating standard, and the fine finish of this quality of silverware make the initial cost greater than the ordinary commercial grades of plate, but the cost is offset by the long-wearing qualities and satisfactory service of the various items.

Hollow Ware. Silver hollow ware items such as serving bowls, platters, sugar bowls, creamers, pitchers, teapots, and coffeepots are made from the same materials as flatware and are plated in a similar manner to varying qualities. The bodies of the various items are die shaped, and the several pieces for each are assembled and hand soldered by expert craftspeople before plating. The quality of materials and workmanship and the design determine cost.

Features to consider in selecting hollow ware include the following: Sharp corners are to be avoided; short spouts are easier to clean than long ones; simple designs are usually more pleasing than ornate ones and are easier to clean. However, plain silverware can become badly scratched with ordinary handling; hence, a pleasing, simple design that breaks the smooth surface may be more practical than plain silver. Simplicity is always the keynote of good taste.

Standard designs and patterns are often made individual by stamping or engraving the name, crest of the organization, or a special decorative motif on the otherwise plain surface. If silverware is to be stamped, the stamping should be done on the back of the item before it is plated. The name of the manufacturer is stamped on the bottom.

Silver hollow ware may seem an extravagance, but when the cost is considered over a period of years, it may be more economical than china or glassware. Furthermore, the satisfaction and prestige gained through its use are not to be discounted.

Care. The care of silverware has much to do with its appearance and wearing qualities. Careful handling prevents many scratches. The following procedure is suggested for cleaning silverware and keeping it in good condition: sort, then wash in a machine to which has been added the proper cleaning compound, at a temperature of 140°F to 150°F, and rinse thoroughly. A final dip in a solution with high-wetting properties prevents spotting of air-dried silver. It is advisable to presoak flatware or wash immediately after use. If washed in flat-bottom racks, the silver should be scattered loosely over the rack surface, sorted after washing, placed into perforated dispensing cylinders, and rewashed to ensure sanitization. If silver is sorted into cylinders before washing, the handles of the utensils are down so that all surfaces of knife blades, fork tines, and bowls of spoons are subjected to the wash and rinse processes. Care must be taken not to over-crowd the containers. The washed silver is left in the cylinders to dry. This system is convenient, especially in self-service units, because clean dispensing cylinders may be inverted over those used in washing, turning the silver upside down so handles are up, and placed on the counter without handling of the clean silver.

Tarnishing of silver occurs readily when exposed to smoke or natural gas, or when it comes in contact with rubber, certain fibers, or sulfur-containing foods. Detarnishing is accomplished quickly and easily by immersing the silver, placed in a wire basket, into a solution of water plus a cleaning compound containing trisodium phosphate in an aluminum kettle reserved for this purpose.

The tarnish (oxide) forms a salt with the aluminum and can be removed through a mild electrolytic action. The cleaning compound also cuts and dissolves any grease or dirt on the silver. The silver is left in the solution only long enough to remove the tarnish. It is then rinsed in boiling water and dipped in a solution of high wetting qualities. Burnishing machines are used for silver polishing in large foodservices. Care must be taken to make sure that the machine is not overloaded and that there are enough steel shots of various sizes in the barrel of the machine to be effective in contacting all surfaces to be polished. Also, the right amount of proper detergent must be added to the water in the burnishing machine to produce the required concentration of the solution. There can be no set rule about the frequency of detarnishing and polishing; each foodservice must set up its own standards.

Stainless Steel Tableware

Stainless steel tableware has gained wide acceptance for heavy-duty tableware in many foodservices. The flatware is fairly inexpensive; is highly resistant to heat, scratches, and wear; and will not rust, stain, peel, chip, or tarnish. It stays bright indefinitely with ordinary washing and offers a wide selection of attractive designs from which to choose. Flatware in stainless steel is available in light, standard, and heavy weights. Cheap-quality stainless steel utensils have appeared on the market, but they are not really suitable for most establishments. These are made from rolled sheets of the metal and are die-stamped into desired shapes. The resulting pieces are the same thickness throughout and have poor balance, and fork tines and bowls of spoons are too thick to pick up food easily. This quality should be avoided.

Good-quality ware is rolled and tapered as needed to give good balance and to be comfortable in the hand. A test for good balance is to place a fork or a spoon at the base of its bowl or tines on an index finger: The utensil should balance equally between handle and bowl or tines. In poor quality, the bowl or tines will overbalance the handle and the utensil will fall off the finger.

Another consideration in selecting stainless steel tableware is the size and shape of the handles. Older persons particularly find it difficult to hold a slim handle and much prefer a wider, easier-to-grasp shape and size.

Water pitchers and individual teapots of stainless steel are considered a lifetime investment, although the initial cost is high in comparison to these items in ordinary glass or pottery. The same methods of sorting, washing, and drying are recommended for stainless steel tableware as for silver.

Amounts of Tableware to Purchase

The menu to be offered determines what items of tableware the foodservice must supply. It is more difficult to calculate the quantities of each piece to stock. As with dinnerware, the trend in use of flatware is toward as few different pieces as possible. For instance, knives and forks of dessert size can be used for many purposes and are usually preferred to knives and forks of dinner size. Dessert spoons can be used for soup and serving spoons as well as for certain desserts.

A good quantity estimate of flatware for cafeterias is twice the seating capacity for all the flatware items required. Should the dishwashing facilities be limited and the turnover of patrons rapid, this quantity might need to be increased to three or even four times the seating capacity. For table or tray service, three teaspoons per cover, three forks, using a dessert fork for all purposes, and two knives per cover usually are sufficient. All other items are estimated on the basis of 1½ per cover, or according to the needs as for banquet or special party service. This may call for limited quantities of specialized items such as oyster or fish forks, bouillon spoons, butter spreaders, or iced tea spoons.

On the basis of total investment in tableware, the average estimate is 2.5 percent of the budget for all foodservice equipment.

Glassware

Glassware is classed as lead or lime glass, depending on the use of lead or lime oxide in the manufacturing process. Lead glass is of better quality, is clearer, and has more brilliance than lime glass, which is less expensive. Articles of glass are made from a molten compound, formed by blowing them into shape by machine or hand processes or by pressing molten glass into molds by means of a machine. The blowing method is more expensive and produces a thinner glass of finer texture, higher luster, and clearer ring. Hand-blown lead glass is superior to all other glassware because of its brilliance, light weight, and variety of styles. Lime-blown glassware possesses these characteristics to a lesser degree, is less expensive, and is used extensively in institutions. It is usually machine blown. The style, color, and decoration determine the cost of manufacture of blown-glass articles.

Pressed lime glass is used in many institutions. It is serviceable, and better qualities of it are comparatively free from bubbles and cloudiness. Moreover, it is relatively inexpensive and can be obtained in many styles. A good quality of glassware should be selected for the institution, regardless of whether pressed glass or blown glass is to be used. Desirable characteristics are clearness, luster, medium weight, freedom from such defects as marks and bubbles, and a clear ring. Also, it should be designed so that it is not easily tipped over.

Glassware must pass boiling and shock tests without showing signs of corrosion, chipping, scumming, or cracking in order to meet federal specifications. In the boiling test, articles are suspended for six hours in boiling water in a closed container with vent. The shock test is made by immersing articles in tap water at 18.5°C ± 2.5° (65°F ± 5°) for a 10-minute period, then suddenly transferring them into boiling water. This procedure is repeated five times. Not all glassware sold meets federal specifications, and there is no labeling to indicate which, if any, is of that quality.

The sizes of glassware used most commonly in institutions are glasses of 5- or 6-ounce capacity for fruit juice, glasses of 9- or 10-ounce capacity for milk and water, and glasses of 12- or 14-ounce capacity for iced tea. A wide range of sizes and shapes must be stocked for bar service.

Goblets and footed dessert dishes are other items of glass selected for some foodservices. The portion size of specific menu items will determine the capacity size required for these items.

Care. Glassware to be washed is sorted and often washed in a separate dishwashing machine from that used for other dishes, or in a glasswasher built for that purpose. If glassware must be washed in the same machine used for dishes, it should be segregated and washed first while the water is entirely free from grease and food particles, or left until after the dishes are finished and the soiled water is replaced by clean. In either case, with a rack machine, all items to be washed are placed upside down in racks after they are transported from the dining room and remain in the same racks to wash and drain. They are then loaded onto carts for transport to the point of storage or use without rehandling.

Glassware should be under constant scrutiny to maintain in service only those pieces that are not chipped, cracked, clouded, or scratched in appearance. Filmed glasses may be caused by low rinse pressure and volume, a rinse cycle that is too short, nonaligned spray jets, and a hard-water precipitate. Tea stains may be removed by using a chlorinated detergent in the glass washing machine. Water spots may be caused by slow drying or the hardness of the rinse water. The effect of an otherwise attractive dining service may be spoiled by damaged or poorly washed glassware on the tables.

The rate of breakage of glassware in institutions is often high and results from careless handling and storage, choice of improper designs for heavy service wear, use of poor quality of glassware, and subjection to high temperature during washing. The shape of the glass has much to do with the breakage anticipated. Straight-sided tumblers that can be stacked are a decided breakage hazard; patented shapes are available that make it impossible to stack tumblers. Many styles of glassware curve in slightly at the top so that the edges do not touch when they are set down together, the contact coming at a reinforced part away from the edge of the glass. Other styles have reinforced edges at the top, advertised as making them more highly resistant to chipping. This feature is also found around the feet of some stemmed ware.

Amounts to Purchase. The amount and kind of glassware to supply vary as for tableware and dinnerware. Choice is based primarily on the menu, type of service, seating capacity and rate of turnover, dishwashing facilities, skill of persons employed in dish handling, and whether scheduling is continuous or intermittent. However, because glassware is more fragile than other tableware, foodservices should have an ample stock on hand of the most frequently used items: tumblers, fruit juice glasses, and sherbet or dessert dishes (if glass ones are used). A suggested rule for quantities to purchase is two pieces for each person to be served: one piece in use and one-half in the dishroom, plus 50 percent of that total in reserve in the stock room.

Cloth Table Covers

In some localities, tablecloths may be rented from local laundries, thus relieving the foodservice of purchasing and storing this item. However, if cloths are to be purchased, there are many materials from which to choose: pure linen, union, rayon, cotton, mercerized cotton, linenized damasks, and polyester-cotton blends.

Cotton fibers may be used in combination with linen or rayon in the union damasks to produce durable and satisfactory table coverings and napkins. Rayon and cotton blend table napkins are highly resistant to wear and often superior to all-cotton or all-linen napkins in appearance and breaking strength. Cotton is used alone in plain cotton, mercerized, or linenized fabrics. After being woven, the last two fabrics are treated such that a permanent finish is produced to give the cloth characteristics similar to linen. Cotton fabrics have better wearing quality than linen, lose less strength during laundering, and do not lint. Linen gives satisfaction in use, is attractive, and lint free.

Because of the high initial and maintenance costs of both linen and cotton cloths, those of a 50–50 blend of polyester and cotton with a no-iron finish are rapidly replacing the former in other than the most sophisticated foodservices. Polyester yarns are used in the making of lace cloths as well as the plain woven ones.

Tablecloths may be purchased in white, in colors, or in white with colored borders or designs. Colored linen is popular as place mats and luncheon cloths for breakfast and luncheon services, as well as to help create "atmosphere" in many dining rooms. Fabrics may be purchased by the yard and made up for the specific size tables of the individual establishment, or the cloths may be purchased ready-made. The size and shape of the tables determine the sizes of cloths needed. The cloth should be large enough to hang 7 to 12 inches below the table top at both sides and ends, with allowances made for shrinkage according to the material selected. The usual sizes of tablecloths are 52 × 52 inches square, 60 × 80 inches, 67 × 90 to 102 inches or longer, depending on the length of banquet tables. Some places use a table-size top over the regular cloth, which allows for frequent changes and reduced laundry costs.

Common sizes for cloth dinner napkins in institutions are 18, 20, or 22 inches square.

Paper Place Mats and Napkins. The range of colors and designs available in paper products is so large that selection of appropriate covers should be relatively easy. Size is dependent on the size of tray for tray service. For use on table tops, 12 × 18-inch mats provide generously for each cover, although the 11 × 14-inch size is frequently used. Often the name, logo, or design of the foodservice is imprinted on the mat and/or napkin, which is good advertising for the establishment.

Index